Rapid Lighting Design and Cost Estimating

Rapid Lighting Design and Cost Estimating

A HANDY, QUICK METHOD FOR LIGHTING DESIGN AND CALCULATION OF INSTALLATION PRICES

Prafulla C. Sorcar, P. E.

McGraw-Hill Book Company New York St. Louis San Francisco Auckland Bogotá Düsseldorf Johannesburg London Madrid Mexico Montreal New Delhi Panama Paris São Paulo Tokyo Singapore Sydney Toronto

Library of Congress Cataloging in Publication Data

Sorcar, Prafulla C
Rapid lighting design and cost estimating.

Includes index.
1. Electric lighting. 2. Electric lighting–
Estimates. I. Title.
TK4169.S64 621.32'2 79–4690
ISBN 0-07-059651-4

1 2 3 4 5 6 7 8 9 0 H D H D 7 8 6 5 4 3 2 1 0 9

*The editors for this book were Tyler G. Hicks and Carolyn Nagy,
the designer was Naomi Auerbach, and the production supervisor
was Sally Fliess. It was set in Times Roman Italic by Florence Lanaro.*

It was printed and bound by Halliday Lithograph.

To my daughter Piya

Table of Contents

PREFACE xiii

HOW TO USE THIS BOOK xix

SECTION A — SURFACE-MOUNT FLUORESCENT ENCLOSED

WRAPAROUND

Corridor, 1 or 2 lamps A-2
Low-Profile, 2 lamps A-4
Low-Profile, 4 lamps A-6
Traditional, 2 lamps A-8
Traditional, 4 lamps A-10
Scissors-Curve, 2 lamps A-12
Premium, 2 or 4 lamps A-14

SPECIAL-PURPOSE WRAPAROUND

Enclosed and Gasketed, 1 or 2 lamps A-16

OPEN-LOUVERED UNITS

With 2 lamps A-18
With 4 lamps A-20

MODULAR UNITS

1- × 4-ft (Acrylic Prismatic Lens), 2 lamps A-22
2- × 2-ft (Acrylic Prismatic Lens), 2 or 3 lamps A-24
2- × 4-ft (Acrylic Prismatic Lens), 2, 3, or 4 lamps A-26
4- × 4-ft (Acrylic Prismatic Lens), 6 or 8 lamps A-28
1- × 4-ft (Dropped-Dish), 2 lamps A-30
2- × 4-ft (Dropped-Dish), 2 or 4 lamps A-32
1- × 4-ft (Plastic-Cube Louvers), 2 lamps A-34
2- × 4-ft (Plastic-Cube Louvers), 2 or 4 lamps A-36

CEILING OUTLETS FOR LUMINAIRES

Installed Cost of Flush-mounted Outlets A-38

SECTION B — RECESSED FLUORESCENT TROFFERS

ACRYLIC PRISMATIC LENS

1- × 4-ft, 2 or 3 lamps	*B-2*
2- × 2-ft, 2 or 3 lamps	*B-4*
2- × 4-ft, 2, 3, or 4 lamps	*B-6*
4- × 4-ft, 6 or 8 lamps	*B-8*

PARABOLIC-LOUVERED

9-in × 8-ft, 1 lamp	*B-10*
1- × 4-ft, 2 lamps	*B-12, B-14*
2- × 2-ft, 2 lamps	*B-16*
2- × 4-ft, 3 lamps	*B-18*
2- × 4-ft, 4 lamps	*B-20*
3- × 3-ft, 6 lamps	*B-22*
4- × 4-ft, 8 lamps	*B-24*

MISCELLANEOUS

2- × 4-ft (Carolite Radialens), 2 Lamps	*B-26*
2- × 4-ft (Carolite Radialens), 3 or 4 Lamps	*B-28*
2- × 4-ft (Day-Brite VIP Lens), 2 Lamps	*B-30*
2- × 4-ft (Day-Brite VIP Lens), 3 Lamps	*B-32*
2- × 4-ft (Day-Brite VIP Lens), 4 Lamps	*B-34*
2- × 4-ft (KSH 3E Lens), 2 Lamps	*B-36*
2- × 4-ft (KSH 3E Lens), 3 Lamps	*B-38*
2- × 4-ft (Gibson EE System), 2 Lamps	*B-40*
2- × 4-ft (Gibson EE System), 3 Lamps	*B-42*
1- × 4-ft (Plastic-Cube Louvers), 2 or 3 Lamps	*B-44*
2- × 4-ft (Plastic-Cube Louvers), 2 or 4 Lamps	*B-46*
1- × 4-ft (Dropped-Dish), 2 or 3 Lamps	*B-48*
2- × 4-ft (Dropped-Dish), 2 or 4 Lamps	*B-50*

CEILING OUTLETS FOR LUMINAIRES

Installed Cost of Outlets above Ceiling	*B-52*

SECTION C — FLUORESCENT STRIPS

GENERAL-PURPOSE

4-ft, 1 Lamp	*C-2*
4-ft, 2 Lamps	*C-4*
8-ft, 1 Lamp	*C-6*
8-ft, 2 Lamps	*C-8*
8-ft, 3 Lamps	*C-10*
8-ft, 4 Lamps	*C-12*

PREMIUM-GRADE

4-ft, 2 Lamps	*C-14*
8-ft, 2 Lamps (HO)	*C-16*
8-ft, 2 Lamps (PG)	*C-18*
8-ft, 3 or 4 Lamps	*C-20*

CEILING OUTLETS FOR LUMINAIRES

Installed Cost of Outlets — C-22

SECTION D — INDUSTRIAL

FLUORESCENT UNITS

General-Purpose Industrial

4-ft, 2 Lamps — D-2
8-ft, 2 Lamps — D-4
8-ft, 3 Lamps — D-6
8-ft, 4 Lamps — D-8

Premium-Grade Industrial

8-ft, 2 Lamps (HO) — D-10
8-ft, 2 Lamps (PG) — D-12

Heavy-Duty-Grade Industrial

8-ft, 2 Lamps (HO) — D-14
8-ft, 2 Lamps (PG) — D-16

HIGH-INTENSITY-DISCHARGE UNITS

Low-Profile Series

Aluminum Reflector, up to 250 W — D-18
Porcelain Enamel Reflector, up to 250 W — D-20
Prismatic Glass Refractor, up to 250 W — D-22

Full-Profile Series

Aluminum Reflector, 400 W — D-24
Prismatic Glass Reflector, 400 W — D-26
Aluminum Reflector, 1000 W — D-28
Prismatic Glass Reflector, 1000 W — D-30

Full-Profile Series: Twin Units

Aluminum Reflector, 400 W — D-32
Prismatic Glass Reflector, 400 W — D-34

CEILING OUTLETS FOR LUMINAIRES

Installed Cost of Ceiling Outlets — D-36

SECTION E — COMMERCIAL HIGH-INTENSITY DISCHARGE UNITS

RECESSED UNITS

Open Downlights

6-in — E-2
8-in — E-4
10-in — E-6
12-in — E-8
16-in — E-10

Ellipsoidal-Reflector Downlights

6-in *E-12*
8-in *E-14*
10-in *E-16*
12-in *E-18*

Miscellaneous Commercial

12- × 12-in Regressed Lensite *E-20*
12- × 12-in Parabolic Louvered *E-22*
2- × 2-ft Regressed Lensite *E-24, E-26*
2- × 2-ft Parabolic Louvered *E-28, E-30*
Round Regressed Lensite (Horizontal Lamp) *E-32*
Round Regressed Lensite (Vertical Lamp) *E-34*
Square Regressed Lensite (Conical Reflector) *E-36*

SURFACE UNITS

Cylindrical Downlight *E-38*
Modular Lensite *E-40*

CEILING OUTLETS FOR LUMINAIRES

Installed Cost of Outlets *E-42*

SECTION F — COMMERCIAL INCANDESCENT

RECESSED UNITS

Open-Reflector Downlights (A-Lamps)

6-in *F-2*
8-in *F-4*
10-in *F-6*

Open-Reflector Downlights (R, PAR Lamps)

6-in *F-8*
7-in *F-10*
9-in *F-12, F-14*

Recessed-Baffle Downlights (R, PAR Lamps)

5-in *F-16*
6-in *F-18*
8-in *F-20*

Ellipsoidal-Reflector Downlights (A-Lamps)

6-in *F-22*
7-in *F-24*
9-in *F-26*
4½-in, Tungsten-Halogen *F-28, F-30*
6-in, Tungsten-Halogen *F-32, F-34*

Miscellaneous Commercial (A-Lamps)

8-in Regressed Round Lensite (Vertical Lamp) F-36
8-in Regressed Round Lensite (Horizontal Lamp) F-38
12- × 12-in Regressed Lensite F-40
12- × 12-in Parabolic-louvered F-42

SURFACE-MOUNTED UNIT

Open-Reflector Downlights (R, PAR Lamps)

6-in F-44
7-in F-46
9-in F-48

Surface-Mounted Baffle Downlights (R, PAR Lamps)

5-in F-50
6-in F-52
8-in F-54

CEILING OUTLETS FOR LUMINAIRE

Installed Cost of Outlets F-56

SECTION G — OUTDOOR LIGHTING

ROADWAY LIGHTING

Post-Top Lighting

Holophane RSL, up to 150 W G-2
Holophane RSL, 175 W G-4
Holophane RSL, 250 W G-6

Pole-Mounted Luminaires

Rectilinear, up to 250 W G-8
Rectilinear, 400 W G-10
Rectilinear, 1000 W G-12
Low-Pressure Sodium, 90 W G-14, G-16
Low-Pressure Sodium, 135 W G-18, G-20

AREA LIGHTING

Holophane Square Post-Top Lighting

175 W G-22
250 W G-24
400 W G-26
1000 W G-28
4 1000 W G-30

Rectilinear Pole-Mounted Luminaires

(1 hd), up to 250 W G-32
(1 hd), 400 W G-34
(1 hd), 1000 W G-36
(2 hds), up to 250 W G-38
(2 hds), 400 W G-40
(2 hds), 1000 W G-42
(4 hds), up to 250 W G-44
(4 hds), 400 W G-46
(4 hds), 1000 W G-48

High-Mast Luminaires:

400 W G-50
1000 W G-52
Installed Cost of Poles G-54

INSTALLED COST OF POLES

Installed Cost of Post-Top and Floodlighting Poles G-56

SECTION H — MISCELLANEOUS

MISCELLANEOUS

Installed Cost of EMT and GRC Conduit with Wire (Indoor) H-2
Installed Cost of GRC and PVC Conduit with Wire in a Trench H-4
Cost-Adjustment Formula H-7
IES Recommended Levels of Illumination, General Lighting H-8
IES Recommended Levels of Illumination, Sports Lighting H-10
IES Recommended Levels of Illumination, Roadway Lighting H-10

LAMP DATA

Incandescent H-11
Fluorescent H-12
Mercury H-13
Metal-Halide H-13
High-Pressure Sodium H-14
Low-Pressure Sodium H-14

INDEX

Preface

With the continuous growth in the building industry, lighting design practitioners today feel increasing pressure to complete jobs in a shorter time. Clients often require a clear picture of the lighting design with cost estimates even before the job gets on the drawing board. Working mainly with the architects, I have found that they like to discuss the various possibilities of lighting design on a particular project before awarding it to the engineer. Esthetics, efficiency, probability of visual comfort, installed cost, etc., are some of the prime considerations in lighting design. To prepare such a design in a conventional manner with all these considerations is extremely time-consuming if accuracy is also a requisite. These requirements established a need, and this book is my answer.

The technique this book advocates avoids the conventional theoretical approach, reduces the whole design procedure to two easy steps, and gives a reasonably accurate result in only about one-tenth the time.

The footcandle values to be calculated are expressed on curves which are functions of the luminaire per occupied area. A set of 10 curves, one for each of the room cavity ratios ranging from 1 to 10, are provided for each indoor type of luminaire. Step 1 is the determination of the room cavity ratio, which identifies the correct curve to be used. Step 2 shows directly the area required per luminaire to maintain a certain illumination level in the room. Several parameters have been carefully considered in determining these curves. A national average shows that the color of the ceiling in any normal working room is either white or of light tint. The wall colors are in the family of white, light yellow, light blue, light green, or light gray. The floors are mostly dark such as gray, blue, green, etc. With all these factors under consideration and realizing that the majority of the luminaires are either surface-mounted or recessed in the ceiling, the effective percentage of reflectances of the ceiling/walls/floor have been treated as 80/50/20. A qualified observer will immediately recognize the fact that these are the most practical figures for determining lighting level with the surroundings mentioned above.

A set of multiplication factors has been provided for all luminaires in the industrial and fluorescent strip sections to convert the effective reflectances to 50/30/20, as an option. This flexibility is provided with the view that warehouses and industrial areas, where most luminaires use a pendant mount (chain-hung or attached to the bottom of joists), generally have low ceiling and wall reflectances.

A wide variety of specification-grade luminaires with incandescent, fluorescent, mercury-vapor, metal halide, low- and high-pressure sodium lamps, ranging from popular old ones to the latest energy-saving ones, have been included in this book. They extend from surface-mount fluorescent enclosed, recessed fluorescent troffers, fluorescent strips, industrial, commercial HID, and commercial incandescent to outdoor pole-mounted street and area lighting. Because the majority of today's popular luminaires are competitively manufactured by several different companies, it was possible to establish curves representing the average. Where a unique but popular luminaire is manufactured by an individual company, the name of the manufacturer and the brand name of the luminaire have been stated for easy identification. It should be noted that the footcandle values for different luminaires determined by this book represent the average only. For a specific application, where accuracy is critical, the designer must consider the photometric data of the specific luminaire under consideration.

For convenience, a useful set of IES recommended illumination levels for indoor and outdoor applications and a set of lamp data have been provided in Section H. Additional design-related information such as consumed power, visual comfort probability, spacing ratio, recommended maintenance factors, life expectancy and lumen output of the lamp have been stated for each individual case.

Another important feature of this book is the inclusion of the contractor's cost and the installed cost for each luminaire. The contractor's cost shown for each luminaire is a typical manufacturer's published contractor's cost, which includes the cost of the lens or louvers and the ballast(s) but not the lamps or any fastening device. The installed cost, however, includes the contractor's cost for the luminaire, lamps, fastening devices, and the labor required for installation and connection of the luminaire.

Because of the labor-rate variation in different parts of the country, an average of \$14.62 (\$11.28 average base rate + approximately 30 percent PRT and fringes) was used as the reference labor rate in this book. This information was based on the Bureau of Labor Statistics report as published in *News* of March 3, 1978. The average base rate, as published, was developed from the individual labor rates in cities of 100,000 inhabitants or more.

One of the inevitable questions in using this type of book is how to compensate for the constantly changing material cost and different labor rates in the country; this is accomplished by the use of a Cost-Adjustment Formula shown in the Miscellaneous section (page H–7). By knowing the labor rate of the specific area and the latest price index for industrial and commercial lighting fixtures (*Electrical Marketing*, McGraw-Hill), this formula can be effectively used to determine a total price multiplier to compensate for such changes. The technique is explained on page H–6.

The labor units in finding the installed costs are as published in the *Manual of Labor Units* by NECA and were modified wherever necessary. In selecting the labor units it has been assumed that the luminaires are of good quality and that the layout is repetitive. It has also been assumed that the job conditions are average. It should be noted that any abnormal situation such as high ceilings, high-rise buildings, or inconvenience in access to job site, will require a job factor to adjust the situation. For the justification of the total sell price, an average of 6 percent tax on material, 10 percent overhead on material, tax, and labor, and 6 percent profit on the total have been considered for each installed cost.

I sincerely believe this book will be of considerable value and assistance to many technical and nontechnical people involved in lighting design. Consulting engineers, designers, draftspersons, electrical contractors, general contractors, mechanical engineers on HVAC design, architects, and interior designers will directly benefit from this book. College and university physical plant administrators and engineers in government agencies such as the Army, Navy, Air Force, General Services Administration, and state and municipal engineering departments will find this book extremely useful.

I would like to thank the following people who with their special knowledge have provided helpful information:

Fred Kohlmeier, *Manufacturer's Representative, Holophane, Denver, Colorado*
Vincent L. Cooke, *Manufacturer's Representative, Gibson, Norelco, Abolite, Denver, Colorado*
Phil W. Smith, *Manufacturer's Representative, Day-Brite, McPhilben, Denver, Colorado*
Frank L. Davenport, Jr., *Manufacturer's Representative, Lightolier, Denver, Colorado*
Ron Johnson, *Manufacturer's Representative, Lithonia, Hi-tek, Denver, Colorado*
Jack Ingwers, *Manufacturer's Representative, Kim, Denver, Colorado*
Don Congdon, *Manufacturer's Representative, Prescolite, Denver, Colorado*
Dennis Underwood, *Manufacturer's Representative, Keystone, McGraw Edison, Globe, Denver, Colorado*
Hal Hebert, *Manufacturer's Representative, Columbia, Gardco, Denver, Colorado*
Casey A. Brown, *K-S-H, Inc., Tuston, California*
Herbert M. Lang, *Estimator, Scott Brothers Elec. Co., Denver, Colorado*
Gregory L. Manning, *Estimator, Intermountain Electric, Inc., Denver, Colorado*

I would also like to thank the following people, who generously gave their time to review the book and provided constructive criticism and helpful suggestions:

Lloyd B. Watts, *Professional Engineer (elec.), U.S. Army Corps of Engineers, Denver Federal Center, Denver, Colorado*
Professor F. R. Bergseth, *Dept. of Electrical Engineering, Graduate School, University of Washington, Seattle, Washington*
R. E. (Russ) Selvy, *Public Works Engineer (elec.), Dept. of Physical Plant, Colorado University, Boulder, Colorado*
John Henderson, *Architect, Indian Technical Assistance Center, Bureau of Indian Affairs, Denver, Colorado*

Special appreciation is extended to my partner, Howard W. Butterweck, for all the valuable suggestions and guidance he has generously provided for this endeavor.

Prafulla C. Sorcar

ACKNOWLEDGMENTS

Where specific products and test results are identified, I would like to thank each of their manufacturers for reviewing and granting permission for use of the material in this book.

How to Use This Book

Indoor Lighting Applications

For the purpose of explaining how to use this book for indoor applications, let us assume that the luminaire type selected is a 2- × 4-ft troffer with acrylic prismatic lens with four F40 T12 rapid-start lamps, suspended on exposed grid tees. Let us also suppose that an average of 80 fc (footcandles) is to be maintained at a maintenance factor = 0.70 in a room with dimensions of length L = 60 ft, width W = 30 ft, and height H = 8 ft. The task level is 4 ft above the finished floor.

Step 1: Determination of Room Cavity Ratio (RCR)

To determine the RCR one needs to know the length L, width W, and depth R under consideration. The cavity depth R is actually the distance in feet between the luminaire and the task level.

Figure 1*a* and *b* shows the cavity depth R, which is the distance between the desk top and the luminaire surface. Note that if the luminaires are surface-mounted or recessed in the ceiling and the task level is the floor, the cavity depth R will be the actual height of the room (Fig. 1*c*).

Knowing the values of L, W, and R, refer to Table 1, the Cavity Ratio Table on page XIV, to determine the RCR. In our example, for L = 60 ft, W = 30 ft, and $R = 8 - 4 =$ 4 ft, the RCR found from the table is 1.0.

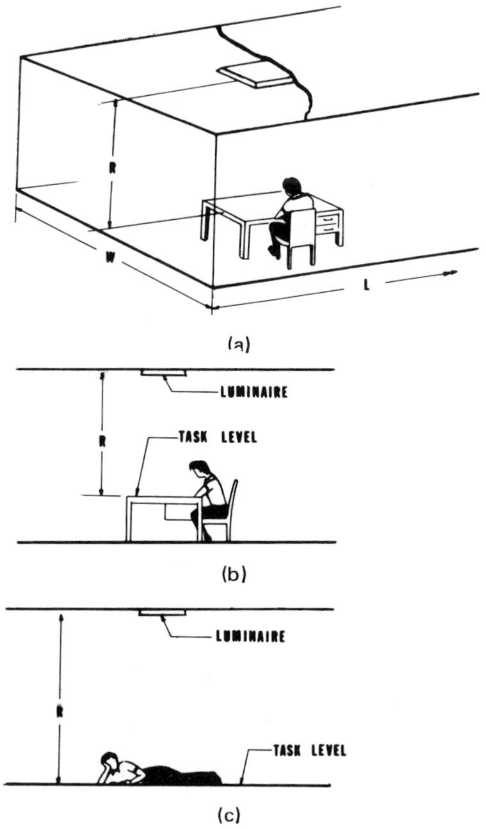

Figure 1

Step 2: Determination of Number of Luminaires

Once the RCR is known, refer directly to the curves assigned for the luminaire under consideration. In our example, we refer to page B–6 in the troffer section. Corresponding to the curve for RCR = 1 and maintained footcandles = 80, we find the area per luminaire required = 80 ft^2; in other words, for the room under consideration, a total of (60 X 30)/80 = 23 such luminaires will be required to maintain 80 fc at a maintenance factor of 0.70.

Note that each curve also offers the option of working with the initial footcandles. Designers who select a maintenance factor other than that shown may use that to determine how many luminaires would be required to maintain a particular footcandle level. For instance, suppose in our example, 80 fc is to be maintained with a maintenance factor of 0.65; then we should look at 80/0.65 = 123 initial footcandles. Corresponding to this initial value of footcandles we find the new square feet per luminaire = 73; a total of (60 X 30)/73 = 25 luminaires will be required.

When room dimensions do not exactly match those shown in Table 1, the RCR values may be interpolated between immediate higher and the lower figures.

Outdoor Lighting Applications

Outdoor street lighting is expressed on curves drawn between average maintained footcandles and corresponding distances in feet. Separate curves have been drawn for different luminaire mounting heights and street widths. The procedure is self-explanatory and is even simpler than the indoor application.

General area lighting is expressed on curves drawn between average footcandle values and spacing distances measured in feet (based on a square array). Again, a set of different curves has been presented for different luminaire mounting heights.

COST ESTIMATING

Indoor Application

To understand how to do indoor lighting cost estimation, consider the example described previously. We found that a total of 23 luminaires was required to maintain 80 fc in a room 60 X 30 X 8 ft.

To maintain symmetry in the lighting pattern in the ceiling, let us consider a total of 24 luminaires instead of 23.

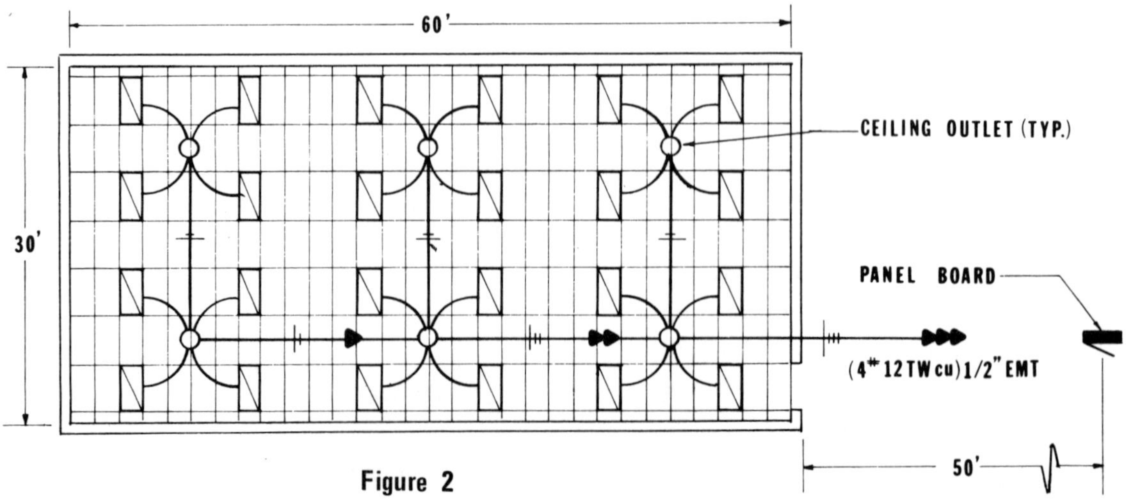

Figure 2

Figure 2 shows the complete floor plan including the circuits. For estimation purposes let us assume that the panel board is located 50 ft away from the room.

1.	From page B-6, installed cost for 24 luminaires = 24 X \$98.00	\$2352.00
2.	From page B-52, installed cost for 6 outlets = \$13.25 X 6	79.50
3.	From page H-3, installed cost for a total of 70 ft of (4 no. 12 TW copper) ½-in EMT at \$1.14 per foot = \$1.14 X 70 . .	79.80
	From page H-3, installed cost for a total of 20 ft of (3 no. 12 TW copper) ½-in EMT at \$1.04 per foot = \$1.04 X 20 . .	20.80
	From page H-3, installed cost for a total of 68 ft of (2 no. 12 TW copper) ½-in EMT at \$0.94 per foot = \$0.94 X 68 . .	63.92
	Total installed cost	\$2596.02

Outdoor Application

The installed costs for the outdoor pole-mounted luminaires are shown in two parts. The first part, which is the installed cost of the luminaire only, consists of the contractor's price for the luminaire, lamp, ballast, and the labor required for the installation and connection on a pole. The second part shows the installed costs of different types of poles, each of which includes the contractor's price for the pole and the labor required to install the pole with a concrete base. For the total installed cost, these figures are to be added together.

In addition, page H-5 shows the installed cost of conduit with wires in a trench. In finding these costs, it has been assumed that the dirt-digging condition is average. For a difficult digging condition, a job factor must be added as necessary.

APPLICATION GUIDE

In general, each luminaire in this book has been described on two facing pages. The right-hand page shows the curves, and the left-hand page describes the luminaire under consideration with related information. For convenience these items will be discussed in the same order as they are presented on each left-hand page.

Description:

This describes the type of luminaire under consideration.

Lamps:

This provides the information on the total number, individual wattage, and type of lamp used to develop the curves shown on the right-hand page. The lumen values are typical manufacturers' claimed initial values corresponding to burning position. The number of hours shown represents the approximate life of each lamp.

Lens or louvers:

These are clearly stated and are self-explanatory.

Spacing ratio:

The values determined by the product of a given spacing ratio and the mounting height represent the maximum spacing between luminaires for an even lighting distribution. Exceeding these values may result in uneven lighting distribution and cause hot spots in the room.

Visual comfort probability (VCP):

This represents a discomfort-glare calculation that predicts the percentage of observers positioned at a specific location (usually 4 ft in front of the center of the rear wall) who would be expected to judge a lighting condition to be comfortable. These figures will vary depending on the size of the room, type and number of lamps per luminaire, and the illumination level in the room. All VCP values shown in this book are based on a room of dimensions 30-ft length, 30-ft width, and 8½-ft height, having a maintained illumination level of 100 fc with the type and number of lamps per luminaire as described under Lamps. The words "length" and "cross" indicate that the luminaires are viewed lengthwise and crosswise, respectively.

Maintenance factors:

The maintenance factor takes into account the fact that the lamp lumens depreciate with time and dirt builds up on the lamp and luminaire. Three values (good/medium/poor) have been provided for each application. The first number is for an application where the air is clean, luminaires are cleaned frequently, and lamps replaced systematically. The second number is for an application where air is less favorable, luminaires cleaned fairly frequently, and lamps are replaced only after burnout. The third number is for an application where the location is dirty and the lamp cleaning and replacing procedures are poor.

Conversion factors:

These are the multiplying factors for the different types of luminaires, to be applied to the "square feet per luminaire," as read from the curves. The result shows the new area per luminaire required to have the same footcandle level for the specific luminaire. For example, on page A–17, for luminaires type A, the area per luminaire required to maintain 20 fc (say RCR = 1) as read from the curve is 150 ft^2. For luminaires type B it will be $150 \times 0.5 = 75.5$ ft^2. For some luminaires in different chapters of this book, an additional set of multiplication factors (one for each of the 10 RCRs) has been shown to convert the ceiling/wall/floor reflectances from average to low. The area per luminaire is to be multiplied by the factor shown for the specific RCR to take this change into account. In the example, the new area per luminaire will be $75 \times 0.87 = 65.25$ ft^2.

Cost details per luminaire:

Type of unit:

These items correspond to the different luminaires described under Conversion Factors.

Input (watts):

Total power in watts required to illuminate the luminaire. This includes the power consumed by the ballast(s).

Contractor's Price:

This is the typical manufacturers' published contractor's book price per luminaire, which includes the lens or louvers and the ballast(s). No lamps or luminaire fastening devices are included in these figures.

Installed cost:

This includes published contractor's book price as described above, lamps as necessary, luminaire fastening devices (a flexible metallic conduit with wires in some luminaires), and the labor required for mounting and connecting the luminaire.

Table 1 Cavity Ratio Table

Room dimensions, ft		Cavity depth, ft																			
Width	Length, ft	1.0	1.5	2.0	2.5	3.0	3.5	4.0	5.0	6.0	7.0	8	9	10	11	12	14	16	20	25	30
8	8	1.2	1.9	2.5	3.1	3.7	4.4	5.0	6.2	7.5	8.8	10.0	11.2	12.5							
	10	1.1	1.7	2.2	2.8	3.4	3.9	4.5	5.6	6.7	7.9	9.0	10.1	11.3	12.4						
	14	1.0	1.5	2.0	2.5	3.0	3.4	3.9	4.9	5.9	6.9	7.8	8.8	9.7	10.7	11.7					
	20	0.9	1.3	1.7	2.2	2.6	3.1	3.5	4.4	5.2	6.1	7.0	7.9	8.8	9.6	10.5	12.2				
	30	0.8	1.2	1.6	2.0	2.4	2.8	3.2	4.0	4.7	5.5	6.3	7.1	7.9	8.7	9.5	11.0				
	40	0.7	1.1	1.5	1.9	2.3	2.6	3.0	3.7	4.5	5.3	5.9	6.5	7.4	8.1	8.8	10.3	11.8			
10	10	1.0	1.5	2.0	2.5	3.0	3.5	4.0	5.0	6.0	7.0	8.0	9.0	10.0	11.0	12.0					
	14	0.9	1.3	1.7	2.1	2.6	3.0	3.4	4.3	5.1	6.0	6.9	7.8	8.6	9.5	10.4	12.0				
	20	0.7	1.1	1.5	1.9	2.3	2.6	3.0	3.7	4.5	5.3	6.0	6.8	7.5	8.3	9.0	10.5	12.0			
	30	0.7	1.0	1.3	1.7	2.0	2.3	2.7	3.3	4.0	4.7	5.3	6.0	6.6	7.3	8.0	9.4	10.6			
	40	0.6	0.9	1.2	1.6	1.9	2.2	2.5	3.1	3.7	4.4	5.0	5.6	6.2	6.9	7.5	8.7	10.0	12.5		
	60	0.6	0.9	1.2	1.5	1.7	2.0	2.3	2.9	3.5	4.1	4.7	5.3	5.9	6.5	7.1	8.2	9.4	11.7		
12	12	0.8	1.2	1.7	2.1	2.5	2.9	3.3	4.2	5.0	5.8	6.7	7.5	8.4	9.2	10.0	11.7				
	16	0.7	1.1	1.5	1.8	2.2	2.5	2.9	3.6	4.4	5.1	5.8	6.5	7.2	8.0	8.7	10.2	11.6			
	24	0.6	0.9	1.2	1.6	1.9	2.2	2.5	3.1	3.7	4.4	5.0	5.6	6.2	6.9	7.5	8.7	10.0	12.5		
	36	0.6	0.8	1.1	1.4	1.7	1.9	2.2	2.8	3.3	3.9	4.4	5.0	5.5	6.0	6.6	7.8	8.8	11.0		
	50	0.5	0.8	1.0	1.3	1.5	1.8	2.1	2.6	3.1	3.6	4.1	4.6	5.1	5.6	6.2	7.2	8.2	10.2		
	70	0.5	0.7	1.0	1.2	1.5	1.7	2.0	2.4	2.9	3.4	3.9	4.4	4.9	5.4	5.8	6.8	7.8	9.7	12.2	
14	14	0.7	1.1	1.4	1.8	2.1	2.5	2.9	3.6	4.3	5.0	5.7	6.4	7.1	7.8	8.5	10.0	11.4			
	20	0.6	0.9	1.2	1.5	1.8	2.1	2.4	3.0	3.6	4.2	4.9	5.5	6.1	6.7	7.3	8.6	9.8	12.3		
	30	0.5	0.8	1.0	1.3	1.6	1.8	2.1	2.6	3.1	3.7	4.2	4.7	5.2	5.8	6.3	7.3	8.4	10.5		
	42	0.5	0.7	1.0	1.2	1.4	1.7	1.9	2.4	2.9	3.3	3.8	4.3	4.7	5.2	5.7	6.7	7.6	9.5	11.9	
	60	0.4	0.7	0.9	1.1	1.3	1.5	1.8	2.2	2.6	3.1	3.5	3.9	4.4	4.8	5.2	6.1	7.0	8.8	10.9	
	90	0.4	0.6	0.8	1.0	1.2	1.4	1.6	2.0	2.5	2.9	3.3	3.7	4.1	4.5	5.0	5.8	6.6	8.3	10.3	12.4
17	17	0.6	0.9	1.2	1.5	1.8	2.1	2.3	2.9	3.5	4.1	4.7	5.3	5.9	6.5	7.0	8.2	9.4	11.7		
	25	0.5	0.7	1.0	1.2	1.5	1.7	2.0	2.5	3.0	3.5	4.0	4.5	5.0	5.5	6.0	7.0	8.0	10.0	12.5	
	35	0.4	0.7	0.9	1.1	1.3	1.5	1.7	2.2	2.6	3.1	3.5	3.9	4.4	4.8	5.2	6.1	7.0	8.7	10.9	
	50	0.4	0.6	0.8	1.0	1.2	1.4	1.6	2.0	2.4	2.8	3.1	3.5	3.9	4.3	4.5	5.4	6.2	7.7	9.7	11.6
	80	0.4	0.5	0.7	0.9	1.1	1.2	1.4	1.8	2.1	2.5	2.9	3.3	3.6	4.0	4.3	5.1	5.8	7.2	9.0	10.9
	120	0.3	0.5	0.7	0.8	1.0	1.2	1.3	1.7	2.0	2.3	2.7	3.0	3.4	3.7	4.0	4.7	5.4	6.7	8.4	10.1
20	20	0.5	0.7	1.0	1.2	1.5	1.7	2.0	2.5	3.0	3.5	4.0	4.5	5.0	5.5	6.0	7.0	8.0	10.0	12.5	–
	30	0.4	0.6	0.8	1.0	1.2	1.5	1.7	2.1	2.5	2.9	3.3	3.7	4.1	4.5	4.9	5.8	6.6	8.2	10.3	12.4
	45	0.4	0.5	0.7	0.9	1.1	1.3	1.4	1.8	2.2	2.5	2.9	3.3	3.6	4.0	4.3	5.1	5.8	7.2	9.1	10.9
	60	0.3	0.5	0.7	0.8	1.0	1.2	1.3	1.7	2.0	2.3	2.7	3.0	3.4	3.7	4.0	4.7	5.4	6.7	8.4	10.1
	90	0.3	0.5	0.6	0.8	0.9	1.1	1.2	1.5	1.8	2.1	2.4	2.7	3.0	3.3	3.6	4.2	4.8	6.0	7.5	9.0
	150	0.3	0.4	0.6	0.7	0.8	1.0	1.1	1.4	1.7	2.0	2.3	2.6	2.9	3.2	3.4	4.0	4.6	5.7	7.2	8.6
24	24	0.4	0.6	0.8	1.0	1.2	1.5	1.7	2.1	2.5	2.9	3.3	3.7	4.1	4.5	5.0	5.8	6.7	8.2	10.3	12.4
	32	0.4	0.5	0.7	0.9	1.1	1.3	1.5	1.8	2.2	2.6	2.9	3.3	3.6	4.0	4.3	5.1	5.8	7.2	9.0	11.0
	50	0.3	0.5	0.6	0.8	0.9	1.1	1.2	1.5	1.8	2.2	2.5	2.8	3.1	3.4	3.7	4.4	5.0	6.2	7.8	9.4
	70	0.3	0.4	0.6	0.7	0.8	1.0	1.1	1.4	1.7	2.0	2.2	2.5	2.8	3.0	3.3	3.8	4.4	5.5	6.9	8.2
	100	0.3	0.4	0.5	0.6	0.8	0.9	1.0	1.3	1.6	1.8	2.1	2.4	2.6	2.9	3.1	3.7	4.2	5.2	6.5	7.9
	160	0.2	0.4	0.5	0.6	0.7	0.8	1.0	1.2	1.4	1.7	1.9	2.1	2.4	2.6	2.8	3.3	3.8	4.7	5.9	7.1
30	30	0.3	0.5	0.7	0.8	1.0	1.2	1.3	1.7	2.0	2.3	2.7	3.0	3.3	3.7	4.0	4.7	5.4	6.7	8.4	10.0
	45	0.3	0.4	0.6	0.7	0.8	1.0	1.1	1.4	1.7	1.9	2.2	2.5	2.7	3.0	3.3	3.8	4.4	5.5	6.9	8.2
	60	0.3	0.4	0.5	0.6	0.7	0.9	1.0	1.2	1.5	1.7	2.0	2.2	2.5	2.7	3.0	3.5	4.0	5.0	6.2	7.4
	90	0.2	0.3	0.4	0.6	0.7	0.8	0.9	1.1	1.3	1.6	1.8	2.0	2.2	2.5	2.7	3.1	3.6	4.5	5.6	6.7
	150	0.2	0.3	0.4	0.5	0.6	0.7	0.8	1.0	1.2	1.4	1.6	1.8	2.0	2.2	2.4	2.8	3.2	4.0	5.0	5.9
	200	0.2	0.3	0.4	0.5	0.6	0.7	0.8	1.0	1.1	1.3	1.5	1.7	1.9	2.0	2.2	2.6	3.0	3.7	4.7	5.6
36	36	0.3	0.4	0.6	0.7	0.8	1.0	1.1	1.4	1.7	1.9	2.2	2.5	2.8	3.0	3.3	3.9	4.4	5.5	6.9	8.3
	50	0.2	0.4	0.5	0.6	0.7	0.8	1.0	1.2	1.4	1.7	1.9	2.1	2.5	2.6	2.9	3.3	3.8	4.8	5.9	7.2
	75	0.2	0.3	0.4	0.5	0.6	0.7	0.8	1.0	1.2	1.4	1.6	1.8	2.0	2.3	2.5	2.9	3.3	4.1	5.1	6.1
	100	0.2	0.3	0.4	0.5	0.6	0.7	0.8	0.9	1.1	1.3	1.5	1.7	1.9	2.1	2.3	2.6	3.0	3.8	4.7	5.7
	150	0.2	0.3	0.3	0.4	0.5	0.6	0.7	0.9	1.0	1.2	1.4	1.6	1.7	1.9	2.1	2.4	2.8	3.5	4.3	5.2
	200	0.2	0.2	0.3	0.4	0.5	0.6	0.7	0.8	1.0	1.1	1.3	1.5	1.6	1.8	2.0	2.3	2.6	3.3	4.1	4.9
42	42	0.2	0.4	0.5	0.6	0.7	0.8	1.0	1.2	1.4	1.6	1.9	2.1	2.4	2.6	2.8	3.3	3.8	4.7	5.9	7.1
	60	0.2	0.3	0.4	0.5	0.6	0.7	0.8	1.0	1.2	1.4	1.6	1.8	2.0	2.2	2.4	2.8	3.2	4.0	5.0	6.0
	90	0.2	0.3	0.3	0.4	0.5	0.6	0.7	0.9	1.0	1.2	1.4	1.6	1.7	1.9	2.1	2.4	2.8	3.5	4.4	5.2
	140	0.2	0.2	0.3	0.4	0.5	0.5	0.6	0.8	0.9	1.1	1.2	1.4	1.5	1.7	1.9	2.2	2.5	3.1	3.9	4.6
	200	0.1	0.2	0.3	0.4	0.4	0.5	0.6	0.7	0.9	1.0	1.1	1.3	1.4	1.6	1.7	2.0	2.3	2.9	3.6	4.3
	300	0.1	0.2	0.3	0.3	0.4	0.5	0.5	0.7	0.8	0.9	1.1	1.3	1.4	1.5	1.7	1.9	2.2	2.8	3.5	4.2
50	50	0.2	0.3	0.4	0.5	0.6	0.7	0.8	1.0	1.2	1.4	1.6	1.8	2.0	2.2	2.4	2.8	3.2	4.0	5.0	6.0
	70	0.2	0.3	0.3	0.4	0.5	0.6	0.7	0.9	1.0	1.2	1.4	1.5	1.7	1.9	2.0	2.4	2.7	3.4	4.3	5.1
	100	0.1	0.2	0.3	0.4	0.4	0.5	0.6	0.7	0.9	1.0	1.2	1.3	1.5	1.6	1.8	2.1	2.4	3.0	3.7	4.5
	150	0.1	0.2	0.3	0.3	0.4	0.5	0.5	0.7	0.8	0.9	1.1	1.2	1.3	1.5	1.6	1.9	2.1	2.7	3.3	4.0
	300	0.1	0.2	0.2	0.3	0.3	0.4	0.5	0.6	0.7	0.8	0.9	1.0	1.1	1.3	1.4	1.6	1.9	2.3	2.9	3.5
60	60	0.2	0.2	0.3	0.4	0.5	0.6	0.7	0.8	1.0	1.2	1.3	1.5	1.7	1.8	2.0	2.3	2.7	3.3	4.2	5.0
	100	0.1	0.2	0.3	0.3	0.4	0.5	0.5	0.7	0.8	0.9	1.1	1.2	1.3	1.5	1.6	1.9	2.1	2.7	3.3	4.0
	150	0.1	0.2	0.2	0.3	0.3	0.4	0.5	0.6	0.7	0.8	0.9	1.0	1.2	1.3	1.4	1.6	1.9	2.3	2.9	3.5
	300	0.1	0.1	0.2	0.2	0.3	0.3	0.4	0.5	0.6	0.7	0.8	0.9	1.0	1.1	1.2	1.4	1.6	2.0	2.5	3.0
75	75	0.1	0.2	0.3	0.3	0.4	0.5	0.5	0.7	0.8	0.9	1.1	1.2	1.3	1.5	1.6	1.9	2.1	2.7	3.3	4.0
	120	0.1	0.2	0.2	0.3	0.3	0.4	0.4	0.5	0.6	0.8	0.9	1.0	1.1	1.2	1.3	1.5	1.7	2.2	2.7	3.3
	200	0.1	0.1	0.2	0.2	0.3	0.3	0.4	0.5	0.5	0.6	0.7	0.8	0.9	1.0	1.1	1.3	1.5	1.8	2.3	2.7
	300	0.1	0.1	0.2	0.2	0.2	0.3	0.3	0.4	0.5	0.6	0.7	0.7	0.8	0.9	1.0	1.2	1.3	1.7	2.1	2.5
100	100	0.1	0.1	0.2	0.2	0.3	0.3	0.4	0.5	0.6	0.7	0.8	0.9	1.0	1.1	1.2	1.4	1.6	2.0	2.5	3.0
	200	0.1	0.1	0.1	0.2	0.2	0.3	0.3	0.4	0.4	0.5	0.6	0.7	0.7	0.8	0.9	1.0	1.2	1.5	1.9	2.2
	300	0.1	0.1	0.1	0.2	0.2	0.2	0.3	0.3	0.4	0.5	0.5	0.6	0.7	0.7	0.8	0.9	1.1	1.3	1.7	2.0
150	150	0.1	0.1	0.1	0.2	0.2	0.2	0.3	0.3	0.4	0.5	0.5	0.6	0.7	0.7	0.8	0.9	1.1	1.3	1.7	2.0
	300		0.1	0.1	0.1	0.1	0.2	0.2	0.2	0.3	0.3	0.4	0.5	0.5	0.6	0.6	0.7	0.8	1.0	1.2	1.5
200	200		0.1	0.1	0.1	0.1	0.2	0.2	0.2	0.3	0.3	0.4	0.5	0.5	0.6	0.6	0.7	0.8	1.0	1.2	1.5
	300		0.1	0.1	0.1	0.1	0.1	0.2	0.2	0.2	0.3	0.3	0.4	0.4	0.5	0.5	0.6	0.7	0.8	1.0	1.2
300	300			0.1	0.1	0.1	0.1	0.1	0.2	0.2	0.2	0.3	0.3	0.3	0.4	0.4	0.5	0.5	0.6	0.7	0.8
500	500					0.1	0.1	0.1	0.1	0.1	0.1	0.2	0.2	0.2	0.2	0.2	0.3	0.3	0.4	0.5	0.6

Rapid Lighting Design and Cost Estimating

A

Surface-Mount Fluorescent Enclosed

WRAPAROUND

Corridor, 1, 2, or 4 Lamps A-2
Low-Profile, 2 or 4 Lamps A-4
Low-Profile, 2, 4, or 8 Lamps A-6
Traditional, 2 or 4 Lamps A-8
Traditional, 4 or 8 Lamps A-10
Scissors-Curve, 2 or 4 Lamps A-12
Premium, 2, 4, or 8 Lamps A-14

SPECIAL-PURPOSE WRAPAROUND

Enclosed and Gasketed, 1 or 2 Lamps A-16

OPEN-LOUVERED UNITS

With 2 Lamps A-18
With 4 Lamps A-20

MODULAR UNITS

1- × 4-ft (Acrylic Prismatic Lens), 2 Lamps A-22
2- × 2-ft (Acrylic Prismatic Lens), 2 or 3 Lamps A-24
2- × 4-ft (Acrylic Prismatic Lens), 2, 3, or 4 Lamps A-26
4- × 4-ft (Acrylic Prismatic Lens), 6 or 8 Lamps A-28
1- × 4-ft (Dropped-Dish), 2 Lamps A-30
2- × 4-ft (Dropped-Dish), 2 or 4 Lamps A-32
1- × 4-ft (Plastic-Cube Louvers), 2 Lamps A-34
2- × 4-ft (Plastic-Cube Louvers), 2 or 4 Lamps A-36

CEILING OUTLETS FOR LUMINAIRES

Installed Cost of Flush-mounted Outlets A-38

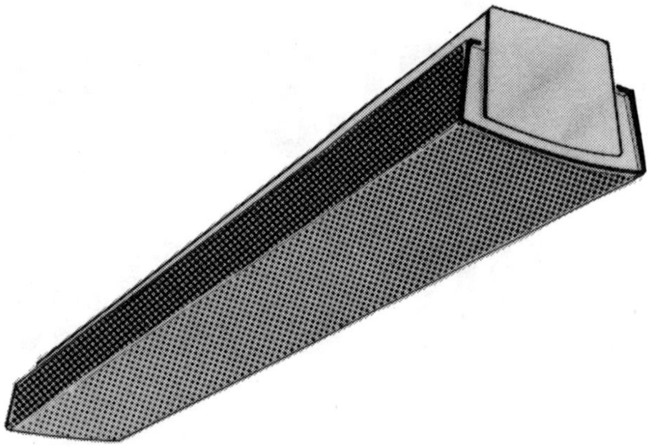

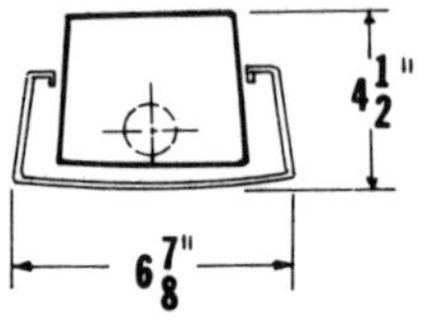

Description	Corridor wraparound
Lamps	One F40 T12, 3200 lm, 20,000 h
Lens	Acrylic prismatic
Spacing ratio	1.4
Visual comfort probability	70 (length)/60 (cross)
Maintenance factors	0.75/0.70/0.65
Conversion factors	A. 4-ft unit with one F40 T12 lamp = 1.0
	B. 4-ft unit with two F40 T12 lamps = 2.0
	C. 8-ft unit with two F40 T12 lamps = 2.0
	D. 8-ft unit with four F40 T12 lamps = 4.0

COST DETAILS PER LUMINAIRE

Type of unit	Input, W	Contractor's price	Installed cost
A	53	$28	$48.50
B	93	29	51.75
C	93	46	76.00
D	186	59	98.75

The installed cost includes published contractor's book price for the luminaire with lens and ballasts, number of lamps as shown, luminaire fastening devices, and the labor required for surface mounting and connection of the luminaire. See page A–38 for a luminaire outlet.

These luminaires are particularly used in hallway, stairway, display, library stacks, and entrance areas where high levels of linear or vertical illumination are required.

SURFACE MOUNT FLUORESCENT—CORRIDOR WRAPAROUND

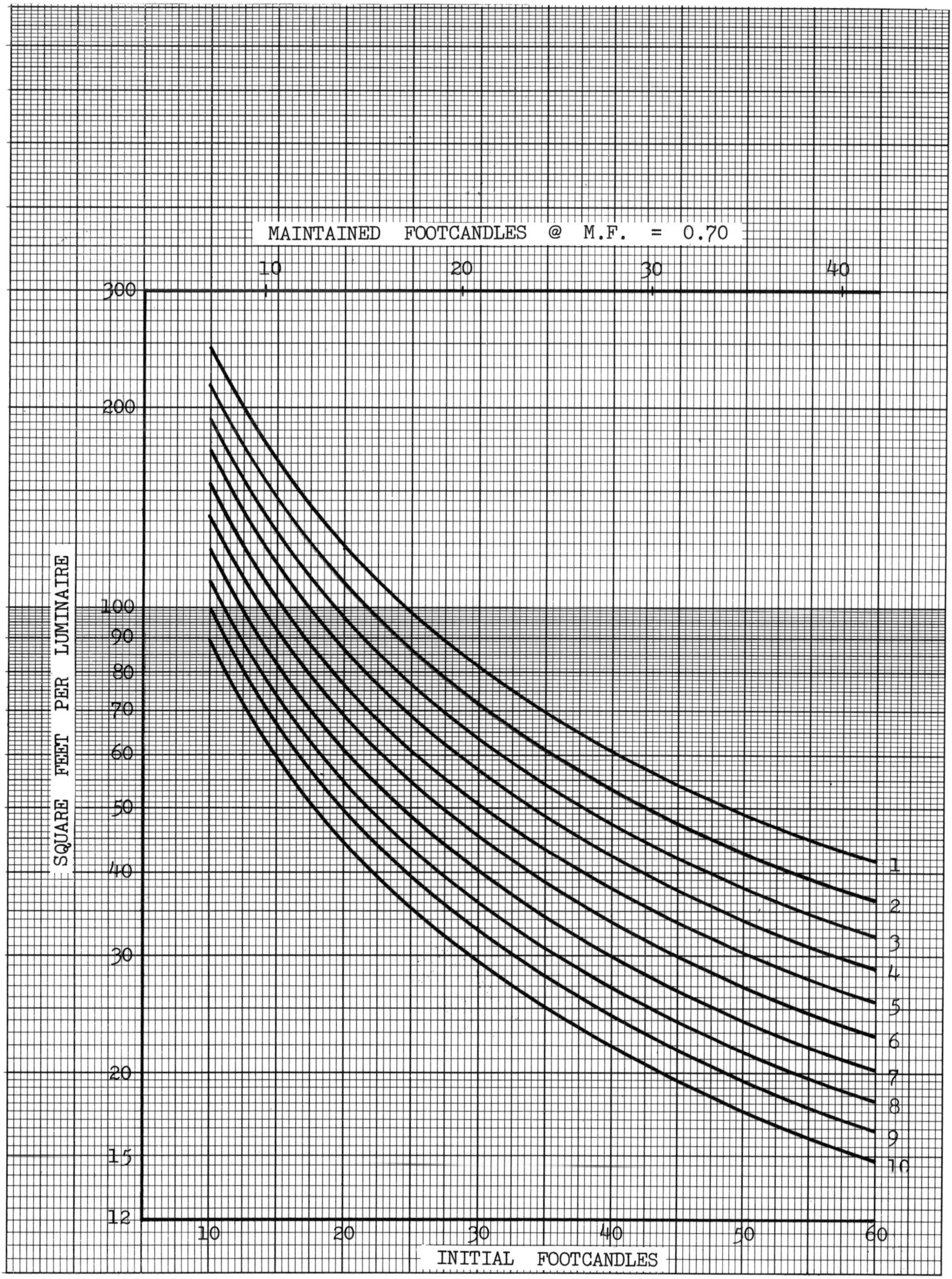

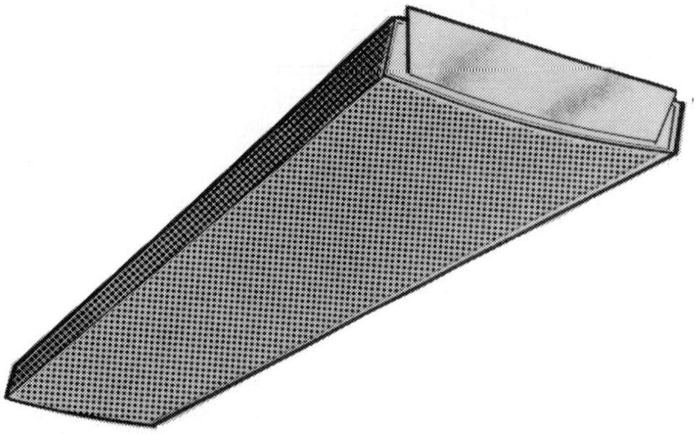

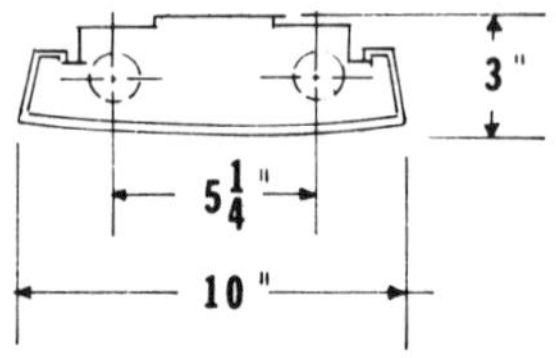

Description	Low-profile wraparound
Lamps	Two F40 T12, 3200 lm each, 20,000 h
Lens	Acrylic prismatic
Spacing ratio	1.4
Visual comfort probability	64 (length)/59 (cross)
Maintenance factors	0.75/0.70/0.65
Conversion factors	A. 4-ft unit with two F40 T12 lamps = 1.0 B. 8-ft unit with four F40 T12 lamps = 2.0

COST DETAILS PER LUMINAIRE

Type of unit	Input, W	Contractor's price	Installed cost
A	93	\$32	\$ 55.50
B	186	64	102.50

The installed cost includes published contractor's book price for the luminaire with lens and ballasts, number of lamps as shown, luminaire fastening devices, and the labor required for surface mounting and connection of the luminaire. See page A–38 to add a luminaire outlet.

This narrow and low-profile line of wraparound luminaire is used mostly in library stacks, corridors, and stairway and entry lighting for institutional and commercial applications.

SURFACE MOUNT FLUORESCENT – LOW PROFILE WRAPAROUND

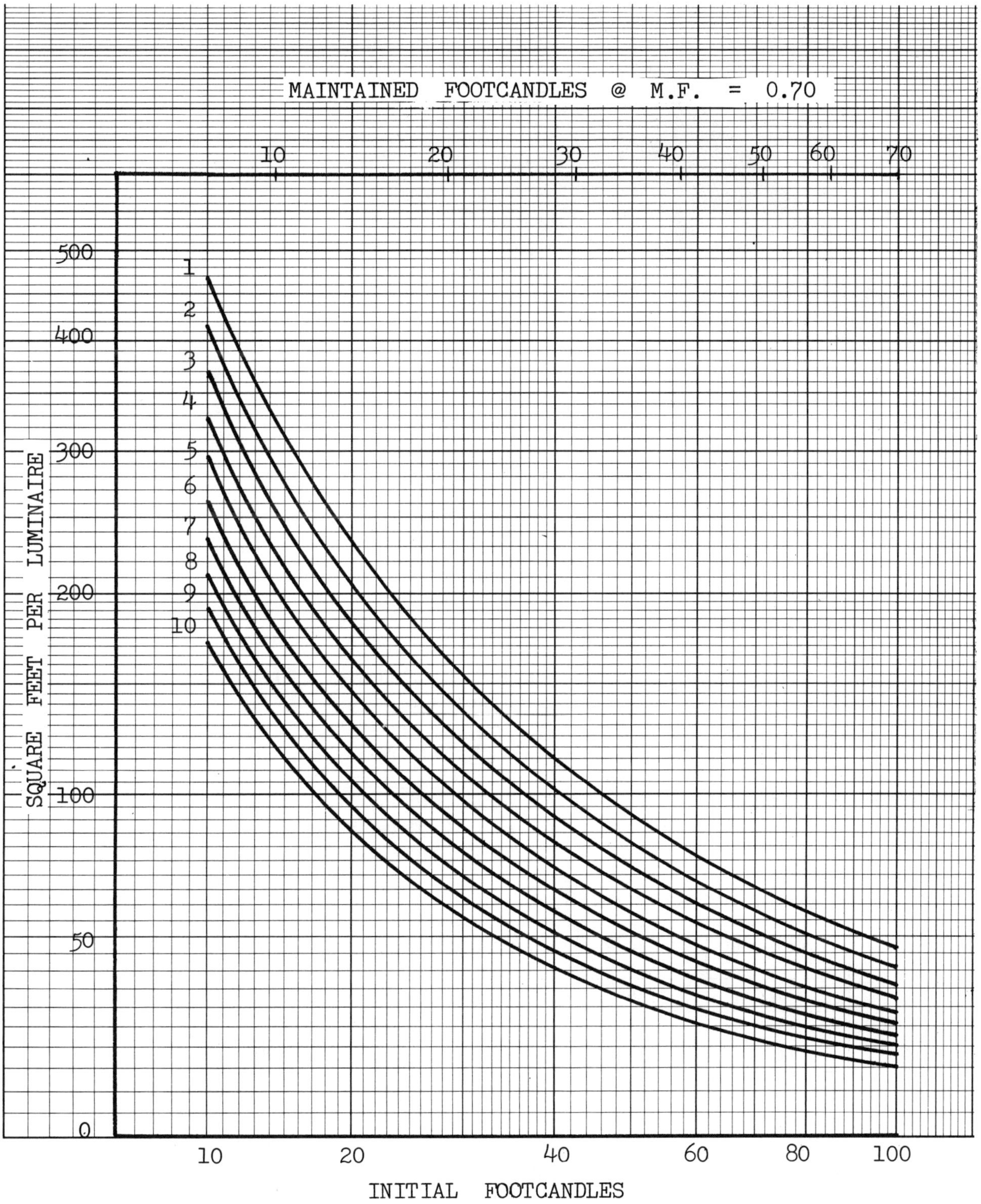

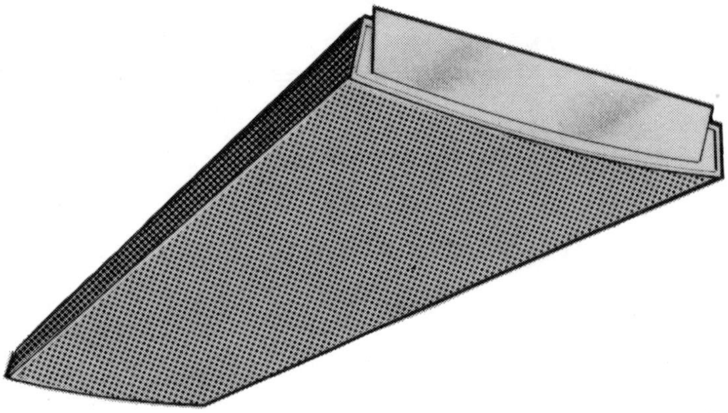

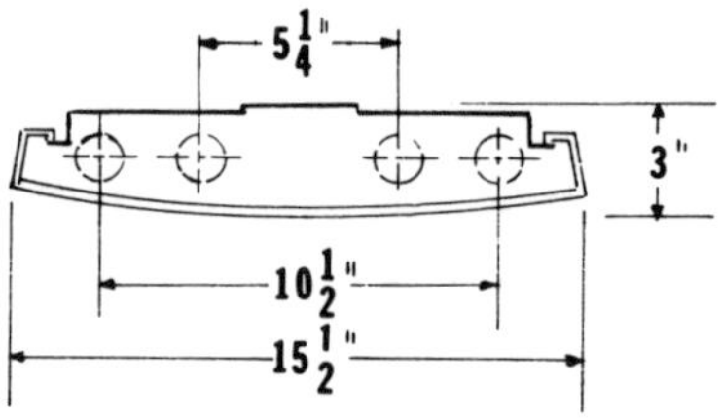

Description	Low-profile wraparound
Lamps	Four F40 T12, 3200 lm each, 20,000 h
Lens	Acrylic prismatic
Spacing ratio	1.4
Visual comfort probability	60 (length)/54 (cross)
Maintenance factors	0.75/0.70/0.65
Conversion factors	A. 4-ft unit with four F40 T12 lamps = 1.0
	B. 4-ft unit with two F40 T12 lamps = 0.5
	C. 8-ft unit with eight F40 T12 lamps = 2.0

COST DETAILS PER LUMINAIRE

Type of unit	Input, W	Contractor's price	Installed cost
A	186	$ 54	$ 88.50
B	93	50	77.75
C	372	108	164.00

The installed cost includes published contractor's book price for the luminaire with lens and ballasts, number of lamps as shown, luminaire fastening devices, and the labor required for surface mounting and connection of the luminaire. *See page A–38 to add a luminaire outlet.*

This narrow and low-profile line of wraparound luminaires is ideally suitable for applications where a high level of illumination is required from limited ceiling space.

SURFACE MOUNT FLUORESCENT – LOW PROFILE WRAPAROUND

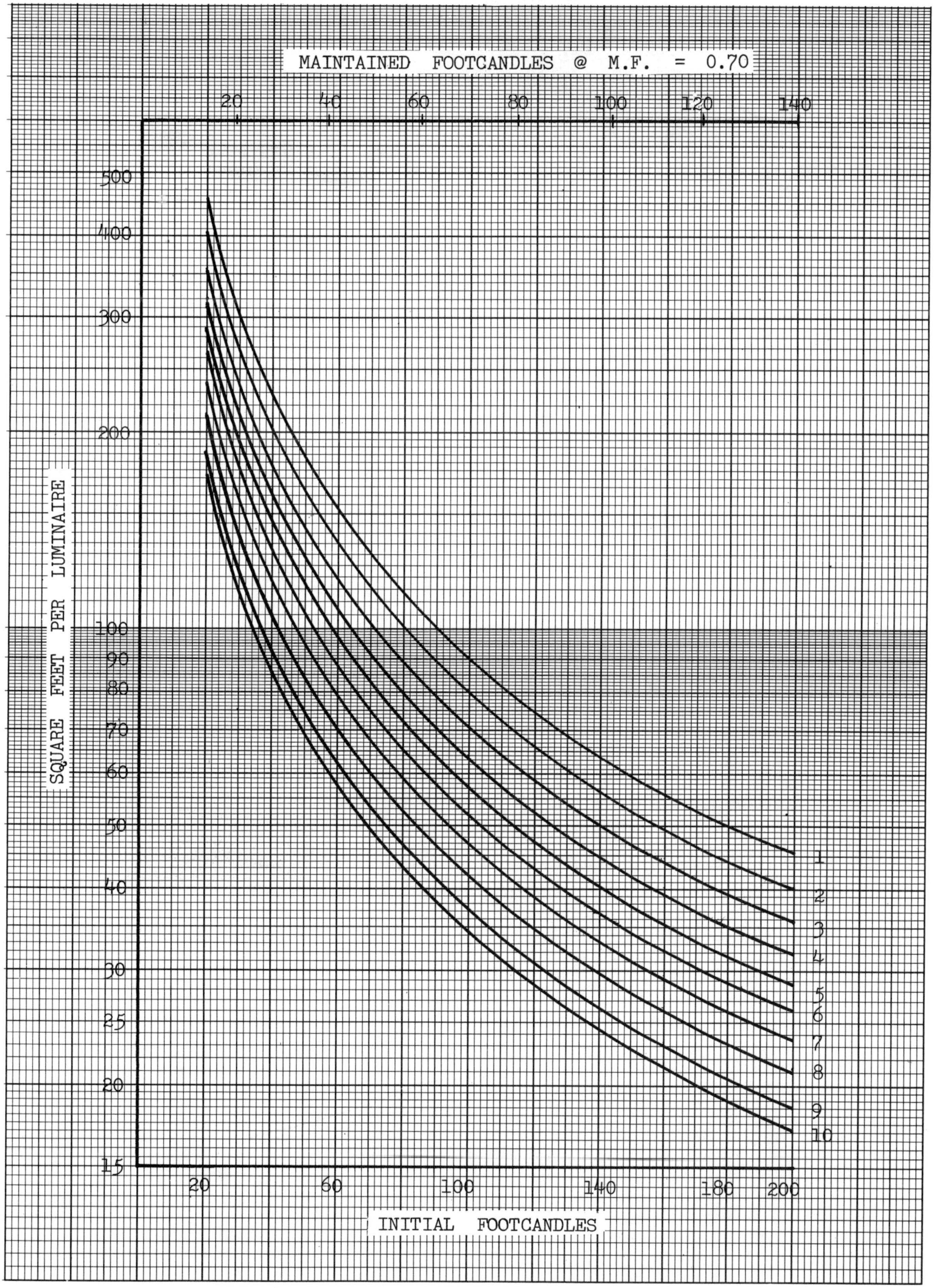

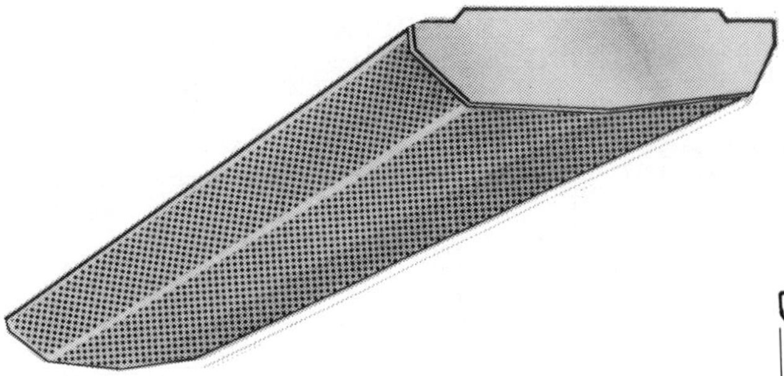

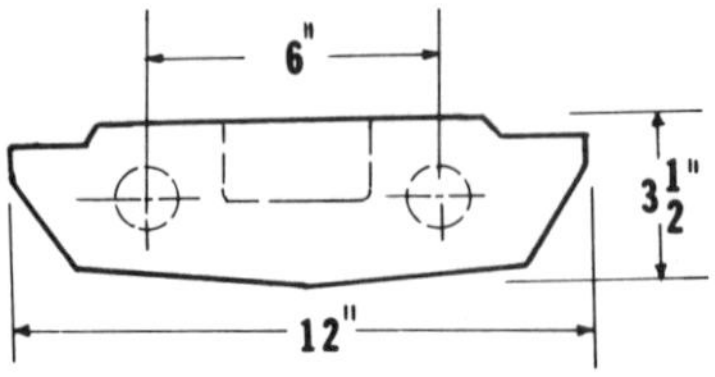

Description	Traditional wraparound
Lamps	Two F40 T12, 3200 lm each, 20,000 h
Lens	Acrylic prismatic
Spacing ratio	1.3
Visual comfort probability	68 (length)/54 (cross)
Maintenance factors	0.75/0.70/0.65
Conversion factors	Unit with polystyrene prismatic lens = 0.98
	A. 4-ft unit with two F40 T12 lamps = 1.00
	B. 8-ft unit with four F40 T12 lamps = 2.00
	C. 8-ft unit with two F96 T12 lamps = 2.00

COST DETAILS PER LUMINAIRE

Type of unit	Input, W	Contractor's price	Installed cost
A	93	$33	$ 56.75
B	186	66	105.00
C	173	66	105.00

The installed cost includes published contractor's book price for the luminaire with lens and ballasts, number of lamps as shown, luminaire fastening devices, and the labor required for surface mounting and connection of the luminaire. *See page A–38 to add a luminaire outlet.*

These closed-top traditional wraparound luminaires are used mostly in offices, schools, and other commercial and institutional applications.

SURFACE MOUNT FLUORESCENT – TRADITIONAL WRAPAROUND

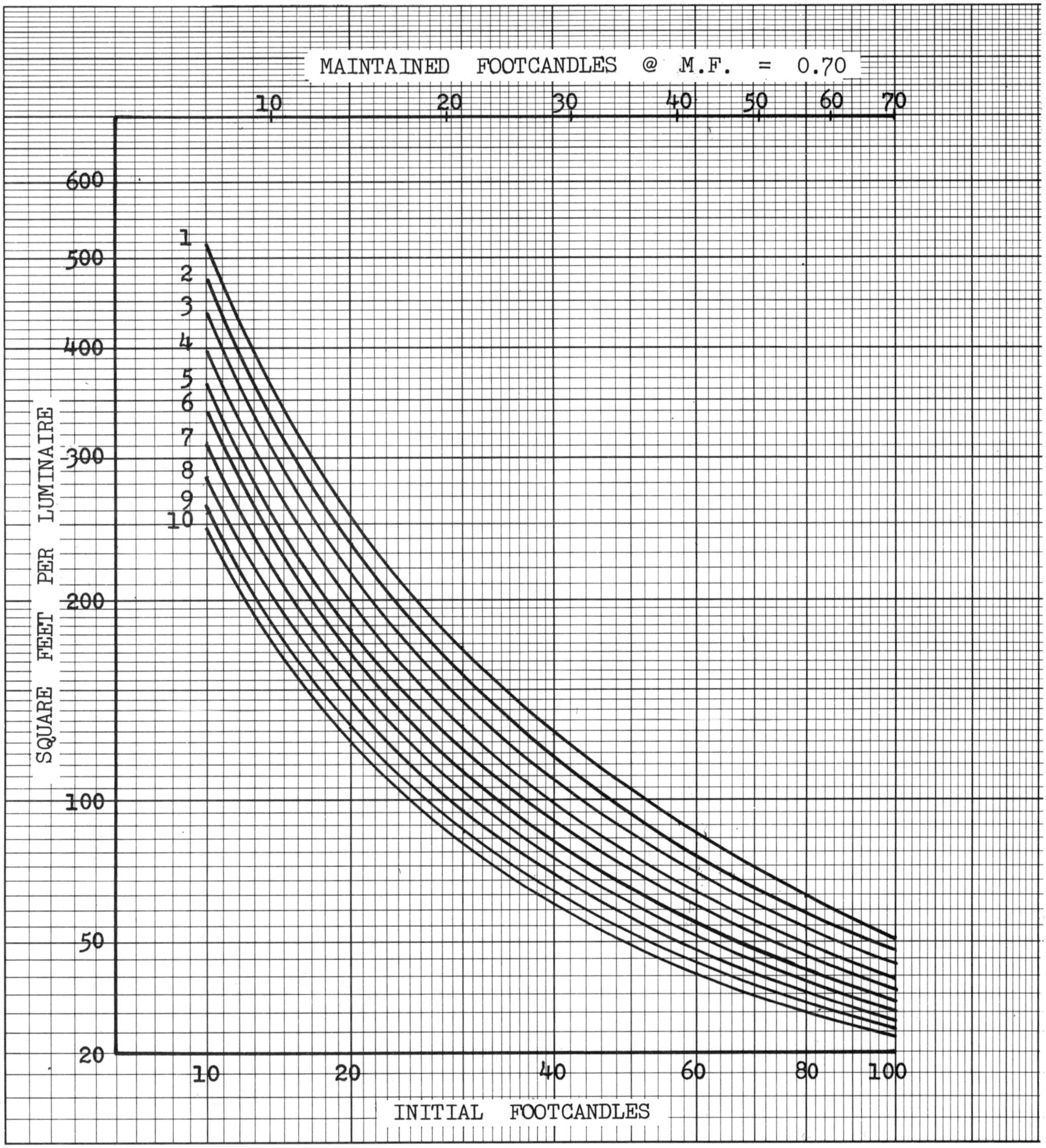

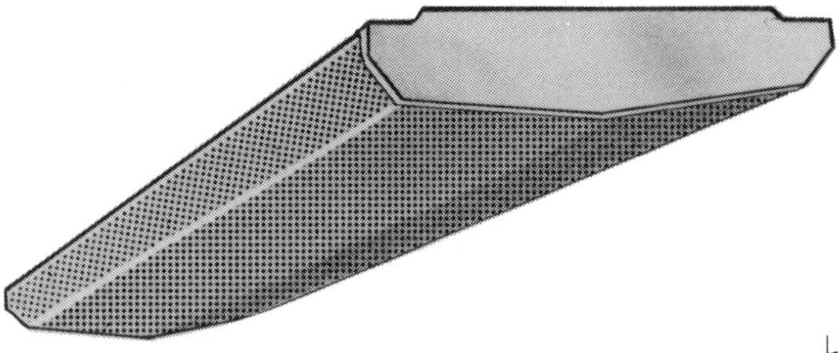

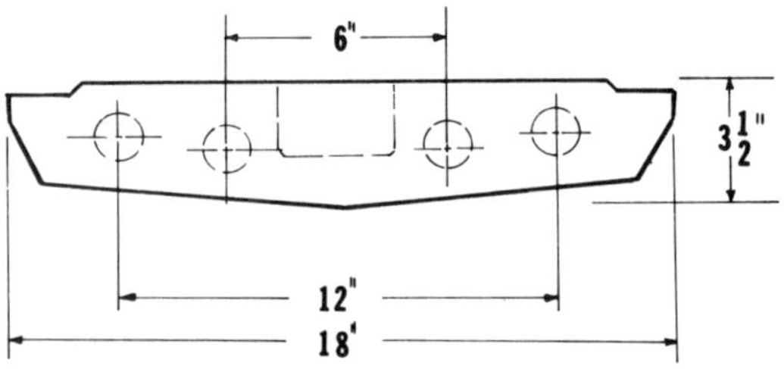

Description	Traditional wraparound
Lamps	Four F40 T12, 3200 lm each, 20,000 h
Lens	Acrylic prismatic
Spacing ratio	1.3
Visual comfort probability	55 (length)/40 (cross)
Maintenance factors	0.75/0.70/0.65
Conversion factors	Unit with polystyrene prismatic lens = 0.98
	A. 4-ft unit with four F40 T12 lamps = 1.00
	B. 8-ft unit with eight F40 T12 lamps = 2.00

COST DETAILS PER LUMINAIRE

Type of unit	Input, W	Contractor's price	Installed cost
A	186	$ 56	$ 91
B	372	112	169

The installed cost includes published contractor's book price for the luminaire with lens and ballasts, number of lamps as shown, luminaire fastening devices, and the labor required for surface mounting and connection of the luminaire. See page A–38 to add a luminaire outlet.

These traditional wraparound luminaires are used mostly in offices, schools, and other commercial and institutional applications.

SURFACE MOUNT FLUORESCENT – TRADITIONAL WRAPAROUND

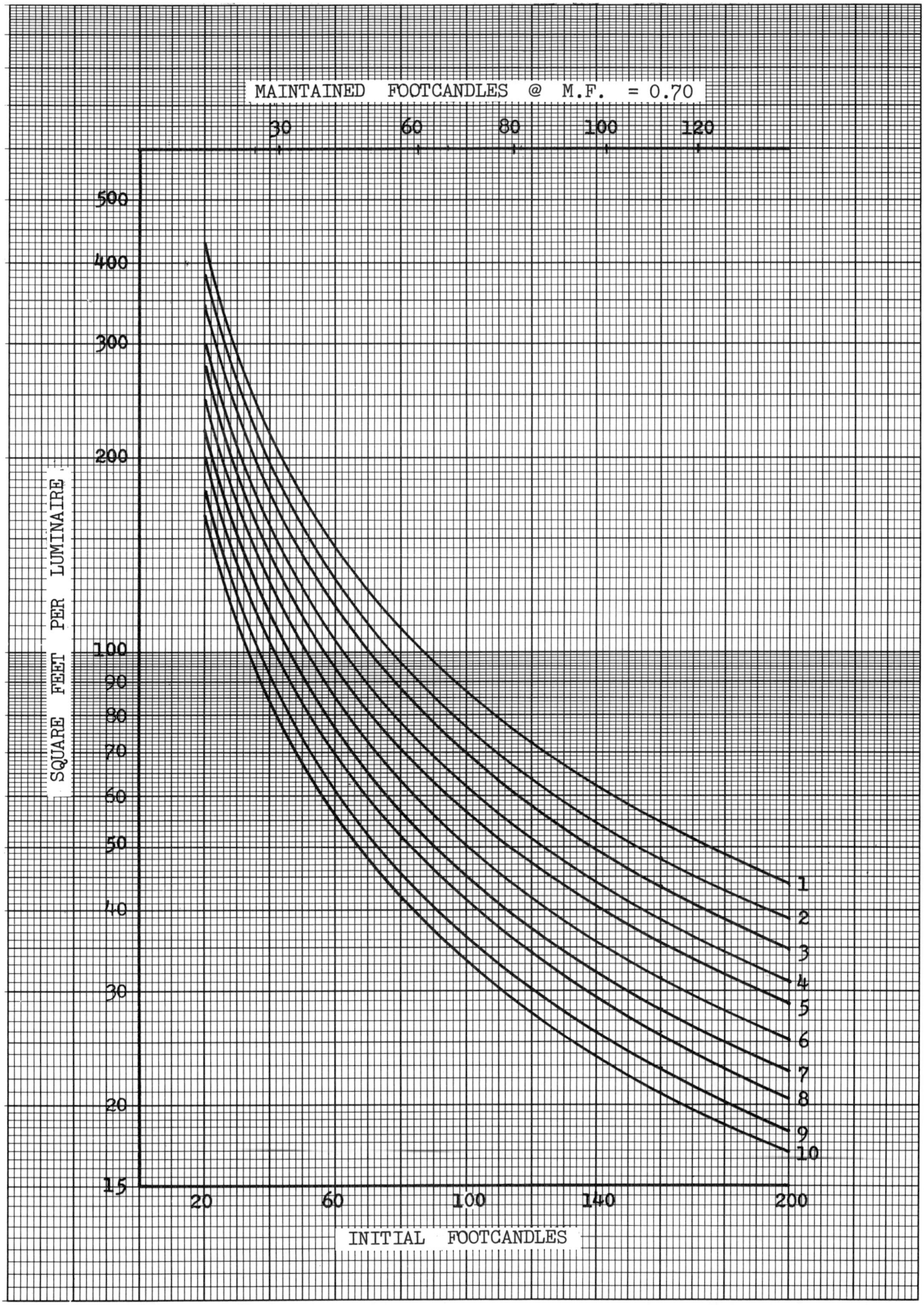

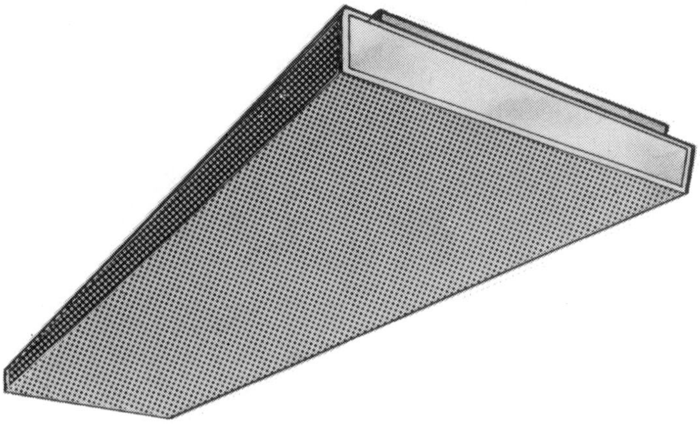

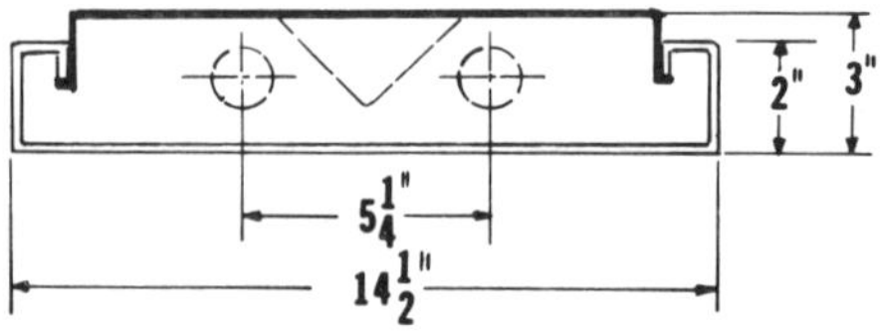

Description	Scissors-curve wraparound
Lamps	Two F40 T12, 3200 lm each, 20,000 h
Lens	Acrylic prismatic (scissors-curve)
Spacing ratio	1.4
Visual comfort probability	82 (length)/77 (cross)
Maintenance factors	0.75/0.70/0.65
Conversion factors	A. 4-ft unit with two F40 T12 lamps = 1.0 B. 8-ft unit with four F40 T12 lamps = 2.0

COST DETAILS PER LUMINAIRE

Type of unit	Input, W	Contractor's price	Installed cost
A	93	$46	$ 72.75
B	186	92	136.75

The installed cost includes published contractor's book price for the luminaire with lens and ballasts, number of lamps as shown, luminaire fastening devices, and the labor required for surface mounting and connection of the luminaire. *See page A–38 to add a luminaire outlet.*

Scissors-curve wraparound luminaires, with high visual comfort probability, are ideally suitable for applications where a high level of illumination is required with minimum distracting glare.

SURFACE MOUNT FLUORESCENT – SCISSORS CURVE WRAPAROUND

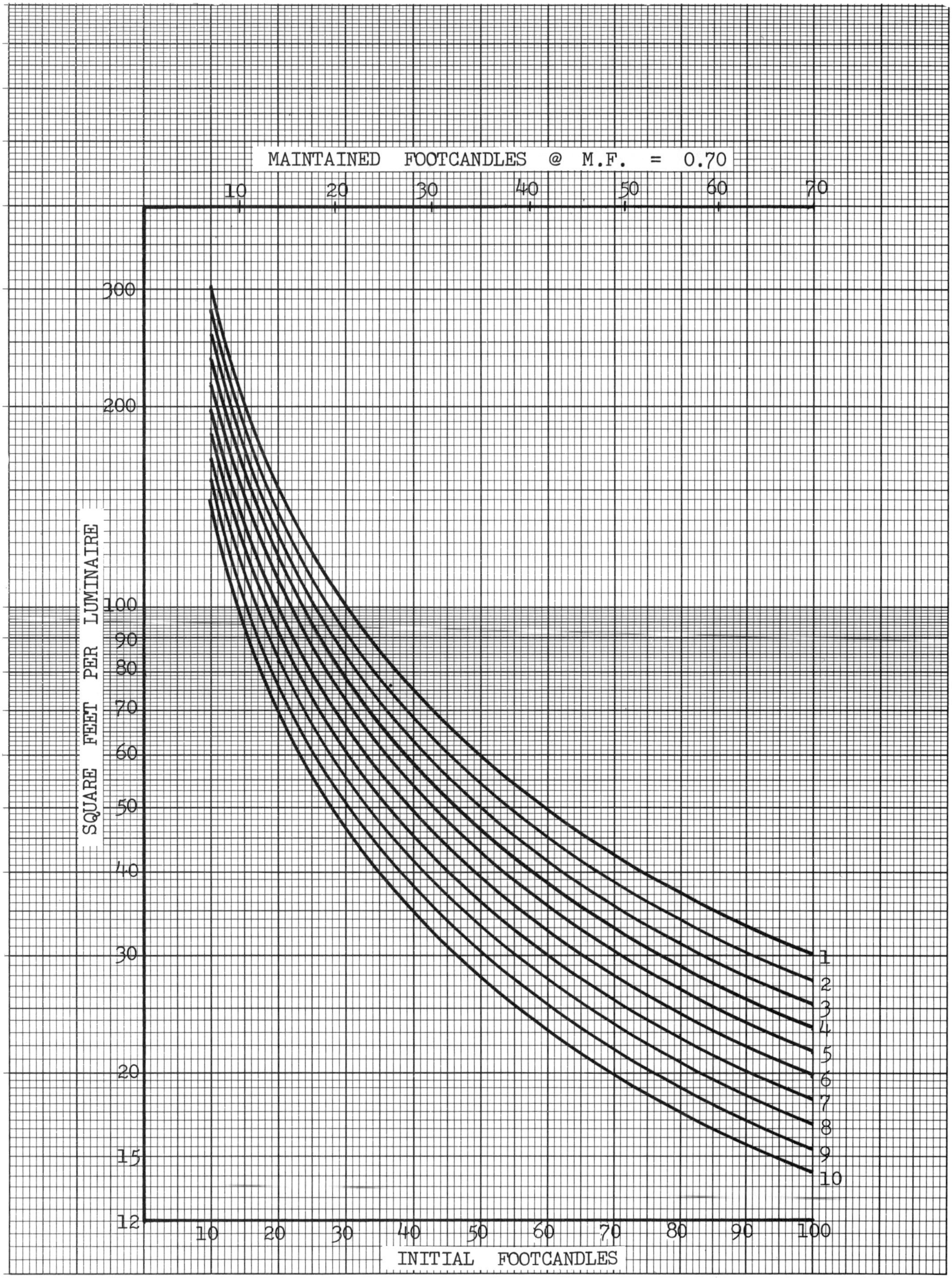

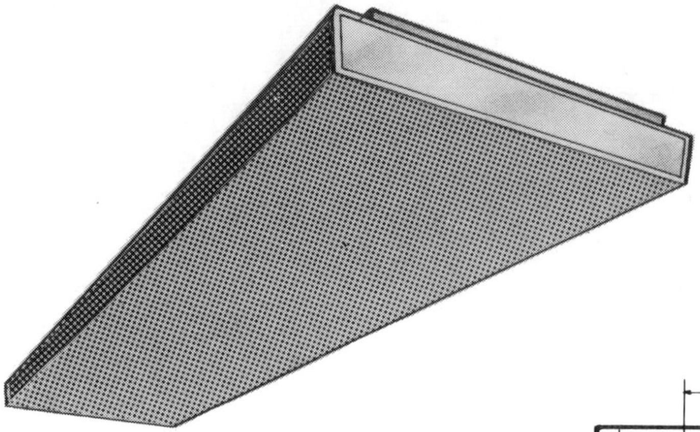

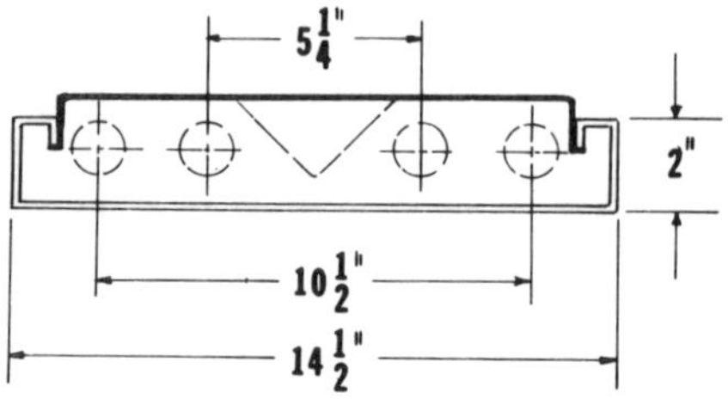

Description	Premium wraparound
Lamps	Four F40 T12, 3200 lm each, 20,000 h
Lens	Acrylic prismatic
Spacing ratio	1.4
Visual comfort probability	67 (length)/62 (cross)
Maintenance factors	0.75/0.70/0.65
Conversion factors	A. 4-ft unit with four F40 T12 lamps = 1.0
	B. 4-ft unit with two F40 T12 lamps = 0.5
	C. 8-ft unit with eight F40 T12 lamps = 2.0

COST DETAILS PER LUMINAIRE

Type of unit	Input, W	Contractor's price	Installed cost
A	186	$ 56	$ 91
B	93	41	66.50
C	372	112	169

The installed cost includes published contractor's book price for the luminaire with lens and ballasts, number of lamps as shown, luminaire fastening devices, and the labor required for surface mounting and connection of the luminaire. *See page A–38 to add a luminaire outlet.*

This narrow and low-profile line of luminaires is ideally suitable for applications where a high level of illumination is required from limited ceiling space.

SURFACE MOUNT FLUORESCENT – PREMIUM WRAPAROUND

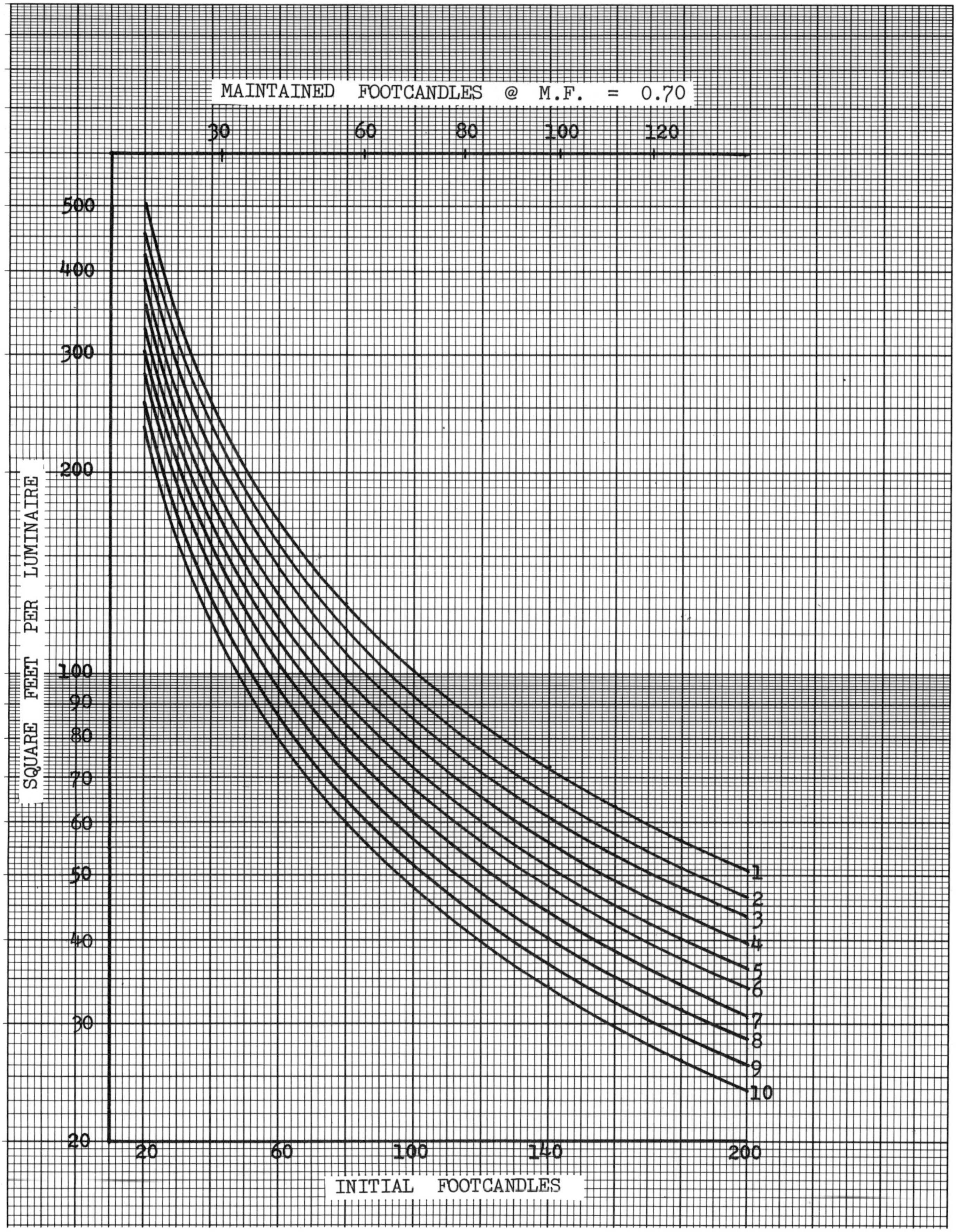

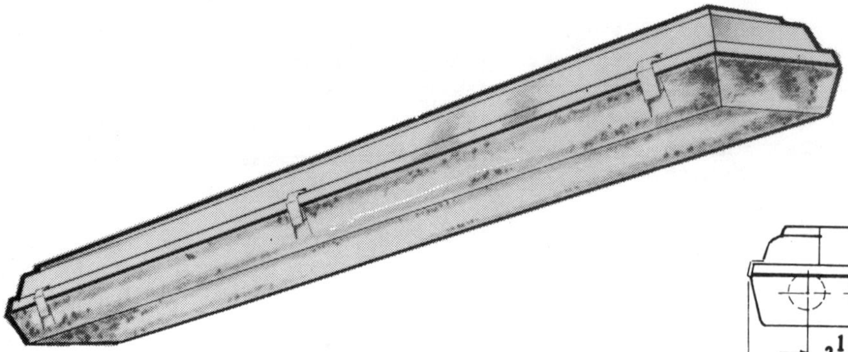

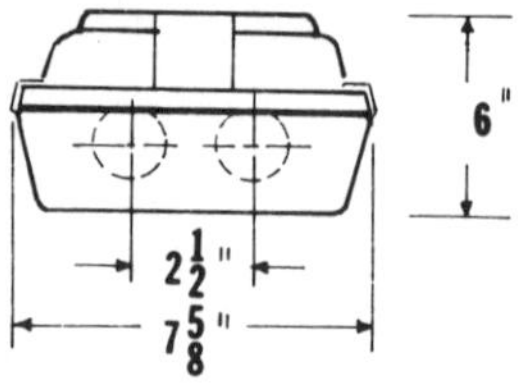

Description	Enclosed and gasketed wraparound
Lamps	Two F40 T12, 3200 lm each, 20,000 h
Lens	High-impact acrylic with stippled interior pattern and smooth exterior
Spacing ratio	1.4
Maintenance factors	0.70/0.65/0.60
Conversion factors	A. 4-ft unit with two F40 T12 lamps = 1.0 B. 4-ft unit with one F40 T12 lamp = 0.5 C. 8-ft unit with two F96 T12 lamps = 2.0 D. 8-ft unit with two F96 T12HO = 2.75

COST DETAILS PER LUMINAIRE

Type of unit	Input, W	Contractor's price	Installed cost
A	93	$ 49	$ 76.50
B	53	49	74.25
C	186	101	144.50
D	241	123	177.50

The installed cost includes published contractor's book price for the luminaire with lens and ballasts, number of lamps as shown, luminaire fastening devices, and labor required for surface mounting and connection of the luminaire. See page A–38 to add a luminaire outlet.

Use the factors shown on page A–18 for an application where the ceiling, wall, and floor reflectances are low.

Enclosed and gasketed luminaires of this line with high-impact acrylic diffuser are ideally suitable for chemical processing, breweries, construction sites, car wash, or any site with dust, moisture, heat, or corrosive abuse. The high-impact lens increases the strength by approximately 8 times over standard acrylic.

SURFACE MOUNT FLUORESCENT – ENCLOSED AND GASKETED

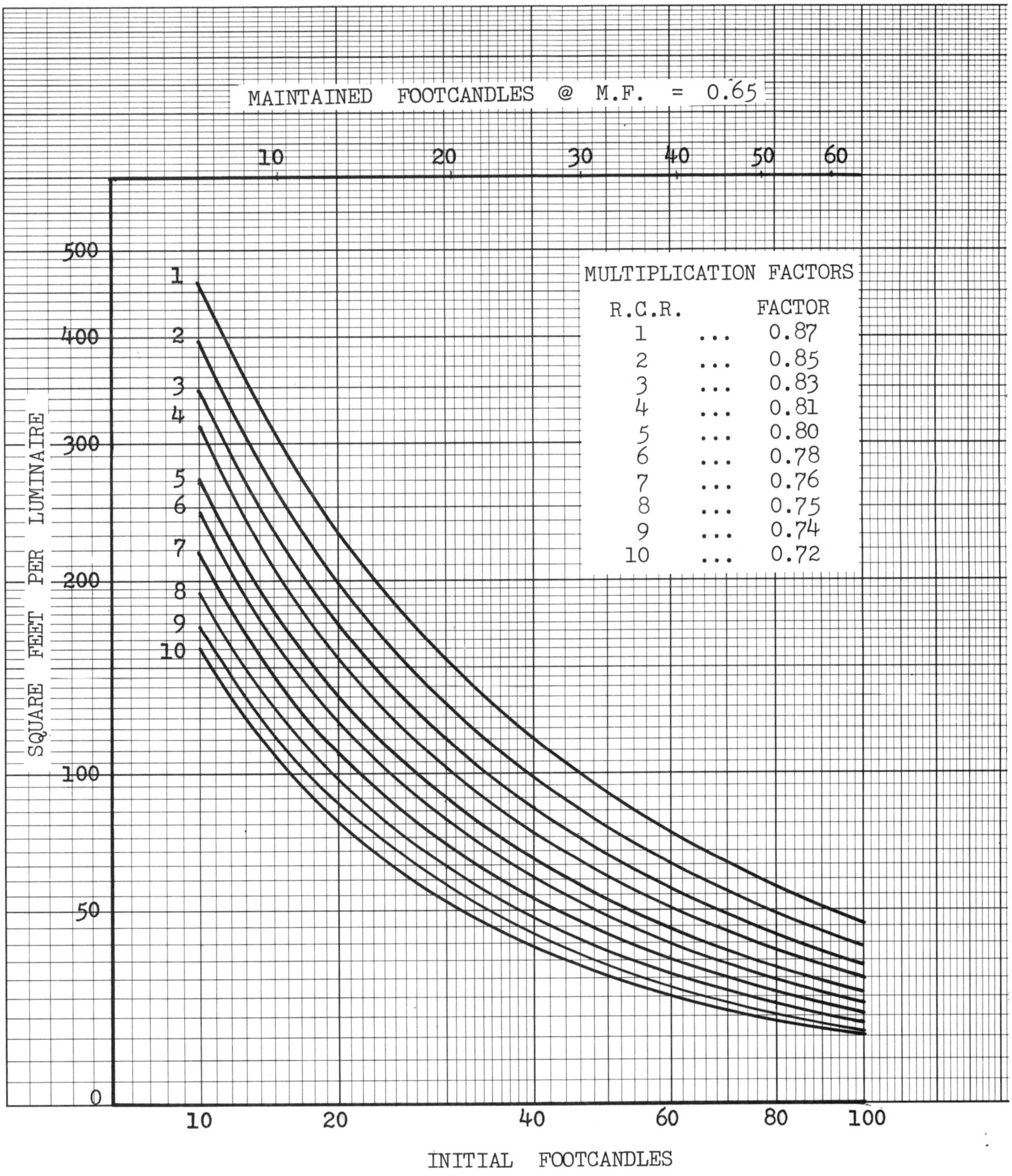

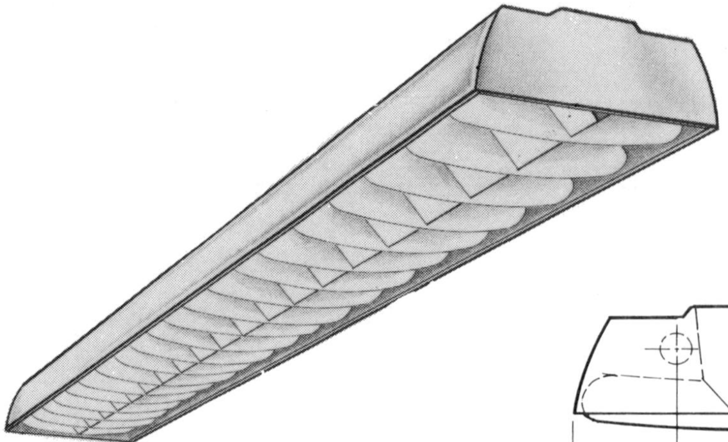

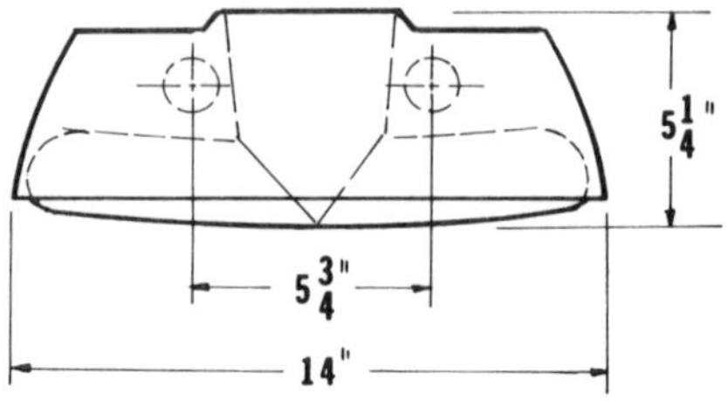

Description	Open-louvered unit
Lamps	Two F40 T12, 3200 lm each, 20,000 h
Louver	35 X 25°
Spacing ratio	1.3 (for 35 X 25° louver) 1.5 (for 35 X 45° louver)
Visual comfort probability	85 (length)/82 (cross)
Maintenance factors	0.75/0.70/0.65
Conversion factors	A. 4-ft unit, metal sides, 35 X 25° louvers = 1.0 B. 4-ft unit, plastic sides, 35 X 25° louvers = 0.98 C. 4-ft unit, metal sides, 35 X 45° louvers = 0.98 D. 4-ft unit, plastic sides, 35 X 45° louvers = 0.97

COST DETAILS PER LUMINAIRE

Type of unit	Input, W	Contractor's price	Installed cost
A	93	$34	$58
B	93	35	59.25
C	93	35	59.25
D	93	36	60.50

The installed cost includes published contractor's book price for the luminaire with louvers and ballasts, number of lamps as shown, luminaire fastening devices, and the labor required for surface mounting and connection of the luminaire. See page A–38 to add a luminaire outlet.

These open-louvered units, with high visual comfort probability, meet the scissors-curve brightness standards for school lighting and are also popular for post office and store lighting.

SURFACE MOUNT FLUORESCENT — OPEN LOUVERED

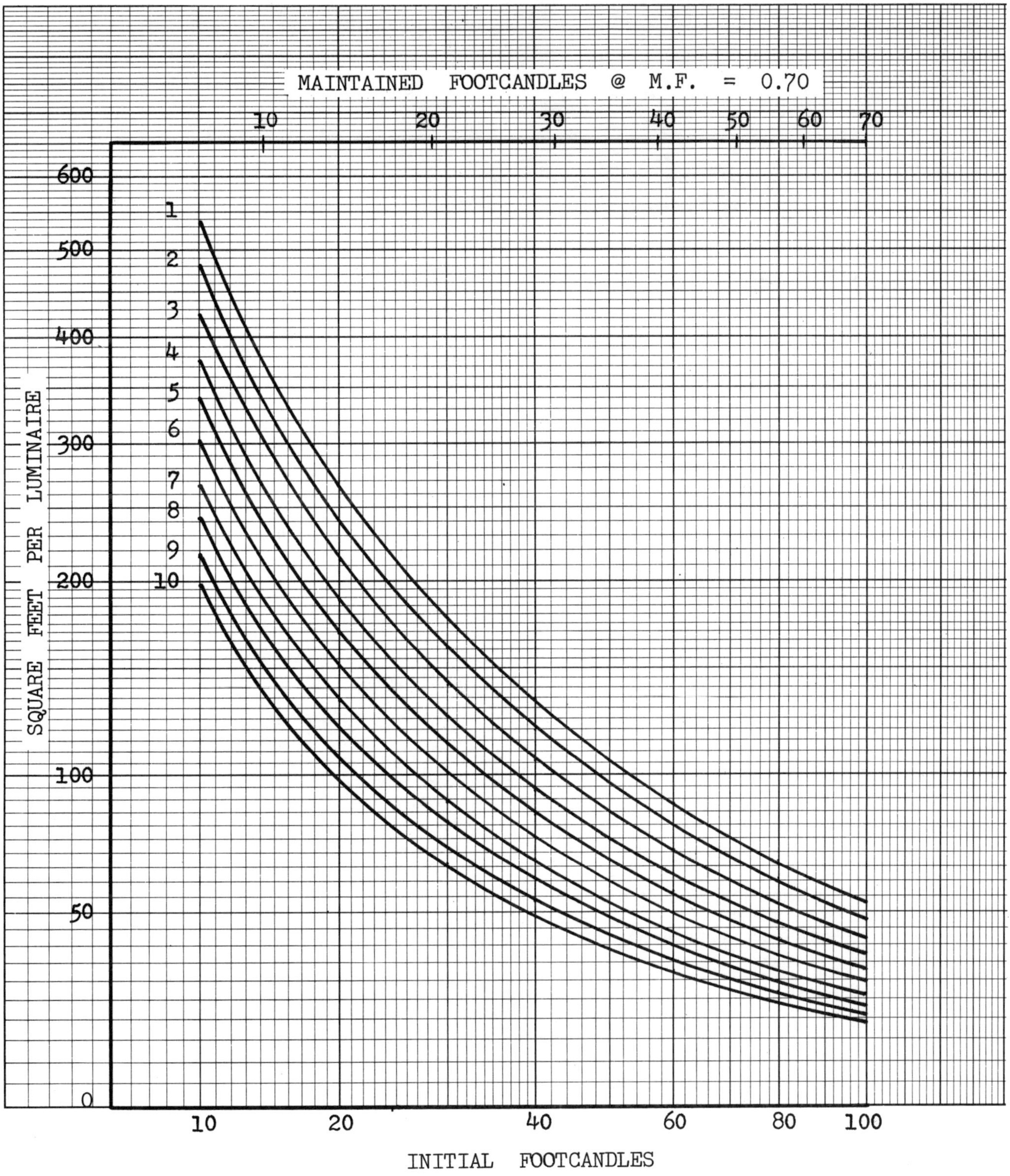

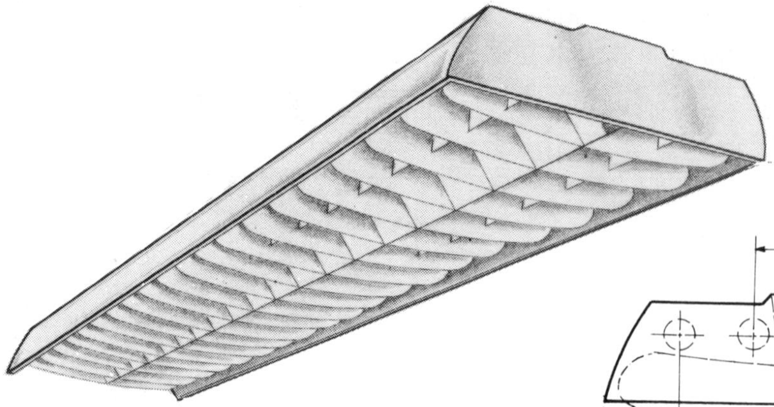

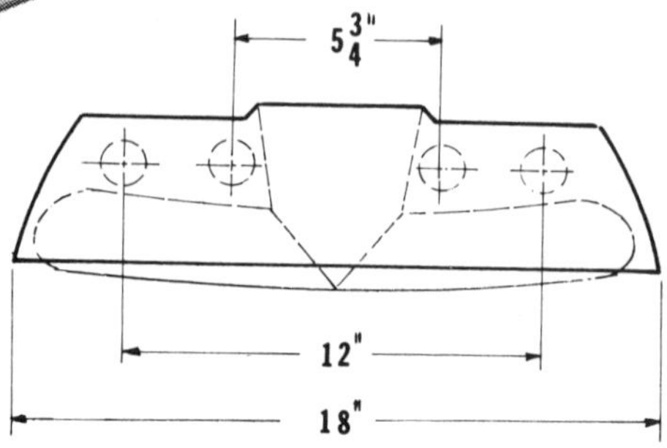

Description	Open-louvered unit
Lamps	Four F40 T12, 3200 lm each, 20,000 h
Louver	35 X 25°
Spacing ratio	1.3 (for 35 X 25° louver) 1.5 (for 35 X 45° louver)
Visual comfort probability	84 (length)/81 (cross)
Maintenance factors	0.75/0.70/0.65
Conversion factors	A. 4-ft unit, metal sides, 35 X 25° louvers = 1.0 B. 4-ft unit, plastic sides, 35 X 25° louvers = 0.98 C. 4-ft unit, metal sides, 35 X 45° louvers = 0.98 D. 4-ft unit, plastic sides, 35 X 45° louvers = 0.97

COST DETAILS PER LUMINAIRE

Type of unit	Input, W	Contractor's price	Installed cost
A	186	$51	$84.75
B	186	52	86
C	186	54	88.50
D	186	56	91

The installed cost includes published contractor's book price for the luminaire with louvers and ballasts, number of lamps as shown, luminaire fastening devices, and the labor required for surface mounting and connection of the luminaire. See page A–38 to add a luminaire outlet.

These open-louvered units, with high visual comfort probability, meet the scissors-curve brightness standards for school lighting and are also popular for post office and store lighting.

SURFACE MOUNT FLUORESCENT – OPEN LOUVERED

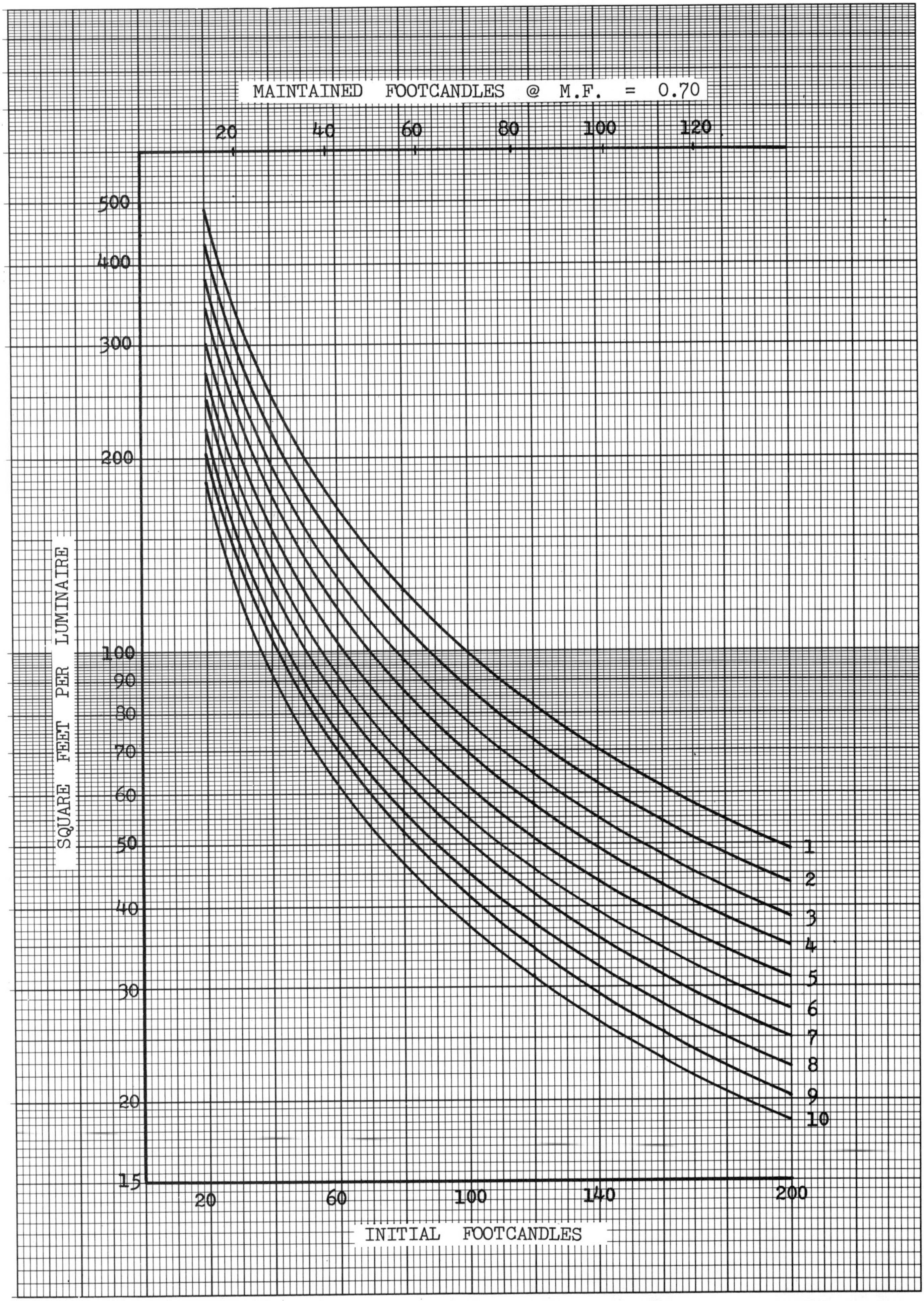

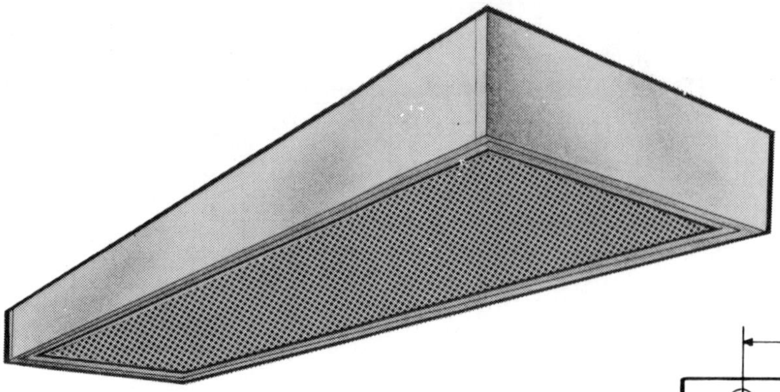

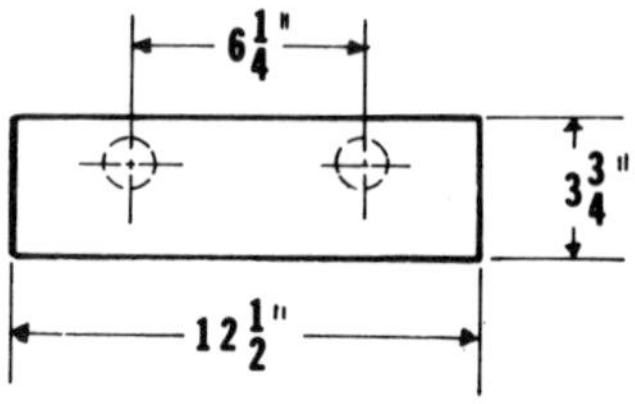

Description	1- X 4-ft modular
Lamps	Two F40 T12, 3200 lm each, 20,000 h
Lens	Acrylic prismatic
Spacing ratio	1.1
Visual comfort probability	63 (length)/62 (cross)
Maintenance factors	0.75/0.70/0.65
Input, W	93

COST DETAILS PER LUMINAIRE

Type of unit	Contractor's price	Installed cost
Metal sides	$45	$71.50
Plastic sides	46	72.75

The installed cost includes contractor's book price for the luminaire with lens and ballast, number of lamps as shown, luminaire fastening devices, and the labor required for surface mounting and connection of the luminaire. See page A–38 to add a luminaire outlet.

1- X 4-ft surface-mounted modules are generally used in corridors and small office areas.

SURFACE MOUNT FLUORESCENT – 1′ × 4′ MODULAR UNIT

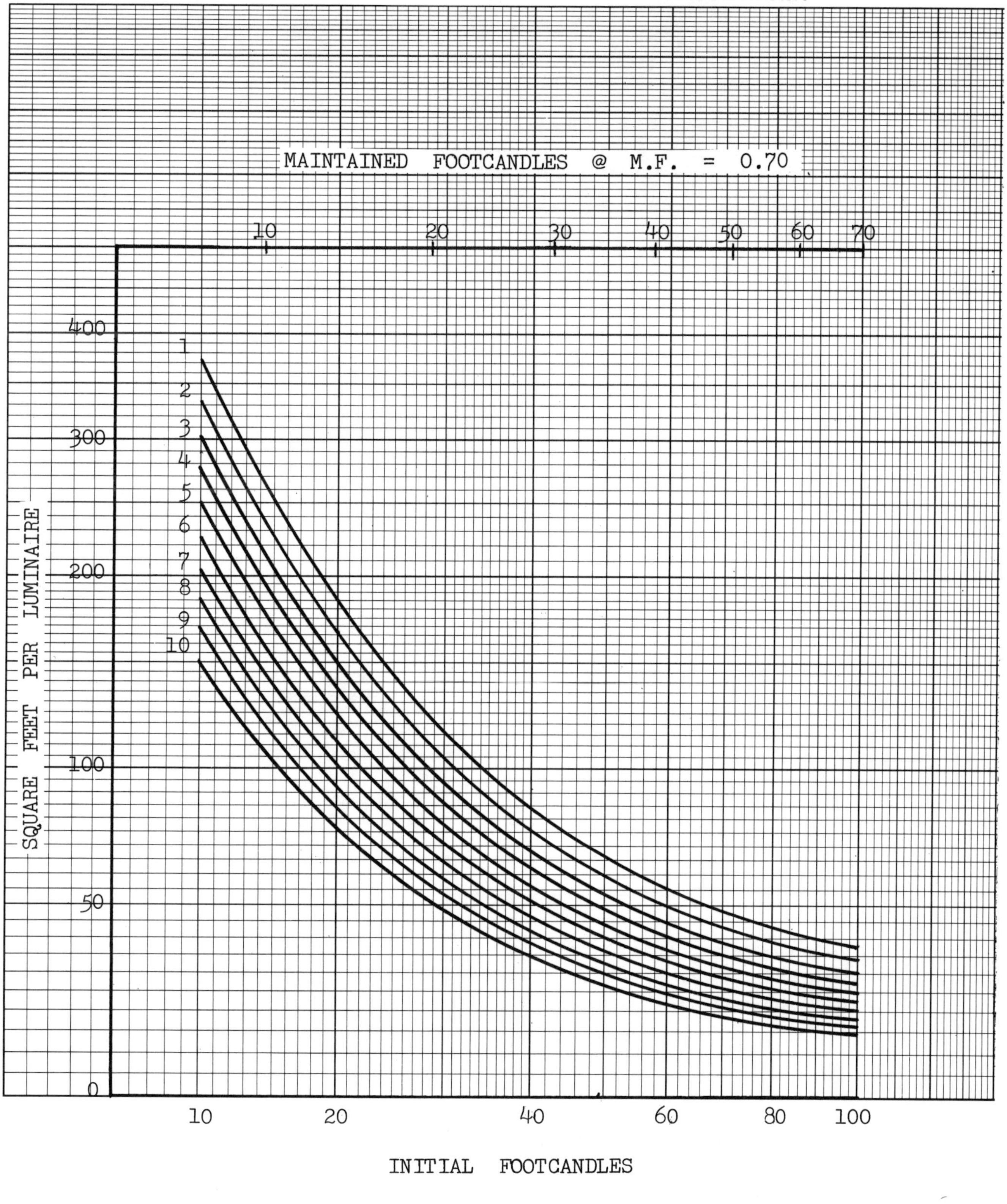

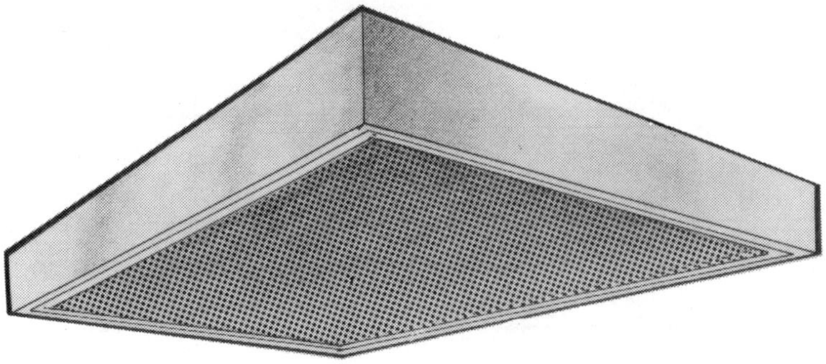

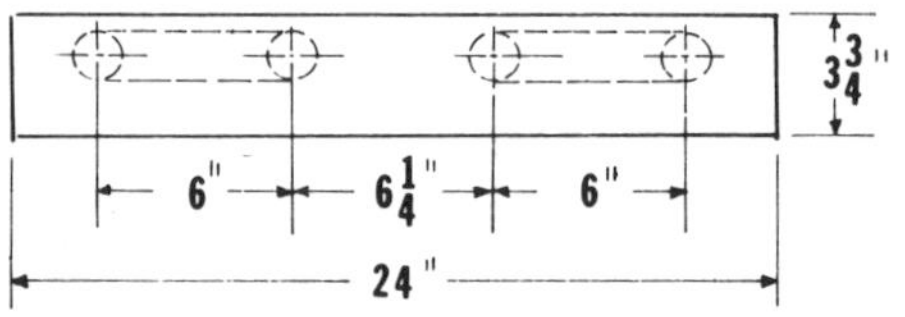

Description	2- × 2-ft modular
Lamps	Two F40/U T12, 3000 lm each, 12,000 h
Lens	Acrylic prismatic
Spacing ratio	1.2
Visual comfort probability	53 (length)/51 (cross)
Maintanance factors	0.75/0.70/0.65
Conversion factors	A. Unit with two F40/U T12 lamps = 1.0 B. Unit with three F40/U T12 lamps = 1.5

COST DETAILS PER LUMINAIRE

Type of unit	Input, W	Contractor's price	Installed cost
A	93	$53	$83
B	146	55	88

The installed cost includes published contractor's book price for the luminaire with lens and ballasts, number of lamps as shown, luminaire fastening devices, and the labor required for surface mounting and connection of the luminaire. *See page A–38 to add a luminaire outlet.*

2- × 2-ft surface-mounted modules are generally used in corridors and small office areas.

SURFACE MOUNT FLUORESCENT – 2′ × 2′ MODULAR UNIT

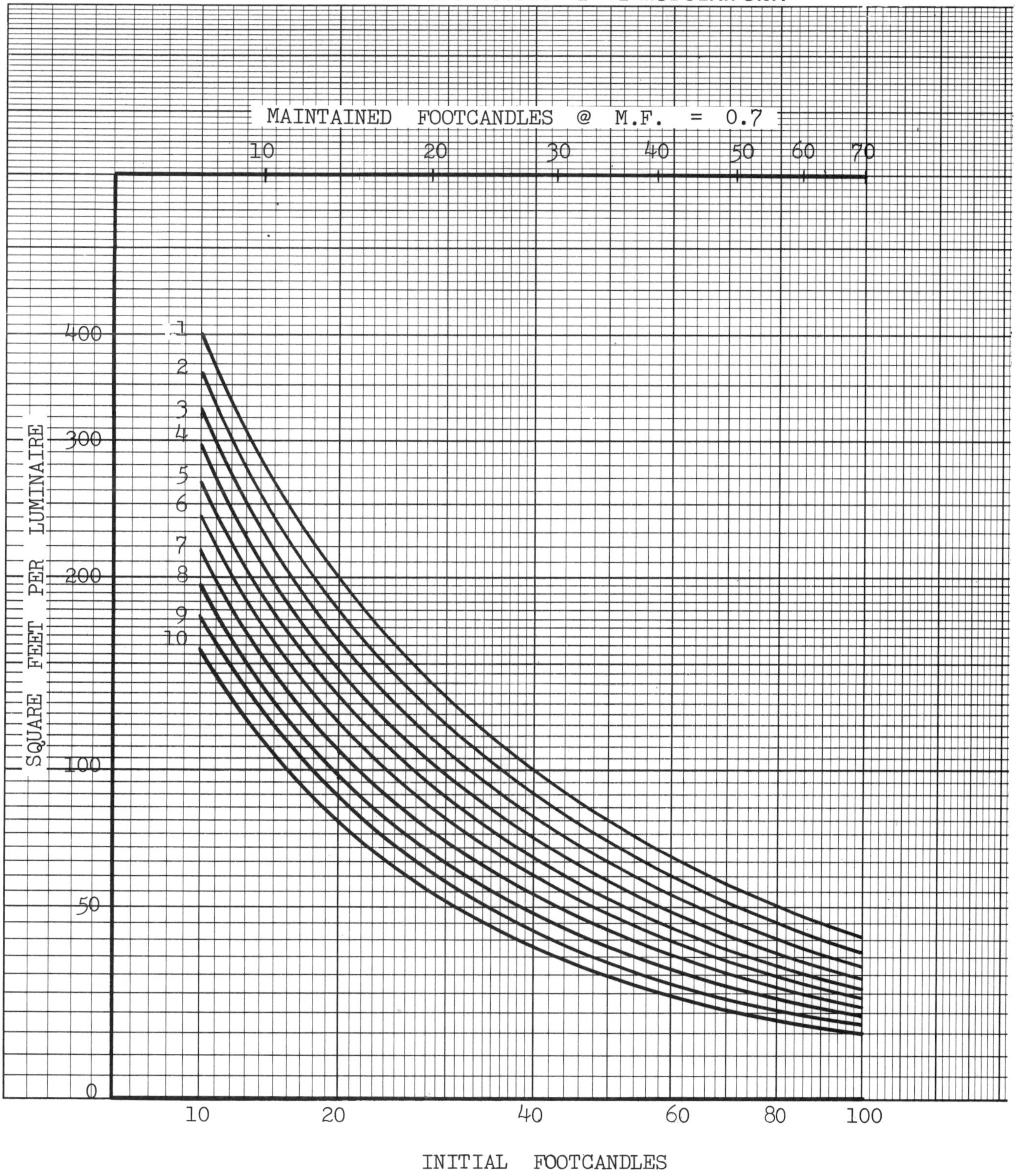

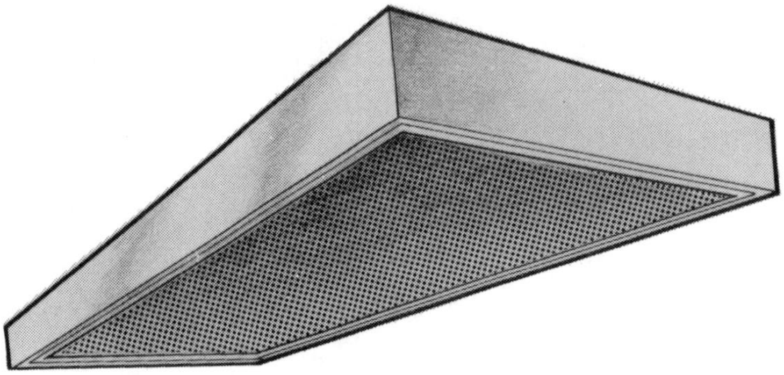

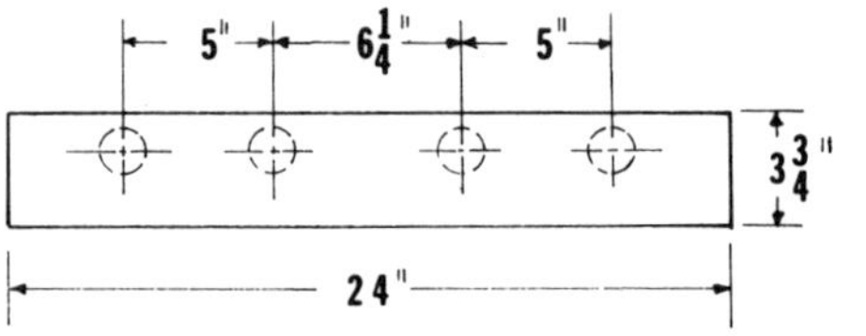

Description	2- X 4-ft modular
Lamps	Four F40 T12, 3200 lm each, 20,000 h
Lens	Acrylic prismatic
Spacing ratio	1.3
Visual comfort probability	60 (length)/59 (cross)
Maintenance factors	0.75/0.70/0.65
Conversion factors	A. Unit with four F40 T12 lamps = 1.0
	B. Unit with three F40 T12 lamps = 0.75
	C. Unit with two F40 T12 lamps = 0.50

COST DETAILS PER LUMINAIRE

Type of unit	Input, W	Contractor's price	Installed cost
A	186	$66	$103.25
B	146	66	100.25
C	93	59	88.75

The installed cost includes published contractor's book price for the luminaire with lens and ballasts, number of lamps as shown, luminaire fastening devices, and the labor required for surface mounting and connection of the luminaire. See page A–38 to add a luminaire outlet.

2- X 4-ft surface mounted modules are generally used in offices, schools, and other commercial and institutional applications.

SURFACE MOUNT FLUORESCENT – 2′ × 4′ MODULAR UNIT

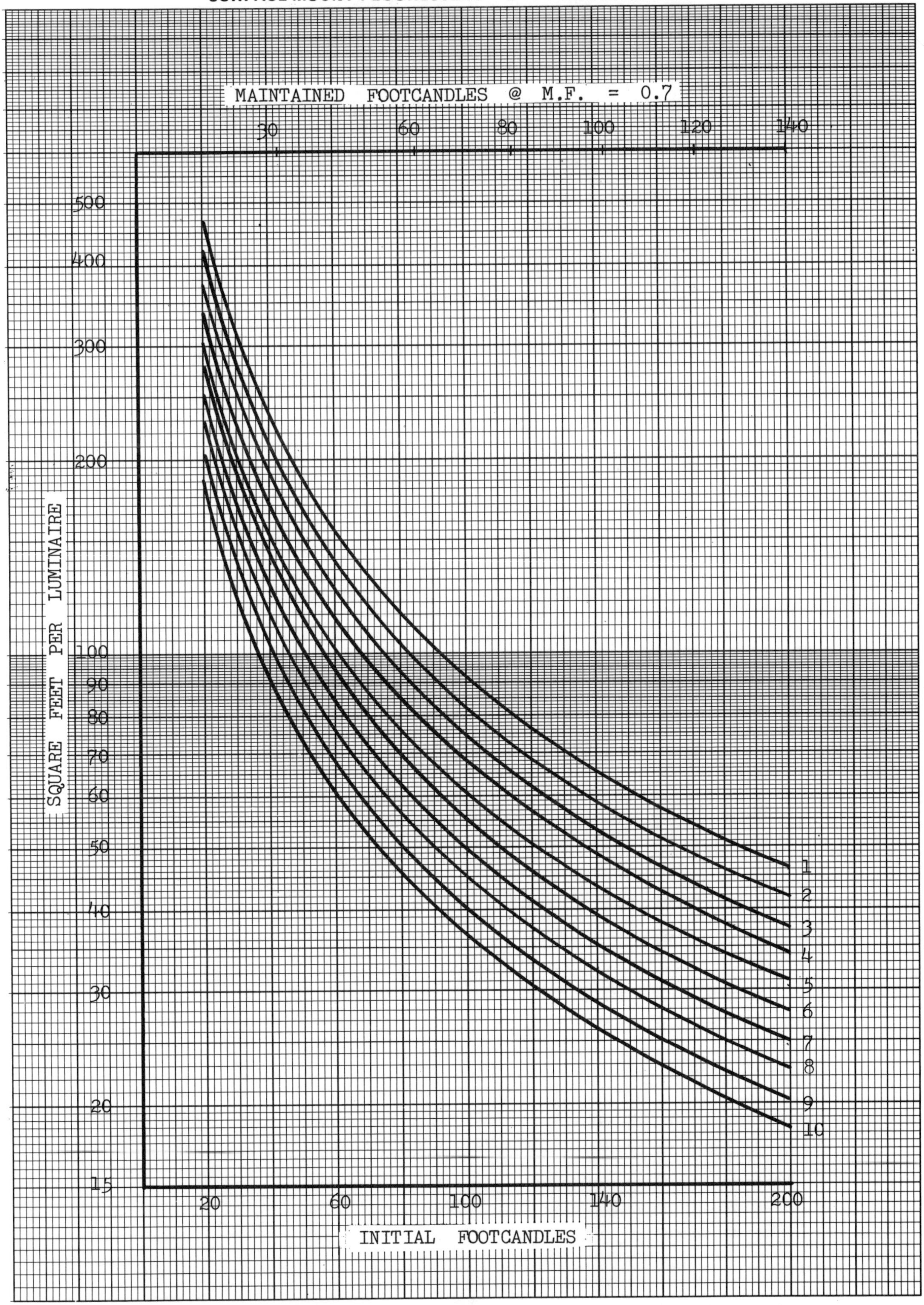

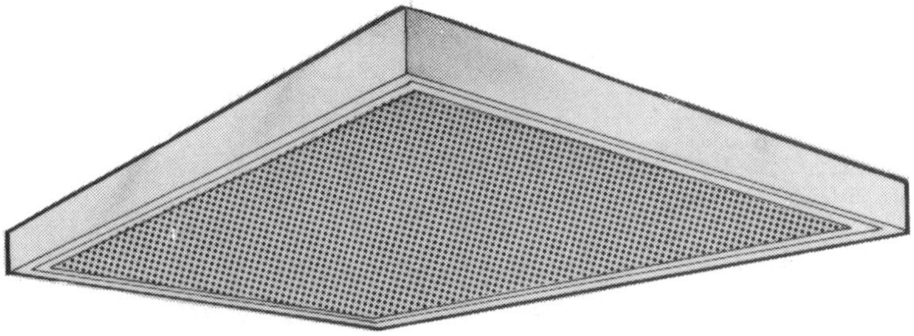

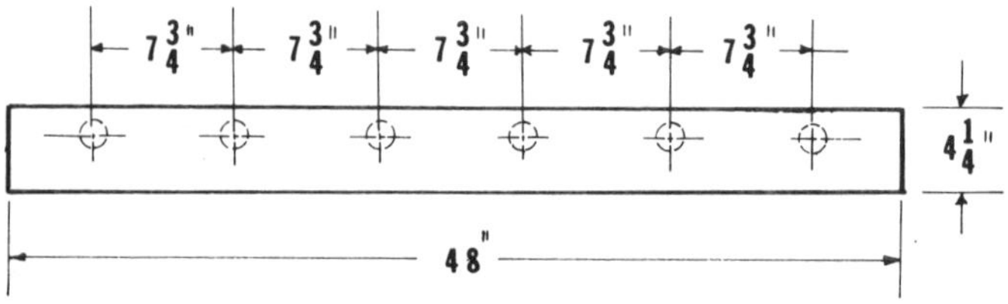

Description	4- X 4-ft modular
Lamps	Six F40 T12, 3200 lm each, 20,000 h
Lens	Acrylic prismatic
Spacing ratio	1.4
Visual comfort probability	58 (length)/56 (cross)
Maintenance factors	0.75/0.70/0.65
Conversion factors	A. Unit with six F40 T12 lamps = 1.0
	B. Unit with eight F40 T12 lamps = 1.2

COST DETAILS PER LUMINAIRE

Type of unit	Input, W	Contractor's price	Installed cost
A	279	$135	$196.50
B	372	145	214.75

The installed cost includes published contractor's book price for the luminaire with lens and ballasts, number of lamps as shown, luminaire fastening devices, and the labor required for surface mounting and connection of the luminaire. *See page A–38 to add a luminaire outlet.*

These large units are used in big conference rooms, retail areas, airport terminals, waiting rooms, etc., where concentrated lighting is required at certain places.

SURFACE MOUNT FLUORESCENT – 4′ × 4′ MODULAR UNIT

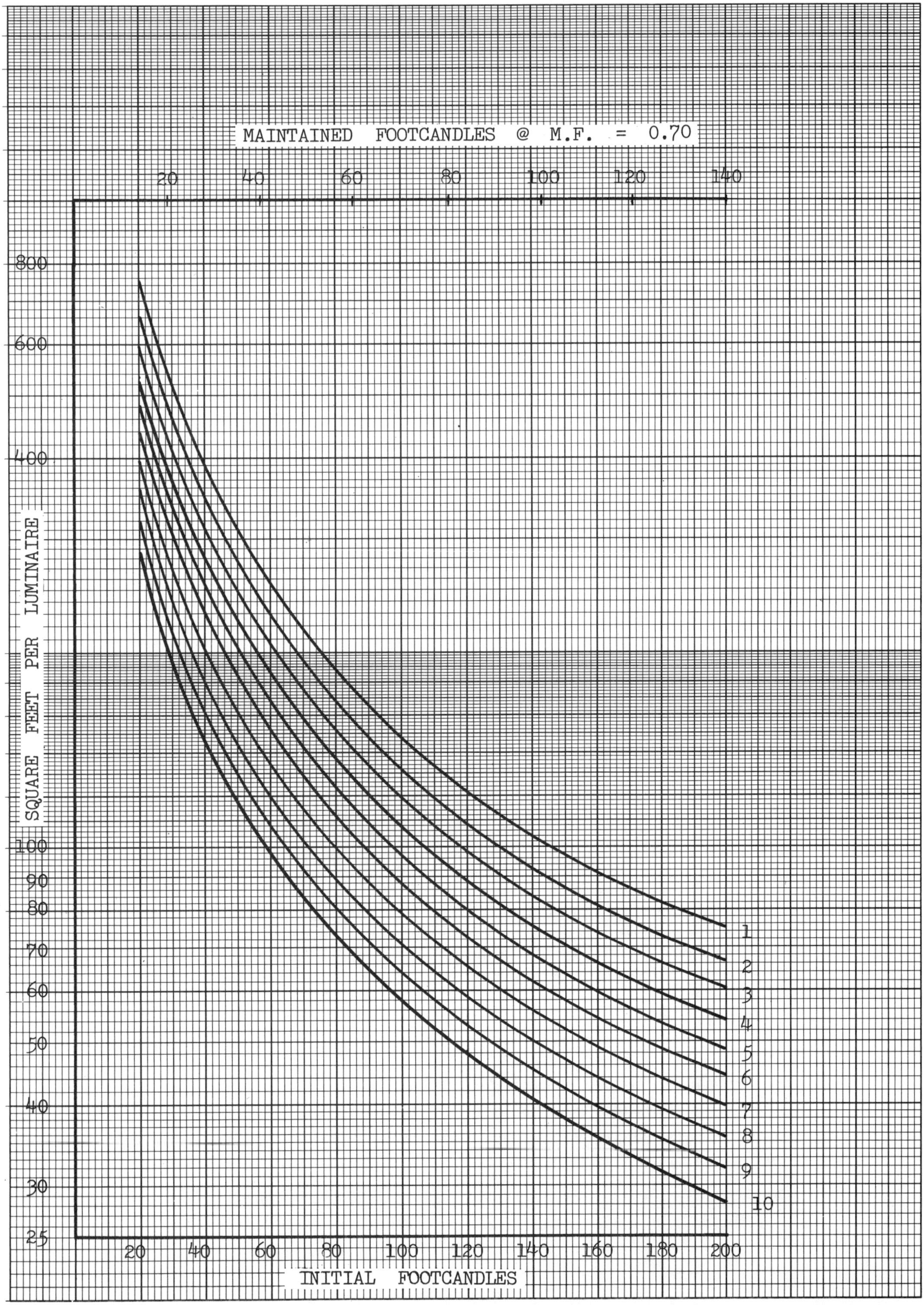

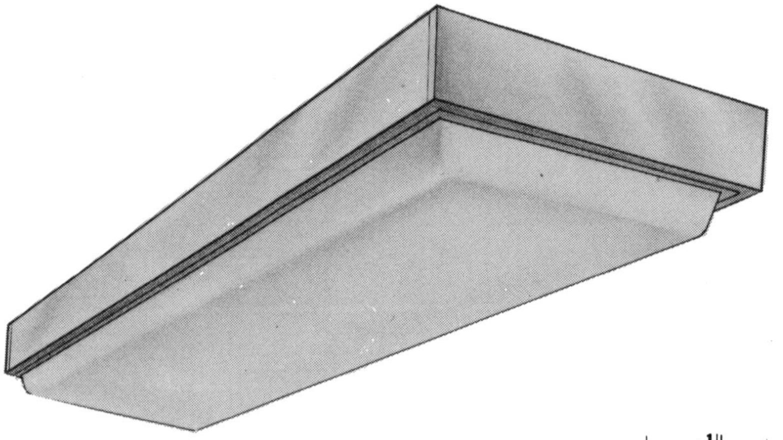

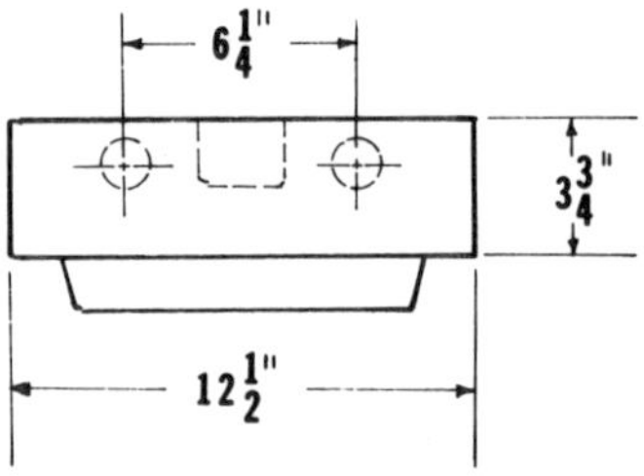

Description	1- X 4-ft dropped-dish modular
Lamps	Two F40 T12, 3200 lm each, 20,000 h
Lens	Dropped-dish acrylic
Spacing ratio	1.3
Visual comfort probability	46 (length)/43 (cross)
Maintenance factors	0.75/0.70/0.65
Input, W	93

COST DETAILS PER LUMINAIRE

Type of unit	Contractor's price	Installed cost
Metal sides	$52	$80
Plastic sides	53	81.25

The installed cost includes published contractor's book price for the luminaire with lens and ballast, number of lamps as shown, luminaire fastening devices, and the labor required for surface mounting and connection of the luminaire. See page A–38 to add a luminaire outlet.

The framed dropped-dish opal acrylic diffuser combines a modern, modular appearance with soft general light distribution. Excellent for high-angle general illumination on high or medium ceilings.

SURFACE MOUNT FLUORESCENT – 1′ × 4′ DROPPED DISH

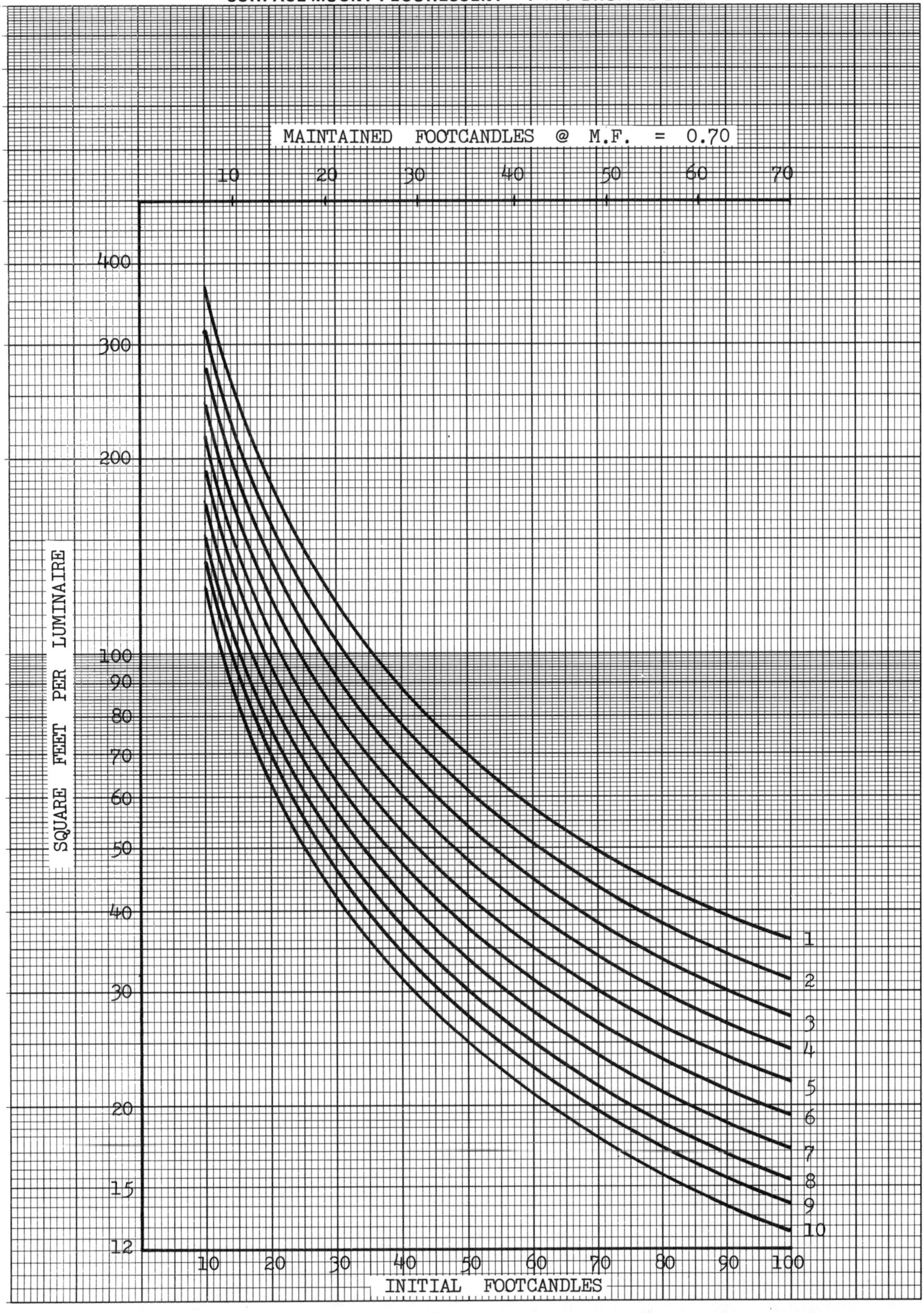

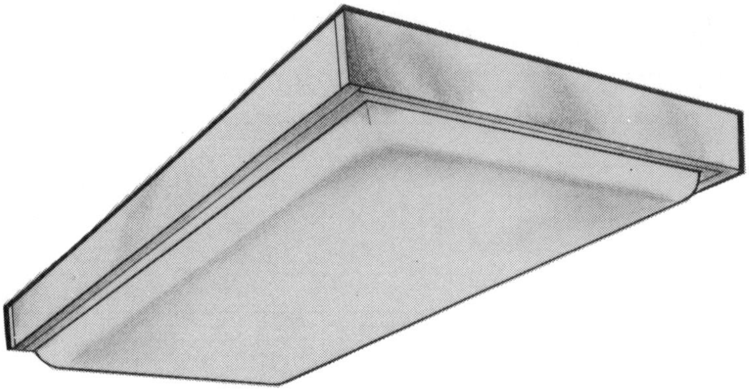

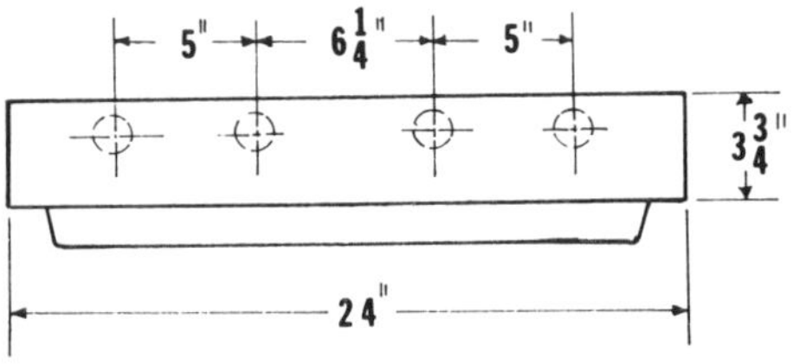

Description	2- × 4-ft dropped-dish modular
Lamps	Four F40 T12, 3200 lm each, 20,000 h
Lens	Dropped-dish acrylic
Spacing ratio	1.3
Visual comfort probability	43 (length)/40 (cross)
Maintenance factors	0.75/0.70/0.65
Conversion factors	A. Unit with four F40 T12 lamps = 1.0 B. Unit with two F40 T12 lamps = 0.5

COST DETAILS PER LUMINAIRE

Type of unit	Input, W	Contractor's price	Installed cost
A	186	$76	$115.50
B	93	74	107

The installed cost includes published contractor's book price for the luminaire with lens and ballasts, number of lamps as shown, luminaire fastening devices, and the labor required for surface mounting and connection of the luminaire. *See page A–38 to add a luminaire outlet.*

The framed dropped-dish opal acrylic diffuser combines a modern, modular appearance with soft general light distribution. Excellent for high-angle general illumination on high or medium ceilings.

SURFACE MOUNT FLUORESCENT – 2′ × 4′ DROPPED DISH

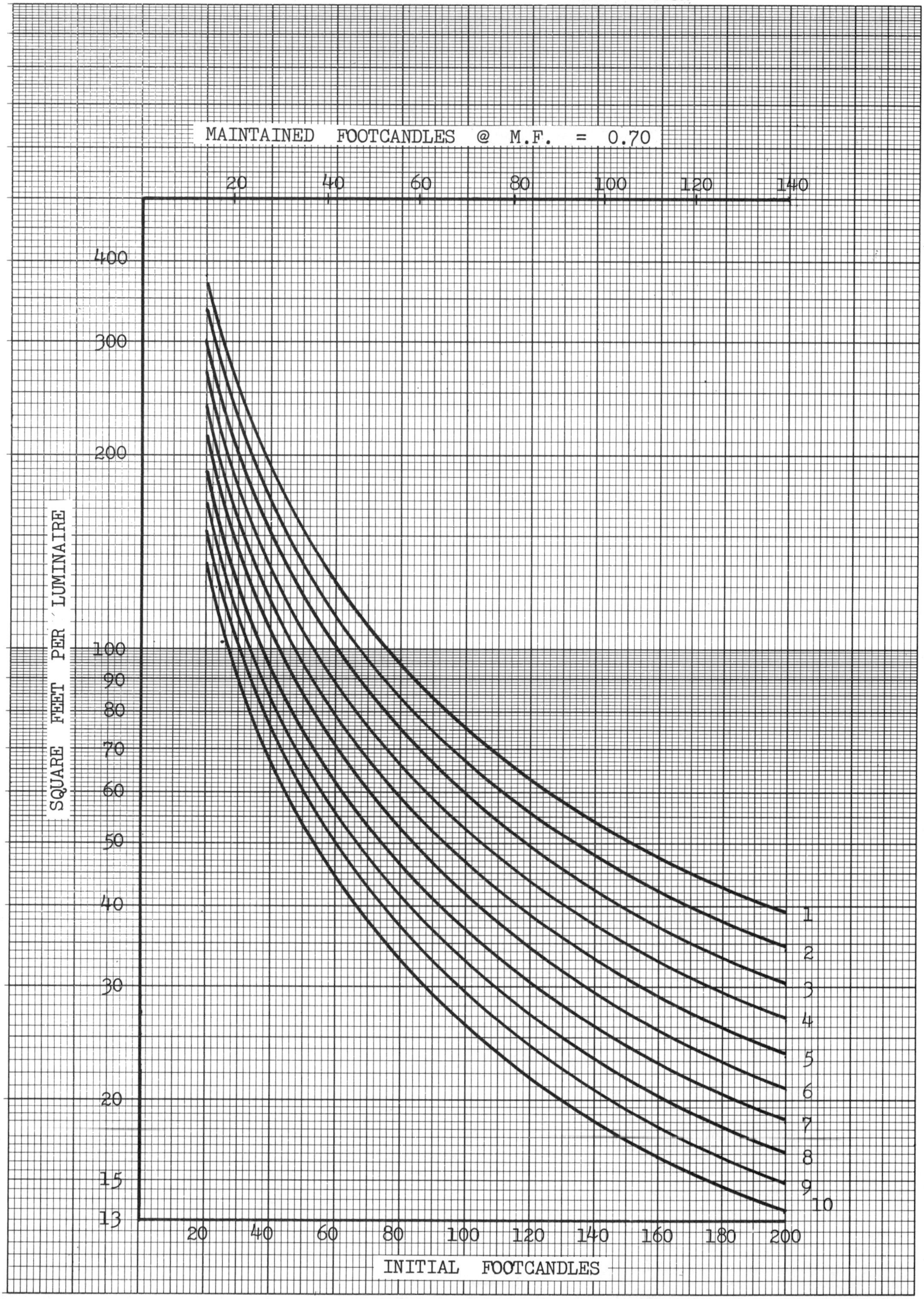

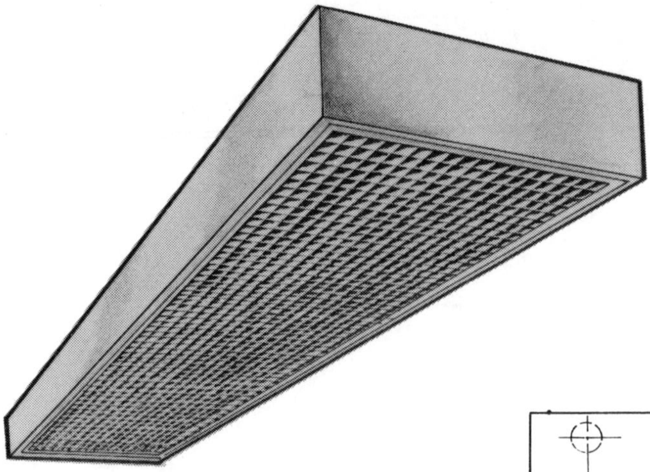

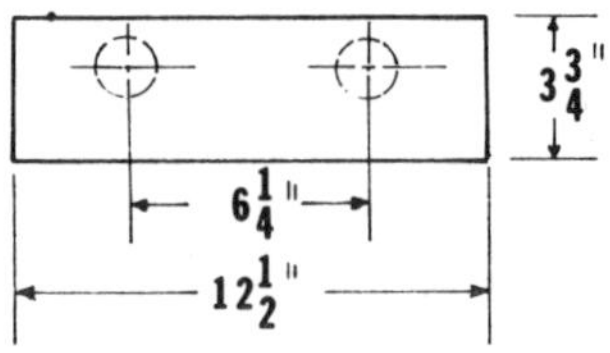

Description	1- X 4-ft plastic-cube modular
Lamps	Two F40 T12, 3200 lm, 20,000 h
Louver	45 X 45° light-stabilized polystyrene plastic egg-crate louver
Spacing ratio	1.0
Visual comfort probability	69 (length)/68 (cross)
Maintenance factors	0.75/0.70/0.65
Input, W	93

COST DETAILS PER LUMINAIRE

Type of unit	Contractor's price	Installed cost
Metal sides	$47	$74
Plastic sides	48	75.25

The installed cost includes published contractor's book price for the luminaire with louver and ballast, number of lamps as shown, luminaire fastening devices, and the labor required for surface mounting and connection of the luminaire. See page A–38 to add a luminaire outlet.

Luminaires with such light-stable luminous open shielding element with 45° (lengthwide and crosswise) cutoff provide a high degree of brightness control in direct-viewing zones.

SURFACE MOUNT FLUORESCENT – 1′ × 4′ PLASTIC–CUBE LOUVER

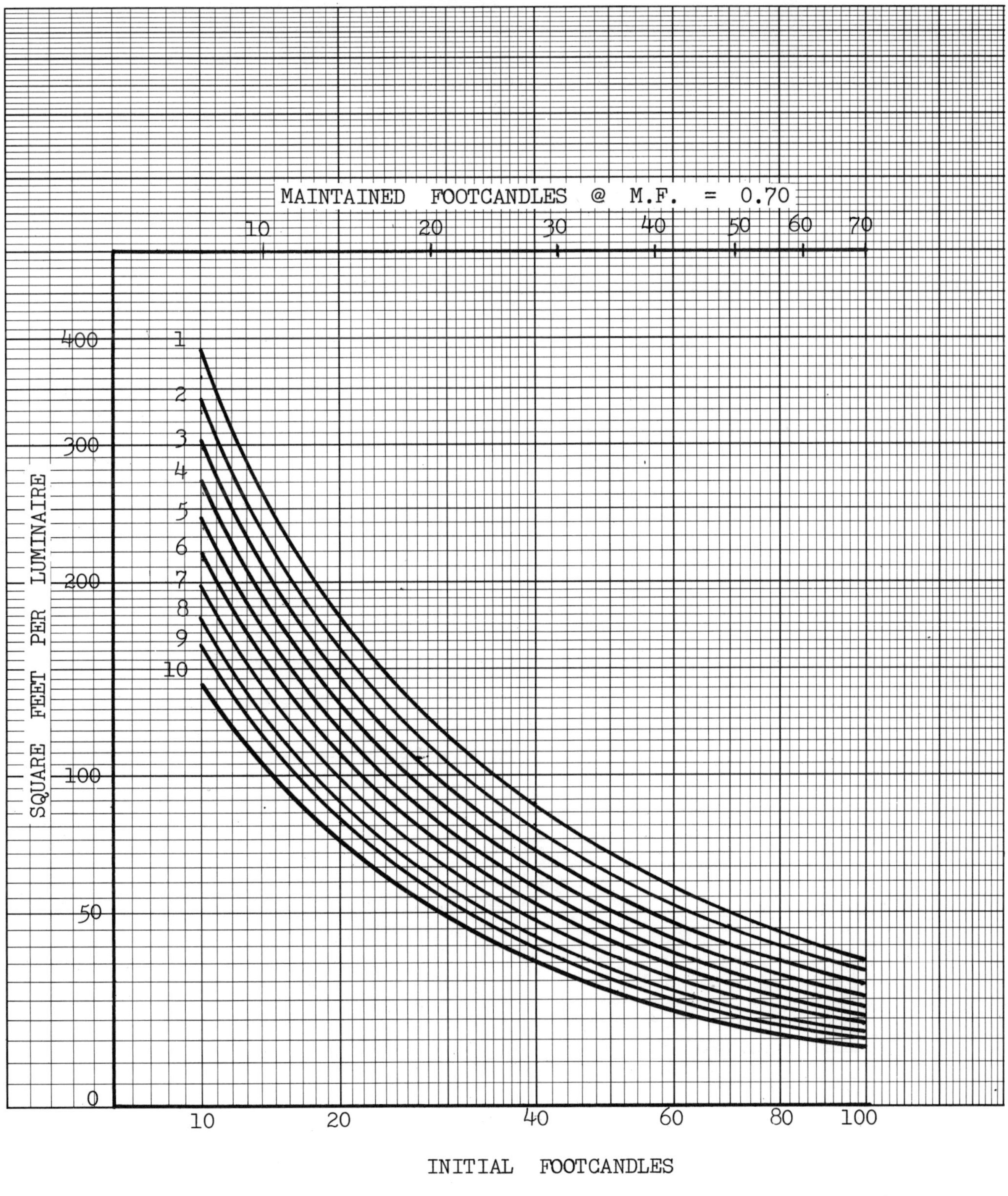

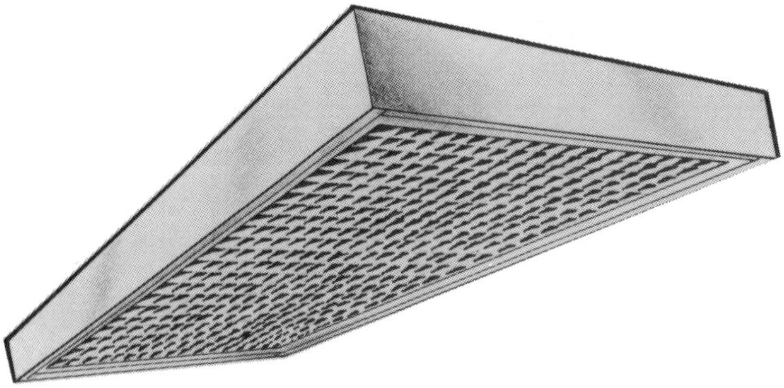

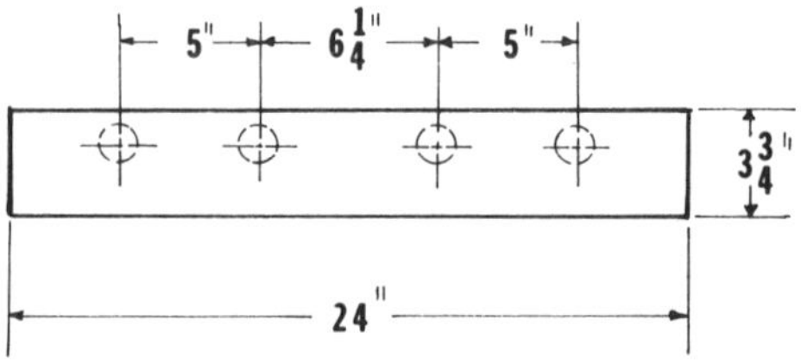

Description	2- X 4-ft plastic-cube modular
Lamps	Four F40 T12, 3200 lm each, 20,000 h
Louvers	45 X 45° light-stabilized polystyrene plastic egg-crate louver
Spacing ratio	1.0
Visual comfort probability	66 (length)/65 (cross)
Maintenance factors	0.75/0.70/0.65
Conversion factors	A. Unit with four F40 T12 lamps = 1.0 B. Unit with two F40 T12 lamps = 0.5

COST DETAILS PER LUMINAIRE

Type of unit	Input, W	Contractor's price	Installed cost
A	186	$72	$110.50
B	93	66	97.25

The installed cost includes published contractor's book price for the luminaire with louver and ballasts, number of lamps as shown, luminaire fastening devices, and the labor required for surface mounting and connection of the luminaire. *See page A–38 to add a luminaire outlet.*

Luminaires with such light-stable luminous open shielding element with 45° (lengthwise and crosswise) cutoff provides a high degree of brightness control in direct-viewing zones.

SURFACE MOUNT FLUORESCENT – 2′ × 4′ PLASTIC–CUBE LOUVER

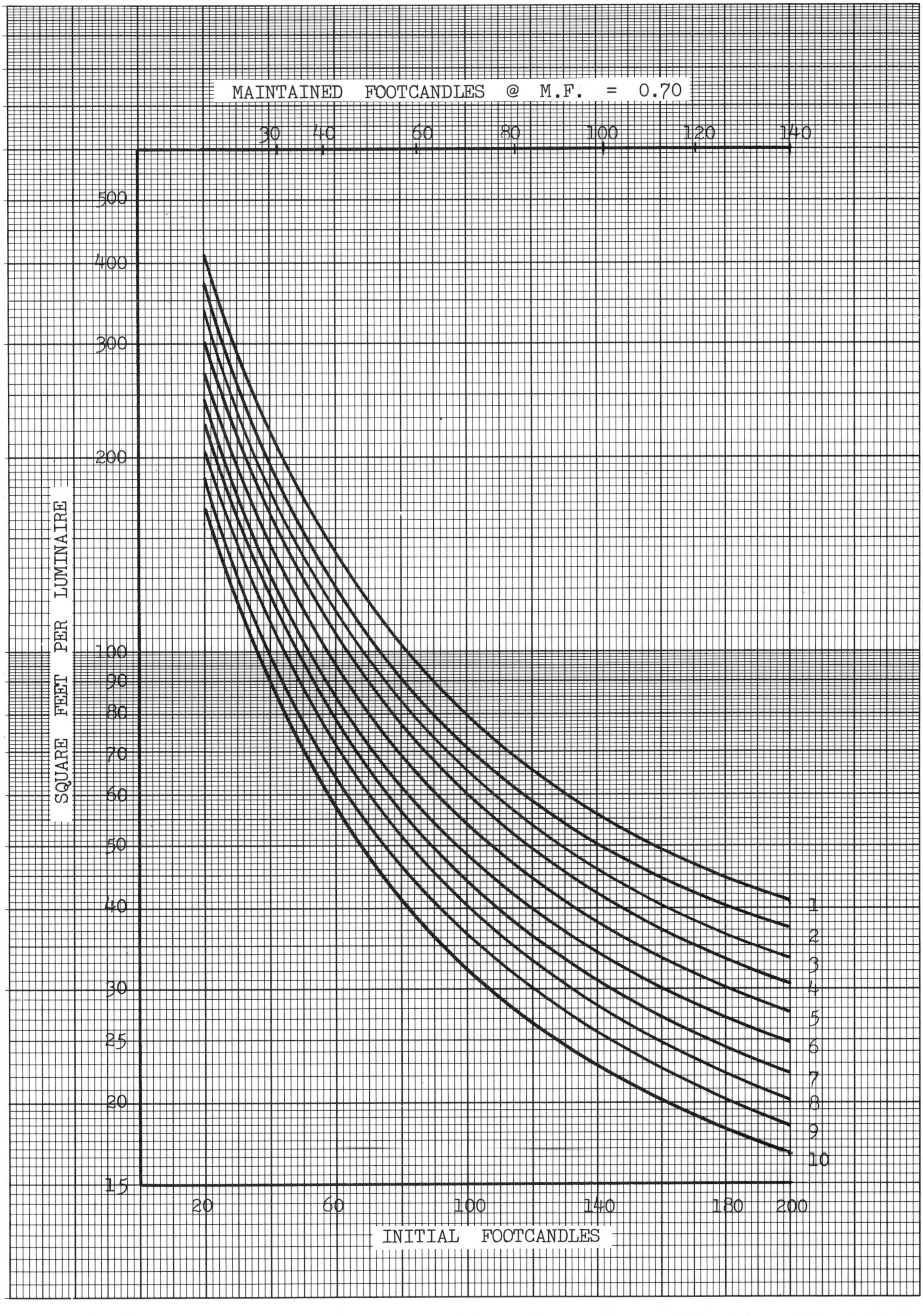

INSTALLED COST OF FLUSH-MOUNTED OUTLETS

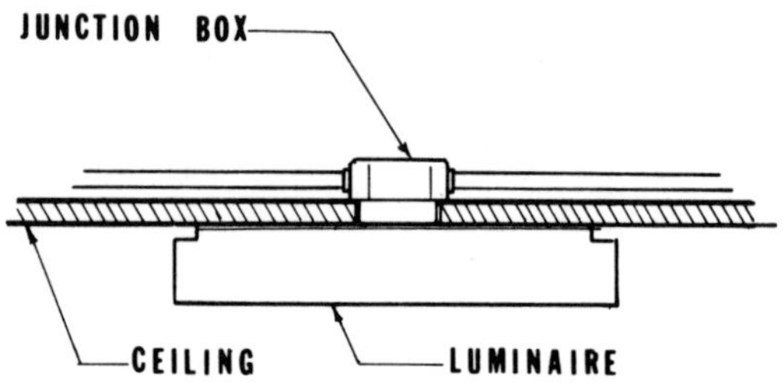

Add

$12.88 for EMT terminal
16.38 for GRC terminal
16.38 for IMS terminal

to the luminaire installed cost for an outlet flush-mounted to a suspended or furred ceiling, which includes a 4-in octagon box, adjustable bar hanger, two connectors, plaster ring, and two wire nuts.

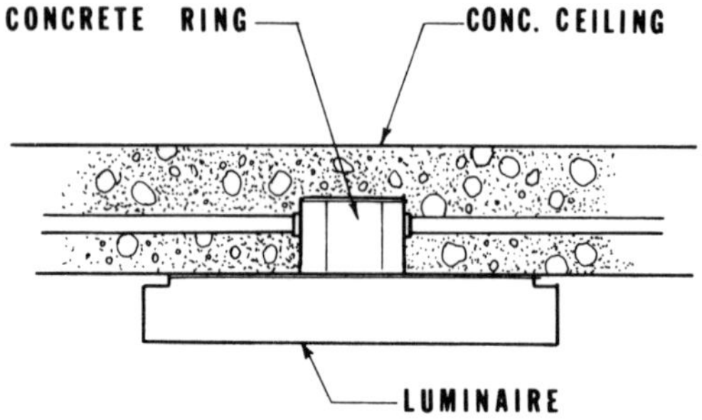

Add

$12.18 for EMT terminal
15.84 for GRC terminal
15.84 for IMS terminal

to the luminaire installed cost for an outlet flush-pan- or deck-mounted in concrete, which includes a 4-in concrete ring, connectors for the type of conduit required, cover plate, and two wire nuts.

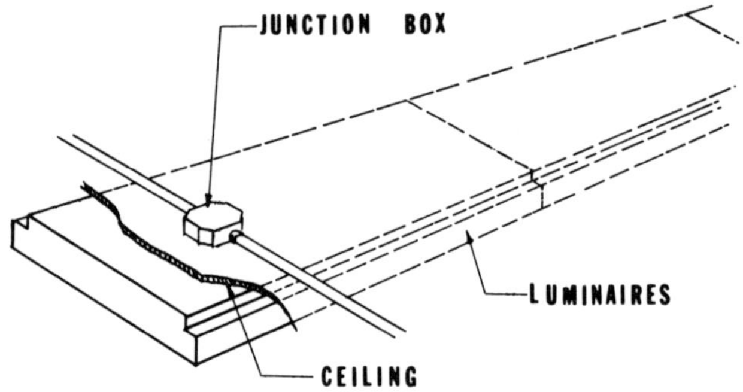

In a series of luminaire connections as on the left, where all luminaires are internally connected and only one outlet is required for service entrance, add all individual luminaire installed costs and one outlet installed cost as necessary, as shown above.

Recessed Fluorescent Troffers

B

ACRYLIC PRISMATIC LENS

1- × 4-ft, 2 or 3 Lamps	*B-2*
2- × 2-ft, 2 or 3 Lamps	*B-4*
2- × 4-ft, 2, 3, or 4 Lamps	*B-6*
4- × 4-ft, 6 or 8 Lamps	*B-8*

PARABOLIC-LOUVERED

9-in × 8-ft, 1 Lamp	*B-10*
1- × 4-ft, 2 Lamps	*B-12, B-14*
2- × 2-ft, 2 Lamps	*B-16*
2- × 4-ft, 3 Lamps	*B-18*
4 Lamps	*B-20*
3- × 3-ft, 6 Lamps	*B-22*
4- × 4-ft, 8 Lamps	*B-24*

MISCELLANEOUS

2- × 4-ft Carolite Radialens, 2 Lamps	*B-26*
3 or 4 Lamps	*B-28*
Day-Brite VIP Lens, 2 Lamps	*B-30*
3 Lamps	*B-32*
4 Lamps	*B-34*
KSH 3E Lens, 2 Lamps	*B-36*
3 Lamps	*B-38*
Gibson EE System, 2 Lamps	*B-40*
3 Lamps	*B-42*
1- × 4-ft, Plastic-Cube Louvers, 2 or 3 Lamps	*B-44*
2- × 4-ft, Plastic-Cube Louvers, 2 or 4 Lamps	*B-46*
1- × 4-ft, Dropped-Dish, 2 or 3 Lamps	*B-48*
2- × 4-ft, Dropped-Dish, 2 or 4 Lamps	*B-50*

CEILING OUTLETS FOR LUMINAIRES

Installed Cost of Outlets above Ceiling	*B-52*

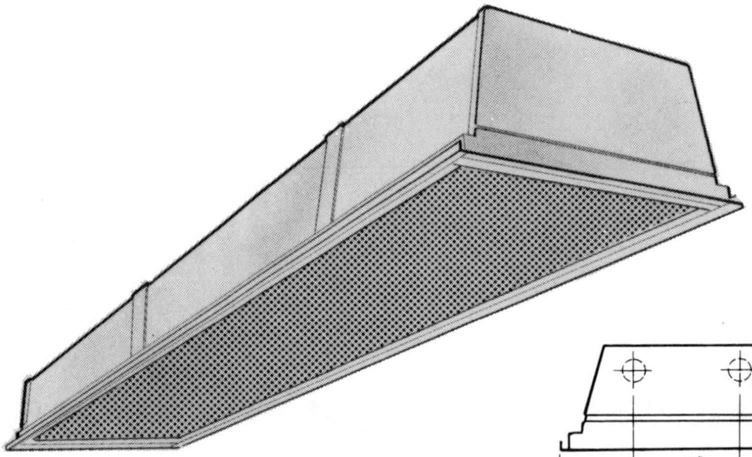

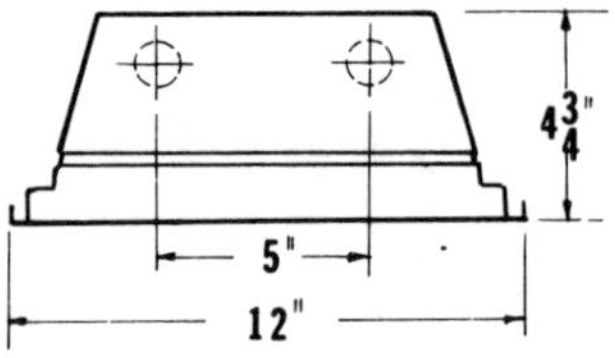

Description	1- X 4-ft troffer
Lamps	Two F40 T12, 3200 lm each, 20,000 h
Lens	Acrylic prismatic lens
Spacing ratio	1.1
Visual comfort probability	62 (length)/61 (cross)
Maintenance factors	0.75/0.70/0.65
Conversion factors	A. Unit with two F40 T12 lamps = 1.0
	B. Unit with three F40 T12 lamps = 1.5

COST DETAILS PER LUMINAIRE

Type of unit	Input, W	Contractor's price		Installed cost	
		Grid	Flange	Grid	Flange
A	93	$44	$45	$74.75	$77.75
B	146	54	55	90	92.75

The installed cost includes published contractor's book price for the luminaire with lens and ballast, number of lamps as showm, luminaire fastening devices, 6-ft length of 3/8-in flexible metallic conduit with two 7-ft lengths of no. 12 AF wire, two connectors, and the labor required for recess mounting and connection of the luminaire. See page B–52 to add a luminaire outlet recessed above ceiling.

1- X 4-ft troffers are used mostly in corridors, between aisles, and in library stack areas.

RECESSED FLUORESCENT –1' X 4' TROFFER (ACRYLIC PRISMATIC LENS)

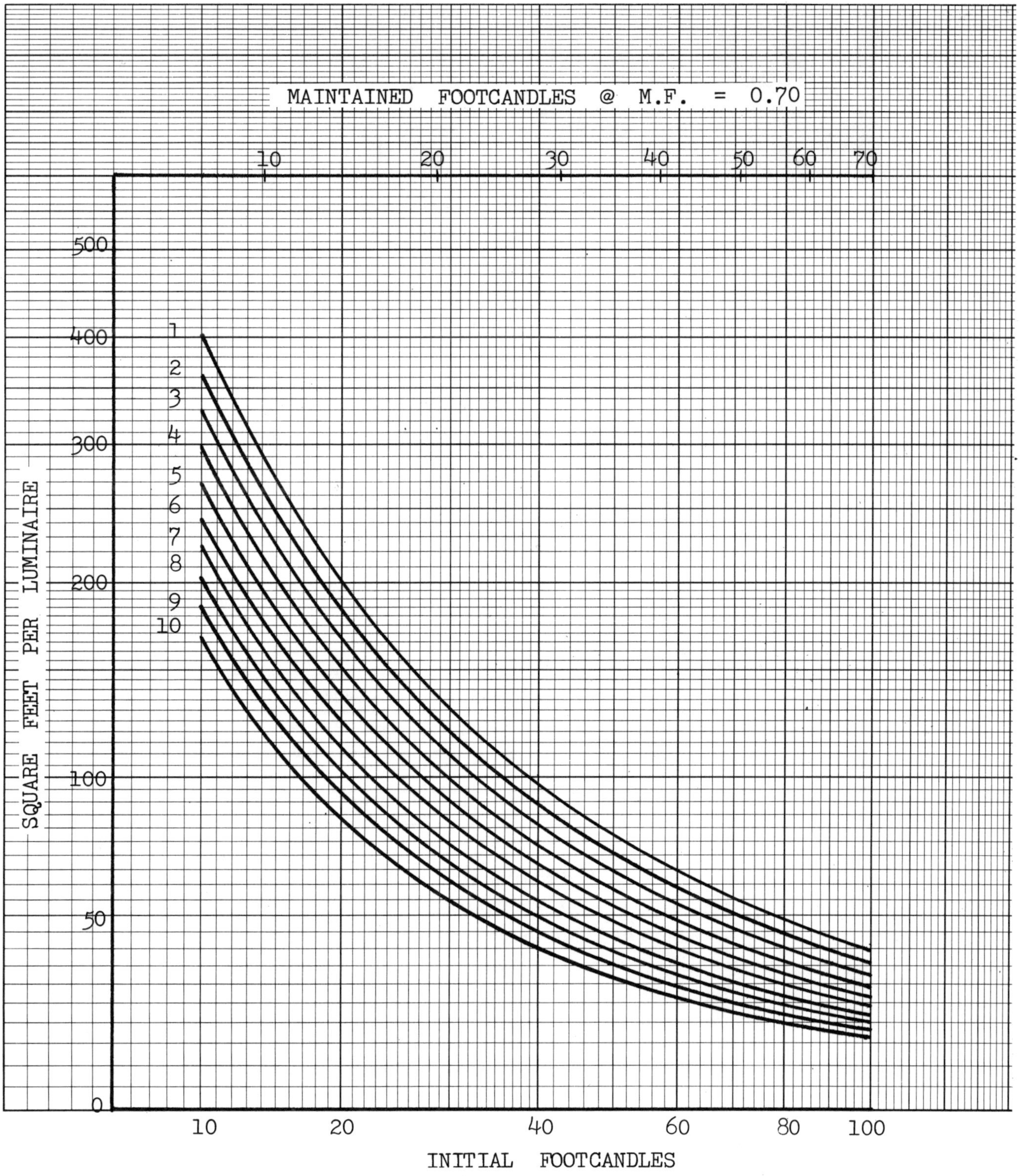

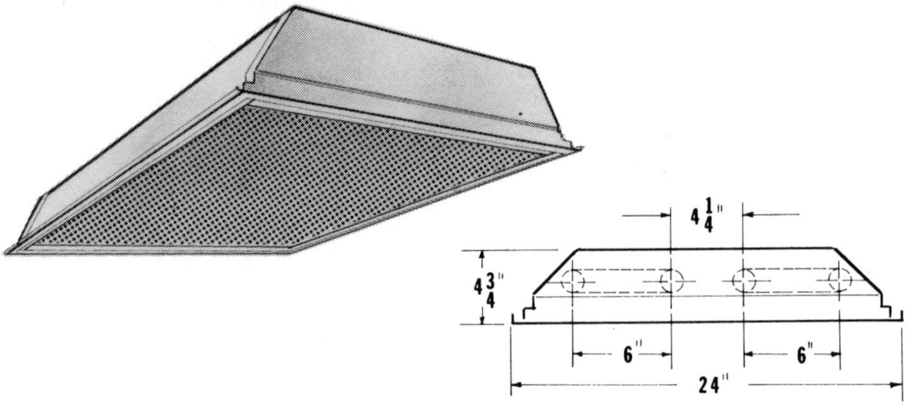

Description	2- X 2-ft troffer
Lamps	Two F40/U T12, 3000 lm each, 12,000 h
Lens	Acrylic prismatic lens
Spacing ratio	1.3
Visual comfort probability	53 (length)/51 (cross)
Maintenance factors	0.75/0.70/0.65
Conversion factors	A. Unit with two F40/U T12 lamps = 1.0
	B. Unit with three F40/U T12 lamps = 1.5

COST DETAILS PER LUMINAIRE

Type of unit	Input, W	Contractor's price		Installed cost	
		Grid	Flange	Grid	Flange
A	93	$53	$56	$84	$ 89.50
B	146	59	66	94.50	104.75

The installed cost includes published contractor's book price for the luminaire with lens and ballast, number of lamps as shown, luminaire fastening devices, 6-ft length of 3/8-in flexible metallic conduit with two 7-ft lengths of no. 12 AF wire, two connectors, and the labor required for recess mounting and connection of the luminaire. *See page B–52 to add a luminaire outlet recessed above ceiling.*

2- X 2-ft ceiling recessed troffers are used mostly in corridors and small office areas.

RECESSED FLUORESCENT – 2' X 2' TROFFER (ACRYLIC PRISMATIC LENS)

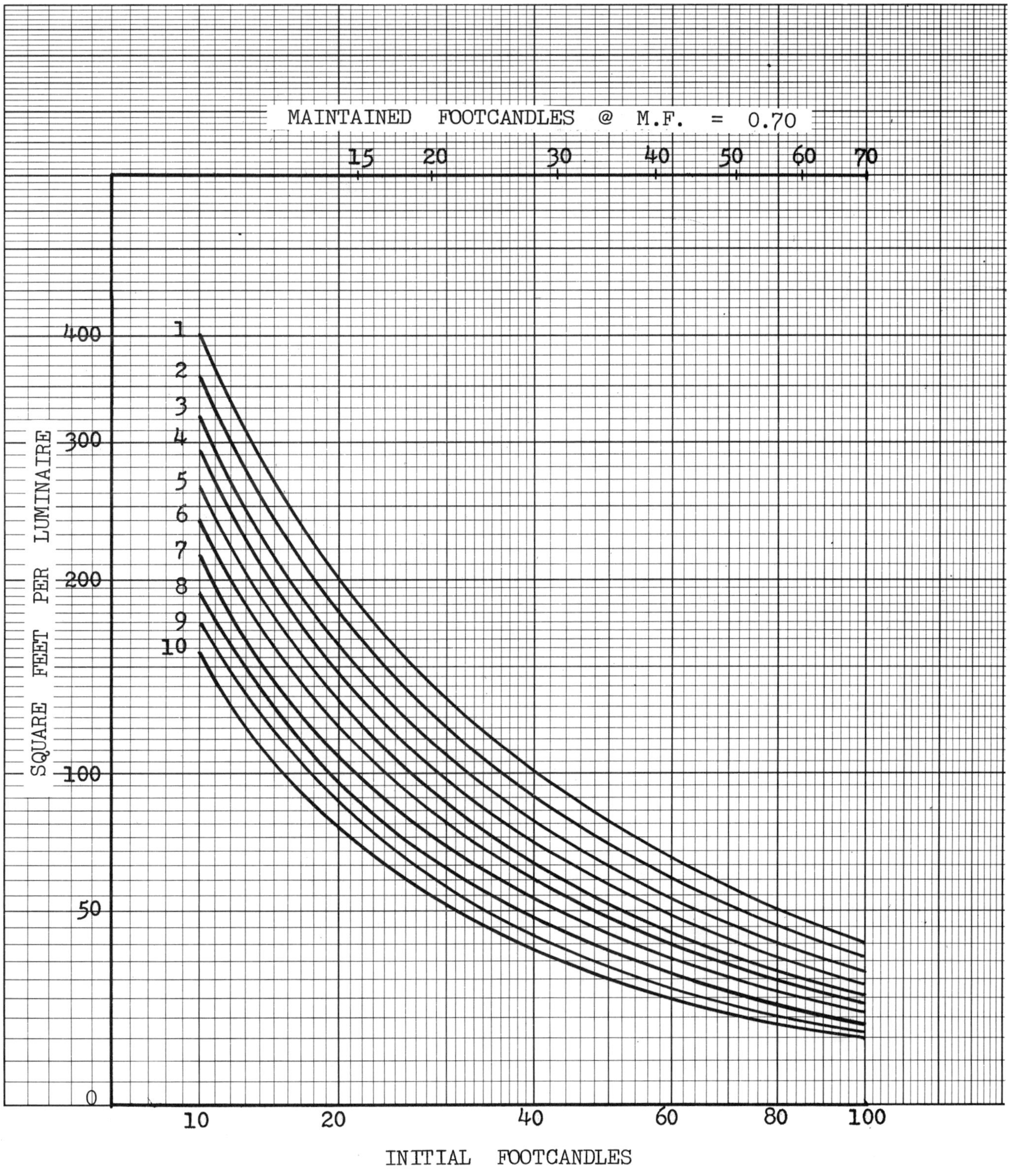

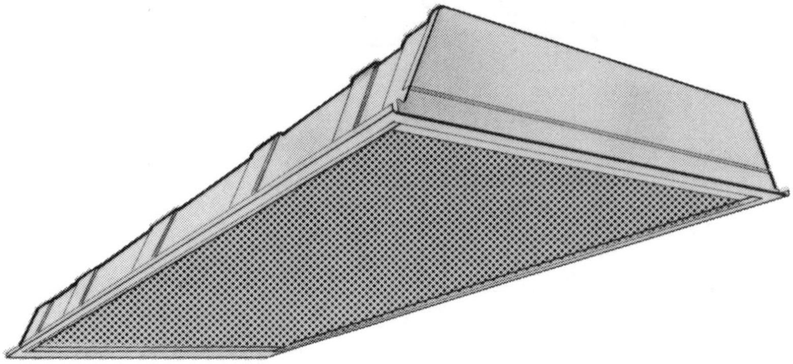

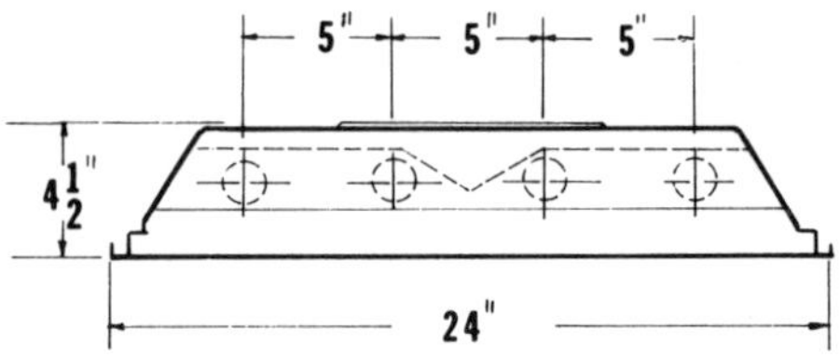

Description	2- X 4-ft troffer
Lamps	Four F40 T12, 3200 lm each, 20,000 h
Lens	Acrylic prismatic lens
Spacing ratio	1.35
Visual comfort probability	61 (length)/59 (cross)
Maintenance factors	0.75/0.70/0.65
Conversion factors	A. Unit with four F40 T12 lamps = 1.0 B. Unit with three F40 T12 lamps = 0.75 C. Unit with two F40 T12 lamps = 0.50

COST DETAILS PER LUMINAIRE

Type of unit	Input, W	Contractor's price		Installed cost	
		Grid	Flange	Grid	Flange
A	186	$58	$62	$98	$103.75
B	146	58	62	95	101.50
C	93	51	54	83.50	88.75

The installed cost includes published contractor's book price for the luminaire with lens and ballasts, number of lamps as shown, luminaire fastening devices, 6-ft length of 3/8-in flexible metallic conduit with two 7-ft lengths of no. 12 AF wire, two connectors, and the labor required for recess mounting and connection of the luminaire. See page B–52 to add a luminaire outlet recessed above ceiling.

2- X 4-ft ceiling-recessed troffers with 4 lamps are the most common luminaires used in office buildings.

RECESSED FLUORESCENT – 2' X 4' TROFFER (ACRYLIC PRISMATIC LENS)

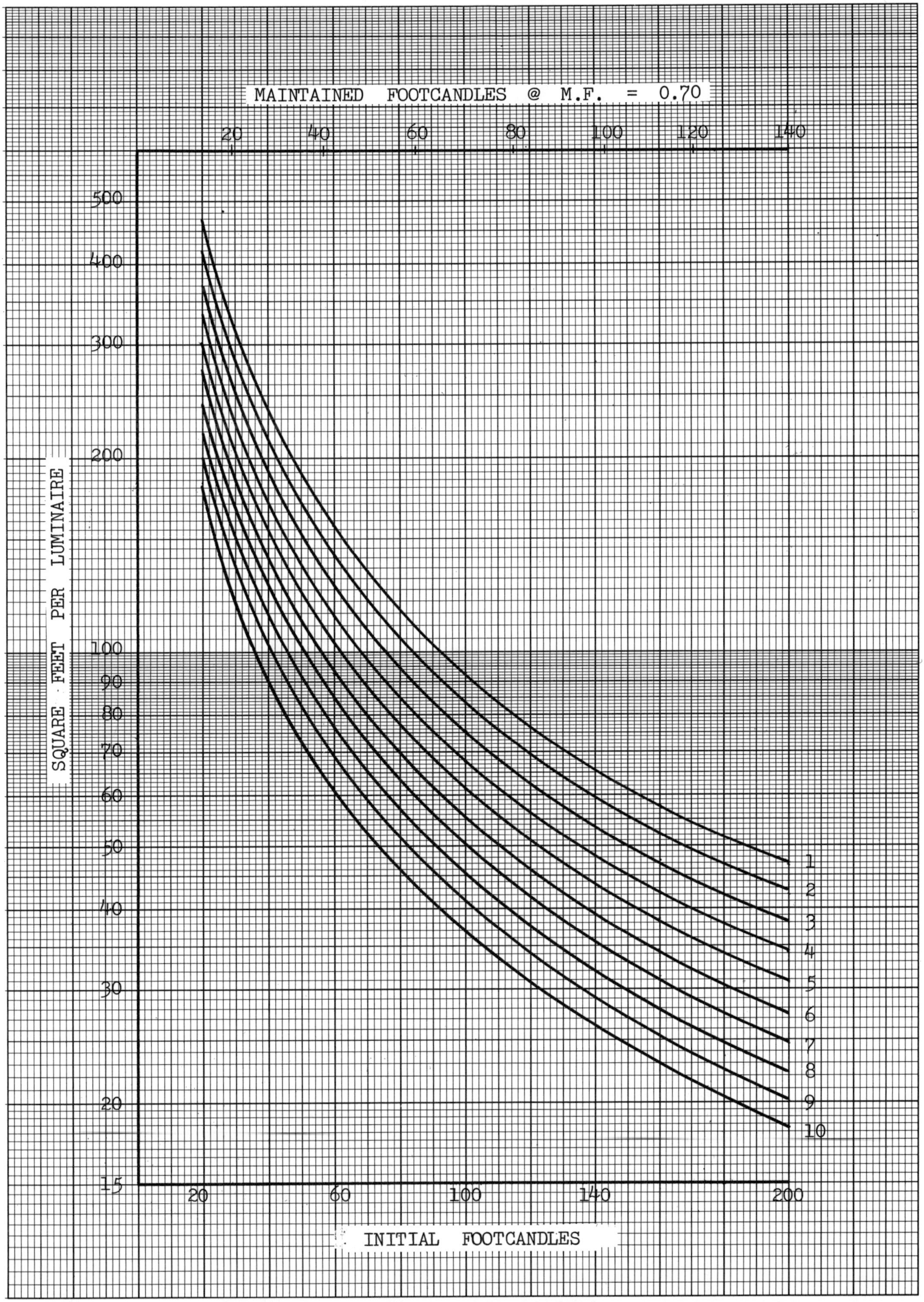

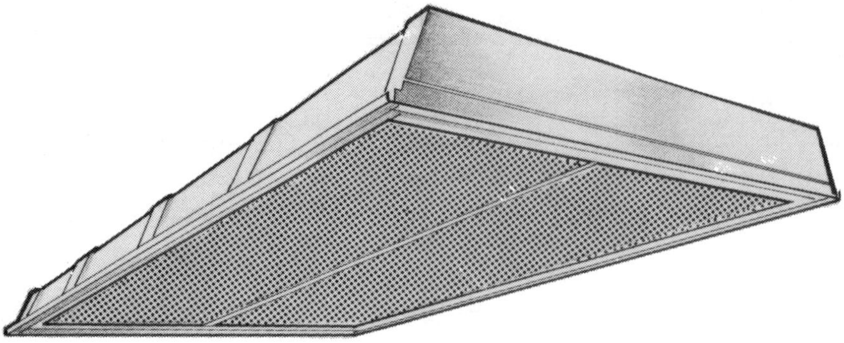

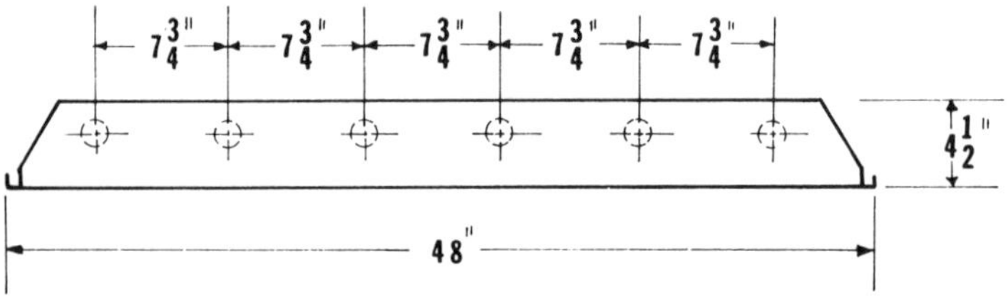

Description	4- X 4-ft troffer
Lamps	Six F40 T12, 3200 lm each, 20,000 h
Lens	Acrylic prismatic lens
Spacing ratio	1.4
Visual comfort probability	58 (length)/56 (cross)
Maintenance factors	0.75/0.70/0.65
Conversion factors	A. Unit with six F40 T12 lamps = 1.0
	B. Unit with eight F40 T12 lamps = 1.2

COST DETAILS PER LUMINAIRE

Type of unit	Input, W	Contractor's price		Installed cost	
		Grid	Flange	Grid	Flange
A	279	$135	$140	$199.50	$204.75
B	372	147	152	219.50	224.50

The installed cost includes published contractor's book price for the luminaire with lens and ballasts, number of lamps as shown, luminaire fastening devices, 6-ft length of 3/8-in flexible metallic conduit with two 7-ft lengths of no. 12 AF wire, two connectors, and the labor required for recess mounting and connection of the luminaire. See page B–52 to add a luminaire outlet recessed above ceiling.

These large units are used in big conference rooms, retail areas, airport terminals, waiting rooms, etc., where concentrated lighting is required at certain places.

RECESSED FLUORESCENT –4' X 4' TROFFER (ACRYLIC PRISMATIC LENS)

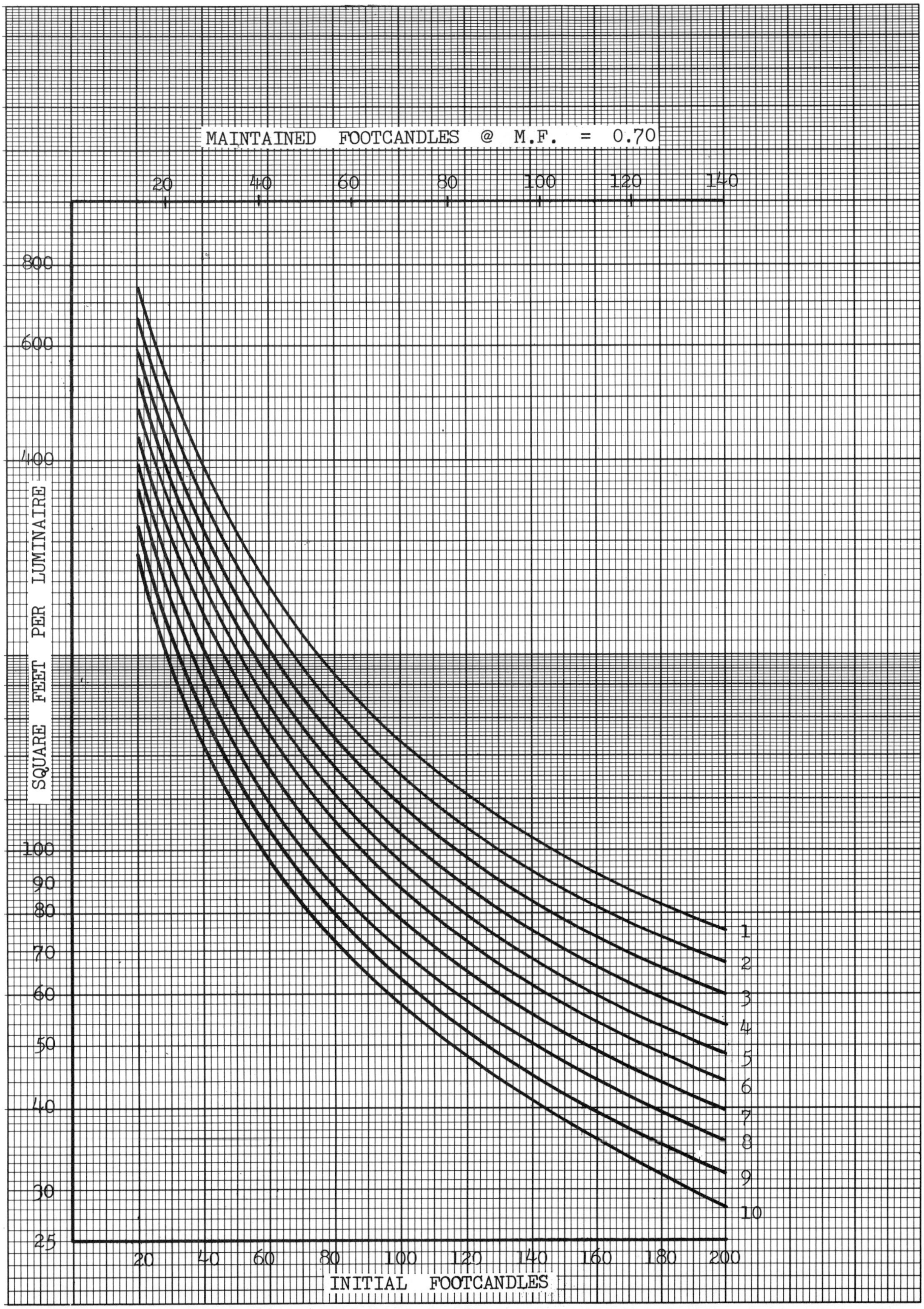

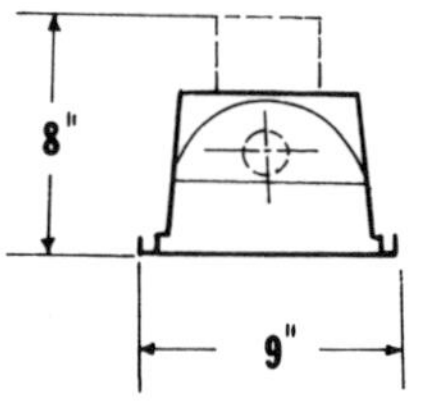

Description	9-in X 8-ft parabolic louvered troffer
Lamp	One F96 T12HO, 9200 lm, 12,000 h
Louvers	Parabolic-reflector cells of specular anodized aluminum
Spacing ratio	1.6
Visual comfort probability	96 (length)/96 (cross)
Maintanance factors	0.90/0.85/0.80
Conversion factors	A. Unit with one F96 T12HO lamp = 1.0 B. Unit with one F96 PG17 lamp = 1.65

COST DETAILS PER LUMINAIRE

Type of unit	Input, Watt	Contractor's price		Installed cost	
		Grid	Flange	Grid	Flange
A	140	$100	$112	$147	$164
B	230	105	117	155	171.25

The installed cost includes published contractor's book price for the luminaire with louvers and ballast, number of lamps as shown, luminaire fastening devices, 6-ft length of 3/8-in flexible metallic conduit with two 7-ft lengths of no. 12 AF wire, two connectors, and the labor required for recess mounting and connection of the luminaire. *See page B–52 to add a luminaire outlet recessed above ceiling.*

This handsome unit with deep parabolic reflector cells of specular anodized aluminum provides illumination with low apparent brightness and extra widespread distribution. Open louvers, having no static charge and no dirt- or grime-collecting surfaces, assure high maintenance factors.

RECESSED FLUORESCENT – 9" X 8' PARABOLIC LOUVERED TROFFER

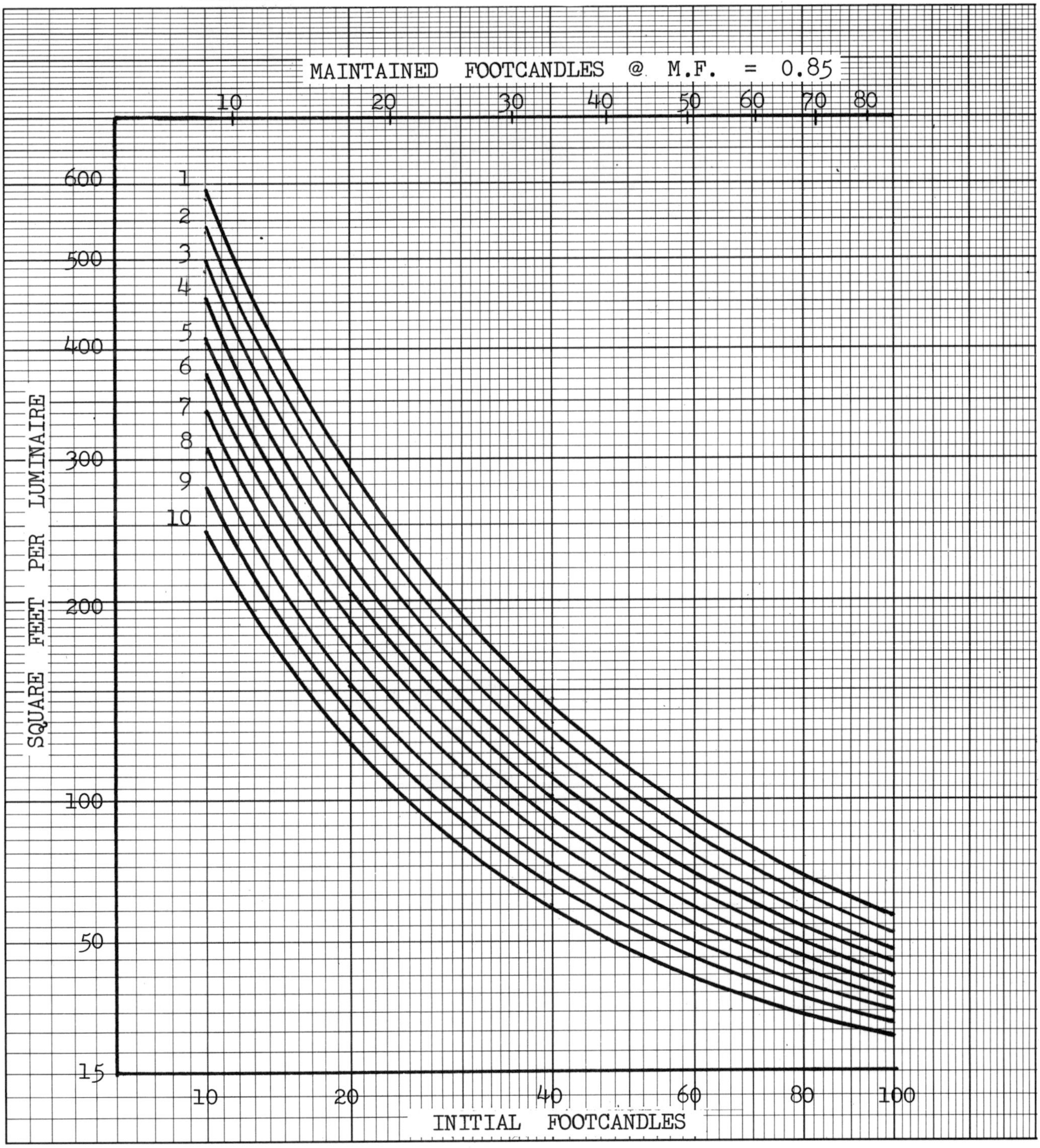

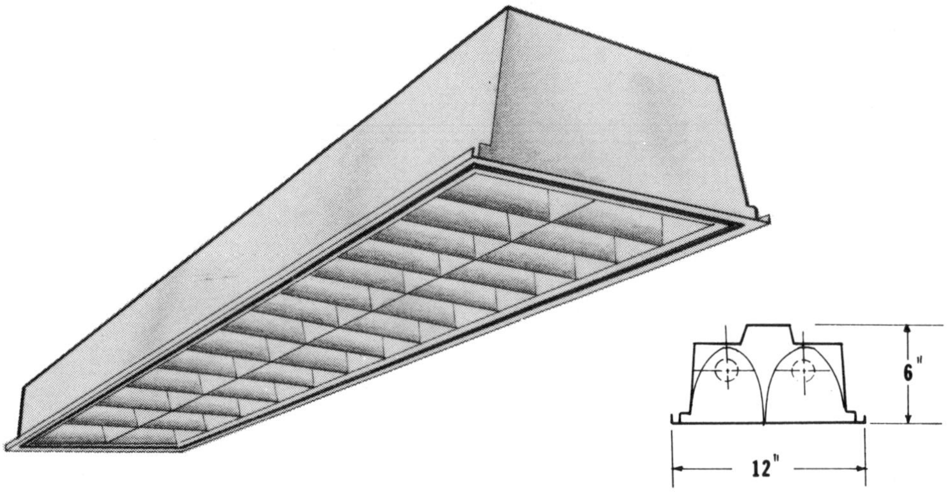

Description	1- × 4-ft parabolic louvered troffer
Lamps	Two F40 T12, 3200 lm each, 20,000 h
Louvers	Parabolic reflector cells of specular anodized aluminum
Spacing ratio	1.6
Visual comfort probability	95 (length)/91 (cross)
Maintenance factors	0.90/0.85/0.80
Input, W	93

COST DETAILS PER LUMINAIRE

Type of unit	Contractor's price	Installed cost
Grid	$64	$ 99.50
Flange	76	116

The installed cost includes published contractor's book price for the luminaire with louvers and ballast, number of lamps as shown, luminaire fastening devices, 6-ft length of 3/8-in flexible metallic conduit with two 7-ft lengths of no. 12 AF wire, two connectors, and the labor required for recess mounting and connection of the luminaire. See page B–52 to add a luminaire outlet recessed above ceiling.

This handsome unit with deep parabolic cells of specular anodized aluminum provides illumination with low apparent brightness and extra widespread distribution. Open louvers, having no static charge and no dirt- or grime-collecting surfaces, assure high maintenance factors.

RECESSED FLUORESCENT – 1' X 4' PARABOLIC LOUVERED TROFFER

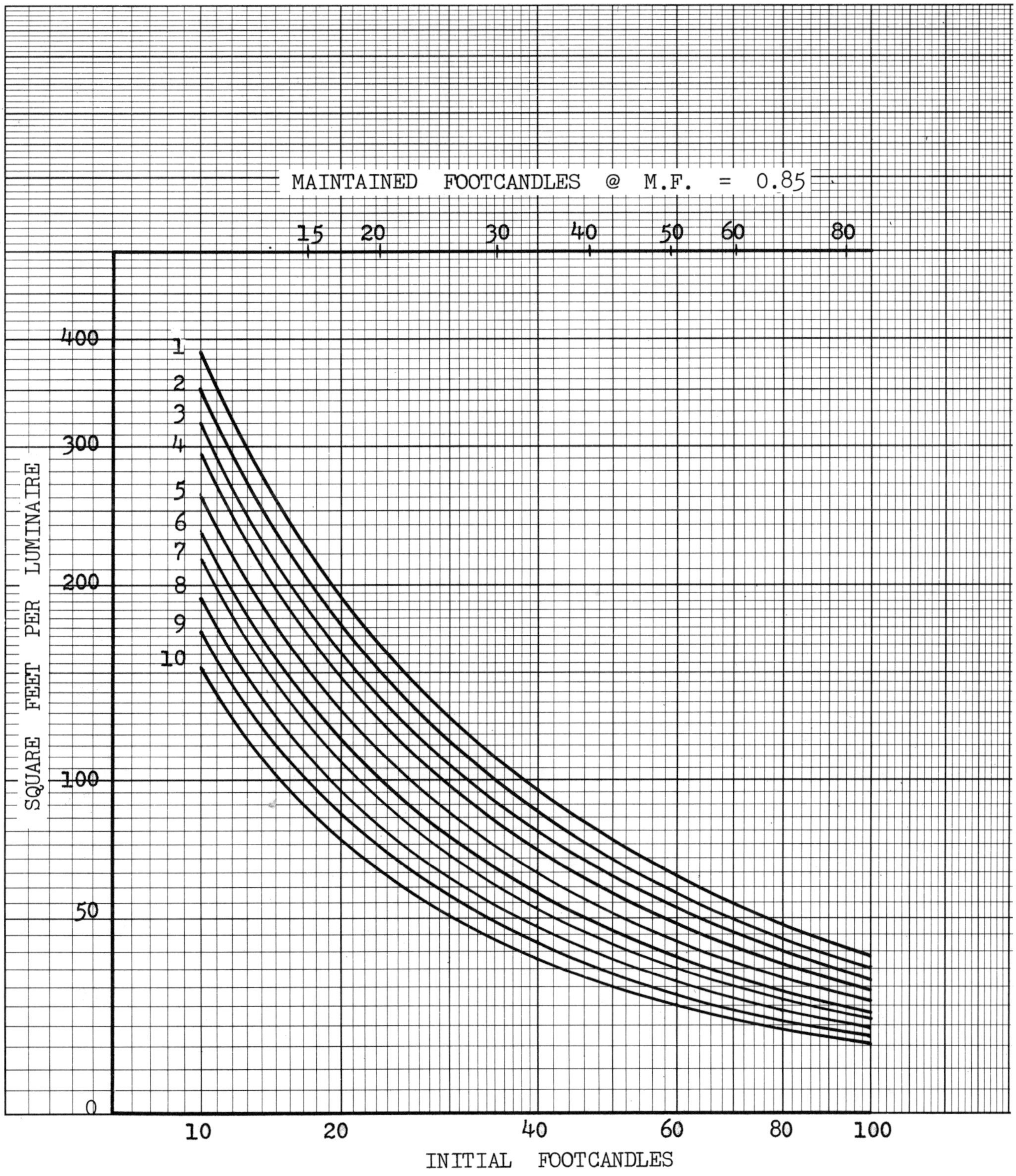

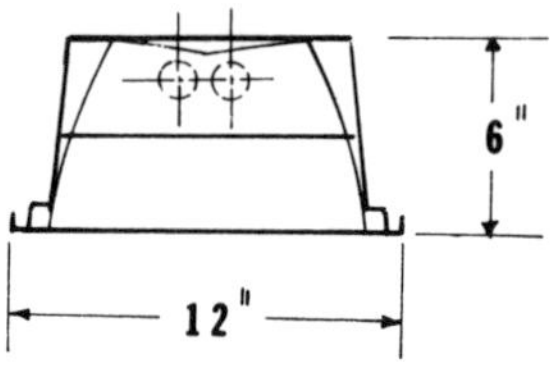

Description	1- × 4-ft parabolic louvered troffer
Lamp	Two F40 T12, 3200 lm each, 20,000 h
Louvers	Parabolic reflector cells of specular anodized aluminum
Spacing ratio	1.8
Visual comfort probability	91 (length)/80 (cross)
Maintenance factors	0.90/0.85/0.80
Input, W	93

COST DETAILS PER LUMINAIRE

Type of unit	Contractor's price	Installed cost
Grid	$61	$ 95.50
Flange	73	112

The installed cost includes published contractor's book price for the luminaire with louvers and ballast, number of lamps as shown, luminaire fastening devices, 6-ft length of 3/8-in flexible metallic conduit with two 7-ft lengths of no. 12 AF wire, two connectors, and the labor required for recess mounting and connection of the luminaire. *See page B–52 to add a luminaire outlet recessed above ceiling.*

This handsome unit with deep parabolic reflector cells of specular anodized aluminum provides illumination with low apparent brightness and extra widespread distribution. Open louvers, having no static charge and no dirt- or grime-collecting surfaces, assure high maintenance factors.

RECESSED FLUORESCENT – 1' X 4' PARABOLIC LOUVERED TROFFER

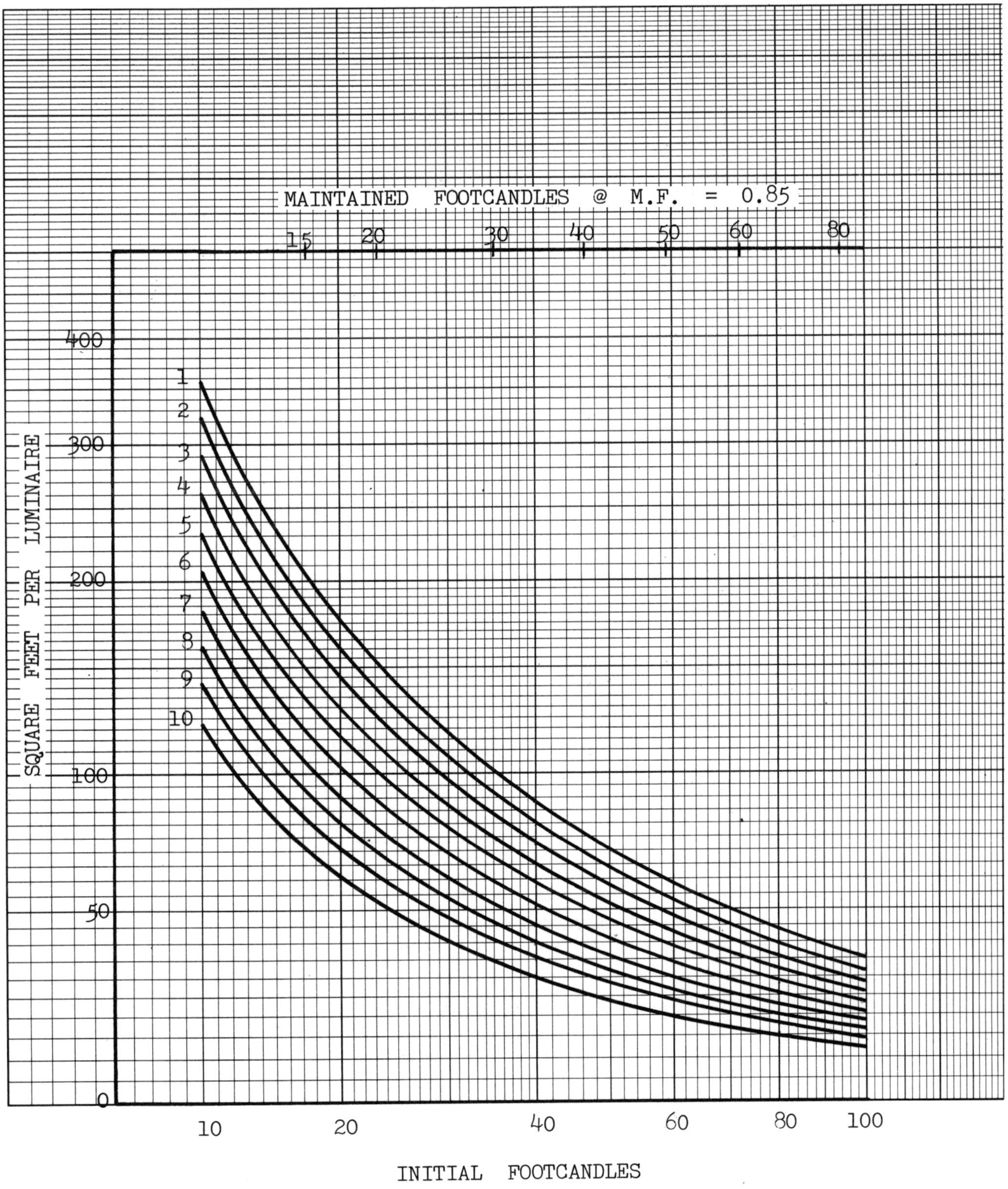

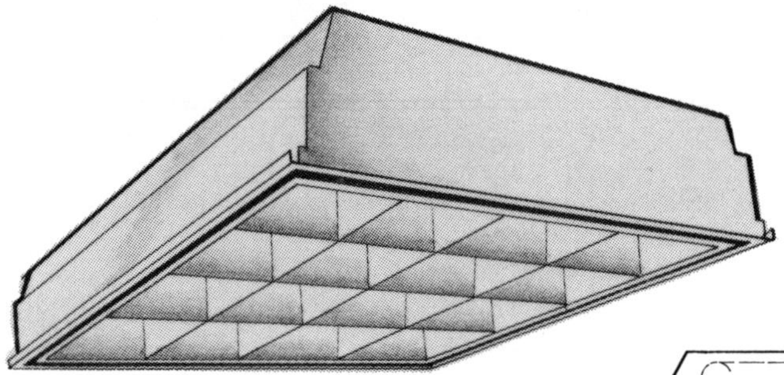

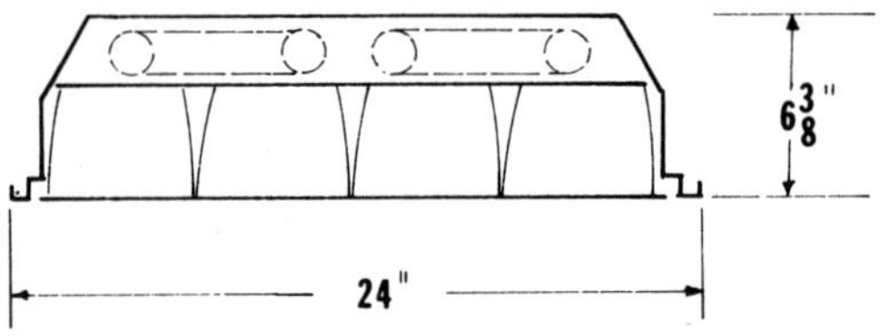

Description	2- X 2-ft parabolic-louvered troffer
Lamps	Two F40/U T12, 3025 lm each, 12,000 h
Louvers	Parabolic reflector cells of specular anodized aluminum
Spacing ratio	1.3
Visual comfort probability	92 (length)/91 (cross)
Maintenance factors	0.90/0.85/0.80
Input, W	93

COST DETAILS PER LUMINAIRE

Type of unit	Contractor's price	Installed cost
Grid	$65	$ 99
Flange	76	114.25

The installed cost includes published contractor's book price for the luminaire with louvers and ballast, number of lamps as shown, luminaire fastening devices, 6-ft length of 3/8-in flexible metallic conduit with two 7-ft lengths of no. 12 AF wire, two connectors, and the labor required for recess mounting and connection of the luminaire. *See paeg B–52 to add a luminaire outlet recessed above ceiling.*

This handsome unit, with deep parabolic reflector cells of specular anodized aluminum, provides illumination with low apparent brightness. Open louvers, having no static charge and no dirt- or grime-collecting surfaces, assure high maintenance factors.

RECESSED FLUORESCENT – 2' X 2' PARABOLIC LOUVERED TROFFER

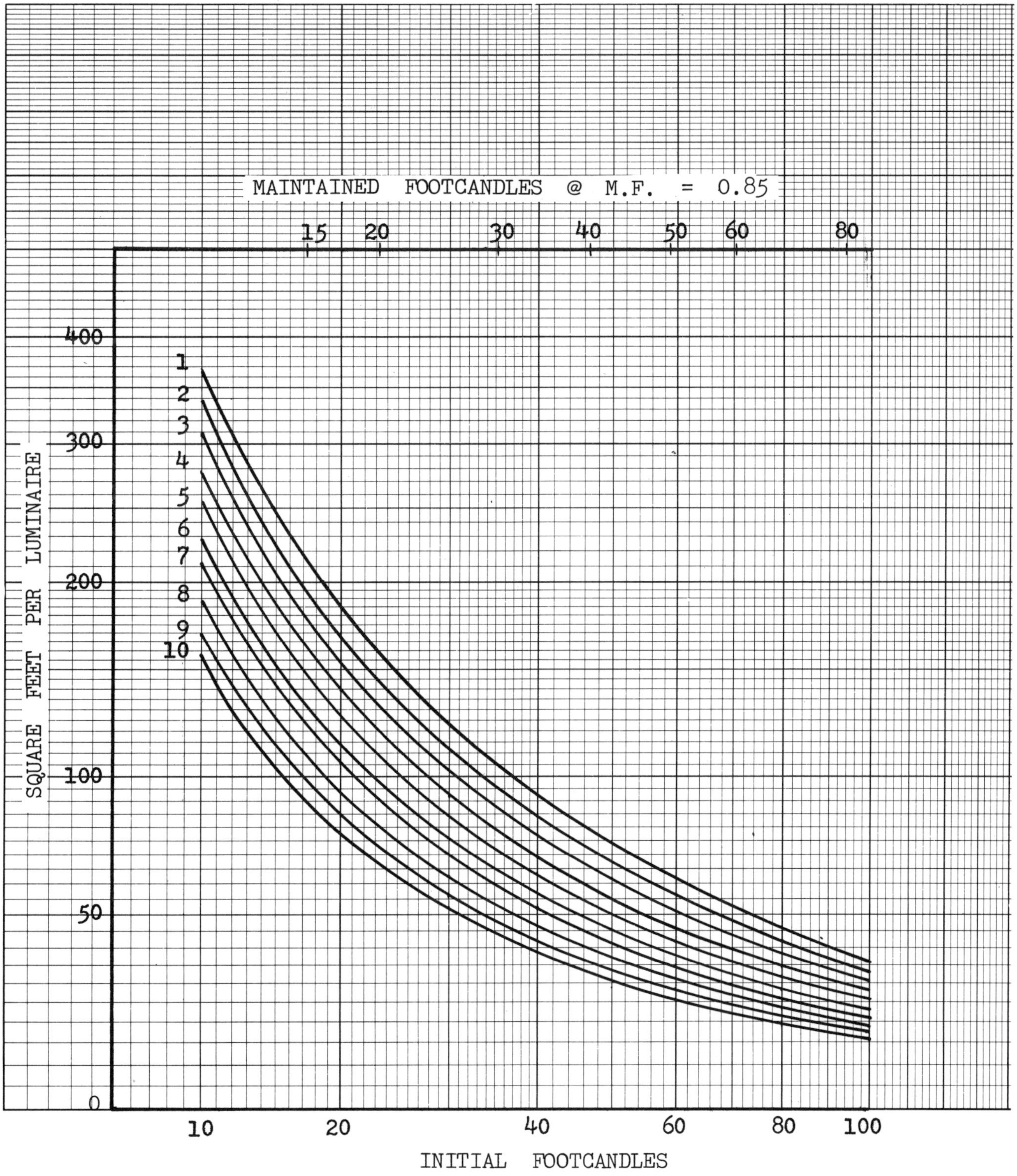

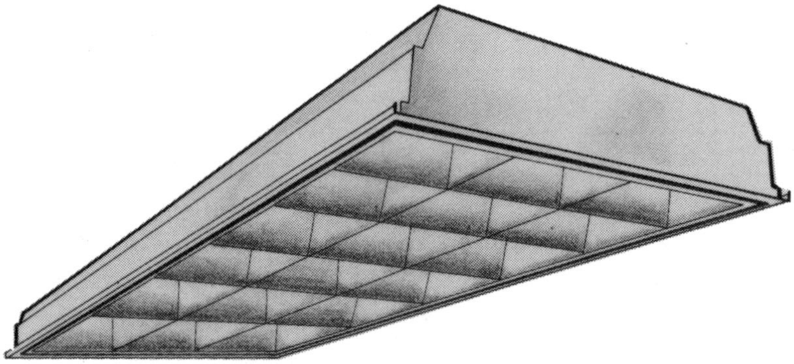

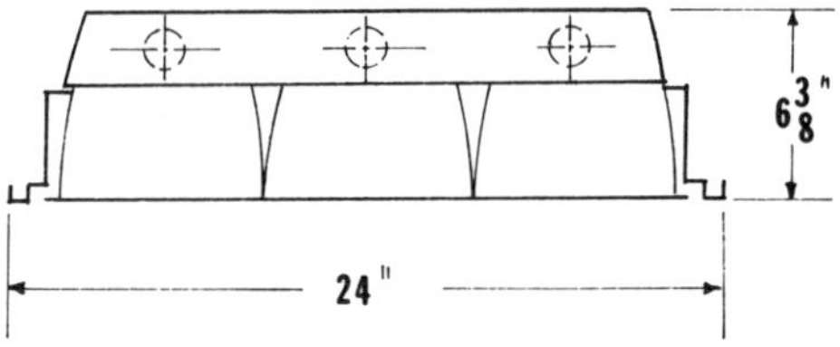

Description	2- × 4-ft parabolic louvered troffer
Lamps	Three F40 T12, 3200 lm each, 20,000 h
Louvers	Parabolic reflector cells of specular anodized aluminum
Spacing ratio	1.5
Visual comfort probability	88 (length)/90 (cross)
Maintenance factors	0.90/0.85/0.80
Input, W	146

COST DETAILS PER LUMINAIRE

Type of unit	Contractor's price	Installed cost
Grid	$86	$129.50
Flange	98	145.75

The installed cost includes published contractor's book price for the luminaire with louvers and ballasts, number of lamps as shown, luminaire fastening devices, 6-ft length of 3/8-in flexible metallic conduit with two 7-ft lengths of no. 12 AF wire, two connectors, and the labor required for recess mounting and connection of the luminaire. See page B–52 to add a luminaire outlet recessed above ceiling.

This handsome unit, with deep parabolic reflector cells of specular anodized aluminum, provides illumination with low apparent brightness and extra widespread distribution. Open louvers, having no static charge and no dirt- or grime-collecting surfaces, assure high maintenance factors.

RECESSED FLUORESCENT – 2′ X 4′ PARABOLIC LOUVERED TROFFER

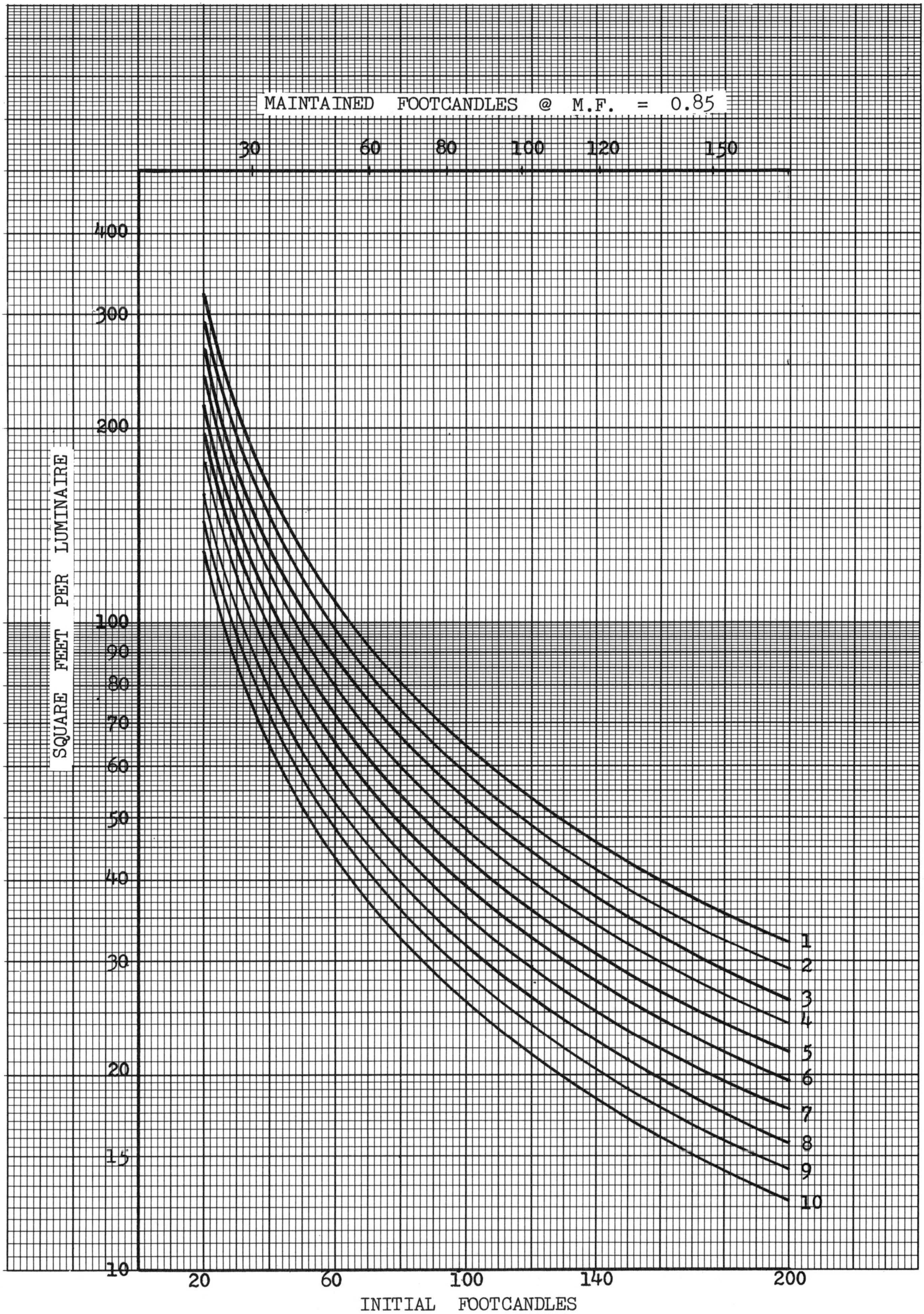

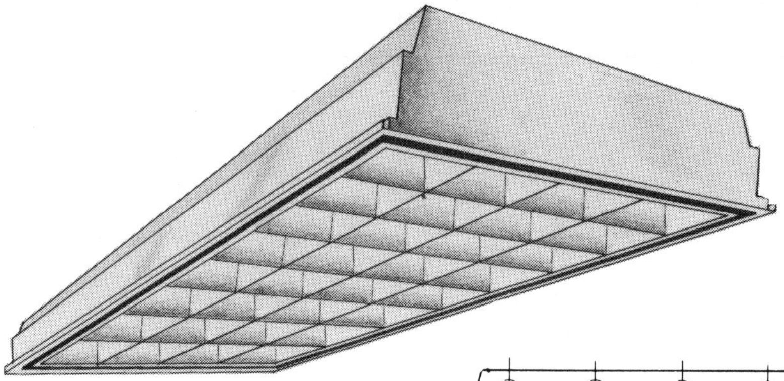

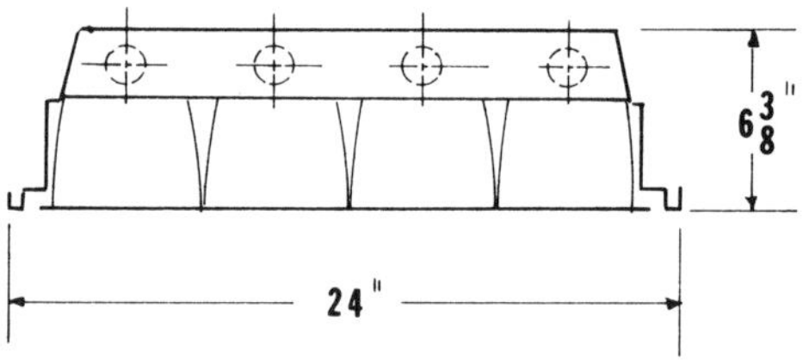

Description	2- X 4-ft parabolic louvered troffer
Lamps	Four F40 T12, 3200 lm each, 20,000 h
Louvers	Parabolic reflector cells of specular anodized aluminum
Spacing ratio	1.3
Visual comfort probability	90 (length)/91 (cross)
Maintenance factors	0.90/0.85/0.80
Input, W	186

COST DETAILS PER LUMINAIRE

Type of unit	Contractor's price	Installed cost
Grid	$ 95	$143.25
Flange	107	159

The installed cost includes published contractor's book price for the luminaire with louvers and ballasts, number of lamps as shown, luminaire fastening devices, 6-ft length of 3/8-in flexible metallic conduit with two 7-ft lengths of no. 12 AF wire, two connectors, and the labor required for recess mounting and connection of the luminaire. See page B–52 to add a luminaire outlet recessed above ceiling.

This handsome unit, with deep parabolic cells of specular anodized aluminum, provides illumination with low apparent brightness. Open louvers, having no static charge and no dirt- or grime-collecting surfaces, assure high maintenance factors.

RECESSED FLUORESCENT – 2′ X 4′ PARABOLIC LOUVERED TROFFER

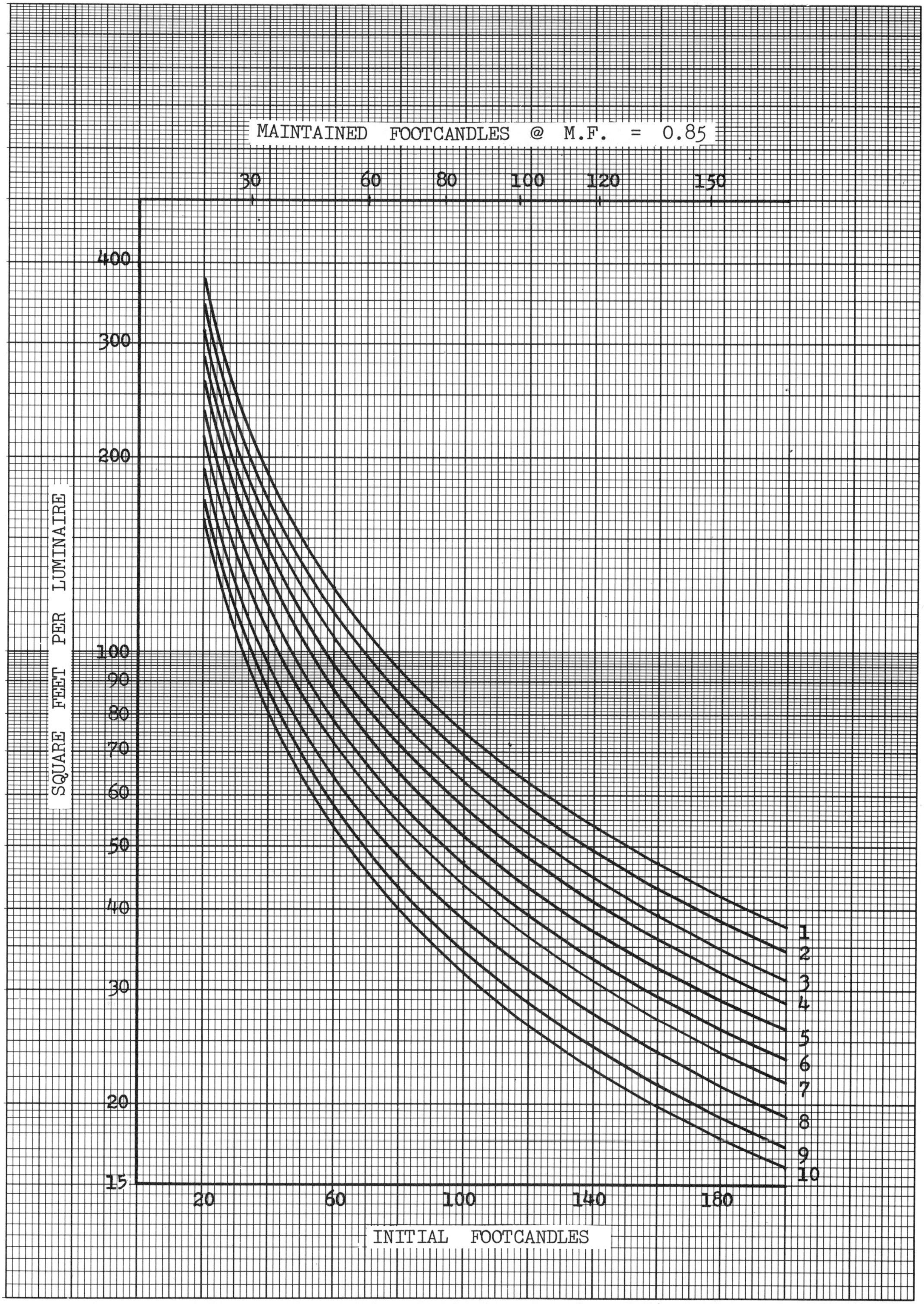

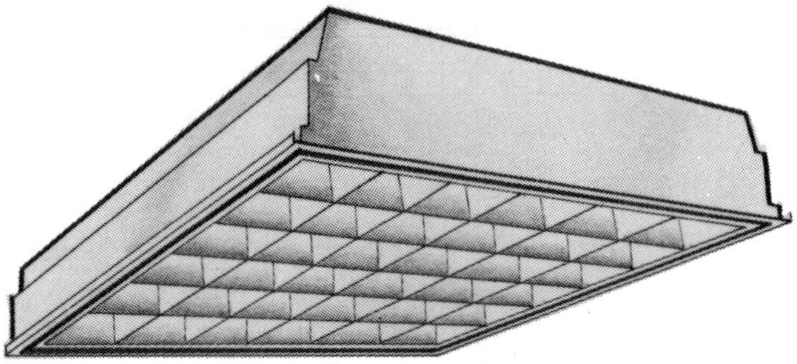

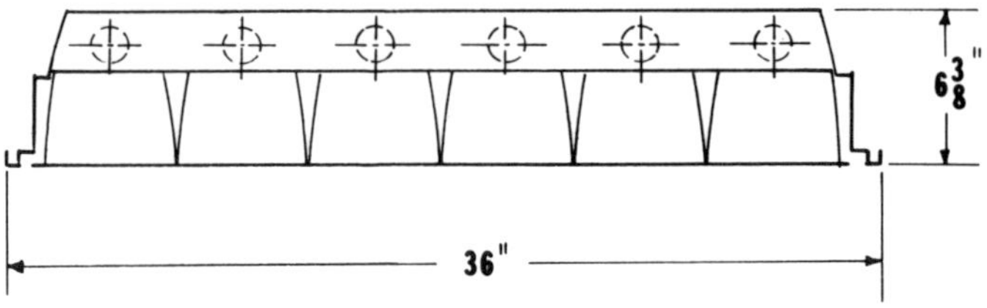

Description	3- X 3-ft parabolic louvered troffer
Lamps	Six F30 T12, 2250 lm each, 18,000 h
Louvers	Parabolic reflector cells of specular anodized aluminum
Spacing ratio	1.3
Visual comfort probability	93 (length)/92 (cross)
Maintenance factors	0.90/0.85/0.80
Input, W	200

COST DETAILS PER LUMINAIRE

Type of unit	Contractor's price	Installed cost
Grid	$120	$176.50
Flange	132	194.75

The installed cost includes published contractor's book price for the luminaire with louvers and ballasts, number of lamps as shown, luminaire fastening devices, 6-ft length of 3/8-in flexible metallic conduit with two 7-ft lengths of no. 12 AF wire, two connectors, and the labor required for recess mounting and connection of the luminaire. *See page B–52 to add a luminaire outlet recessed above ceiling.*

This handsome unit, with deep parabolic reflector cells of specular anodized aluminum, provides illumination with low apparent brightness. Open louvers, having no static charge and no dirt- or grime-collecting surfaces, assure high maintenance factors.

RECESSED FLUORESCENT – 3' X 3' PARABOLIC LOUVERED TROFFER

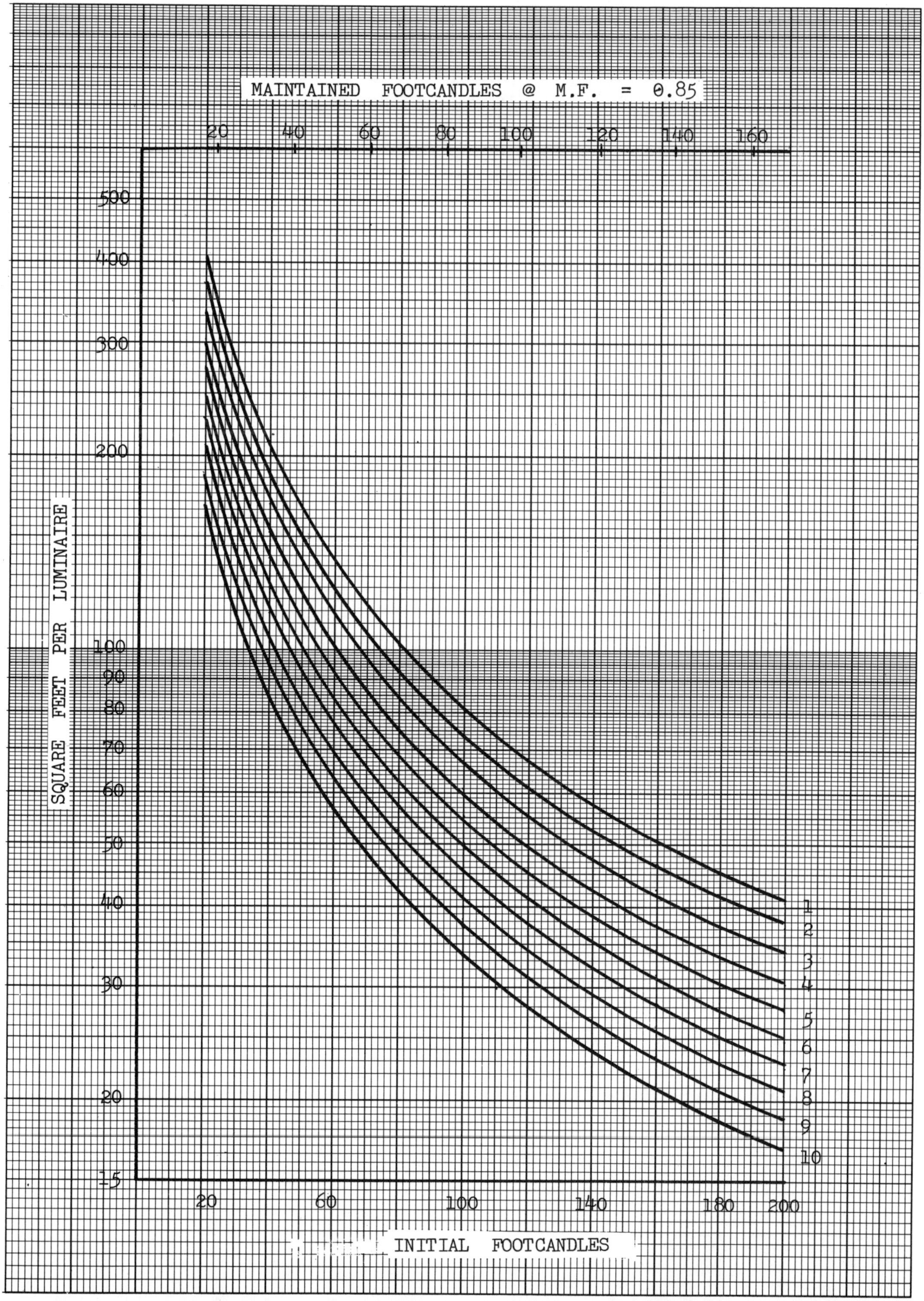

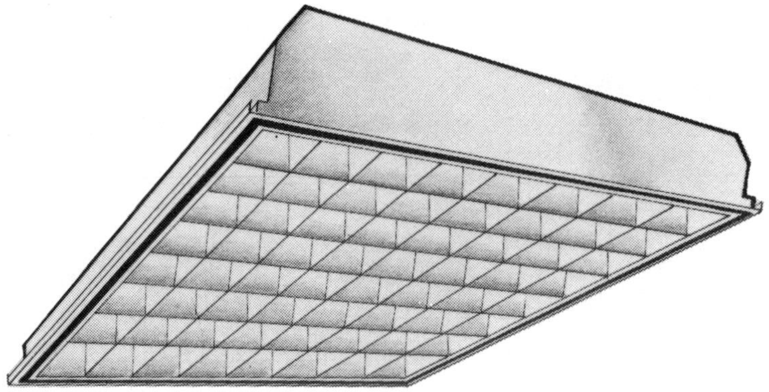

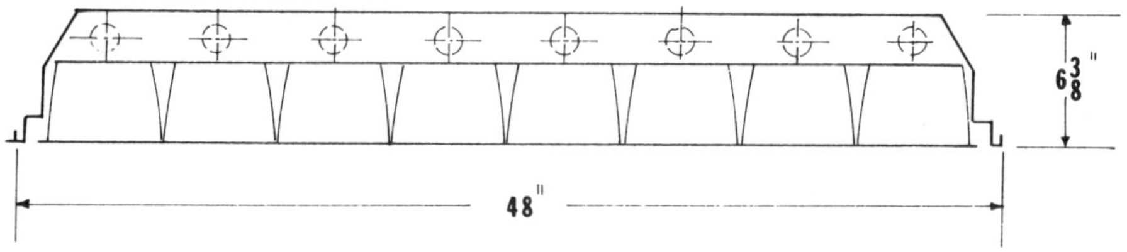

Description	4- X 4-ft parabolic louvered troffer
Lamps	Eight F40 T12, 3200 lm each, 20,000 h
Louvers	Parabolic reflector cells of specular anodized aluminum
Spacing ratio	1.4
Visual comfort probability	89 (length)/88 (cross)
Maintenance factors	0.90/0.85/0.80
Input, W	372

COST DETAILS PER LUMINAIRE

Type of unit	Contractor's price	Installed cost
Grid	$160	$234.25
Flange	172	244.50

The installed cost includes published contractor's book price for the luminaire with louvers and ballasts, number of lamps as shown, luminaire fastening devices, 6-ft length of 3/8-in flexible metallic conduit with two 7-ft lengths of no. 12 AF wire, two connectors, and the labor required for recess mounting and connection of the luminaire. *See page B–52 to add a luminaire outlet recessed above ceiling.*

This handsome unit, with deep parabolic reflector cells of specular anodized aluminum, provides illumination with low apparent brightness. Open louvers, having no static charge and no dirt- or grime-collecting surfaces, assure high maintenance factors.

RECESSED FLUORESCENT – 4′ X 4′ PARABOLIC LOUVERED TROFFER

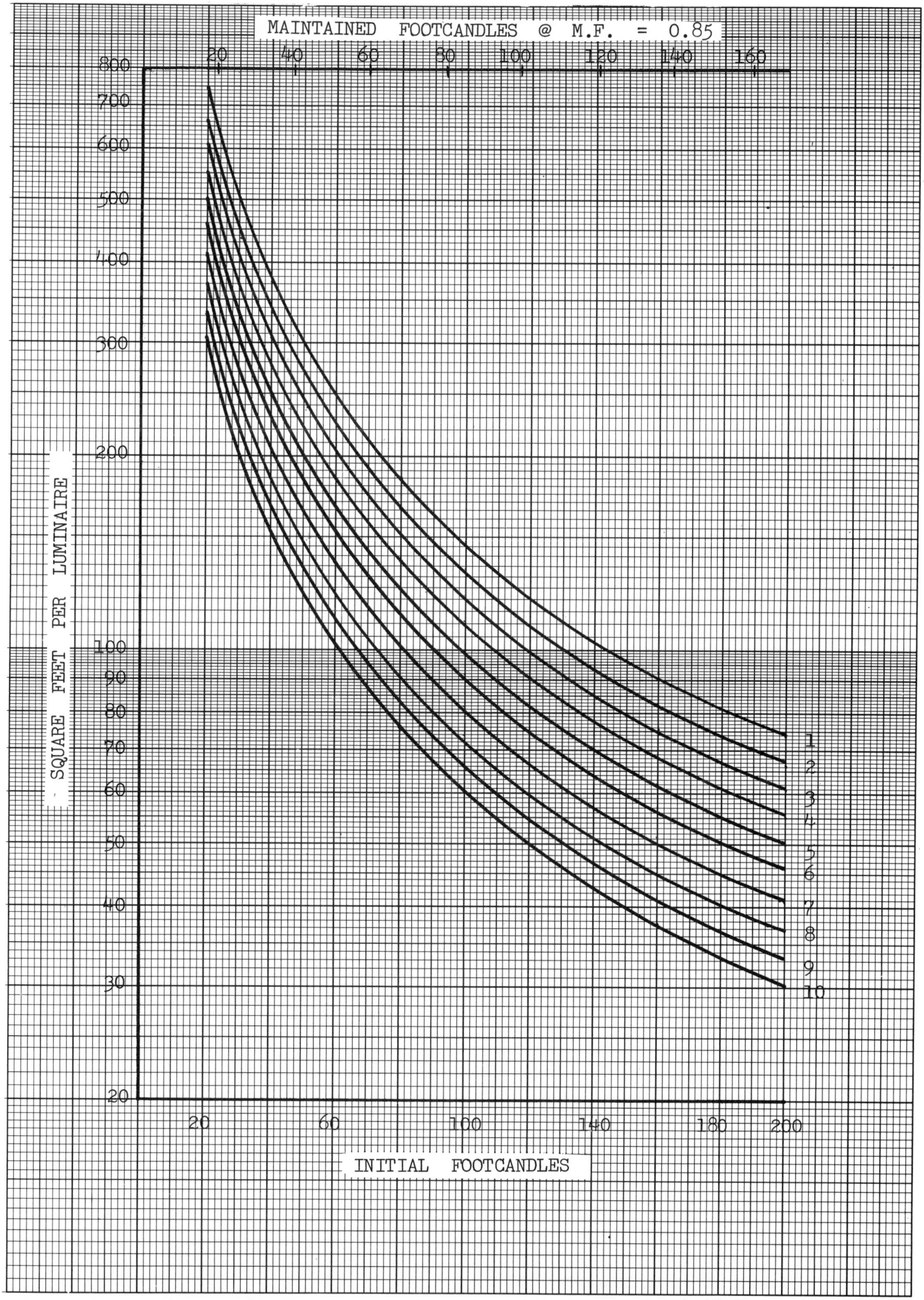

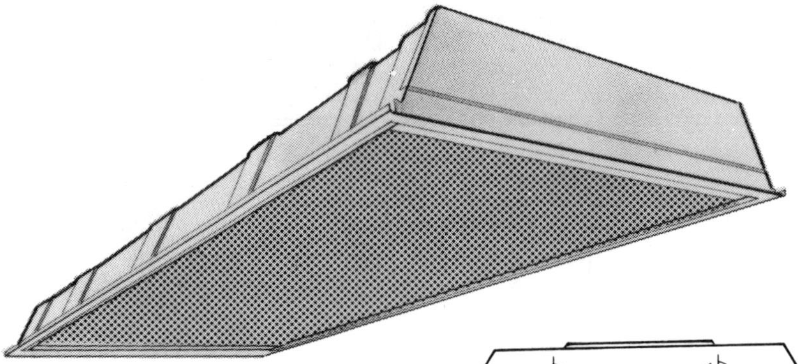

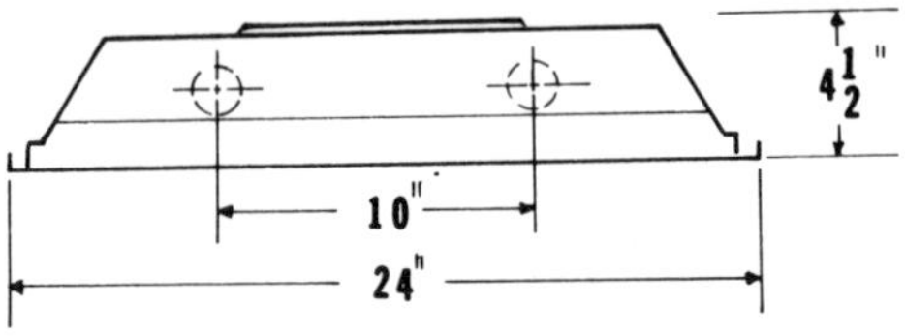

Description	2- X 4-ft troffer with Carolite Radialens
Lamps	Two F40 T12, 3200 lm each, 20,000 h
Lens	Carolite Radialens with overlay
Spacing ratio	1.75
Visual comfort probability	59 (length)/57 (cross)
Maintenance factors	0.75/0.70/0.65
Input, W	93
Conversion factor	Same unit without overlay = 1.05

COST DETAILS PER LUMINAIRE

Type of unit	Contractor's price	Installed cost
Grid	$60	$ 94.50
Flange	67	104.75

The installed cost includes published contractor's book price for the luminaire with lens and ballast, number of lamps as shown, luminaire fastening devices, 6-ft length of 3/8-in flexible metallic conduit with two 7-ft lengths of no. 12 AF wire, two connectors, and the labor required for recess mounting and connection of the luminaire. See page B–52 to add a luminaire outlet above ceiling.

Luminaires with this special diffusing medium provide uniform lighting with extra widespread distribution. These luminaires are widely used in office buildings.

This information was based on test 5941, as prepared by Day-Brite Lighting Division, Emerson Electric.

RECESSED FLUORESCENT – 2′ X 4′ TROFFER (CAROLITE RADIALENS)

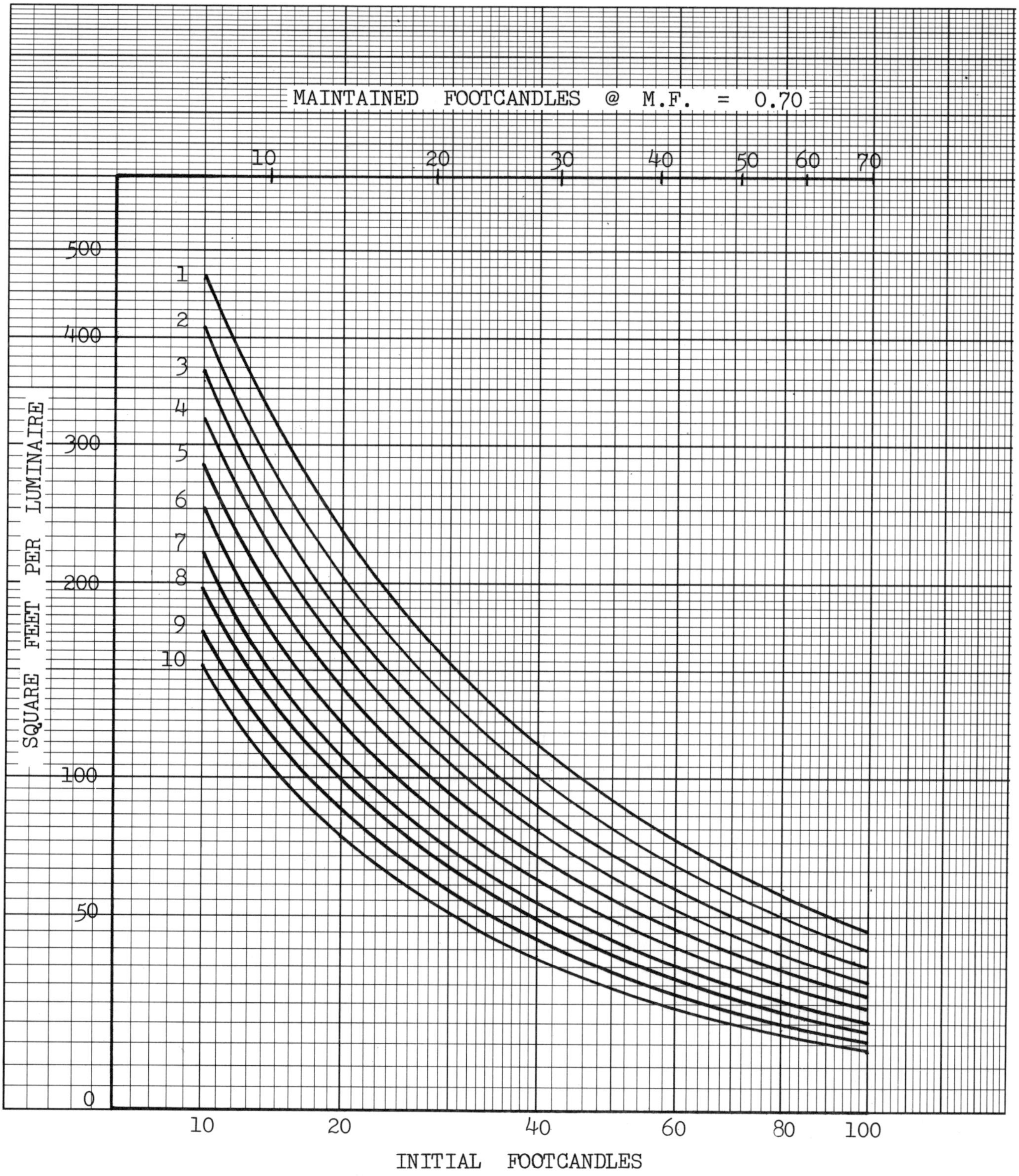

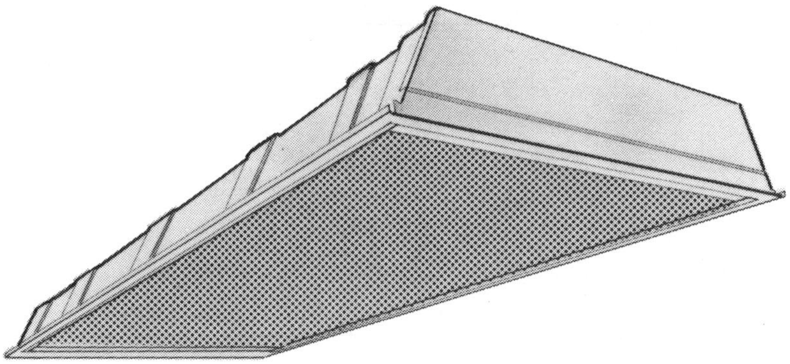

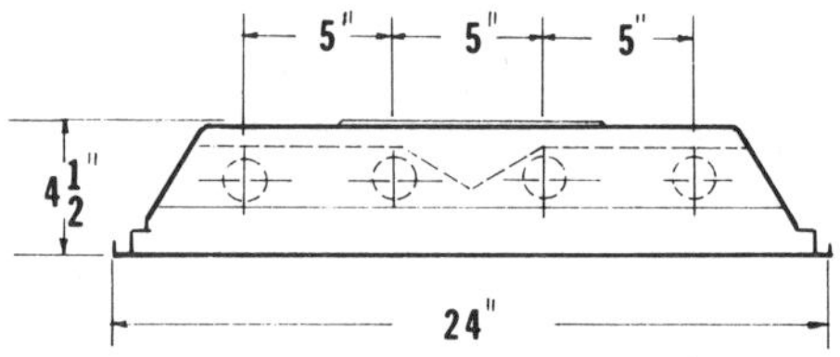

Description	2- X 4-ft troffer with Carolite Radialens
Lamps	Four F40 T12, 3200 lm each, 20,000 h
Lens	Carolite Radialens (with overlay)
Spacing ratio	1.8
Visual comfort probability	45 (length)/45 (cross)
Maintenance factor	0.75/0.70/0.65
Conversion factors	A. Unit with four F40 T12 lamps = 1.0
	B. Unit with three F40 T12 lamps = 0.75

COST DETAILS PER LUMINAIRE

Type of unit	Input, W	Contractor's price		Installed cost	
		Grid	Flange	Grid	Flange
A	186	$68	$75	$110.25	$119.75
B	146	68	75	107.25	117.50

The installed cost includes published contractor's book price for the luminaire with lens and ballasts, number of lamps as shown, luminaire fastening devices, 6-ft length of 3/8-in flexible metallic conduit with two 7-ft lengths of no. 12 AF wire, two connectors, and the labor required for recess mounting and connection of the luminaire. *See page B–52 to add a luminaire outlet recessed above ceiling.*

Luminaires with this special diffusing medium provide uniform lighting with extra-widespread distribution. These luminaires are widely used in office buildings.

This information was based on test 16630, prepared by ITL, for Lithonia Lighting, Georgia.

RECESSED FLUORESCENT – 2' X 4' TROFFER (CAROLITE RADIALENS)

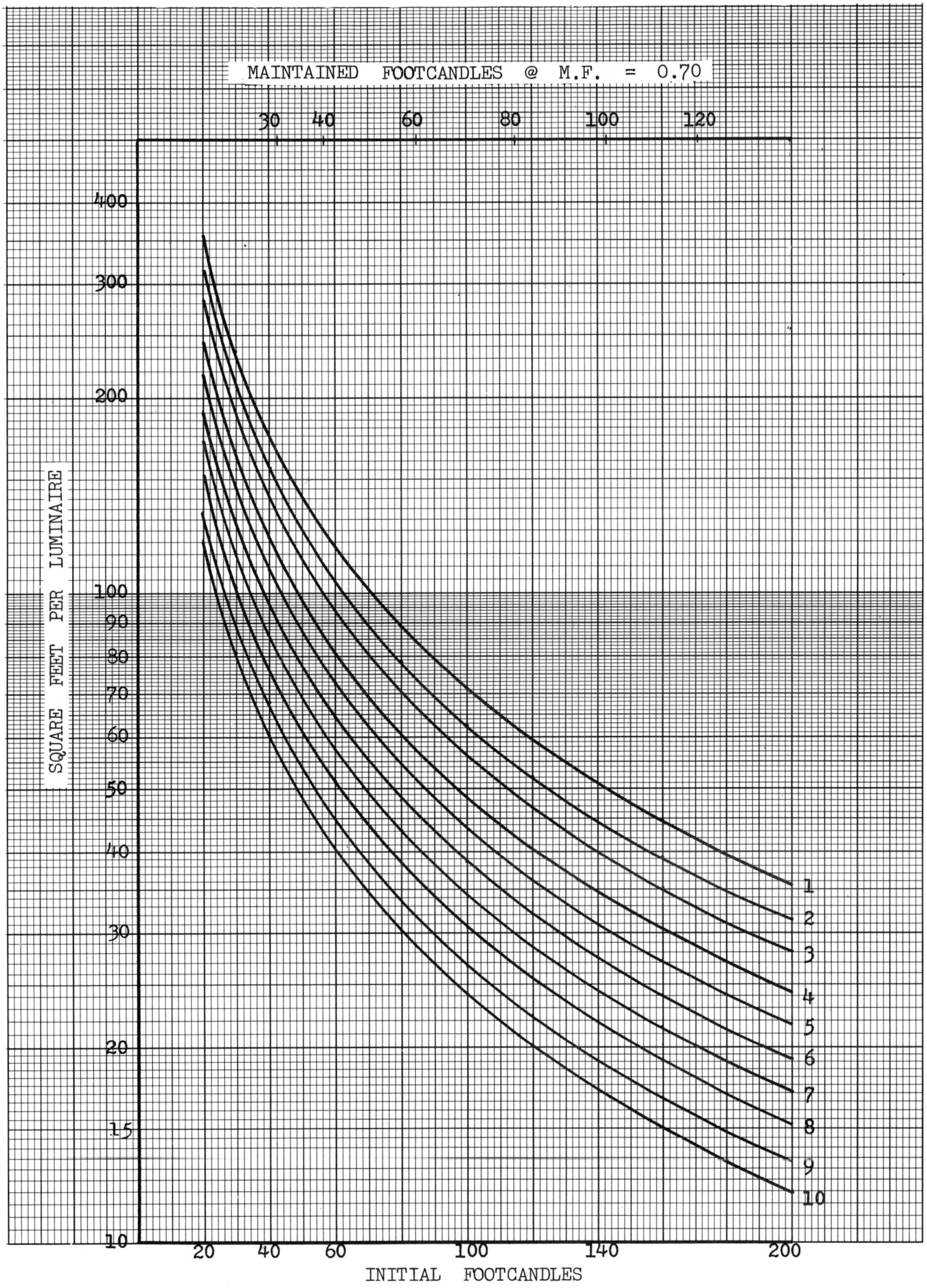

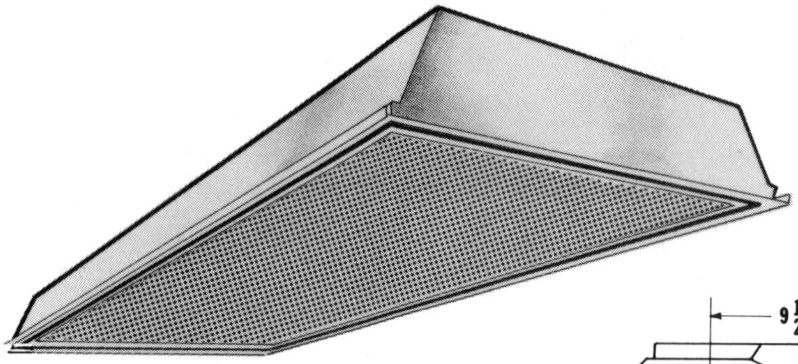

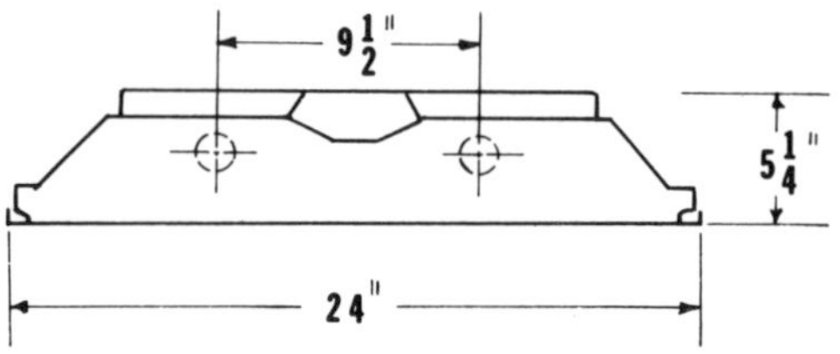

Description	2- × 4-ft troffer with Day-Brite VIP lens
Lamps	Two F40 T12, 3200 lm each, 20,000 h
Lens	Day-Brite VIP lens
Spacing ratio	1.79
Visual comfort probability	66 (length)/65 (cross)
Maintenance factors	0.75/0.70/0.65
Input, W	93

COST DETAILS PER LUMINAIRE

Type of unit	Contractor's price	Installed cost
Grid	\$72	\$109.50
Flange	79	119.50

The installed cost includes published contractor's book price for the luminaire with lens and ballast, number of lamps as shown, luminaire fastening devices, 6-ft length of 3/8-in flexible metallic conduit with two 7-ft lengths of no. 12 AF wire, two connectors, and the labor required for recess mounting and connection of the luminaire. See page B–52 to add a luminaire outlet above ceiling.

Luminaires with this special diffusing medium provide uniform lighting with extra-widespread distribution. These luminaires are widely used in office buildings.

The reference luminaire is as manufactured by Day-Brite, Mobilex unit.

This information was based on test 6300, prepared by Day-Brite Lighting Division, Emerson Electric.

RECESSED FLUORESCENT – 2′ X 4′ TROFFER (DAY-BRITE VIP LENS)

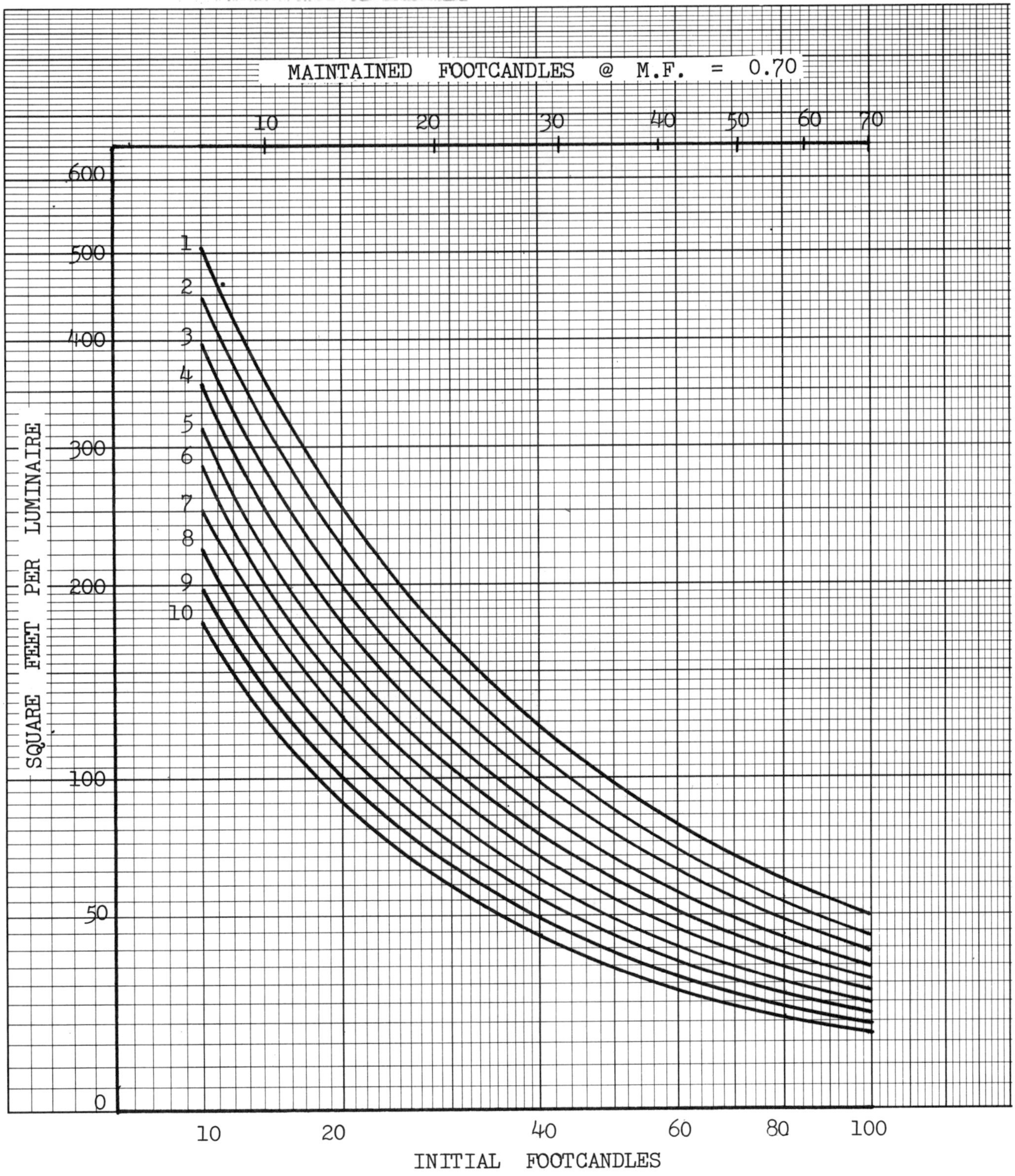

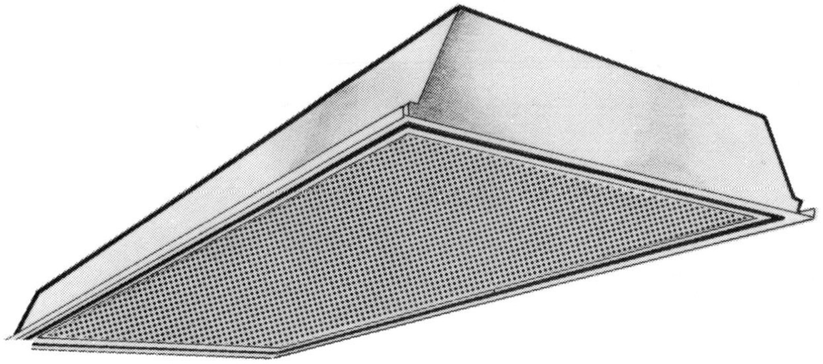

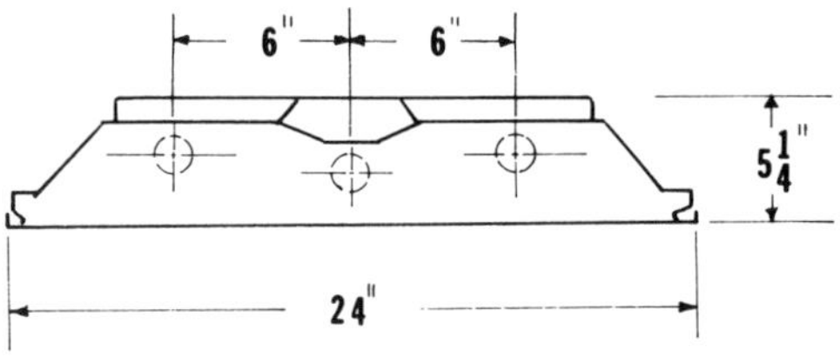

Description	2- X 4-ft troffer with Day-Brite VIP lens
Lamps	Three F40 T12, 3200 lm each, 20,000 h
Lens	Day-Brite VIP lens
Spacing ratio	1.81
Visual comfort probability	59 (length)/57 (cross)
Maintenance factors	0.75/0.70/0.65
Input, W	146

COST DETAILS PER LUMINAIRE

Type of unit	Contractor's price	Installed cost
Grid	$82	$124.50
Flange	89	134.75

The installed cost includes published contractor's book price for the luminaire with lens and ballasts, number of lamps as shown, luminaire fastening devices, 6-ft length of 3/8-in flexible metallic conduit with two 7-ft lengths of no. 12 AF wire, two connectors, and the labor required for recess mounting and connection of the luminaire. See page B–52 to add a luminaire outlet recessed above ceiling.

Luminaires with this special diffusing medium provide uniform lighting with extra-widespread distribution. These luminaires are widely used in office buildings.

The reference luminaire is as manufactured by Day-Brite, Mobilex unit.

This information was based on test 6297, prepared by Day-Brite Lighting Division, Emerson Electric.

RECESSED FLUORESCENT – 2' X 4' TROFFER (DAY-BRITE VIP LENS)

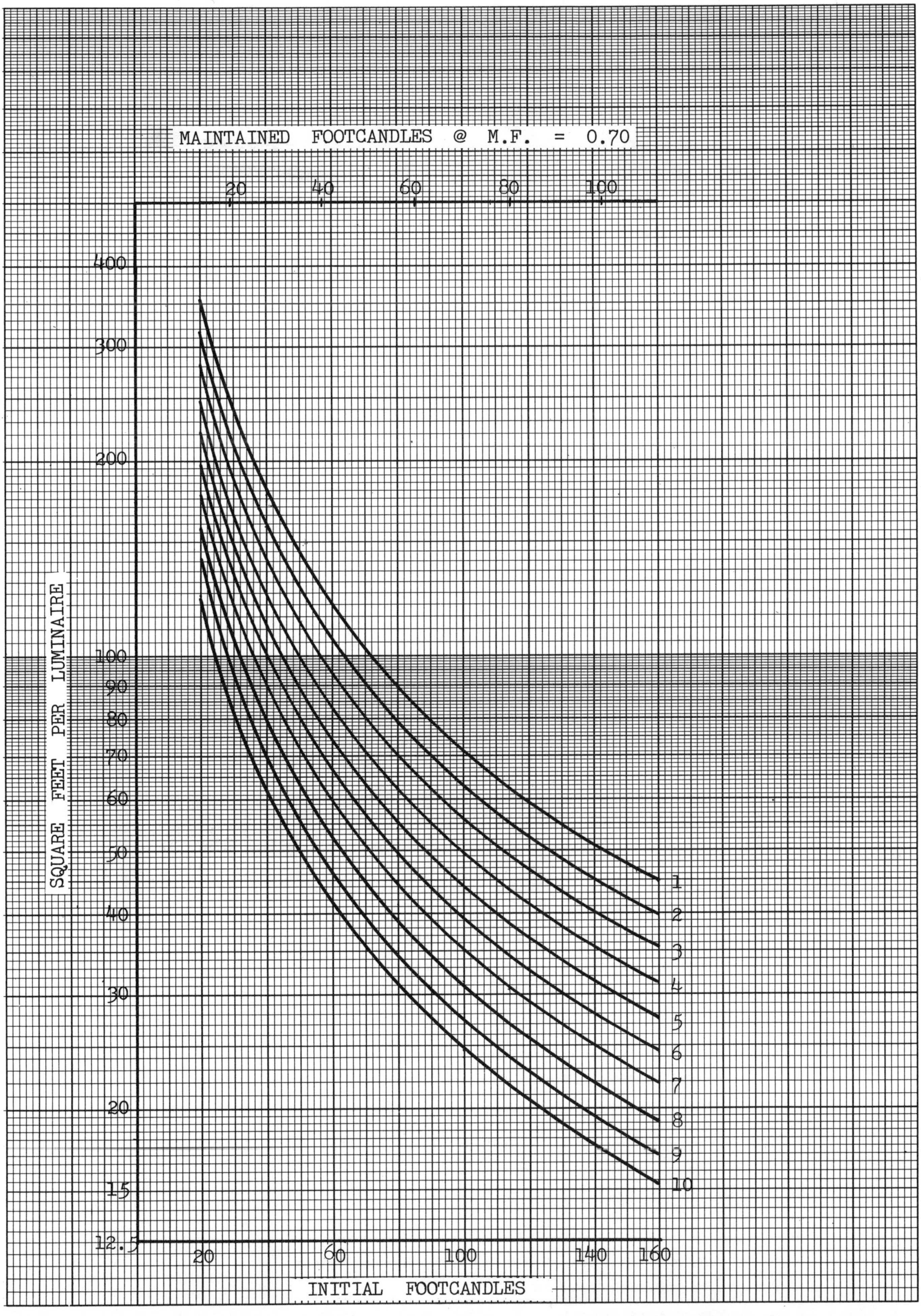

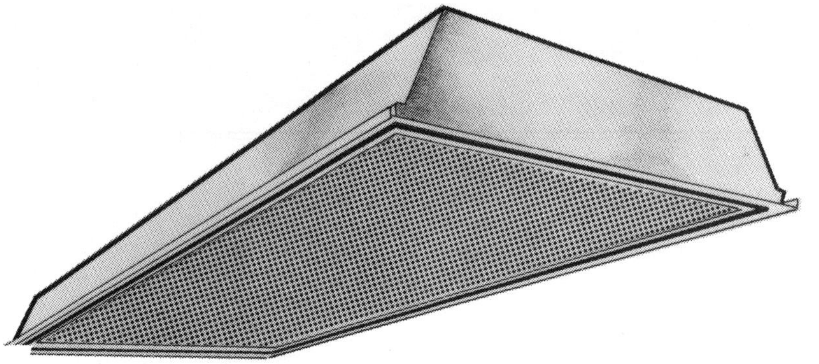

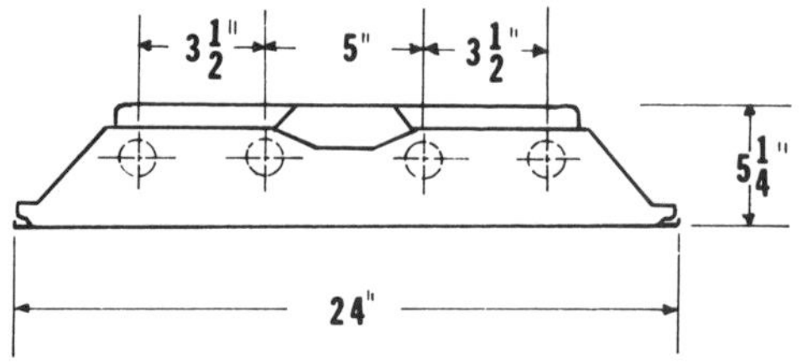

Description	2- X 4-ft troffer with Day-Brite VIP lens
Lamps	Four F40 T12, 3200 lm each, 20,000 h
Lens	Day-Brite VIP lens
Spacing ratio	1.77
Visual comfort probability	53 (length)/52 (cross)
Maintenance factors	0.75/0.70/0.65
Input, W	186

COST DETAILS PER LUMINAIRE

Type of unit	Contractor's price	Installed cost
Grid	$82	$127.50
Flange	89	136.75

The installed cost includes published contractor's book price for the luminaire with lens and ballasts, number of lamps as shown, luminaire fastening devices, 6-ft length of 3/8-in flexible metallic conduit with two 7-ft lengths of no. 12 AF wire, two connectors, and the labor required for recess mounting and connection of the luminaire. See page B–52 to add a luminaire outlet above ceiling.

Luminaires with this special diffusing medium provide uniform lighting with extra-widespread distribution. These luminaires are widely used in office buildings.

The reference luminaire is as manufactured by Day-Brite, Mobilex unit.

This information was based on test 6289, prepared by Day-Brite Lighting Division, Emerson Electric.

RECESSED FLUORESCENT – 2′ X 4′ TROFFER (DAY-BRITE VIP LENS)

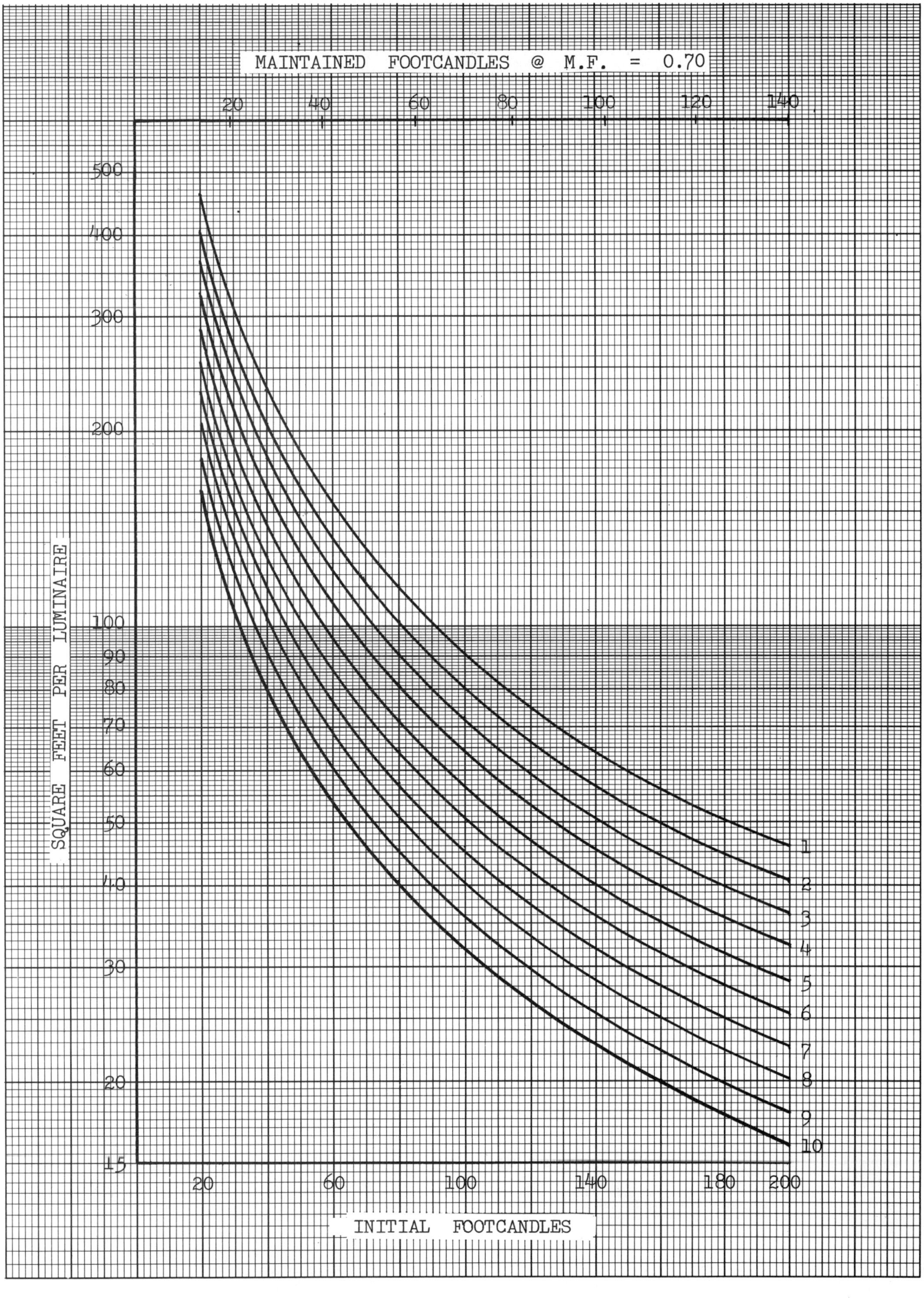

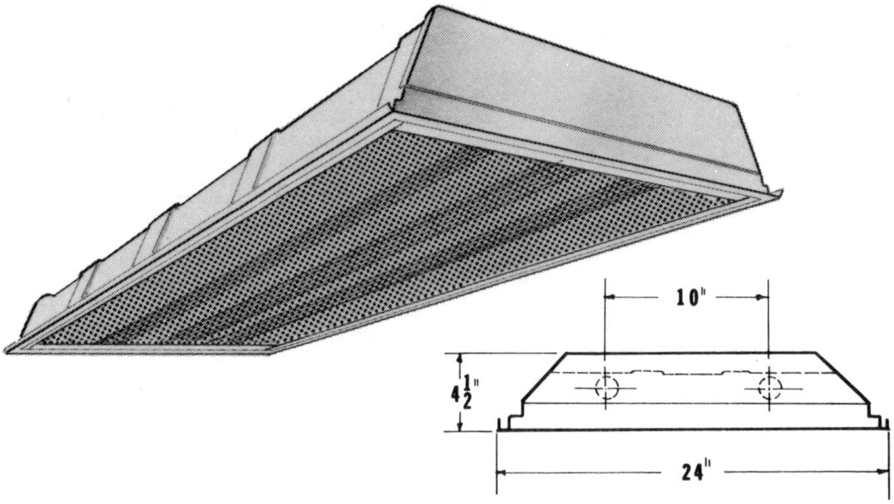

Description	2- X 4-ft troffer with 3-E lens
Lamps	Two F40 T12, 3200 lm each, 20,000 h
Lens	KSH 3-E (trade mark)
Spacing ratio	1.8
Visual comfort probability	64 (length)/63 (cross)
Maintenance factors	0.75/0.70/0.65
Input, W	93

COST DETAILS PER LUMINAIRE

Type of unit	Contractor's price	Installed cost
Grid	$58	$ 92
Flange	64	101

The installed cost includes published contractor's book price for the luminaire with lens and ballast, number of lamps as shown, luminaire fastening devices, 6-ft length of 3/8-in flexible metallic conduit with two 7-ft lengths of no. 12 AF wire, two connectors, and the labor required for recess mounting and connection of the luminaire. See page B–52 to add a luminaire outlet recessed above ceiling.

Luminaires with this special diffusing medium provide uniform lighting with extra-widespread distribution. These luminaires are widely used in institutions and office buildings.

This information was based on ERL report 1274, prepared for KSH, Inc., St. Louis, Missouri.

RECESSED FLUORESCENT – 2' X 4' TROFFER (KSH 3-E LENS)

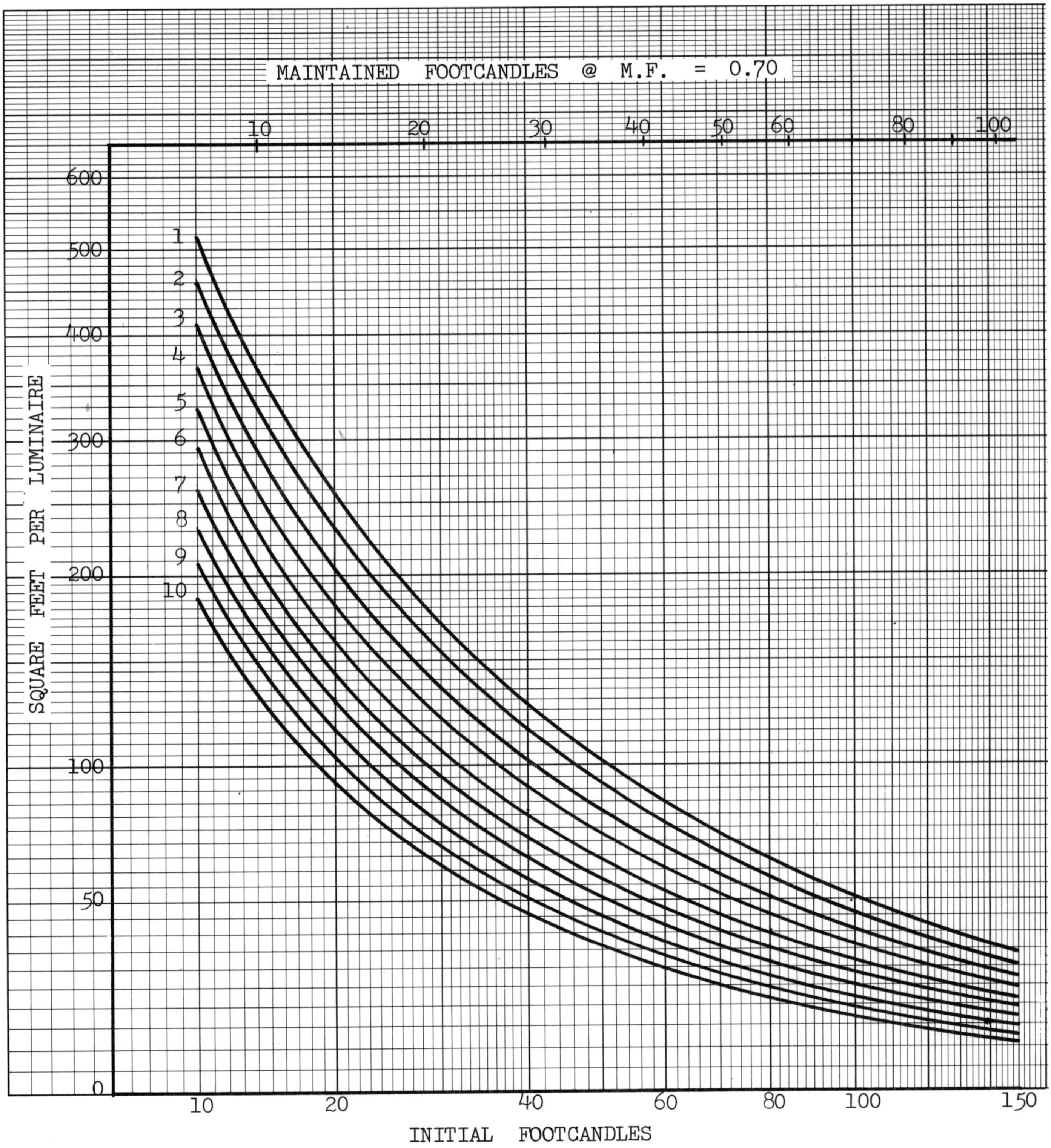

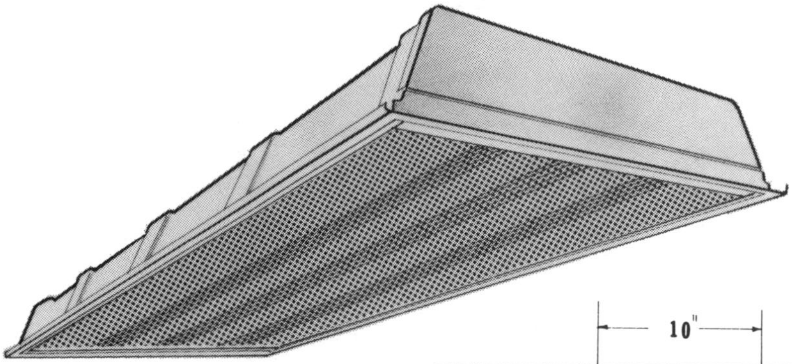

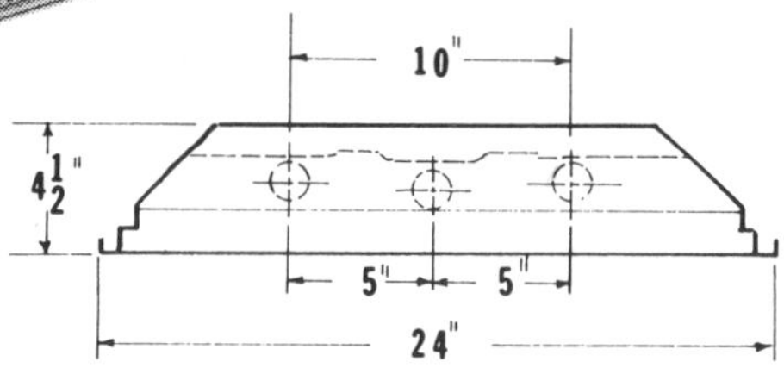

Description	2- X 4-ft troffer with 3-E lens
Lamps	Three F40 T12, 3200 lm each, 20,000 h
Lens	KSH 3-E (trade mark)
Spacing ratio	1.8
Visual comfort probability	55 (length)/55 (cross)
Maintenance factors	0.75/0.70/0.65
Input, W	146

COST DETAILS PER LUMINAIRE

Type of unit	Contractor's price	Installed cost
Grid	$65	$103.50
Flange	71	112.75

The installed cost includes published contractor's book price for the luminaire with lens and ballasts, number of lamps as shown, luminaire fastening devices, 6-ft length of 3/8-in flexible metallic conduit with two 7-ft lengths of no. 12 AF wire, two connectors, and the labor required for recess mounting and connection of the luminaire. See page B–52 to add a luminaire outlet recessed above ceiling.

Luminaires with this special diffusing medium provide uniform lighting with extra-widespread distribution. These luminaires are widely used in institutions and office buildings.

This information was based on ERL report 1271, prepared for KSH, Inc., St. Louis, Missouri.

RECESSED FLUORESCENT – 2' X 4' TROFFER (KSH 3-E LENS)

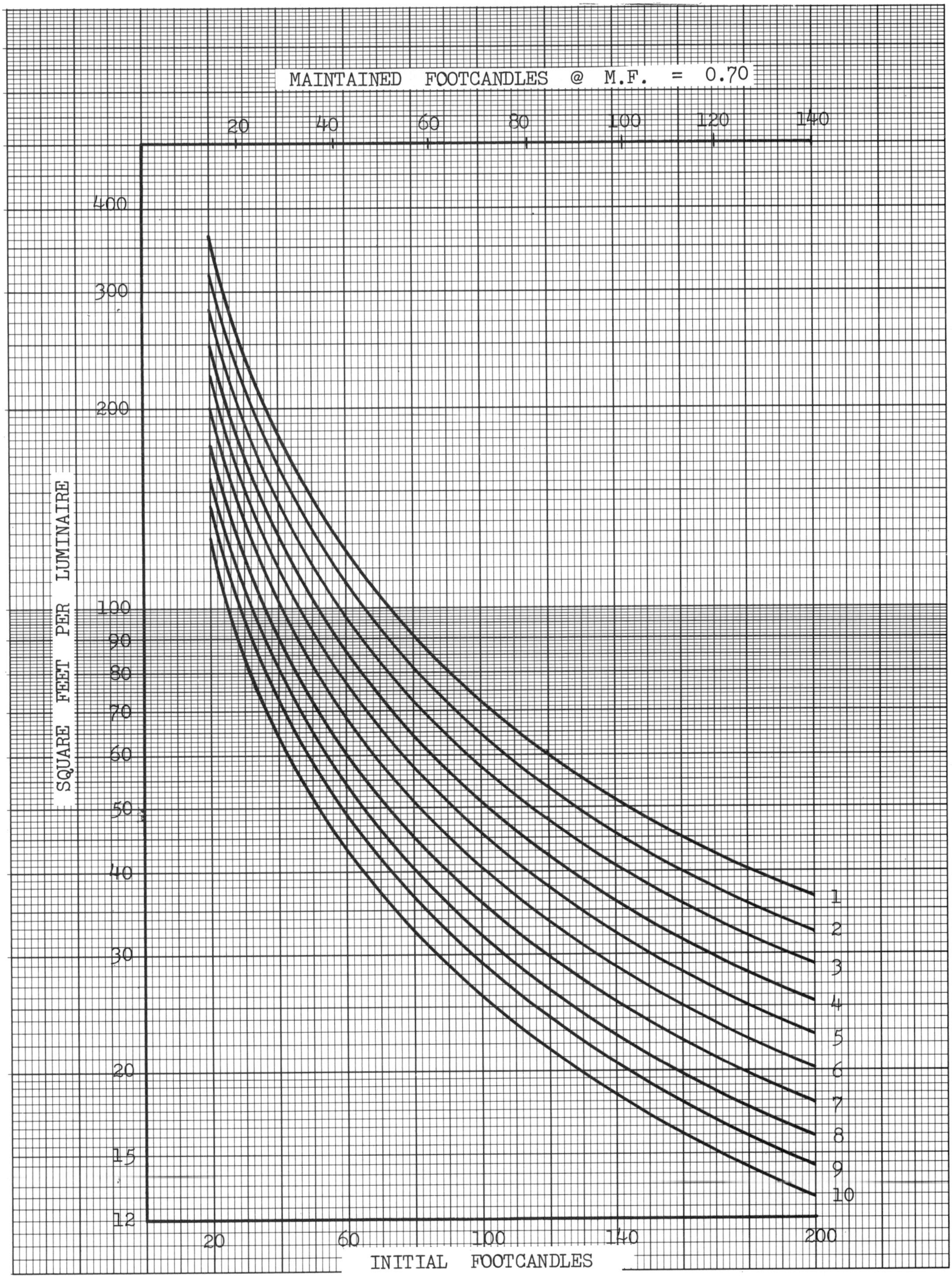

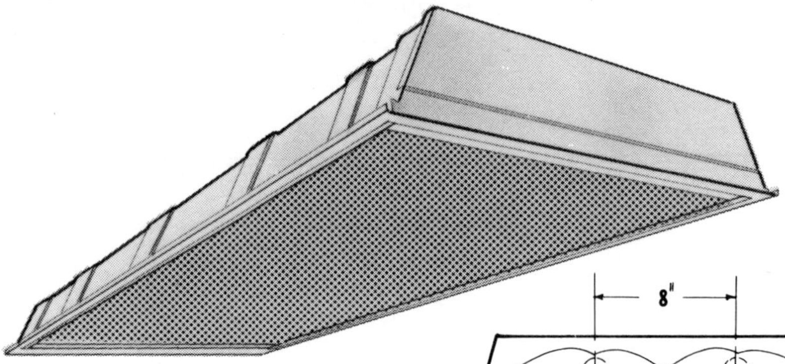

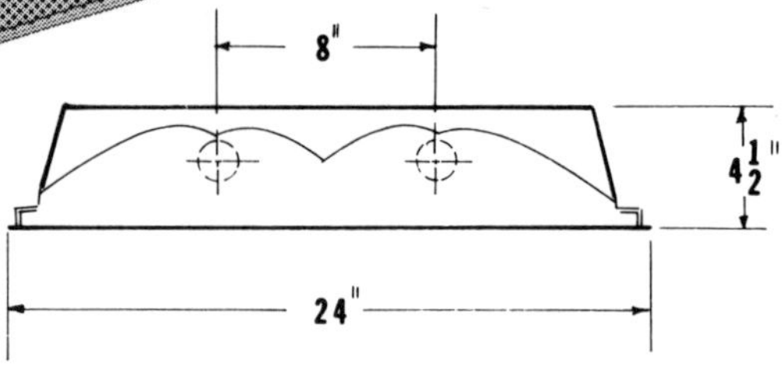

Description	2- X 4-ft troffer (Gibson EE system)
Lamps	Two F40 T12, 3200 lm each, 20,000 h
Lens	Gibson EE lens
Reflector	Specular anodized aluminum
Spacing ratio	1.8
Visual comfort probability	63 (length)/54 (cross)
Maintenance factors	0.75/0.70/0.65
Input, W	93

COST DETAILS PER LUMINAIRE

Type of unit	Contractor's price	Installed cost
Grid	$85	$125.25
Flange	92	135.50

The installed cost includes published contractor's book price for the luminaire with lens and ballast, number of lamps as shown, luminaire fastening devices, 6-ft length of 3/8-in flexible metallic conduit with two 7-ft lengths of no. 12 AF wire, two connectors, and labor required for recess mounting and connection of the luminaire. See page B–52 to add a luminaire outlet recessed above ceiling.

Luminaires with this special reflecting surface and the diffusing medium provide uniform illumination with extra-widespread distribution. These luminaires are widely used in institutions and office buildings.

This information was based on ERL report 1925, prepared for Gibson Lighting, Americus, Georgia.

RECESSED FLUORESCENT – 2′ X 4′ TROFFER (GIBSON EE SYSTEM)

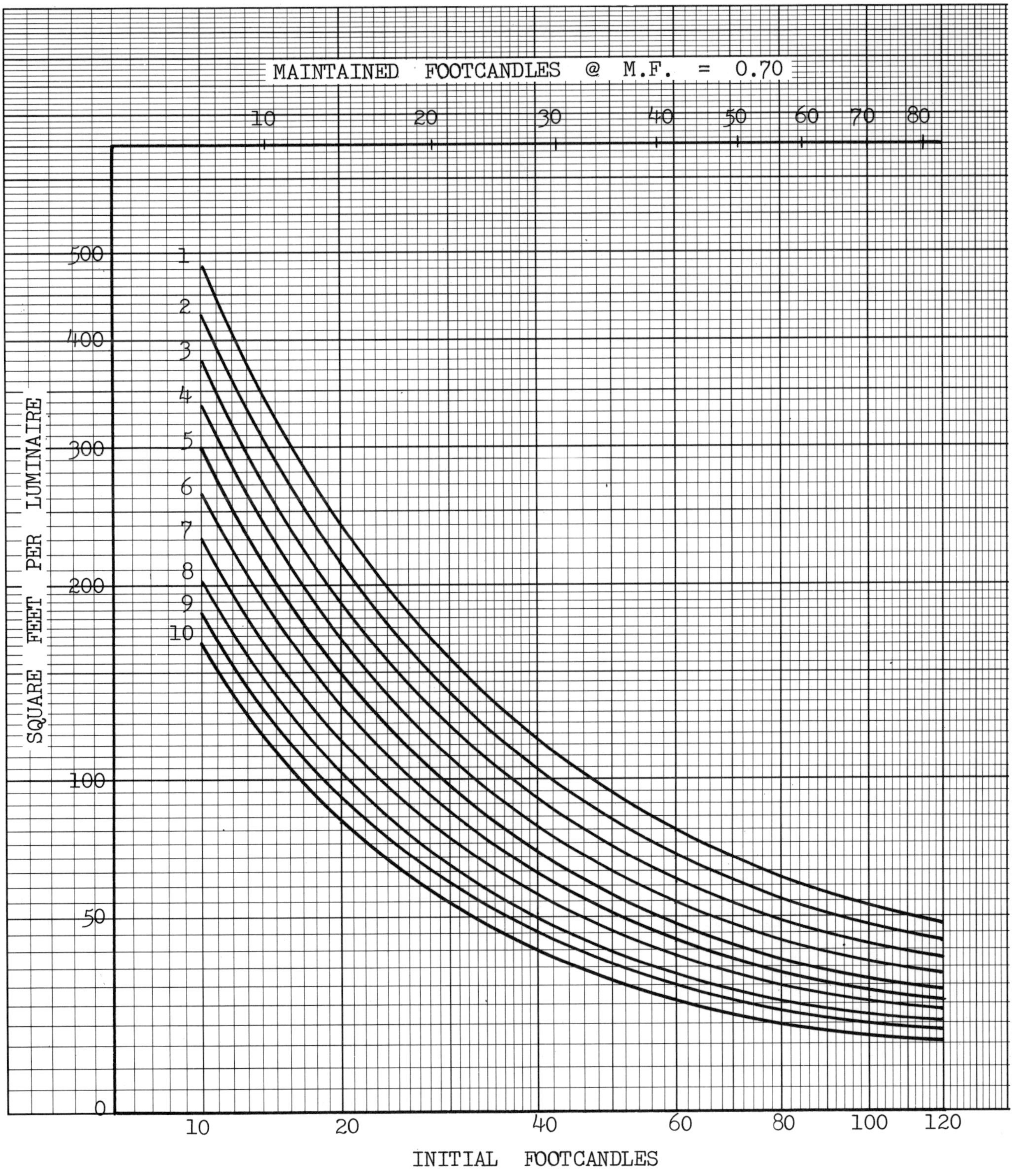

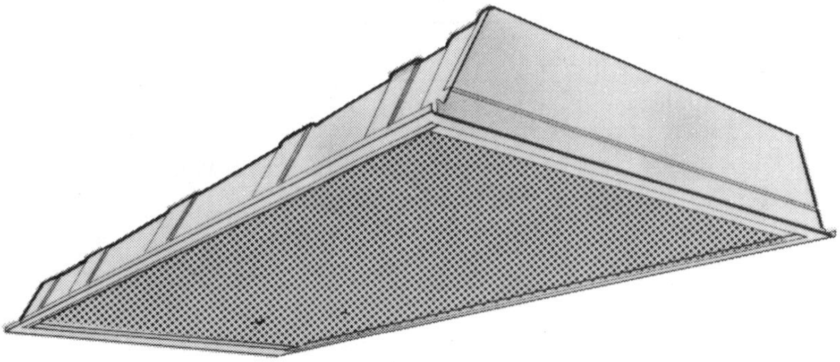

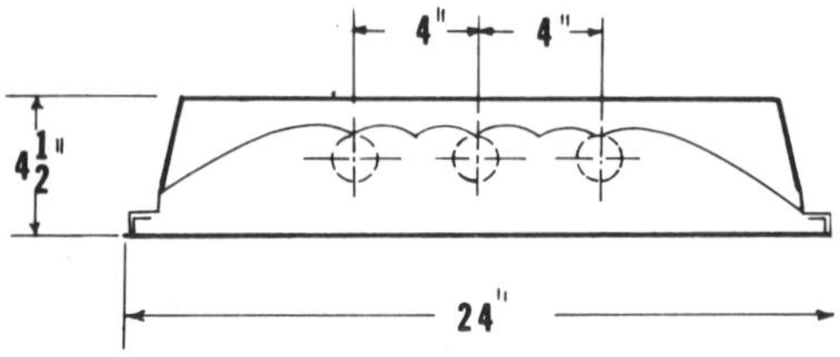

Description	2- X 4-ft troffer (Gibson EE system)
Lamps	Three F40 T12, 3200 lm each, 20,000 h
Lens	Gibson EE lens
Reflector	Specular anodized aluminum
Spacing ratio	1.7
Visual comfort probability	56 (length)/47 (cross)
Maintenance factors	0.75/0.70/0.65
Input, W	146

COST DETAILS PER LUMINAIRE

Type of unit	Contractor's price	Installed cost
Grid	$ 96	$141.50
Flange	103	152

The installed cost includes published contractor's book price for the luminaire with lens and ballasts, number of lamps as shown, luminaire fastening devices, 6-ft length of 3/8-in flexible metallic conduit with two 7-ft lengths of no. 12 AF wire, two connectors, and the labor required for recess mounting and connection of the luminaire. See page B–52 to add a luminaire outlet recessed above ceiling.

Luminaires with this special reflecting surface and the diffusing medium provide uniform illumination with extra-widespread distribution. These luminaires are widely used in institutions and office buildings.

This information was based on ERL report 2134, prepared for Gibson Lighting, Americus, Georgia.

RECESSED FLUORESCENT – 2′ X 4′ TROFFER (GIBSON EE SYSTEM)

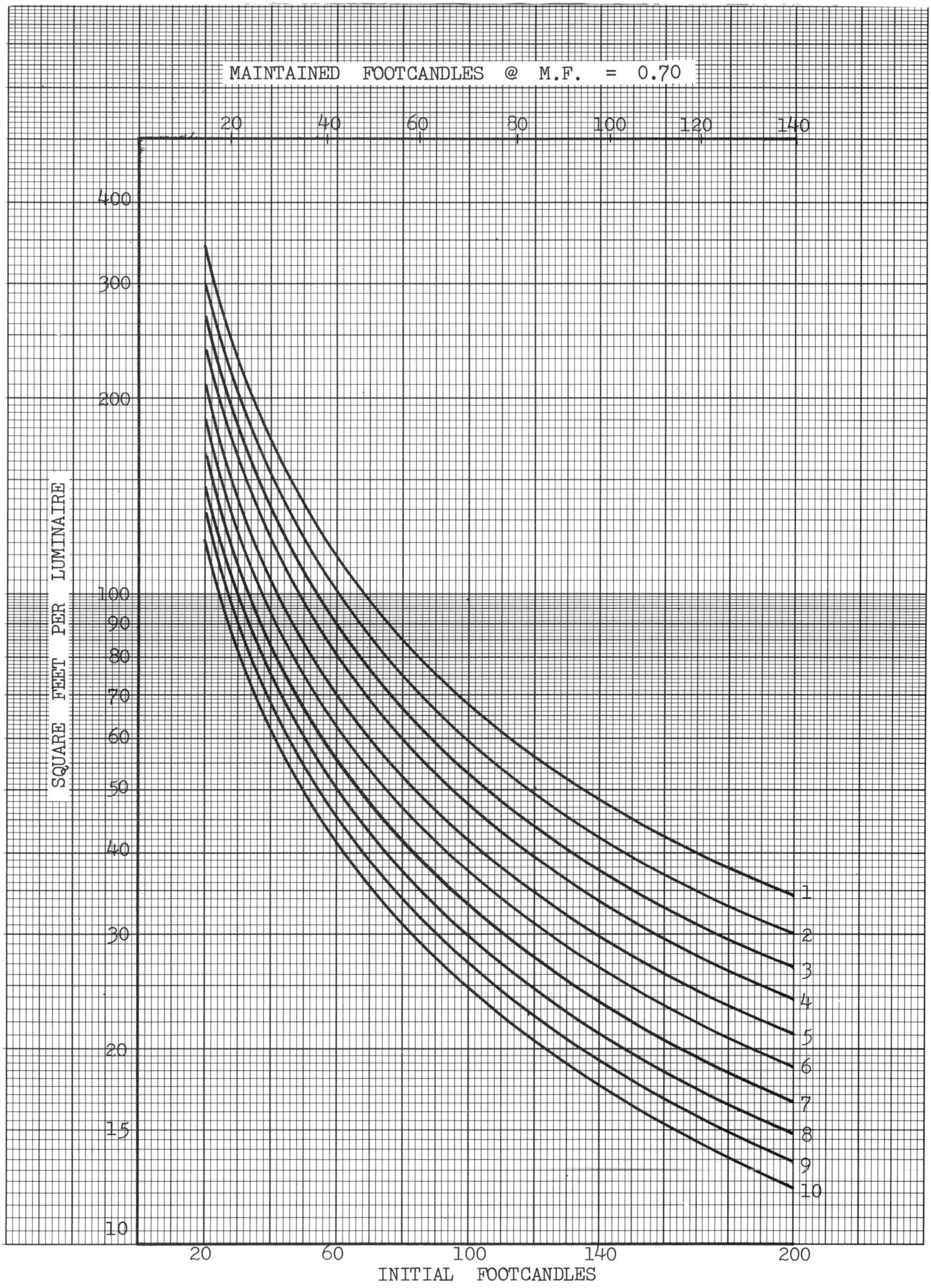

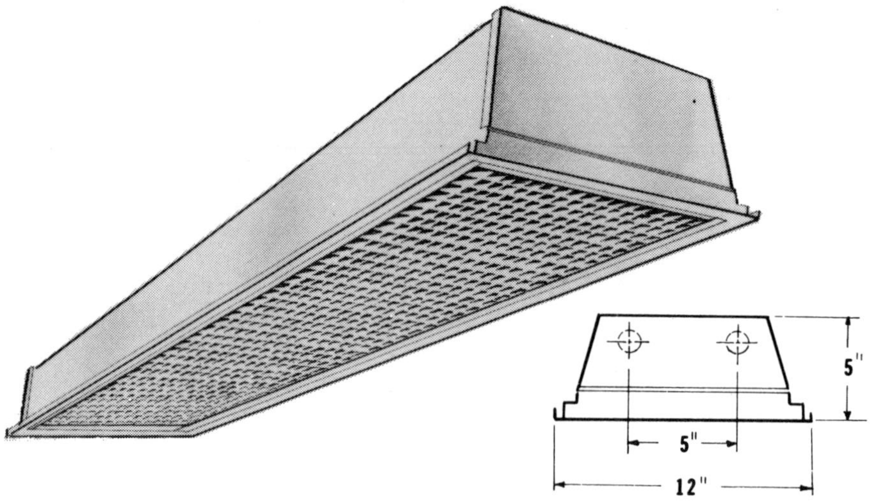

Description	1- X 4-ft troffer (plastic-cube)
Lamps	Two F40 T12, 3200 lm each, 20,000 h
Louver	45 X 45° light-stabilized polystyrene plastic egg-crate louver
Spacing ratio	1.0
Visual comfort probability	69 (length)/68 (cross)
Maintenance factors	0.75/0.70/0.65
Conversion factors	A. Unit with two F40 T12 lamps = 1.0 B. Unit with three F40 T12 lamps = 1.5

COST DETAILS PER LUMINAIRE

Type of unit	Input, W	Contractor's price		Installed cost	
		Grid	Flange	Grid	Flange
A	93	$42	$48	$72.25	$82.25
B	146	47	51	81.50	88

The installed cost includes published contractor's book price for the luminaire with louver and ballast, number of lamps as shown, luminaire fastening devices, 6-ft length of 3/8-in flexible metallic conduit with two 7-ft lengths of no. 12 AF wire, two connectors, and the labor required for recess mounting and connection of the luminaire. *See page B–52 to add a luminaire outlet recessed above ceiling.*

Luminaires with such light-stable luminous open shielding elements with 45° (lengthwise and crosswise) cutoff provide a high degree of brightness control in direct-viewing zones.

RECESSED FLUORESCENT – 1' X 4' TROFFER (PLASTIC-CUBE LOUVERS)

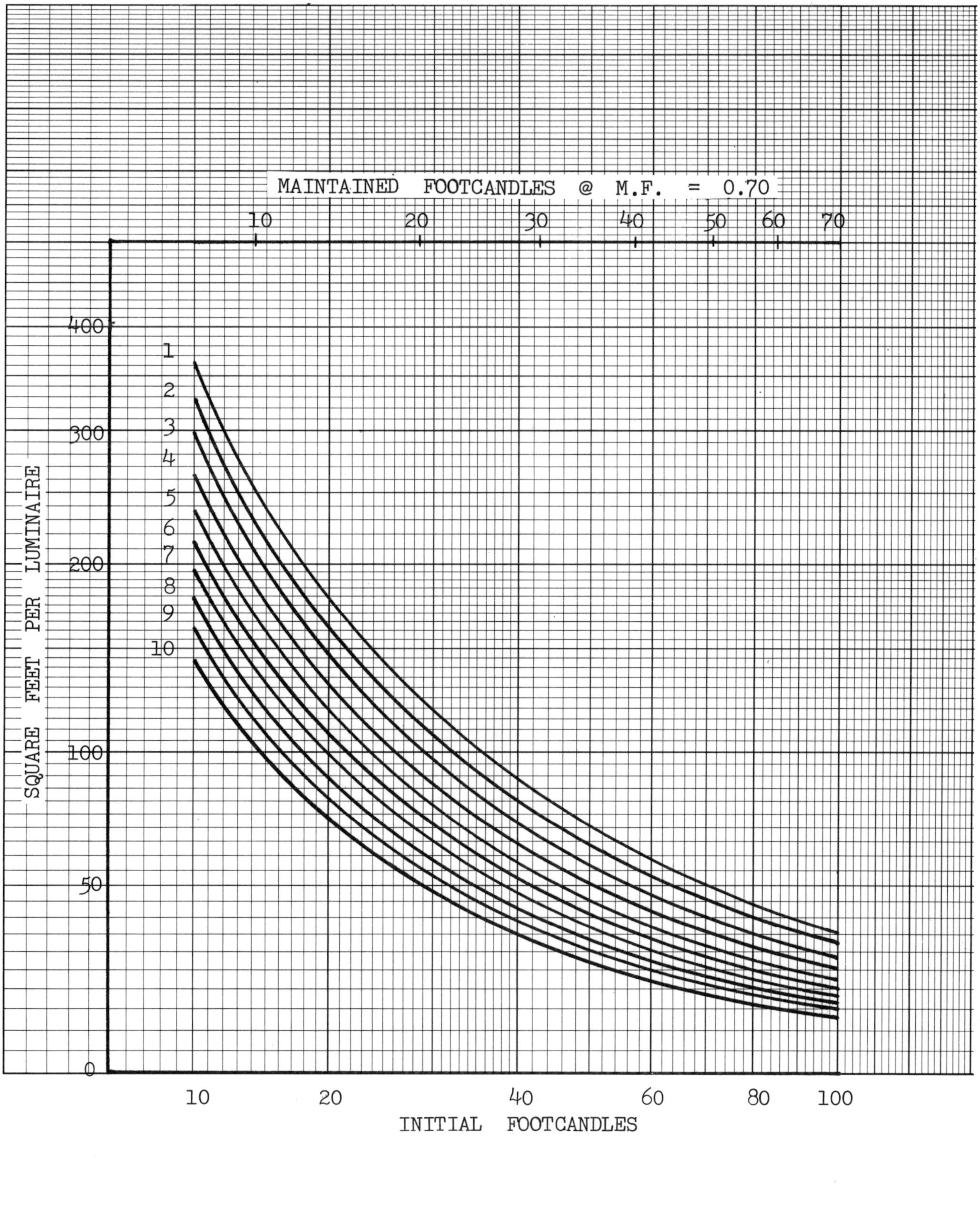

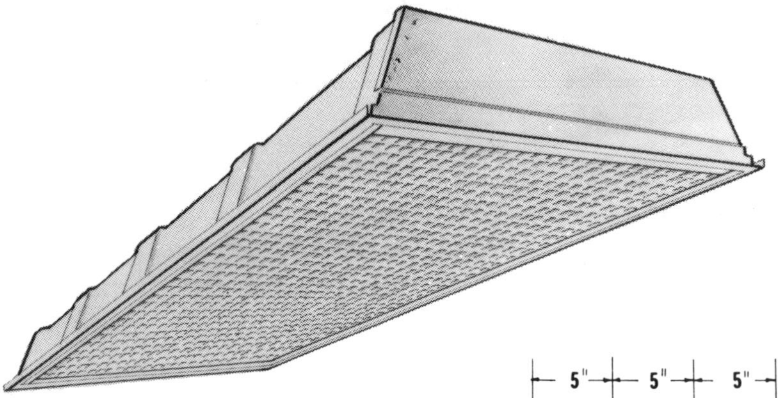

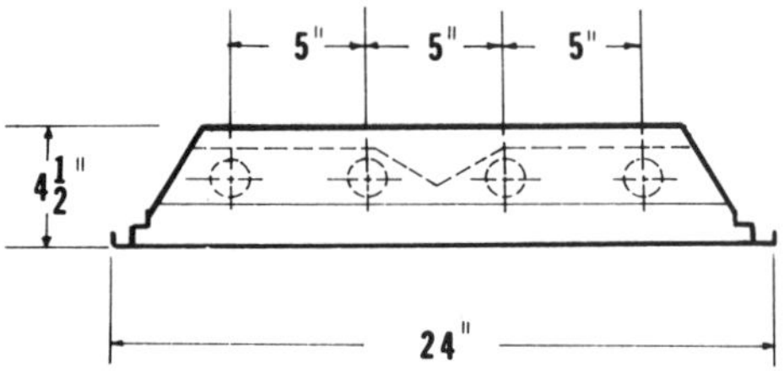

Description	2- X 4-ft troffer (plastic-cube)
Lamps	Four F40 T12, 3200 lm each, 20,000 h
Louver	45 X 45° light-stabilized polystyrene plastic egg-crate louver
Spacing ratio	1.1
Visual comfort probability	66 (length)/65 (cross)
Maintenance factors	0.75/0.70/0.65
Conversion factors	A. Unit with four F40 T12 lamps = 1.0 B. Unit with two F40 T12 lamps = 0.5

COST DETAILS PER LUMINAIRE

Type of unit	Input, W	Contractor's price		Installed cost	
		Grid	Flange	Grid	Flange
A	186	$55	$61	$ 94.25	$102.50
B	93	65	70	100.75	108.50

The installed cost includes contractor's book price for the luminaire with louver and ballasts, number of lamps as shown, luminaire fastening devices, 6-ft length of 3/8-in flexible metallic conduit with two 7-ft lengths of no. 12 AF wire, two connectors, and the labor required for recess mounting and connection of the luminaire. *See page B–52 to add a luminaire outlet recessed above ceiling.*

Luminaires with such light-stable luminous open shielding element with 45° (lengthwide and crosswise) cutoff provide a high degree of brightness control in direct-viewing zones.

RECESSED FLUORESCENT – 2′ X 4′ TROFFER (PLASTIC-CUBE LOUVER)

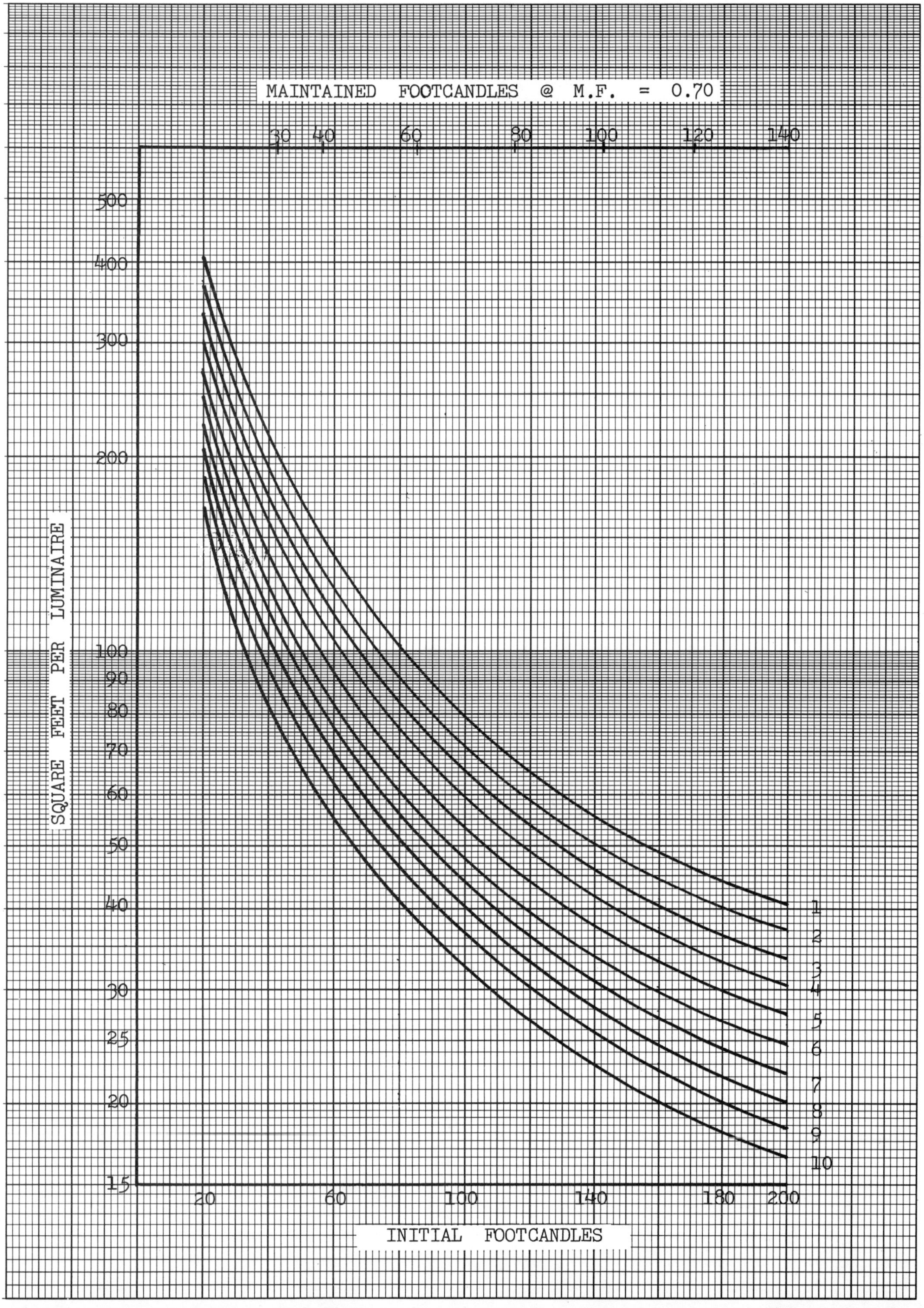

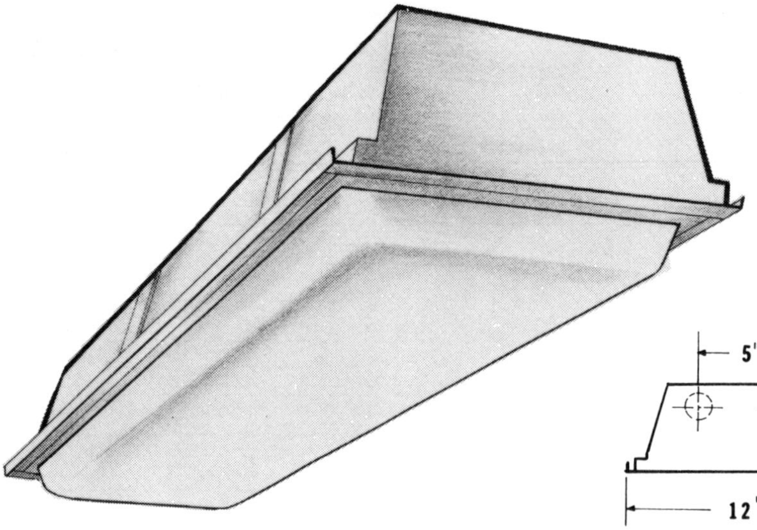

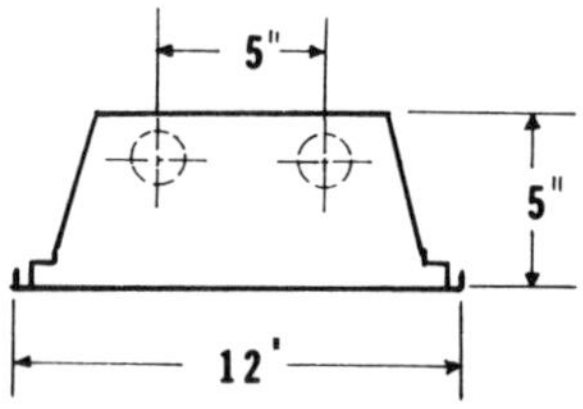

Description	1- X 4-ft troffer (dropped-dish)
Lamps	Two F40 T12, 3200 lm each, 20,000 h
Lens	Dropped-dish acrylic
Spacing ratio	1.2
Visual comfort probability	46 (length)/43 (cross)
Maintenance factors	0.75/0.70/0.65
Conversion factors	A. Unit with two F40 T12 lamps = 1.0 B. Unit with three F40 T12 lamps = 1.5

COST DETAILS PER LUMINAIRE

Type of unit	Input, W	Contractor's price		Installed cost	
		Grid	Flange	Grid	Flange
A	93	$51	$56	$83.50	$ 91.25
B	146	61	66	98.50	106.50

The installed cost includes published contractor's book price for the luminaire with lens and ballast, number of lamps as shown, luminaire fastening devices, 6-ft length of 3/8-in flexible metallic conduit with two 7-ft lengths of no. 12 AF wire, two connectors, and the labor required for recess mounting and connection of the luminaire. See page B–52 to add a luminaire outlet above ceiling.

The framed dropped-dish opal acrylic diffuser combines a modern, modular appearance with soft general light distribution. Excellent for high-angle general illumination on high or medium ceilings.

RECESSED FLUORESCENT – 1' X 4' TROFFER (DROPPED DISH)

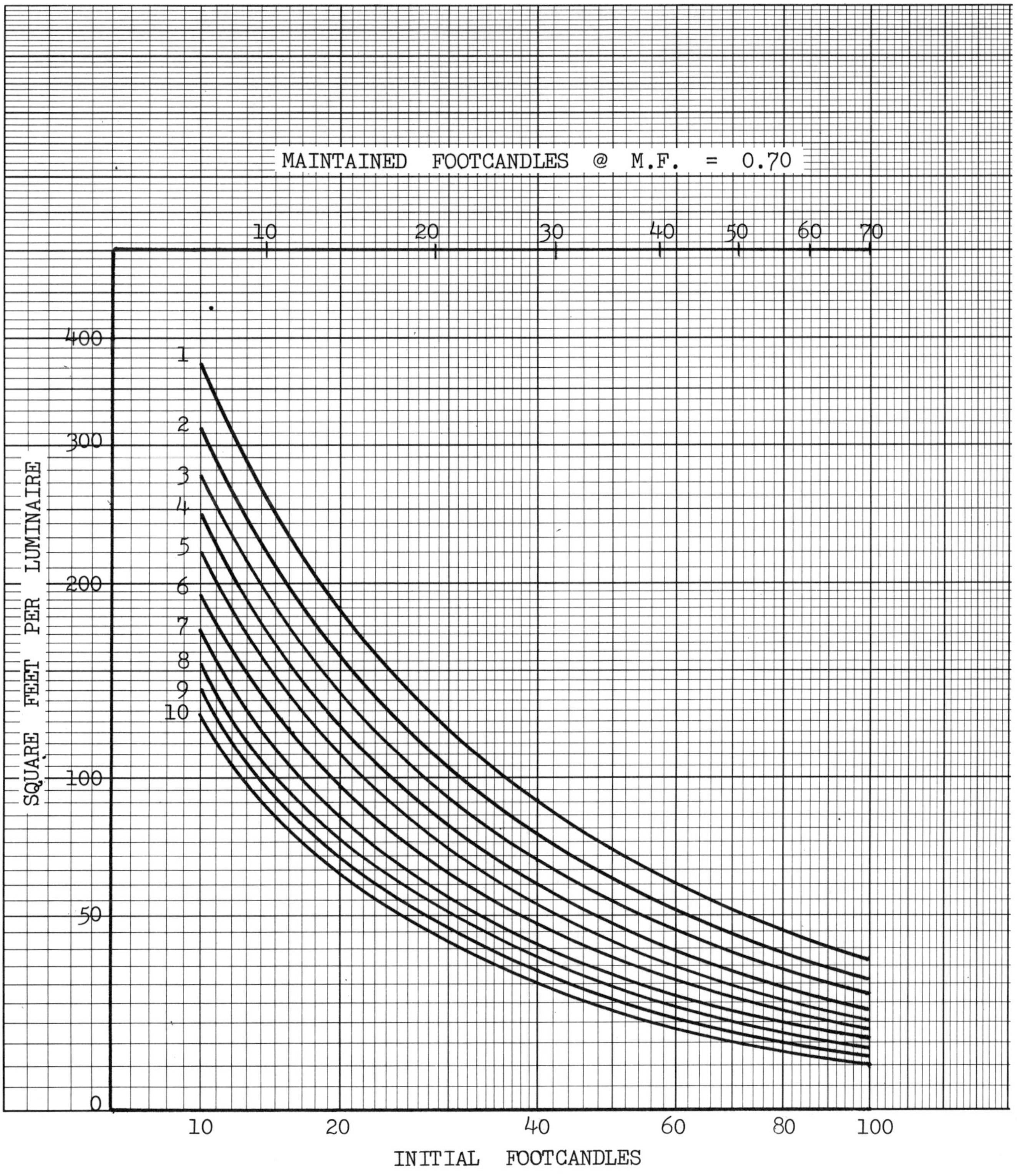

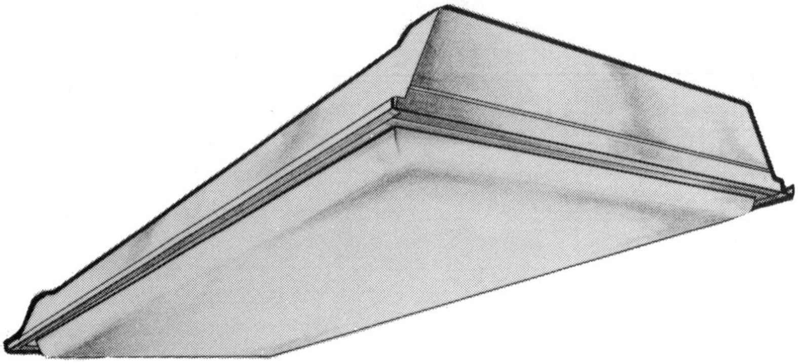

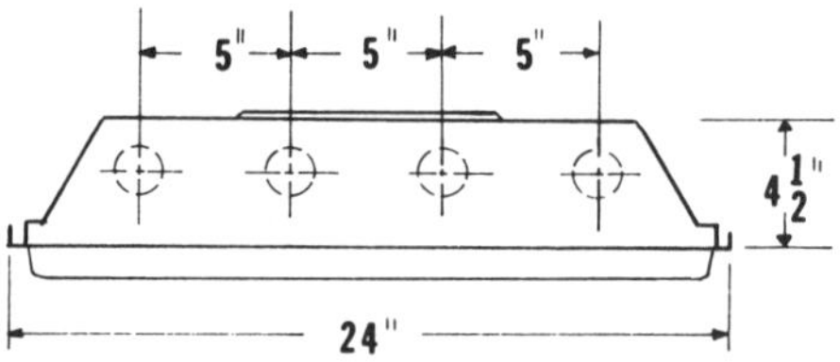

Description	2- X 4-ft troffer (dropped-dish)
Lamps	Four F40 T12, 3200 lm each, 20,000 h
Lens	Dropped-dish acrylic
Spacing ratio	1.3
Visual comfort probability	43 (length)/40 (cross)
Maintenance factors	0.75/0.70/0.65
Conversion factors	A. Unit with four F40 T12 lamps = 1.0
	B. Unit with two F40 T12 lamps = 0.5

COST DETAILS PER LUMINAIRE

Type of unit	Input, W	Contractor's price		Installed cost	
		Grid	Flange	Grid	Flange
A	186	$70	$75	$112	$119.50
B	93	62	67	97	104.75

The installed cost includes published contractor's book price for the luminaire with lens and ballasts, number of lamps as shown, luminaire fastening devices, 6-ft length of 3/8-in flexible metallic conduit with two 7-ft lengths of no. 12 AF wire, two connectors, and the labor required for recess mounting and connection of the luminaire. *See page B–52 to add a luminaire outlet recessed above ceiling.*

The framed dropped-dish opal acrylic diffuser combines a modern, modular appearance with soft general light distribution. Excellent for high-angle general illumination on high or medium ceilings.

RECESSED FLUORESCENT – 2′ X 4′ TROFFER (DROPPED DISH)

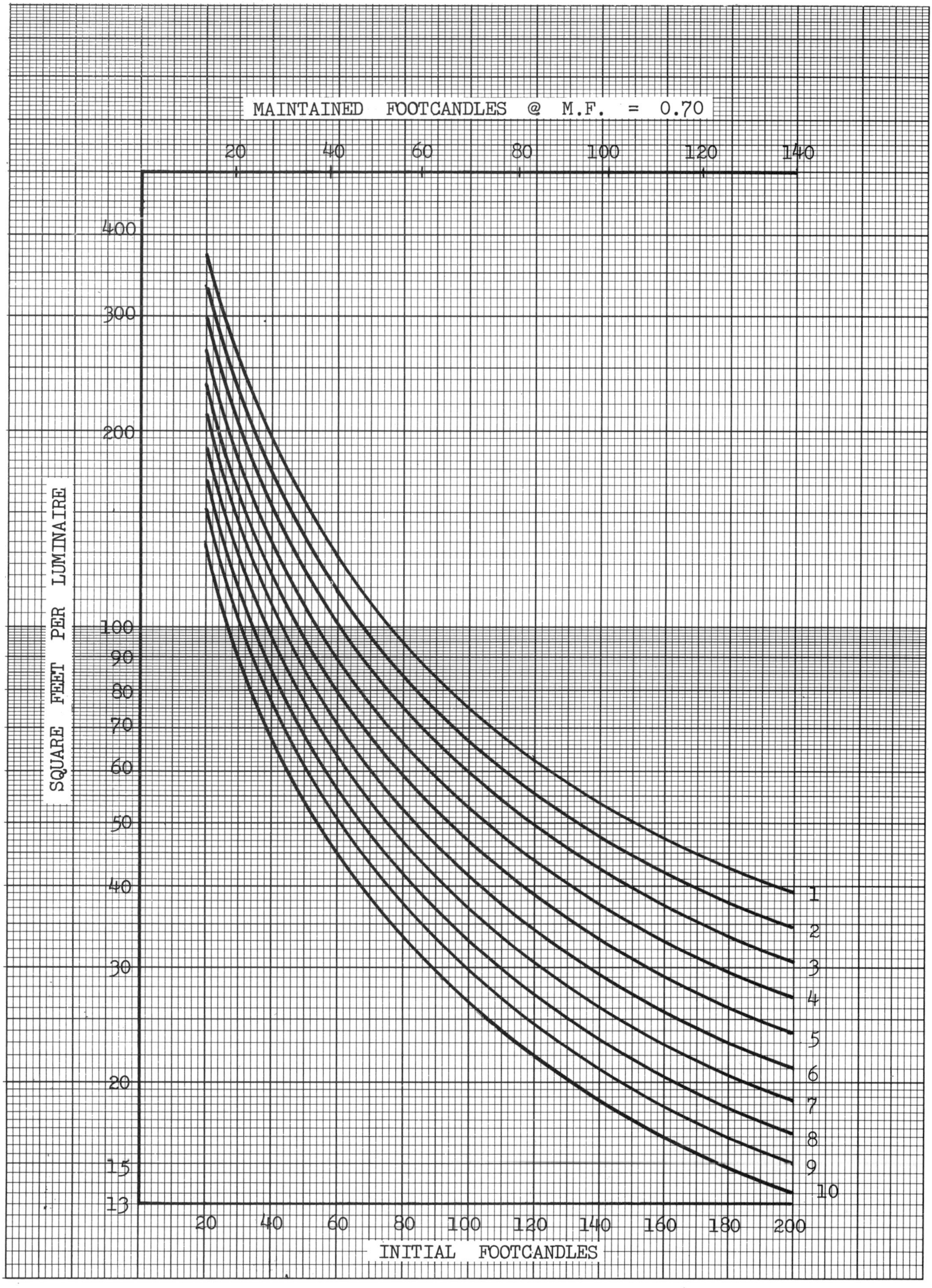

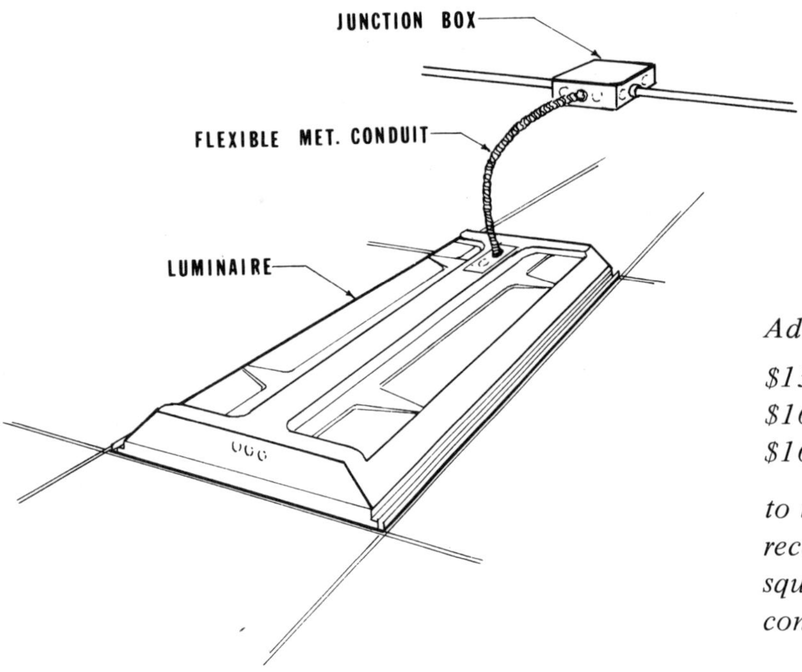

Add

$13.25 for EMT terminal
$16.70 for GRC terminal
$16.70 for IMS terminal

to the luminaire installed cost for an outlet recessed above ceiling, which includes a 4-in square box, blank cover, bar hanger, two connectors for conduit, and two wire nuts.

Fluorescent Strips

C

GENERAL-PURPOSE

4-ft, 1 Lamp	*C-2*
2 Lamps	*C-4*
8-ft, 1 Lamp	*C-6*
2 Lamps	*C-8*
3 Lamps	*C-10*
4 Lamps	*C-12*

PREMIUM-GRADE

4-ft, 2 Lamps	*C-14*
8-ft, 2 Lamps, HO	*C-16*
PG	*C-18*
3 or 4 Lamps	*C-20*

CEILING OUTLETS FOR LUMINAIRES

Installed Cost of Outlets	*C-22*

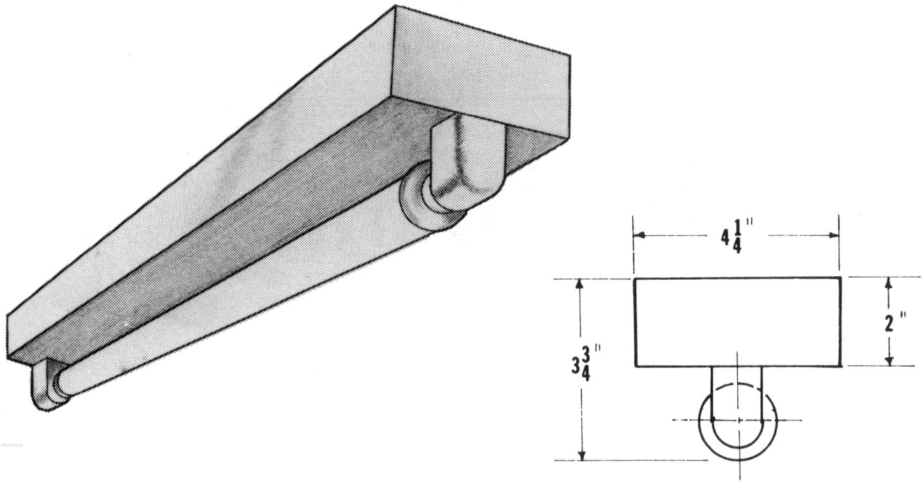

Description	4-ft long fluorescent strip
Lamp	One F40 T12, 3200 lm, 20,000 h
Spacing ratio	1.6
Maintenance factors	0.85/0.80/0.75
Conversion factors	A. Unit with one F40 T12 lamp = 1.0
	B. Unit with one F48 T12HO lamp = 1.35
	C. Unit with one F48 PG17 lamp = 2.35

COST DETAILS PER LUMINAIRE

Type of unit	Input, W	Contractor's price	Installed cost
A	53	$15	$30
B	85	32	52
C	138	44	68.75

The installed cost includes published contractor's book price for the luminaire, number of lamps as shown, luminaire fastening devices, and the labor required for the installation and connections of the luminaire. *See page C–22 to add an outlet as required.*

Use the conversion factors shown on page C–3 for an area where the ceiling, wall, and floor reflectances are low.

GENERAL PURPOSE FLUORESCENT STRIP – 4' LONG, 1 LAMP

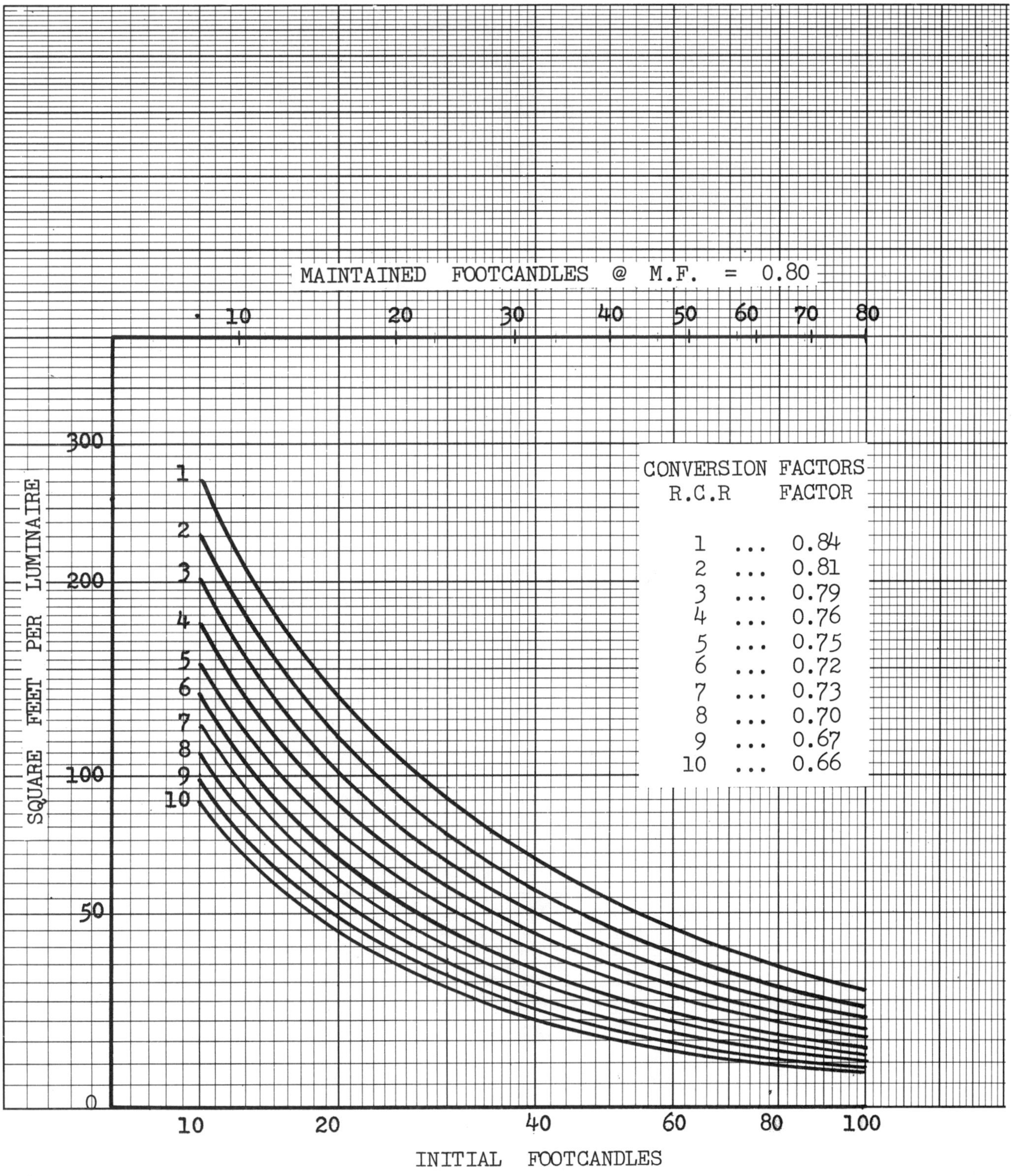

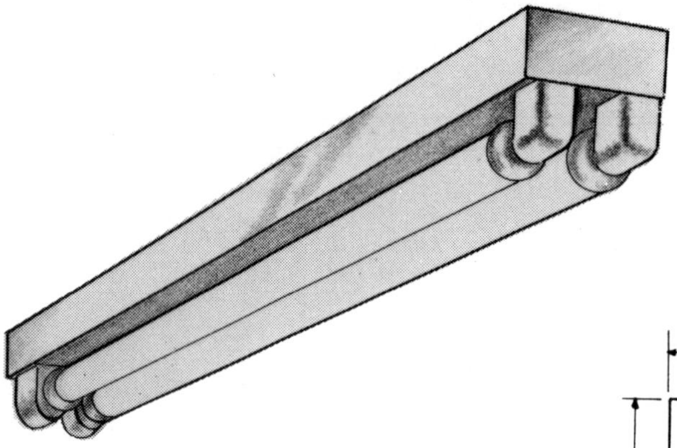

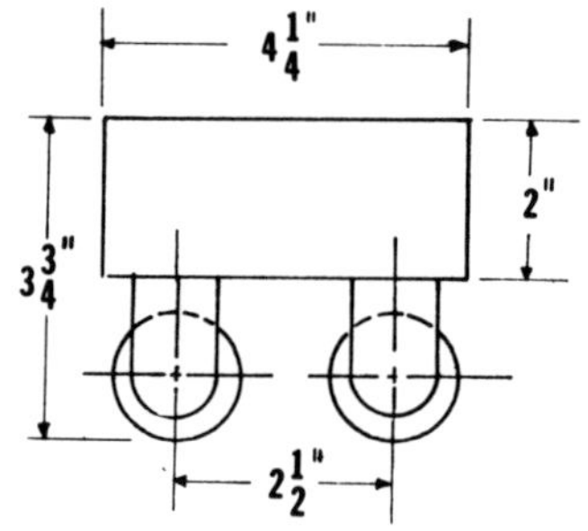

Description — 4-ft long fluorescent strip
Lamps — Two F40 T12, 3200 lm each, 20,000 h
Spacing ratio — 1.6
Maintenance factors — 0.85/0.80/0.75
Conversion factors —
A. Unit with two F40 T12 lamps = 1.0
B. Unit with two F48 T12HO lamps = 1.35

COST DETAILS PER LUMINAIRE

Type of unit	Input, W	Contractor's price	Installed cost
A	93	$15	$33
B	150	32	56.25

The installed cost includes published contractor's book price for the luminaire, number of lamps as shown, luminaire fastening devices, and the labor required for the installation and connections of the luminaire. *See page C–22 to add an outlet as required.*

Use the conversion factors shown on page C–5 for an area where the ceiling, wall, and floor reflectances are low.

GENERAL PURPOSE FLUORESCENT STRIP – 4′ LONG, 2 LAMPS

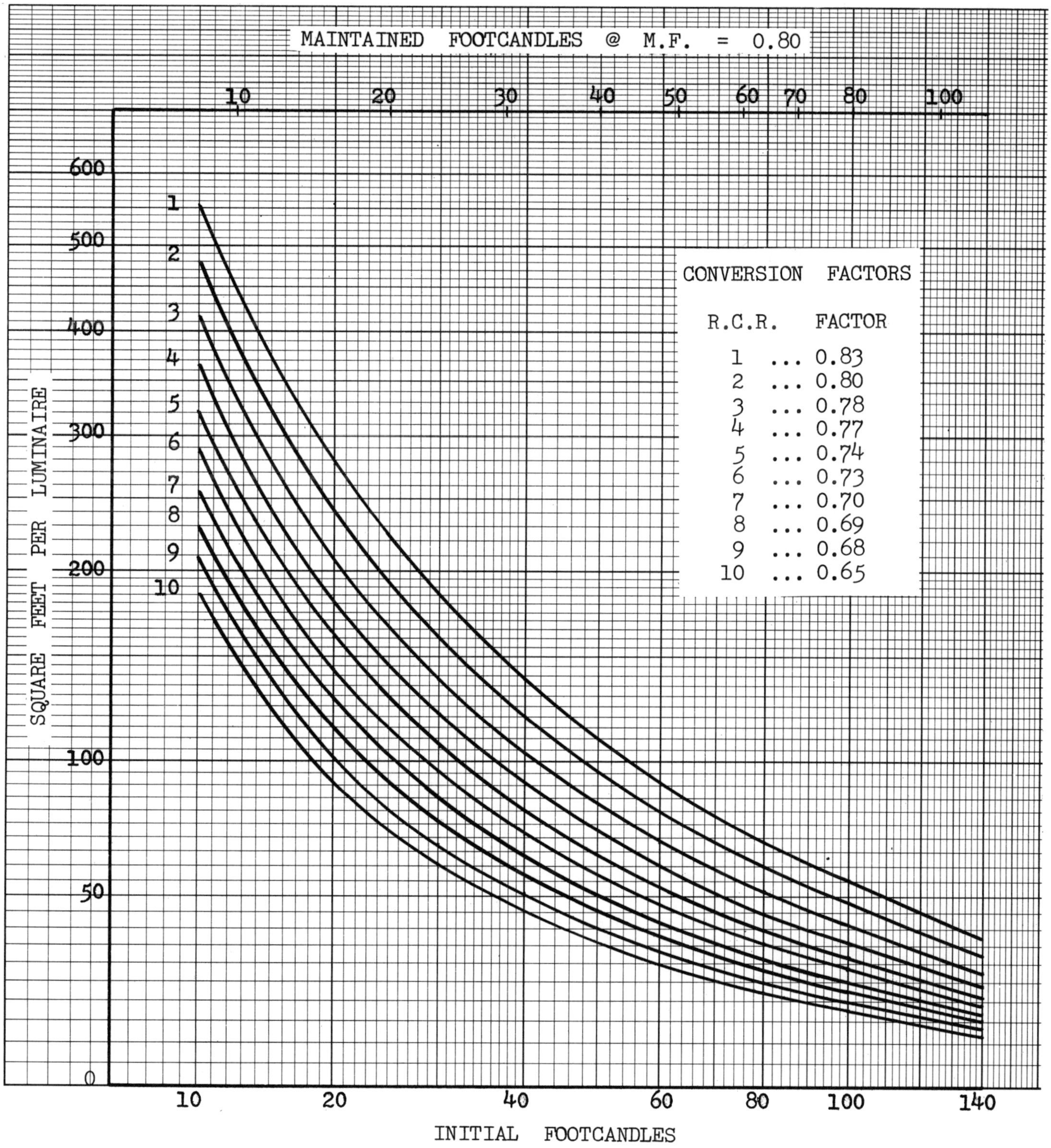

R.C.R.	FACTOR
1	... 0.83
2	... 0.80
3	... 0.78
4	... 0.77
5	... 0.74
6	... 0.73
7	... 0.70
8	... 0.69
9	... 0.68
10	... 0.65

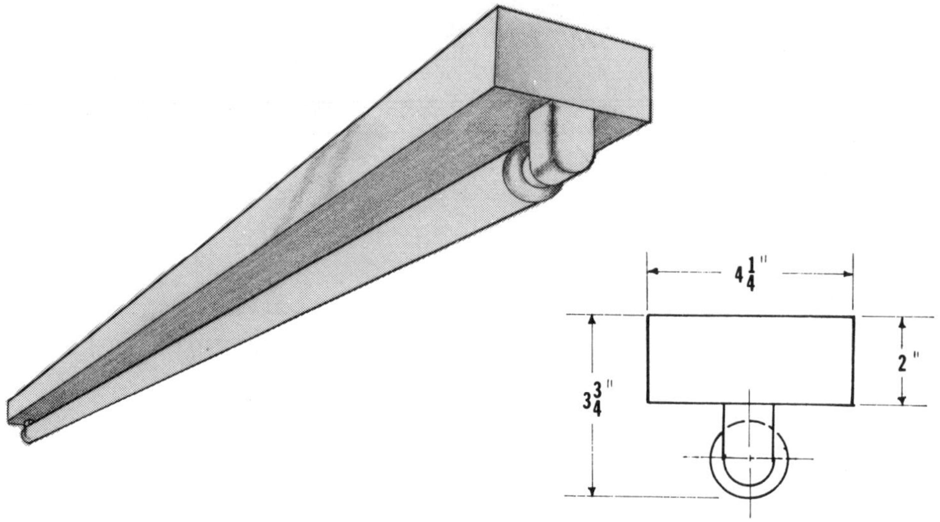

Description	8-ft long fluorescent strip
Lamp	One F96 T12, 6400 lm, 12,000 h
Spacing ratio	1.6
Maintenance factors	0.85/0.80/0.75
Conversion factors	A. Unit with one F96 T12 lamp = 1.0
	B. Unit with one F96 T12HO lamp = 1.43
	C. Unit with one F96 PG17 lamp = 2.5

COST DETAILS PER LUMINAIRE

Type of unit	Input, W	Contractor's price	Installed cost
A	98	$22	$45
B	140	33	59.75
C	230	44	74.50

The installed-cost includes published contractor's book price for the luminaire, number of lamps as shown, luminaire fastening devices, and the labor required for the installation and connections of the luminaire. See page C–22 to add an outlet as required.

Use the conversion factors shown on page C–7 for an area where the ceiling, wall, and floor reflectances are low.

GENERAL PURPOSE FLUORESCENT STRIP—8′ LONG, 1 LAMP

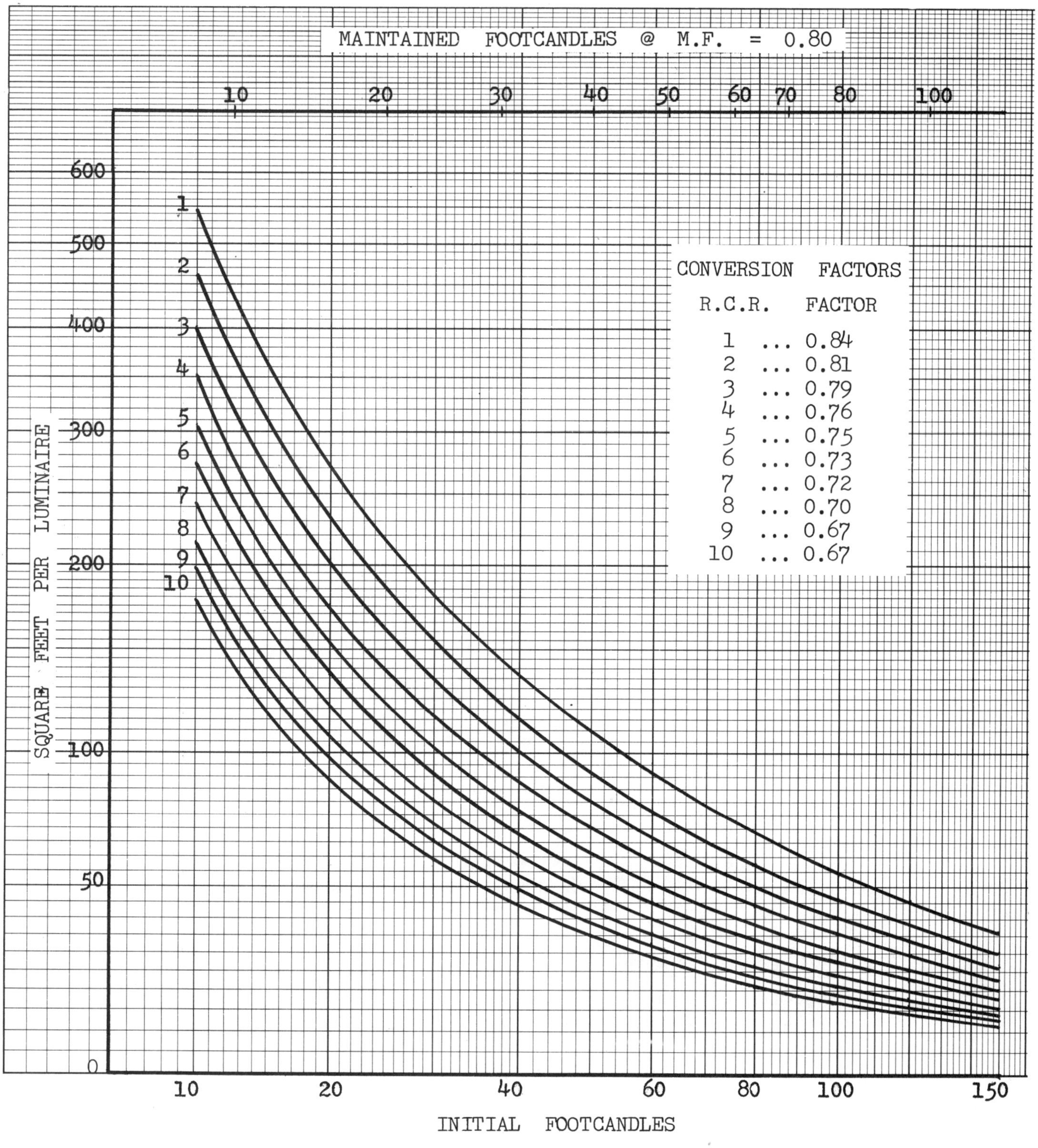

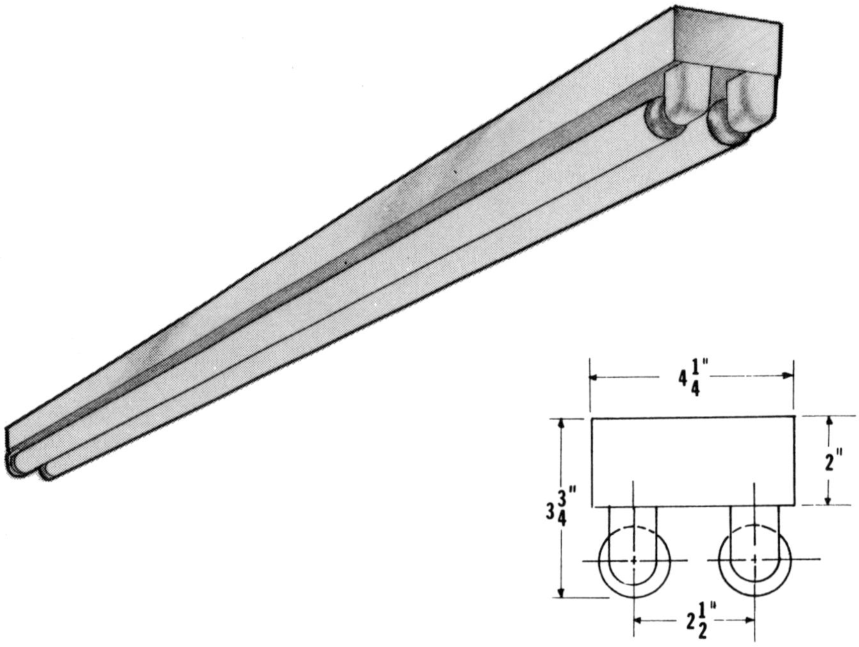

Description	8-ft long fluorescent strip
Lamps	Two F96 T12, 6400 lm each, 12,000 h
Spacing ratio	1.6
Maintenance factors	0.85/0.80/0.75
Conversion factors	A. Unit with two F96 T12 lamps = 1.0
	B. Unit with two F96 T12HO lamps = 1.43

COST DETAILS PER LUMINAIRE

Type of unit	Input, W	Contractor's price	Installed cost
A	173	$22	$49
B	241	33	65

The installed cost includes published contractor's book price for the luminaire, number of lamps as shown, luminaire fastening devices, and the labor required for the installation and connection of the luminaire. *See page C–22 to add an outlet as required.*

Use the conversion factors shown on page C–9 for an area where the ceiling, wall, and floor reflectances are low.

GENERAL PURPOSE FLUORESCENT STRIP – 8′ LONG, 2 LAMPS

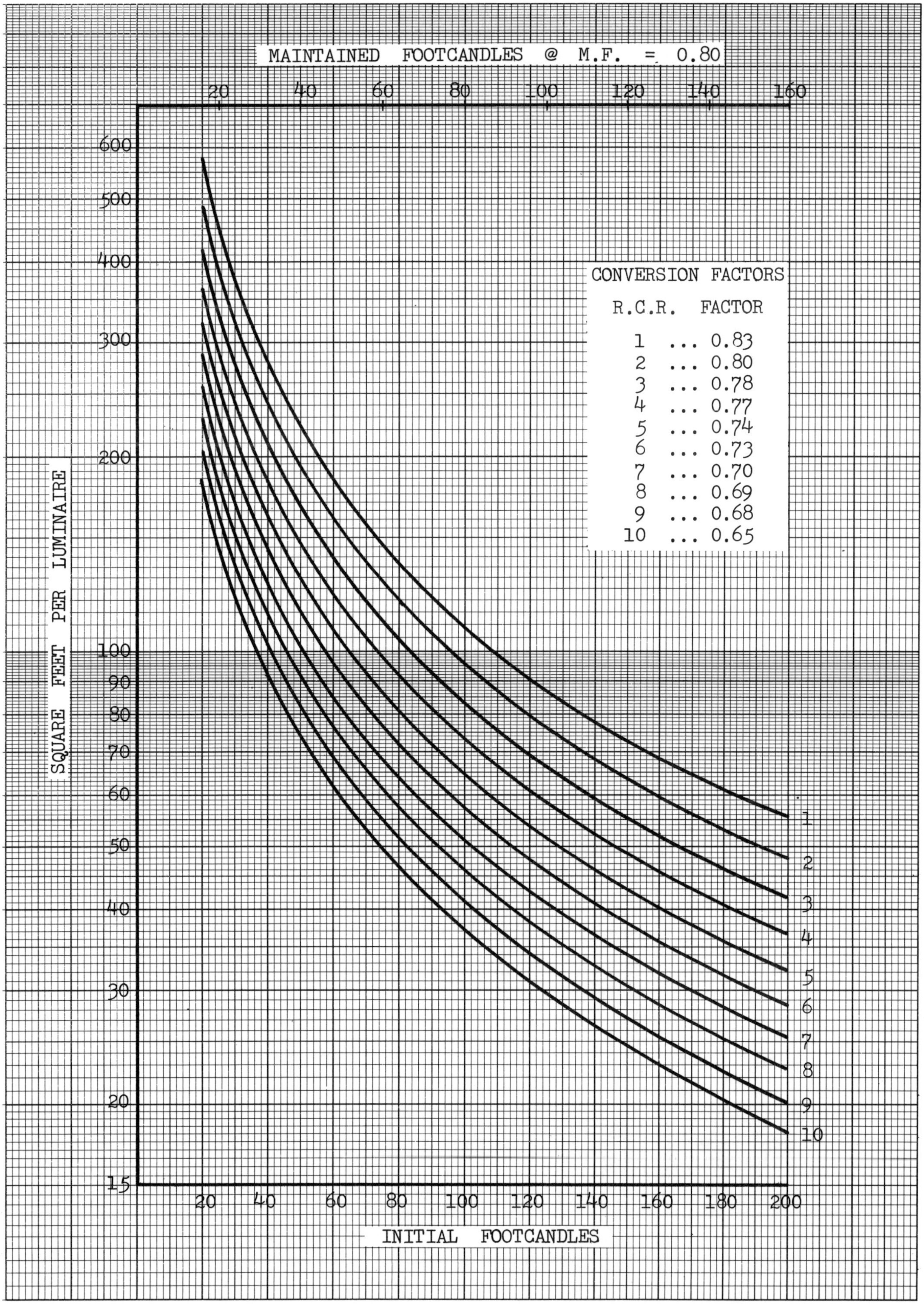

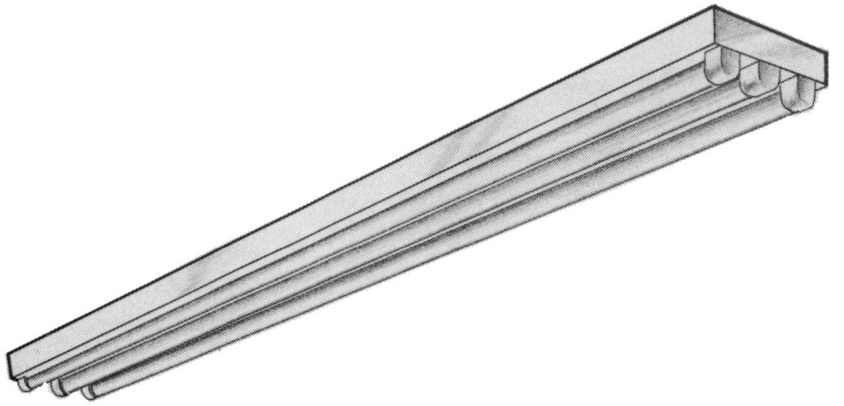

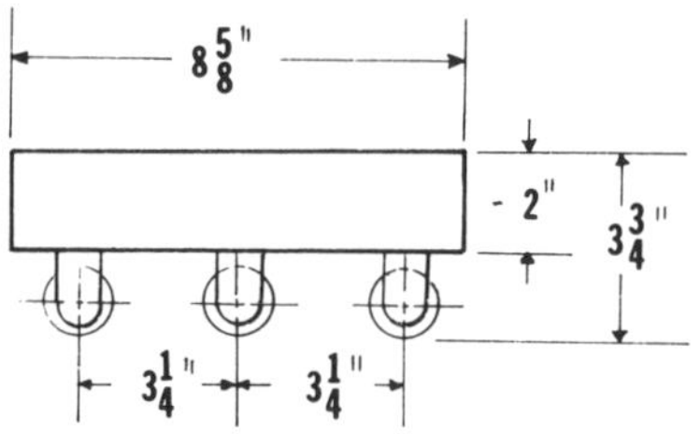

Description	8-ft long fluorescent strip
Lamps	Three F96 T12, 6400 lm each, 12,000 h
Spacing ratio	1.6
Maintenance factors	0.85/0.80/0.75
Input, W	281
Cost details per luminaire	Contractor's price = $43
	Installed cost = $79

The installed cost includes published contractor's book price for the luminaire, number of lamps as shown, luminaire fastening devices, and the labor required for the installation and connection of the luminaire. See page C–22 to add an outlet as required.

Use the conversion factors shown on page C–13 for an area where the ceiling, wall, and floor reflectances are low.

GENERAL PURPOSE FLUORESCENT STRIP – 8′ LONG, 3 LAMPS

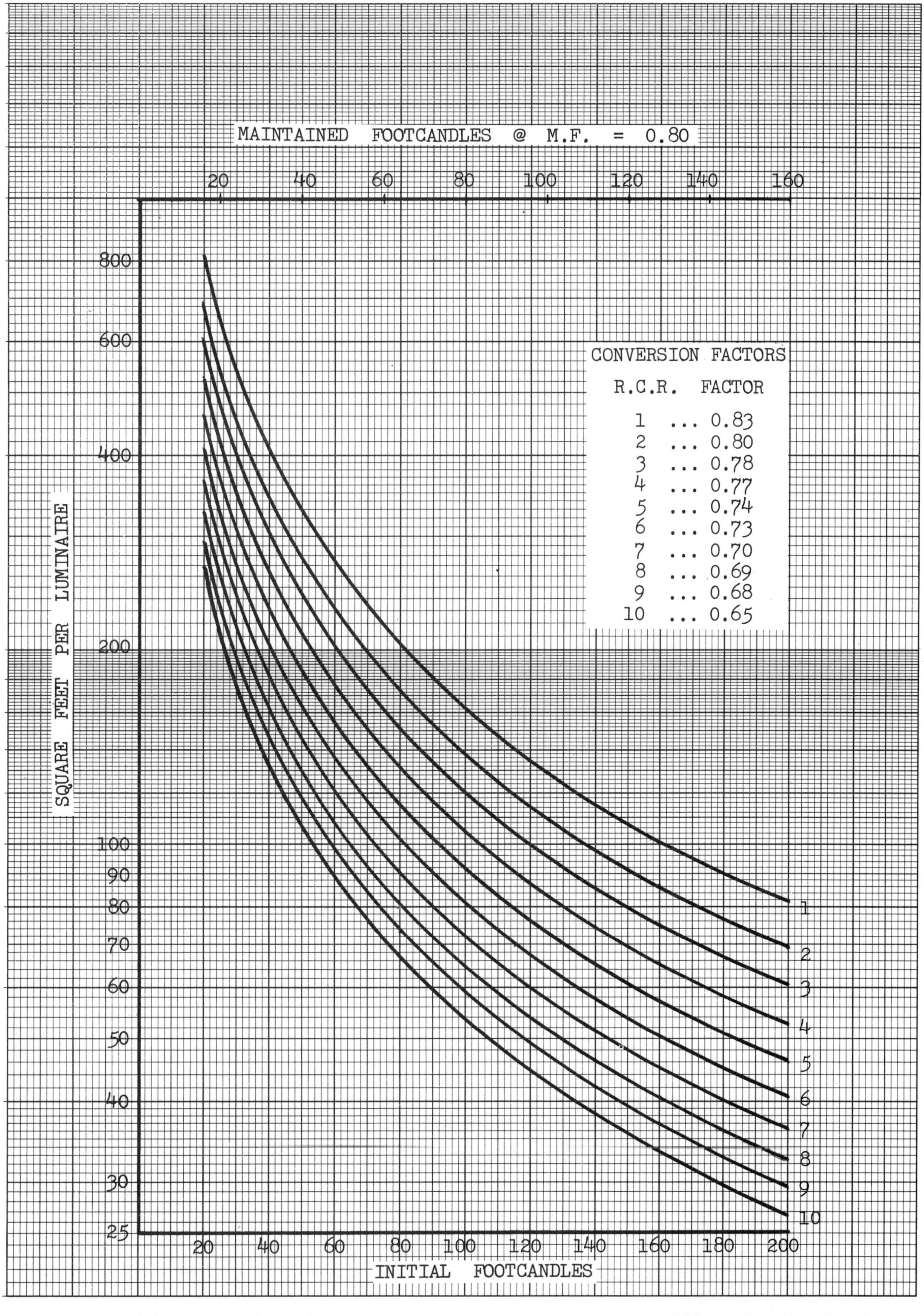

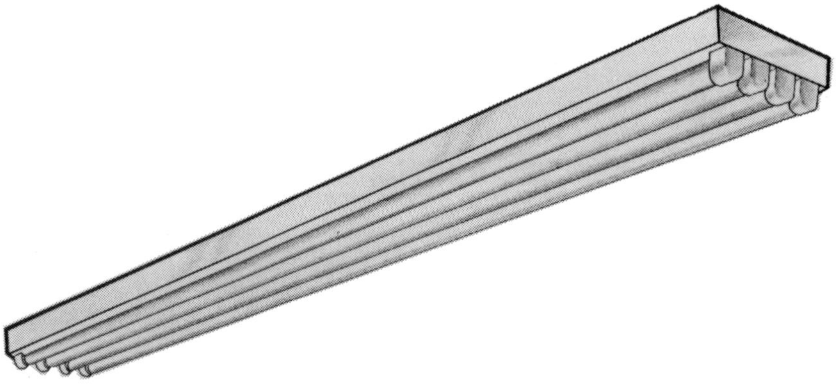

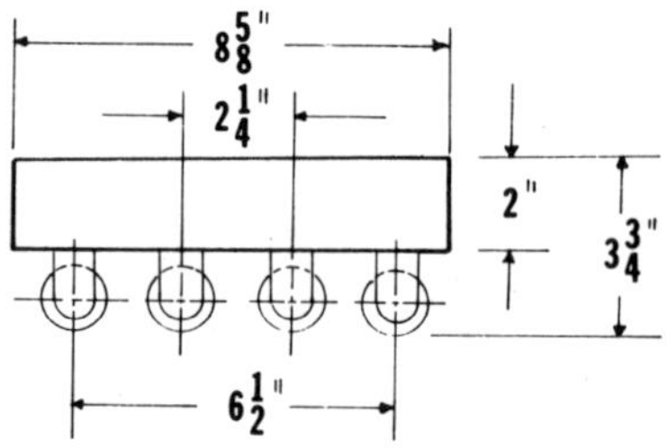

Description	8-ft long fluorescent strip
Lamps	Four F96 T12, 6400 lm each, 12,000 h
Spacing ratio	1.6
Maintenance factors	0.85/0.80/0.75
Input, W	346
Cost Details per Luminaire	Contractor's price = $43
	Installed cost = $82.50

The installed cost includes published contractor's book price for the luminaire, number of lamps as shown, luminaire fastening devices, and the labor required for the installation and connection of the luminaire. See page C–22 to add an outlet as required.

Use the conversion factors shown on page C–13 for an area where the ceiling, wall, and floor reflectances are low.

GENERAL PURPOSE FLUORESCENT STRIP – 8′ LONG, 4 LAMPS

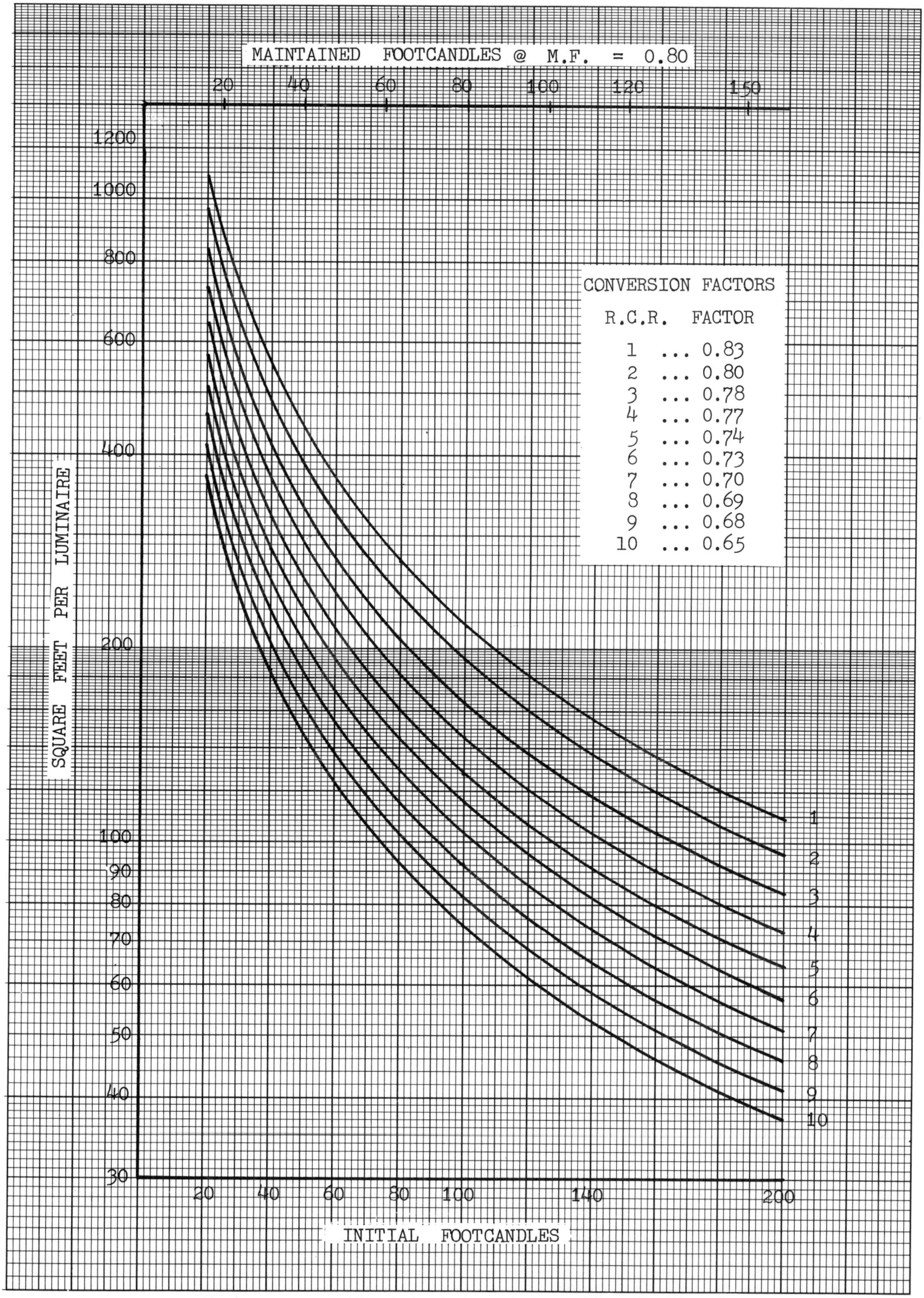

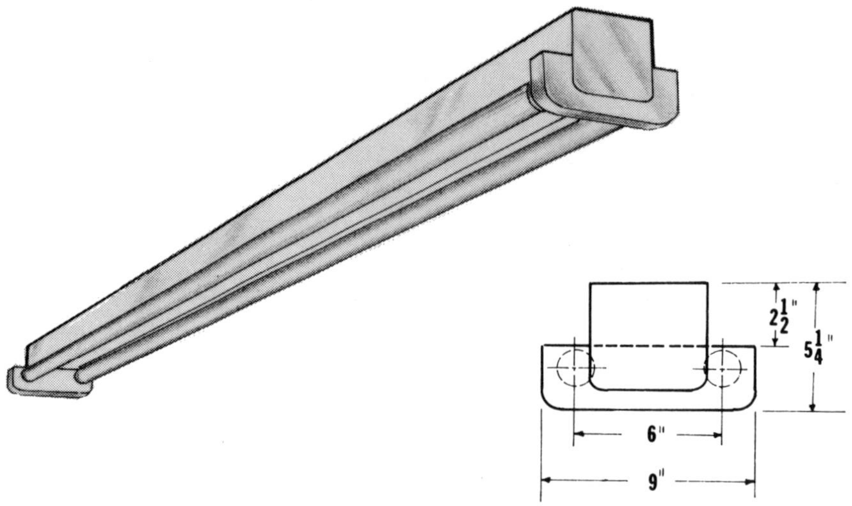

Description	4-ft long premium fluorescent strip
Lamps	Two F40 T12, 3200 lm each, 20,000 h
Spacing ratio	1.4
Maintenance factors	0.85/0.80/0.75
Conversion factors	A. Unit with two F40 T12 lamps = 1.0
	B. Unit with two F48 T12HO lamps = 1.35
	C. Unit with two F48 PG17 lamps = 2.35

COST DETAILS PER LUMINAIRE

Type of unit	Input, W	Contractor's price	Installed cost
A	93	$22	$41.50
B	150	39	64.75
C	235	58	92

The installed cost includes published contractor's book price for the luminaire, number of lamps as shown, luminaire fastening devices, and the labor required for the installation and connection of the luminaire. See page C–22 to add an outlet as required.

Use the conversion factors shown on page C–15 for an application where the ceiling, wall, and floor reflectances are low.

FLUORESCENT STRIP – 4′ LONG, PREMIUM GRADE, 2 LAMPS

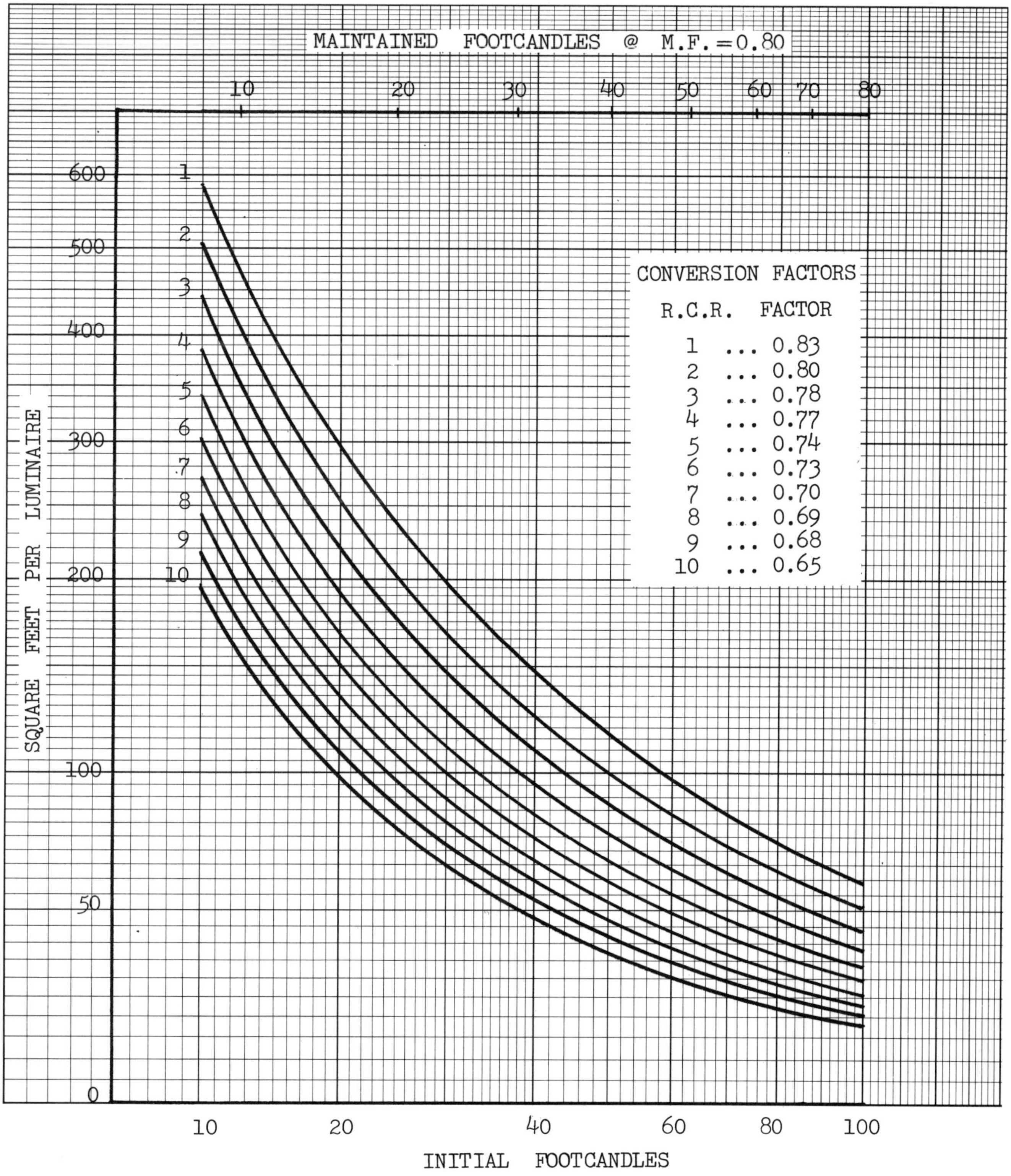

CONVERSION FACTORS

R.C.R.	FACTOR
1	... 0.83
2	... 0.80
3	... 0.78
4	... 0.77
5	... 0.74
6	... 0.73
7	... 0.70
8	... 0.69
9	... 0.68
10	... 0.65

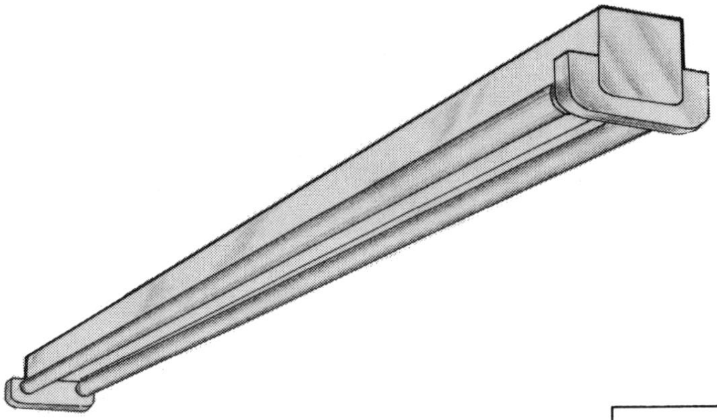

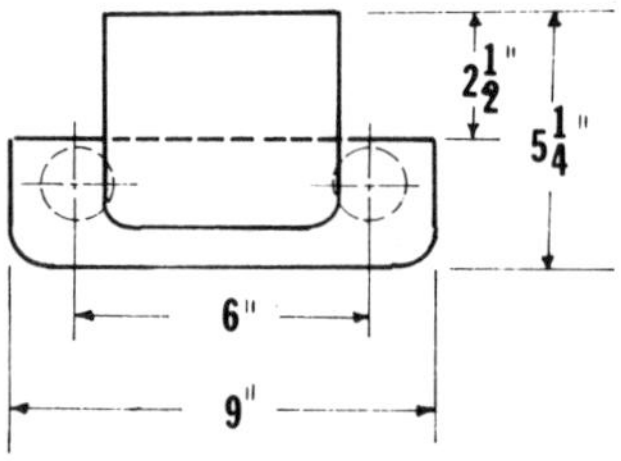

Description	8-ft long premium fluorescent strip
Lamps	Two F96 T12HO, 9150 lm each, 12,000 h
Spacing ratio	1.5
Maintenance factors	0.85/0.80/0.75
Conversion factors	A. Unit with two F96 T12HO lamps = 1.0 B. Unit with two F96 T12 lamps = 0.7

COST DETAILS PER LUMINAIRE

Type of unit	Input, W	Contractor's price	Installed cost
A	241	$39	$72.50
B	173	33	62.50

The installed cost includes published contractor's book price for the luminaire, number of lamps as shown, luminaire fastening devices, and the labor required for the installation and connection of the luminaire. *See page C–22 to add an outlet as required.*

Use the conversion factors shown on page C–17 for an application where the ceiling, wall, and floor reflectances are low.

FLUORESCENT STRIP — 8′ LONG, PREMIUM GRADE, 2 LAMPS

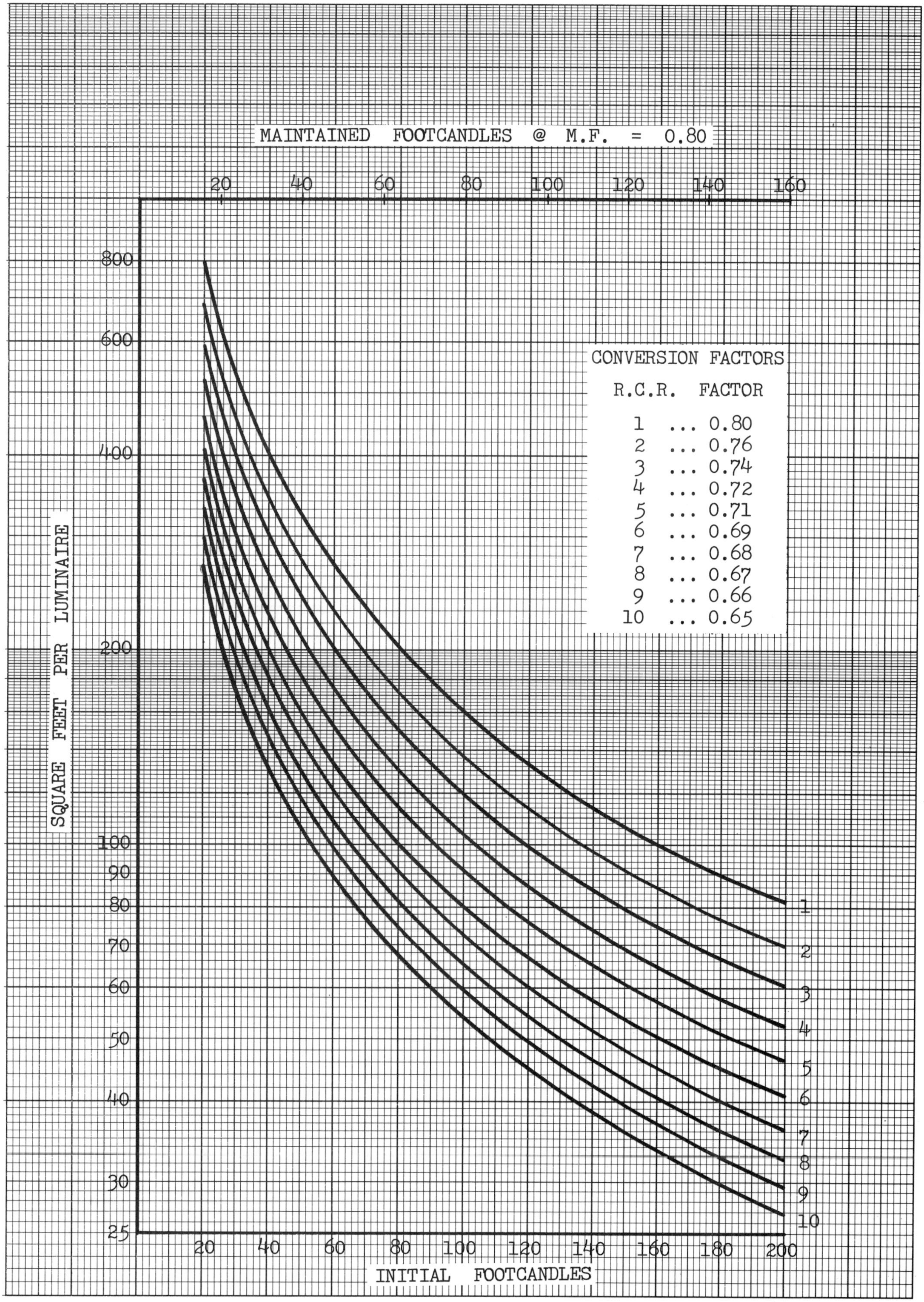

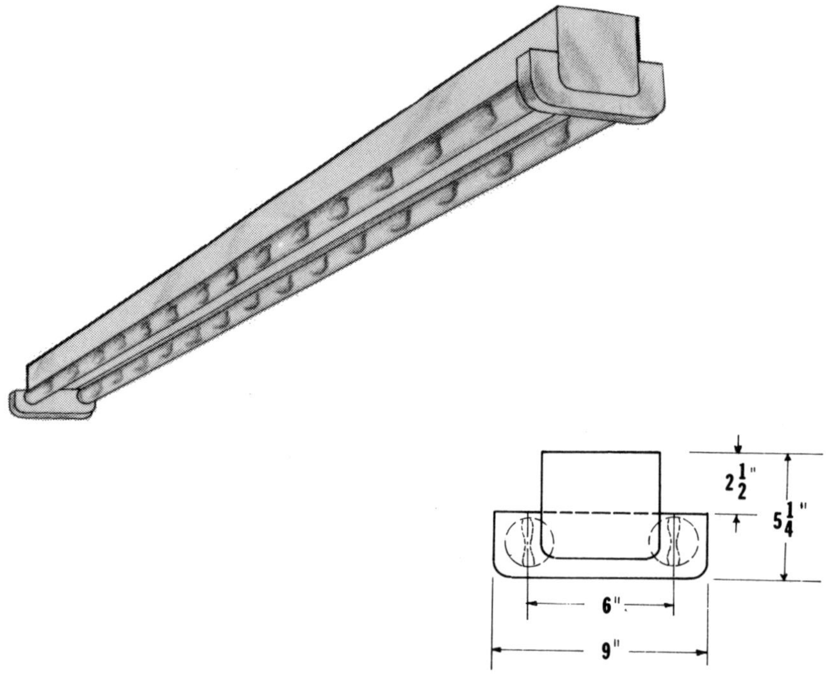

Description	8-ft long premium fluorescent strip
Lamps	Two F96 PG17, 16,000 lm each, 12,000 h
Spacing ratio	1.6
Maintenance factors	0.85/0.80/0.75
Input, W	455
Cost Details per Luminaire	Contractor's price = \$67
	Installed cost = \$109.25

The installed cost includes published contractor's book price for the luminaire, number of lamps as shown, luminaire fastening devices, and the labor required for the installation and connection of the luminaire. See page C–22 to add an outlet as required.

Use the conversion factors shown on page C–19 for an area where the ceiling, wall, and floor reflectances are low.

FLUORESCENT STRIP – 8′ LONG, PREMIUM GRADE, 2 LAMPS

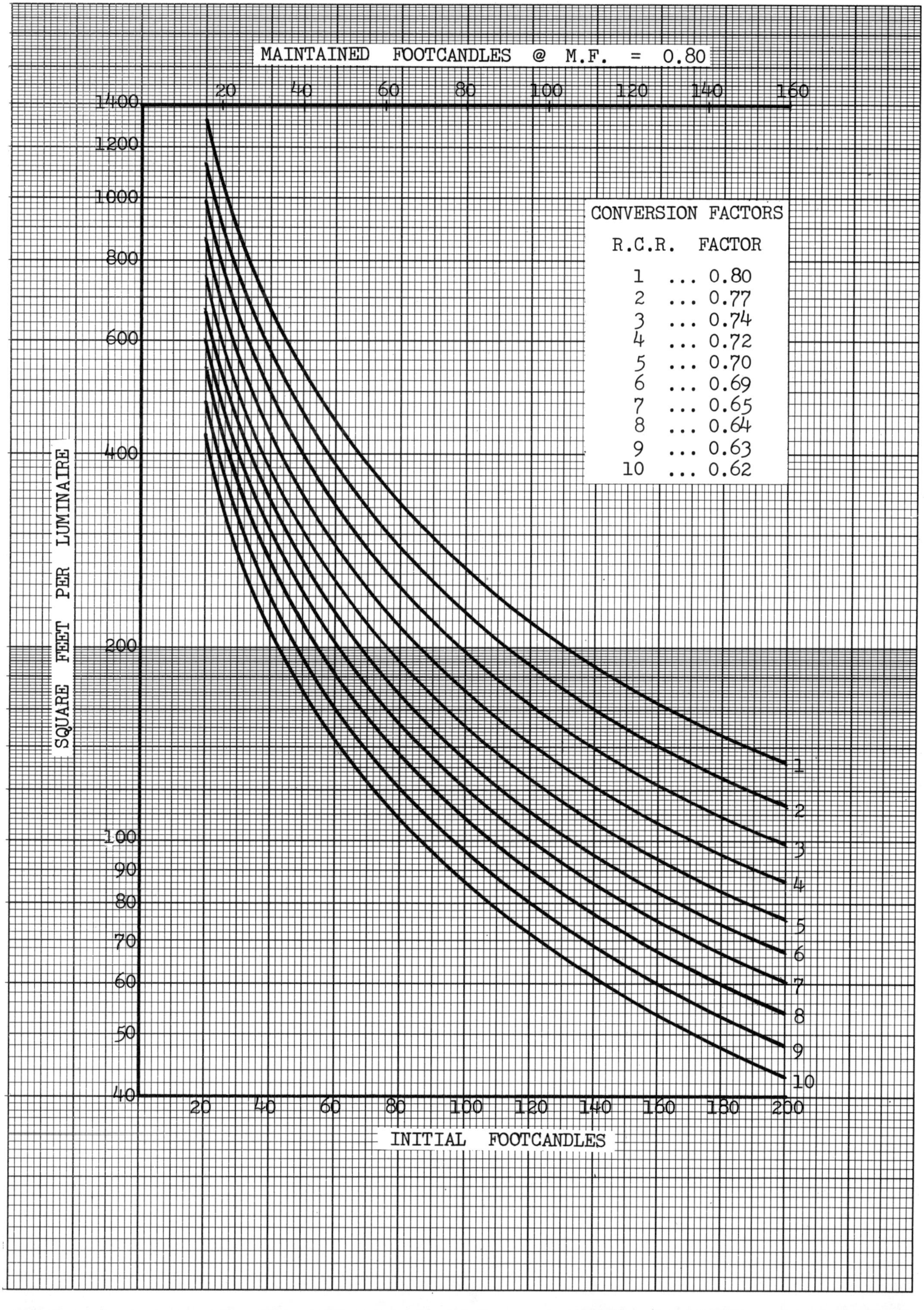

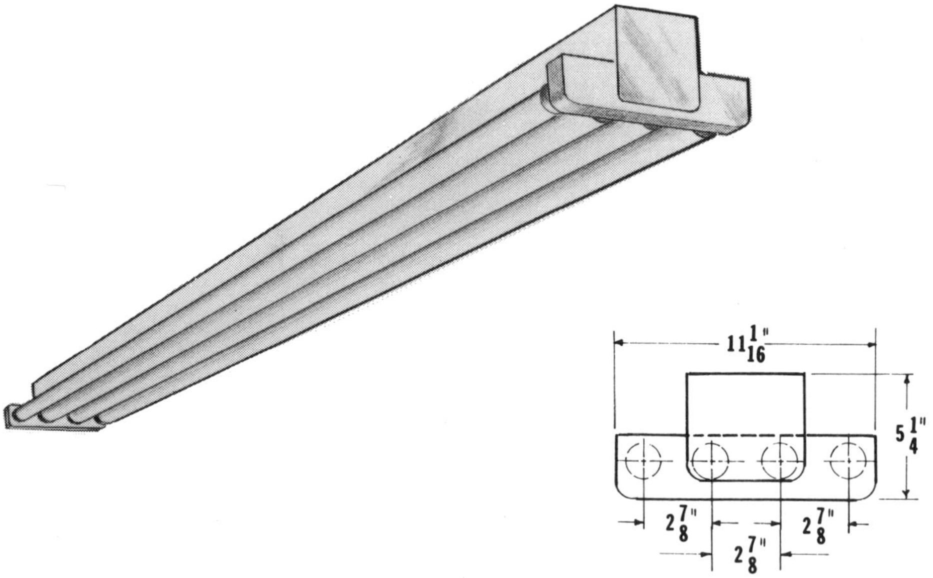

Description	8-ft long premium fluorescent strip
Lamps	Four F96 T12, 6400 lm each, 12,000 h
Spacing ratio	1.5
Maintenance factors	0.85/0.80/0.75
Conversion factors	A. Unit with four F96 T12 lamps = 1.0 B. Unit with three F96 T12 lamps = 0.75

COST DETAILS PER LUMINAIRE

Type of unit	Input, W	Contractor's price	Installed cost
A	346	$57	$99.50
B	281	54	92.50

The installed cost includes published contractor's book price for the luminaire, number of lamps as shown, luminaire fastening devices, and the labor required for the installation and connection of the luminaire. *See page C–22 to add an outlet as required.*

Use the conversion factors shown on page C–21 for an application where the ceiling, wall, and floor reflectances are low.

FLUORESCENT STRIP – 8′ LONG, PREMIUM GRADE. 3, 4 LAMPS

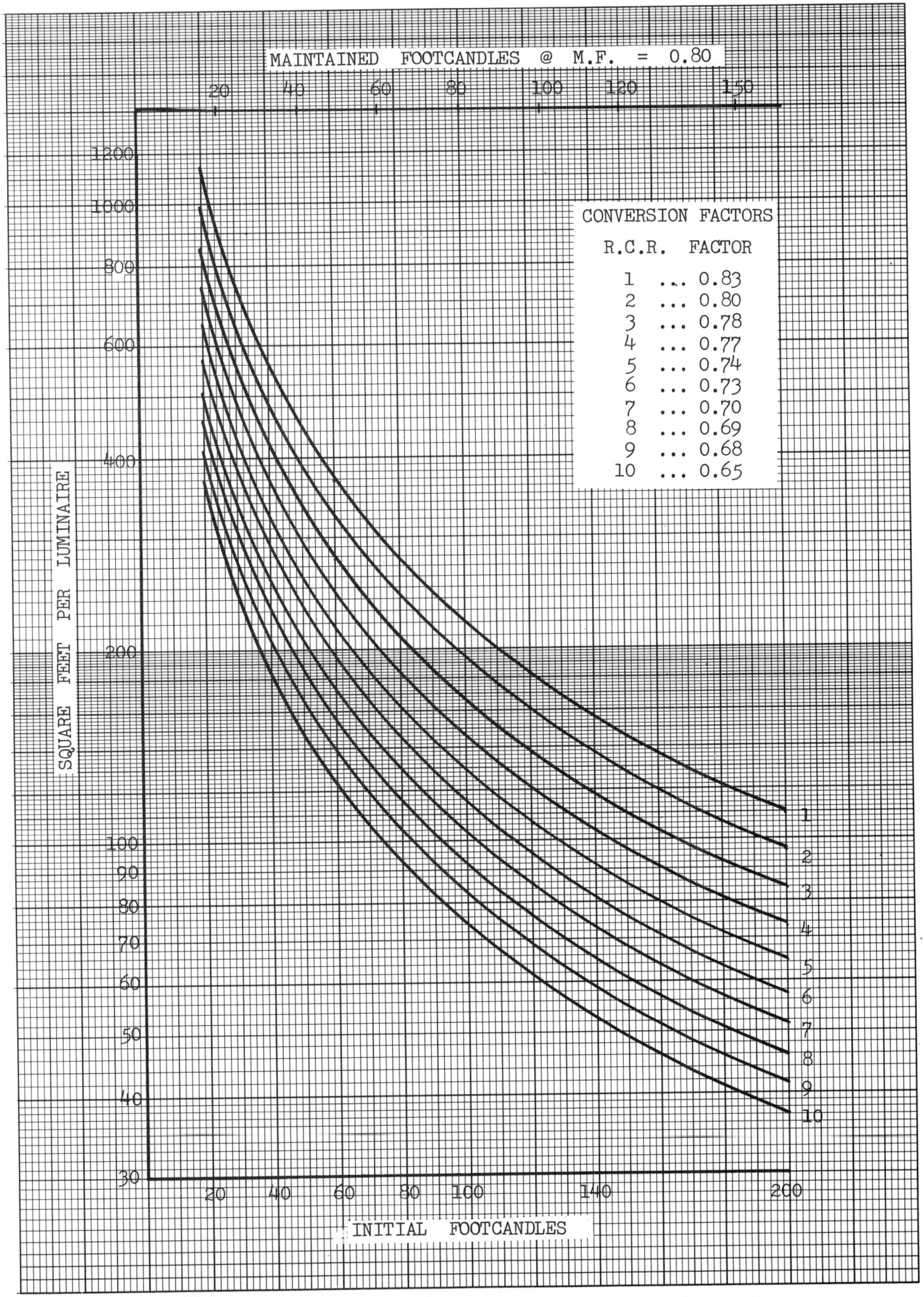

Direct-mount

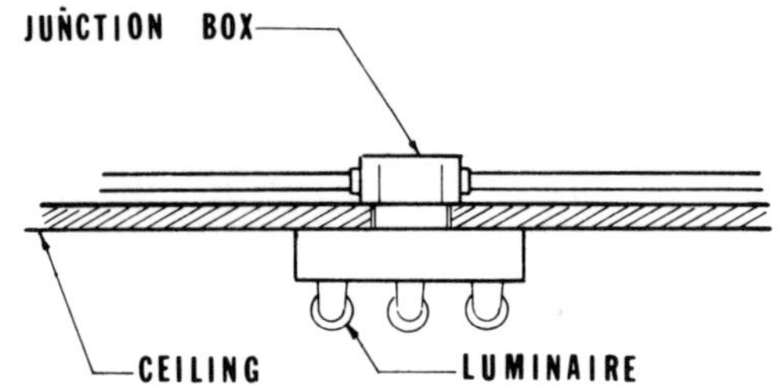

Add

$12.88 for EMT terminal
16.38 for GRC terminal
16.38 for IMS terminal

to the luminaire installed cost for an outlet flush-mounted to a suspended or furred ceiling, which includes a 4-in octagon box, adjustable bar hanger, two connectors, plaster ring, and two wire nuts.

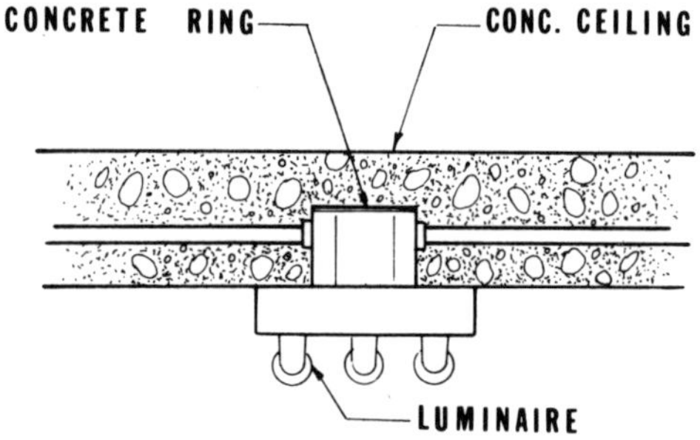

Add

$12.18 for EMT terminal
15.84 for GRC terminal
15.84 for IMS terminal

to the luminaire installed cost for an outlet flush-pan- or deck-mounted in concrete, which includes a 4-in concrete ring, connectors for the type of conduit required, cover plate, and two wire nuts.

Chain-suspended

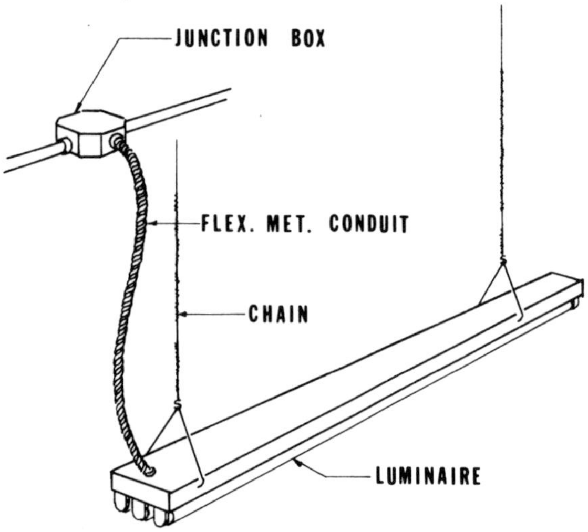

Add

$4.50 for each chain suspension which includes a 3-ft chain, two S hooks, and a Y hook. Add $0.50 for each additional 1-ft length of chain.

For a surface-mounted outlet to feed the chain-suspended luminaire add as shown below:

Type terminal	Type of construction		
	Steel	Wood	Concrete
EMT	13.78	$13.60	$16.33
GRC	18.88	18.70	21.43
IMS	18.88	18.70	21.43

This includes an octagon outlet box with a 6-ft length of flexible metallic conduit having 8-ft long 2 no. 12 AF wire, two connectors, and two wire nuts.

Industrial

FLUORESCENT UNITS

General-Purpose

4-ft, 2 Lamps D-2
8-ft, 2 Lamps D-4
3 Lamps D-6
4 Lamps D-8

Premium-Grade

8-ft, 2 Lamps, HO D-10
PG D-12

Heavy-Duty-Grade

8-ft, 2 Lamps, HO D-14
2 Lamps, PG D-16

HIGH-INTENSITY DISCHARGE UNITS

Low-Profile Series

Aluminum Reflector, up to 250 W D-18
Porcelain Enamel Reflector, up to 250 W D-20
Prismatic Glass Refractor, up to 250 W D-22

Full-Profile Series

Aluminum Reflector, 400 W D-24
Prismatic Glass Reflector, 400 W D-26
Aluminum Reflector, 1000 W D-28
Prismatic Glass Reflector, 1000 W D-30

Full-Profile Series: Twin Units

Aluminum Reflector, 400 W D-32
Prismatic Glass Reflector, 400 W D-34

CEILING OUTLETS FOR LUMINAIRES

Installed Cost of Luminaire Outlets D-36

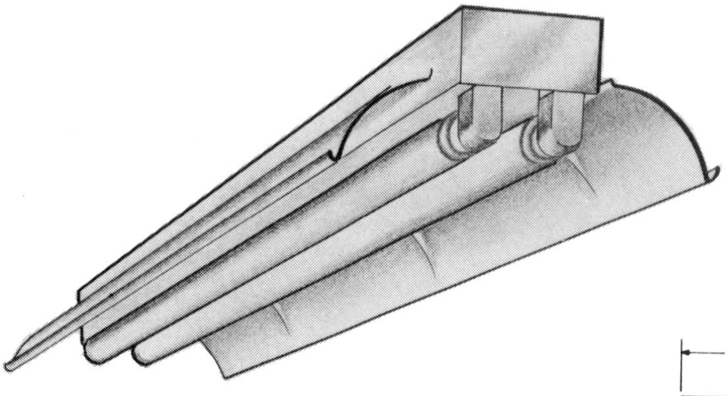

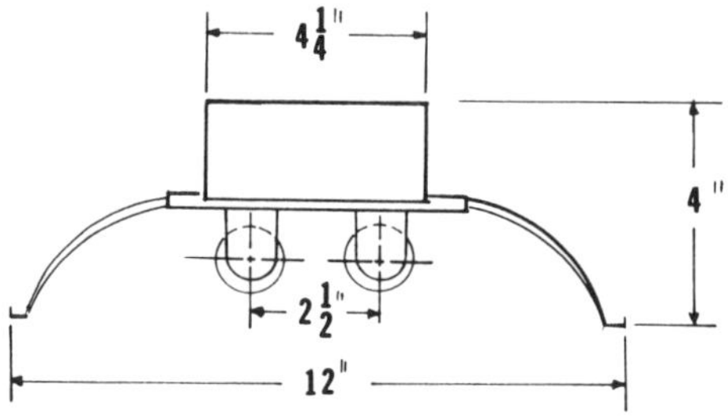

Description	4-ft general-purpose industrial
Lamps	Two F40 T12, 3200 lm each, 20,000 h
Spacing ratio	1.5
Reflector	Apertured or closed-top
Maintenance factors	0.85/0.80/0.75 (apertured unit) 0.80/0.75/0.70 (closed-top unit)
Conversion factors	A. Unit with two F40 T12 lamps = 1.0 B. Unit with two F48 T12HO lamps = 1.35 C. Unit with two F48 PF17 lamps = 2.35

COST DETAILS PER LUMINAIRE

Type of unit	Input, W	Contractor's price	Installed cost
A	93	$18	$37
B	150	34	59.50
C	235	50	83

The installed cost includes published contractor's book price for the luminaire with ballast and reflector, number of lamps as shown, and labor required for fastening to an existing suspension system. No hanging or fastening materials are included. See page D–36 for an outlet and hanging or fastening installed cost.

Apertured units, due to their flow-through chimney effect, carry dirt from the reflector, assuring a better maintenance factor. Use the conversion factors shown on page D–3 for an application where the ceiling, wall, and floor reflectances are low. Use the lower maintenance factor if necessary.

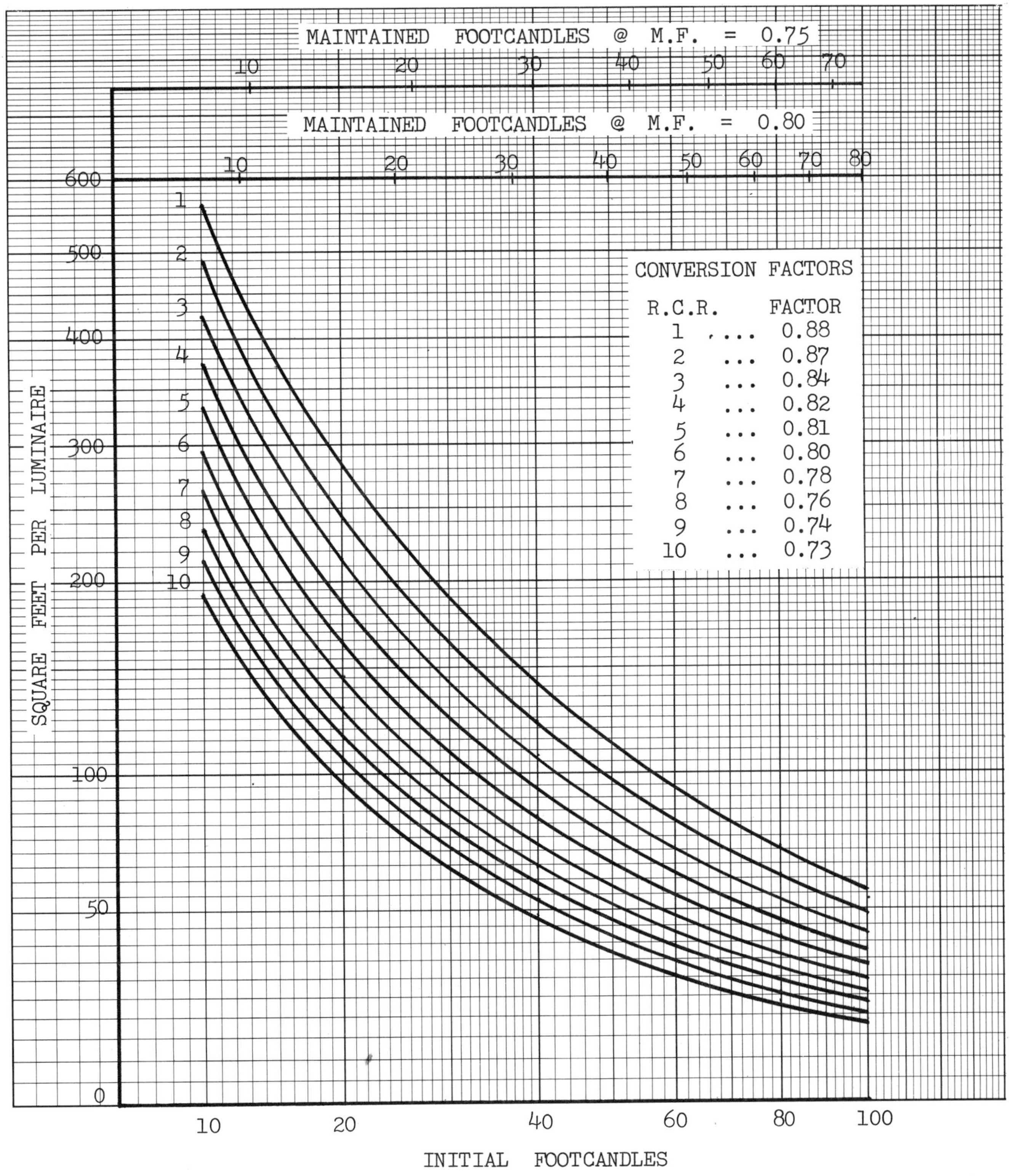
MAINTAINED FOOTCANDLES @ M.F. = 0.75
10 20 30 40 50 60 70
MAINTAINED FOOTCANDLES @ M.F. = 0.80
10 20 30 40 50 60 70 80
SQUARE FEET PER LUMINAIRE
600 500 400 300 200 100 50 0
1 2 3 4 5 6 7 8 9 10
CONVERSION FACTORS
R.C.R. FACTOR
1 .... 0.88
2 ... 0.87
3 ... 0.84
4 ... 0.82
5 ... 0.81
6 ... 0.80
7 ... 0.78
8 ... 0.76
9 ... 0.74
10 ... 0.73
10 20 40 60 80 100
INITIAL FOOTCANDLES

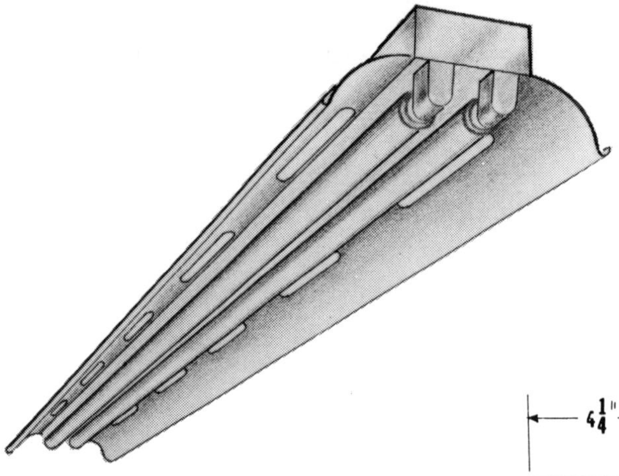

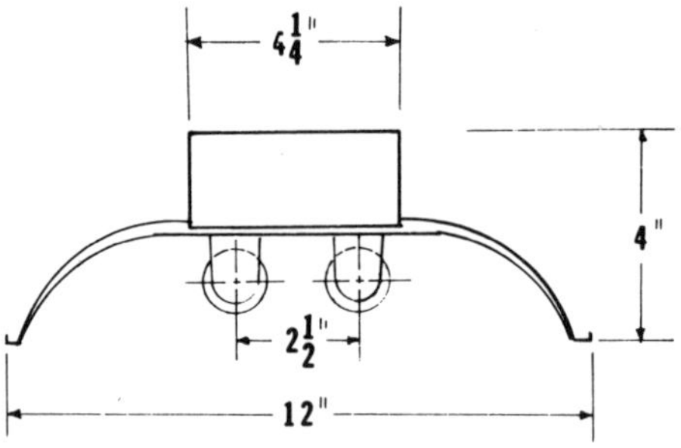

Description	8-ft general-purpose industrial
Lamps	Two F96 T12, 6400 lm each, 12,000 h
Spacing ratio	1.5
Reflector	Apertured or closed-top
Maintenance factors	0.85/0.80/0.75 (apertured unit) 0.80/0.75/0.70 (closed-top unit)
Conversion factors	A. Unit with two F96 T12 lamps = 1.0 B. Unit with two F96 T12HO lamps = 1.43

COST DETAILS PER LUMINAIRE

Type of unit	Input, W	Contractor's price	Installed cost
A	173	$29	$57.75
B	241	39	72.50

The installed cost includes published contractor's book price for the luminaire with ballast and reflector, number of lamps as shown, and the labor required for fastening to an existing suspension system. No hanging or fastening materials are included. See page D–36 for an outlet and hanging or fastening installed cost.

Apertured units, due to their flow-through chimney effect, carry dirt from the reflector, assuring a better maintenance factor. Use the conversion factors shown on page D–5 for an application where the ceiling, wall, and floor reflectances are low. Use the lower maintenance factor if necessary.

INDUSTRIAL FLUORESCENT, GENERAL PURPOSE – 8′ LONG, 2 LAMPS

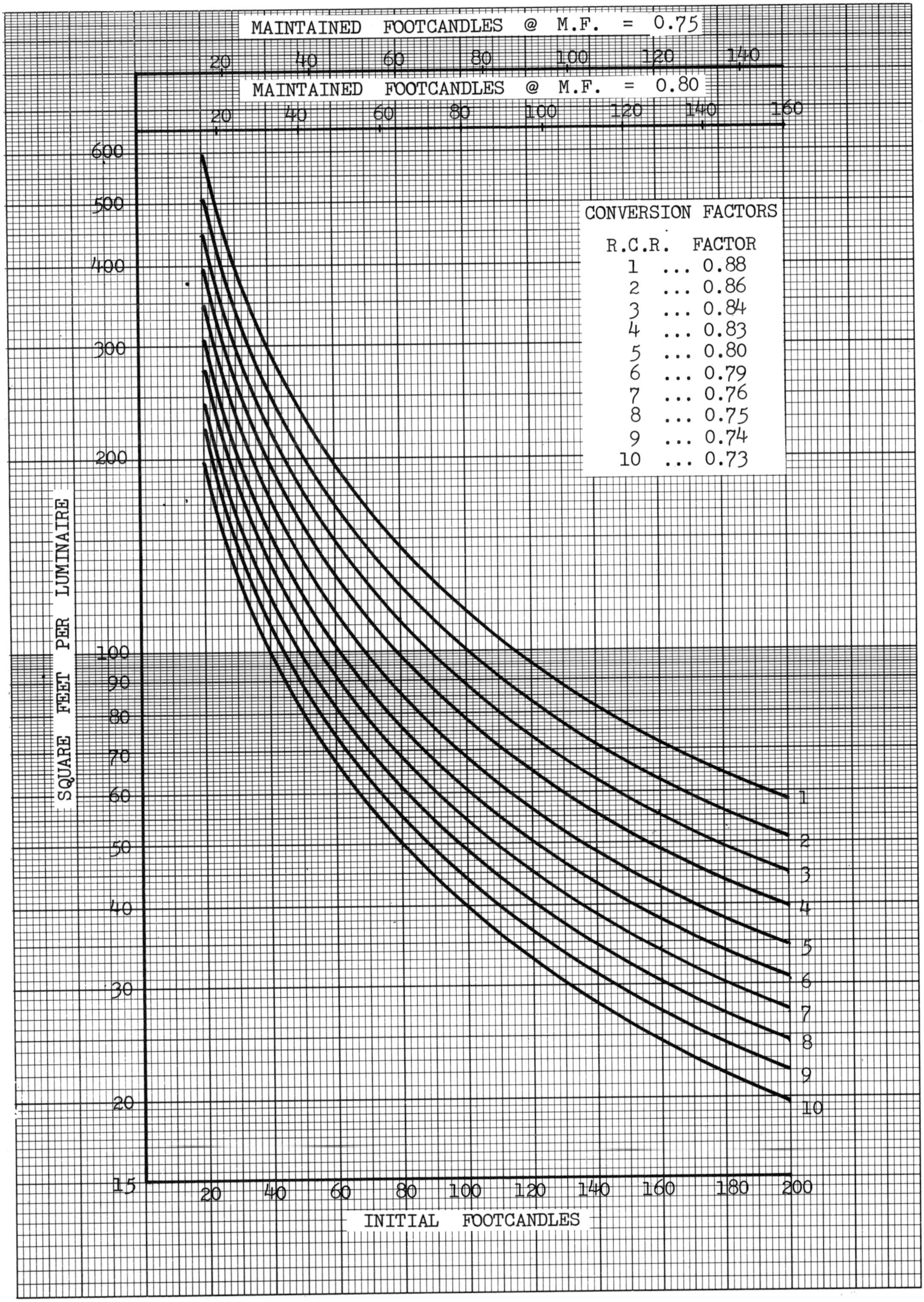

D

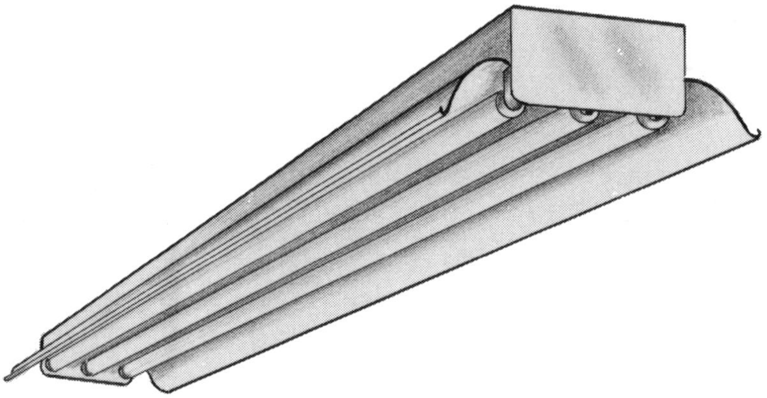

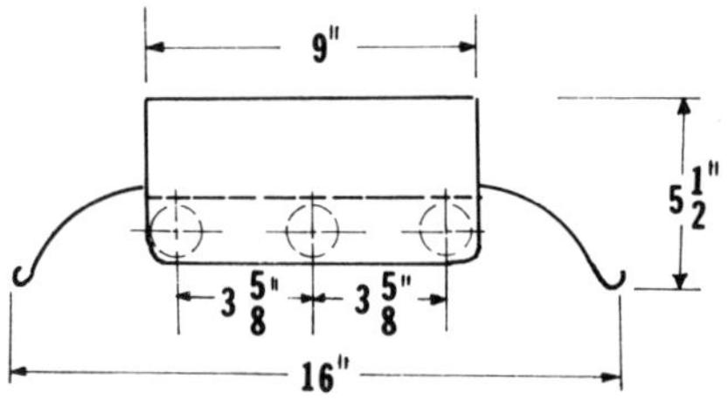

D-6

Description	8-ft general-purpose industrial
Lamps	Three F96 T12, 6400 lm each, 12,000 h
Spacing ratio	1.5
Reflector	Apertured or closed-top
Maintenance factors	0.85/0.80/0.75 (apertured units) 0.80/0.75/0.70 (closed-top units)
Input, W	281
Cost details per luminaire	Contractor's price = \$58 Installed cost = \$97.50

The installed cost includes published contractor's book price for the luminaire with ballasts and reflector, number of lamps as shown, and the labor required for fastening to an existing suspension system. No hanging or fastening materials are included. See page D–36 for an outlet and hanging or fastening installed cost.

Apertured units due to their flow-through chimney effect, carry dirt from the reflector, assuring a better maintenance factor. Use the conversion factors shown on page D–7 for an application where the ceiling, wall, and floor reflectances are low. Use the lower maintenance factor if necessary.

INDUSTRIAL FLUORESCENT, GENERAL PURPOSE – 8′ LONG, 3 LAMPS

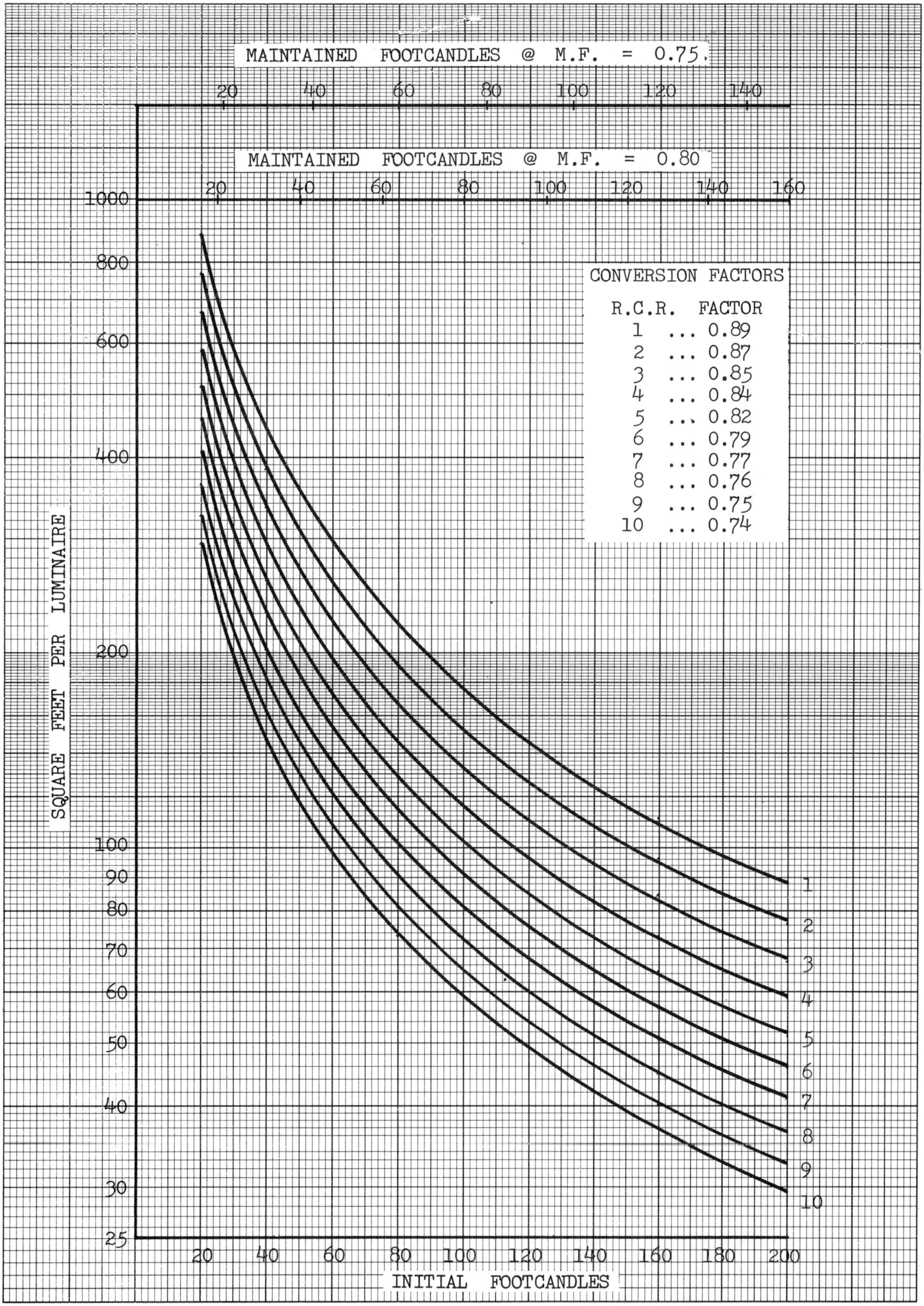

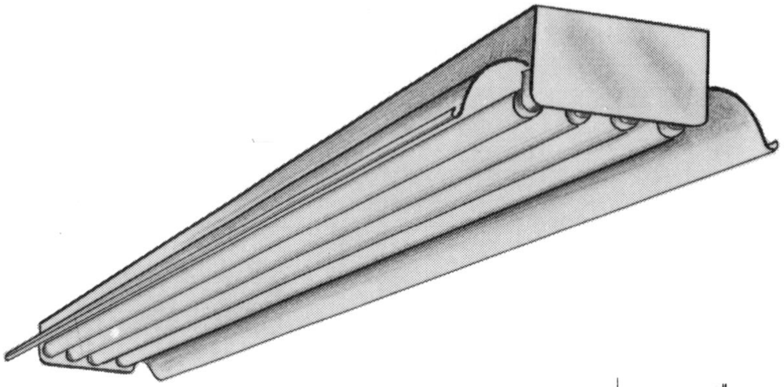

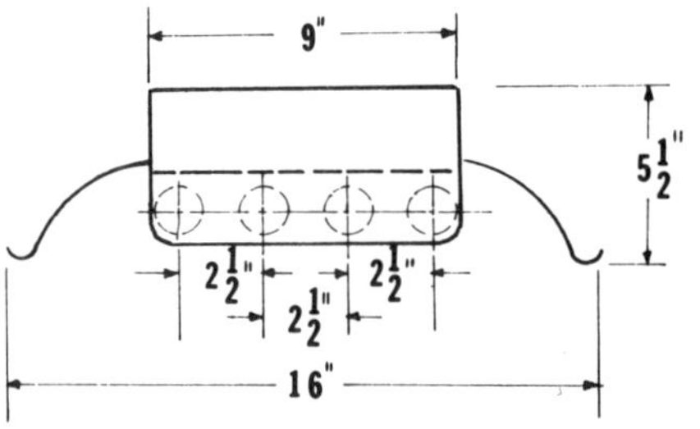

Description	8-ft general-purpose industrial
Lamps	Four F96 T12, 6400 lm each, 12,000 h
Spacing ratio	1.5
Reflector	Apertured or closed-top
Maintenance factors	0.85/0.80/0.75 (apertured units)
	0.80/0.75/0.70 (closed-top units)
Input, W	346
Cost details per luminaire	Contractor's price = \$58
	Installed cost = \$100.75

The installed cost includes published contractor's book price for the luminaire with ballasts and reflector, number of lamps as shown, and the labor required for fastening to an existing suspension system. No hanging or fastening materials are included. See page D–36 for an outlet and hanging or fastening installed cost.

Apertured units due to their flow-through chimney effect, carry dirt from the reflector, assuring a better maintenance factor. Use the conversion factors shown on page D–9 for an application where the ceiling, wall, and floor reflectances are low. Use the lower maintenance factor if necessary.

INDUSTRIAL FLUORESCENT, GENERAL PURPOSE – 8′ LONG, 4 LAMPS

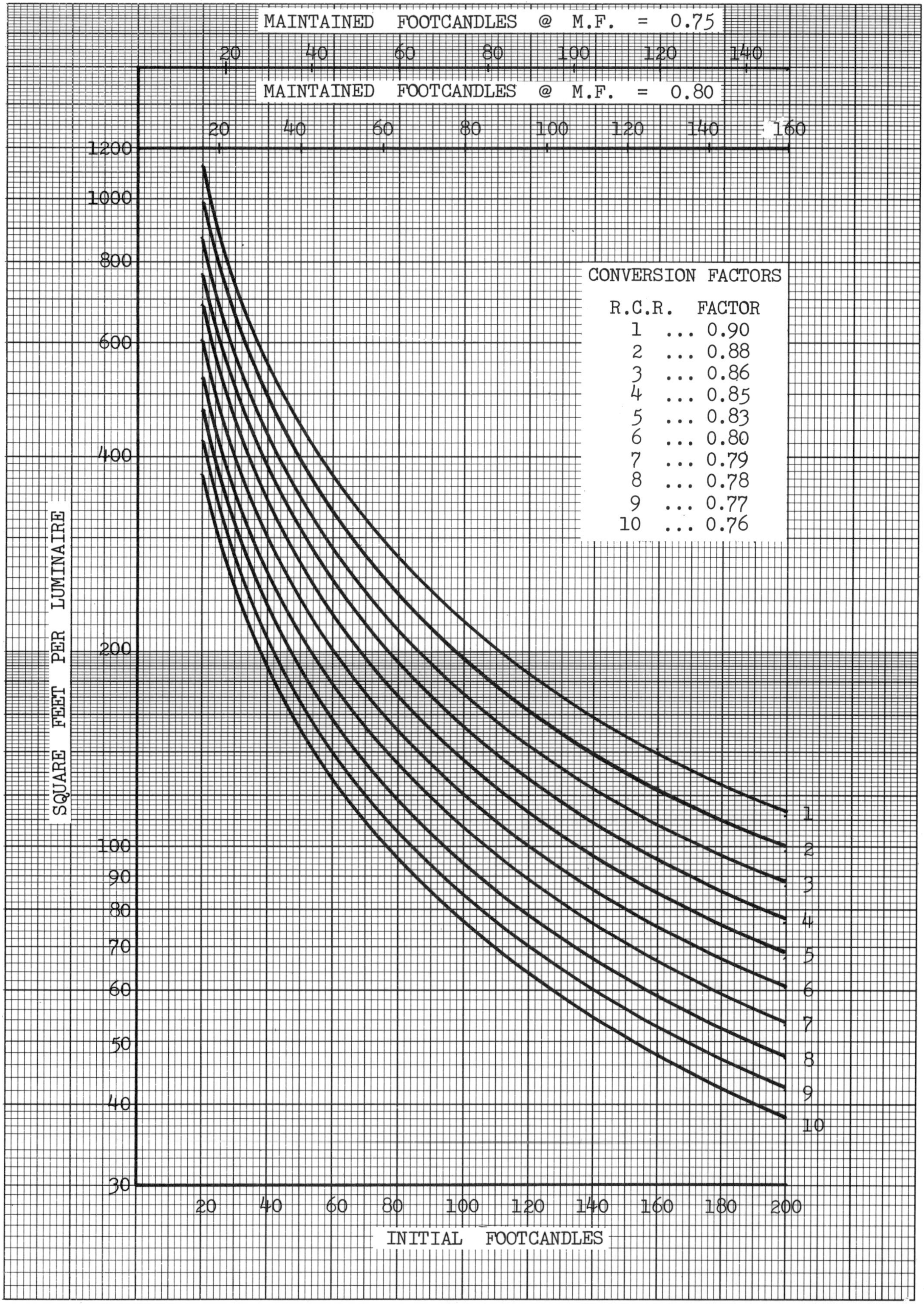

D

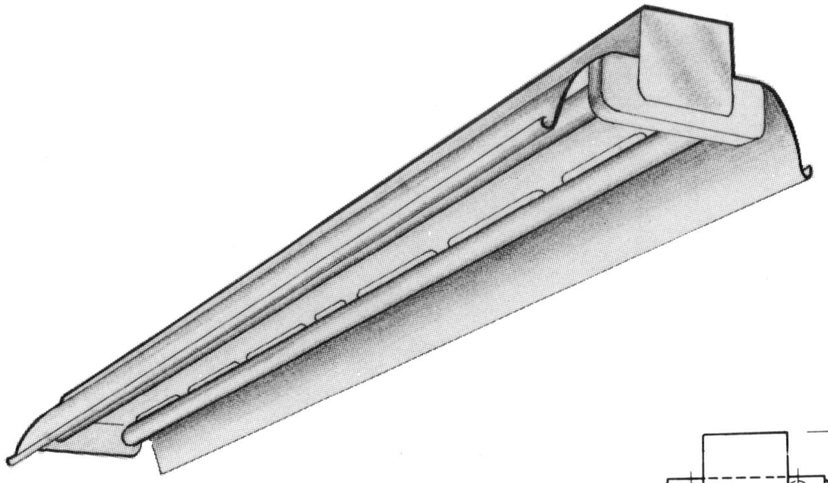

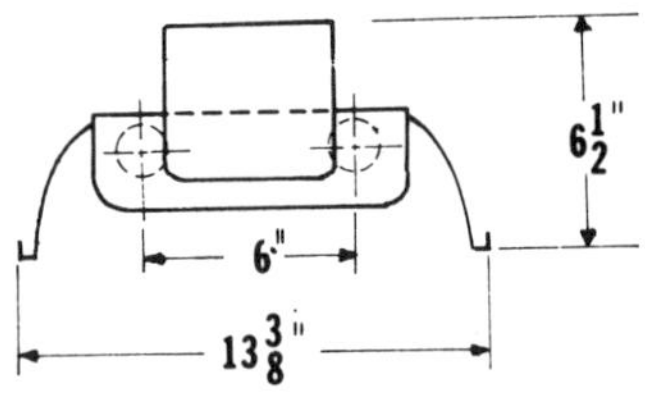

Description	8-ft premium industrial
Lamps	Two F96 T12HO, 9200 lm each, 12,000 h
Spacing ratio	1.5
Reflector	25% uplight
Maintenance factors	0.85/0.80/0.75
Conversion factors	A. Unit with two F96 T12HO lamps = 1.0
	B. Unit with two F96 T12 lamps = 0.7

COST DETAILS PER LUMINAIRE

Type of unit	Input, W	Contractor's price	Installed cost
A	241	$55	$92
B	173	44	76

The installed cost includes published contractor's book price for the luminaire with ballast and reflector, number of lamps as shown, and the labor required for fastening to an existing suspension system. No hanging or fastening materials are included. See page D–36 for an outlet and hanging or fastening installed cost.

Apertured units, due to their flow-through chimney effect, carry dirt from the reflector, assuring a better maintenance factor. Use the conversion factors shown on page D–11 for an application where the ceiling, wall, and floor reflectances are low. Use the lower maintenance factor if necessary.

INDUSTRIAL FLUORESCENT – 8′ LONG, PREMIUM GRADE, 2 LAMPS

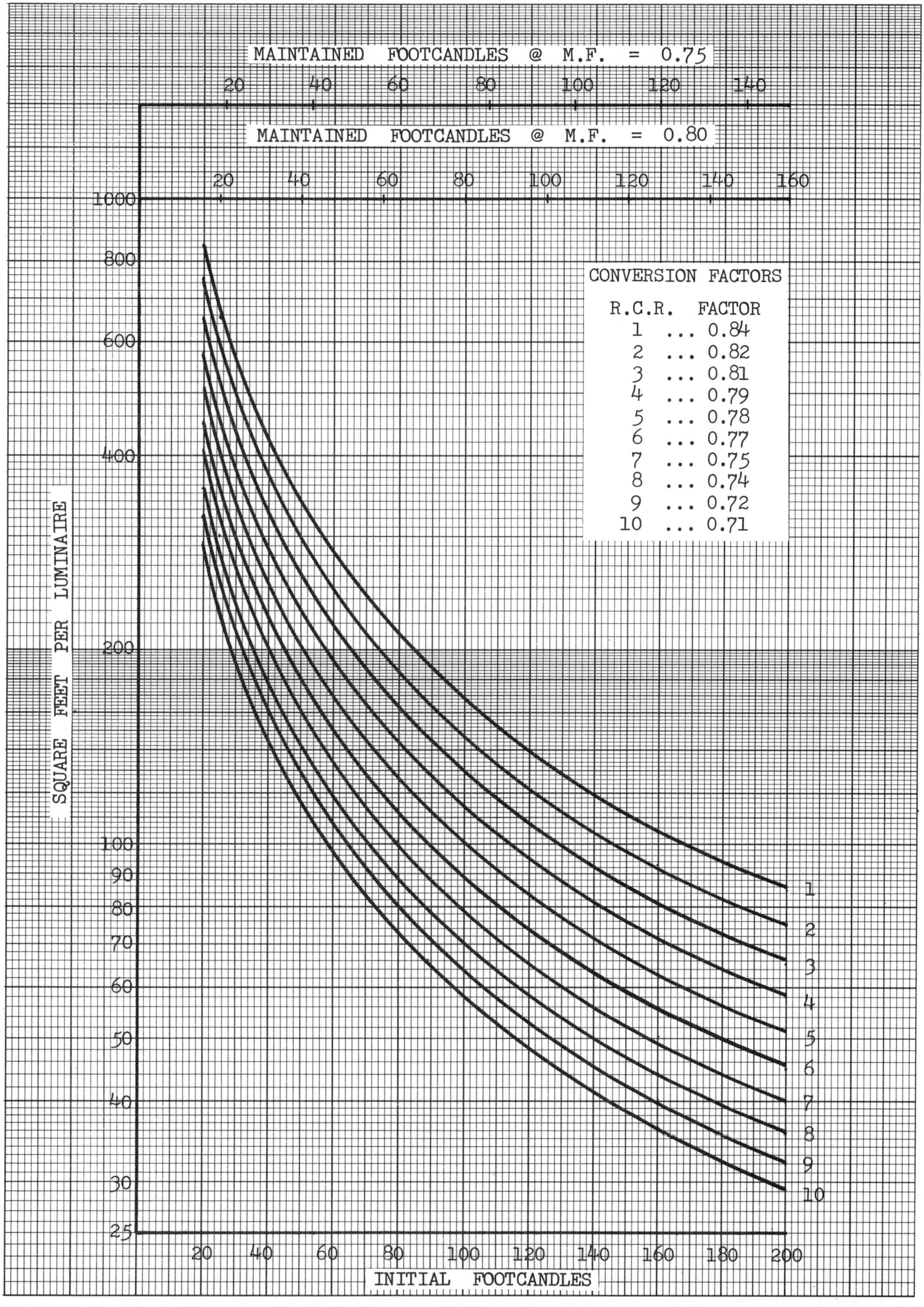

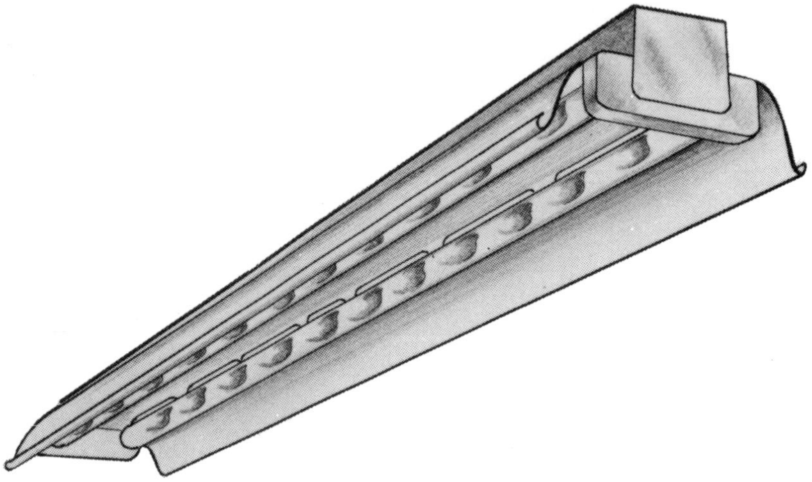

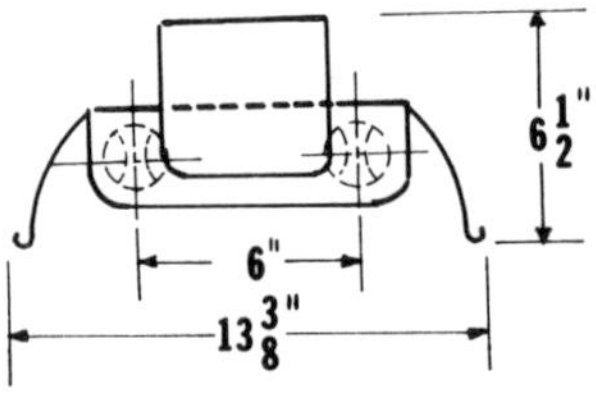

Description	8-ft premium industrial
Lamps	Two F96 PG17, 16000 lm each, 12,000 h
Spacing ratio	1.6
Reflector	25% uplight
Maintenance factors	0.85/0.80/0.75
Input, W	455
Cost details per luminaire	Contractor's price = \$75
	Installed cost = \$119

The installed cost includes published contractor's book price for the luminaire with ballast and reflector, number of lamps as shown, and the labor required for fastening to an existing suspension system. No hanging or fastening materials are included. See page D–36 for an outlet and hanging or fastening installed cost.

Apertured units, due to their flow-through chimney effect, carry dirt from the reflector, assuring a better maintenance factor. Use the conversion factors shown on page D–13 for an application where the ceiling, wall, and floor reflectances are low. Use the lower maintenance factor, if necessary.

INDUSTRIAL FLUORESCENT – 8′ LONG, PREMIUM GRADE, 2 LAMPS

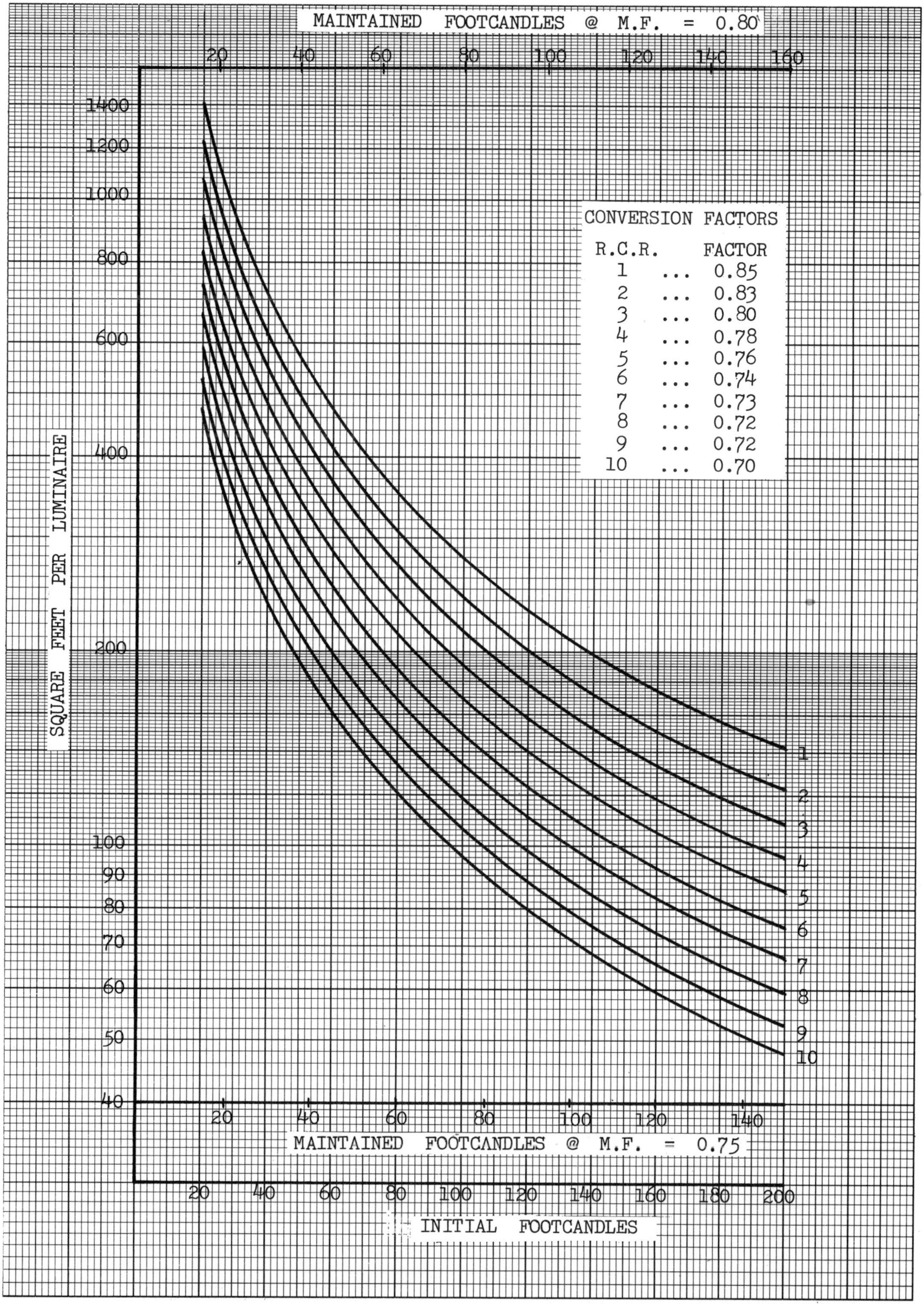

CONVERSION FACTORS

R.C.R.		FACTOR
1	...	0.85
2	...	0.83
3	...	0.80
4	...	0.78
5	...	0.76
6	...	0.74
7	...	0.73
8	...	0.72
9	...	0.72
10	...	0.70

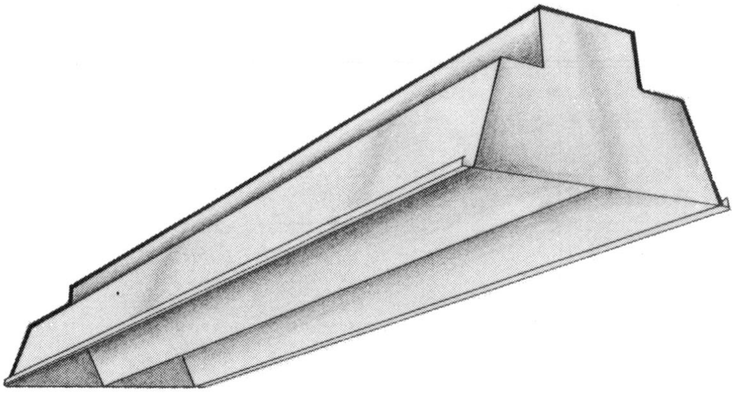

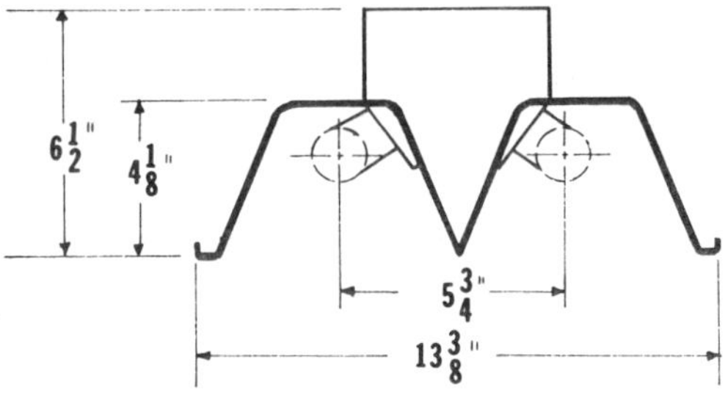

D-14

Description	8-ft heavy-duty industrial
Lamps	Two F96 T12HO, 9200 lm each, 12,000 h
Spacing ratio	1.3
Reflector	20% uplight
Maintenance factors	0.85/0.80/0.75
Conversion factors	A. Unit with two F96 T12HO lamps = 1.0
	B. Unit with two F96 T12 lamps = 0.7

COST DETAILS PER LUMINAIRE

Type of unit	Input, W	Contractor's price	Installed cost
A	241	$60	$98
B	173	56	90.75

The installed cost includes published contractor's book price for the luminaire with ballast and reflector, number of lamps as shown, and the labor required for fastening to an existing suspension system. No hanging or fastening materials are included. See page D–36 for an outlet and hanging or fastening installed cost.

Apertured units, due to their flow-through chimney effect, carry dirt from the reflector, assuring a better maintenance factor. Use the conversion factors shown on page D–15 for an application where the ceiling, wall, and floor reflectances are low. Use the lower maintenance factor if necessary.

INDUSTRIAL FLUORESCENT – 8′ LONG, HEAVY–DUTY GRADE, 2 LAMPS

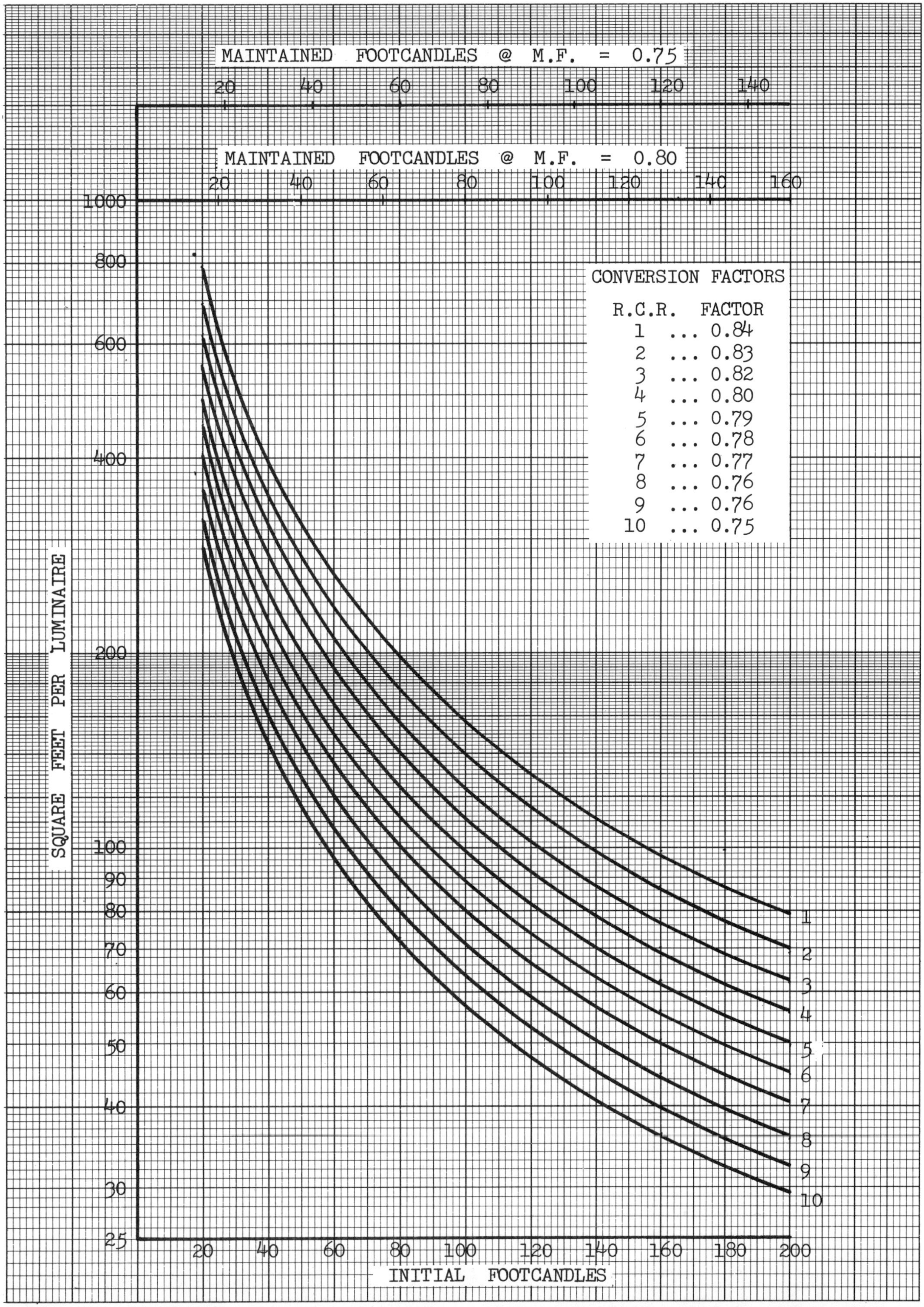

D

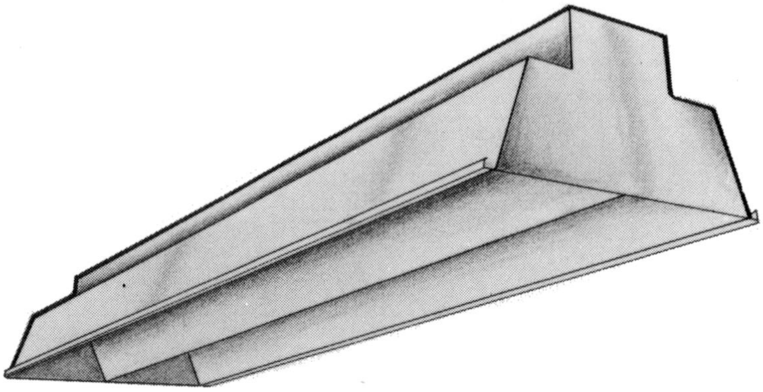

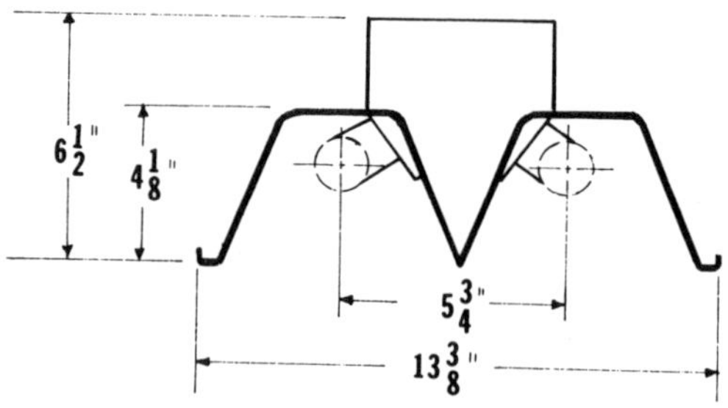

D-16

Description	8-ft heavy-duty industrial
Lamps	Two F96 PG12, 16000 lm each, 12,000 h
Spacing ratio	1.3
Reflector	20% uplight
Maintenance factors	0.85/0.80/0.75
Input, W	455
Cost details per luminaire	Contractor's price = \$80 Installed cost = \$125.25

The installed cost includes published contractor's book price for the luminaire with ballast and reflector, number of lamps as shown, and the labor required for fastening to an existing suspension system. No hanging or fastening materials are included. See page D–36 for an outlet and hanging or fastening installed cost.

Apertured units, due to their flow-through chimney effect, carry dirt from the reflector, assuring a better maintenance factor. Use the conversion factors shown on page D–17 for an application where the ceiling, wall, and floor reflectances are low. Use the lower maintenance factor if necessary.

INDUSTRIAL FLUORESCENT – 8′ LONG, HEAVY–DUTY GRADE, 2 LAMPS

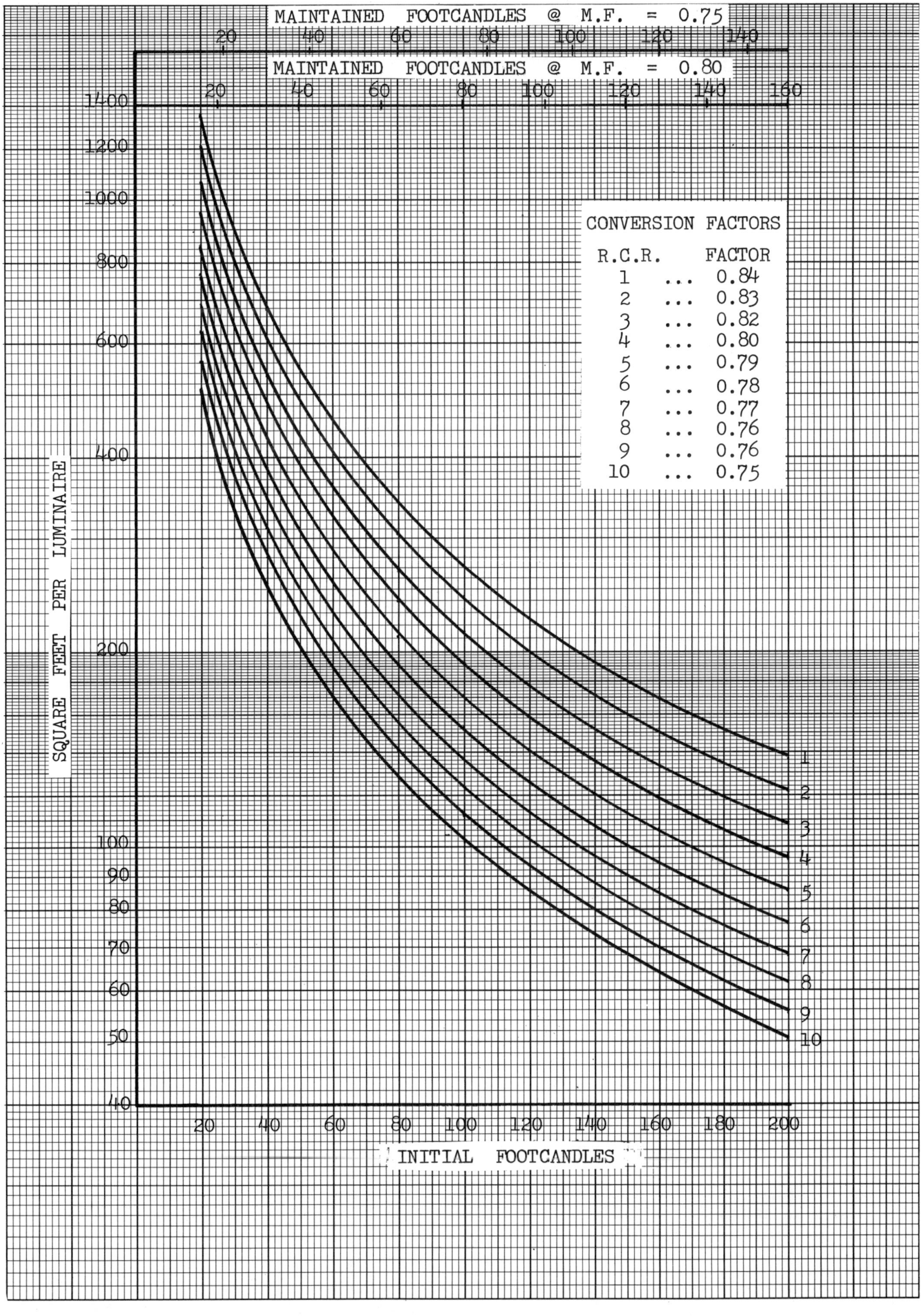

CONVERSION FACTORS		
R.C.R.		FACTOR
1	...	0.84
2	...	0.83
3	...	0.82
4	...	0.80
5	...	0.79
6	...	0.78
7	...	0.77
8	...	0.76
9	...	0.76
10	...	0.75

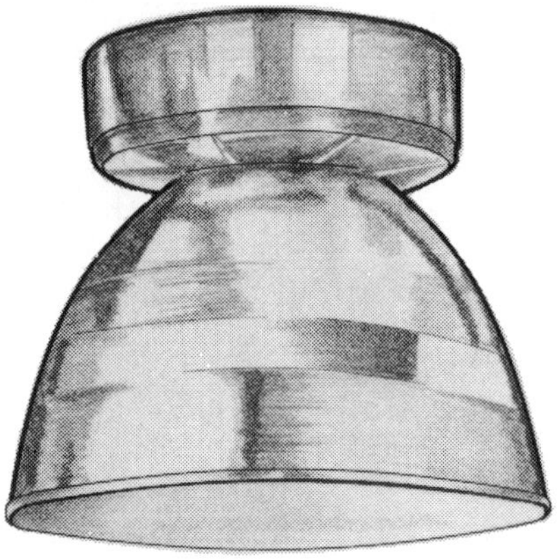

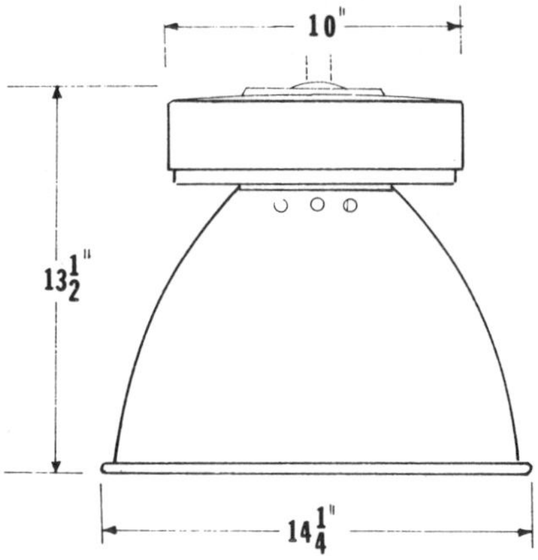

Description	Low-profile Alzak aluminum reflector
Lamp	One 175-W mercury (DX), 8150 lm, 24,000 h
Spacing ratio	1.3
Maintenance factors	0.85/0.80/0.75
Conversion factors	A. Unit with one 175-W mercury (DX) = 1.0
	B. Unit with one 100-W mercury (DX) = 0.51
	C. Unit with one 250-W mercury (DX) = 1.48

COST DETAILS PER LUMINAIRE

Type of unit	Input, W	Contractor's price	Installed cost
A	200	$51	$ 90.75
B	120	49	95.75
C	290	53	100.75

The installed cost includes published contractor's book price for the luminaire with ballast, lamp as shown, and the labor required for installation and connection to an existing outlet. See page D–36 for an outlet installed cost.

These units represent the family of low-budget lighting for protected areas where the ceiling heights are relatively low. Spread distribution from low-brightness industrial Alzak aluminum reflector provides uniform coverage when even lighting levels are required.

Use the conversion factors shown on page D–19 for an application, where the ceiling, wall, and floor reflectances are low. Use the lower maintenance factor if necessary.

The reference luminaires are as manufactured by Abolite.

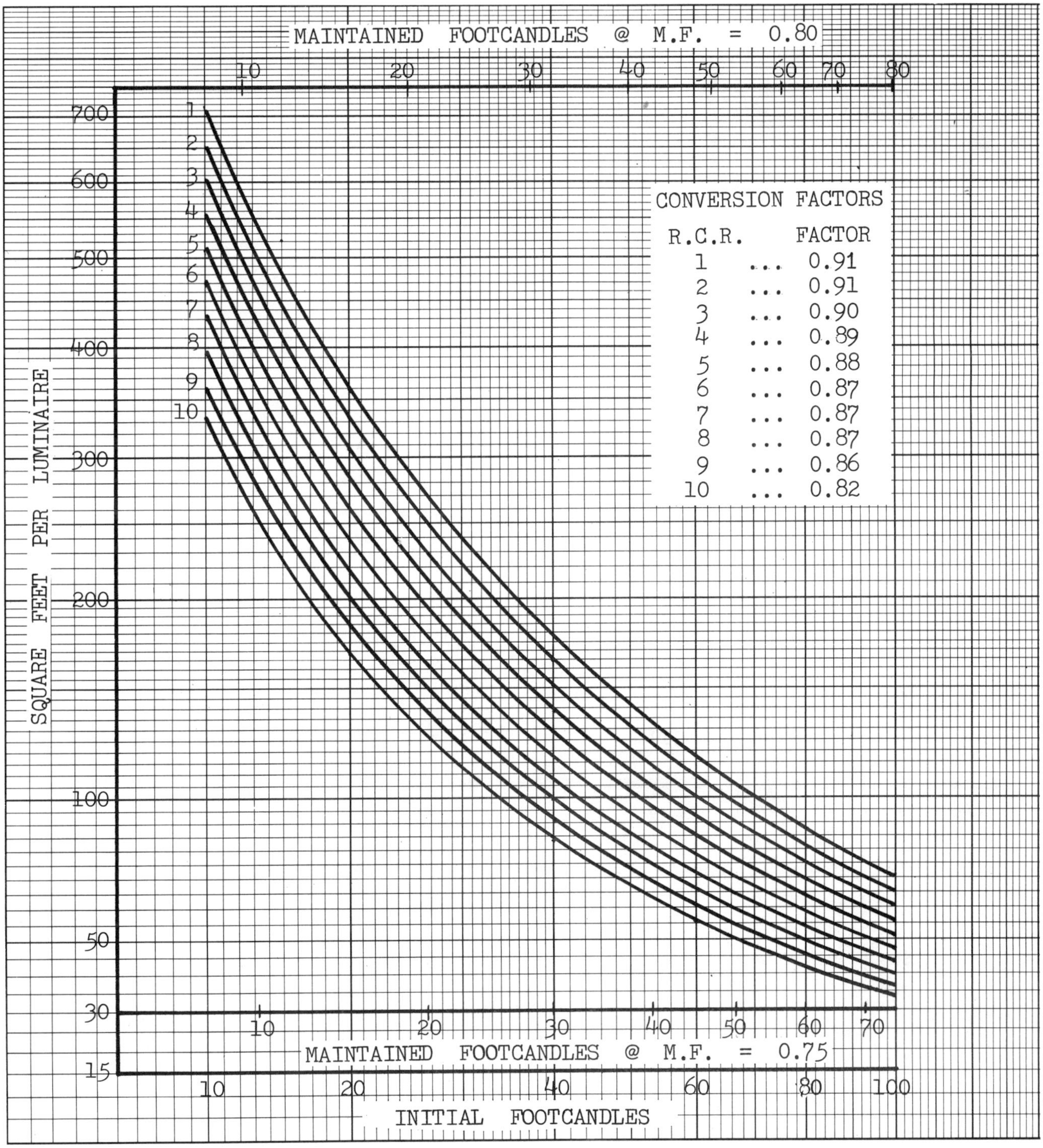
MAINTAINED FOOTCANDLES @ M.F. = 0.80
10
20
30
40
50
60
70
80
SQUARE FEET PER LUMINAIRE
700
600
500
400
300
200
100
50
30
15
1
2
3
4
5
6
7
8
9
10
CONVERSION FACTORS
R.C.R. FACTOR
1 ... 0.91
2 ... 0.91
3 ... 0.90
4 ... 0.89
5 ... 0.88
6 ... 0.87
7 ... 0.87
8 ... 0.87
9 ... 0.86
10 ... 0.82
MAINTAINED FOOTCANDLES @ M.F. = 0.75
10
20
30
40
50
60
70
INITIAL FOOTCANDLES
10
20
40
60
80
100

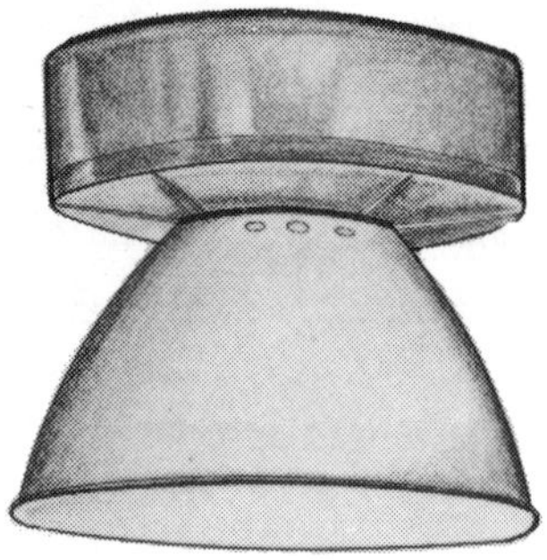

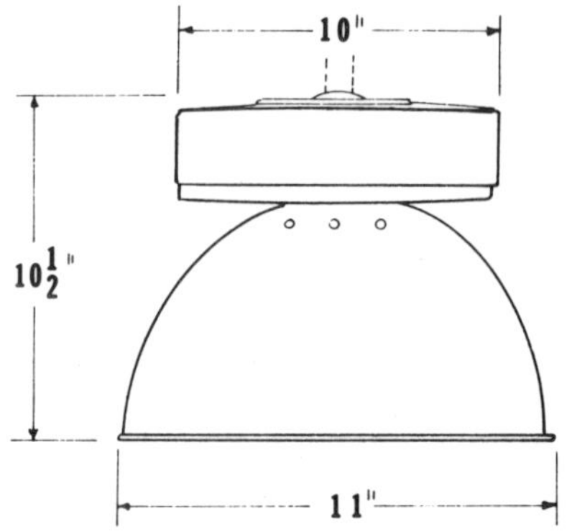

Description	Low-profile porcelain enamel reflector
Lamp	One 175-W mercury (DX), 8150 lm, 24,000 h
Spacing ratio	1.3
Maintenance factors	0.85/0.80/0.75
Conversion factors	A. Unit with one 175-W mercury (DX) = 1.0 B. Unit with one 100-W mercury (DX) = 0.51 C. Unit with one 250-W mercury (DX) = 1.48

COST DETAILS PER LUMINAIRE

Type of unit	Input, W	Contractor's price	Installed cost
A	200	$46	$84.75
B	120	45	90.75
C	290	49	95.75

The installed cost includes published contractor's book price for the luminaire with ballast, lamp as shown, and the labor required for installation and connection to an existing outlet. *See page D–36 for an outlet installed cost.*

These units represent the family of low-budget lighting for protected areas where the ceiling heights are relatively low. Porcelain enamel reflectors resist acids, fumes, and heat.

Use the conversion factors shown on page D–21 for an application, where the ceiling, wall, and floor reflectances are low. Use the lower maintenance factor if necessary.

The reference luminaires are as manufactured by Abolite.

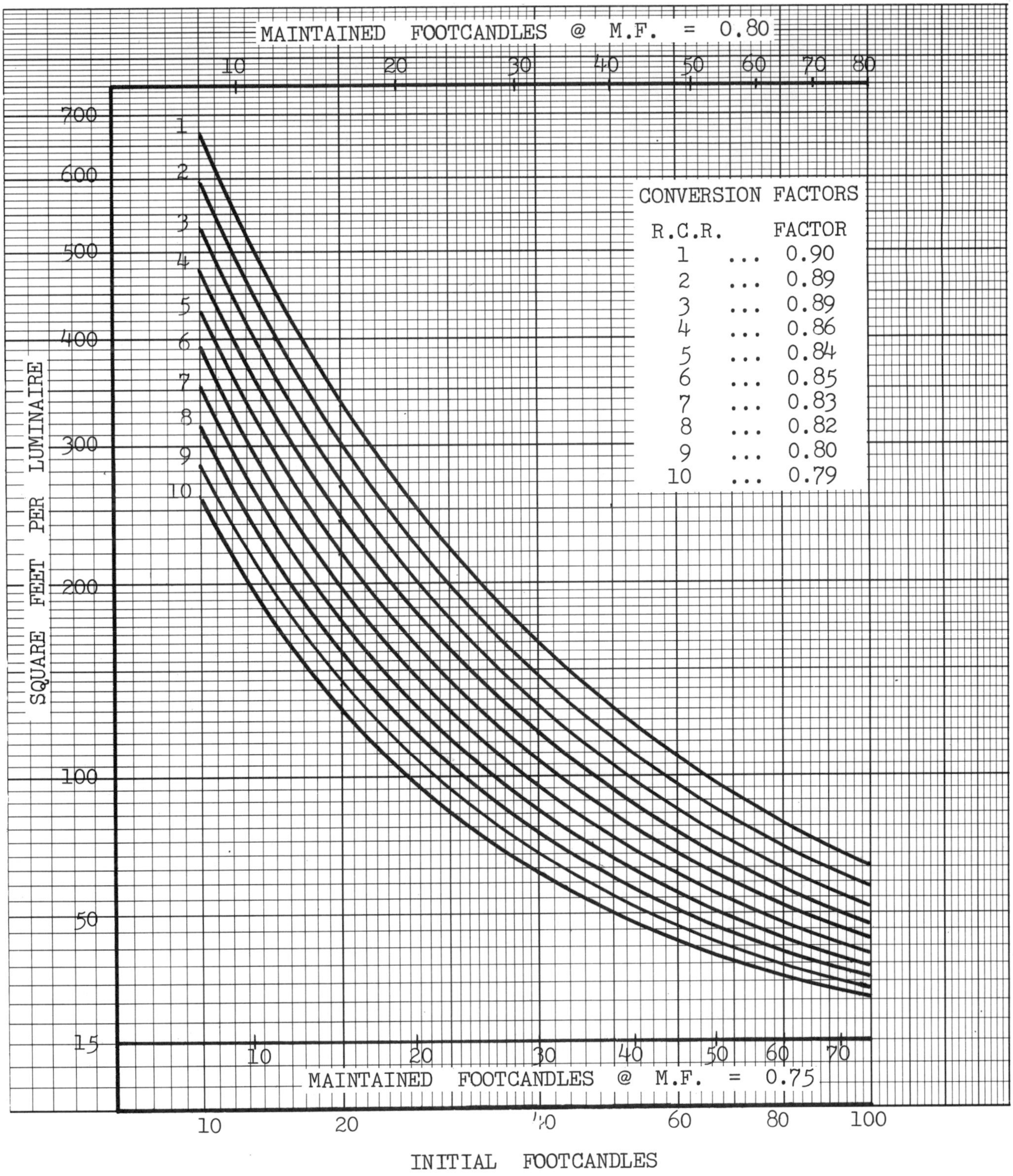
MAINTAINED FOOTCANDLES @ M.F. = 0.80
10
20
30
40
50
60
70
80
700
600
500
400
300
200
100
50
15
SQUARE FEET PER LUMINAIRE
1
2
3
4
5
6
7
8
9
10
CONVERSION FACTORS
R.C.R. FACTOR
1 ... 0.90
2 ... 0.89
3 ... 0.89
4 ... 0.86
5 ... 0.84
6 ... 0.85
7 ... 0.83
8 ... 0.82
9 ... 0.80
10 ... 0.79
10
20
30
40
50
60
70
MAINTAINED FOOTCANDLES @ M.F. = 0.75
10
20
40
60
80
100
INITIAL FOOTCANDLES

D

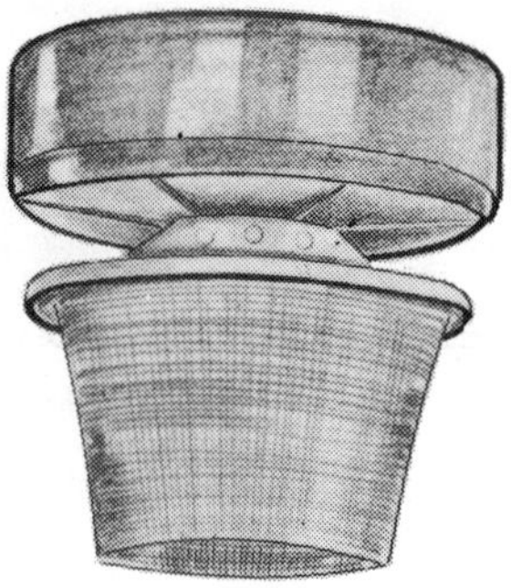

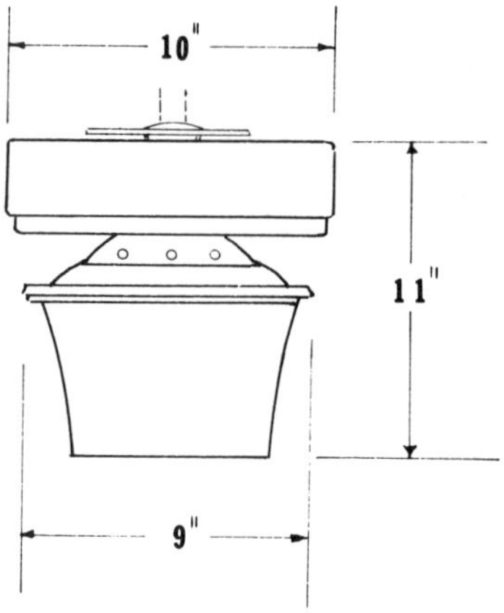

Description	Low-profile prismatic glass refractor
Lamp	One 175-W mercury (DX), 8150 lm, 24,000 h
Spacing ratio	1.4
Maintenance factors	0.85/0.80/0.75
Conversion factors	A. Unit with one 175-W mercury (DX) = 1.0 B. Unit with one 100-W mercury (DX) = 0.51 C. Unit with one 250-W mercury (DX) = 1.48

COST DETAILS PER LUMINAIRE

Type of unit	Input, W	Contractor's price	Installed cost
A	200	$54	$ 94.50
B	120	52	99.50
C	290	56	104.50

The installed cost includes published contractor's book price for the luminaire with ballast, lamp as shown, and the labor required for installation and connection to an existing outlet. *See page D–36 for an outlet installed cost.*

These units represent the family of low-budget lighting for protected areas where the ceiling heights are relatively low. These units are available in different types of light distribution. The reference luminaire is of type V, symmetrical distribution.

Use the conversion factors shown on page D–23 for an application where the ceiling, wall, and floor reflectances are low. Use the lower maintenance factor if necessary.

The reference luminaires are as manufactured by Abolite.

INDUSTRIAL H.I.D. – LOW PROFILE PRISMATIC GLASS REFRACTOR

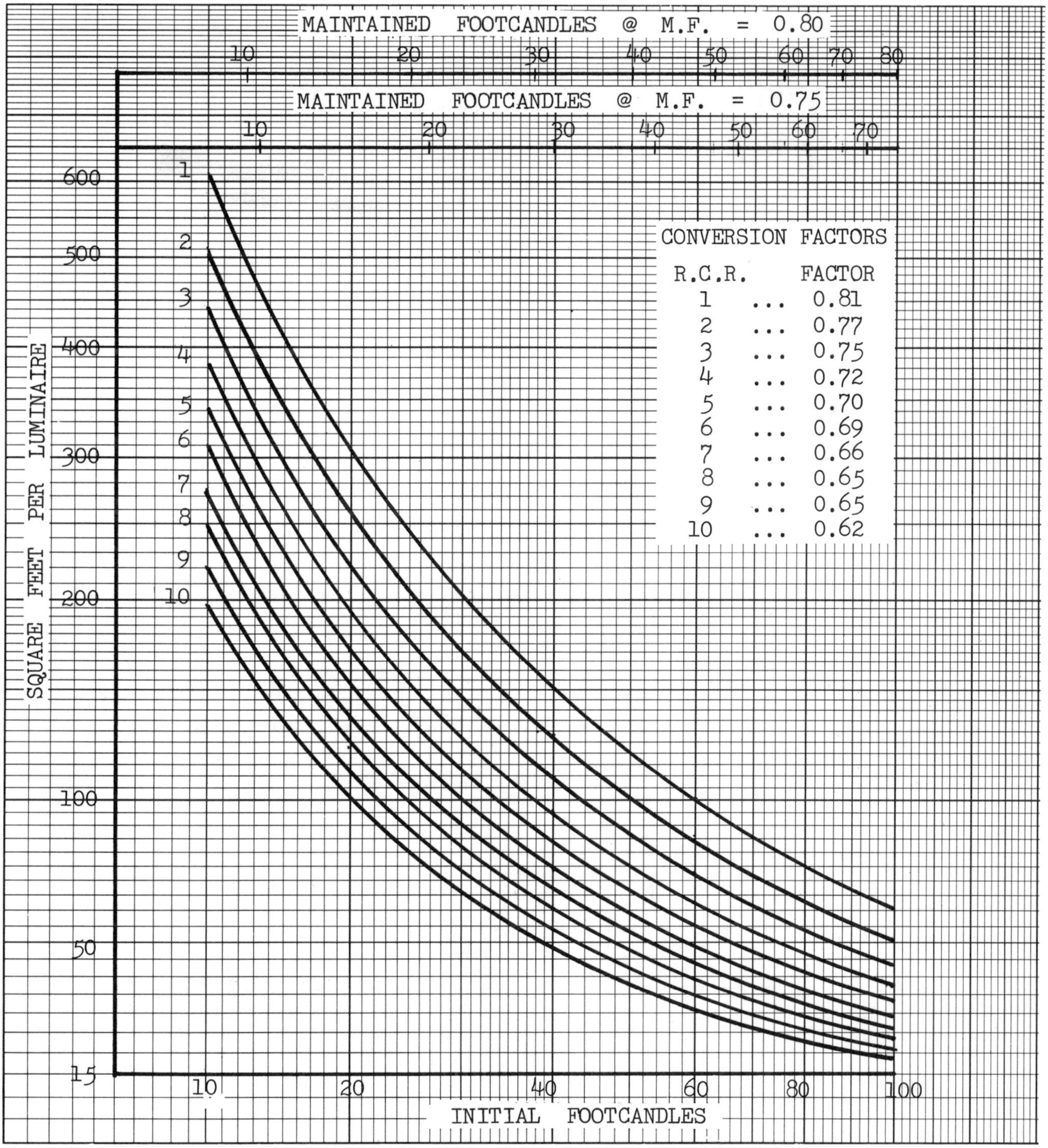

R.C.R.		FACTOR
1	...	0.81
2	...	0.77
3	...	0.75
4	...	0.72
5	...	0.70
6	...	0.69
7	...	0.66
8	...	0.65
9	...	0.65
10	...	0.62

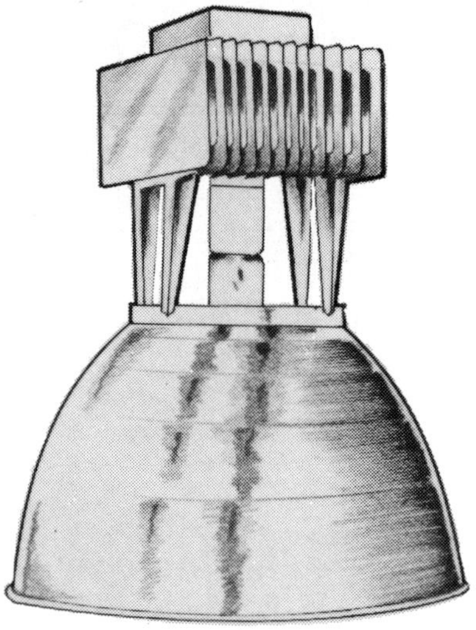

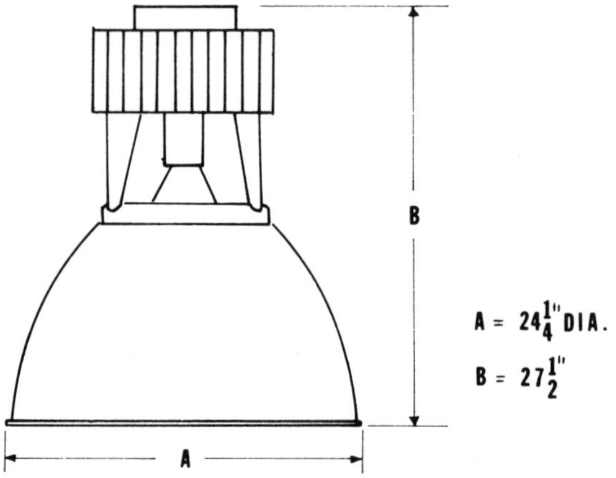

Description	400-W, aluminum reflector
Lamp	One 400-W mercury (DX), 22,500 lm, 24,000 h
Reflector	Open top (uplight)
Spacing ratio	1.3
Maintenance factors	0.85/0.80/0.75
Conversion factors	A. Unit with one 400-W mercury (DX) = 1.0
	B. Unit with one 400-W metal halide (coated) = 1.54
	C. Unit with one 400-W high-pressure sodium = 2.28

COST DETAILS PER LUMINAIRE

Type of unit	Input, W	Contractor's price	Installed cost
A	445	$ 70	$122.25
B	460	88	170
C	470	147	258.75

The installed cost includes published contractor's book price for the luminaire with ballast, lamp as shown, and the labor required for the installation and connection of the luminaire to an existing outlet. *See page D–36 for an outlet installed cost.*

Uplight units, due to their flow-through chimney effect, carry dirt from the reflector, assuring a good maintenance factor. A wide variety of lighting distribution is available in this type of luminaire. A medium distribution has been selected for the reference luminaire.

Use the conversion factors shown on page D–25 for an application where the ceiling, wall, and the floor reflectances are low. Use the lower maintanance factor if necessary.

INDUSTRIAL H.I.D. – ALUMINUM REFLECTOR, 400W

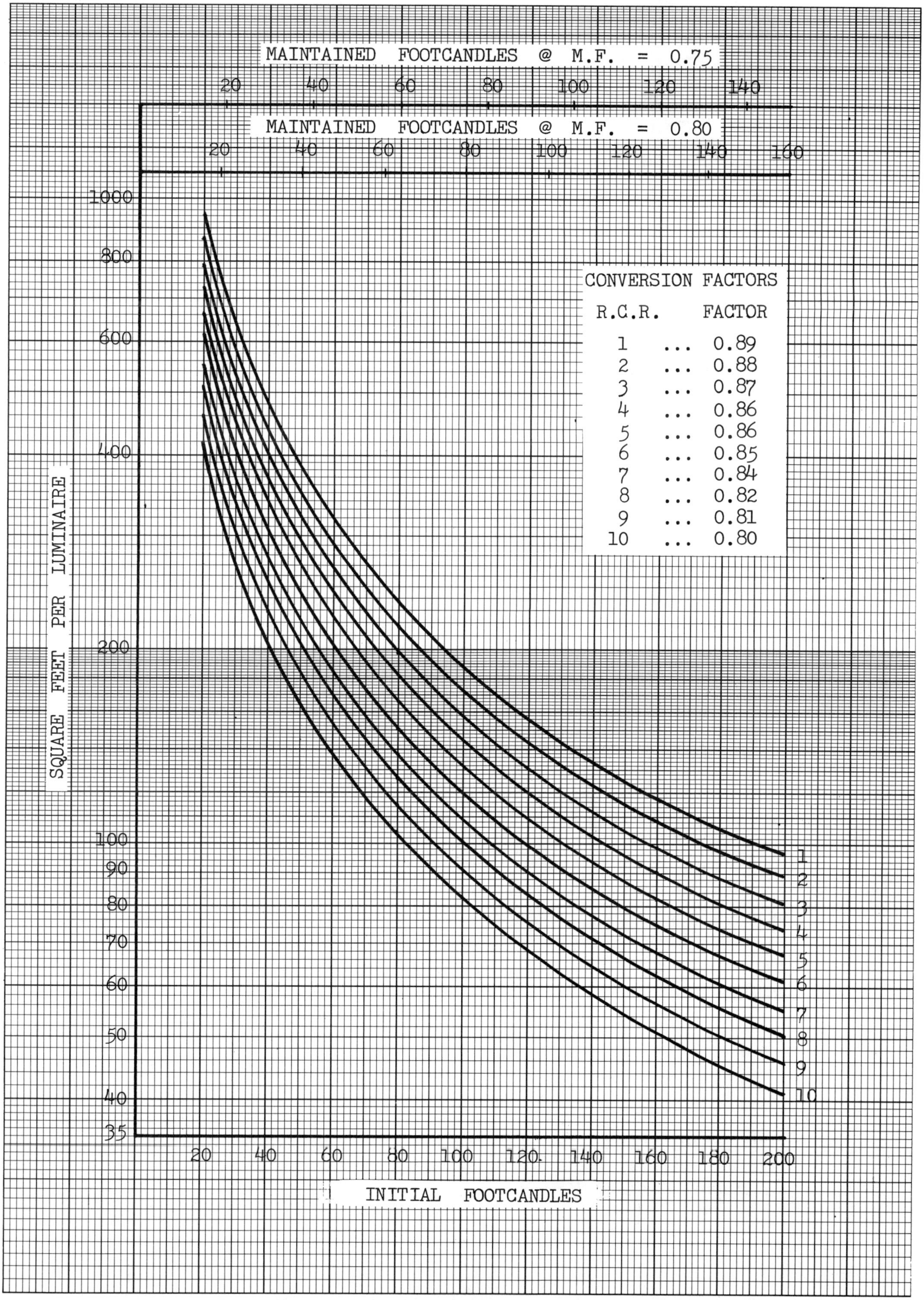

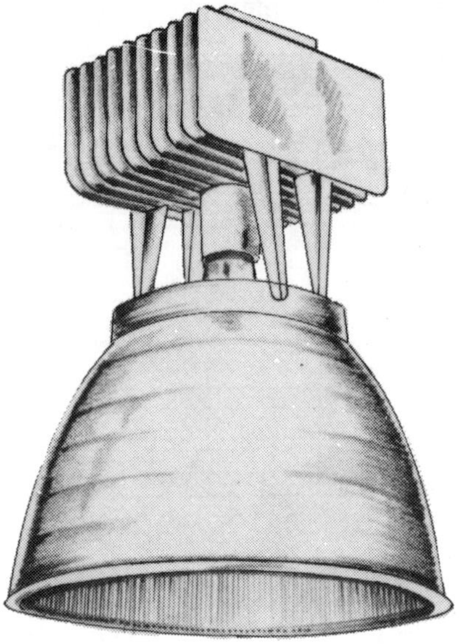

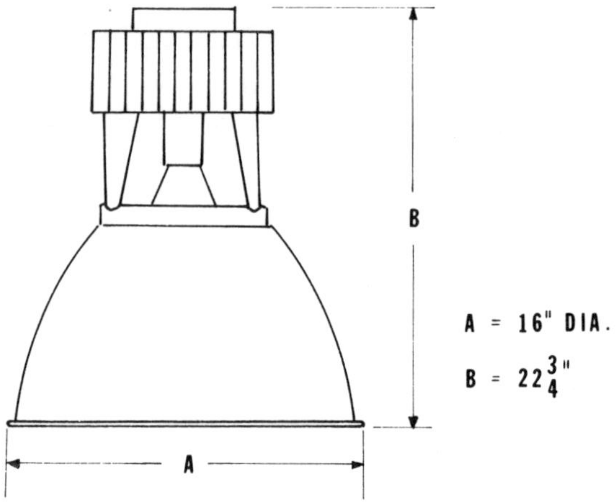

Description	400-W, prismatic glass reflector
Lamp	One 400-W mercury (DX), 22,500 lm, 24,000 h
Reflector	Open top (uplight)
Spacing ratio	1.3
Maintenance factors	0.85/0.80/0.75
Conversion factors	A. Unit with one 400-W mercury (DX) = 1.0 B. Unit with one 400-W metal halide (coated) = 1.54 C. Unit with one 400-W high-pressure sodium = 2.4

COST DETAILS PER LUMINAIRE

Type of unit	Input, W	Contractor's price	Installed cost
A	445	$ 87	$143
B	460	102	187.50
C	470	155	268.50

The installed cost includes published contractor's book price for the luminaire with ballast, lamp as shown, and the labor required for the installation and connection of the luminaire to an existing outlet. See page D–36 for an outlet installed cost.

Uplight units, due to their flow-through chimney effect, carry dirt from the reflector, assuring a good maintenance factor. A wide variety of lighting distribution is available in this type of luminaire. A medium distribution has been selected for the reference luminaire.

Use the conversion factors shown on page D–27 for an application where the ceiling, wall, and the floor reflectances are low. Use the lower maintenance factor if necessary.

INDUSTRIAL H.I.D. – PRISMATIC GLASS REFLECTOR, 400W

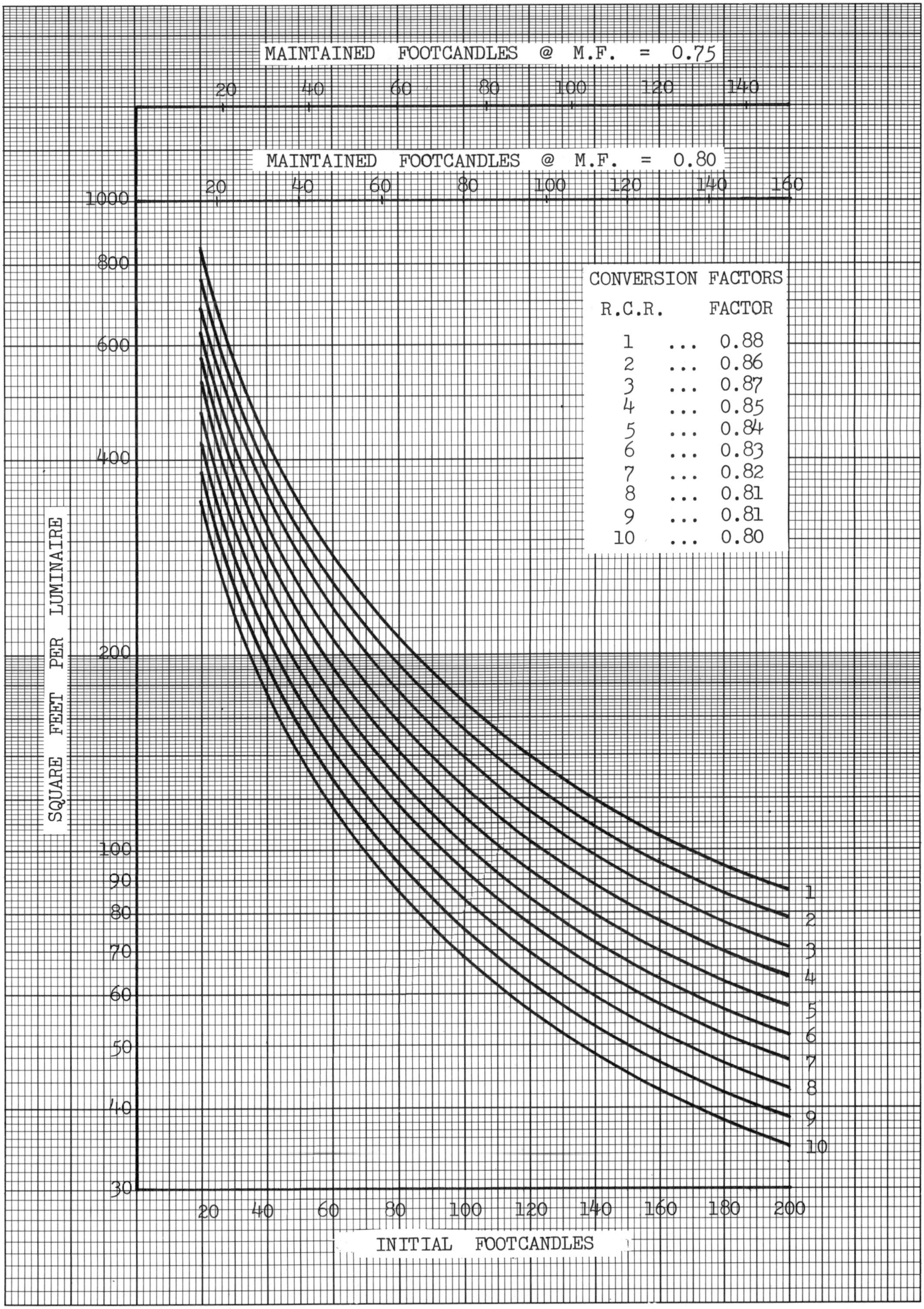

D

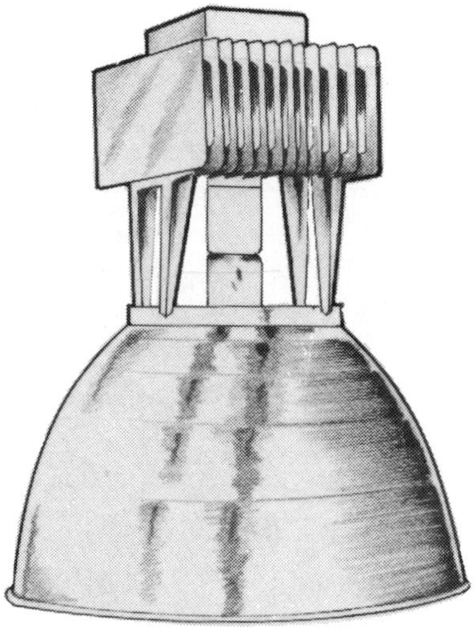

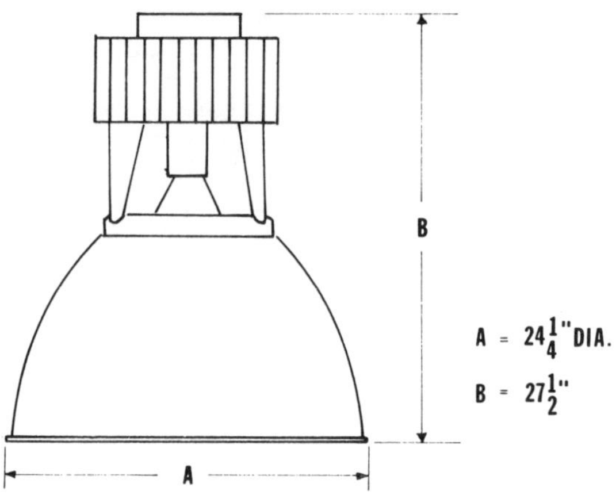

Description	1000-W, aluminum reflector
Lamp	One 1000-W mercury (DX), 63,000 lm, 24,000 h
Reflector	Open top (uplight)
Spacing ratio	1.3
Maintenance factors	0.85/0.80/0.75
Conversion factors	A. Unit with one 1000-W mercury (DX) = 1.0 B. Unit with one 1000-W metal halide (coated) = 1.7

COST DETAILS PER LUMINAIRE

Type of unit	Input, W	Contractor's price	Installed cost
A	1065	$110	$194
B	1085	137	282

The installed cost includes published contractor's book price for the luminaire with ballast, lamp as shown, and the labor required for the installation and connection of the luminaire to an existing outlet. *See page D–36 for an outlet installed cost.*

Uplight units, due to their flow-through chimney effect, carry dirt from the reflector, assuring a good maintenance factor. A wide variety of lighting distribution is available in this type of luminaire. A medium distribution has been selected for the reference luminaire.

Use the conversion factors shown on page D–29 for an application where the ceiling, wall, and the floor reflectances are low. Use the lower maintenance factor if necessary.

INDUSTRIAL H.I.D. – ALUMINUM REFLECTOR, 1000W

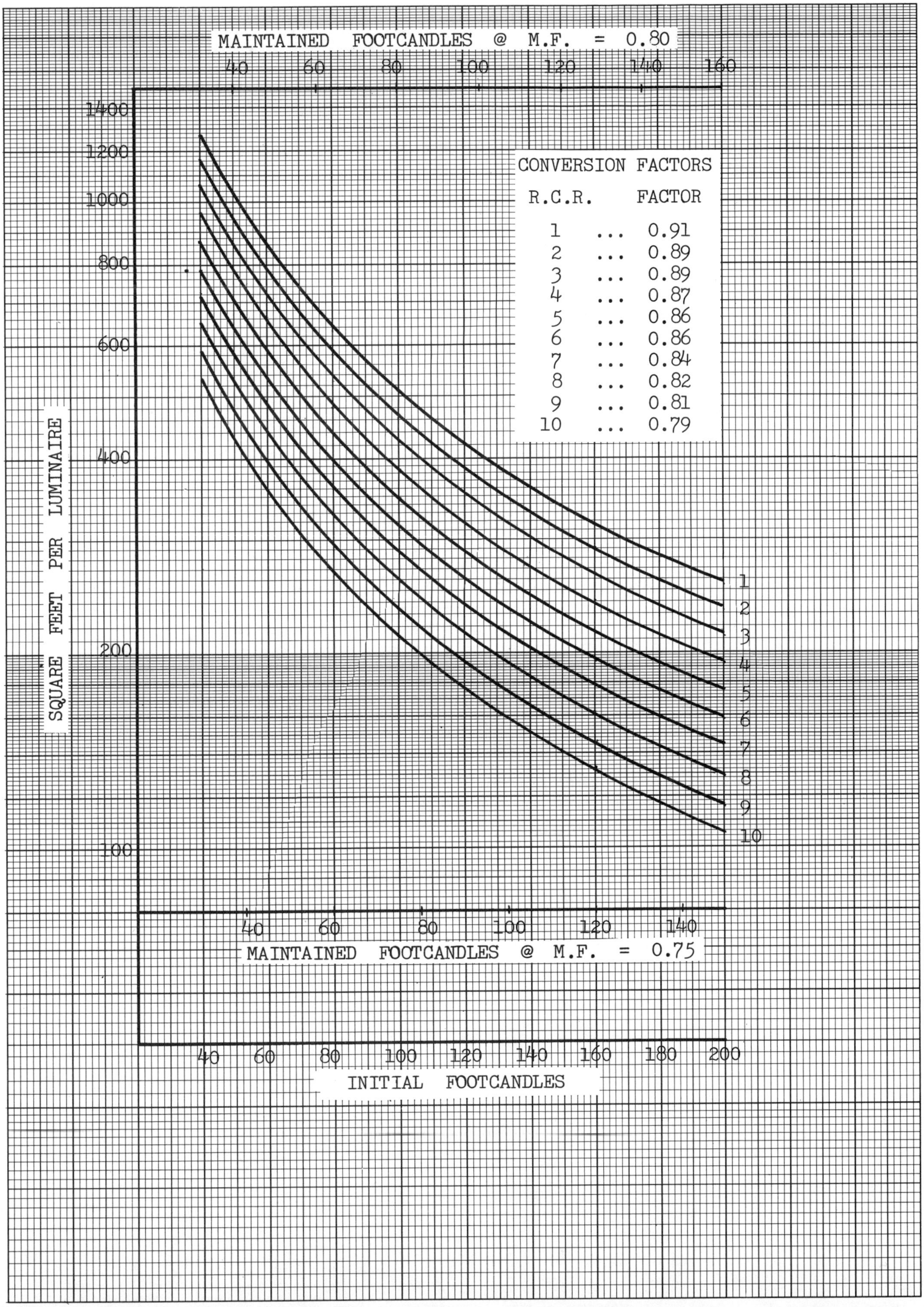

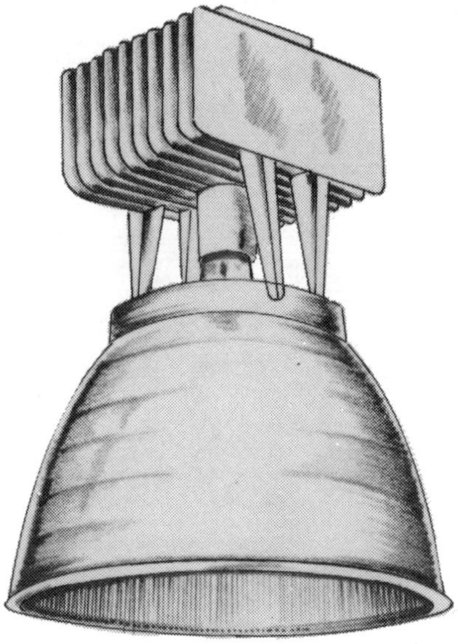

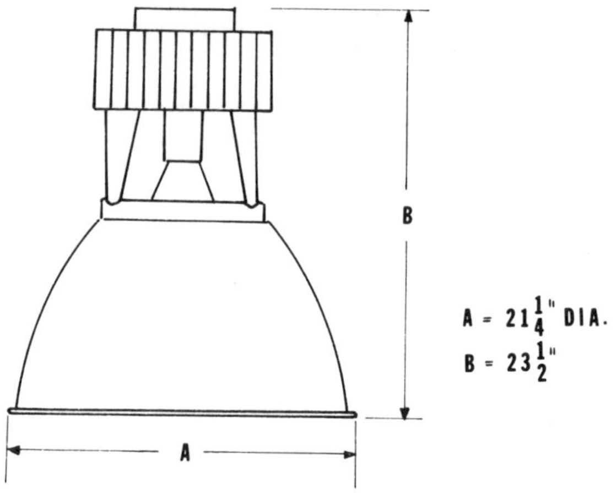

Description	1000-W, prismatic glass reflector
Lamp	One 1000-W mercury (DX), 63,000 lm, 24,000 h
Reflector	Open top (uplight)
Spacing ratio	1.3
Maintenance factors	0.85/0.80/0.75
Conversion factors	A. Unit with one 1000-W mercury (DX) = 1.0
	B. Unit with one 1000-W metal halide (coated) = 1.7

COST DETAILS PER LUMINAIRE

Type of unit	Input, W	Contractor's price	Installed cost
A	1065	$129	$217.50
B	1085	160	311

The installed cost includes published contractor's book price for the luminaire with ballast, lamp as shown, and the labor required for the installation and connection of the luminaire to an existing outlet. *See page D–36 for an outlet installed cost.*

Uplight units, due to their flow-through chimney effect, carry dirt from the reflector, assuring a good maintenance factor. A wide variety of lighting distribution is available in this type of luminaire. A medium distribution has been selected for the reference luminaire.

Use the conversion factors shown on page D–31 for an application where the ceiling, wall, and the floor reflectances are low. Use the lower maintenance factor if necessary.

INDUSTRIAL H.I.D. – PRISMATIC GLASS REFLECTOR, 1000W

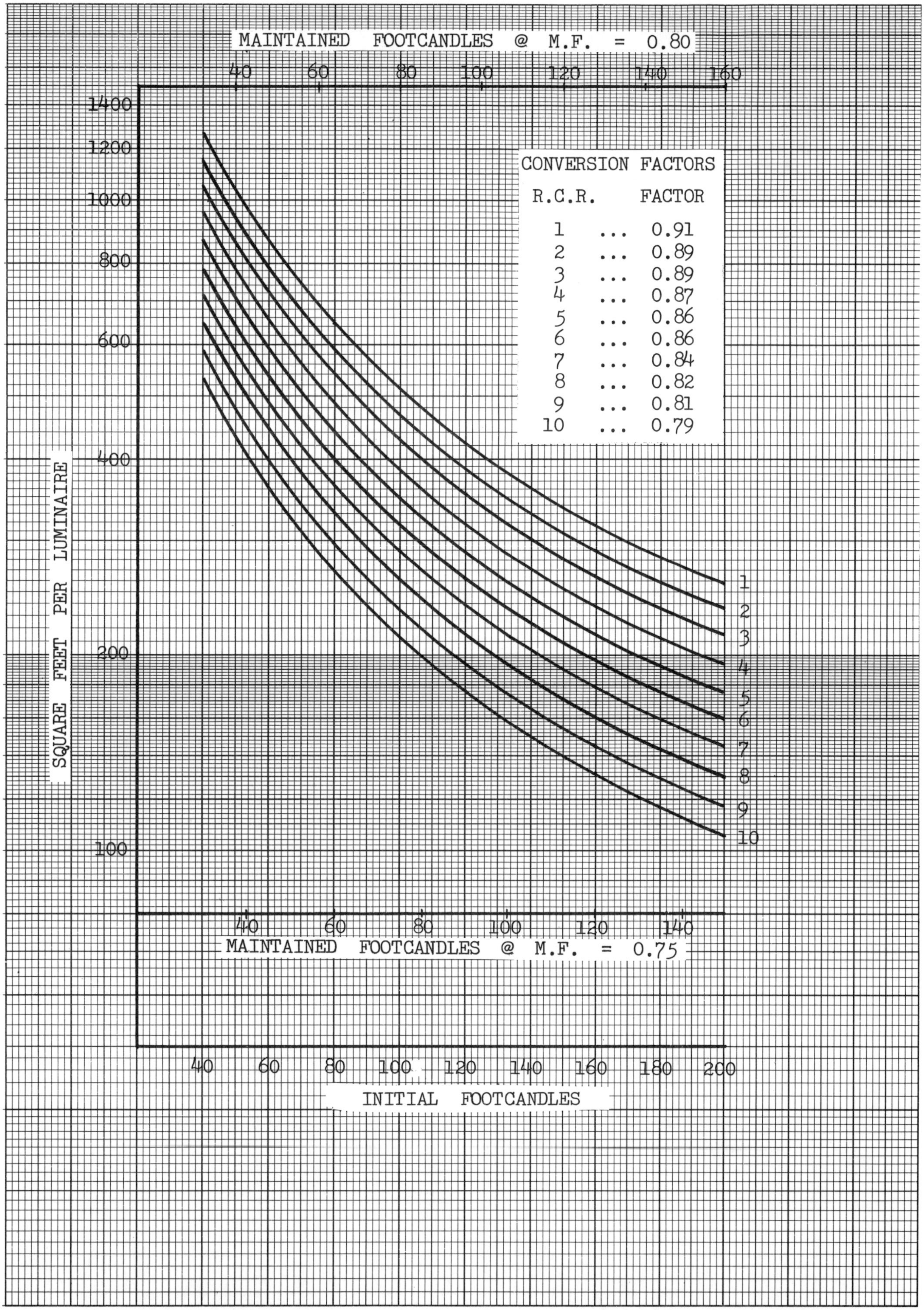

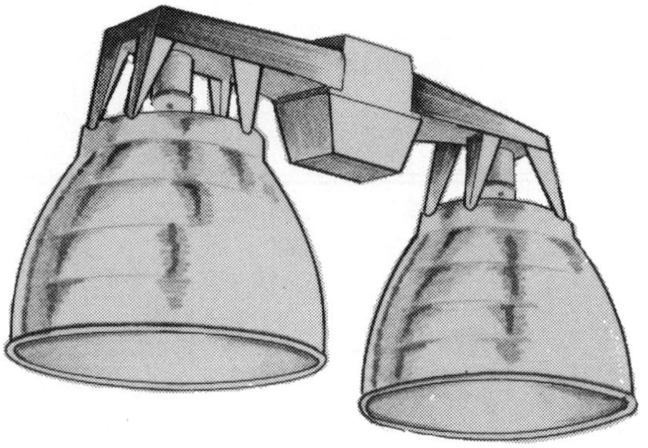

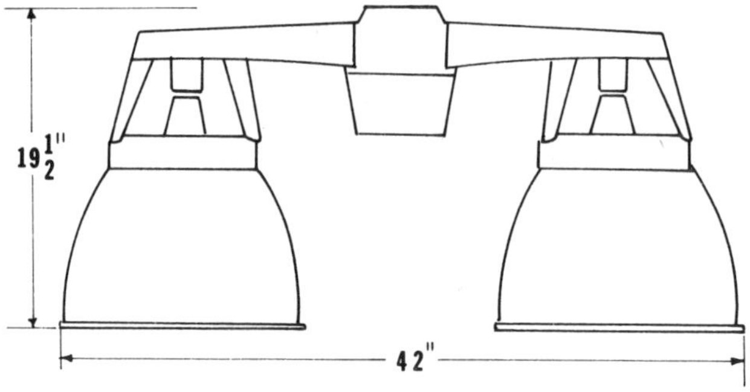

Description	Aluminum reflector (twin unit)
Lamp	Two 400-W mercury (DX), 22,500 lm, 24,000 h
Reflectors	Open top (uplight)
Spacing ratio	1.3
Maintenance factors	0.85/0.80/0.75
Conversion factors	A. Unit with two 400-W mercury (DX) = 1.0 B. Unit with two 400-W metal halide (coated) = 1.54

COST DETAILS PER LUMINAIRE

Type of unit	Input, W	Contractor's price	Installed cost
A	880	$130	$218.75
B	910	170	328.25

The installed cost includes published contractor's book price for the luminaire with ballast, lamps as shown, and the labor required for the installation and connection of the luminaire to an existing outlet. See page D–36 for an outlet installed cost.

Uplight units, due to their flow-through chimney effect, carry dirt from the reflector, assuring a good maintenance factor. A wide variety of lighting distribution is available in this type of luminaire. A medium distribution has been selected for the reference luminaire.

Use the conversion factors shown on page D–33 for an application where the ceiling, wall, and the floor reflectances are low. Use the lower maintenance factor if necessary.

INDUSTRIAL H.I.D. – ALUMINUM REFLECTOR, TWIN UNIT, 400W

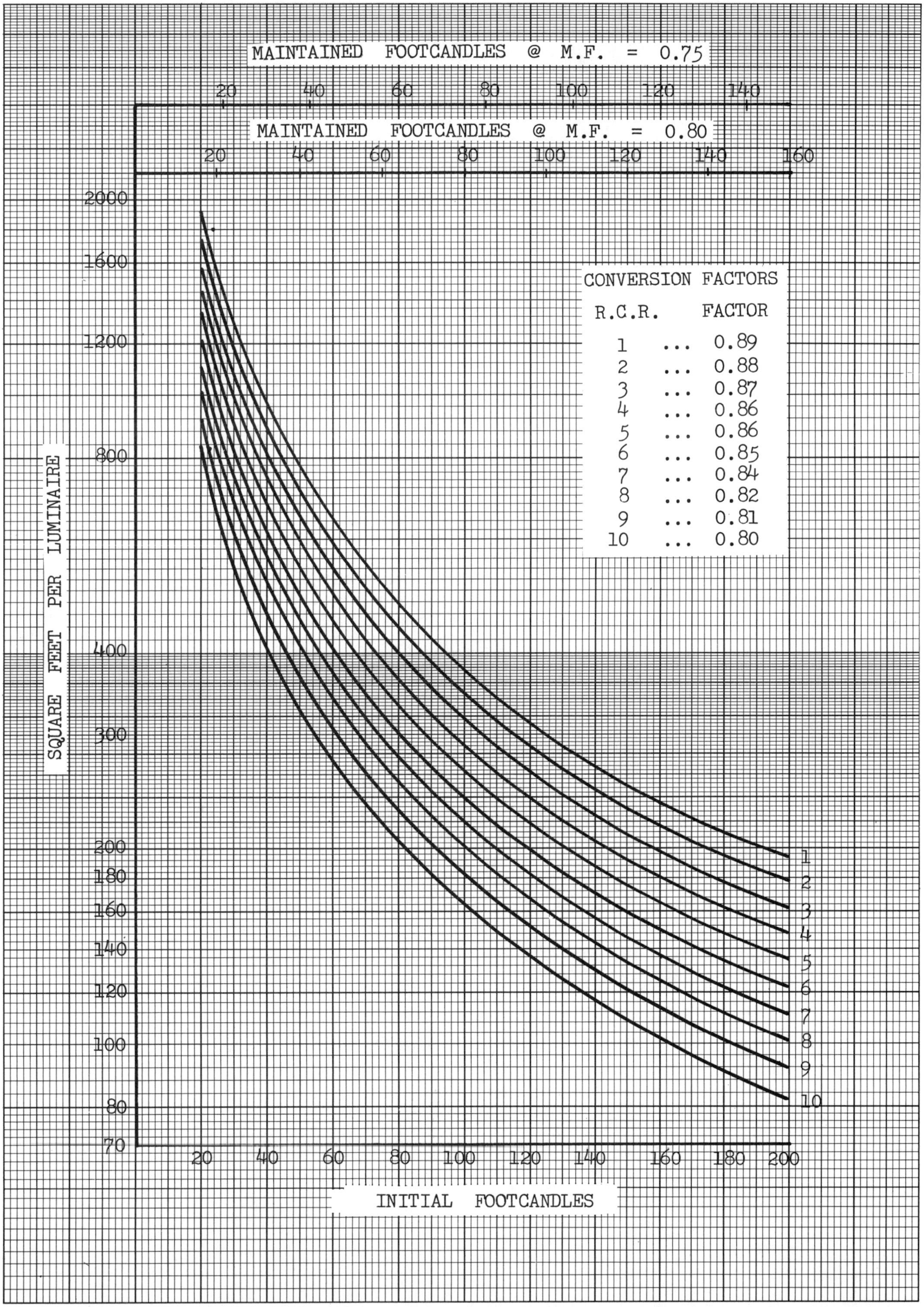

D

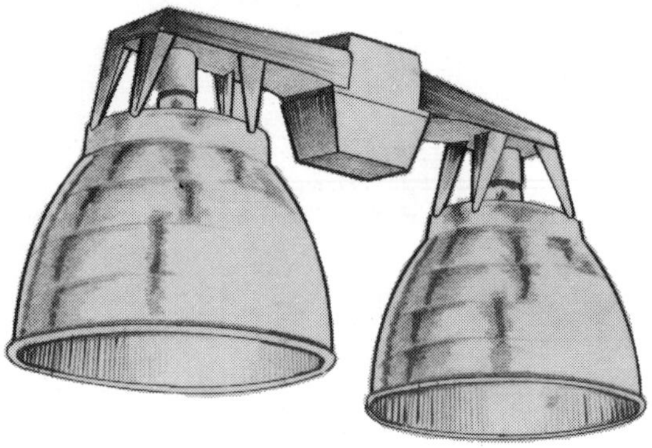

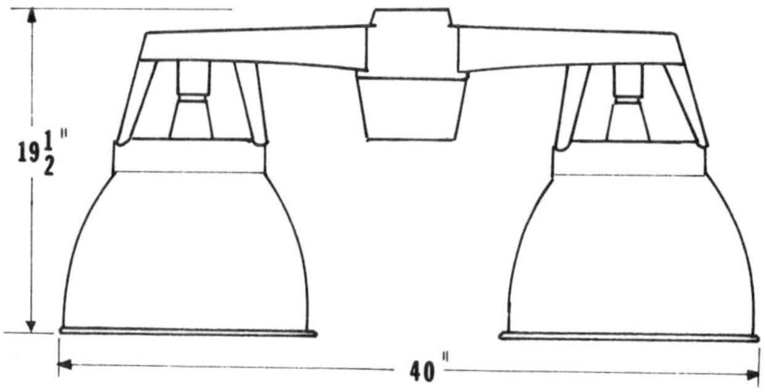

Description	Prismatic glass reflector (twin unit)
Lamps	Two 400-W mercury (DX), 22,500 lm, 24,000 h
Reflectors	Open top (uplight)
Spacing ratio	1.3
Maintenance factors	0.85/0.80/0.75
Conversion factors	A. Unit with two 400-W mercury (DX) = 1.0 B. Unit with two 400-W metal halide (coated) = 1.54

COST DETAILS PER LUMINAIRE

Type of unit	Input, W	Contractor's price	Installed cost
A	880	$177	$289.25
B	910	217	390

The installed cost includes published contractor's book price for the luminaire with ballasts, lamps as shown, and the labor required for the installation and connection of the luminaire to an existing outlet. See page D–36 for an outlet installed cost.

Uplight units, due to their flow-through chimney effect, carry dirt from the reflector, assuring a good maintenance factor. A wide variety of lighting distribution is available in this type of luminaire. A medium distribution has been selected for the reference luminaire.

Use the conversion factors shown on page D–35 for an application where the ceiling, wall, and the floor reflectances are low. Use the lower maintenance factor if necessary.

INDUSTRIAL H.I.D. – PRISMATIC GLASS REFLECTOR, TWIN UNIT, 400W

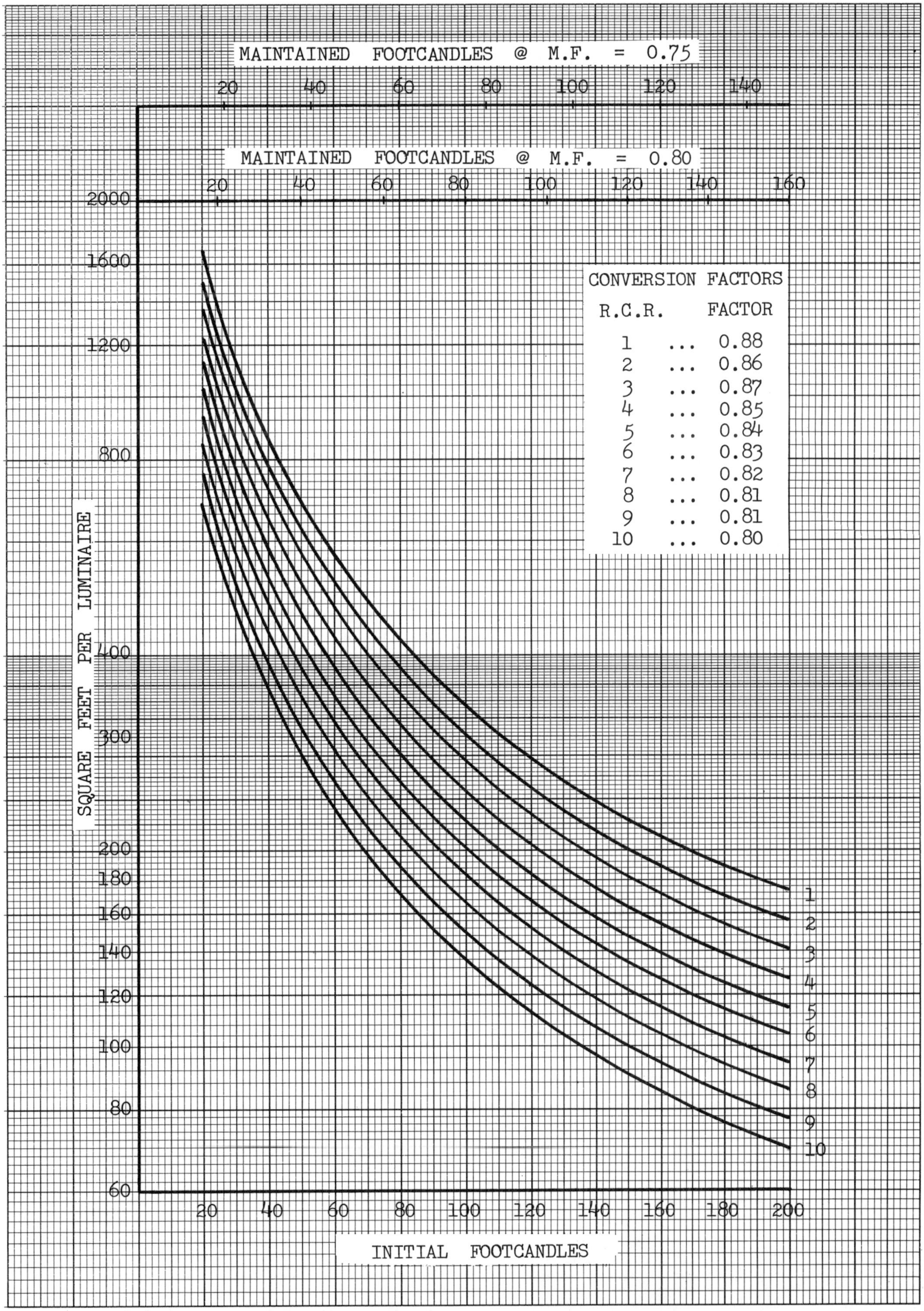

CONVERSION FACTORS

R.C.R.	FACTOR
1	... 0.88
2	... 0.86
3	... 0.87
4	... 0.85
5	... 0.84
6	... 0.83
7	... 0.82
8	... 0.81
9	... 0.81
10	... 0.80

D

Chain-suspended

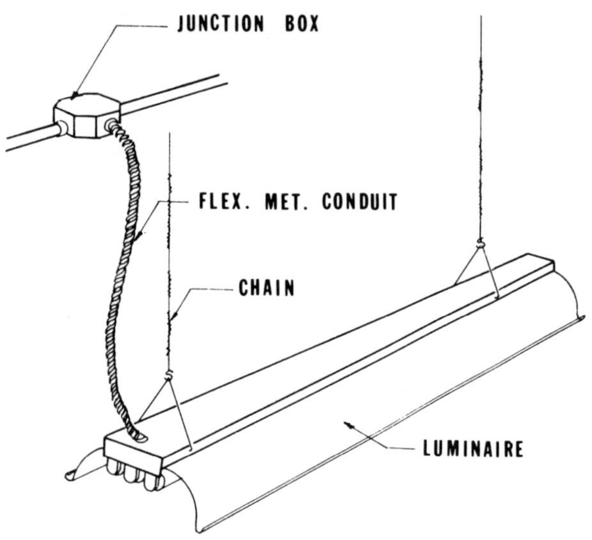

Add

$4.50 for each chain suspension which includes a 3-ft chain, two S hooks, and a Y hook. Add $0.50 for each additional 1-ft length of chain.

For a surface-mounted outlet to feed the chain-suspended luminaire add as shown below:

Type of terminal	Type of construction		
	Steel	Wood	Concrete
EMT	$13.78	$13.60	$16.33
GRC	18.88	18.70	21.43
IMS	18.88	18.70	21.43

This includes an octagon outlet box, a 6-ft length of flexible metallic conduit with 8-ft long 2 no. 12 AF wire, two connectors, and two wire nuts.

Direct-mounting

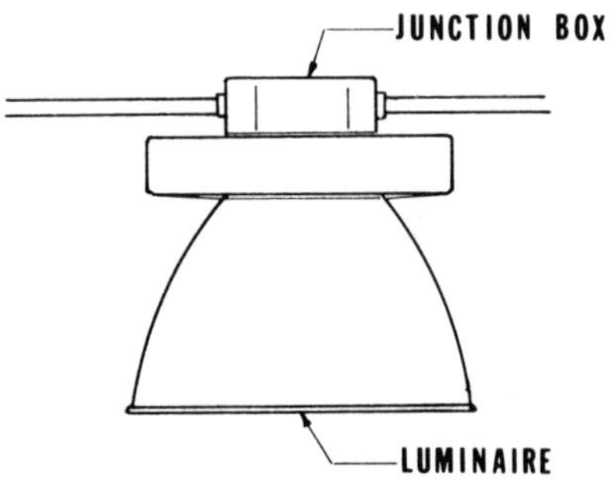

For an exposed mounted outlet for direct connection to the luminaire add as shown below:

Type of terminal	Type of construction		
	Steel	Wood	Concrete
EMT	$10.48	$10.30	$13.0
GRC	15.58	15.40	18.10
IMS	15.58	15.40	18.10

This includes a 4-in square box, mounting plate, two connectors, and two wire nuts.

Power-hook-mounted

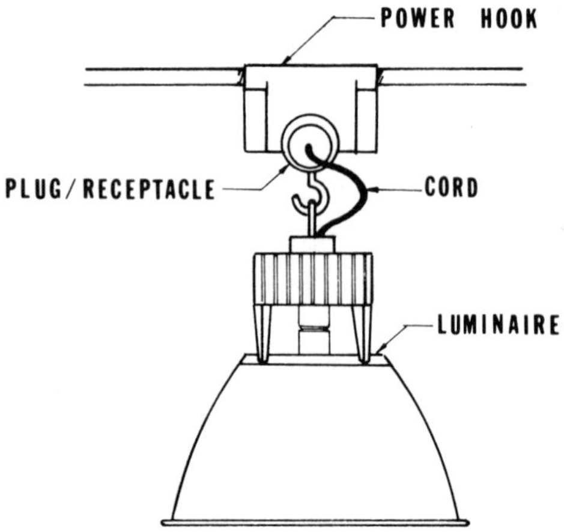

For a luminaire mounted on a power hook add as shown below:

Type of terminal	Type of construction		
	Steel	Wood	Concrete
EMT	$33.78	$33.50	$36.33
GRC	38.0	37.80	41.43
IMS	38.0	37.80	41.43

This includes a prewired power hook with cord, twist-lock plug and receptacle, a loop and connectors, as required. No fusing is included in the power hook.

Commercial High-Intensity Discharge Units

RECESSED UNITS

Open Downlights

6-in E-2
8-in E-4
10-in E-6
12-in E-8
16-in E-10

Ellipsoidal-Reflector Downlights

6-in E-12
8-in E-14
10-in E-16
12-in E-18

Miscellaneous Commercial

12- × 12-in Regressed Lens E-20
Parabolic-Louvered E-22
2- × 2-ft Regressed Lens E-24, E-26
Parabolic-Louvered E-28, E-30
Round Regressed Lens, horizontal Lamp E-32
Vertical Lamp E-34
Square Regressed Lens E-36

SURFACE UNITS

Cylindrical Downlight E-38
Modular Lens Unit E-40

CEILING OUTLETS FOR LUMINAIRES

Installed Cost of Outlets E-42

E

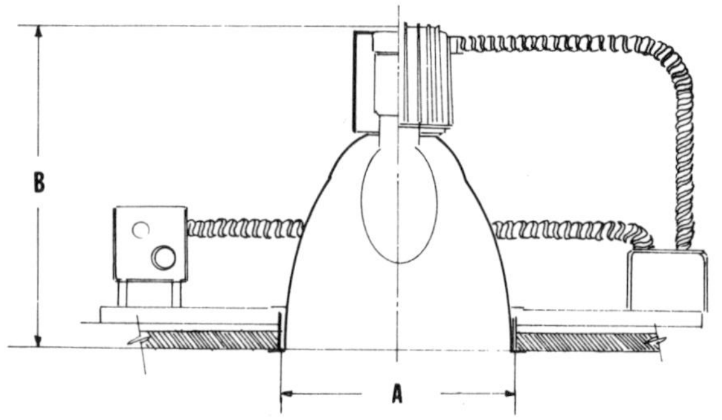

E-2

Description	6-in open downlight
Lamp	One 75-W E-17 mercury (DX), 2800 lm, 16,000 h
Reflector	Clear specular aluminum
Spacing ratio	1.2
Maintenance factors	0.85/0.80/0.75
Input, W	90
Conversion Factors	Unit with specular gold reflector, multiply footcandle values by 0.90
Cost details per luminaire	Contractor's price = \$83 Installed cost = \$135.75

The installed cost includes published contractor's book price for the luminaire with ballast, lamp as shown, luminaire fastening devices, and the labor required for recess mounting and connection of the luminaire. No separate outlet is required since the unit is supplied with an attached outlet ready to accept supply leads.

These luminaires are recommended for ceiling heights of 8 to 14 ft.

COMMERCIAL RECESSED H.I.D.–6" OPEN DOWNLIGHT

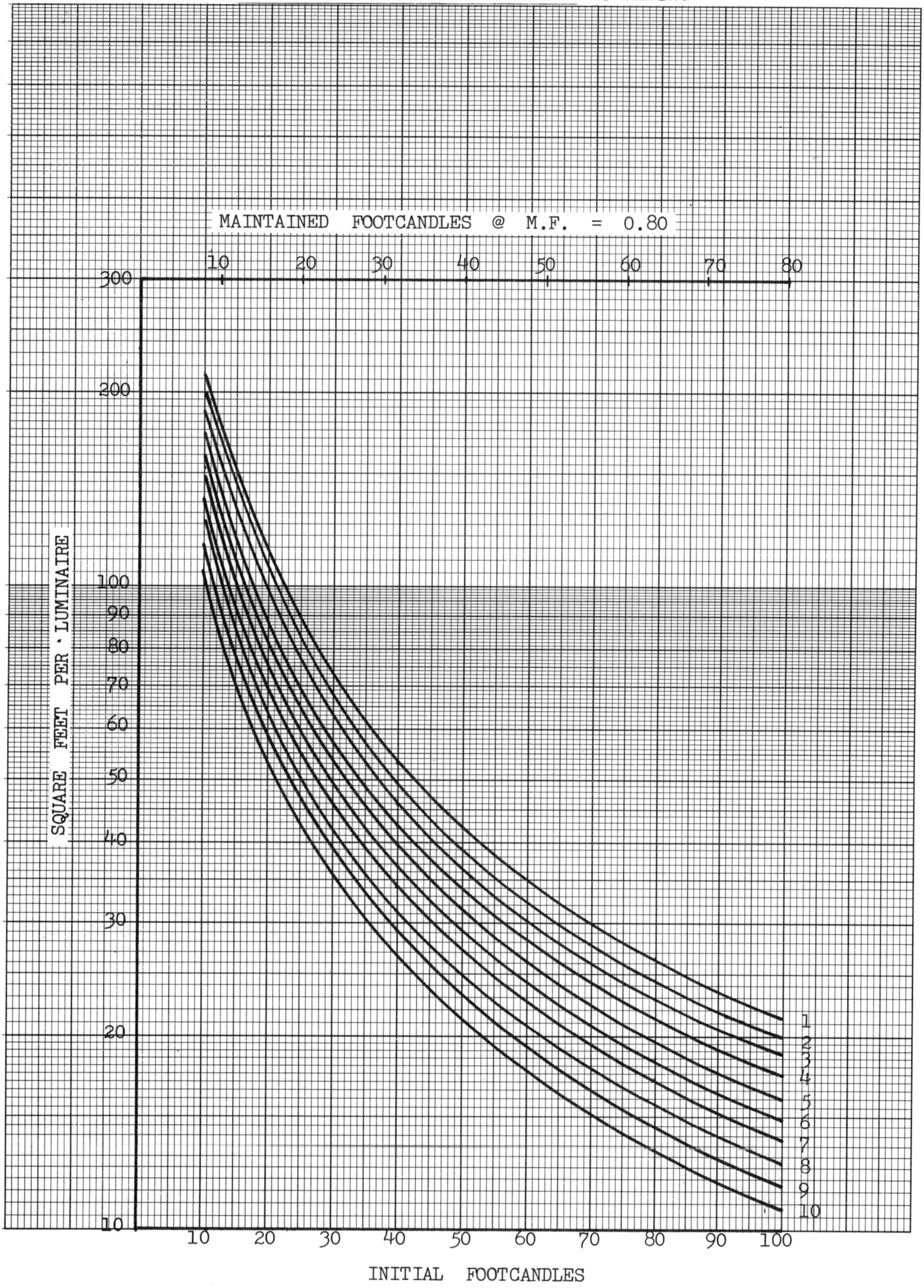

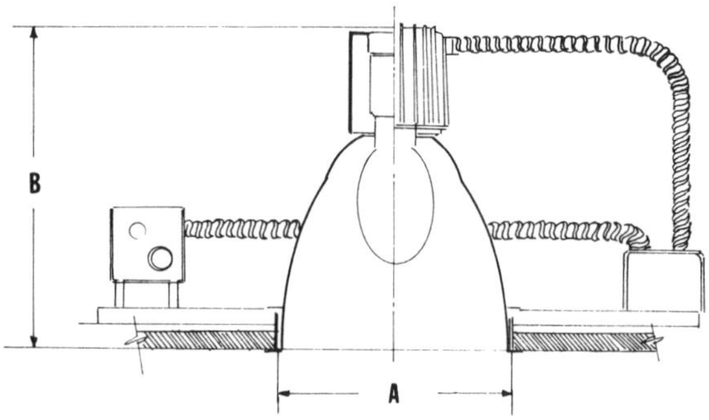

E-4

Description	8-in open downlight
Lamp	One 75-W E-17 mercury (DX), 2800 lm, 16,000 h
Reflector	Clear specular aluminum
Spacing ratio	1.3
Maintenance factors	0.85/0.80/0.75
Conversion factors	A. Unit with one 75-W E-17 mercury (DX) = 1.0 B. Unit with one 100-W A-23 mercury (DX) = 1.3 For specular gold reflector, multiply footcandle values by 0.90

COST DETAILS PER LUMINAIRE

Type of unit	Input, W	Contractor's price	Installed cost
A	90	$95	$150.50
B	120	97	159.25

The installed cost includes published contractor's book price for the luminaire with ballast, lamp as shown, required fastening devices, and the labor required for recess mounting and connection of the luminaire. No separate outlet is required since the unit is supplied with an attached outlet ready to accept supply leads.

These luminaires are recommended for ceiling heights of 8 to 16 ft.

COMMERCIAL RECESSED H.I.D.– 8" OPEN DOWNLIGHT

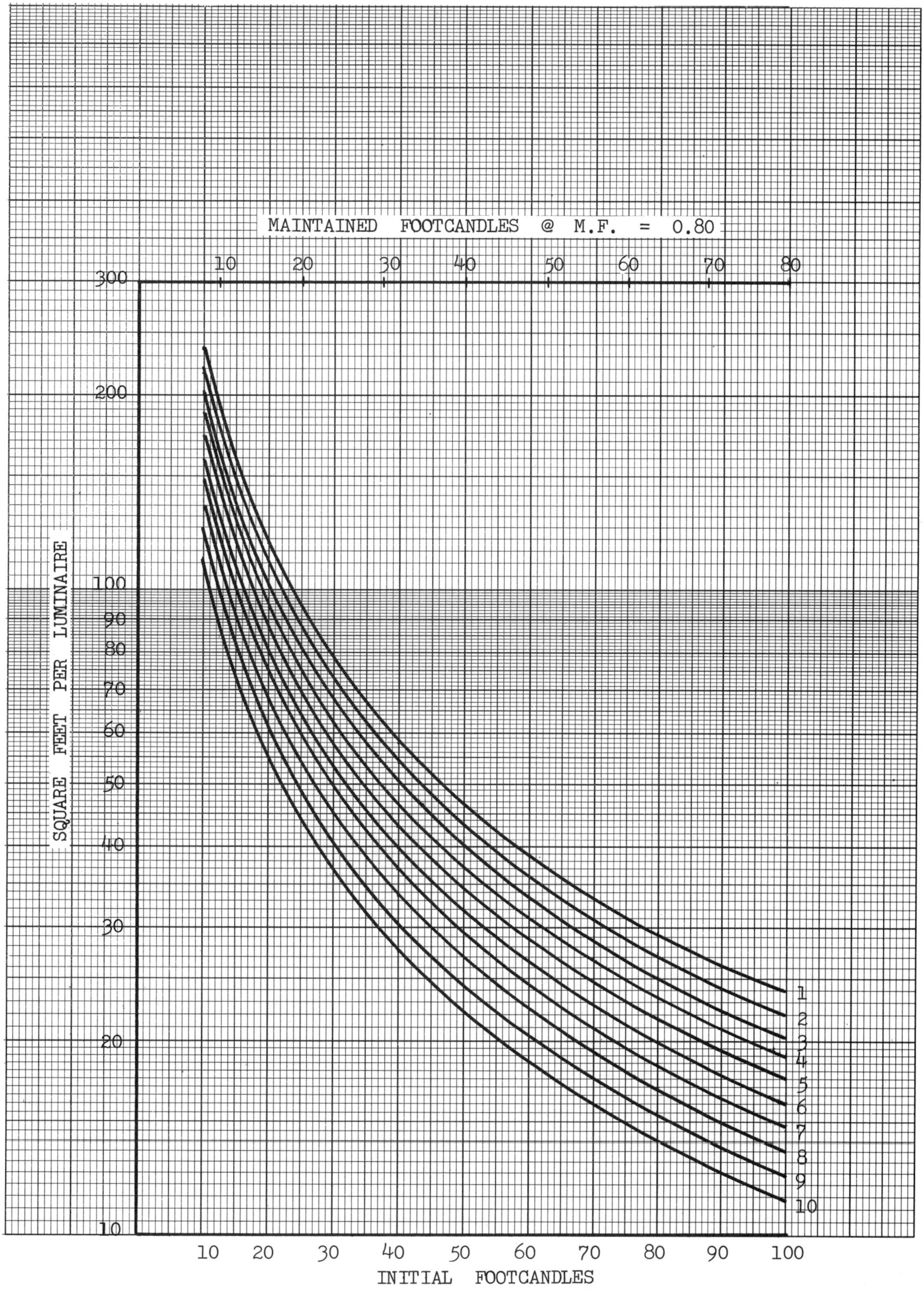

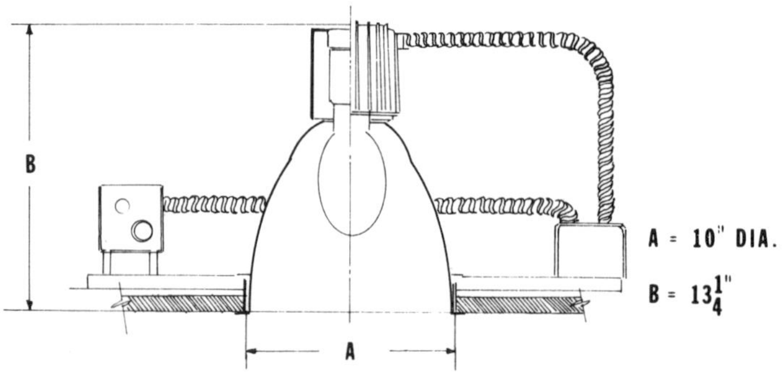

E-6

Description	10-in open downlight
Lamp	One 100-W E-23½ mercury (DX), 4200 1m, 24,000 h
Reflector	Clear specular aluminum
Spacing ratio	1.3
Maintanance factors	0.85/0.80/0.75
Conversion factors	A. Unit with one 100-W E-23½ mercury (DX) = 1.0 B. Unit with one 70-W E-23½ high-pressure sodium = 1.5 C. Unit with one 100-W E-23½ high-pressure sodium = 2.3

COST DETAILS PER LUMINAIRE

Type of unit	Input, W	Contractor's price	Installed cost
A	120	$104	$167.75
B	88	168	240.25
C	128	170	248.75

The installed cost includes published contractor's book price for the luminaire with ballast, lamp as shown, required fastening devices, and the labor required for recess mounting and connection of the luminaire. No separate outlet is required since the unit is supplied with an attached outlet ready to accept supply leads.

These luminaires are recommended for ceiling heights of 10 to 16 ft for mercury-vapor lamps and 14 to 25 ft for high-pressure sodium lamps.

COMMERCIAL RECESSED H.I.D.–10" OPEN DOWNLIGHT

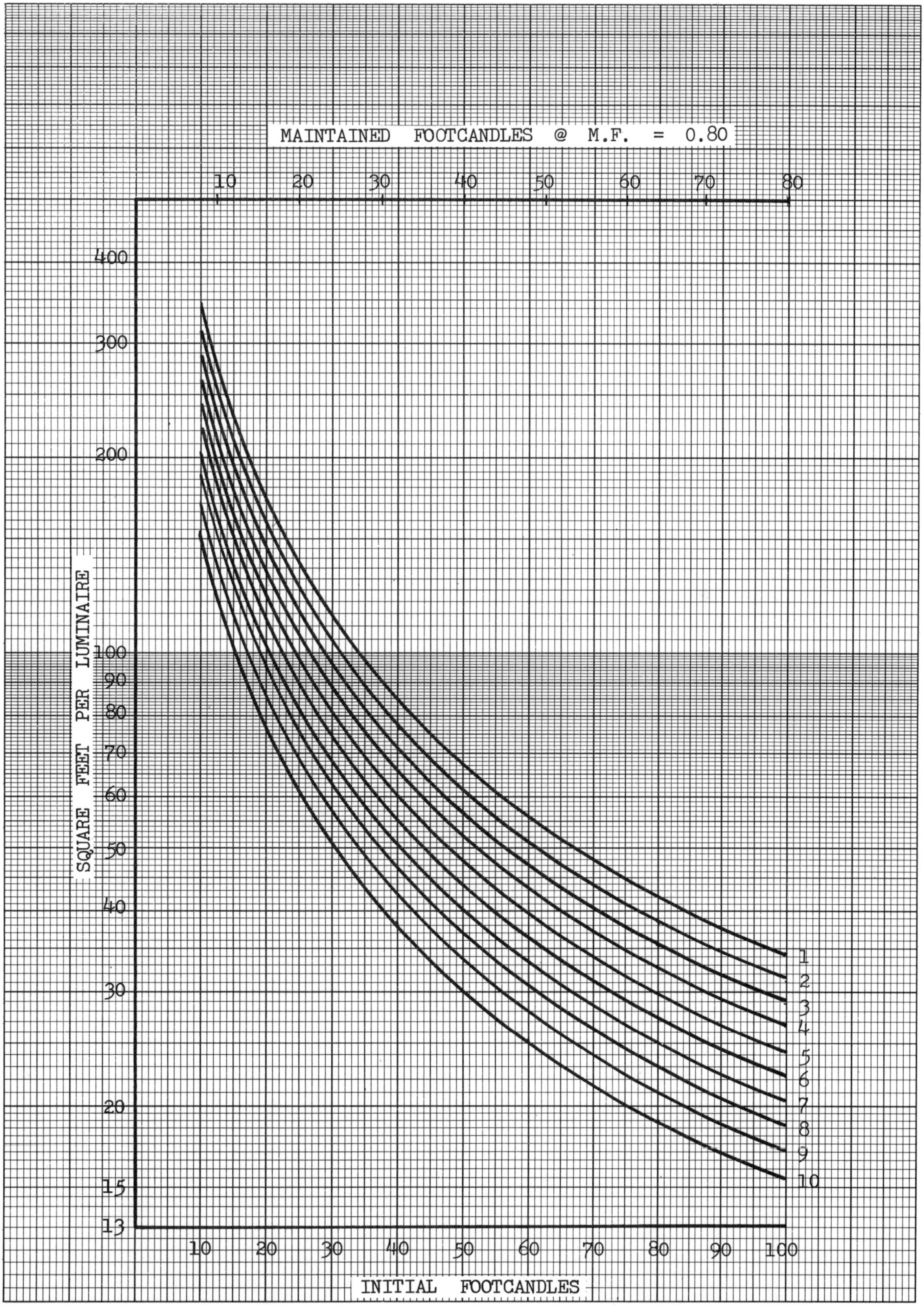

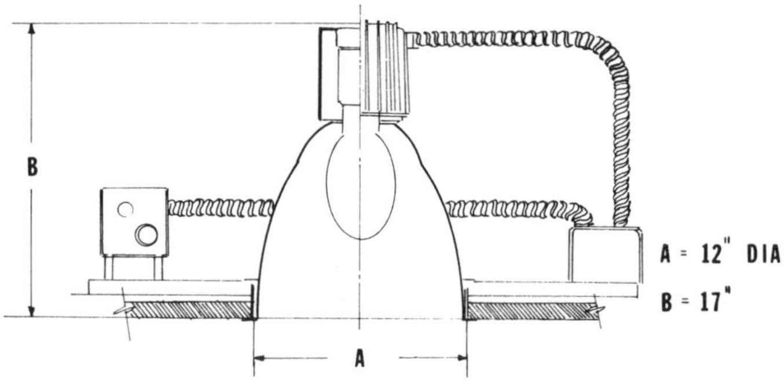

Description	12-in open downlight
Lamp	One 250-W E-28 mercury (DX), 12,100 1m, 24,000 h
Reflector	Clear specular aluminum
Spacing ratio	1.15
Maintenance factors	0.85/0.80/0.75
Conversion factors	A. Unit with one 250-W E-28 mercury (DX) = 1.0 B. Unit with one 175-W E-28 mercury (DX) = 0.71 C. Unit with one 250-W E-18 high-pressure sodium = 2.0 For specular gold reflector multiply footcandle values by 0.90

COST DETAILS PER LUMINAIRE

Type of unit	Input, W	Contractor's price	Installed cost
A	290	$134	$207.25
B	200	123	184.50
C	295	246	381.90

The installed cost includes published contractor's book price for the luminaire with ballast, lamp as shown, required fastening devices, and the labor required for recess mounting and connection of the luminaire. No separate outlet is required since the unit is supplied with an attached outlet ready to accept supply leads.

These luminaires are recommended for ceiling heights of 10 to 25 ft for mercury-vapor lamps and 20 to 40 ft for high-pressure sodium lamps.

COMMERCIAL RECESSED H.I.D.–12" OPEN DOWNLIGHT

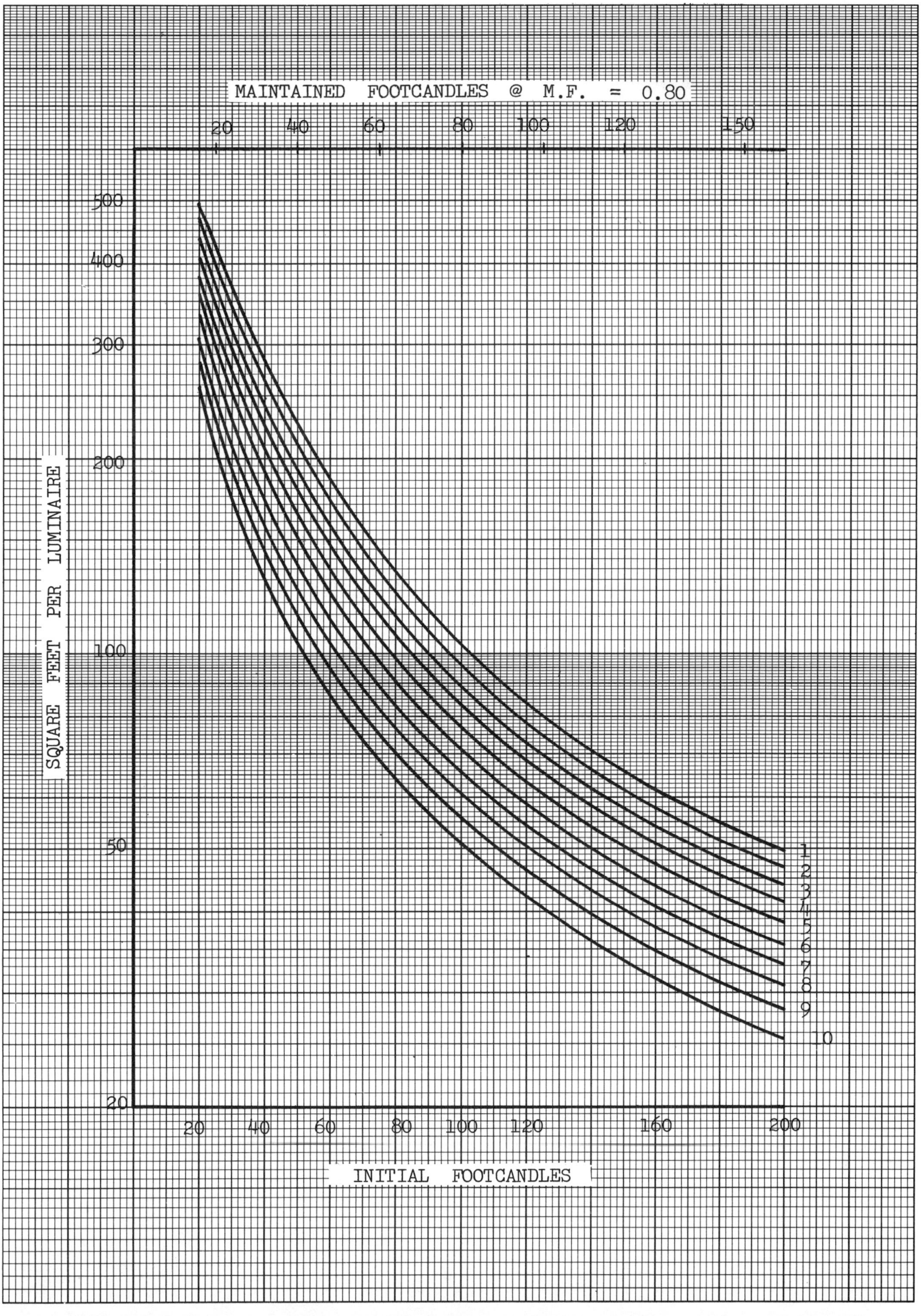

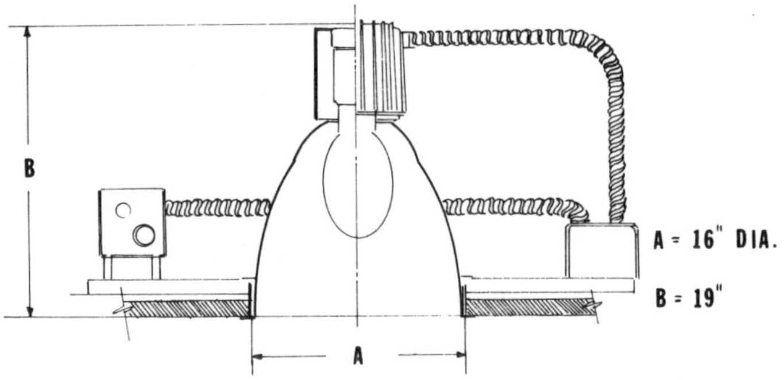

Description	16-in open downlight
Lamp	One 400-W E-37 mercury (DX), 22,500 1m, 24,000 h
Reflector	Clear specular aluminum
Spacing ratio	1.0
Maintenance factors	0.85/0.80/0.75
Conversion factors	A. Unit with one 400-W E-37 mercury (DX) = 1.0
	B. Unit with one 400-W BT-37 metal halide (coated) = 1.5
	For specular gold reflector multiply footcandle values by 0.90

COST DETAILS PER LUMINAIRE

Type of unit	Input, W	Contractor's price	Installed cost
A	445	$159	$236
B	460	172	277.75

The installed cost includes published contractor's book price for the luminaire with ballast, lamp as shown, required fastening devices, and the labor required for recess mounting and connection of the luminaire. No separate outlet is required since the unit is supplied with an attached outlet ready to accept supply leads.

These luminaires are recommended for ceiling heights of 16 to 40 ft.

COMMERCIAL RECESSED H.I.D.–16" OPEN DOWNLIGHT

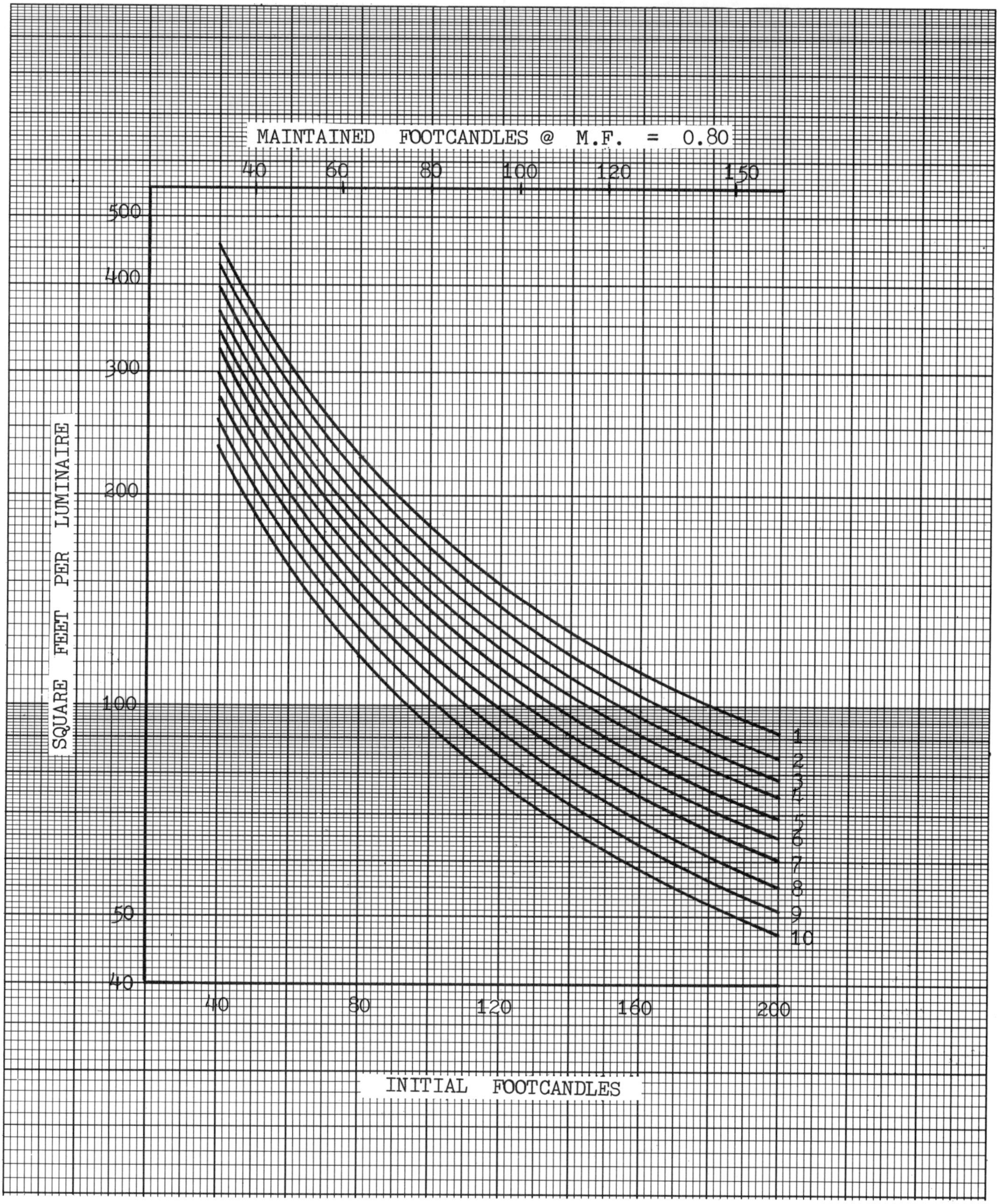

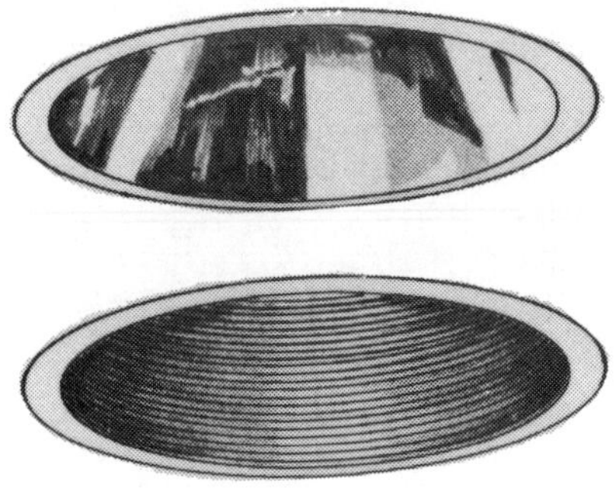

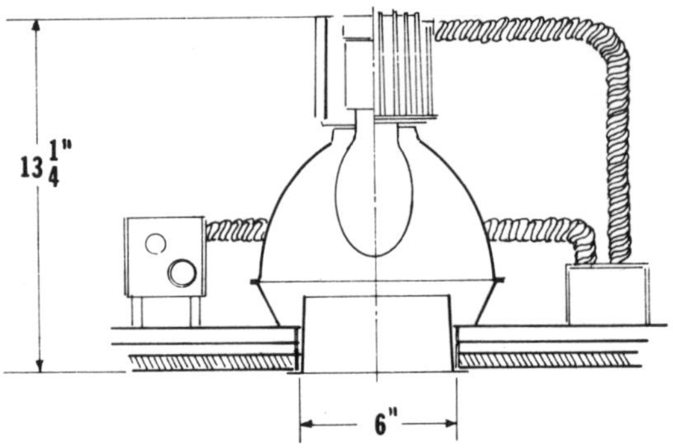

Description	6-in ellipsoidal-reflector downlight
Lamp	One 100-W E-23½ mercury (DX), 4200 1m, 24,000 h
Reflector	Clear specular aluminum
Spacing ratio	1.2
Maintenance factors	0.85/0.80/0.75
Conversion factors	A. Unit with one 100-W E-23½ mercury (DX) = 1.0
	B. Unit with one 70-W E-23½ high-pressure sodium (clear) = 1.7
	For units with black milligroove baffle aperture, multiply footcandle values by 0.80

COST DETAILS PER LUMINAIRE

Type of unit	Input, W	Contractor's price	Installed cost
A	120	$120	$175.25
B	88	168	277.25

The installed cost includes published contractor's book price for the luminaire with ballast, lamp as shown, required fastening devices, and the labor required for recess mounting and connection of the luminaire. No separate outlet is required since the unit is supplied with an attached outlet ready to accept supply leads.

These low-brightness downlights are recommended for ceiling heights of 8 to 10 ft for mercury lamps and up to 16 ft for high-pressure sodium lamps.

COMMERCIAL RECESSED H.I.D.—6" ELLIPSOIDAL REFLECTOR DOWNLIGHT

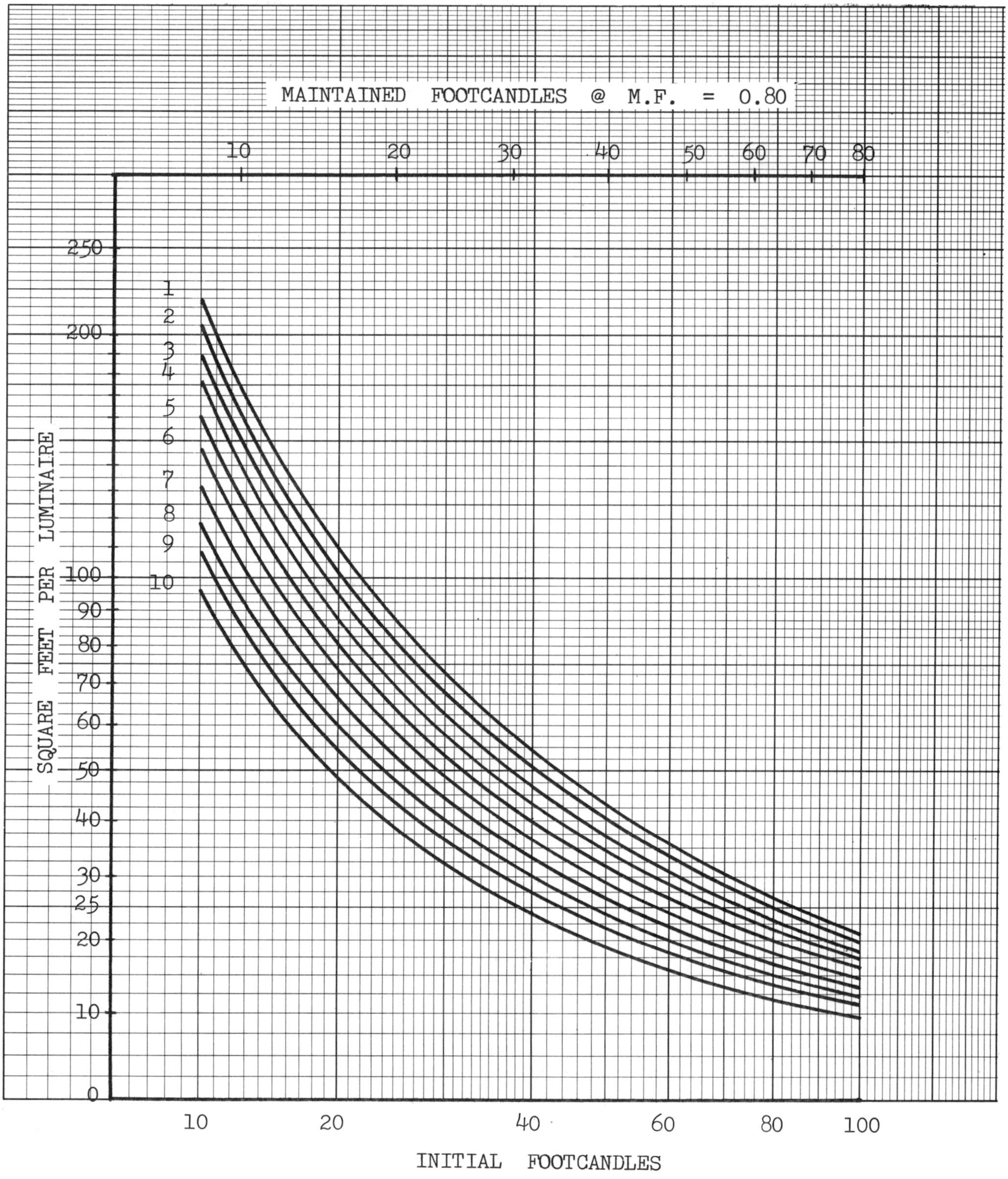

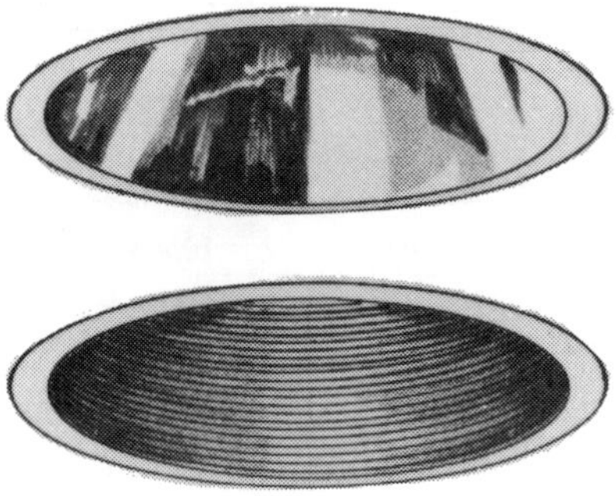

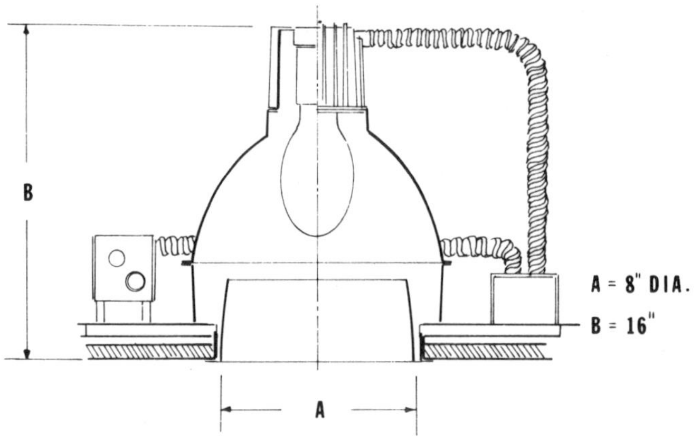

E-14

Description	8-in ellipsoidal-reflector downlight
Lamp	One 250-W E-28 mercury (DX), 12,100 1m, 24,000 h
Reflector	Clear specular aluminum
Spacing ratio	1.2
Maintenance factors	0.85/0.80/0.75
Conversion factors	A. Unit with one 250-W E-28 mercury (DX) = 1.0 B. Unit with one 175-W E-28 mercury (DX) = 0.71 For units with black milligroove baffle aperture, multiply footcandle values by 0.80

COST DETAILS PER LUMINAIRE

Type of unit	Input, W	Contractor's price	Installed cost
A	290	$130	$202.25
B	200	120	180.25

The installed cost includes published contractor's book price for the luminaire with ballast, lamp as shown, required fastening devices, and the labor required for recess mounting and connection of the luminaire. No separate outlet is required since the unit is supplied with an attached outlet ready to accept supply leads.

These low-brightness downlights are recommended for ceiling heights of 10 to 16 ft.

COMMERCIAL RECESSED H.I.D.– 8″ ELLIPSOIDAL REFLECTOR DOWNLIGHT

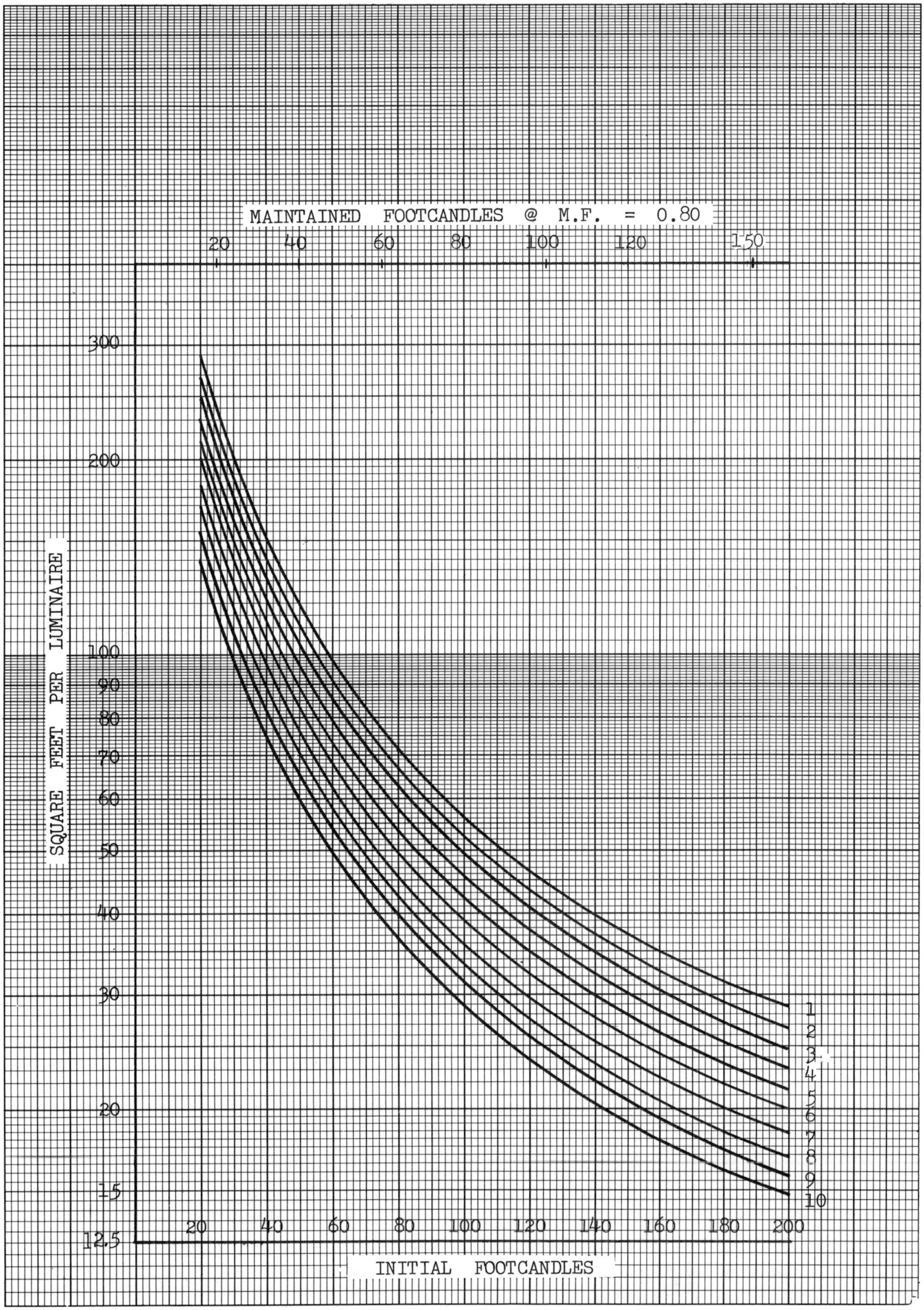

E

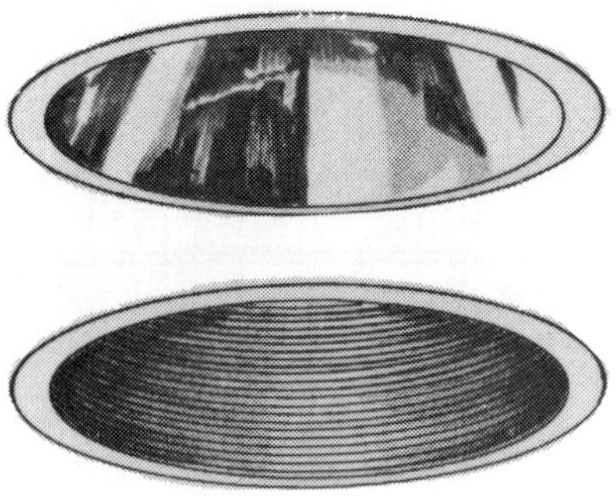

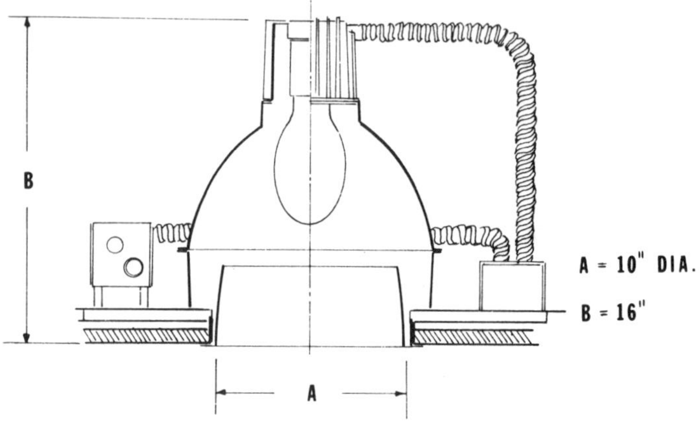

Description	10-in ellipsoidal-reflector downlight
Lamp	One 250-W E-28 mercury (DX), 12,100 1m, 24,000 h
Reflector	Clear specular aluminum
Spacing ratio	1.2
Maintenance factors	0.85/0.80/0.75 0.80/0.75/0.70 (for metal halide lamp only)
Conversion factors	A. Unit with one 250-W E-28 mercury (DX) = 1.0 B. Unit with one 175-W E-28 mercury (DX) = 0.71 C. Unit with one 175-W BT-28 metal halide (coated) = 1.0 D. Unit with one 250-W E-18 high-pressure sodium (clear) = 2.2 For units with black milligroove baffle aperture, multiply footcandle values by 0.80

COST DETAILS PER LUMINAIRE

Type of unit	Input, W	Contractor's price	Installed cost
A	290	$138	$216.75
B	200	127	189.50
C	210	154	248.50
D	295	252	389.25

The installed cost includes published contractor's book price for the luminaire with ballast, lamp as shown, required fastening devices, and the labor required for recess mounting and connection of the luminaire. No separate outlet is required since the unit is supplied with an attached outlet ready to accept supply leads.

These low-brightness downlights are recommended for ceiling heights of 16 to 25 ft for high-pressure sodium lamps and 10 to 16 ft for other lamps. As recommended by the lamp manufacturer, a lamp guard is to be used for all metal halide lamps under 400 W. This causes a reduction in maintenance factor. Use the lower set of recommended maintenance factors for the metal halide lamps.

COMMERCIAL RECESSED H.I.D.–10" ELLIPSOIDAL REFLECTOR DOWNLIGHT

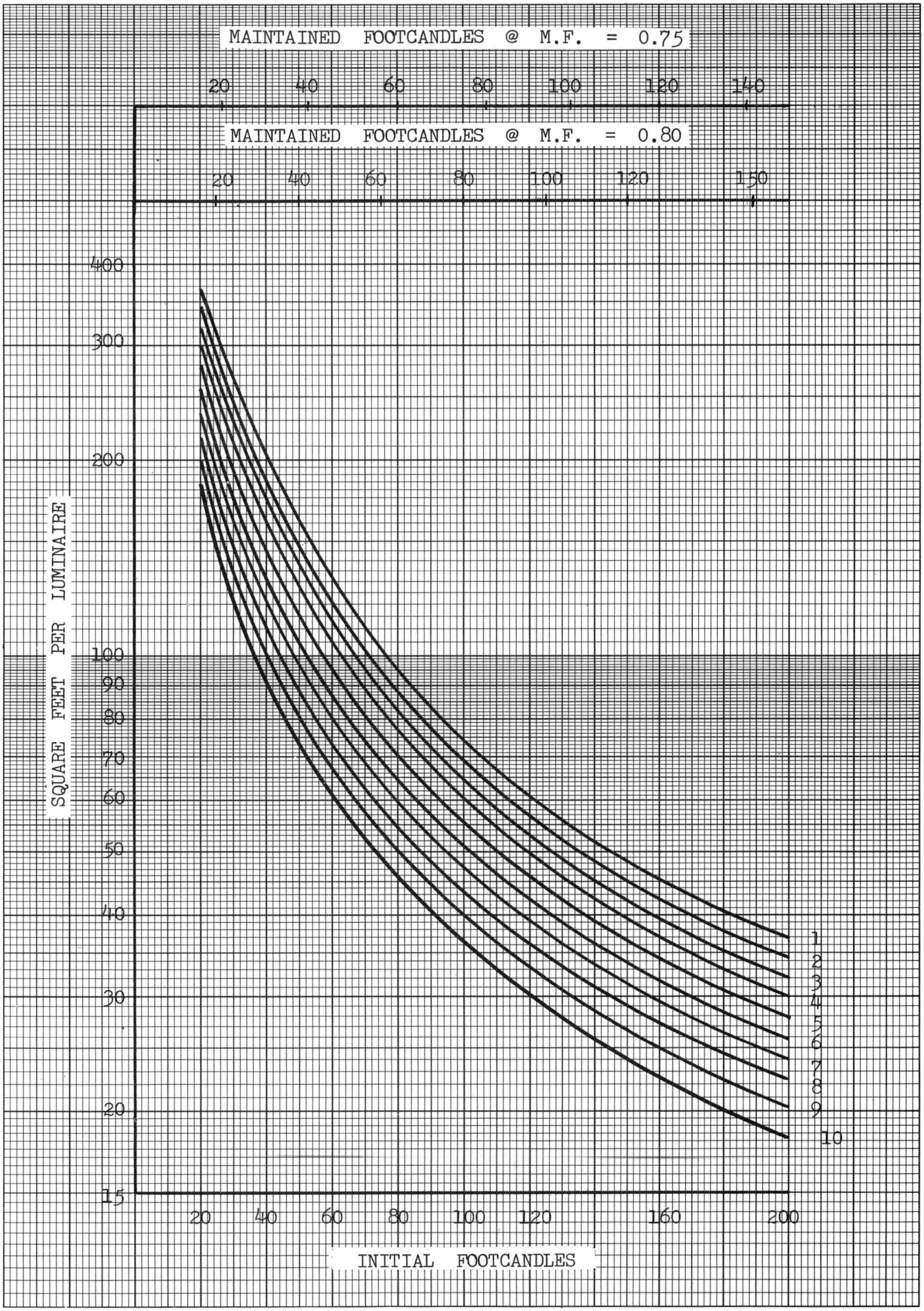

E

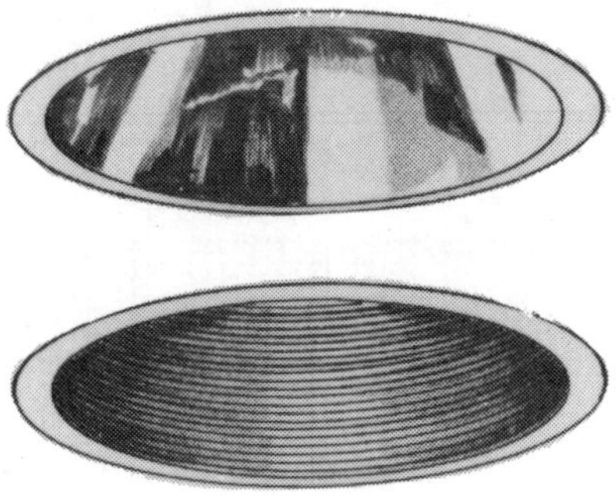

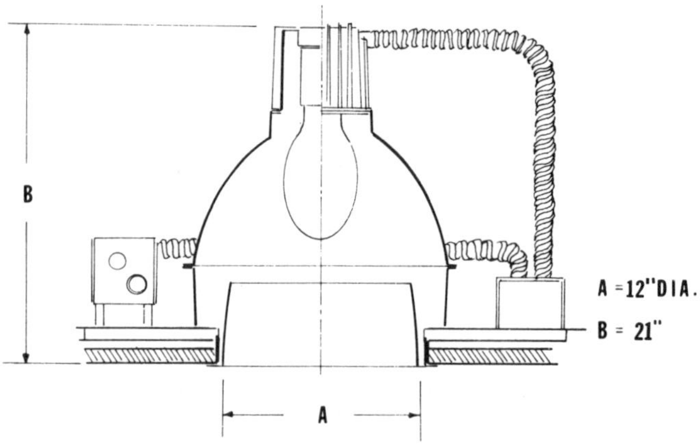

E-18

Description	12-in ellipsoidal-reflector downlight
Lamp	One 400-W E-37 mercury (DX), 22,500 1m, 24,000 h
Reflector	Clear specular aluminum
Spacing ratio	1.1
Maintenance factors	0.85/0.80/0.75
Conversion factors	A. Unit with one 400-W E-37 mercury (DX) = 1.0 B. Unit with one 400-W BT-37 metal halide (coated) = 1.7 C. Unit with one 400-W E-18 high-pressure sodium (clear) = 2.5 For units with black milligroove baffle aperture, multiply footcandle values by 0.80

COST DETAILS PER LUMINAIRE

Type of unit	Input, W	Contractor's price	Installed cost
A	445	$180	$261.75
B	460	194	304.75
C	470	278	424.25

The installed cost includes published contractor's book price for the luminaire with ballast, lamp as shown, required fastening devices, and the labor required for recess mounting and connection of the luminaire. No separate outlet is required since the unit is supplied with an attached outlet ready to accept supply leads.

These low-brightness downlights are recommended for ceiling heights of 20 to 35 ft for high-pressure sodium lamps and 12 to 20 ft for other lamps.

COMMERCIAL RECESSED H.I.D.—12" ELLIPSOIDAL REFLECTOR DOWNLIGHT

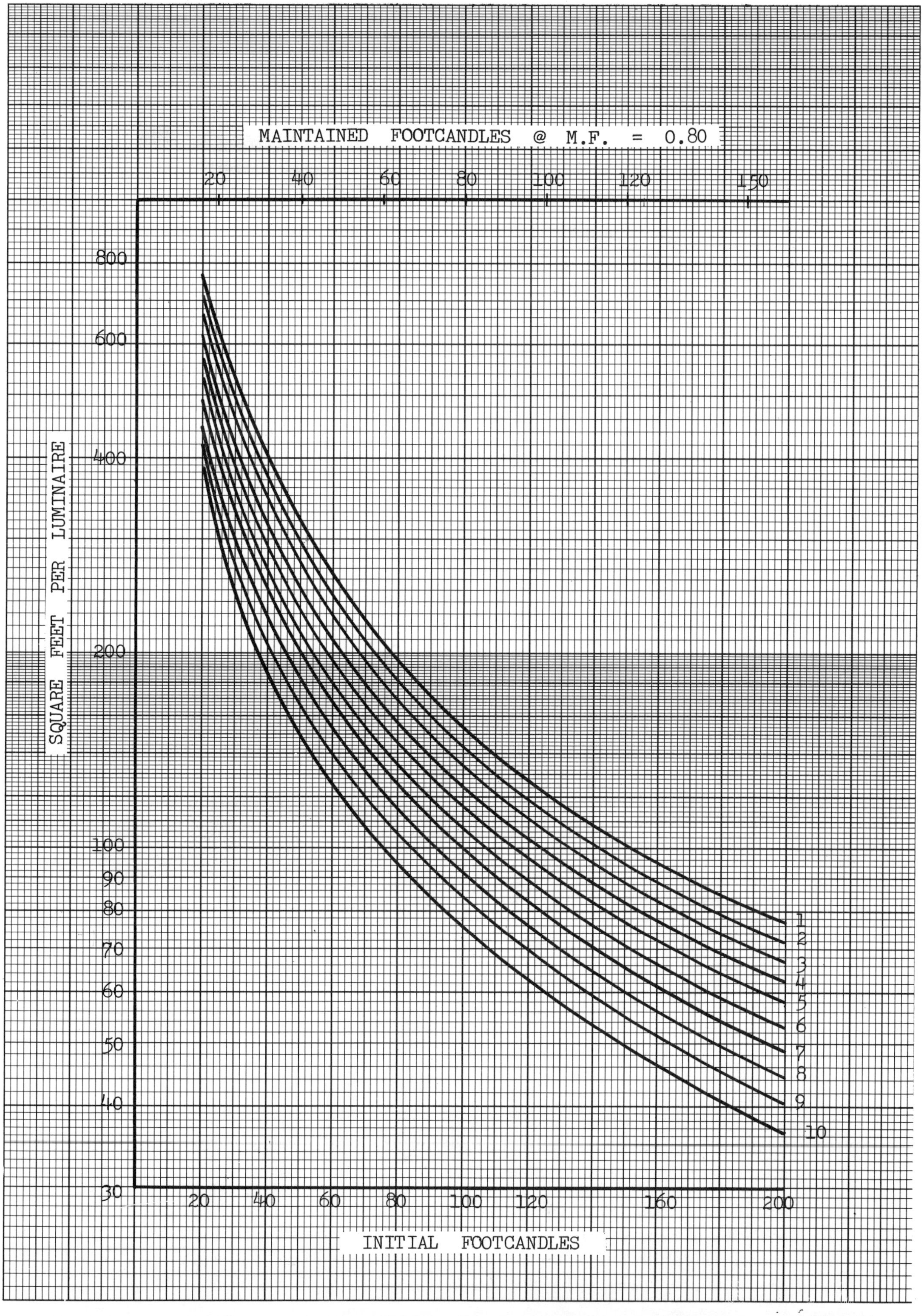

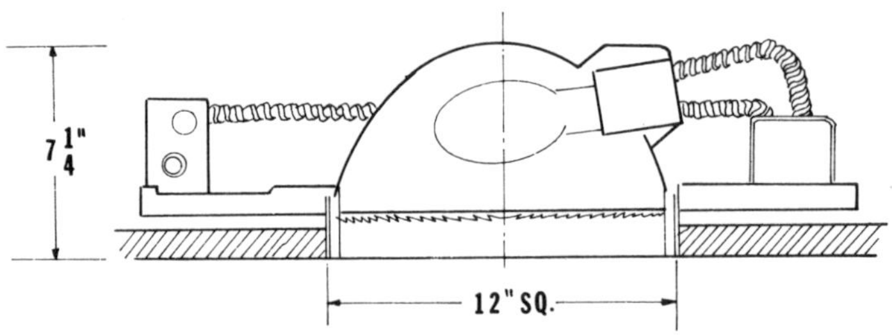

E-20

Description	12- X 12-in regressed lens
Lamp	One 100-W E-23½ mercury (DX), 4000 1m, 24,000 h
Lens	Regressed Fresnel lens
Reflector	Semispecular aluminum
Spacing ratio	1.0
Maintenance factors	0.75/0.70/0.65
Conversion factors	A. Unit with one 100-W E-23½ mercury (DX) = 1.0
	B. Unit with one 175-W E-28 mercury (DX) = 1.8

COST DETAILS PER LUMINAIRE

Type of unit	Input, W	Contractor's price	Installed cost
A	120	$105	$168.75
B	200	107	164

The installed cost includes published contractor's book price for the luminaire with ballast, lamp as shown, required fastening devices, plaster frame, and labor required for recess mounting and connection of the luminaire. No separate outlet is required since unit is supplied with an attached outlet ready to accept supply leads.

Horizontal mercury lamps generally provide 4.5 percent fewer lumens initially and 22 percent fewer lumens at 70 percent rated life than vertical lamps. This causes a reduction in maintenance factor. These luminaires are suitable for rooms with ceiling heights of 8 to 16 ft.

COMMERCIAL RECESSED H.I.D.–12" X 12" REGRESSED LENS

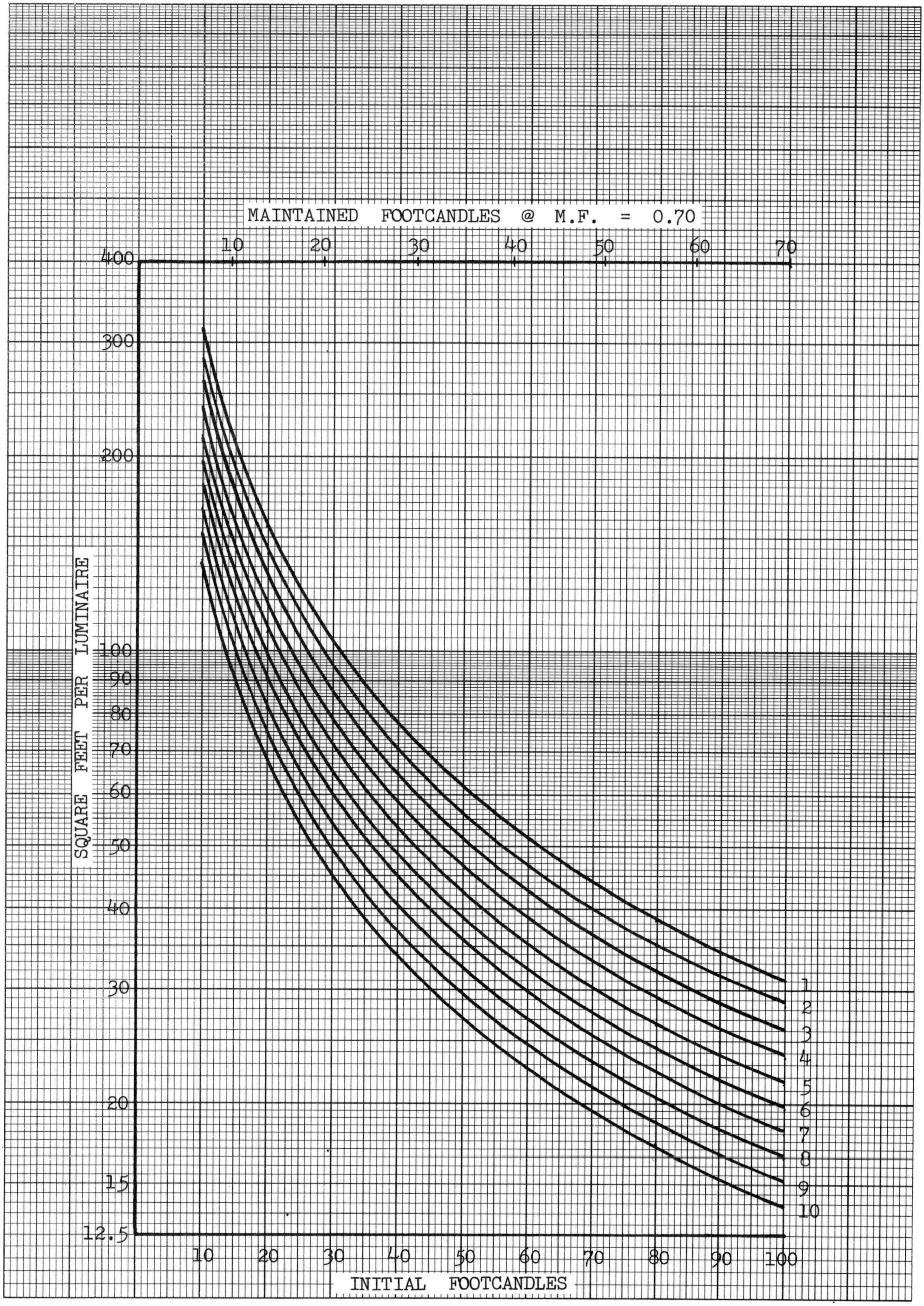

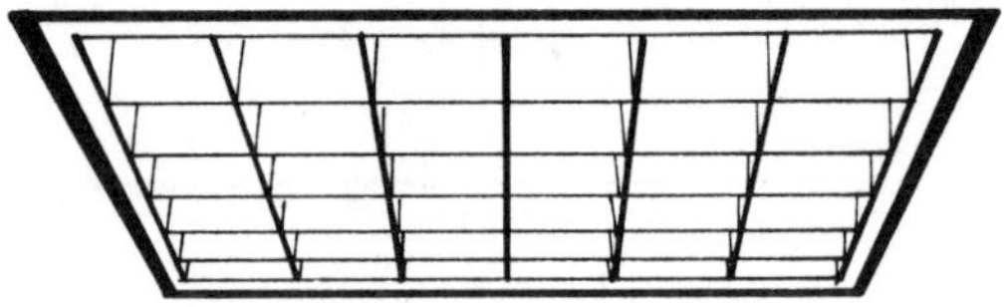

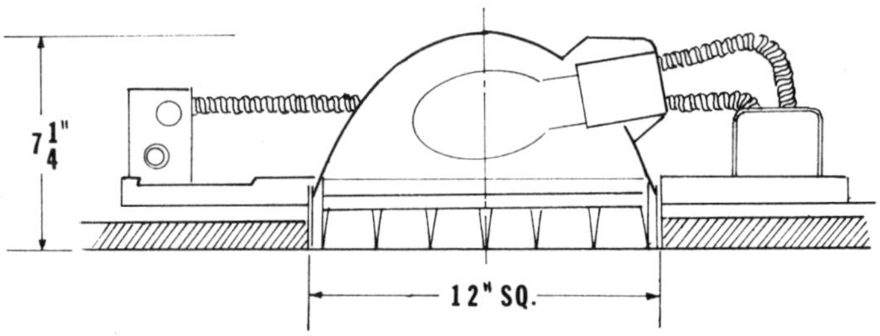

Description	12- X 12-in parabolic louvered
Lamp	One 100-W E-23½ mercury (DX), 4000 1m (horizontal) 24,000 h
Louvers	Parabolic reflector cells of specular anodized aluminum
Spacing ratio	1.0
Maintenance factors	0.85/0.80/0.75
Conversion factors	A. Unit with one 100-W E-23½ mercury (DX) = 1.0 B. Unit with one 175-W E-28 mercury (DX) = 1.8

COST DETAILS PER LUMINAIRE

Type of unit	Input, W	Contractor's price	Installed cost
A	120	$111	$176.25
B	200	114	173.50

The installed cost includes published contractor's book price for the luminaire with louvers and ballast, lamp as shown, required fastening devices, plaster frame, and the labor required for recess mounting and connection of the luminaire. No separate outlet is required since unit is supplied with an attached outlet ready to accept supply leads.

This handsome unit with parabolic reflector cells of specular anodized aluminum provides illumination with low apparent brightness. Horizontal mercury lamps have fewer lumens and cause a light loss; open louvers, having no static charge and dirt- or grime-collecting surfaces, assure good maintenance factors.

The reference luminaire is as manufactured by Lightolier.

This information was based on test 14216, prepared by ITL for Lightolier.

COMMERCIAL RECESSED H.I.D.–12" X 12" PARABOLIC LOUVERED

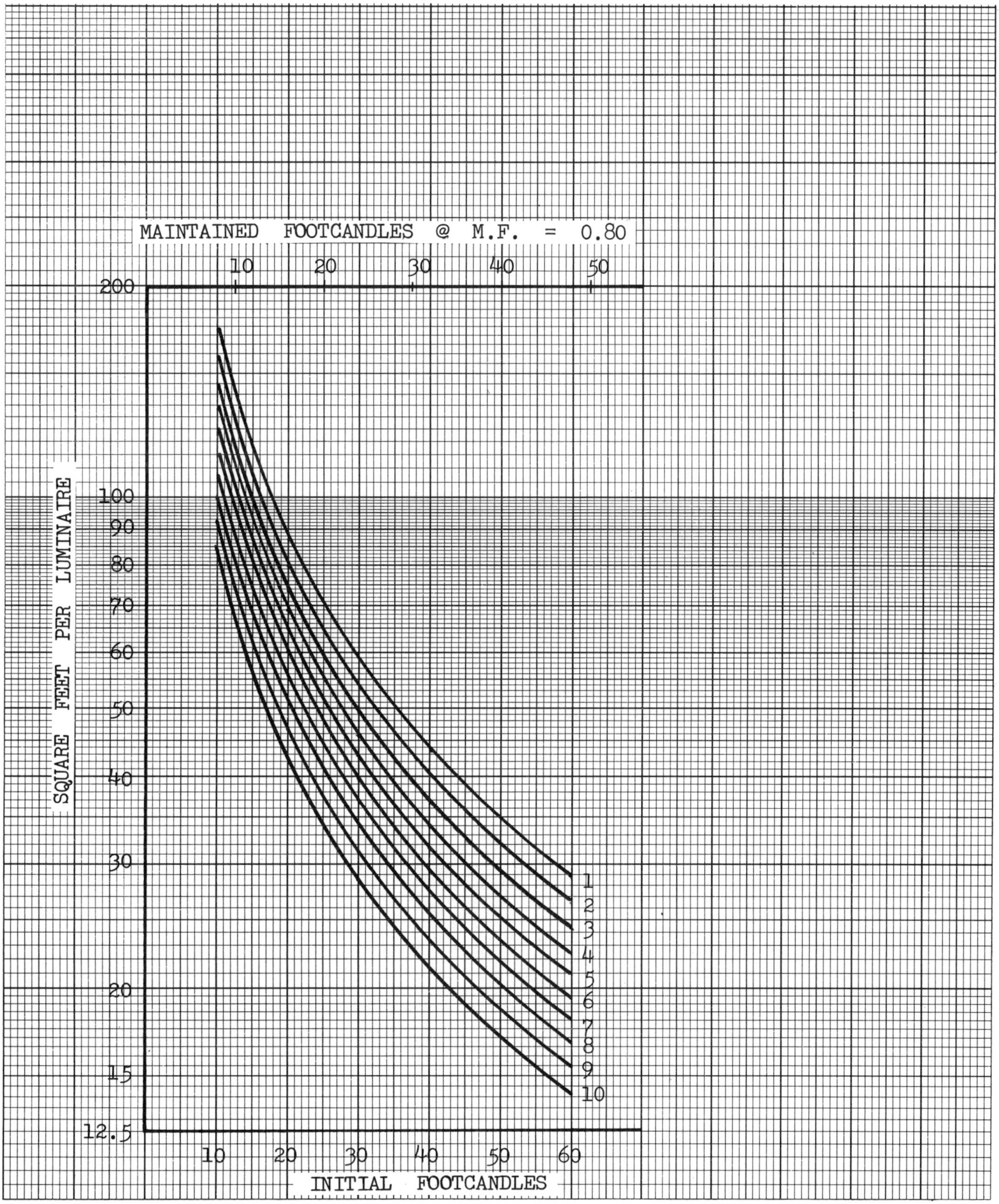

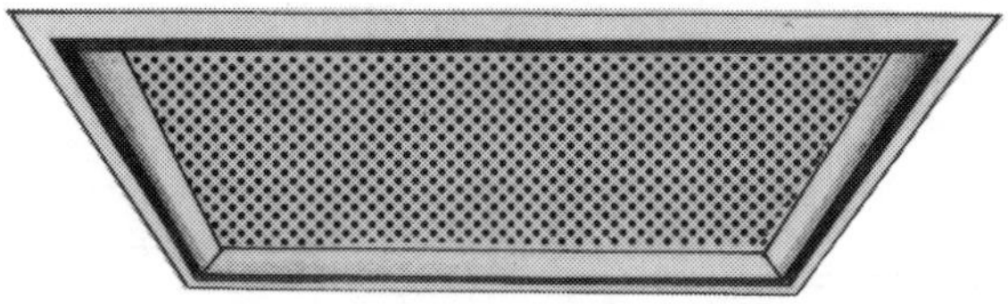

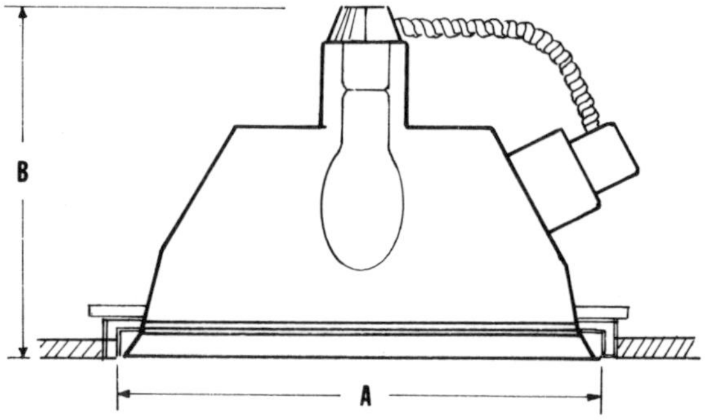

Description	2- X 2-ft regressed lens
Lamp	One 250-W E-28 mercury (DX), 12,100 1m, 24,000 h
Lens	100 percent virgin acrylic with diagonal array of female conical prisms
Spacing ratio	1.2
Maintenance factors	0.80/0.75/0.70
Conversion factors	A. Unit with one 250-W E-28 mercury (DX) = 1.0 B. Unit with one 175-W E-28 mercury (DX) = 0.7 C. Unit with one 250-W BT-28 metal halide (coated) = 1.7 D. Unit with one 175-W E-28 metal halide (coated) = 1.15

COST DETAILS PER LUMINAIRE

Type of Unit	Input, W	Contractor's price		Installed cost	
		Lay-in	Fit-in	Lay-in	Fit-in
A	290	$101	$103	$170.25	$174.75
B	200	97	99	152.50	160.75
C	294	107	109	119.25	205
D	210	103	105	189.25	194.75

The installed cost includes published contractor's book price for the luminaire with lens and ballast, lamp as shown, required fastening devices, 4-ft length of 3/8-in flexible metallic conduit with 6-ft length of 2 no. 12 AF wire, two connectors, and the labor required for recess mounting and connection of the luminaire. See page E–42 for an outlet above ceiling.

This recess luminaire with low brightness prismatic lens is suitable for ceilings ranging from 10 to 16 ft.

The reference luminaire is as manufactured by Lightolier.

This information was based on test 16084, as prepared by ITL for Lightolier.

COMMERCIAL RECESSED H.I.D.–2' X 2' REGRESSED LENS

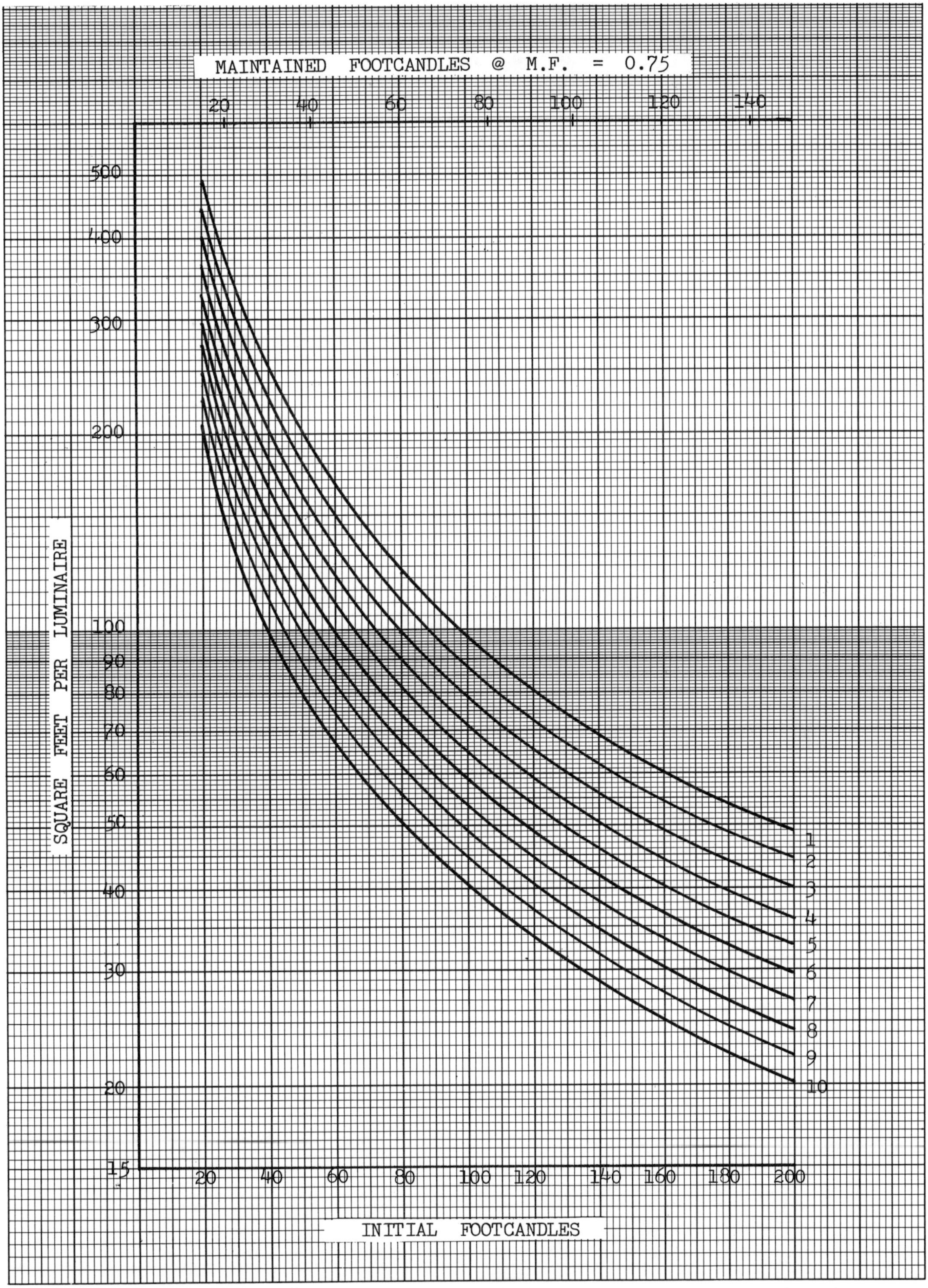

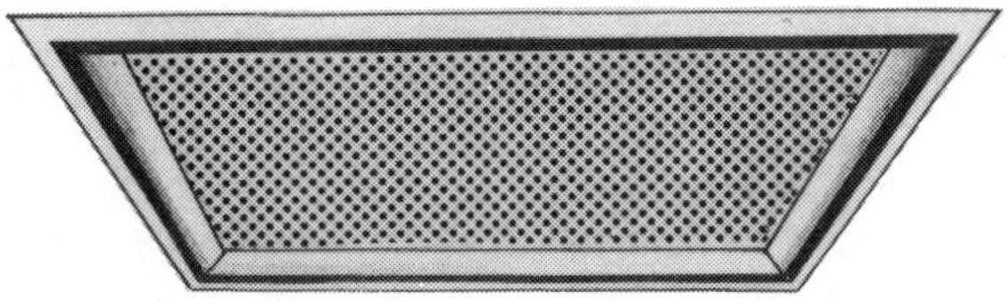

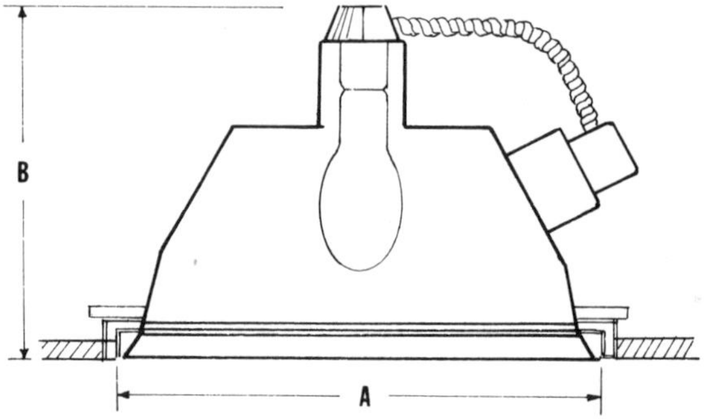

Description	2- X 2-ft regressed lens
Lamp	One 400-W E-37 mercury (DX), 22,500 lm, 24,000 h
Lens	100 percent virgin acrylic with diagonal array of female conical prisms
Spacing ratio	1.2
Maintenance factors	0.80/0.75/0.70
Conversion factors	A. Unit with one 400-W E-37 mercury (DX) = 1.0 B. Unit with one 400-W BT-37 metal halide (coated) = 1.5

COST DETAILS PER LUMINAIRE

Type of Unit	Input, W	Contractor's price		Installed cost	
		Lay-in	Fit-in	Lay-in	Fit-in
A	445	$123	$125	$195.25	$200.50
B	460	130	132	229.75	234.50

The installed cost includes published contractor's book price for the luminaire with lens and ballast, lamp as shown, required fastening devices, 4-ft length of 3/8-in flexible metallic conduit with 6-ft length of 2 no. 12 AF wire, two connectors, and the labor required for recess mounting and connection of the luminaire. See page E–42 for an outlet above ceiling.

This recessed luminaire with low-brightness prismatic lens is suitable for high ceiling areas.

The reference luminaire is as manufactured by Lightolier.

This report was based on test 16084, as prepared by ITL for Lightolier.

COMMERCIAL RECESSED H.I.D.–2′ X 2′ REGRESSED LENS

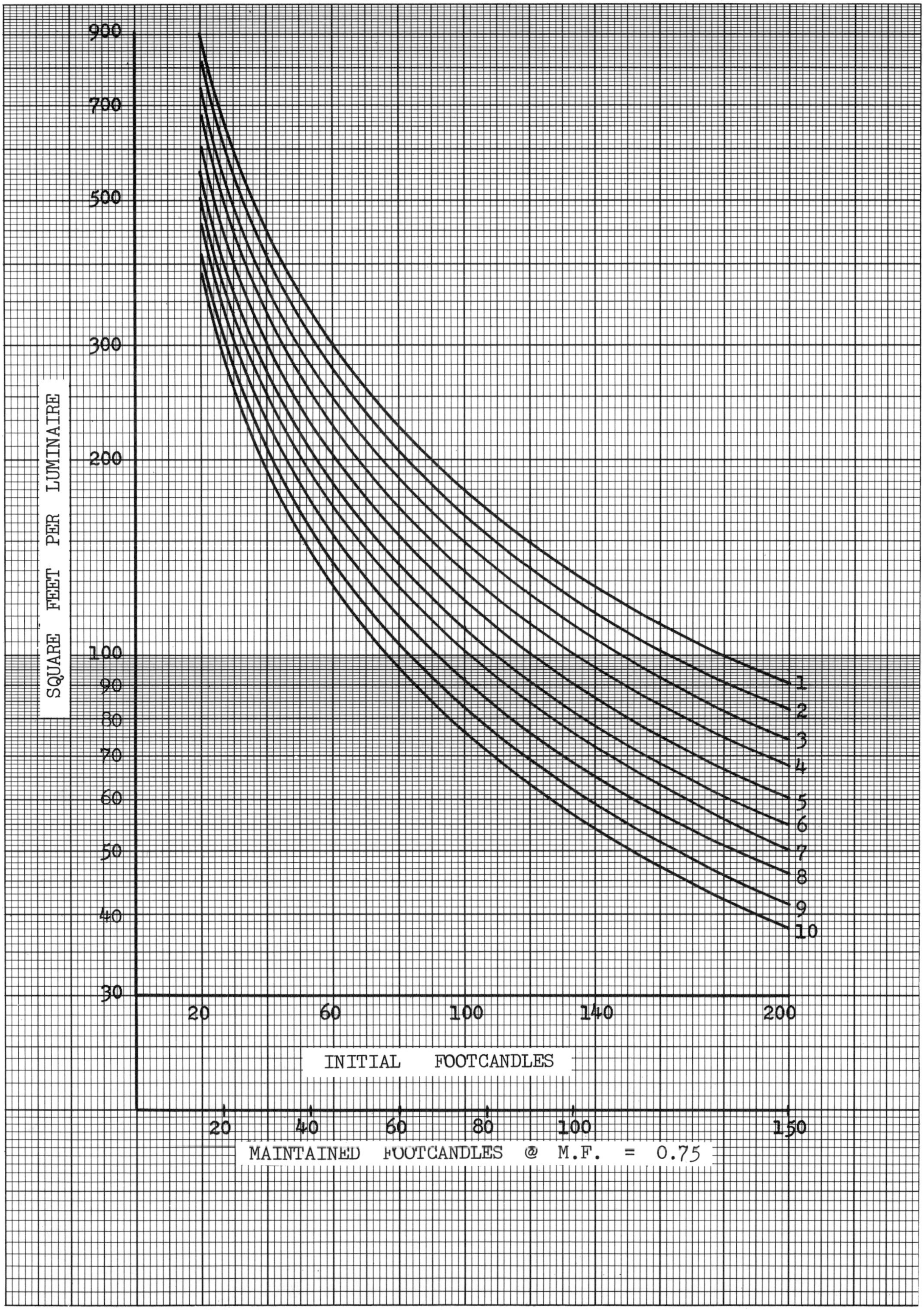

E

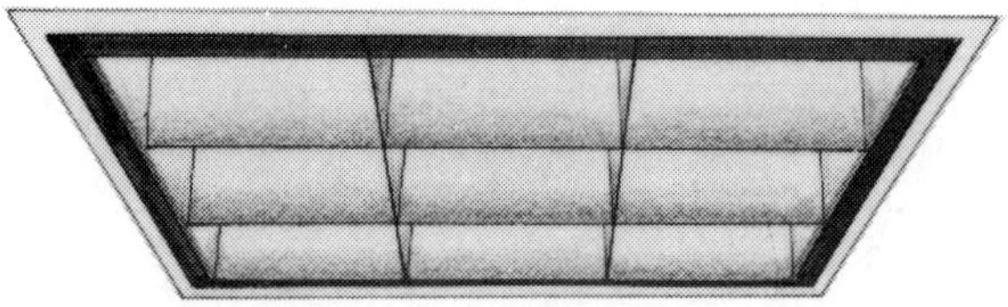

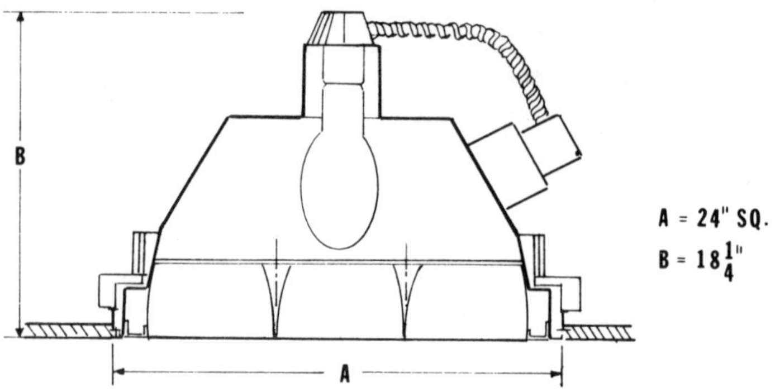

Description	2- × 2-ft parabolic-louvered
Lamp	One 250-W E-28 mercury (DX), 12,100 1m, 24,000 h
Louvers	Parabolic reflector cells of semispecular anodized aluminum
Spacing ratio	1.3
Visual comfort probability	84 (length)/84 (cross)
Maintenance factors	0.90/0.85/0.80 (mercury lamps) 0.80/0.75/0.70 (metal halide lamps)
Conversion factors	A. Unit with one 250-W E-28 mercury (DX) = 1.0 B. Unit with one 175-W E-28 mercury (DX) = 0.7 C. Unit with one 250-W BT-28 metal halide (coated) = 1.57 D. Unit with one 175-W BT-28 metal halide (coated) = 1.1

COST DETAILS PER LUMINAIRE

Type of unit	Input, W	Contractor's price		Installed cost	
		Lay-in	Fit-in	Lay-in	Fit-in
A	290	$114	$116	$186.25	$191
B	200	110	112	172.25	177
C	294	121	123	217	221.50
D	210	117	119	206.75	211

E-28

The installed cost includes published contractor's book price for the luminaire with louvers and ballast, lamp as shown, required fastening devices, 4-ft length of 3/8-in flexible metallic conduit with 6-ft length of 2 no. 12 AF wire, two connectors and the labor required for recess mounting and connection of the luminaire. See page E–42 for an outlet above ceiling.

This handsome unit with deep parabolic reflector cells of semispecular anodized aluminum provides illumination with low apparent brightness. Open louvers, having no static charge and no dirt- or grime-collecting surfaces, assure a better maintenance factor. For the metal halide lamps, however, a lamp-guarding shield is used, and thus the lower set of recommended maintenance factors is more appropriate.

The reference luminaire is as manufactured by Lightolier.

This report was based on test 19733, prepared by ITL for Lightolier.

COMMERCIAL RECESSED H.I.D.—2' X 2' PARABOLIC LOUVERED

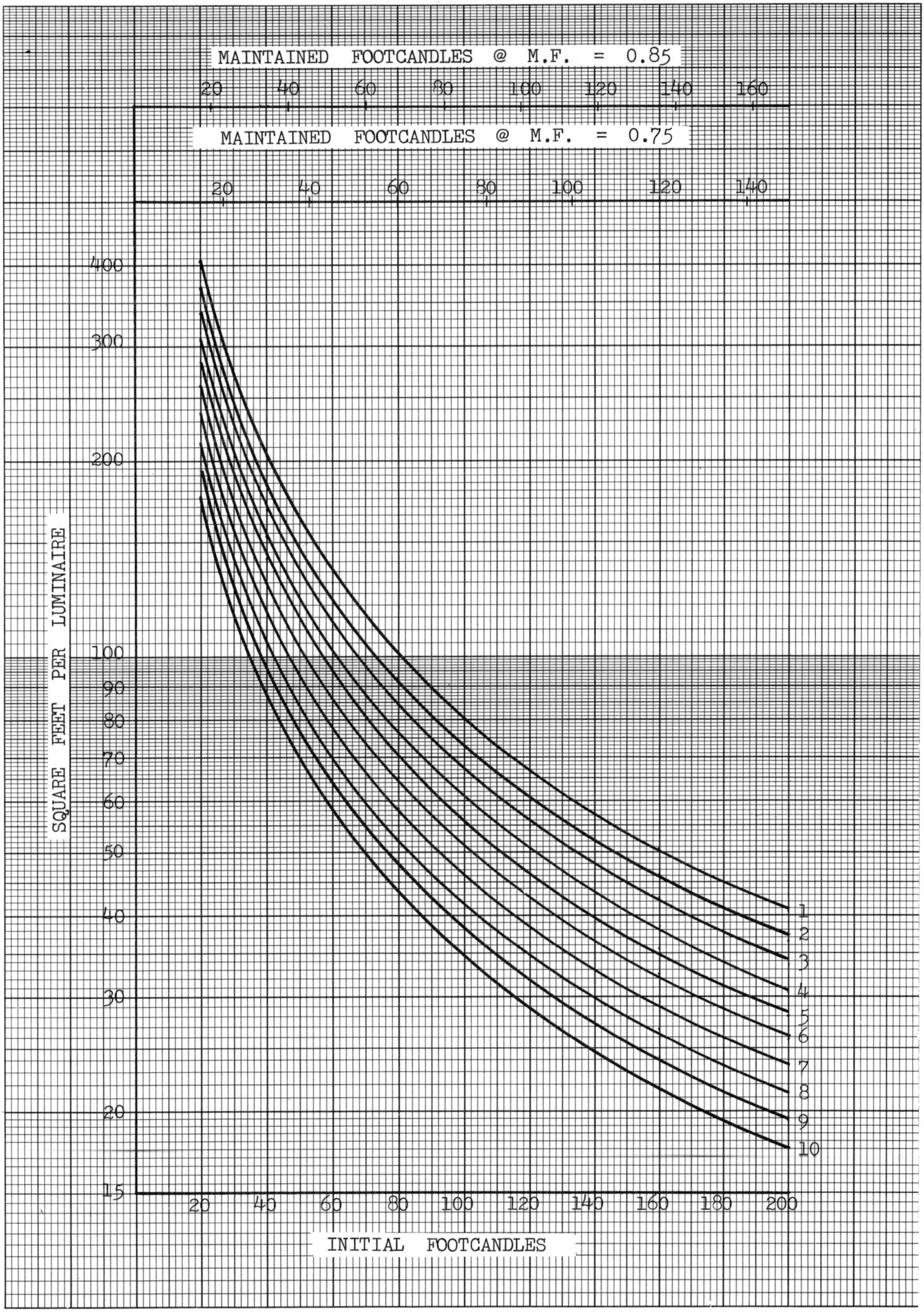

E

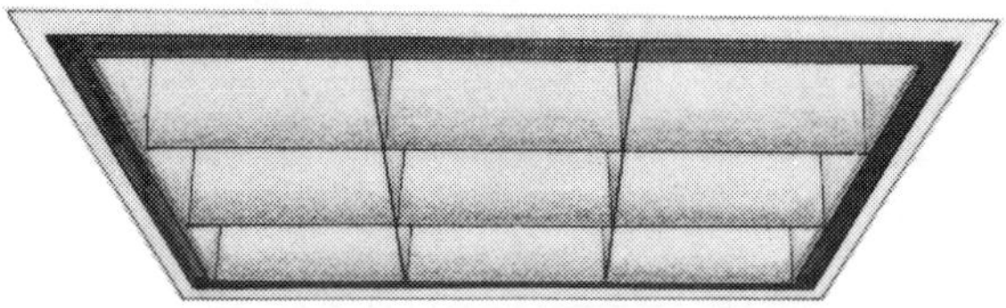

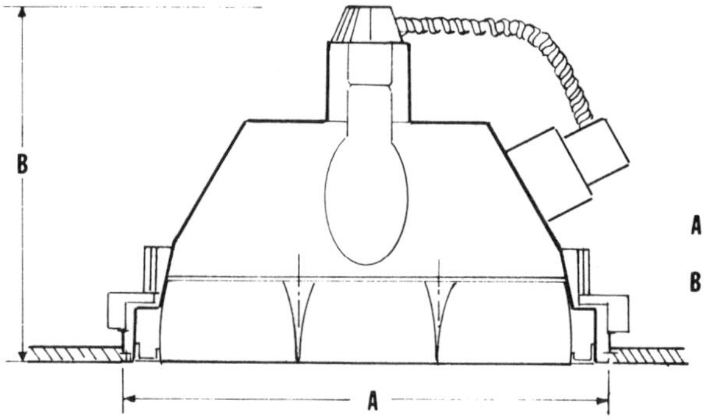

Description	2- X 2-ft parabolic-louvered
Lamp	One 400-W E-37 mercury (DX), 22,500 lm, 24,000 h
Louvers	Parabolic reflector cells of semispecular anodized aluminum
Spacing ratio	1.3
Visual comfort probability	82 (length)/83 (cross)
Maintenance factors	0.90/0.85/0.80
Conversion factors	A. Unit with one 400-W E-37 mercury (DX) = 1.0 B. Unit with one 400-W BT-37 metal halide (coated) = 1.5

COST DETAILS PER LUMINAIRE

Type of unit	Input, W	Contractor's price		Installed cost	
		Lay-in	Fit-in	Lay-in	Fit-in
A	445	$136	$138	$211.25	$217
B	460	143	145	245.75	251

The installed cost includes published contractor's book price for the luminaire with louvers and ballast, lamp as shown, required fastening devices, 4-ft length of 3/8-in flexible metallic conduit with 6-ft length of 2 no. 12 AF wire, two connectors, and the labor required for recess mounting and connection of the luminaire. *See page E–42 for an outlet above the ceiling.*

This handsome unit with deep parabolic reflector cells of semispecular anodized aluminum provides illumination with low apparent brightness. Open louvers, having no static charge and dirt- or grime-collecting surfaces, assure high maintenance factors.

The reference luminaire is as manufactured by Lightolier.

This report was based on test 19733, prepared by ITL for Lightolier.

COMMERCIAL RECESSED H.I.D.—2' X 2' PARABOLIC LOUVERED

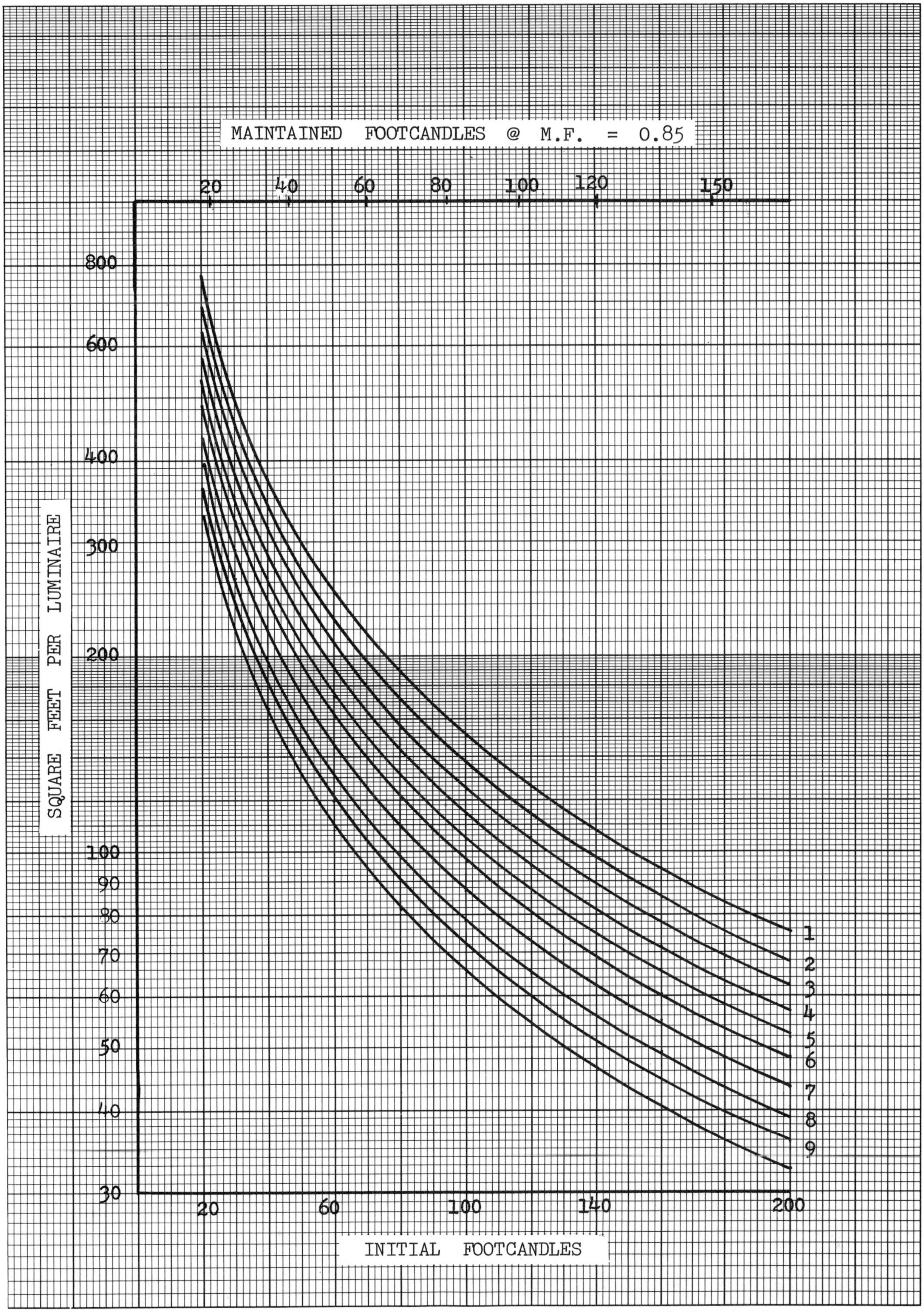

E

E-32

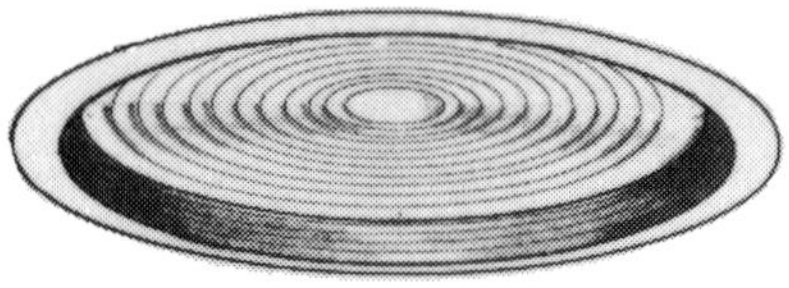

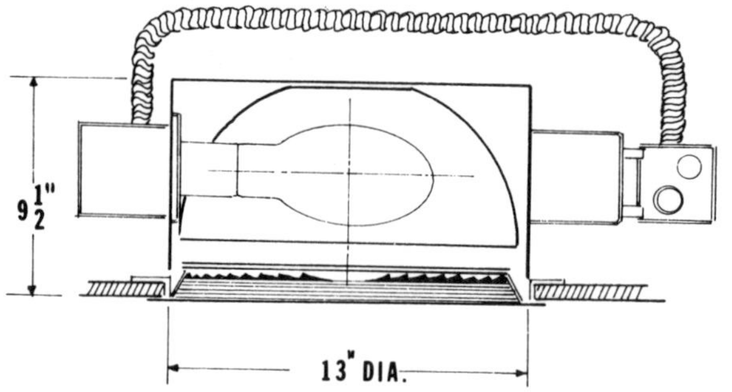

Description	Round regressed lens (horizontal lamp)
Lamp	One 175-W E-28 mercury (DX), 7750 lm, 24,000 h
Lens	Fresnel lens
Reflector	Clear specular aluminum
Spacing ratio	1.0
Maintenance factors	0.75/0.70/0.65
Input, W	200
Cost details per luminaire	Contractor's price = \$98
	Installed cost = \$153.75

The installed cost includes published contractor's book price for the luminaire with ballast and lens, lamp as shown, required fastening devices, and the labor required for recess mounting and connection of the luminaire. No separate outlet is required since the unit is supplied with an attached outlet ready to accept supply leads.

Horizontal mercury lamps generally provide 4.5 percent fewer lumens initially and 22 percent fewer lumens at 70 percent rated life than vertical lamps. This causes a reduction in maintenance factor. These luminaires are suitable for rooms with ceiling heights of 8 to 16 ft.

COMMERCIAL RECESSED H.I.D.–ROUND REGRESSED LENS (HORIZONTAL LAMP)

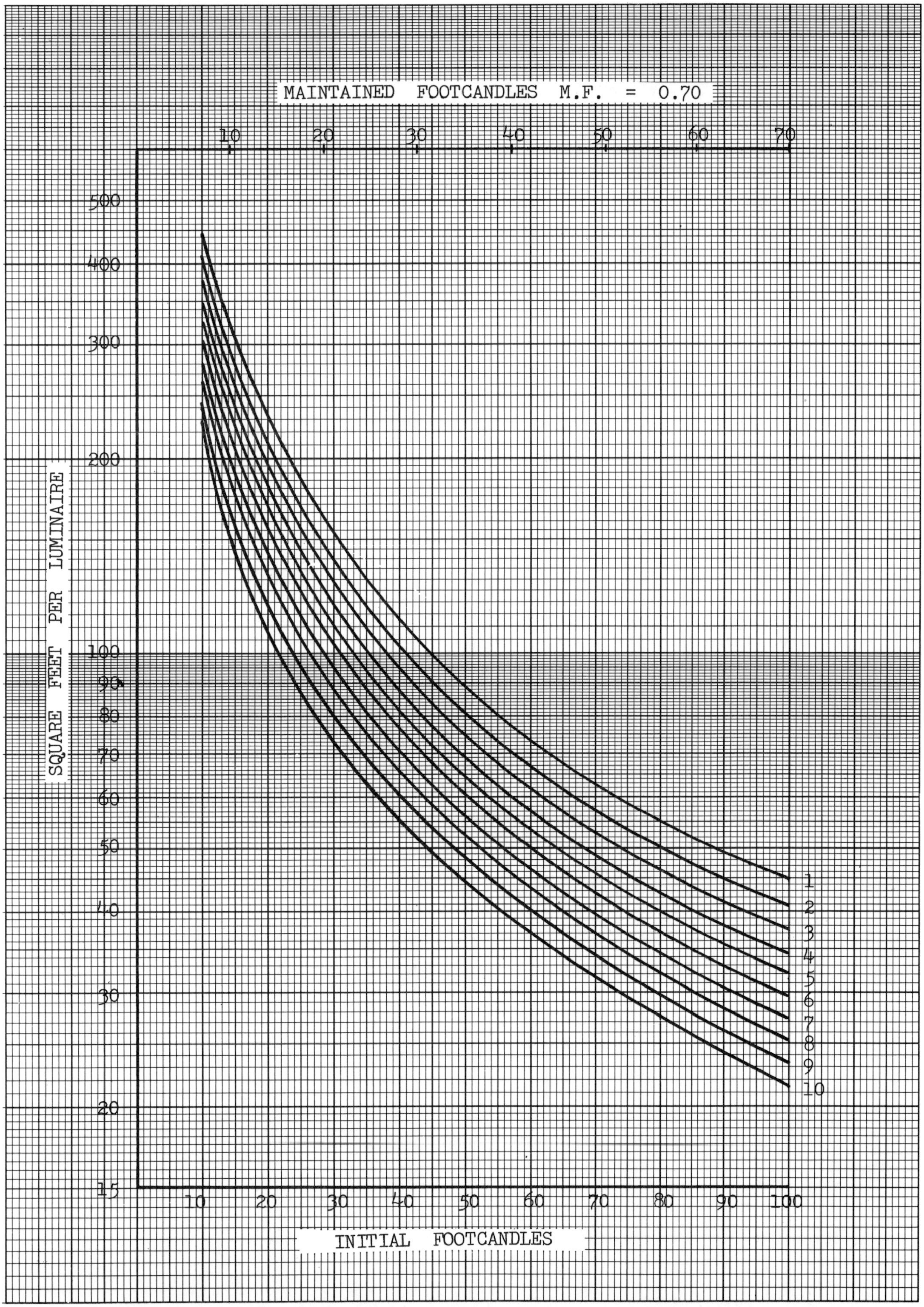

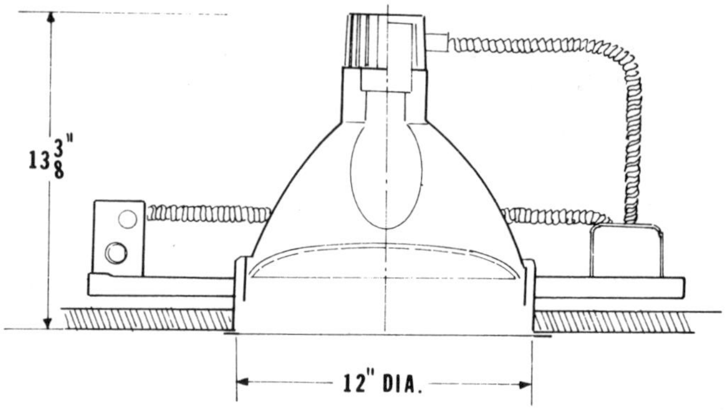

Description	Round regressed lens (vertical lamp)
Lamp	One 175-W E-28 mercury (DX), 8150 lm, 24,000 h
Lens	Holophane prismatic lens
Reflector	Clear specular aluminum
Spacing ratio	1.0
Maintenance factors	0.80/0.75/0.70
Conversion factors	A. Unit with one 175-W E-28 mercury (DX) = 1.0
	B. Unit with one 250-W E-28 mercury (DX) = 1.5
	C. Unit with one 175-W BT-28 metal halide (coated) = 1.7

COST DETAILS PER LUMINAIRE

Type of unit	Input, W	Contractor's price	Installed cost
A	200	$130	$193
B	290	143	218.25
C	210	143	209.25

The installed cost includes published contractor's book price for the luminaire with ballast and lens, lamp as shown, required fastening devices, and the labor required for recess mounting and connection of the luminaire. No separate outlet is required since the unit is supplied with an attached outlet ready to accept supply leads.

These low-brightness luminaires are suitable for rooms with ceiling heights of 8 to 14 ft.

COMMERCIAL RECESSED H.I.D.–ROUND REGRESSED LENS (VERTICAL LAMP)

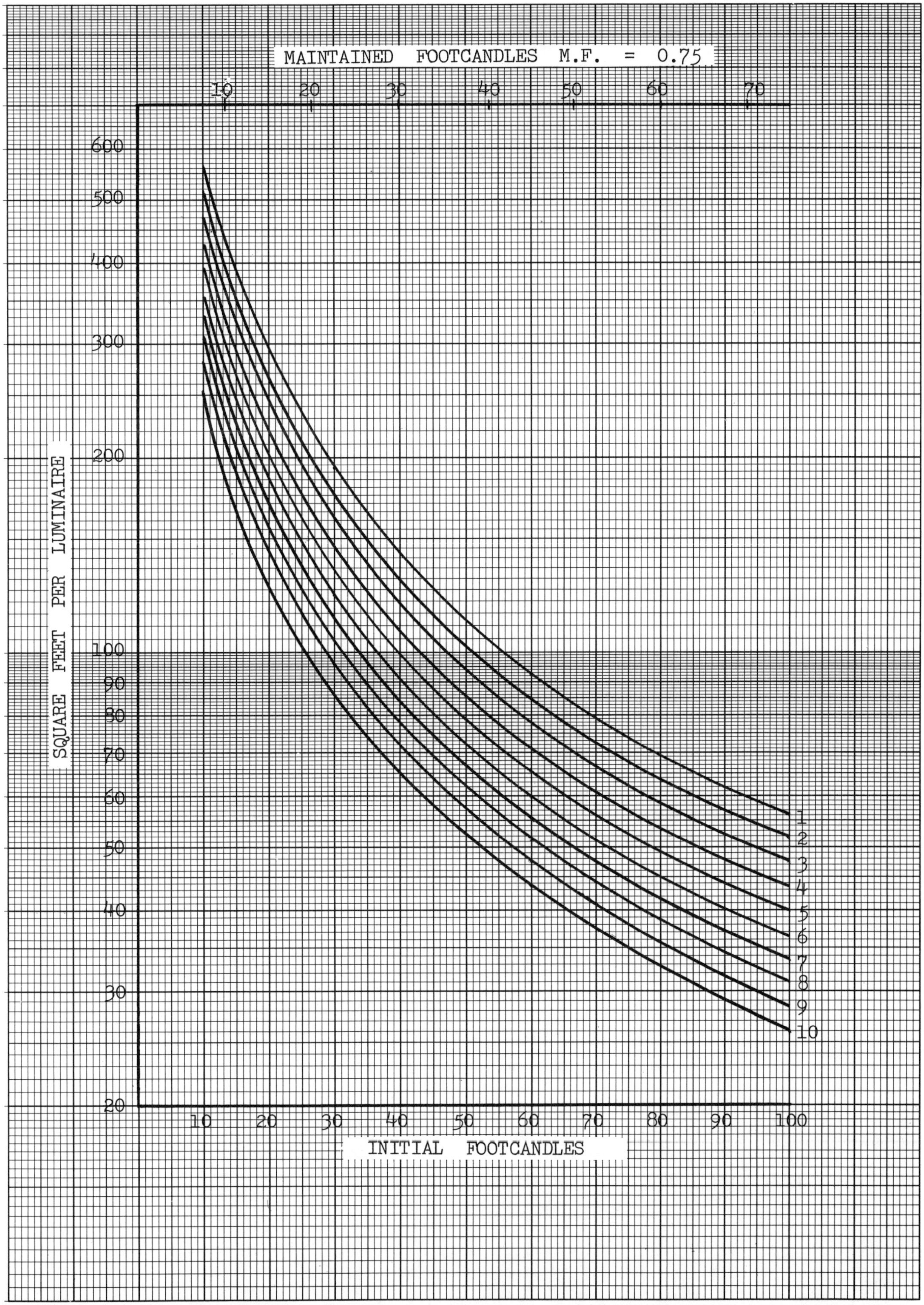

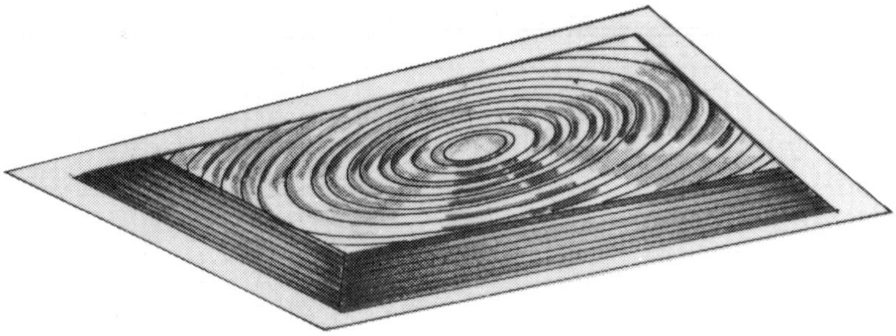

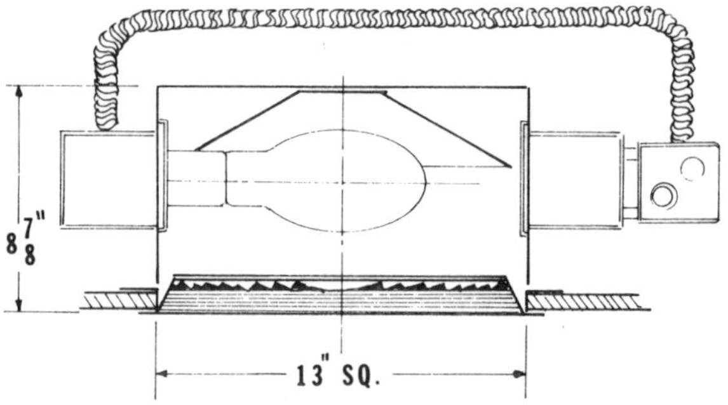

E-36

Description	Square regressed lens (conical reflector)
Lamp	One 175-W E-28 mercury (DX), 7750 lm, 24,000 h
Lens	Fresnel lens
Reflector	Specular clear aluminum (conical)
Spacing ratio	1.0
Maintenance factors	0.75/0.70/0.65
Input, W	200
Cost details per luminaire	Contractor's price = $101
	Installed cost = $157.50

The installed cost includes published contractor's book price for the luminaire with ballast and lens, lamp as shown, required fastening devices, and the labor required for recess mounting and connection of the luminaire. No separate outlet is required since the unit is supplied with an attached outlet ready to accept supply leads.

Horizontal mercury lamps generally provide 4.5 percent fewer lumens initially and 22 percent fewer lumens at 70 percent rated life than vertical lamps. This causes a reduction in maintenance factor. These luminaires are suitable for rooms with ceiling heights of 8 to 16 ft.

COMMERCIAL RECESSED H.I.D.–SQUARE REGRESSED LENS (CONICAL REFLECTOR)

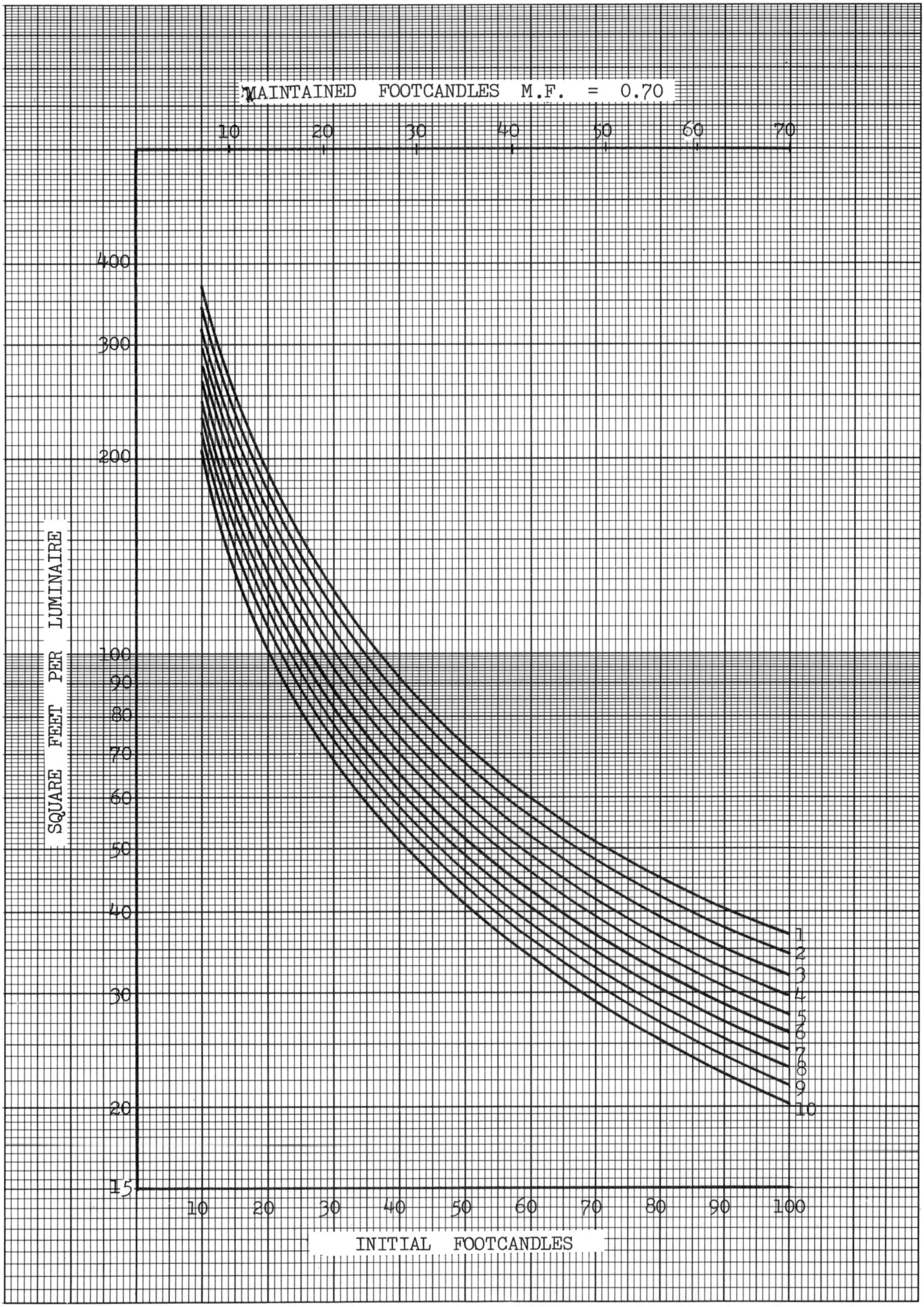

E

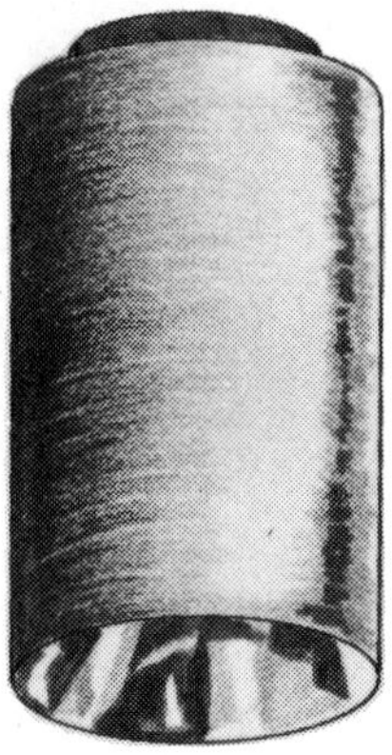

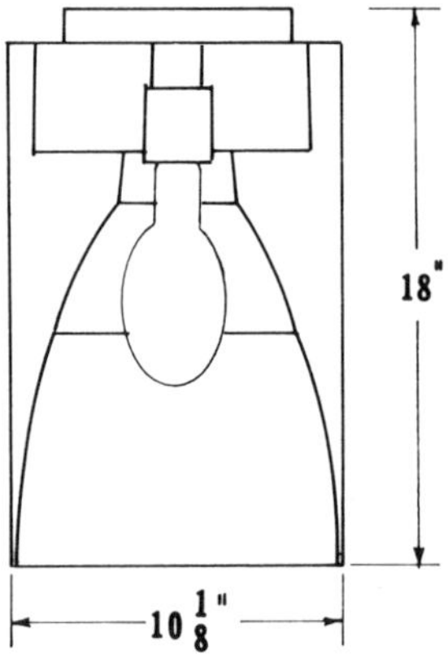

Description	Cylindrical downlight
Lamp	One 250-W E-28 mercury (DX), 12,100 lm, 24,000 h
Reflector	Specular clear aluminum
Spacing ratio	1.4
Maintenance factors	0.86/0.80/0.75
Conversion factors	A. Unit with one 250-W E-28 mercury (DX) = 1.0 B. Unit with one 175-W E-28 mercury (DX) = 0.7 For units with specular aluminum (gold), multiply footcandle values by 0.9

COST DETAILS PER LUMINAIRE

Type of unit	Input, W	Contractor's price	Installed cost
A	290	$186	$272
B	200	182	258

The installed cost includes published contractor's book price for the luminaire with ballast, lamp as shown, required fastening devices, and the labor required for surface mounting and connection of the luminaire. See page E–42 for an outlet as required.

A widespread type of luminaire has been selected here. These luminaires are recommended for rooms with 12- to 18-ft ceilings.

COMMERCIAL SURFACE MOUNT H.I.D.–CYLINDRICAL DOWNLIGHT

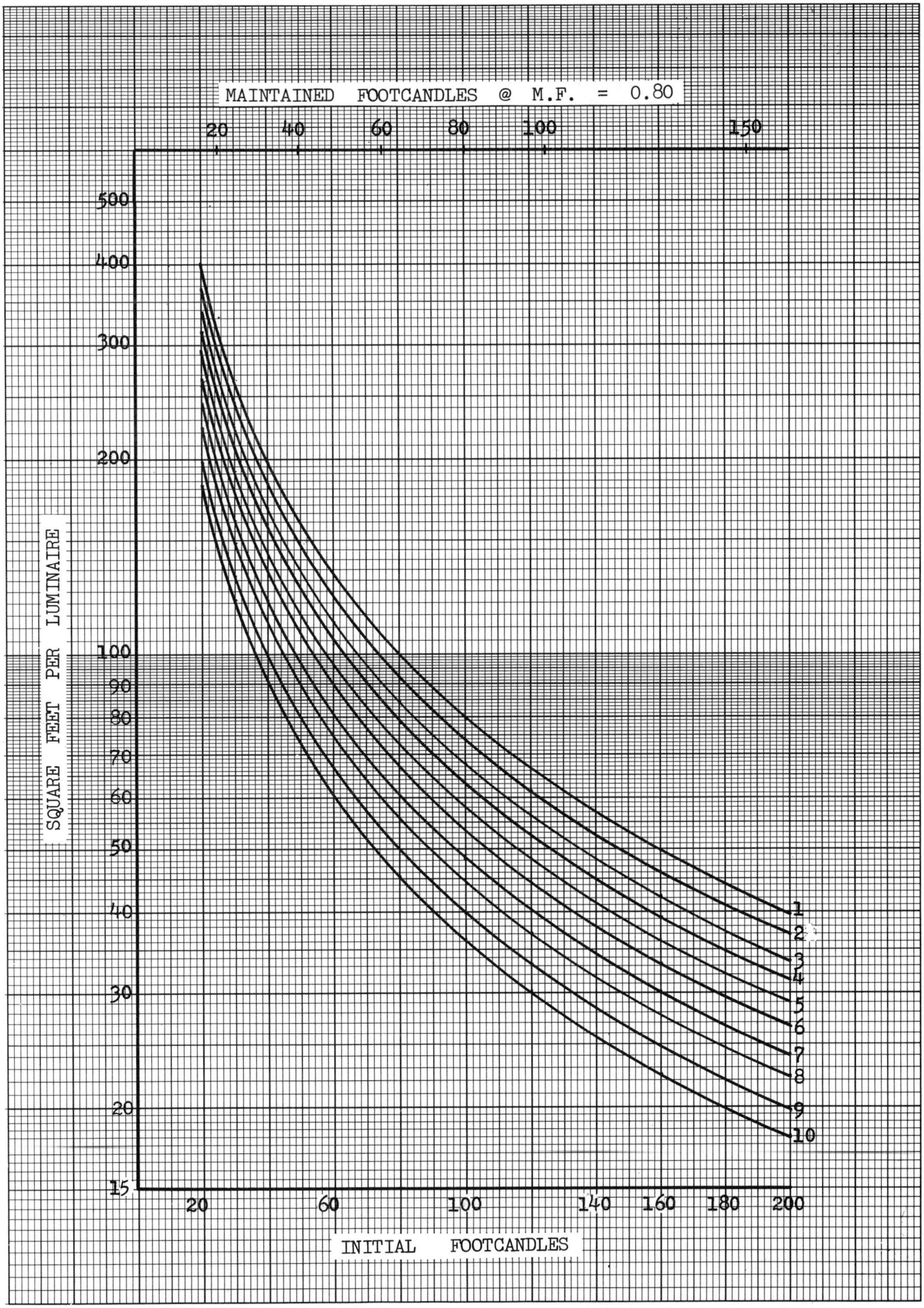

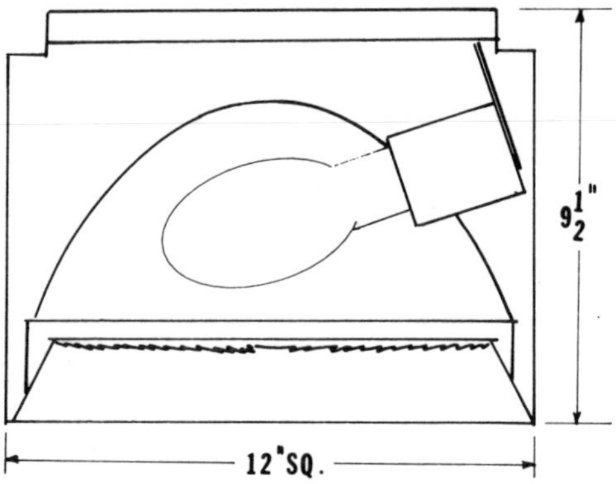

Description	12- X 12-in modular lens unit
Lamp	One 100-W E23½ mercury (DX), 4000 lm (horizontal), 24,000 h
Lens	Regressed Fresnel lens
Spacing ratio	1.0
Maintenance factors	0.75/0.70/0.65
Conversion factors	A. Unit with one 100-W E23½ mercury (DX) = 1.0 B. Unit with one 175-W E-28 mercury (DX) = 1.8

COST DETAILS PER LUMINAIRE

Type of unit	Input, W	Contractor's price	Installed cost
A	120	$126	$195.75
B	200	130	194

The installed cost includes published contractor's book price for the luminaire with ballast, lamp as shown, required fastening devices, and the labor required for surface mounting and connection of the luminaire. *See page E–42 for an outlet as required.*

Horizontal mercury lamps generally provide 4.5 percent fewer lumens initially and 22 percent fewer lumens at 70 percent rated life than vertical lamps. This causes a reduced maintenance factor. These luminaires are suitable for rooms with 8- to 16-ft ceilings.

COMMERCIAL SURFACE MOUNT H.I.D.–MODULAR LENS UNIT

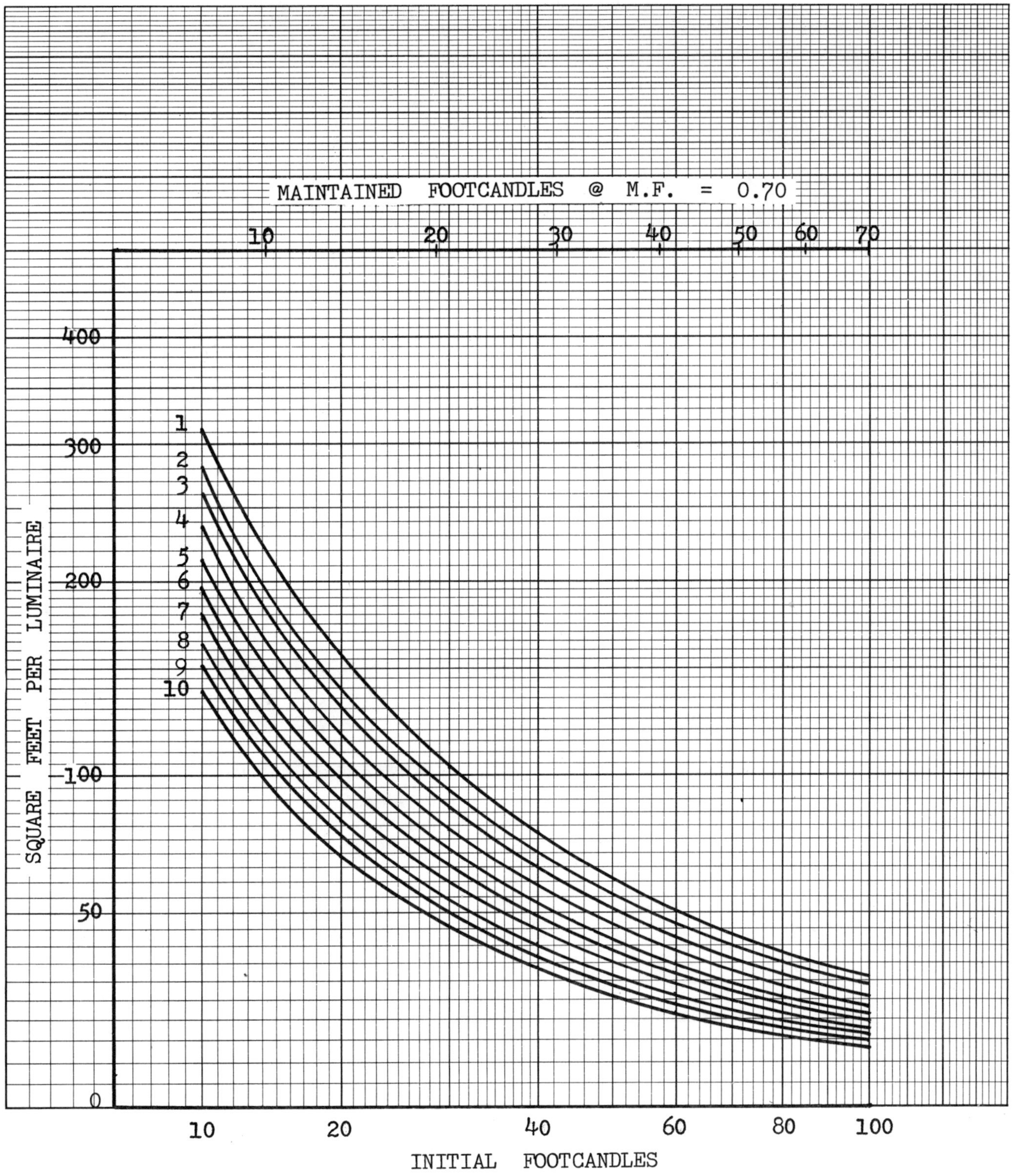

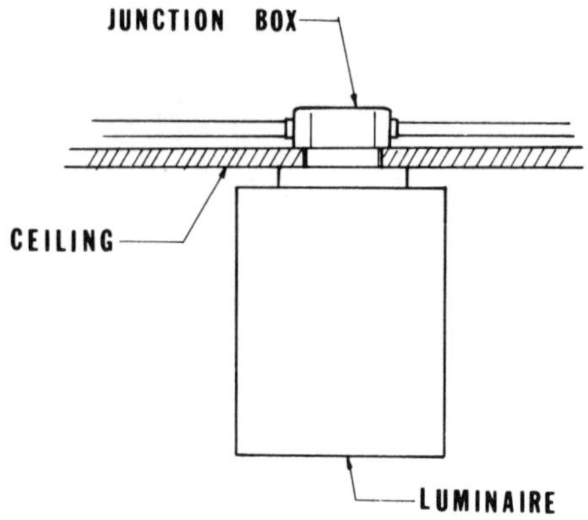

Add

$12.88 for EMT terminal
16.38 for GRC terminal
16.38 for IMS terminal

to the luminaire installed cost for an outlet flush-mounted to a suspended or furred ceiling. This includes a 4-in octagon box, adjustable bar hanger, two connectors, plaster ring, and two wire nuts.

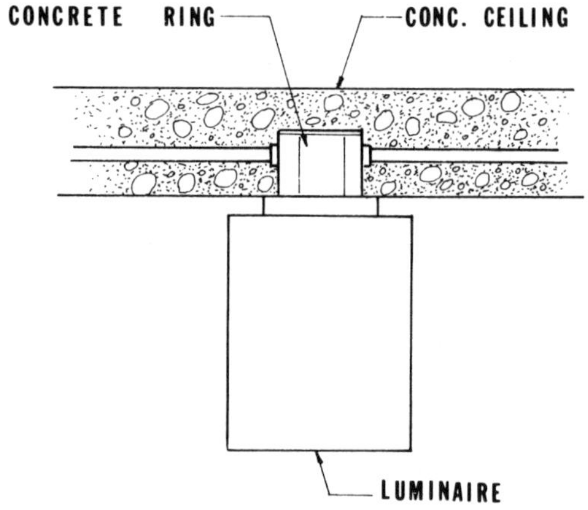

Add

$12.18 for EMT terminal
15.84 for GRC terminal
15.84 for IMS terminal

to the luminaire installed cost for an outlet flush-pan- or deck-mounted in concrete. This includes a 4-in concrete ring, two connectors as required, cover plate, and two wire nuts.

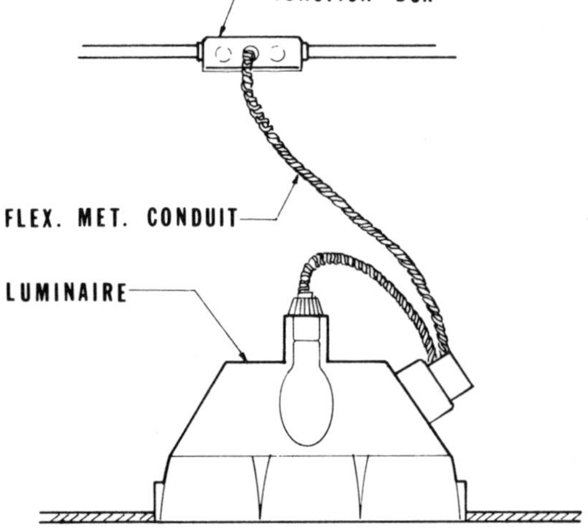

Add

$13.29 for EMT terminal
16.73 for GRC terminal
16.73 for IMS terminal

to the luminaire installed cost for an outlet recessed above ceiling. This includes a 4-in square box, blank cover, bar hanger, two connectors, and two wire nuts.

Commercial Incandescent

RECESSED UNITS

Open-Reflector Downlights (A-Lamps)

6-in	*F-2*
8-in	*F-4*
10-in	*F-6*

Open-Reflector Downlights (R, PAR Lamps)

6-in	*F-8*
7-in	*F-10*
9-in	*F-12, F-14*

Recessed Baffle Downlights (R, PAR Lamps)

5-in	*F-16*
6-in	*F-18*
8-in	*F-20*

Ellipsoidal-Reflector Downlights (A-Lamps)

6-in	*F-22*
7-in	*F-24*
9-in	*F-26*

Ellipsoidal-Reflector Downlights (Tungsten-Halogen)

4½-in	*F-28, F-30*
6-in	*F-32, F-34*

Miscellaneous Commercial (A-Lamps)

8-in Regressed Round Lens, Vertical Lamp	*F-36*
Horizontal Lamp	*F-38*
12- × 12-in Regressed Lens	*F-40*
12- × 12-in Parabolic-Louvered	*F-42*

SURFACE-MOUNTED UNITS

Open-Reflector Downlights (R, PAR Lamps)

6-in	*F-44*
7-in	*F-46*
9-in	*F-48*

Baffle Downlights (R, PAR Lamps)

5-in	*F-50*
6-in	*F-52*
8-in	*F-54*

CEILING OUTLETS FOR LUMINAIRES

Installed Cost of Outlets	*F-56*

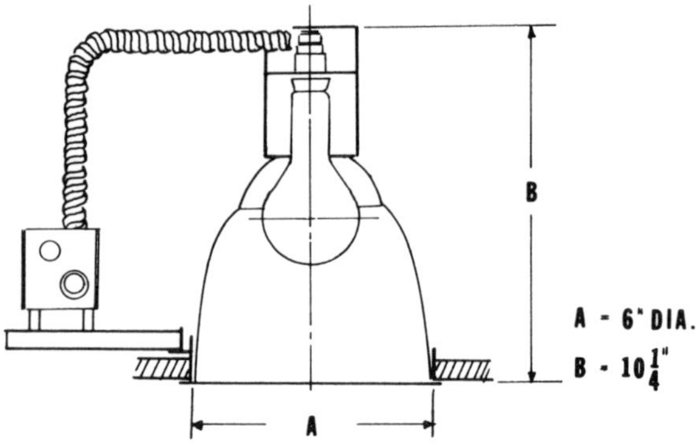

Description	6-in reflector downlight
Lamp	One 100-W A-19, 1750 lm, 750 h
Reflector	Clear specular aluminum
Spacing ratio	1.3
Maintenance factors	0.80/0.75/0.70
Input, W	100
Conversion factor	Unit with one 150-W A-21 = 1.64
Cost details per luminaire	Contractor's price = \$38
	Installed cost = \$61.50

The installed cost includes published contractor's book price for the luminaire, lamp as shown, required fastening devices, and the labor required for recess mounting and connection of the luminaire. No separate outlet is required since the unit is supplied with an attached outlet ready to accept supply leads.

This line of luminaires provides widespread distribution with very low brightness. Low-cost, high-luman-output general-service lamps combine with precise, full reflectors, resulting in higher overall efficiency than most other downlights.

RECESSED INCANDESCENT - 6" OPEN REFLECTOR DOWNLIGHT (A-LAMP)

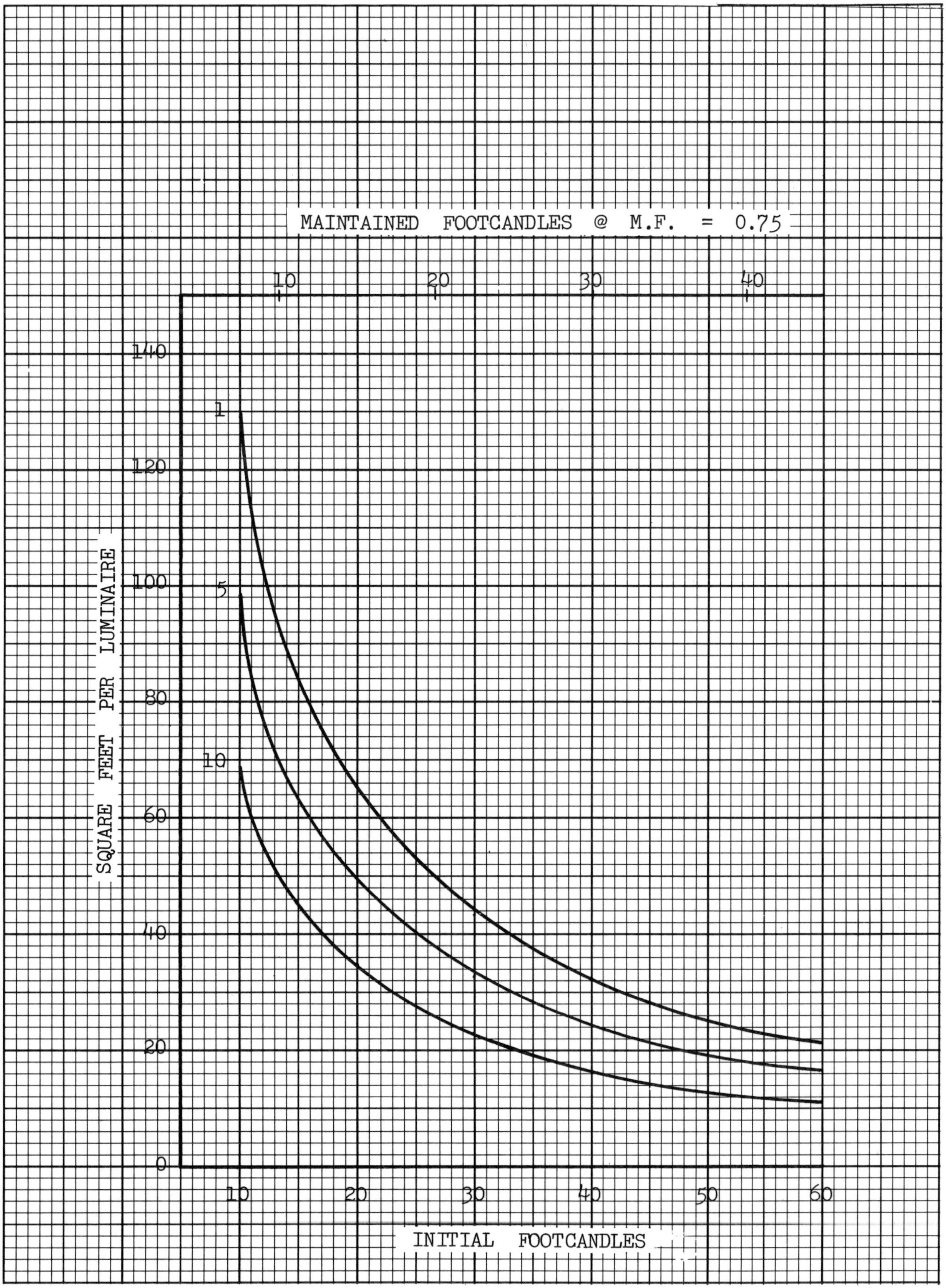

F

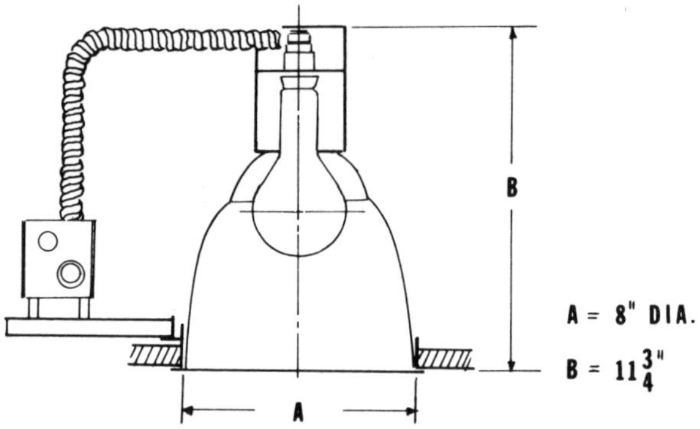

Description	8-in reflector downlight
Lamp	One 150-W A-21, 2880 lm, 750 h
Reflector	Clear specular aluminum
Spacing ratio	1.5
Maintenance factors	0.80/0.75/0.70
Input, W	150
Conversion factors	Unit with one 200-W A-23 = 1.4
Cost details per luminaire	Contractor's price = $42
	Installed cost = 68

The installed cost includes published contractor's book price for the luminaire, lamp as shown, required fastening devices, and the labor required for recess mounting and connection of the luminaire. No separate outlet is required since the unit is supplied with an attached outlet ready to accept supply leads.

This line of luminaires provides widespread distribution with very low brightness. Low-cost, high-lumen-output general-service lamps combine with precise, full reflectors, resulting in higher overall efficiency than most other downlights.

RECESSED INCANDESCENT – 8" OPEN REFLECTOR DOWNLIGHT (A-LAMP)

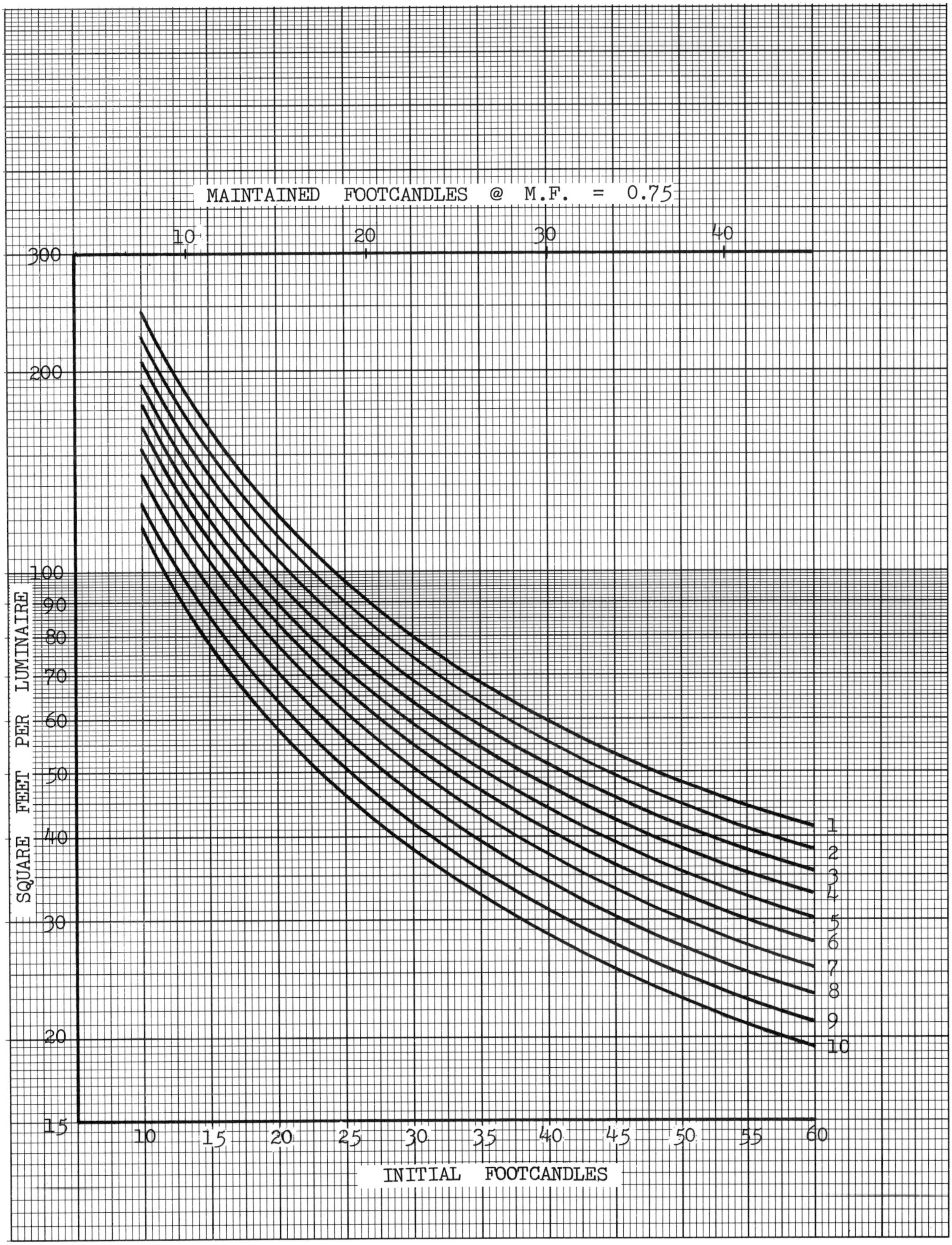

F

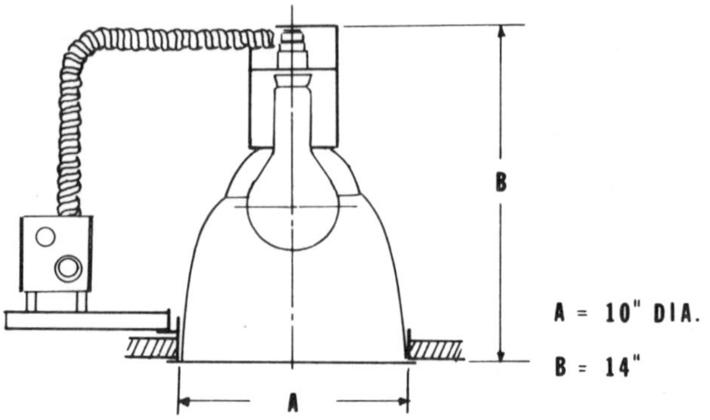

Description	10-in reflector downlight
Lamp	One 300-W PS-25, 6360 lm, 750 h
Reflector	Clear specular aluminum
Spacing ratio	1.3
Maintenance factors	0.80/0.75/0.70
Input, W	300
Conversion factors	Unit with one 300-W PS-30 = 0.8
Cost details per luminaire	Contractor's price = $53
	Installed cost = $83.75

The installed cost includes published contractor's book price for the luminaire, lamp as shown, required fastening devices, and the labor required for recess mounting and connection of the luminaire. No separate outlet is required since the unit is supplied with an attached outlet ready to accept supply leads.

This line of luminaires provides widespread distribution with very low brightness. Low-cost, high-lumen-output general-service lamps combine with precise, full reflectors, resulting in higher overall efficiency than most other downlights.

RECESSED INCANDESCENT–10" OPEN REFLECTOR DOWNLIGHT (A-LAMP)

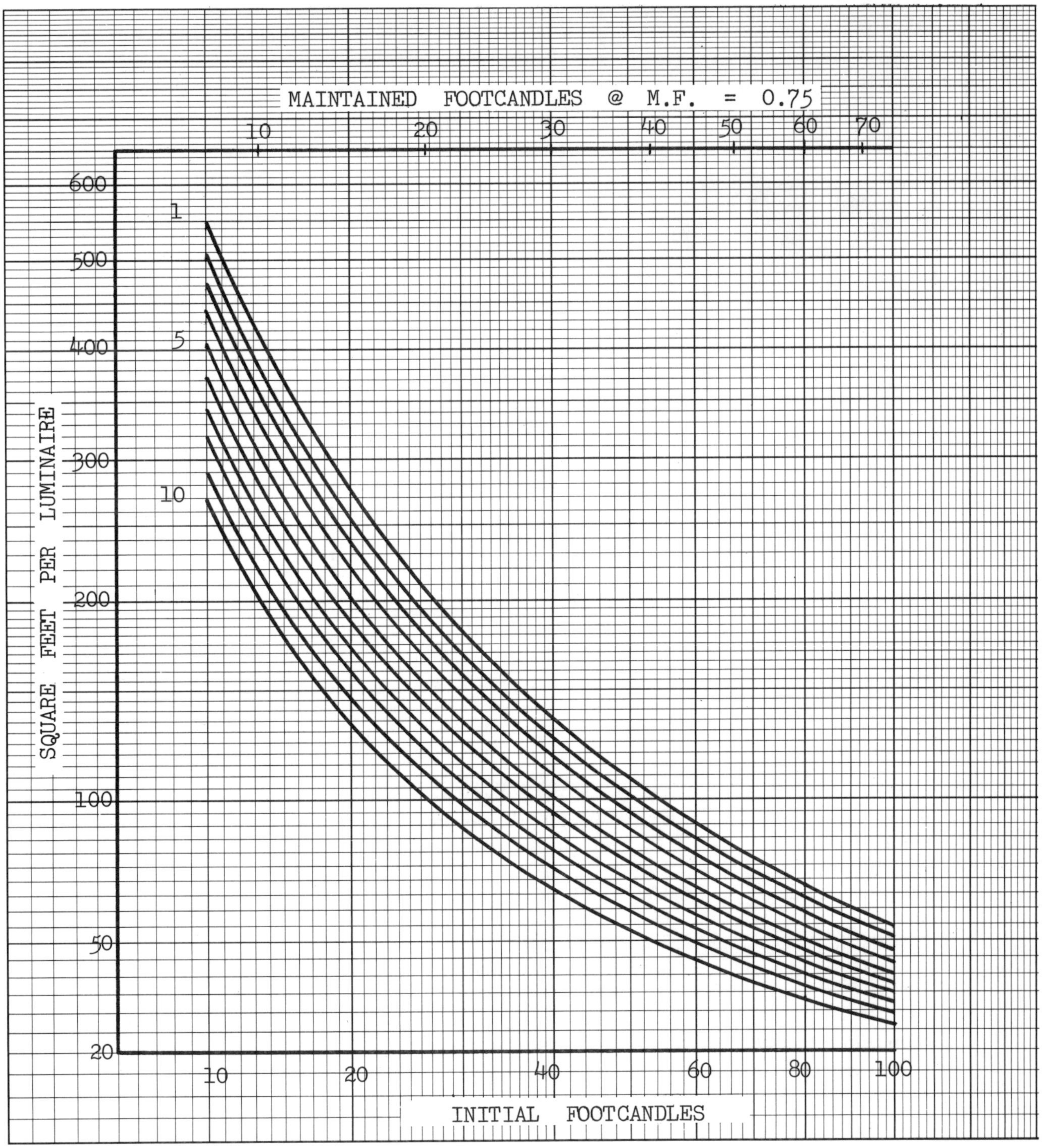

F

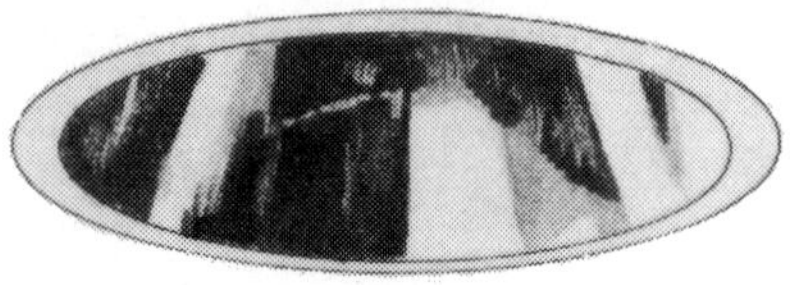

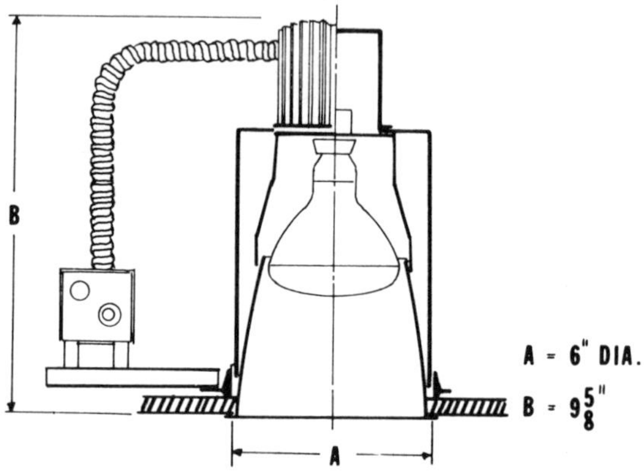

Description	6-in open-reflector downlight
Lamp	One 75-W R-30 (FL), 860 lm, 2000 h
Reflector	Clear specular aluminum
Spacing ratio	0.7
Maintenance factors	0.80/0.75/0.70
Input, W	75
Cost details per luminaire	Contractor's price = $29
	Installed cost = $52.25

F-8

The installed cost includes published contractor's book price for the luminaire, lamp as shown, required fastening devices, and the labor required for recess mounting and connection of the luminaire. No separate outlet is required since the unit is supplied with an attached outlet ready to accept supply leads.

Open-reflector downlights are compact and efficient and provide concentrated distribution with very low brightness. This luminaire is suitable for rooms with ceiling heights of 8 to 14 ft.

RECESSED INCANDESCENT – 6" OPEN REFLECTOR DOWNLIGHT

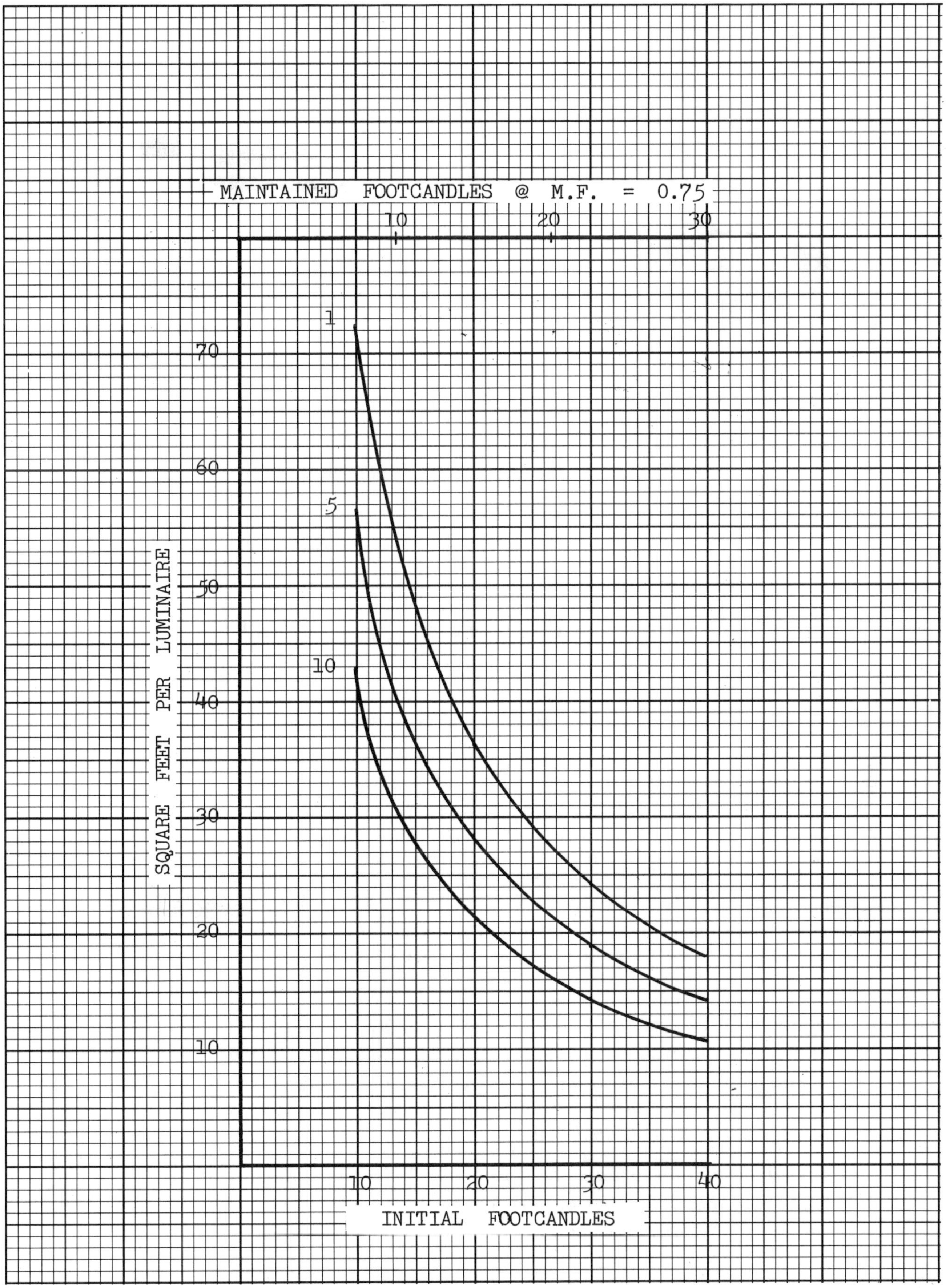

F

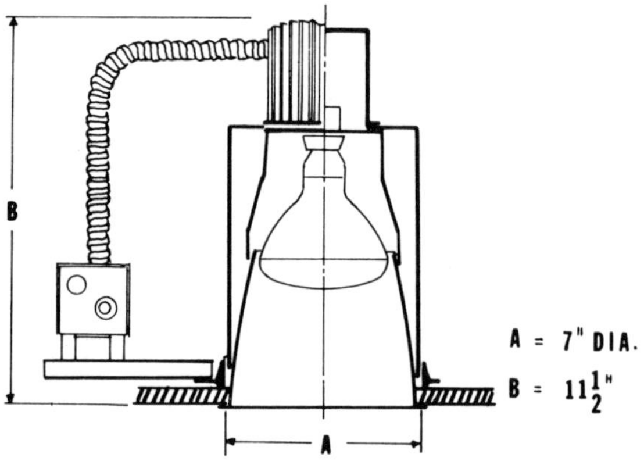

Description	7-in open-reflector downlight
Lamp	One 150-W R-40 (FL), 1900 lm, 2000 h
Reflector	Clear specular aluminum
Spacing ratio	0.5
Maintenance factors	0.80/0.75/0.70
Input, W	150
Cost details per luminaire	Contractor's price = \$34 Installed cost = \$59.50

F-10

The installed cost includes published contractor's book price for the luminaire, lamp as shown, required fastening devices, and the labor required for recess mounting and connection of the luminaire. No separate outlet is required since the unit is supplied with an attached outlet ready to accept supply leads.

Open-reflector downlights are compact and efficient and provide concentrated distribution with very low brightness. This luminaire is suitable for rooms with ceiling heights of 10 to 20 ft.

RECESSED INCANDESCENT–7" OPEN REFLECTOR DOWNLIGHT

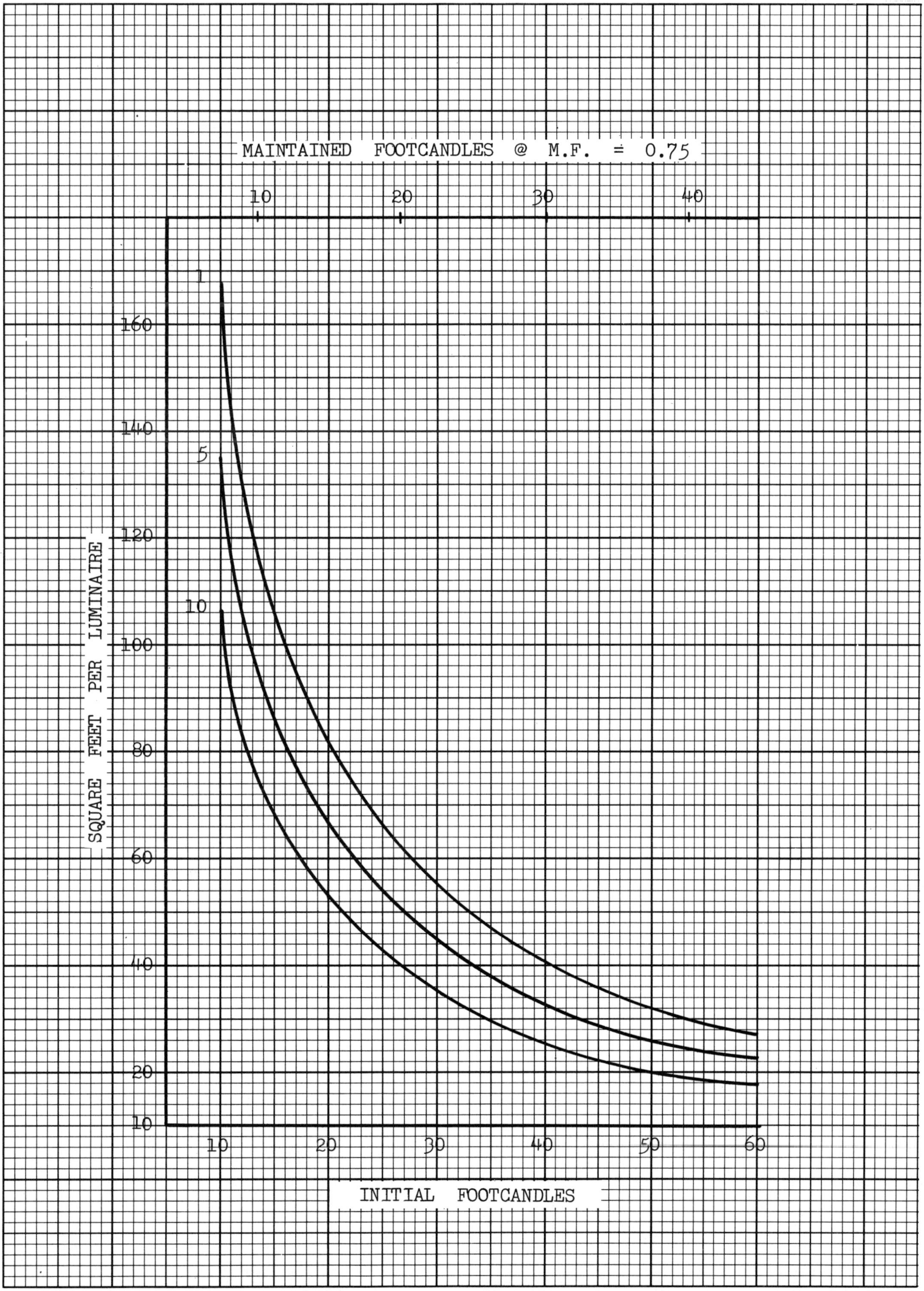

F

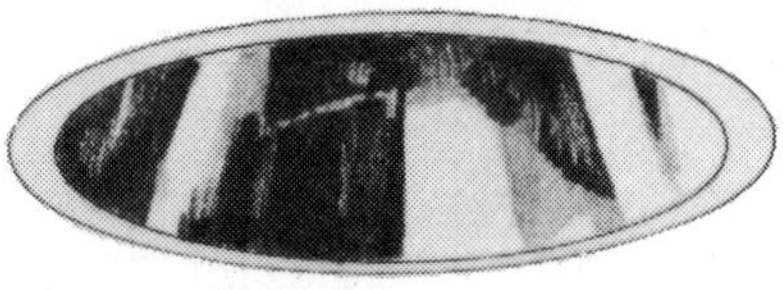

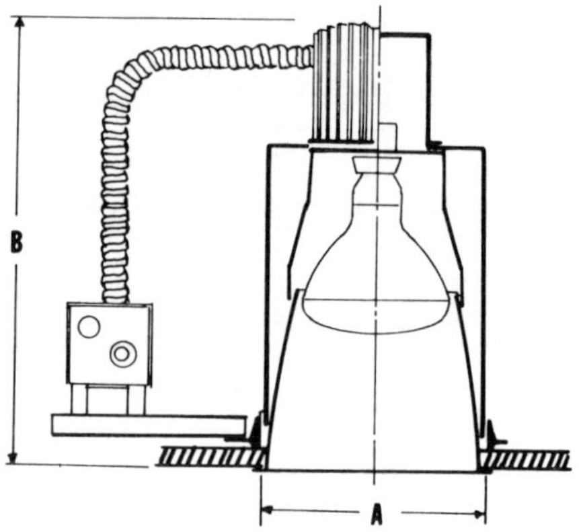

Description	9-in open-reflector downlight
Lamp	One 500-W R-40 (FL), 6500 lm, 2000 h
Reflector	Clear specular aluminum
Spacing ratio	0.4
Maintenance factors	0.80/0.75/0.70
Input, W	500
Conversion factor	Unit with one 300-W R-40 (FL) = 0.55
Cost details per luminaire	Contractor's price = $54 Installed cost = $93.35

The installed cost includes published contractor's book price for the luminaire, lamp as shown, required fastening devices, and the labor required for recess mounting and connection of the luminaire. No separate outlet is required since the unit is supplied with an attached outlet ready to accept supply leads.

Open-reflector downlights are compact and efficient and provide concentrated distribution with very low brightness. These luminaires are suitable for rooms with ceiling heights of 16 to 30 ft.

RECESSED INCANDESCENT–9″ OPEN REFLECTOR DOWNLIGHT

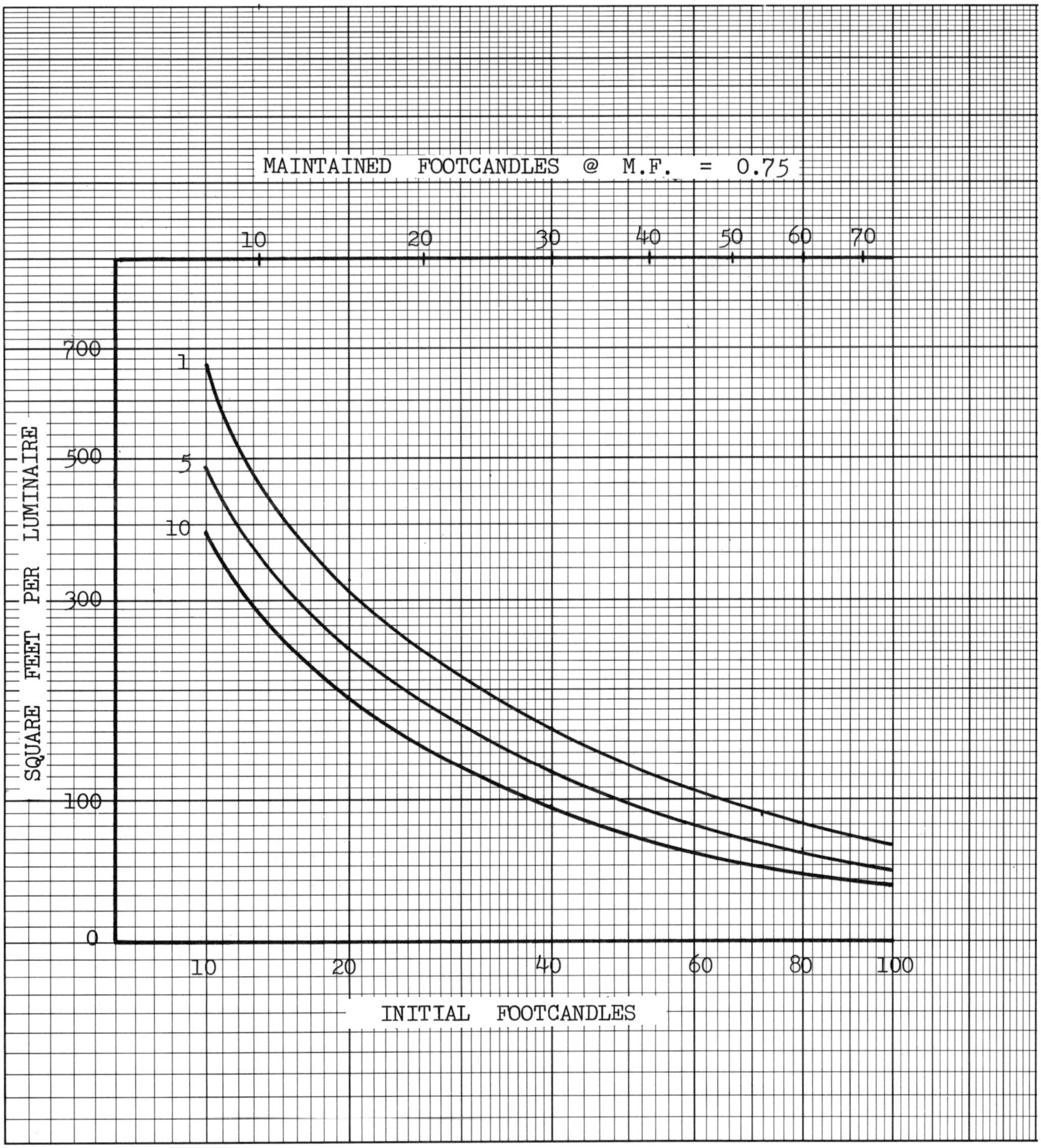

F

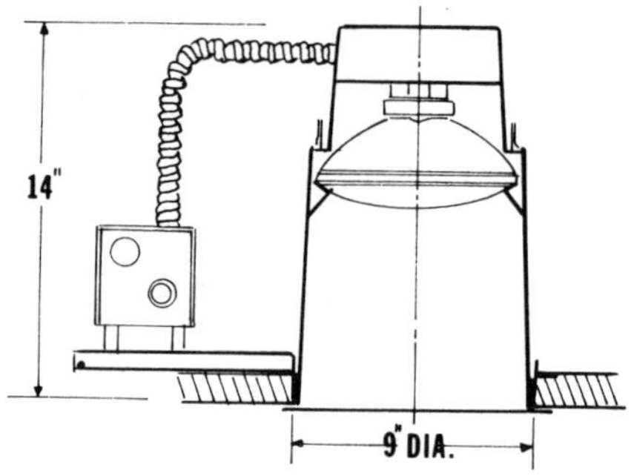

Description	9-in open-reflector downlight
Lamp	One 300-W PAR-56 (MFL), 3840 lm, 2000 h
Reflector	Clear specular aluminum
Spacing ratio	0.3
Maintenance factors	0.80/0.75/0.70
Input, W	300
Cost details per luminaire	Contractor's price = $68
	Installed cost = $110.75

The installed cost includes published contractor's book price for the luminaire, lamp as shown, required fastening devices, and the labor required for recess mounting and connection of the luminaire. No separate outlet is required since the unit is supplied with an attached outlet ready to accept supply leads.

Open-reflector downlights are compact and efficient and provide concentrated distribution with very low brightness. This luminaire can be rotated to give desired orientation of elliptical beam pattern and locked in place. Suitable for rooms with ceiling heights of 18 to 30 ft.

RECESSED INCANDESCENT–9" OPEN REFLECTOR DOWNLIGHT

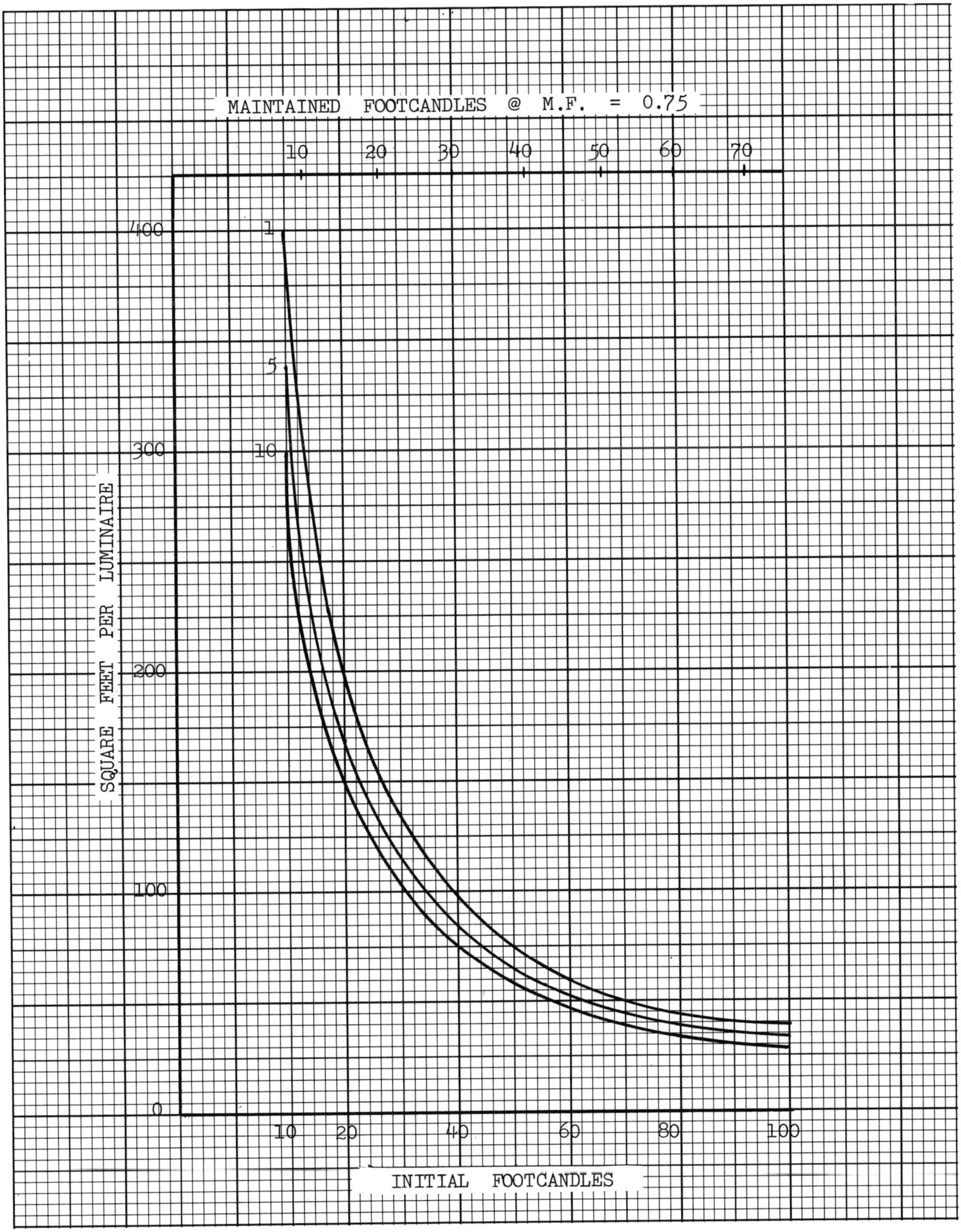

F

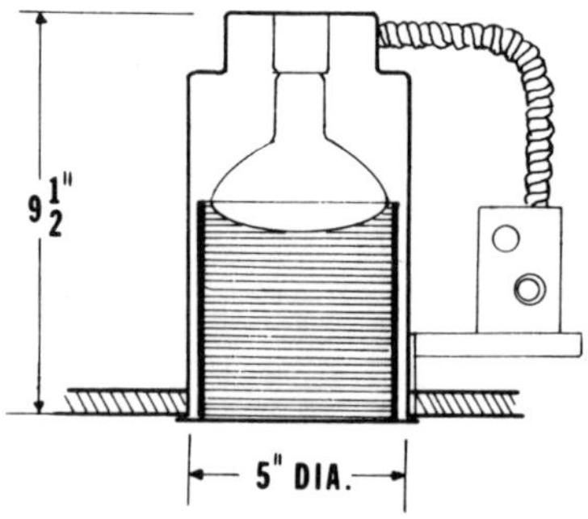

Description	5-in recessed baffle downlight
Lamp	One 75-W R-30 (SP), 860 lm, 2000 h
Reflector	Multigroove baffle
Spacing ratio	0.4
Maintenance factors	0.80/0.75/0.70
Input, W	75
Cost details per luminaire	Contractor's price = \$25 Installed cost = \$47.50

The installed cost includes published contractor's book price for the luminaire, lamp as shown, required fastening devices, and the labor required for recess mounting and connection of the luminaire. No separate outlet is required since the unit is supplied with an attached outlet ready to accept supply leads.

These ultra-low-brightness downlights provide concentrated distribution and are suitable for rooms with ceiling heights of 8 to 14 ft. Black multigrooves minimize aperture brightness.

RECESSED INCANDESCENT – 5" BAFFLE DOWNLIGHT

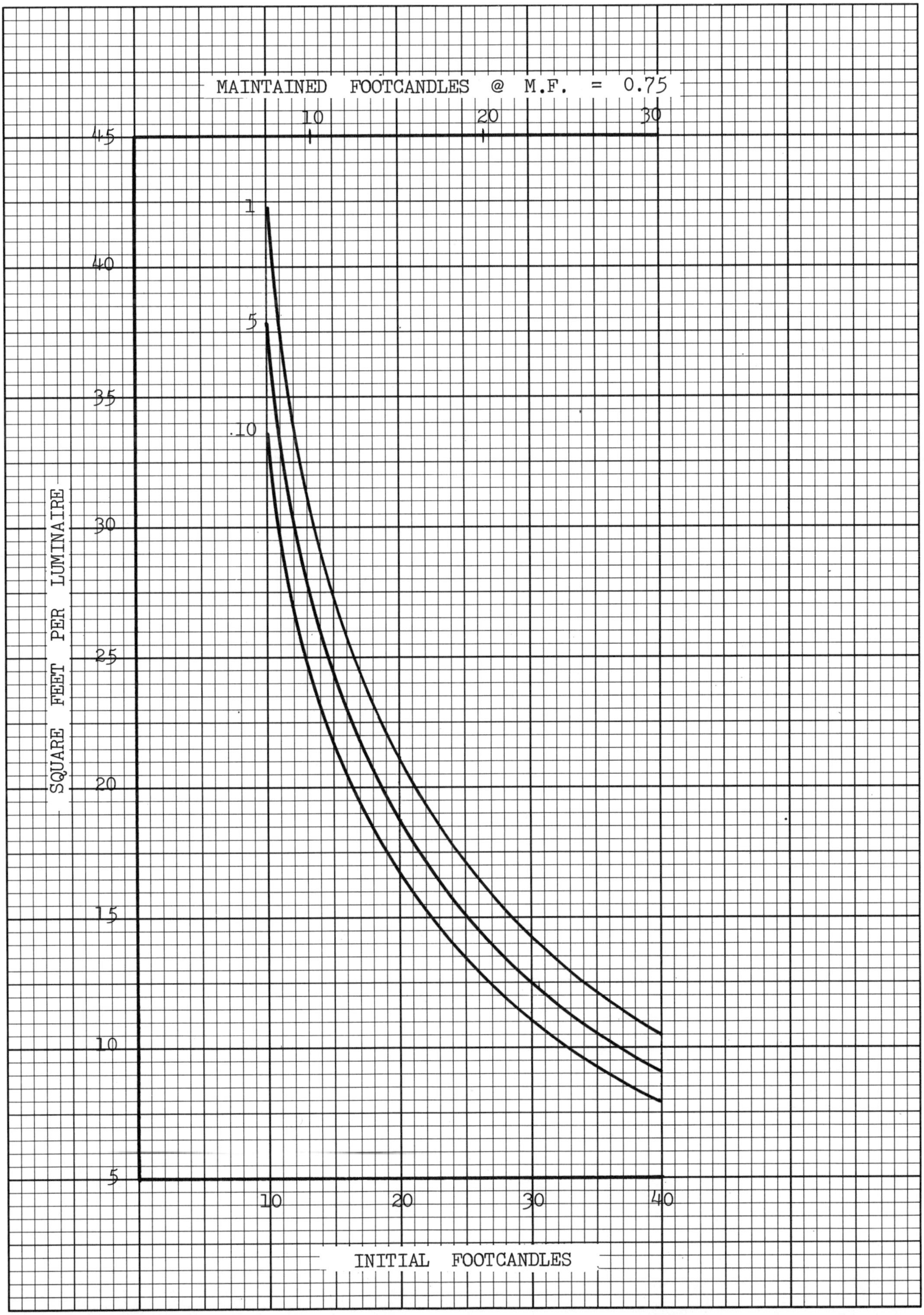

F

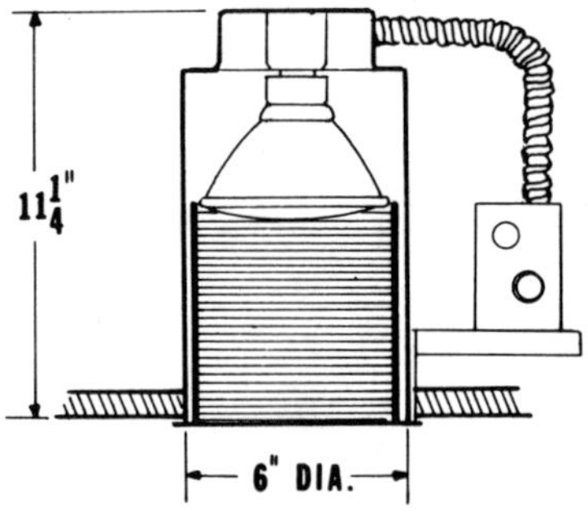

Description	6-in recessed baffle downlight
Lamp	One 150-W PAR-38 (SP), 1730 lm, 2000 h
Reflector	Multigroove baffle
Spacing ratio	0.4
Maintenance factors	0.80/0.75/0.70
Input, W	150
Cost details per luminaire	Contractor's price = $26
	Installed cost = $50.75

The installed cost includes published contractor's book price for the luminaire, lamp as shown, required fastening devices and the labor required for recess mounting and connection of the luminaire. No separate outlet is required since the unit is supplied with an attached outlet ready to accept supply leads.

These ultra-low-brightness downlights provide concentrated distribution and are suitable for rooms with ceiling heights of 10 to 20 ft. Black multigrooves minimize aperture brightness.

RECESSED INCANDESCENT—6" BAFFLE DOWNLIGHT

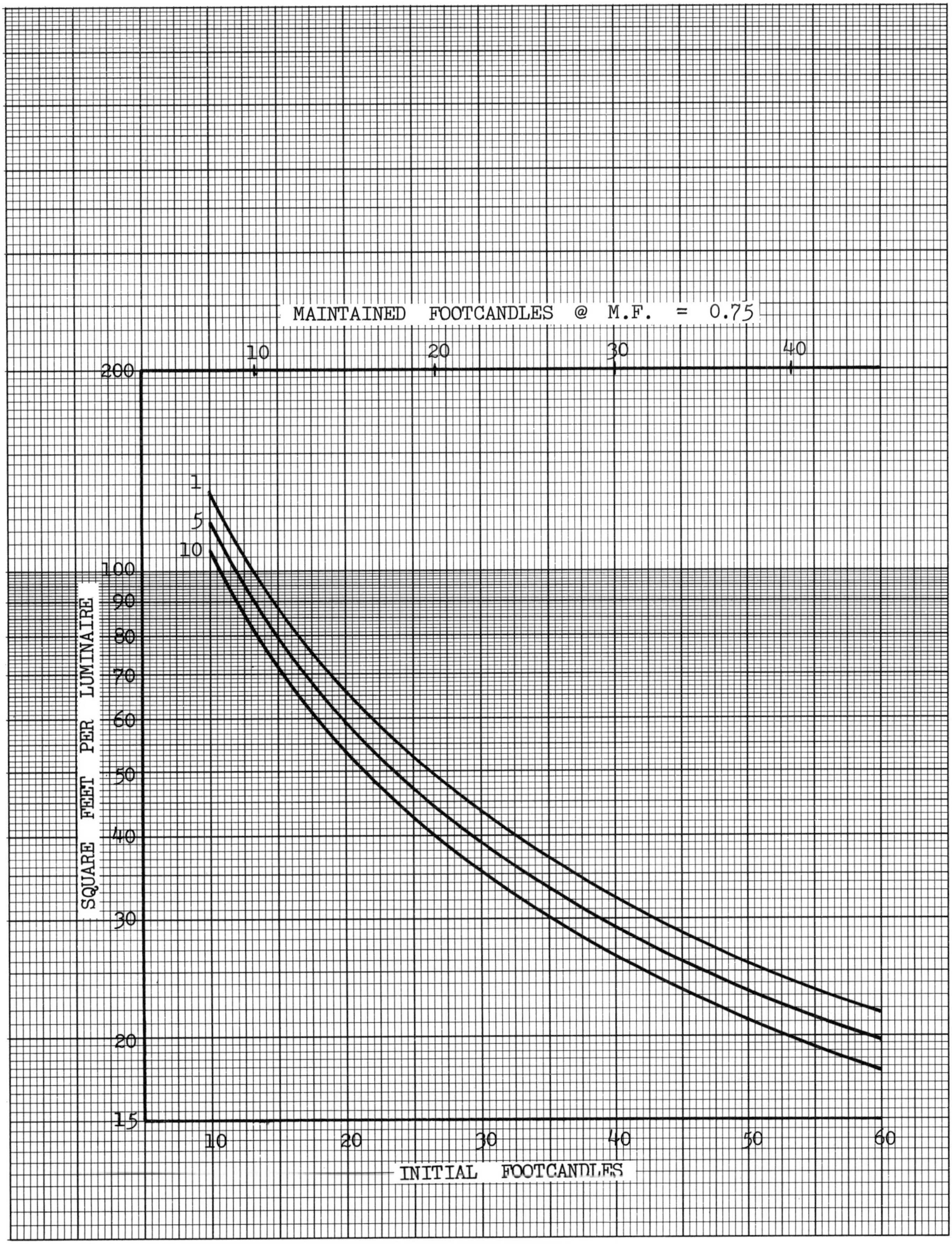

F

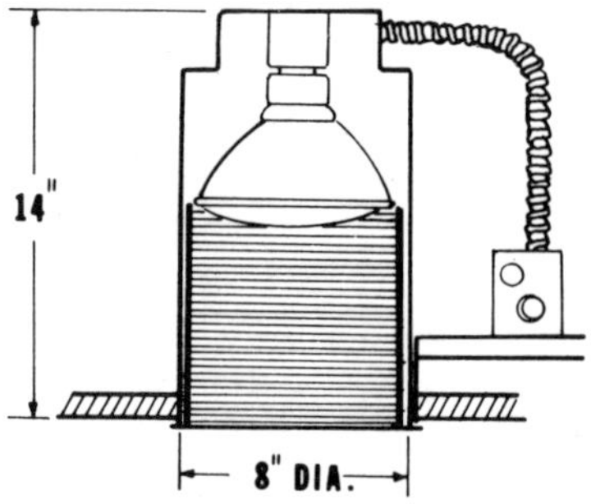

Description	8-in recessed baffle downlight
Lamp	One 300-W PAR-56 (MFL), 3840 lm, 2000 h
Reflector	Multigroove baffle
Spacing ratio	0.4
Maintenance factors	0.80/0.75/0.70
Input, W	300
Cost details per luminaire	Contractor's price = $54
	Installed cost = $93.50

F-20

The installed cost includes published contractor's book price for the luminaire, lamp as shown, required fastening devices, and the labor required for recess mounting and connection of the luminaire. No separate outlet is required since the unit is supplied with an attached outlet ready to accept supply leads.

These ultra-low-brightness downlights provide concentrated distribution and are suitable for rooms with ceiling heights of 14 to 26 ft. Black multigrooves minimize aperture brightness.

RECESSED INCANDESCENT– 8" BAFFLE DOWNLIGHT

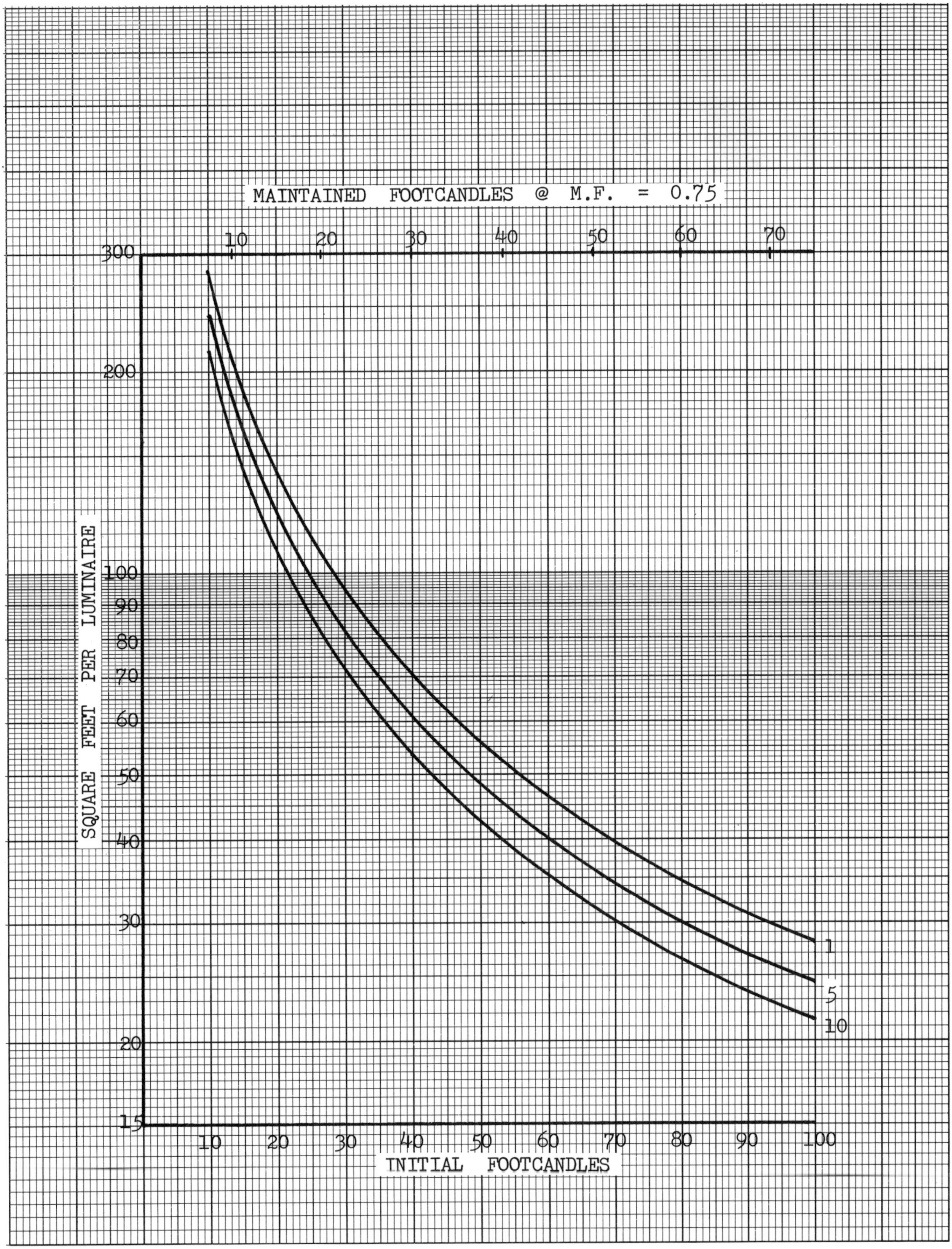

F

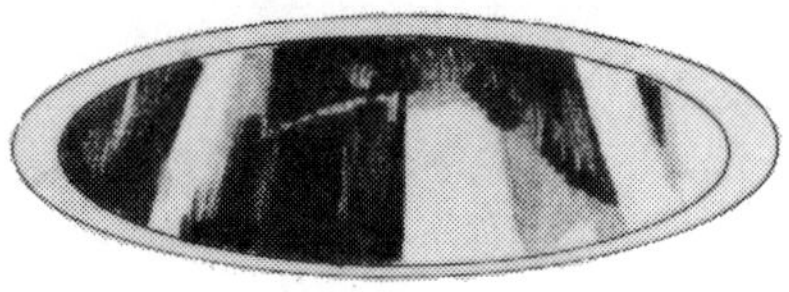

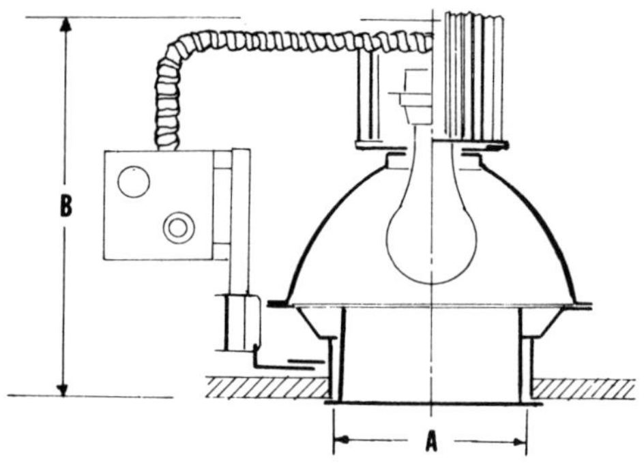

Description	6-in ellipsoidal-reflector downlight
Lamp	One 150-W A-21, 2880 lm, 750 h
Reflector	Clear specular aluminum
Spacing ratio	1.1
Maintenance factor	0.80/0.75/0.70
Input, W	150
Cost details per luminaire	Contractor's price = $43 Installed cost = $69.25

The installed cost includes published contractor's book price for the luminaire, lamp as shown, required fastening devices and the labor required for recess mounting and connection of the luminaire. No separate outlet is required since the unit is supplied with an attached outlet ready to accept supply leads.

These low-brightness downlights are suitable for ceiling heights of 8 to 14 ft.

RECESSED INCANDESCENT – 6" ELLIPSOIDAL REFLECTOR DOWNLIGHT

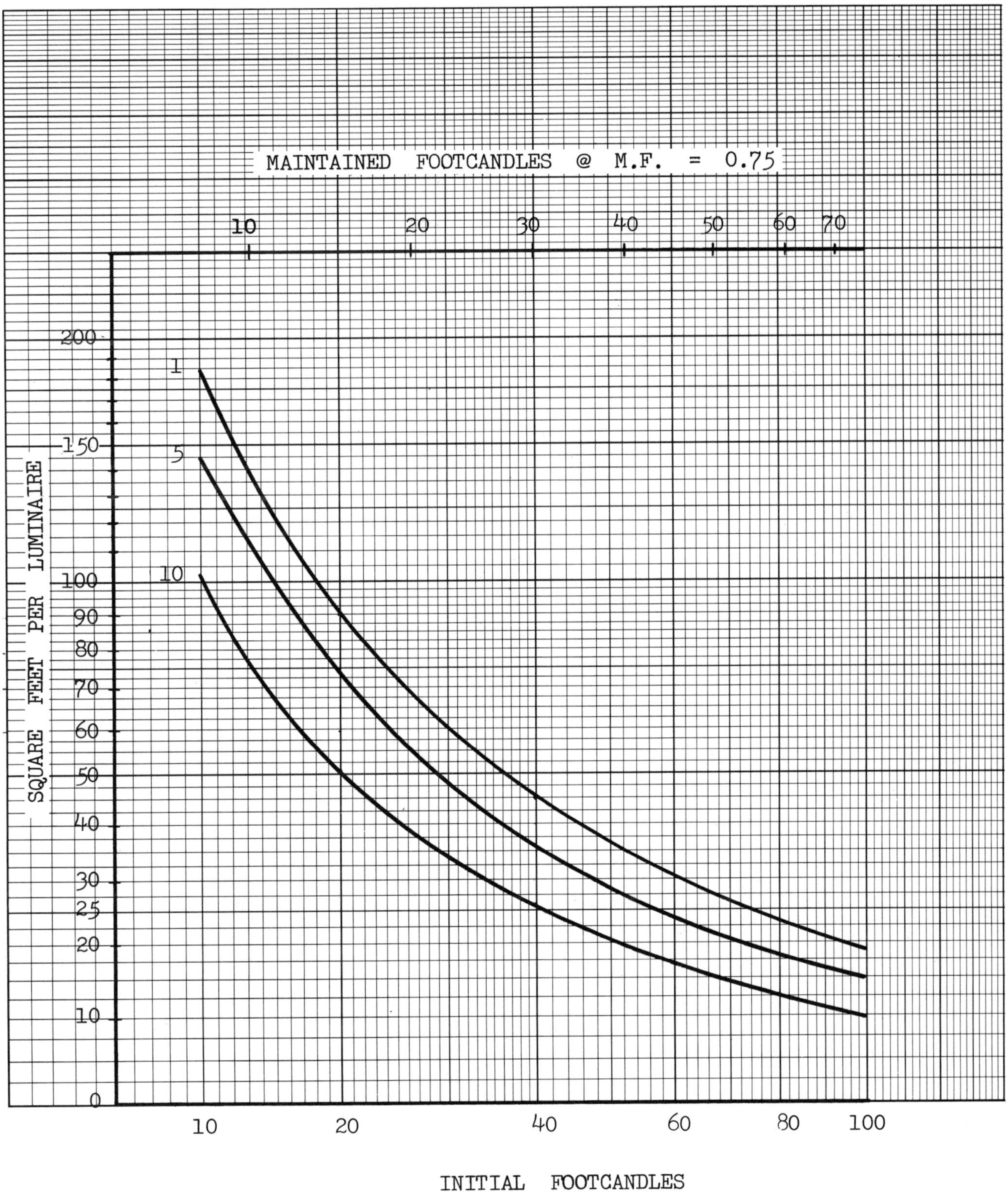

F

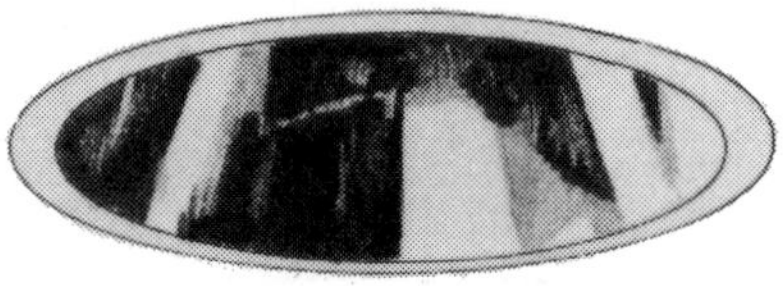

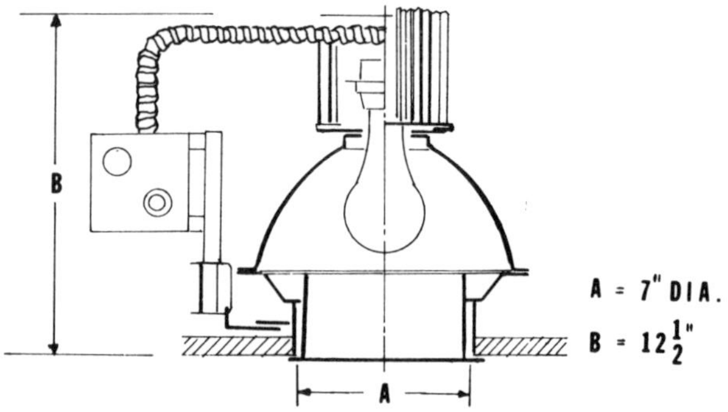

Description	7-in ellipsoidal-reflector downlight
Lamp	One 200-W A-23, 4010 lm,
Reflector	Clear specular aluminum
Spacing ratio	1.1
Maintenance factors	0.80/0.75/0.70
Input, W	200
Cost details per luminaire	Contractor's price = $54 Installed cost = $83.50

F-24

The installed cost includes published contractor's book price for the luminaire, lamp as shown, required fastening devices, and the labor required for recess mounting and connection of the luminaire. No separate outlet is required since the unit is supplied with an attached outlet ready to accept supply leads.

These low-brightness downlights are suitable for ceiling heights of 8 to 16 ft.

RECESSED INCANDESCENT– 7" ELLIPSOIDAL REFLECTOR DOWNLIGHT

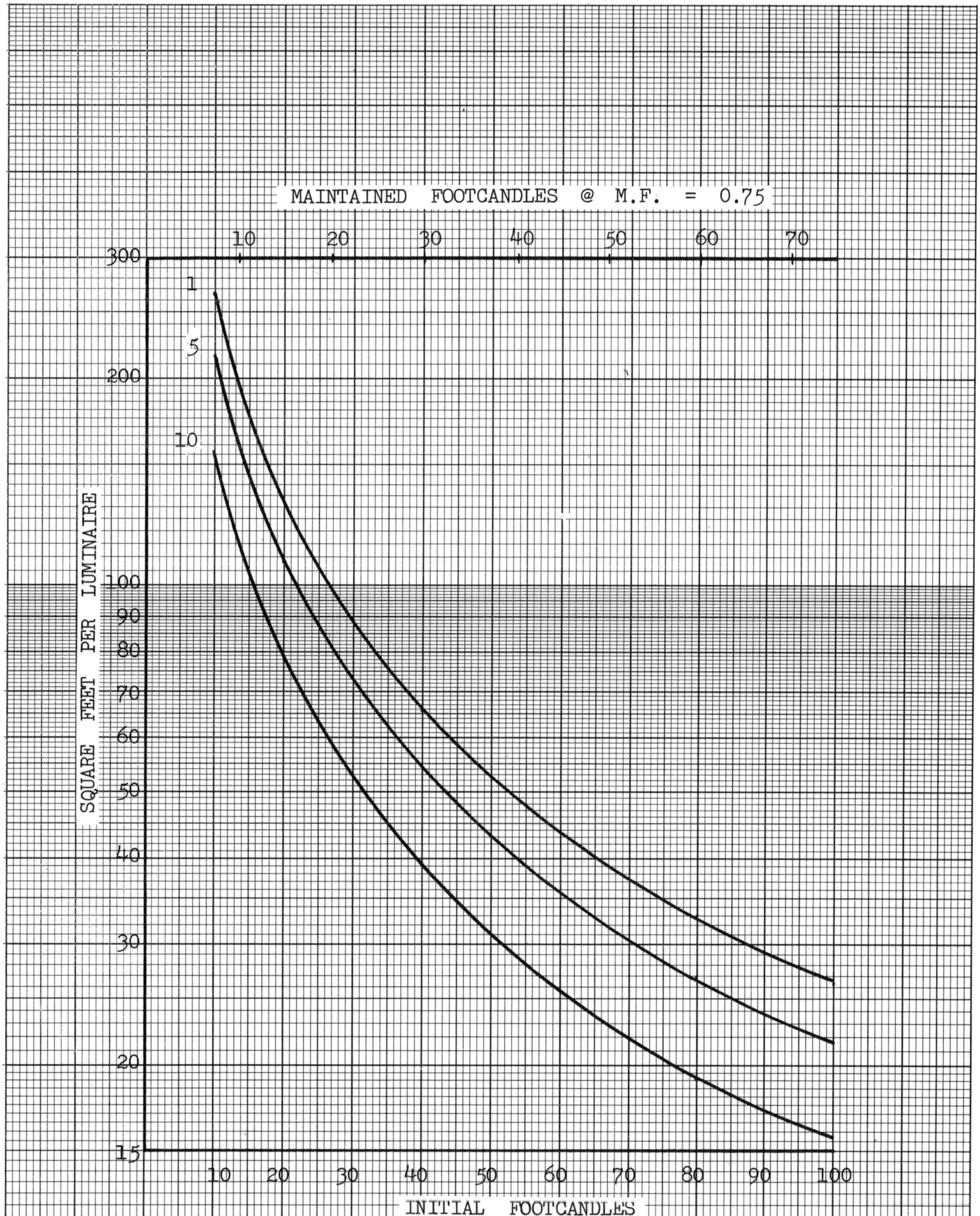

F

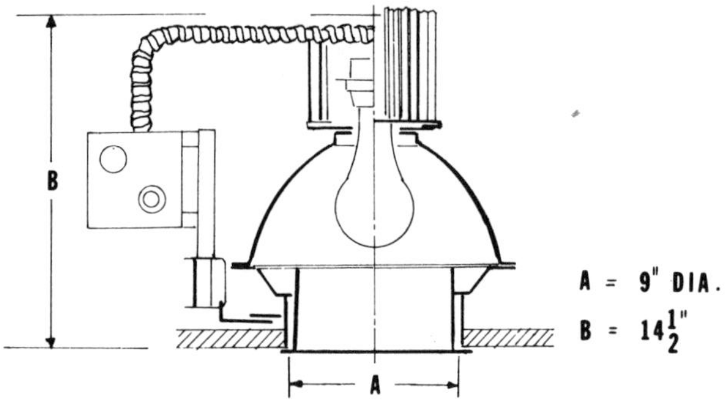

Description	9-in ellipsoidal-reflector downlight
Lamp	One 300-W PS-25, 6360 lm,
Reflector	Clear specular aluminum
Spacing ratio	1.3
Maintenance factors	0.80/0.75/0.70
Input, W	300
Cost details per luminaire	Contractor's price = $61
	Installed cost = $93.50

The installed cost includes published contractor's book price for the luminaire, lamp as shown, required fastening devices, and the labor required for recess mounting and connection of the luminaire. No separate outlet is required since the unit is supplied with an attached outlet ready to accept supply leads.

These low-brightness downlights are suitable for ceiling heights of 10 to 20 ft.

RECESSED INCANDESCENT—9" ELLIPSOIDAL REFLECTOR DOWNLIGHT

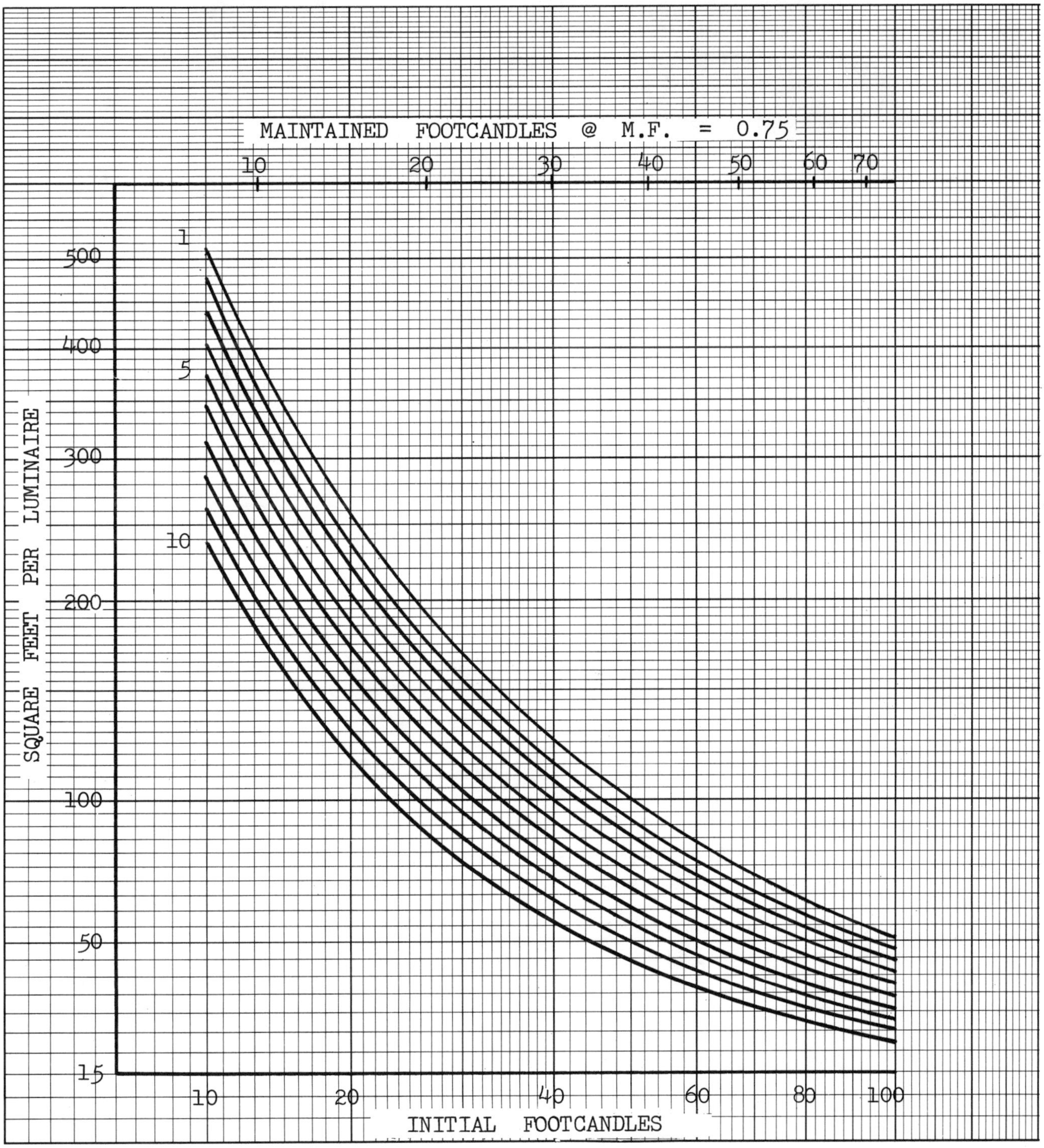

F

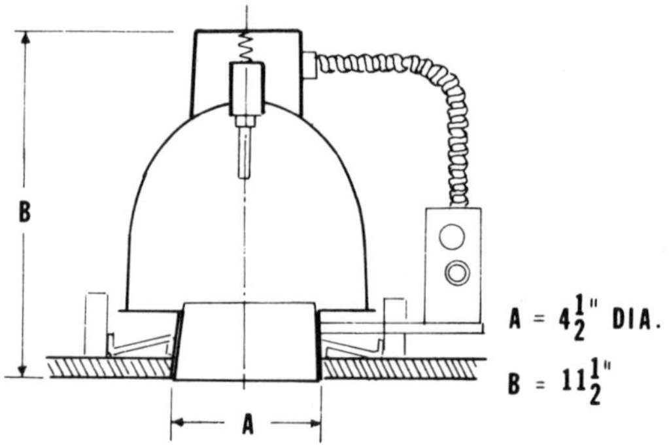

Description	4½-in ellipsoidal-reflector downlight
Lamp	One 250-W T-4 (tungsten-halogen), 4800 lm, 2000 h
Reflector	Clear specular aluminum
Spacing ratio	1.4 (socket in low position)
	0.4 (socket in high position)
Maintenance factors	0.80/0.75/0.70
Input, W	250
Cost details per luminaire	Contractor's price = $70
	Installed cost = $127.75

The installed cost includes published contractor's book price for the luminaire, lamp as shown, required fastening devices, and the labor required for recess mounting and connection of the luminaire. No separate outlet is required since the unit is supplied with an attached outlet ready to accept supply leads.

These low-brightness downlights for general illumination are for medium- to high-ceiling areas. The Mini Can base socket is recessed within an adjustable aluminum sleeve which is preset to provide wide distribution and can be reset in the field to provide narrow distribution.

Curves shown on page F–29 are based on the socket in low position. See page F–31 for socket in high position.

The reference luminaire is as manufactured by Lightolier.

This information was based on test 12323/12425, prepared by ITL for Lightolier.

4½" ELLIPSOIDAL REFLECTOR DOWNLIGHT (TUNGSTEN-HALOGEN)

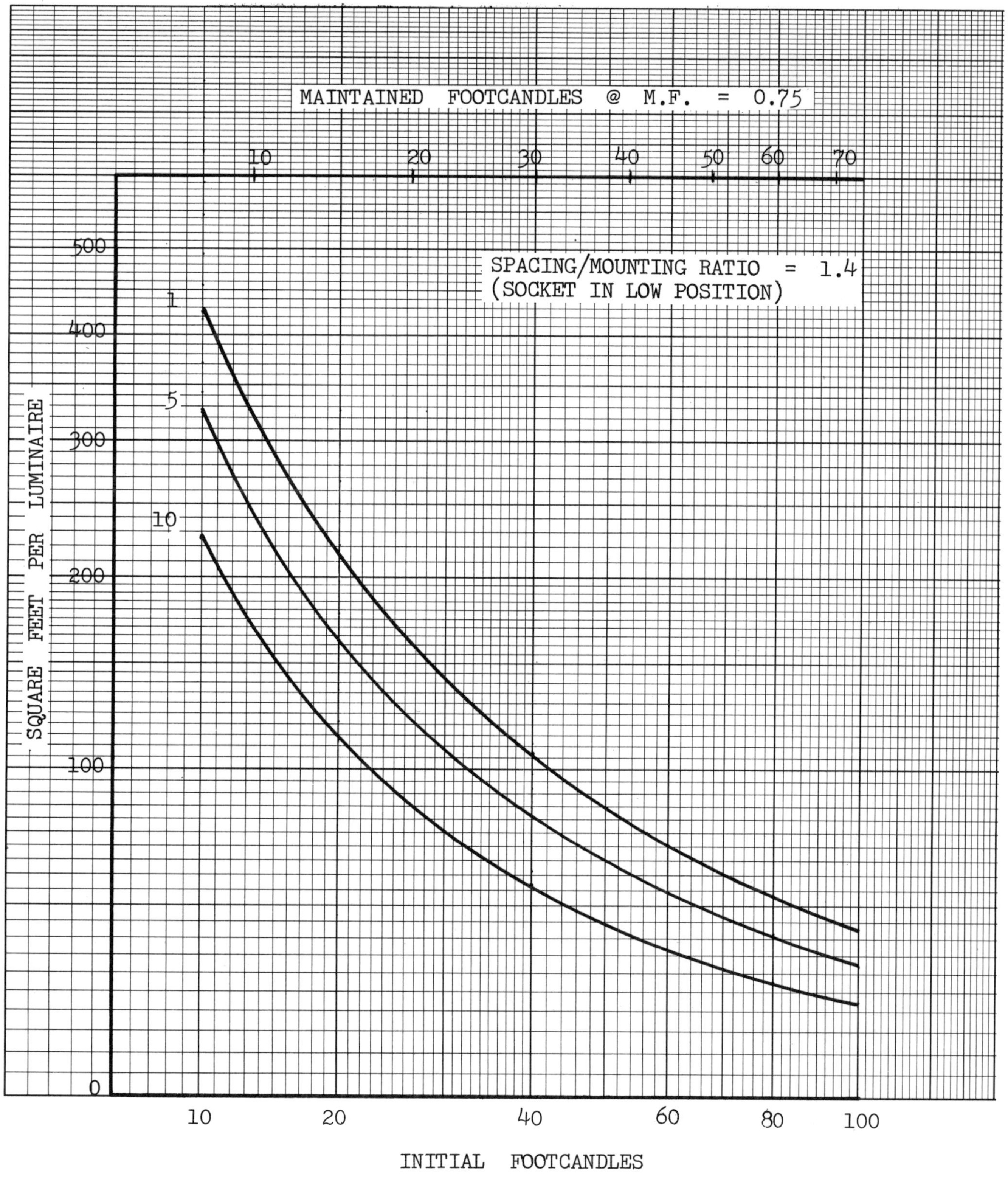

F

4½-in Ellipsoidal-Reflector Downlight with a 250-W T-4 Tungsten-Halogen Lamp (continued from page F-28)

Curves shown on page F-31 are based on socket in high position. With this socket position the spacing-to-mounting ratio is 0.4. For other details, see page F-28.

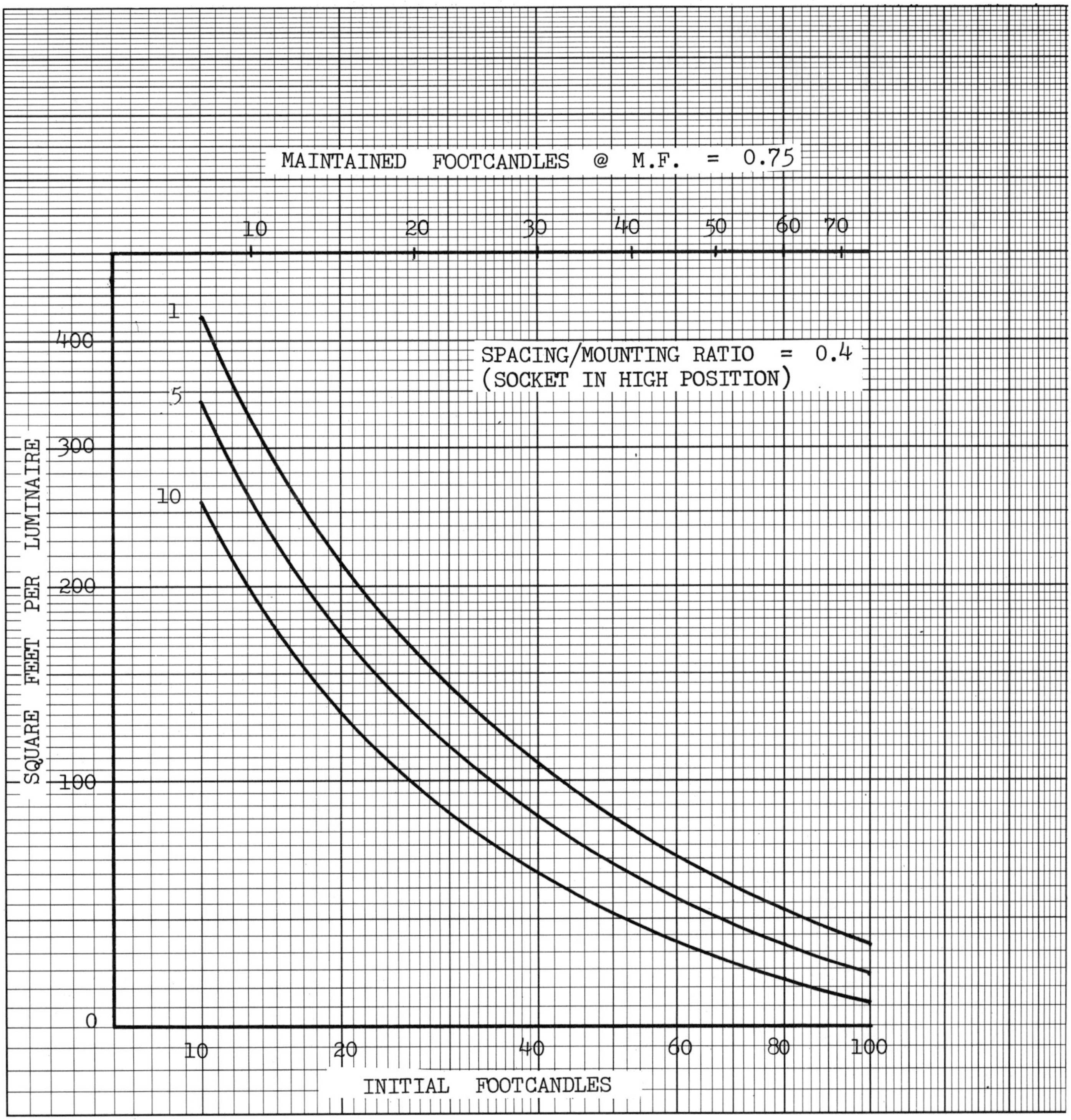
MAINTAINED FOOTCANDLES @ M.F. = 0.75
10
20
30
40
50
60
70
SPACING/MOUNTING RATIO = 0.4
(SOCKET IN HIGH POSITION)
1
5
10
400
300
200
100
0
SQUARE FEET PER LUMINAIRE
10
20
40
60
80
100
INITIAL FOOTCANDLES

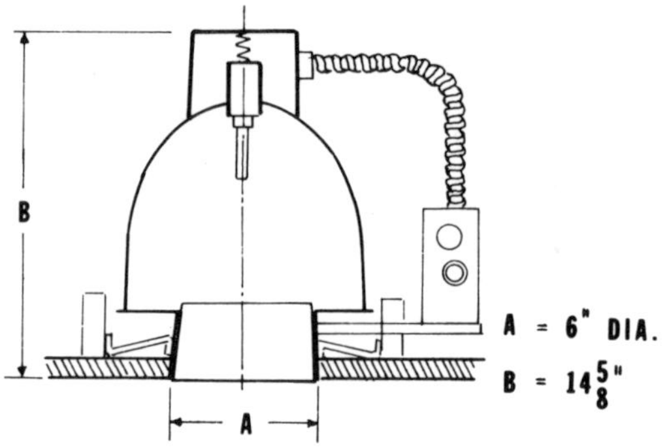

Description	6-in ellipsoidal-reflector downlight
Lamp	One 500-W T-4 (tungsten-halogen), 9500 lm, 2000 h
Reflector	Clear specular aluminum
Spacing ratio	1.0 (socket in low position) 0.3 (socket in high position)
Maintenance factors	0.80/0.75/0.70
Input, W	500
Cost details per luminaire:	Contractor's price = \$80 Installed cost = \$142.50

The installed cost includes published contractor's book price for the luminaire, lamp as shown, required fastening devices, and the labor required for recess mounting and connection of the luminaire. No separate outlet is required since the unit is supplied with an attached outlet ready to accept supply leads.

These low-brightness downlights for general illumination are for medium- to high-ceiling areas. The Mini Can base socket is recessed within an adjustable aluminum sleeve which is preset to provide wide distribution and can be reset in the field to provide narrow distribution.

Curves shown on page F–33 are based on the socket in low position. See page F–35 for socket in high position.

The reference luminaire is as manufactured by Lightolier.

This information was based on test 12327/12328, prepared by ITL for Lightolier.

6" ELLIPSOIDAL REFLECTOR DOWNLIGHT (TUNGSTEN-HALOGEN)

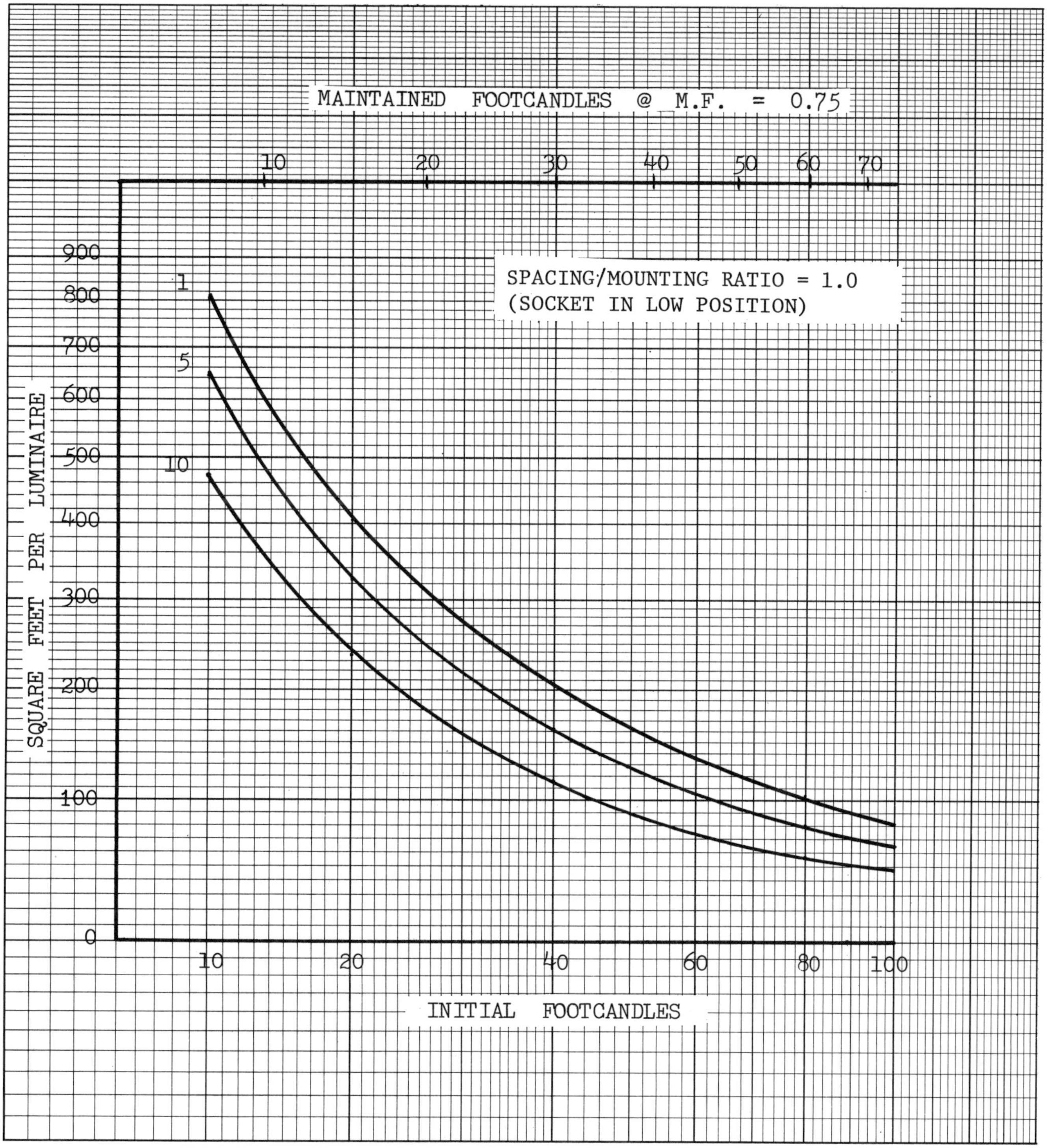

F

6-in Ellipsoidal-Reflector Downlight with a 500 W T-4 Tungsten-Halogen Lamp (continued from page F–32)

Curves shown on page F–35 are based on socket in high position. With this socket position, the spacing-to-mounting ratio is 0.3. For other details, see page F–32.

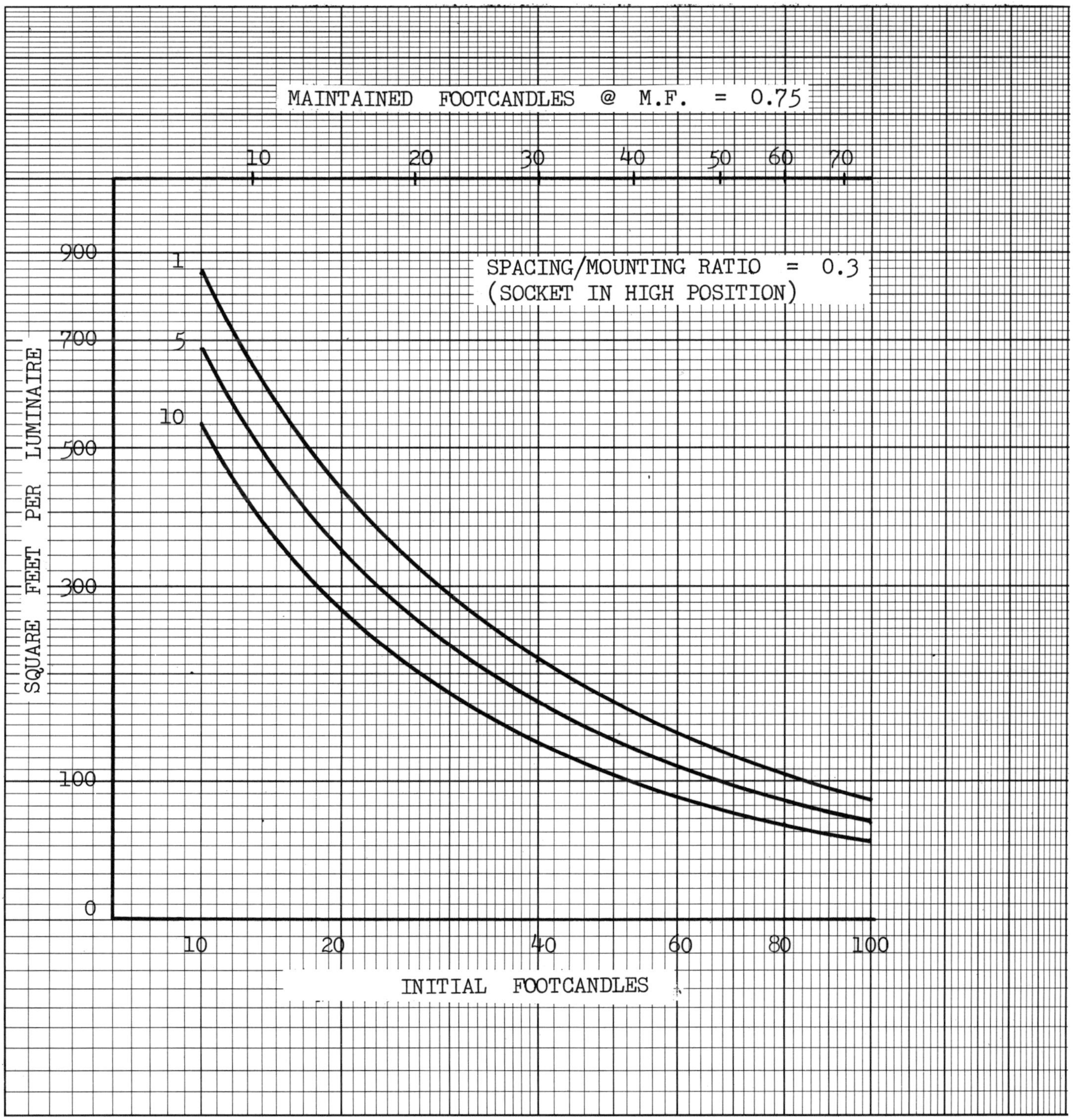
MAINTAINED FOOTCANDLES @ M.F. = 0.75
10
20
30
40
50
60
70
SPACING/MOUNTING RATIO = 0.3
(SOCKET IN HIGH POSITION)
1
5
10
900
700
500
300
100
0
SQUARE FEET PER LUMINAIRE
10
20
40
60
80
100
INITIAL FOOTCANDLES

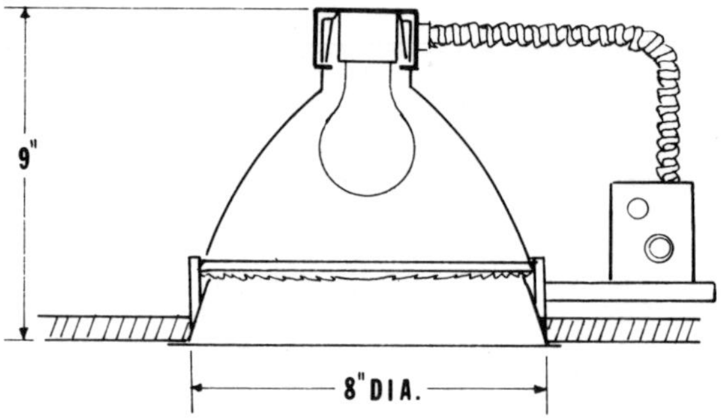

Description	8-in regressed lens (vertical lamp)
Lamp	One 100-W A-19, 1750 lm, 750 h
Lens	Fresnel lens
Spacing ratio	1.3
Maintenance factors	0.75/0.70/0.65
Input, W	100
Conversion factors	Unit with one 150-W A-21 = 1.4
Cost details per luminaire	Contractor's price = $13
	Installed cost = $30.75

The installed cost includes published contractor's book price for the luminaire, lamp as shown, required fastening devices, and the labor required for recess mounting and connection of the luminaire. No separate outlet is required since the unit is supplied with an attached outlet ready to accept supply leads.

Luminaires of this family with a Fresnel lens diffuse the light, filtering out the high-angle glare component. The luminaire selected here is a wide-distribution type.

RECESSED INCANDESCENT—8" REGRESSED ROUND LENS (VERTICAL LAMP)

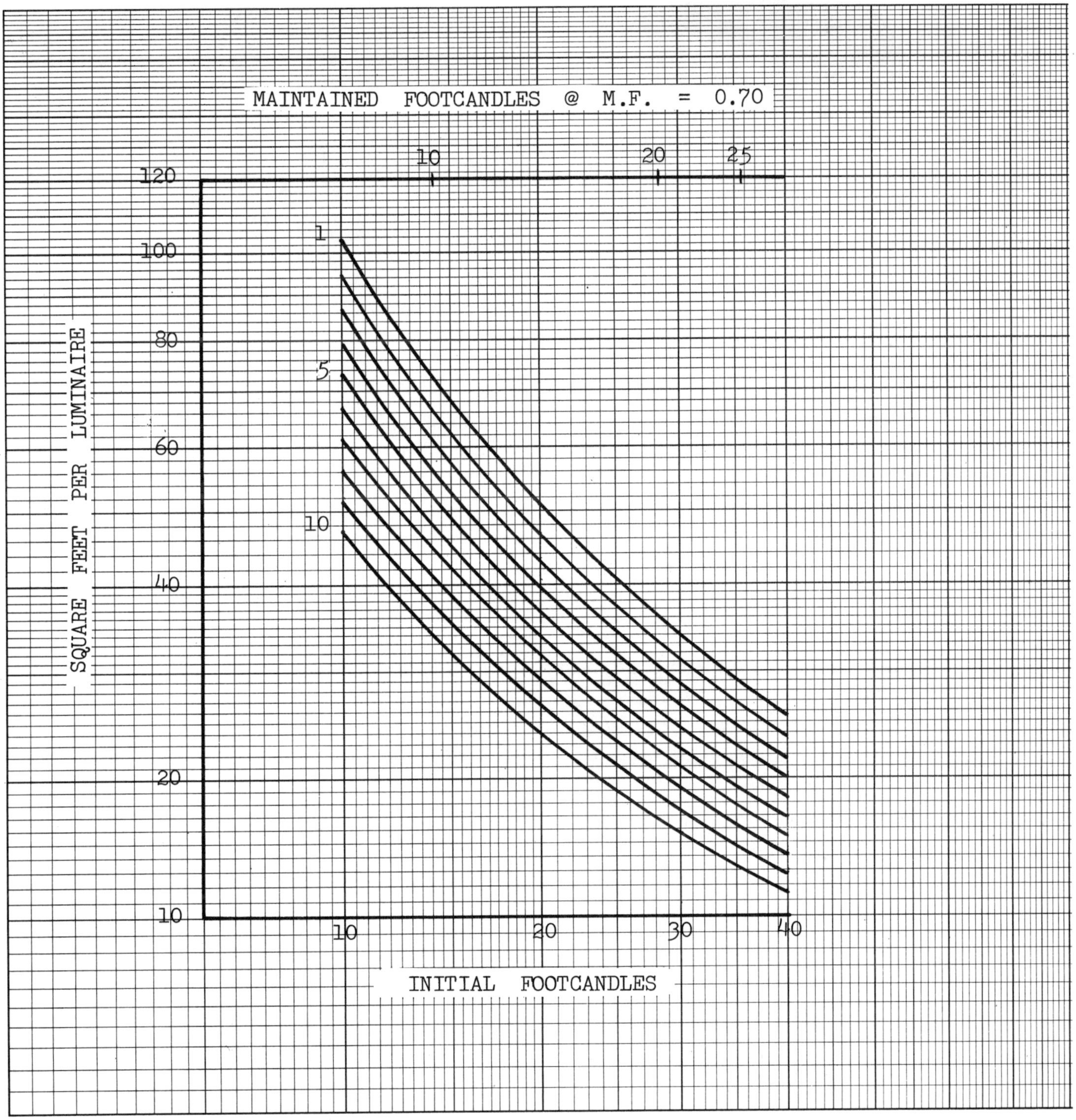

F

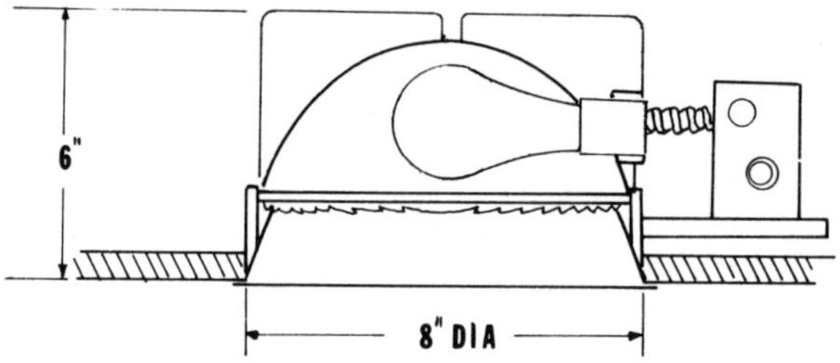

Description	8-in regressed lens (horizontal lamp)
Lamp	One 100-W A-19, 1750 lm, 750 h
Lens	Fresnel lens
Spacing ratio	1.1
Maintenance factors	0.75/0.70/0.65
Input, W	100
Cost details per luminaire	Contractor's price = $16
	Installed cost = $34.50

The installed cost includes published contractor's book price for the luminaire, lamp as shown, required fastening devices, and the labor required for recess mounting and connection of the luminaire. No separate outlet is required since the unit is supplied with an attached outlet ready to accept supply leads.

Luminaires of this family with a Fresnel lens diffuse the light, filtering out the high-angle glare component. Because of the shallow height (horizontal lamp) these luminaires are used where the recessed depth is limited.

RECESSED INCANDESCENT–8" REGRESSED ROUND LENS (HORIZONTAL LAMP)

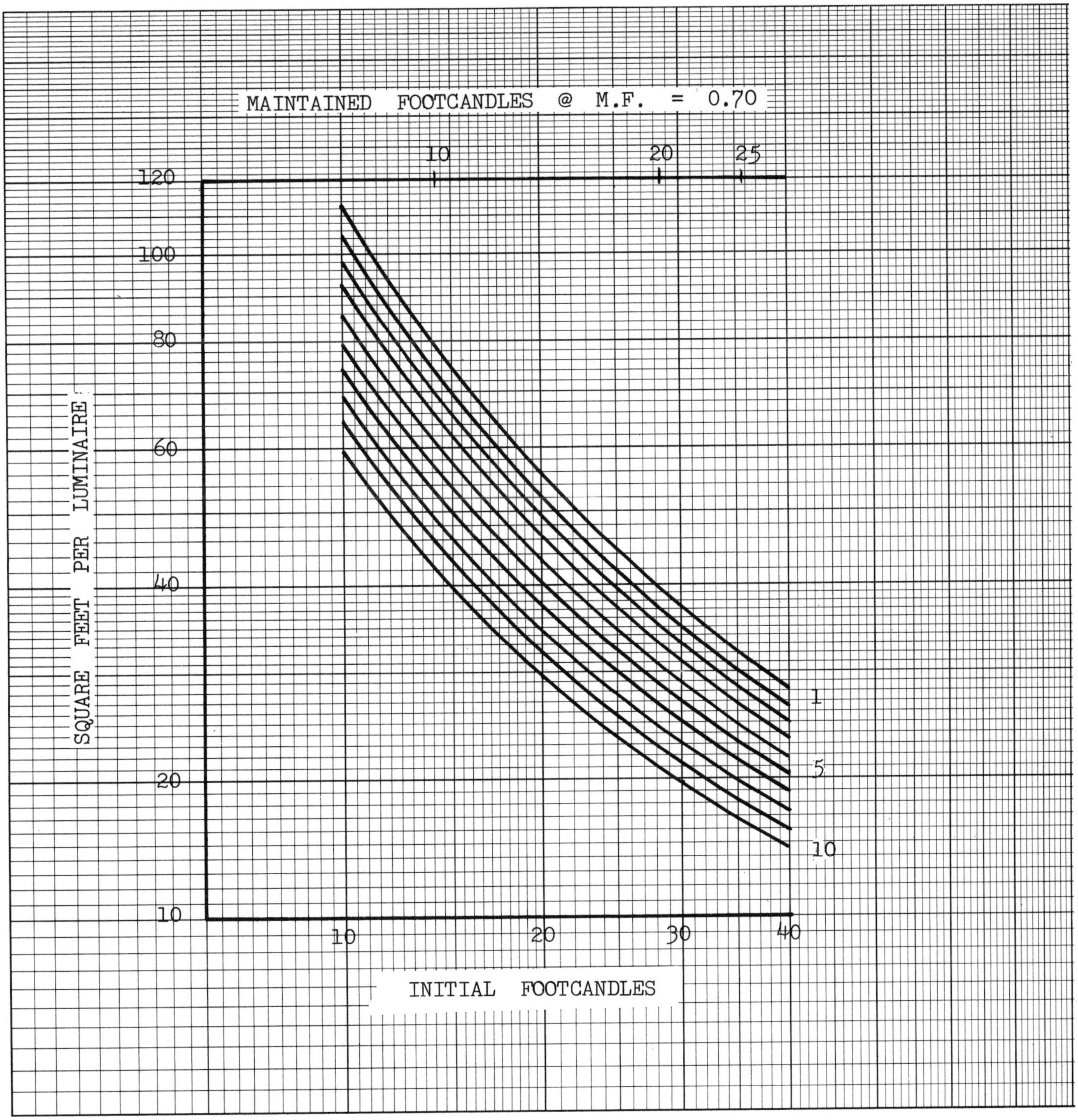

F

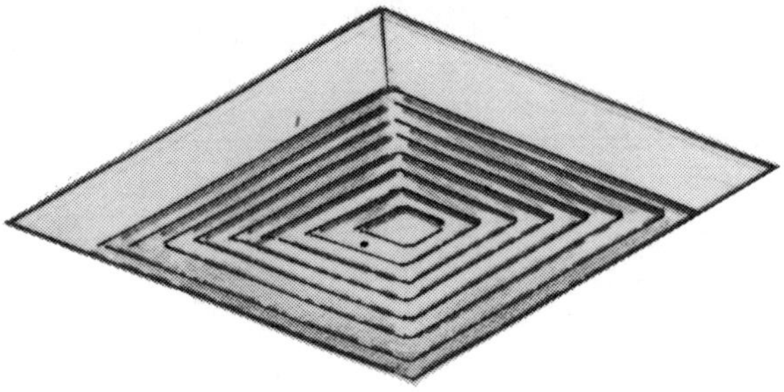

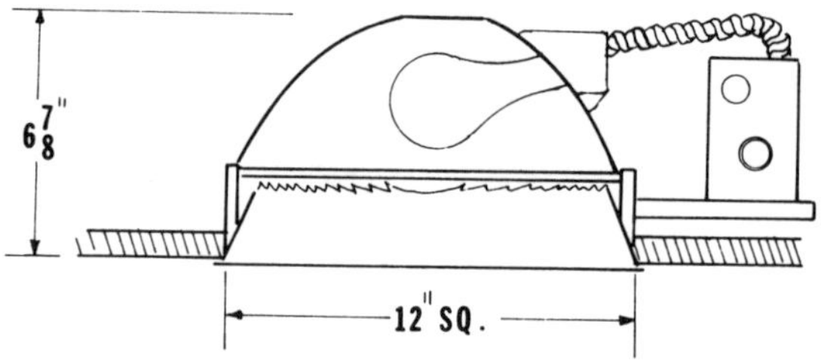

Description	12- X 12-in regressed lens
Lamp	One 200-W A-23, 3940 lm, 750 h
Lens	Fresnel lens
Spacing ratio	1.2
Maintenance factors	0.75/0.70/0.65
Conversion factors	A. Unit with one 200-W A-23 = 1.0
	B. Unit with one 300-W PS-25 = 1.6

COST DETAILS PER LUMINAIRE

Type of unit	Input, W	Contractor's price	Installed cost
A	200	$46	$73.75
B	300	46	75

The installed cost includes published contractor's book price for the luminaire, lamp as shown, required fastening devices, and the labor required for recess mounting and connection of the luminaire. No separate outlet is required since the unit is supplied with an attached outlet ready to accept supply leads.

These high-efficiency downlights with Fresnel lens diffuse the light, filtering out the high-angle glare component. Deep splay assures subtle brightness transition and visual cutoff to shielding at shallow angles.

RECESSED INCANDESCENT–12" X 12" REGRESSED LENS

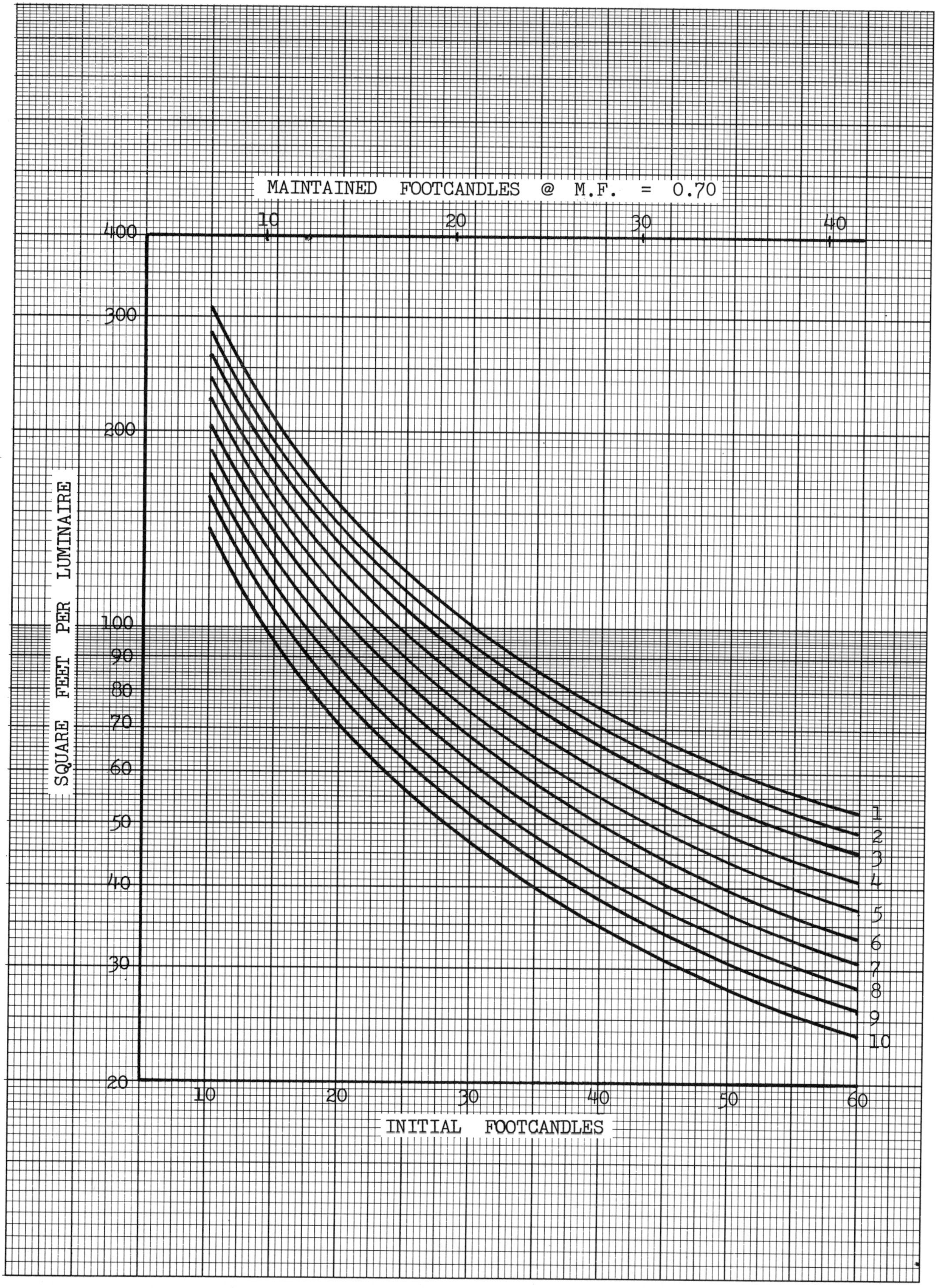

F

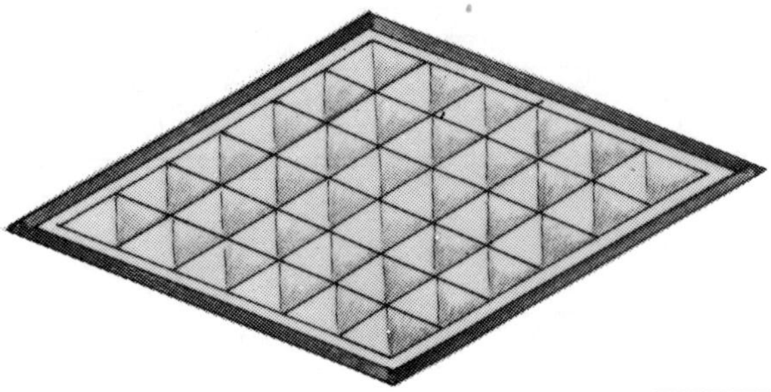

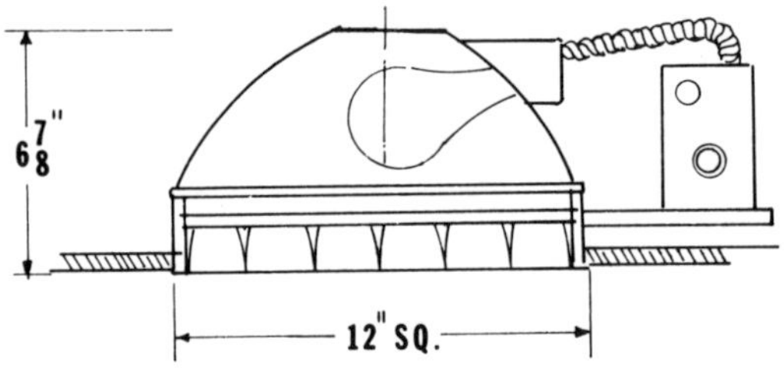

Description	12- X 12-in parabolic-louvered
Lamp	One 200-W A-23, 3940 lm, 750 h
Louvers	Parabolic reflector cells of specular anodized aluminum
Spacing ratio	1.3
Maintenance factors	0.80/0.75/0.70
Conversion factors	A. Unit with one 200-W A-23 = 1.0
	B. Unit with one 300-W PS-25 = 1.6

COST DETAILS PER LUMINAIRE

Type of unit	Input, W	Contractor's price	Installed cost
A	200	$53	$82.50
B	300	53	83.75

The installed cost includes published contractor's book price for the luminaire, lamp as shown, required fastening devices, and the labor required for recess mounting and connection of the luminaire. No separate outlet is required since the unit is supplied with an attached outlet ready to accept supply leads.

These handsome luminaires with parabolic reflector cells of specular anodized aluminum provide a soft-edged beam (medium distribution) with very low brightness.

The reference luminaire is as manufactured by Lightolier.

This information was based on test 12294, prepared by ITL for Lightolier.

RECESSED INCANDESCENT—12" X 12" PARABOLIC LOUVERED

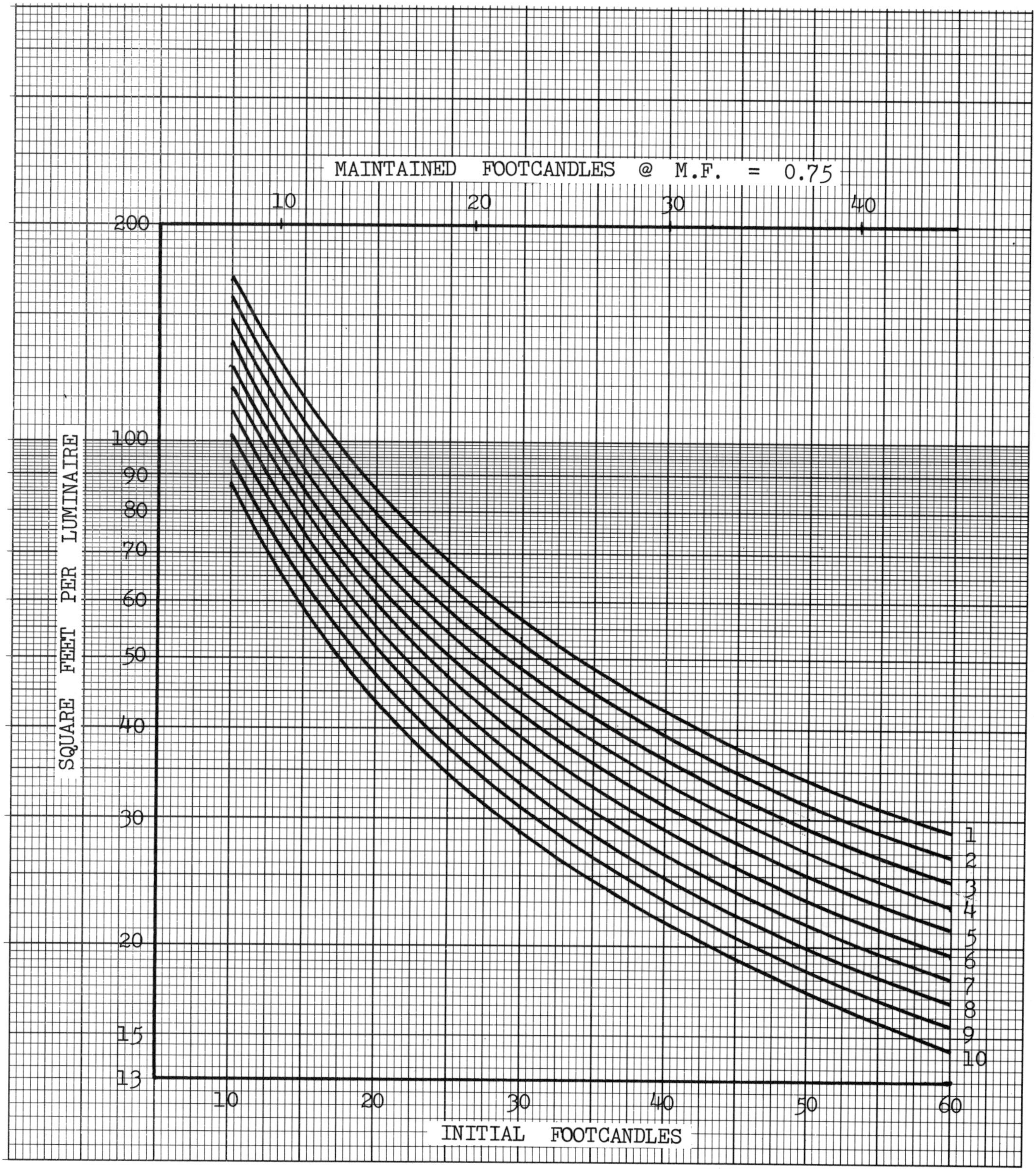

F

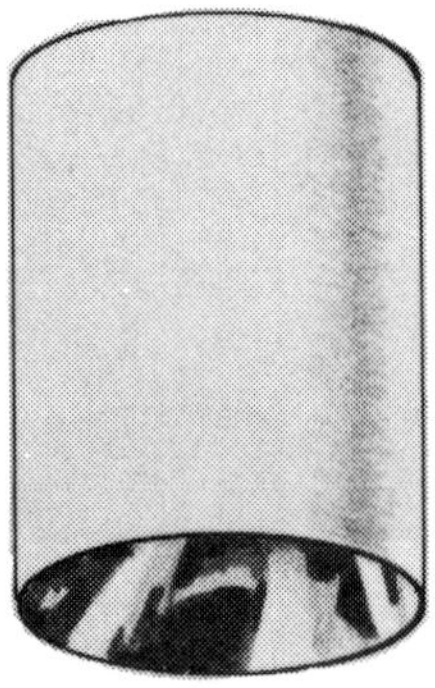

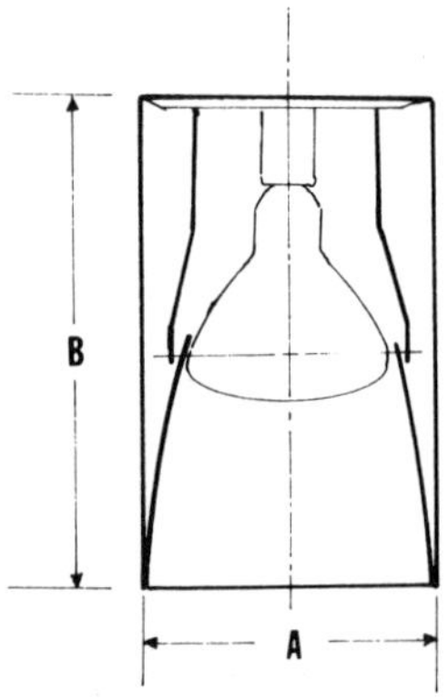

A = 6" DIA.

B = $9\frac{7}{8}$"

Description	6-in surface-mounted open-reflector downlight
Lamp	One 75-W R-30 (FL), 860 lm, 2000 h
Reflector	Clear specular aluminum
Spacing ratio	0.7
Maintenance factors	0.80/0.75/0.70
Input, W	75
Cost details per luminaire	Contractor's price = \$27 Installed cost = \$49.75

The installed cost includes published contractor's book price for the luminaire, lamp as shown, required fastening devices, and the labor required for surface mounting and connection of the luminaire. See page F–56 for a luminaire outlet above the ceiling.

Open-reflector downlights are compact and efficient and provide concentrated distribution with very low brightness. These luminaires are suitable for rooms with ceiling heights of 8 to 14 ft.

SURFACE MOUNT INCANDESCENT– 6" OPEN REFLECTOR DOWNLIGHT

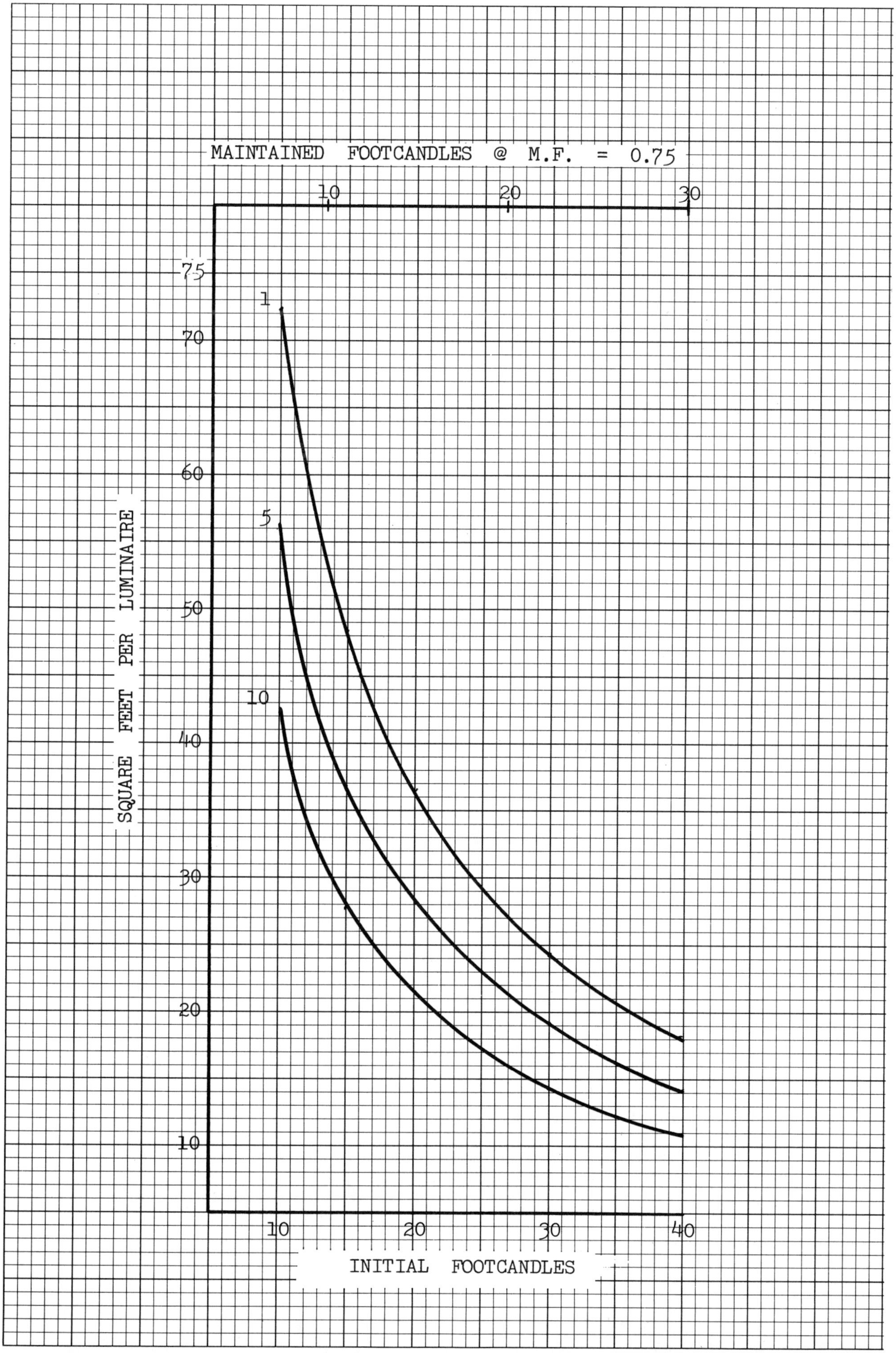

F

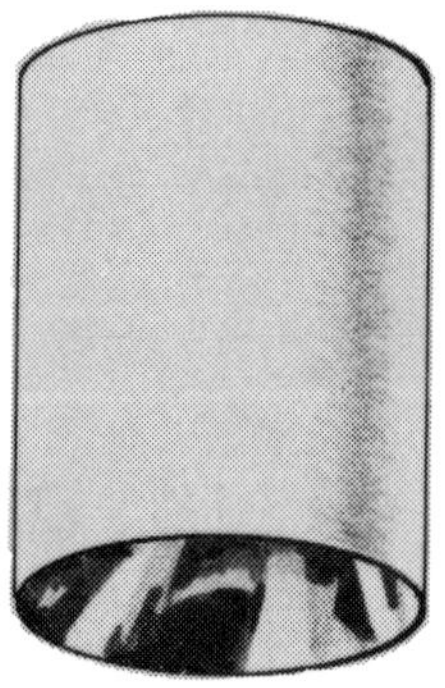

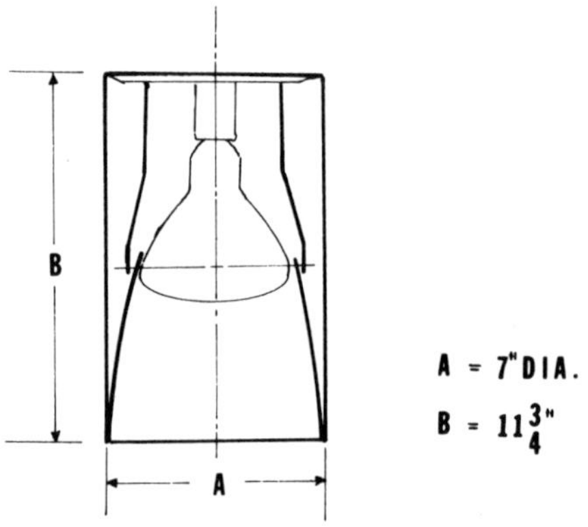

Description	7-in surface-mounted open-reflector downlight
Lamp	One 150-W R-40 (FL), 1900 lm, 2000 h
Reflector	Clear specular aluminum
Spacing ratio	0.5
Maintenance factors	0.80/0.75/0.70
Input, W	150
Cost details per luminaire	Contractor's price = $32 Installed cost = $57

The installed cost includes published contractor's book price for the luminaire, lamp as shown, required fastening devices, and the labor required for surface mounting and connection of the luminaire. See page F–56 for a luminaire outlet above ceiling.

Open-reflector downlights are compact and efficient and provide concentrated distribution with very low brightness. This luminaire is suitable for rooms with ceiling heights of 10 to 20 ft.

SURFACE MOUNT INCANDESCENT – 7" OPEN REFLECTOR DOWNLIGHT

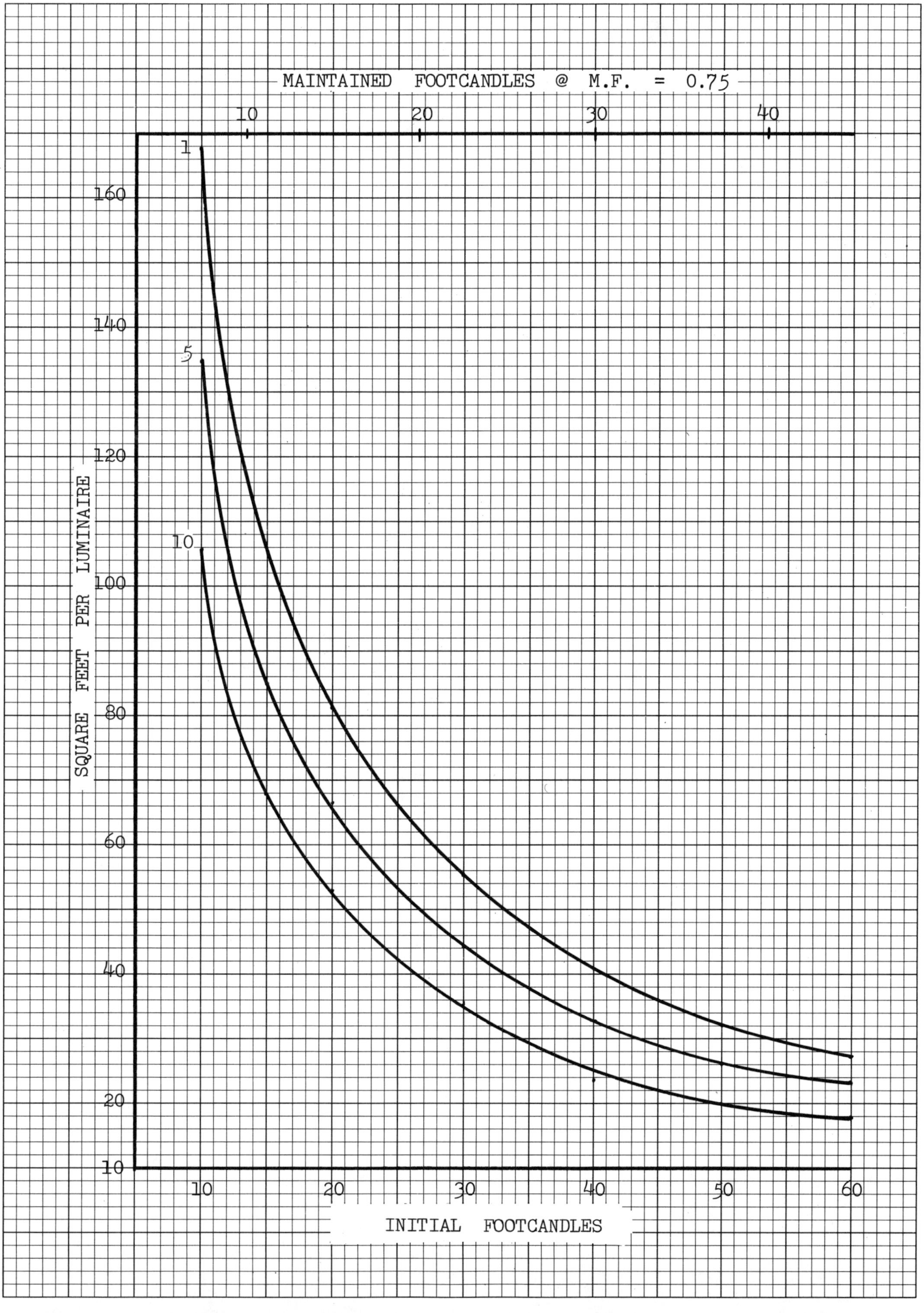

F

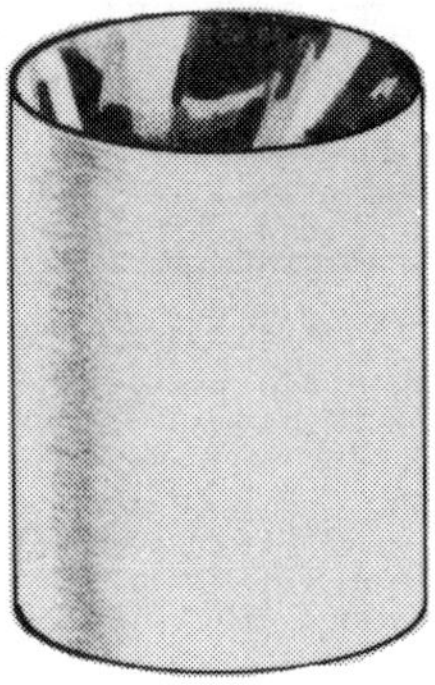

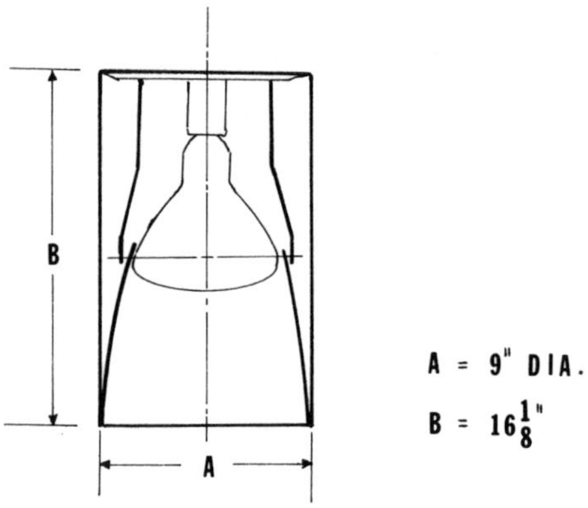

Description	9-in surface-mount open-reflector downlight
Lamp	One 500-W R-40 (FL), 6500 lm, 2000 h
Reflector	Clear specular aluminum
Spacing ratio	0.4
Maintenance factors	0.80/0.75/0.70
Input, W	500
Conversion factors	Unit with one 300-W R-40 (FL) = 0.55
Cost details per luminaire	Contractor's price = \$50 Installed cost = \$88.50

The installed cost includes published contractor's book price for the luminaire, lamp as shown, required fastening devices, and the labor required for surface mounting and connection of the luminaire. See page F–56 for a luminaire outlet above ceiling.

Open-reflector downlights are compact and efficient and provide concentrated distribution with very low brightness. This luminaire is suitable for rooms with ceiling heights of 16 to 30 ft.

SURFACE MOUNT INCANDESCENT– 9" OPEN REFLECTOR DOWNLIGHT

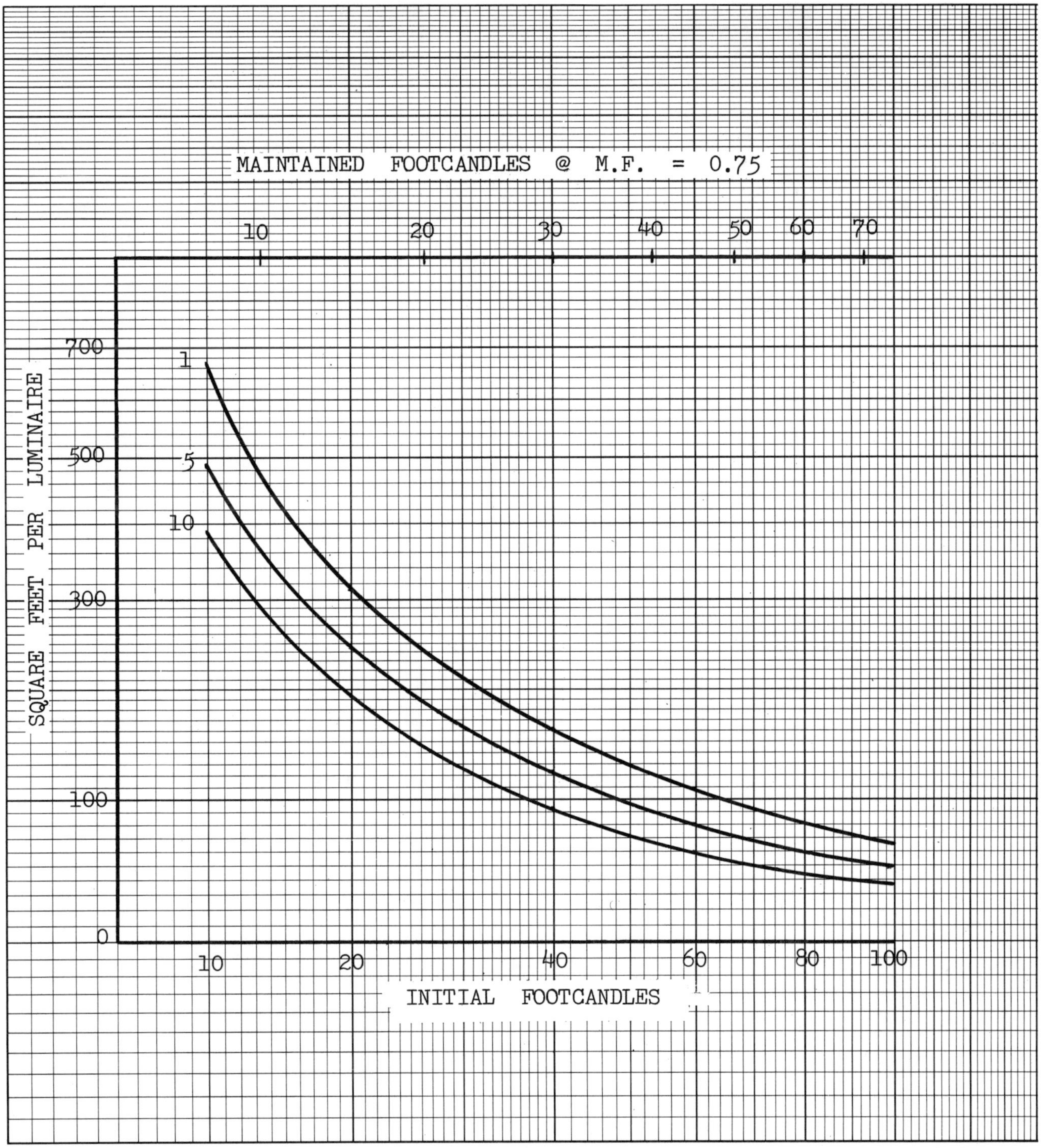

F

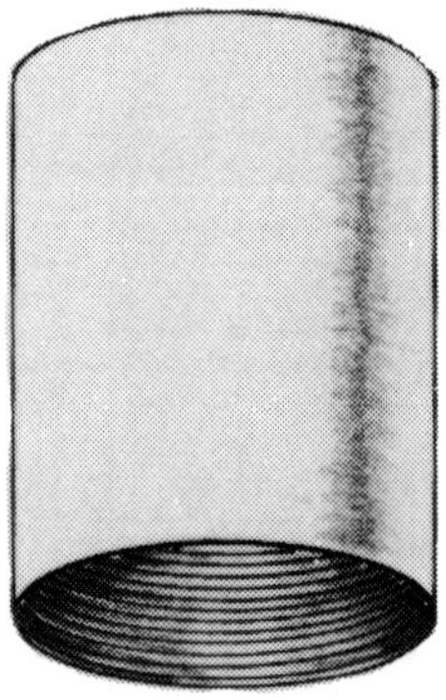

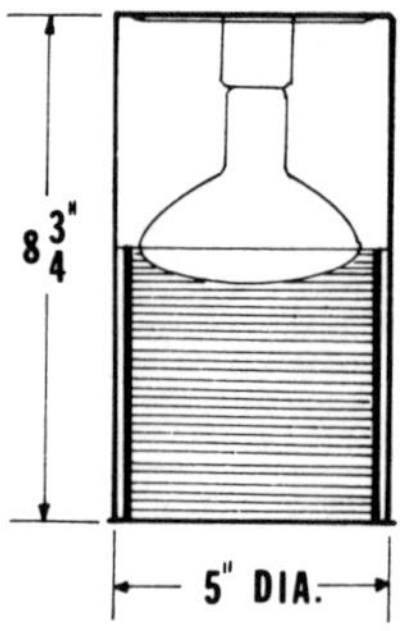

Description	5-in surface-mount baffle downlight
Lamp	One 75-W R-30 (SP), 860 lm, 2000 h
Reflector	Multigroove baffle
Spacing ratio	0.4
Maintenance factors	0.80/0.75/0.70
Input, W	75
Cost details per luminaire	Contractor's price = \$20
	Installed cost = \$41.25

The installed cost includes published contractor's book price for the luminaire, lamp as shown, required fastening devices, and the labor required for surface mounting and connection of the luminaire. See page F–56 for an outlet as required.

These ultra-low-brightness downlights provide concentrated distribution and are suitable for rooms with ceiling heights of 8 to 14 ft. Black multigrooves minimize aperture brightness.

SURFACE MOUNT INCANDESCENT– 5" BAFFLE DOWNLIGHT

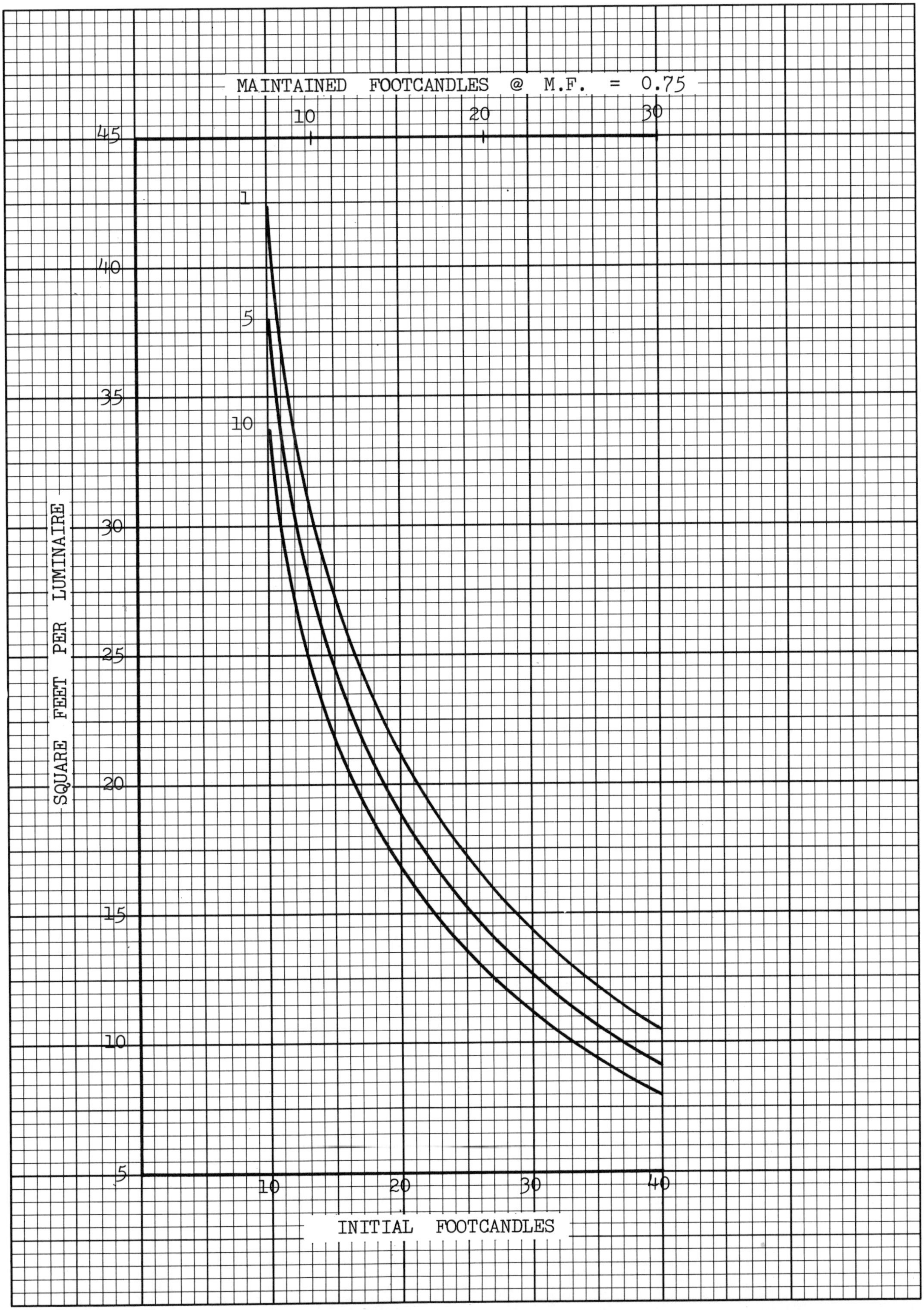

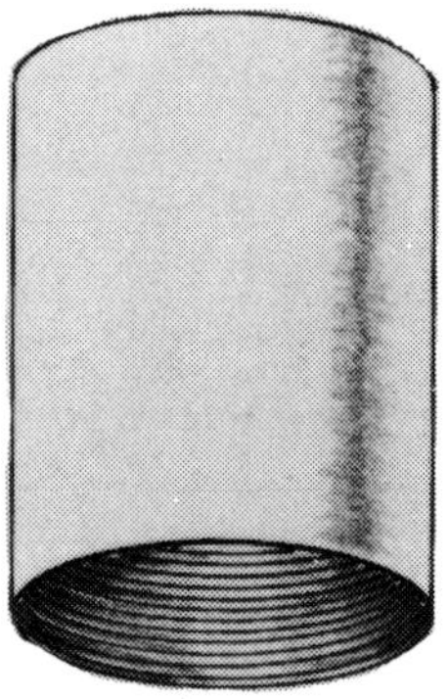

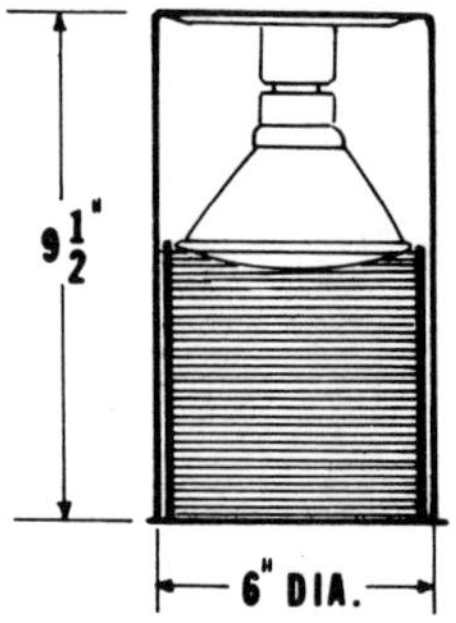

Description	6-in surface-mount baffle downlight
Lamp	One 150-W PAR-38 (SP), 1730 lm, 2000 h
Reflector	Multigroove baffle
Spacing ratio	0.4
Maintenance factors	0.80/0.75/0.70
Input, W	150
Cost details per luminaire	Contractor's price = \$22
	Installed cost = \$45.75

The installed cost includes published contractor's book price for the luminaire, lamp as shown, required fastening devices, and the labor required for surface mounting and connection of the luminaire. See page F–56 for an outlet in the ceiling as required.

These ultra-low-brightness downlights provide concentrated distribution and are suitable for rooms with ceiling heights of 10 to 20 ft. Black multigrooves minimize aperture brightness.

SURFACE MOUNT INCANDESCENT – 6" BAFFLE DOWNLIGHT

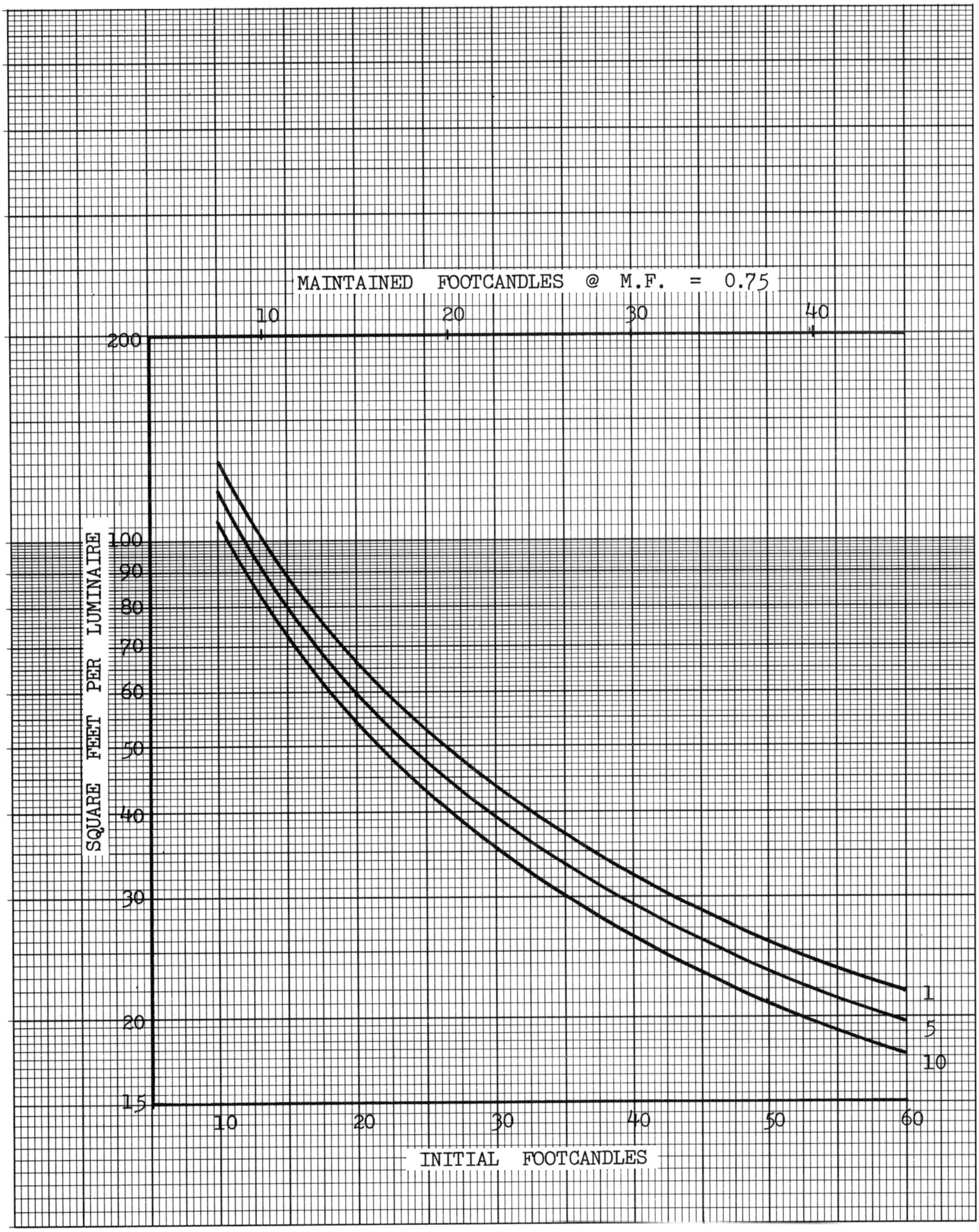

F

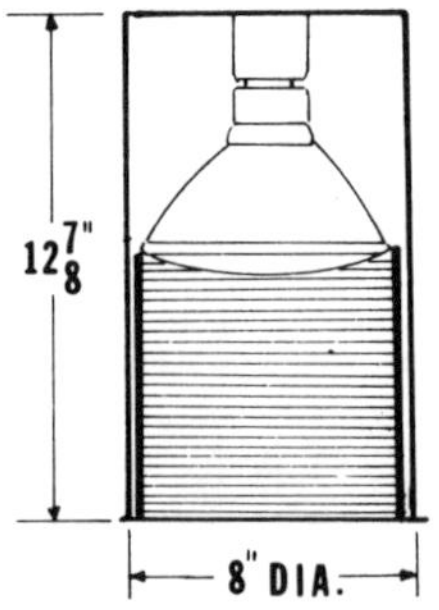

Description	8-in surface-mount baffle downlight
Lamp	One 300-W PAR-56 (MFL), 3840 lm, 2000 h
Reflector	Multigroove baffle
Spacing ratio	0.4
Maintenance factors	0.80/0.75/0.70
Input, W	300
Cost details per luminaire	Contractor's price = $51 Installed cost = $89.75

The installed cost includes published contractor's book price for the luminaire, lamp as shown, required fastening devices, and the labor required for surface mounting and connection of the luminaire. See page F–56 for an outlet in ceiling as required.

These ultra-low-brightness downlights provide concentrated distribution and are suitable for rooms with ceiling heights of 14 to 26 ft. Black multigrooves minimize aperture brightness.

SURFACE MOUNT INCANDESCENT – 8" BAFFLE DOWNLIGHT

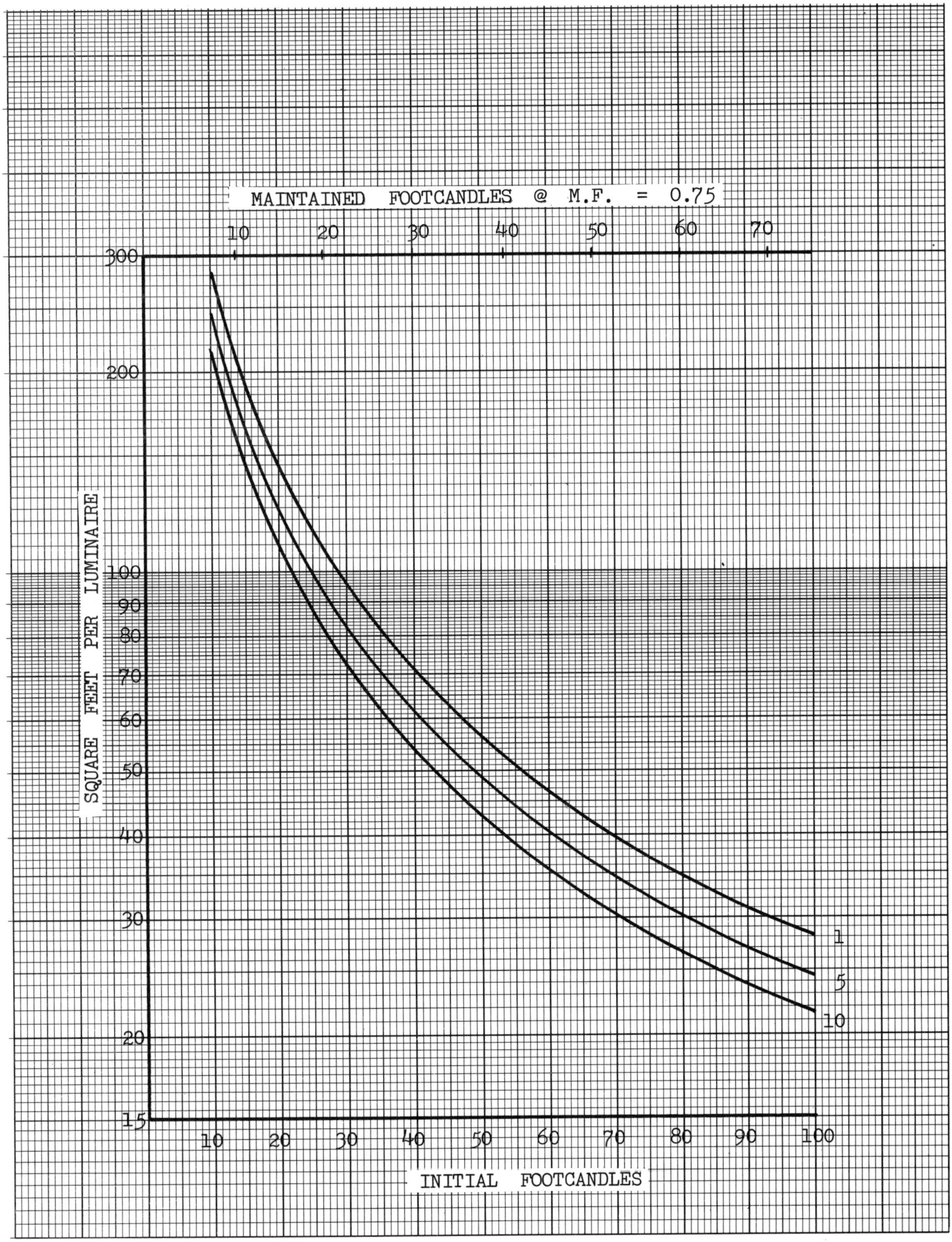

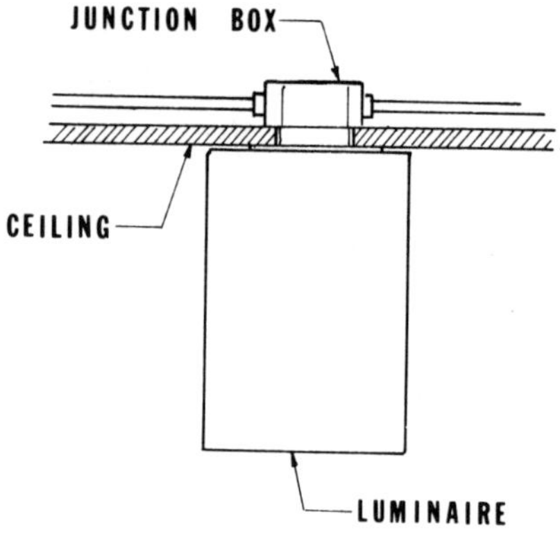

Add

$12.88 for EMT terminal
16.38 for GRC terminal
16.38 for IMS terminal

to the luminaire installed cost for an outlet flush-mounted to a suspended or furred ceiling. This includes a 4-in octagon box, adjustable bar hanger, two connectors, plaster ring, and two wire nuts.

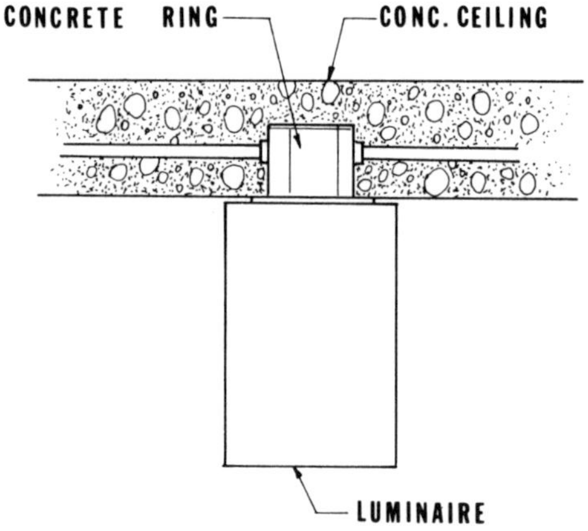

Add

$12.18 for EMT terminal
15.84 for GRC terminal
15.84 for IMS terminal

to the luminaire installed cost for an outlet flush-pan- or deck-mounted in concrete. This includes a 4-in concrete ring, two connectors as required, cover plate, and two wire nuts.

Outdoor Lighting

ROADWAY LIGHTING

Holophane RSL Post-Top Lighting

Up to 150 W	*G-2*
175 W	*G-4*
250 W	*G-6*

Pole-Mounted Luminaires

Rectilinear, up to 250 W	*G-8*
up to 400 W	*G-10*
up to 1000 W	*G-12*
Low-Pressure Sodium, 90 W	*G-14, G-16*
135 W	*G-18, G-20*

AREA LIGHTING

Holophane Square Post-Top Lighting

175 W	*G-22*
250 W	*G-24*
400 W	*G-26*
1000 W	*G-28*
4-1000-W	*G-30*

Pole-Mounted Rectilinear Luminaires

1 Head, up to 250 W	*G-32*
up to 400 W	*G-34*
up to 1000 W	*G-36*
2 Heads, up to 250 W	*G-38*
up to 400 W	*G-40*
up to 1000 W	*G-42*
4 Heads, up to 250 W	*G-44*
up to 400 W	*G-46*
up to 1000 W	*G-48*

High-Mast Luminaires

400 W	*G-50*
1000 W	*G-52*

INSTALLED COST OF POLES

Installed Cost of High-Mast Poles	*G-55*
Installed Cost of Post-Top and Floodlighting Poles	*G-57*

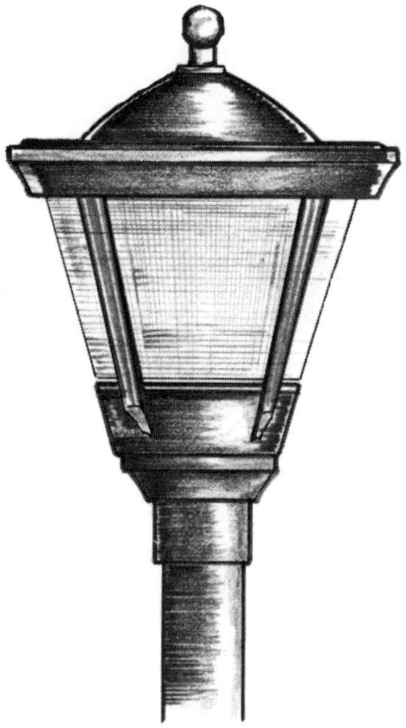

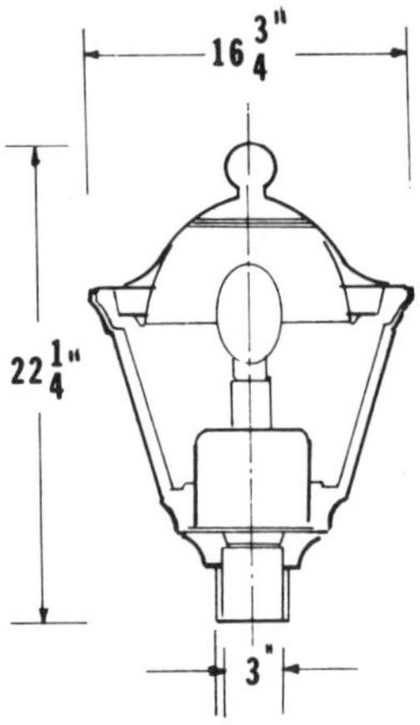

Description	Residential street lights (Holophane RSL)
Lamp	One 70-W high-pressure sodium, 5800 lm, 20,000 h
Construction	Cast-aluminum house with prismatic refractor
Distribution	Type III
Maintenance factor	0.7
Conversion factors	A. Unit with one 70-W high-pressure sodium lamp = 1.0 B. Unit with one 100-W high-pressure sodium lamp = 1.5 C. Unit with one 150-W high-pressure sodium lamp = 2.6

COST DETAILS PER LUMINAIRE

Type of unit	Input, W	Contractor's price	Installed cost
A	88	$162	$282.46
B	128	174	297.22
C	185	174	300.90

The installed cost includes published contractor's book price for the luminaire, lamp as shown, fastening devices, and the labor required for installation and connection on a pole. See page G–57 for the installed cost of a pole.

These popular post-top residential luminaires can be spaced up to 12 times the mounting height and achieve 6 : 1 uniformity. Completely sealed and gasketed optical section reduces dirt depreciation.

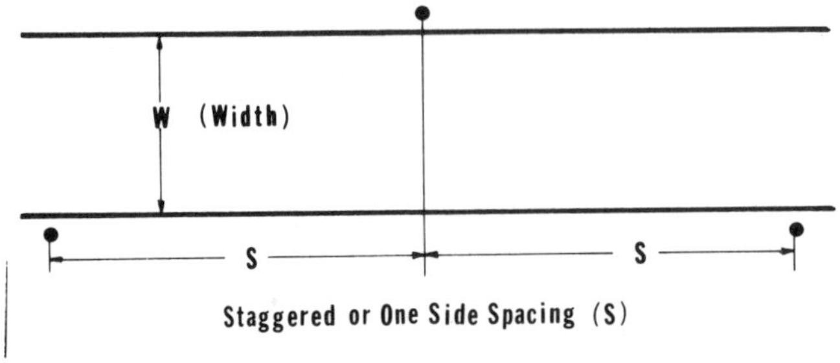

This information was based on isolux chart (test 28284), published by Holophane, Johns-Manville Sales Corp.

ROADWAY LIGHTING – HOLOPHANE RSL POSTOP, UP TO 150W

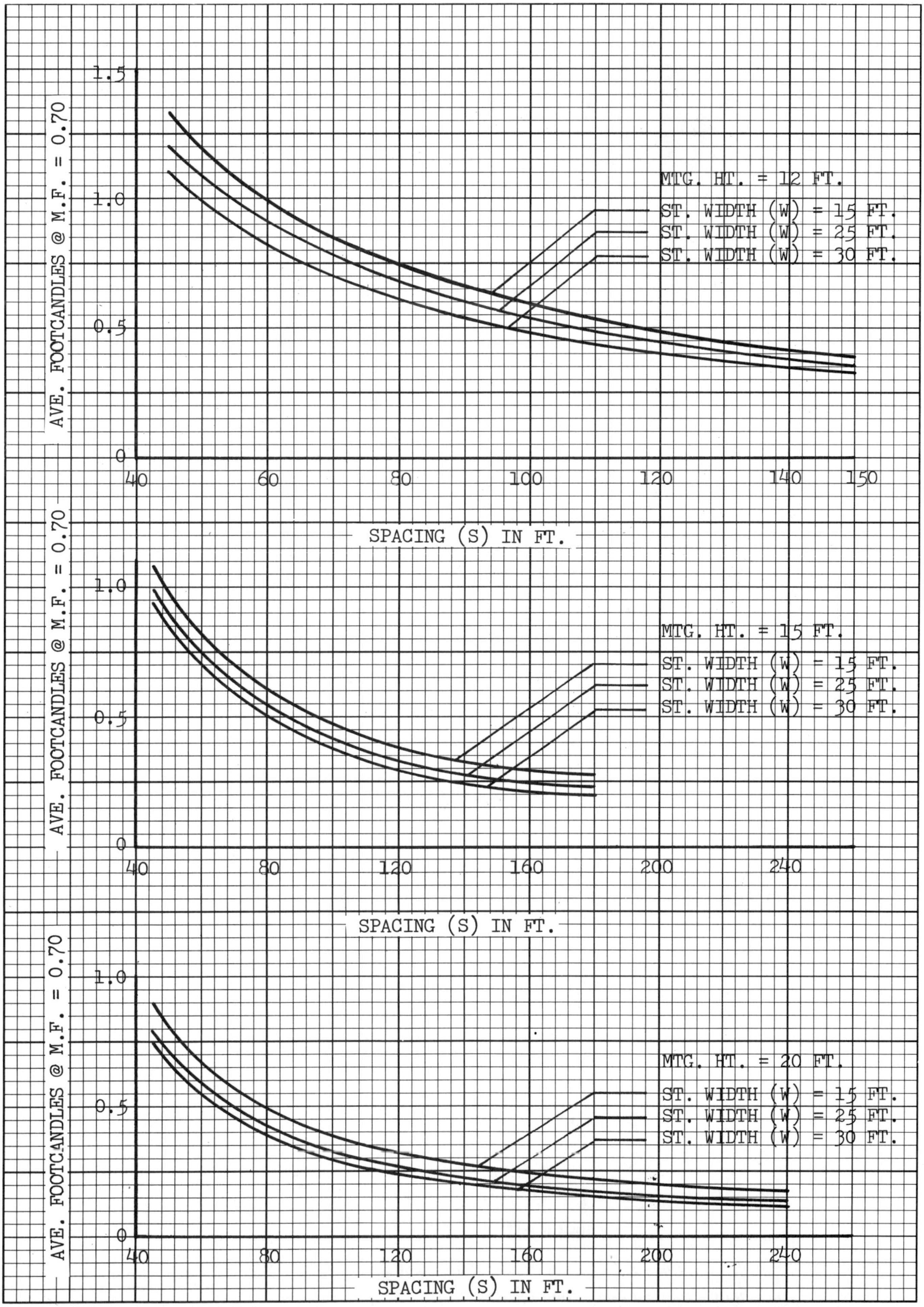

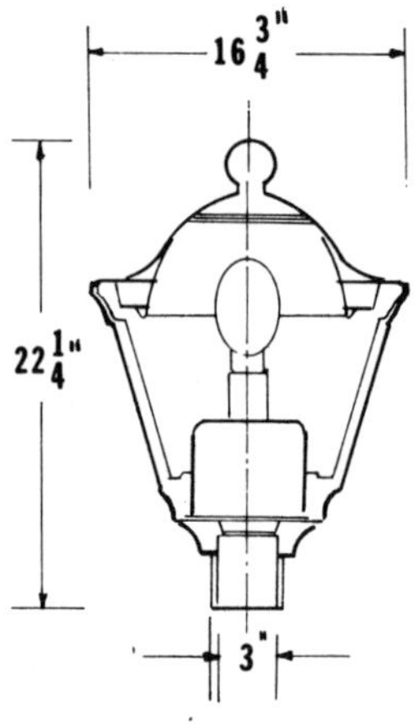

Description	Residential street lights (Holophane RSL)
Lamp	One 175-W E-28 metal halide (coated), 14,000 lm, 7500 h
Construction	Cast-aluminum house with prismatic refractor
Distribution	Type III
Maintenance factor	0.7
Conversion factors	A. Unit with one 175-W E-28 metal halide (coated) = 1.0
	B. Unit with one 175-W E-28 mercury (clear) = 0.56

COST DETAILS PER LUMINAIRE

Type of unit	Input, W	Contractor's price	Installed cost
A	210	$149.64	$254.95
B	200	131.24	206.50

The installed cost includes published contractor's book price for the luminaire, lamp as shown, fastening devices, and the labor required for installation and connection on a pole. See page G–57 for the installed cost of a pole.

These popular post-top residential luminaires can be spaced up to 12 times the mounting height and achieve 6 : 1 uniformity. Completely sealed and gasketed optical section reduces dirt depreciation.

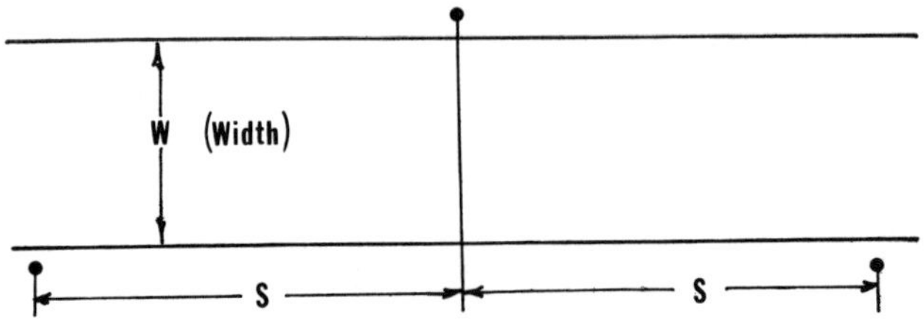

Staggered or One Side Spacing (S)

This information was based on isolux chart (test 23444), published by Holophane, Johns-Manville Sales Corp.

ROADWAY LIGHTING – HOLOPHANE RSL POSTOP, 175W

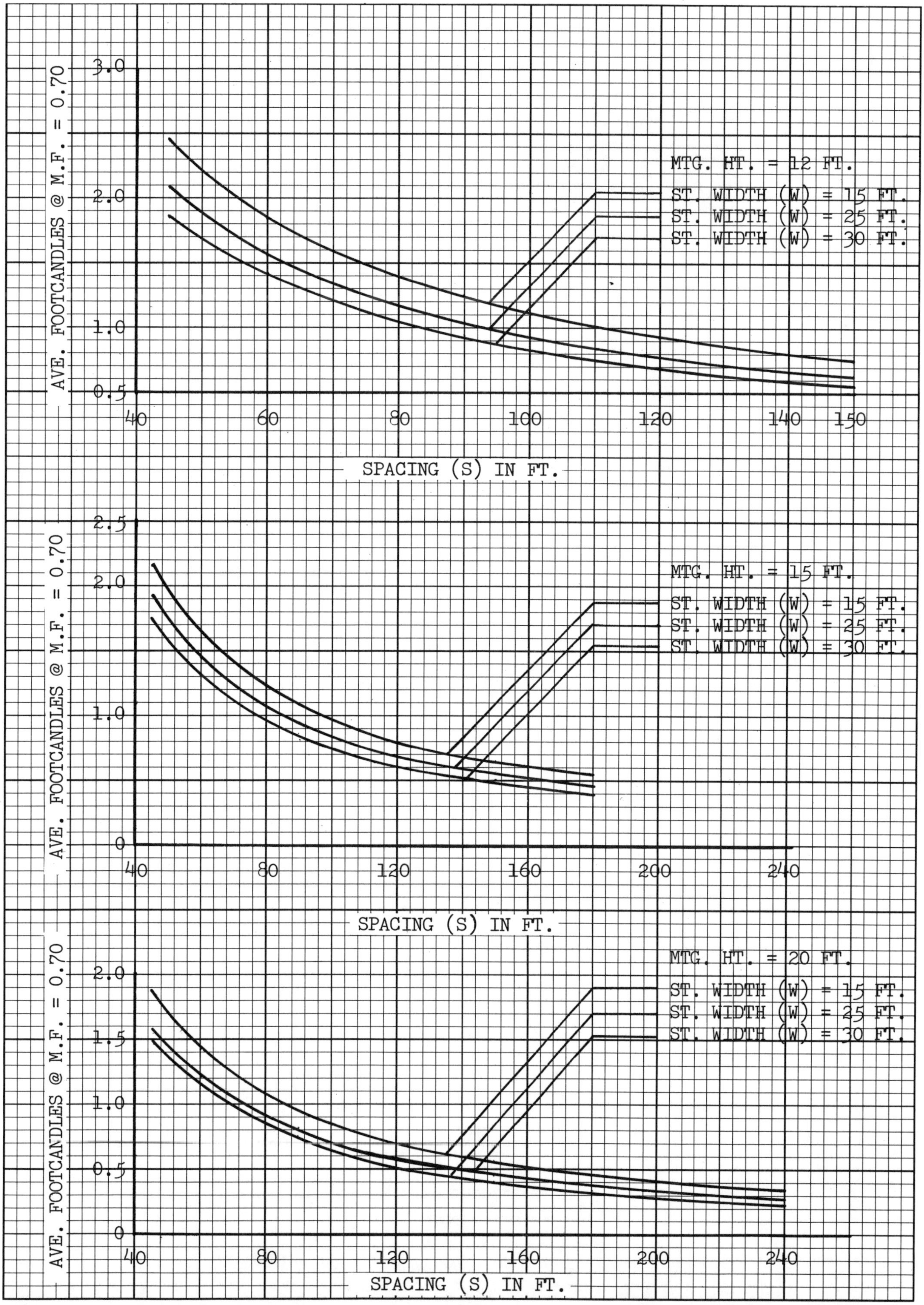

G

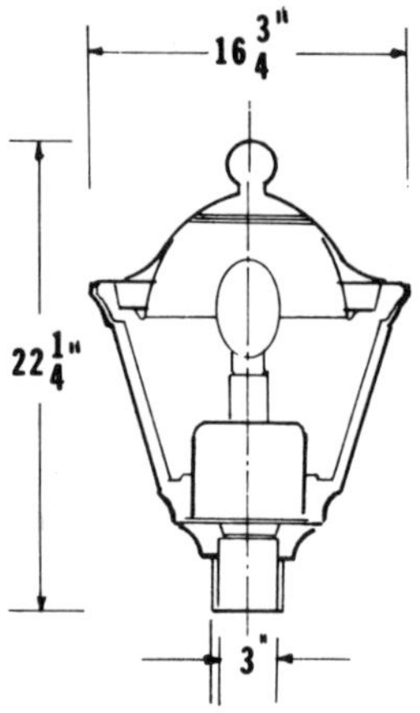

Description	Residential street lights (Holophane RSL)
Lamp	One 250-W E-28 mercury (DX), 11,200 lm, 24,000 h
Construction	Cast-aluminum house with prismatic refractor
Distribution	Type III
Maintenance factor	0.7
Input, W	285
Cost details per luminaire	Contractor's price = \$142.24 Installed cost = \$227.40

The installed cost includes published contractor's book price for the luminaire, lamp as shown, fastening devices, and the labor required for installation and connection on a pole. See page G–57 for the installed cost of a pole.

These popular post-top residential luminaires can be spaced up to 12 times the mounting height and achieve 6 : 1 uniformity. Completely sealed and gasketed optical section reduces dirt depreciation.

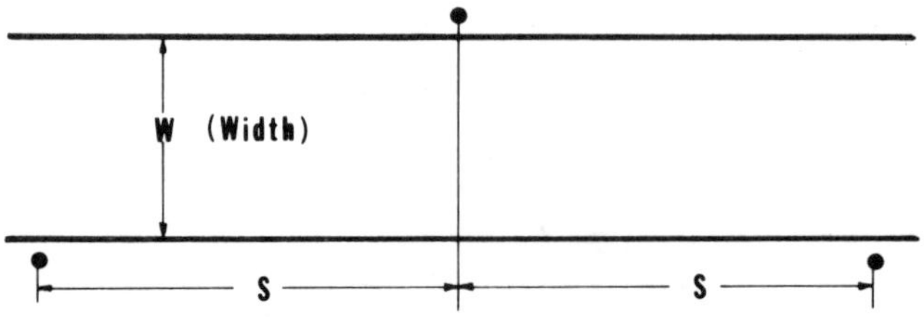

Staggered or One Side Spacing (S)

This information was based on isolux chart (test 24006), published by Holophane, Johns-Manville Sales Corp.

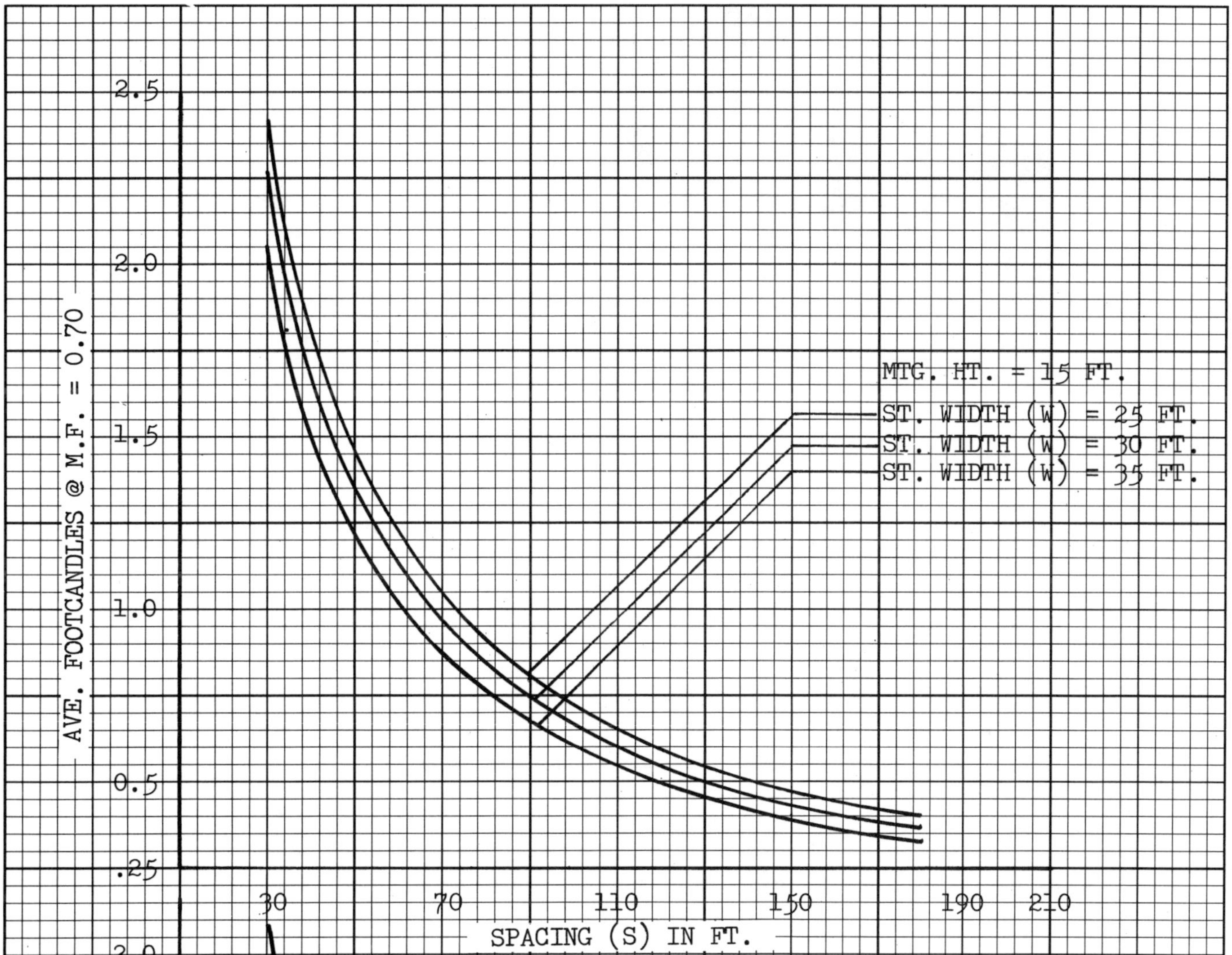
AVE. FOOTCANDLES @ M.F. = 0.70
2.5
2.0
1.5
1.0
0.5
.25
30
70
110
150
190
210
SPACING (S) IN FT.
MTG. HT. = 15 FT.
ST. WIDTH (W) = 25 FT.
ST. WIDTH (W) = 30 FT.
ST. WIDTH (W) = 35 FT.

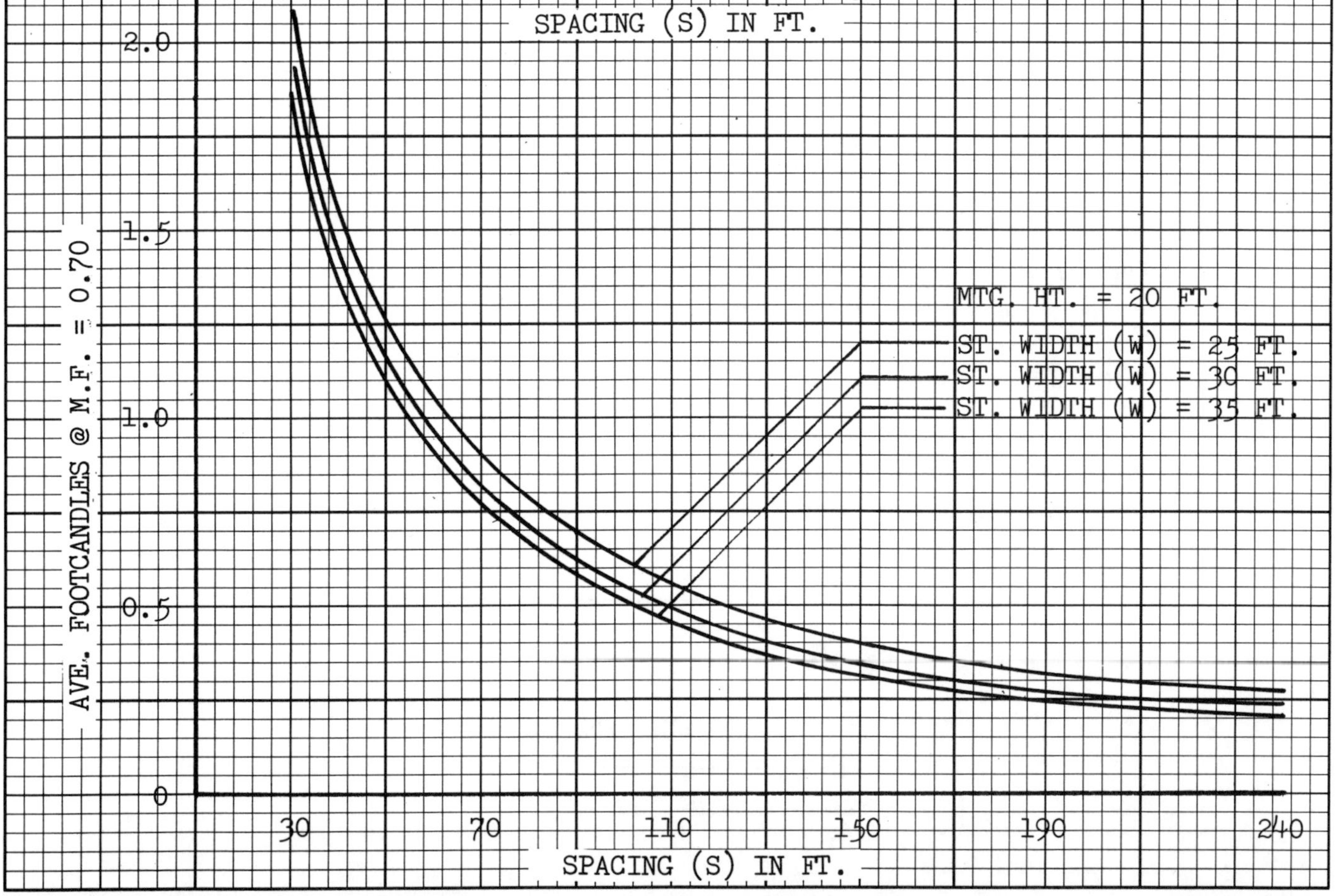
AVE. FOOTCANDLES @ M.F. = 0.70
2.0
1.5
1.0
0.5
0
30
70
110
150
190
240
SPACING (S) IN FT.
MTG. HT. = 20 FT.
ST. WIDTH (W) = 25 FT.
ST. WIDTH (W) = 30 FT.
ST. WIDTH (W) = 35 FT.

G

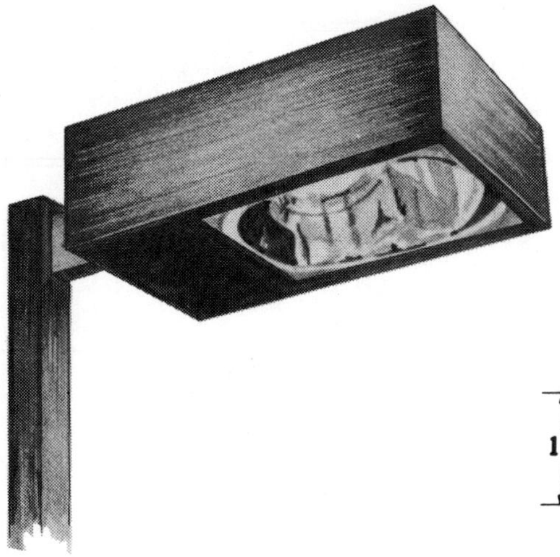

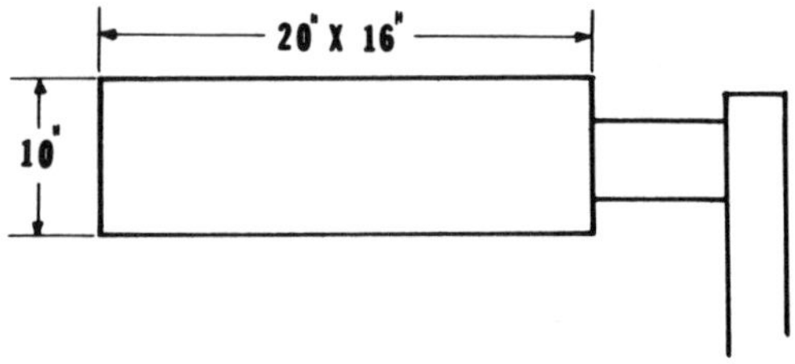

Description	Rectilinear luminaire
Lamp	One 175-W mercury (DX), 7750 lm, 24,000 h
Reflector	Clear specular aluminum
Distribution	Type III
Maintenance factor	0.7
Conversion factors	A. Unit with one 175-W mercury (DX) = 1.0
	B. Unit with one 250-W mercury (DX) = 1.48
	C. Unit with one 175-W metal halide (clear) = 1.93
	D. Unit with one 150-W high-pressure sodium = 2.0

COST DETAILS PER LUMINAIRE

Type of unit	Input, W	Contractor's price	Installed cost
A	200	$240	$340.27
B	290	245	358.00
C	200	254	383.30
D	185	289	442.35

The installed cost includes published contractor's book price for the luminaire, lamp as shown, fastening devices, and the labor required for installation and connection on a pole. See page G–57 for the installed cost of a pole.

Luminaires of this rectilinear family represent today's popular residential street lighting. For uniformity, refer to the isolux chart of the specific luminaire under consideration.

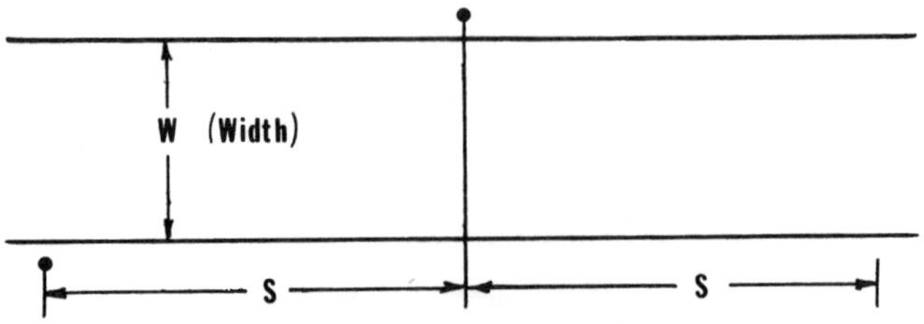

Staggered or One Side Spacing (S)

ROADWAY LIGHTING – RECTILINEAR LUMINAIRES, UP TO 250W

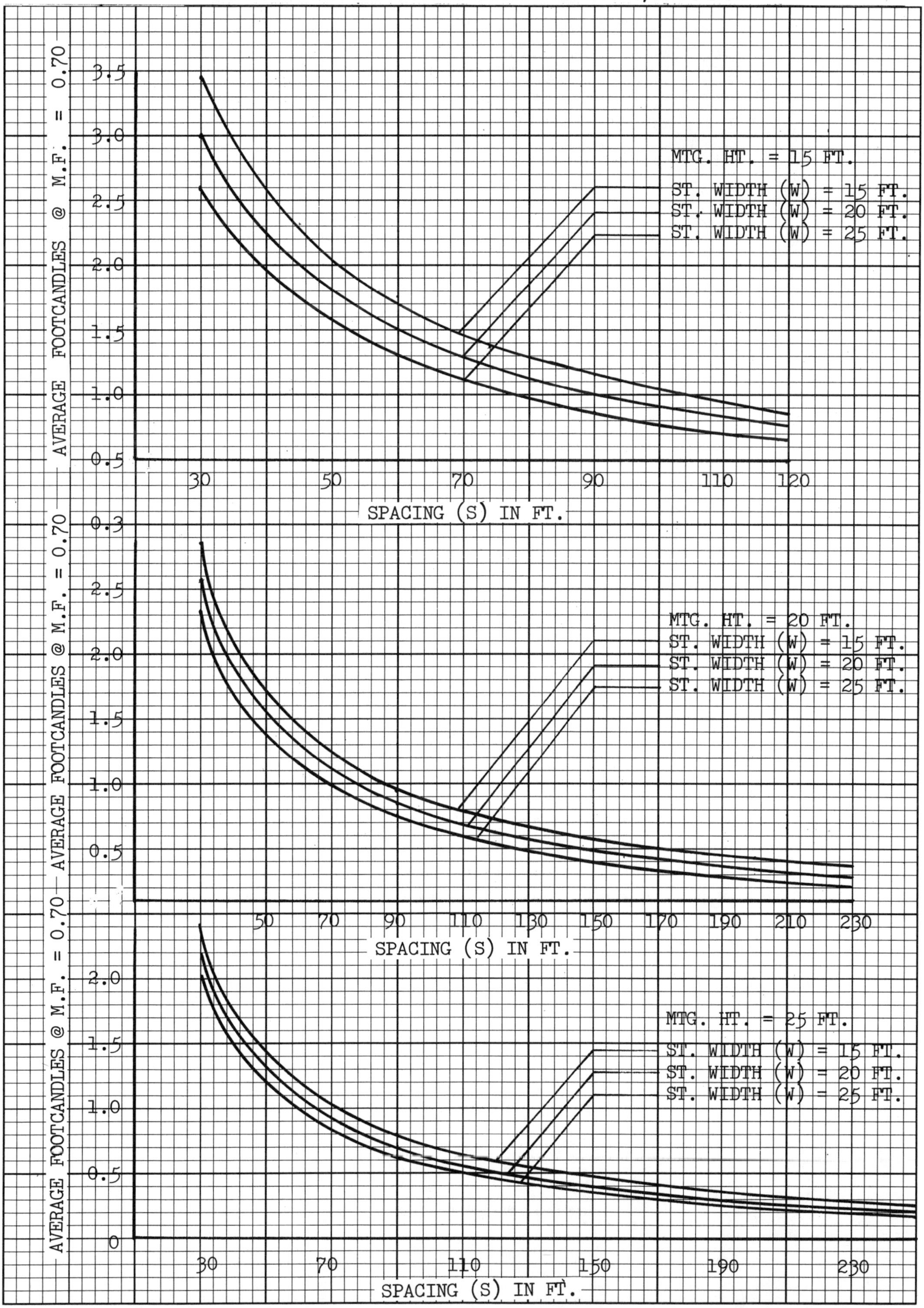

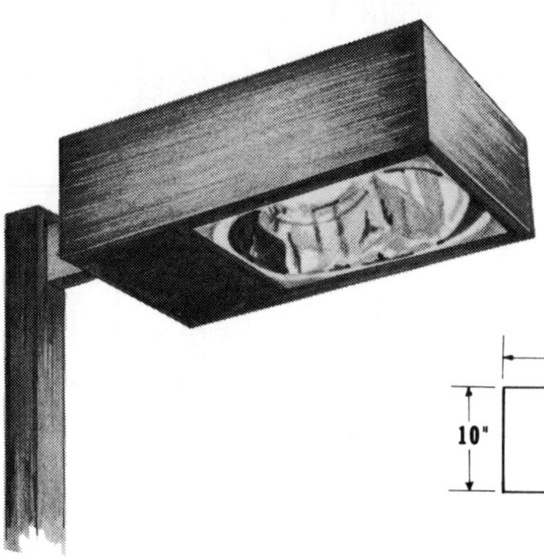

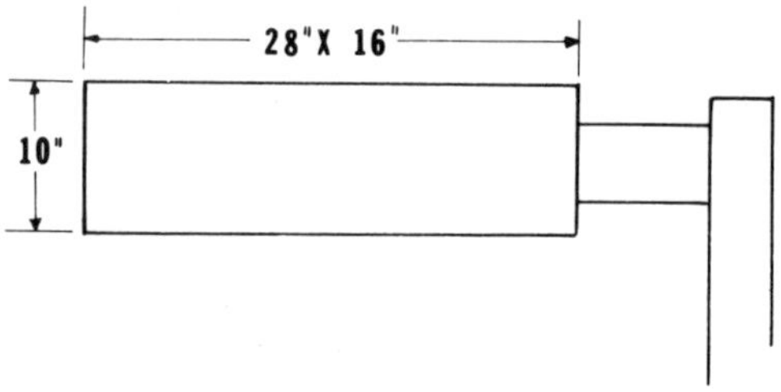

Description	Rectilinear luminaire
Lamp	One 400-W mercury (DX), 21,500 lm, 24,000 h
Reflector	Clear specular aluminum
Distribution	Type III
Maintenance factor	0.7
Conversion factors	A. Unit with one 400-W mercury (DX) = 1.0
	B. Unit with one 400-W metal halide (clear) = 1.8
	C. Unit with one 250-W high-pressure sodium = 1.92
	D. Unit with one 400-W high-pressure sodium = 2.9

COST DETAILS PER LUMINAIRE

Type of unit	Input, W	Contractor's price	Installed cost
A	445	$313	$446.50
B	465	331	494.47
C	295	340	511.80
D	450	380	570.70

The installed cost includes published contractor's book price for the luminaire, lamp as shown, fastening devices, and the labor required for installation and connection on a pole. *See page G–57 for the installed cost of a pole.*

Luminaires of this rectilinear family represent today's popular residential street lighting. For uniformity, refer to the isolux chart of the specific luminaire under consideration.

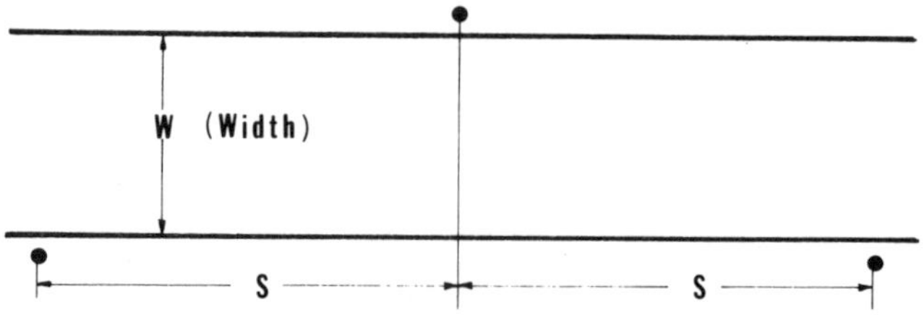

Staggered or One Side Spacing (S)

ROADWAY LIGHTING – RECTILINEAR LUMINAIRE, 400W

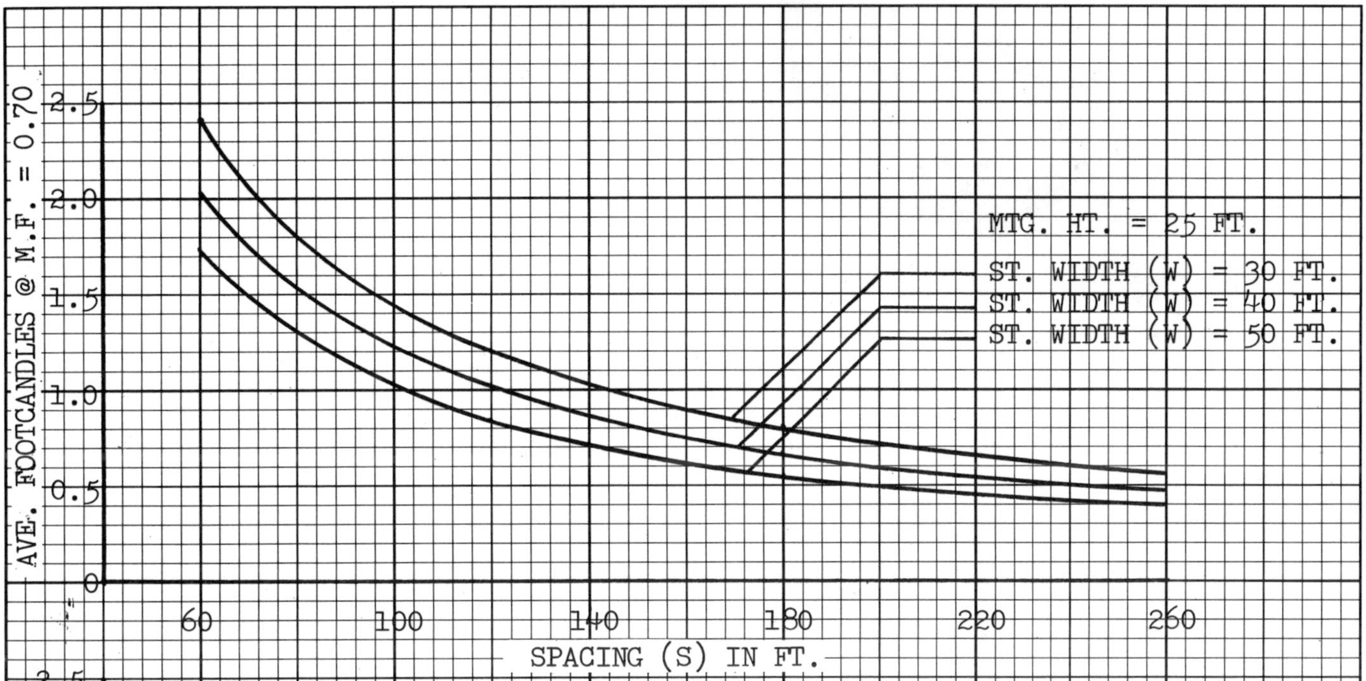

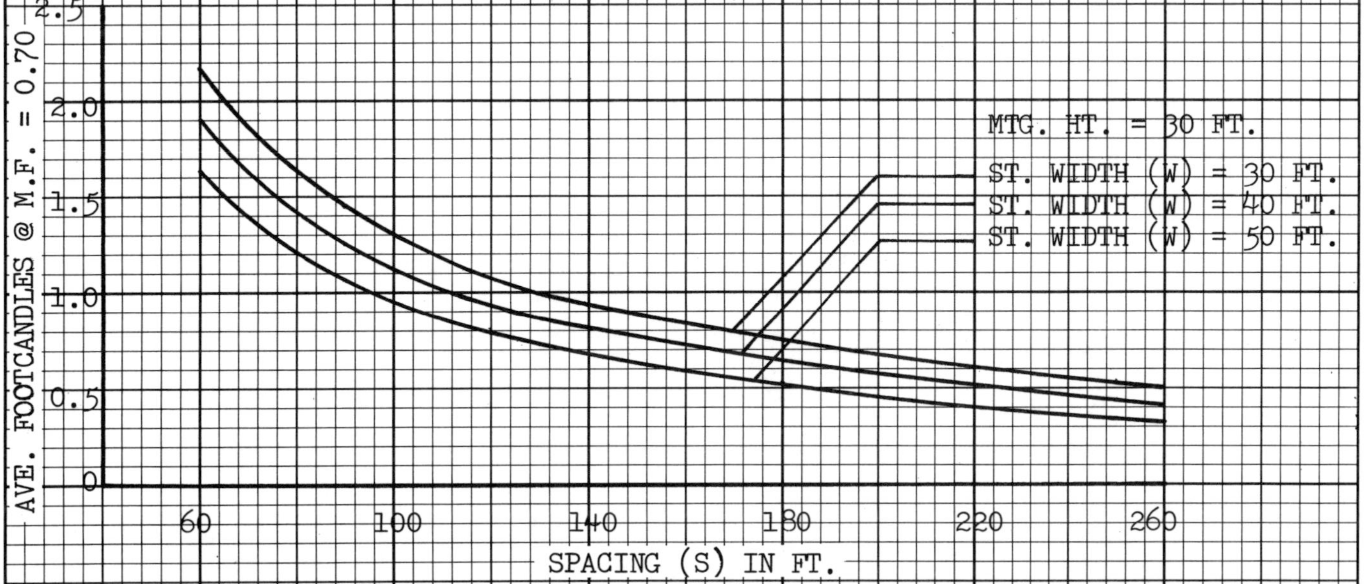

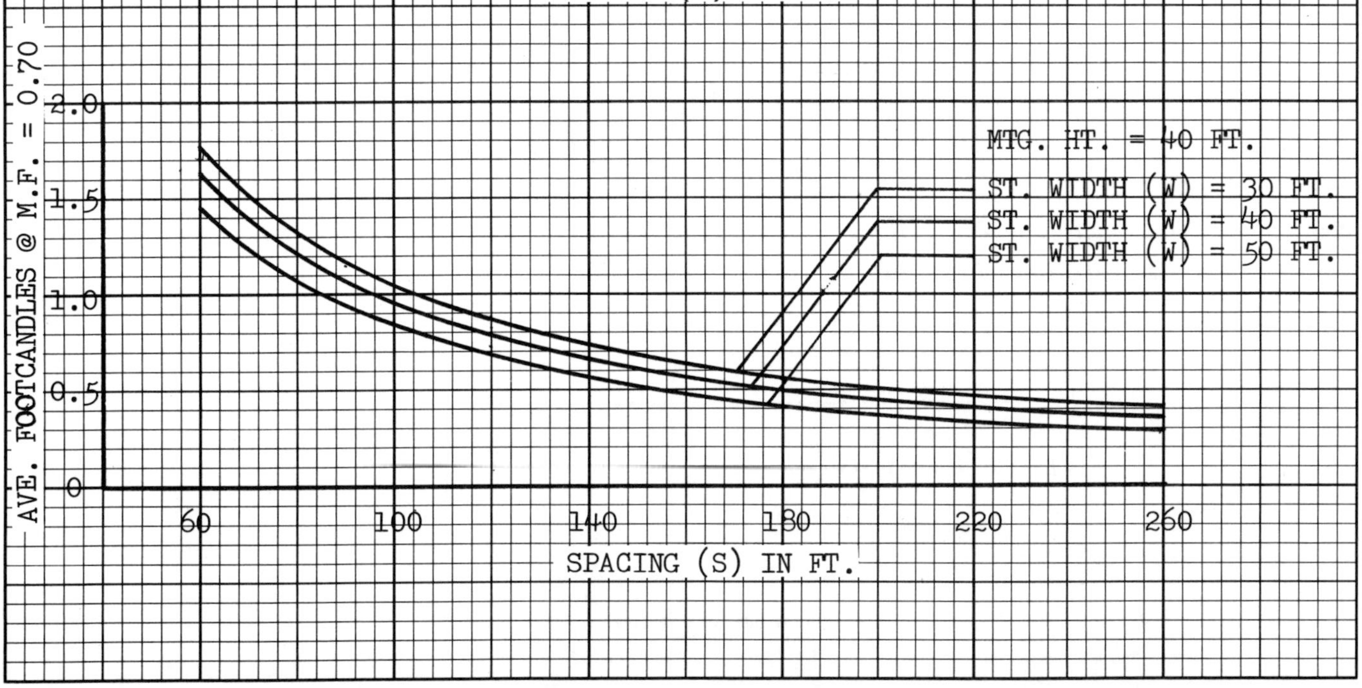

G

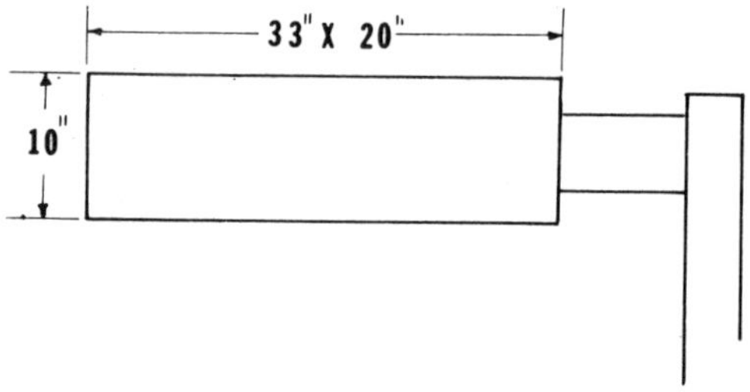

Description	Rectilinear luminaire
Lamp	One 1000-W mercury (DX), 60,000 lm, 24,000 h
Reflector	Clear specular aluminum
Distribution	Type III
Maintenance factor	0.7
Conversion factors	A. Unit with one 1000-W mercury (DX) = 1.0
	B. Unit with one 1000-W metal halide (clear) = 2.0
	C. Unit with one 1000-W high-pressure sodium = 2.4

COST DETAILS PER LUMINAIRE

Type of unit	Input, W	Contractor's price	Installed cost
A	1065	$377	$566.70
B	1085	405	656.50
C	1068	580	914.80

The installed cost includes published contractor's book price for the luminaire, lamp as shown, fastening devices, and the labor required for installation and connection on a pole. See page G–57 for the installed cost of a pole.

Luminaires of this rectilinear family represent today's popular residential street lighting. For uniformity, refer to the isolux chart of the specific luminaire under consideration.

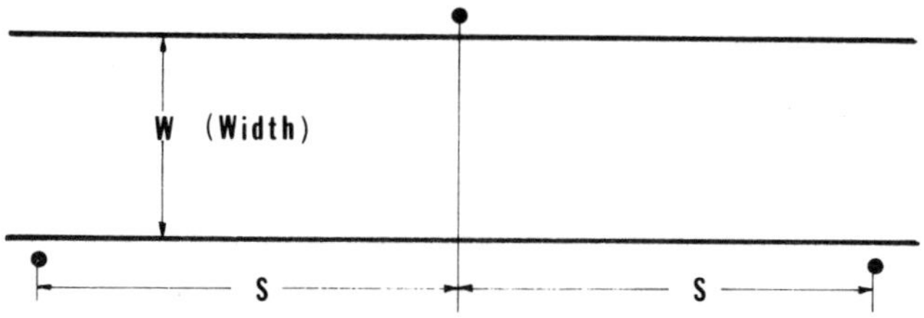

Staggered or One Side Spacing (S)

ROADWAY LIGHTING – RECTILINEAR LUMINAIRE, 1000W

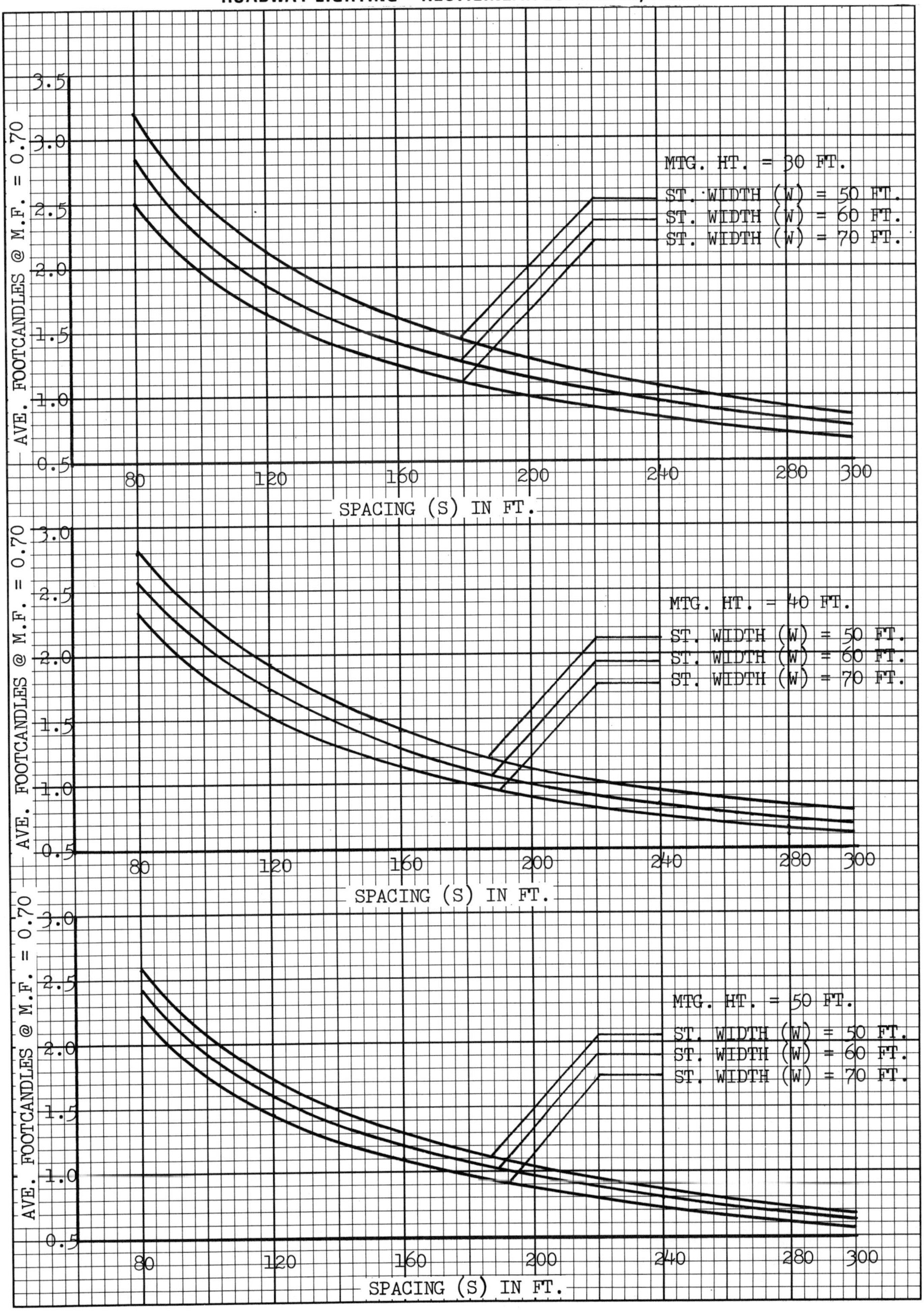

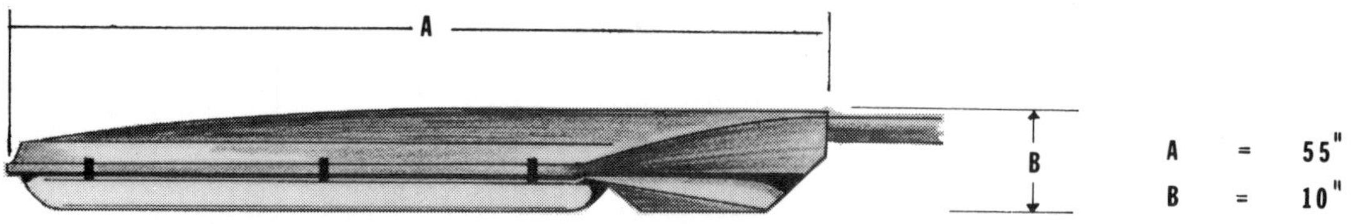

Description	Low-pressure sodium luminaire (Norelco)
Lamp	One 90-W low-pressure sodium, 13,500 lm, 18,000 h
Refractor	Injection-moulded acrylic prismatic lens
Reflector	ABS gloss-white surface with 88 percent reflectance No. 1
Socket position	No. 1
Distribution	Type IV, medium semicutoff, maximum candlepower at 70°
Maintenance factor	0.95
Input, W	125
Cost details per luminaire	Contractor's price = \$231 Installed cost = \$359.75

The installed cost includes published contractor's book price for the luminaire with ballast, lamp as shown, fastening devices, and the labor required for installation and connection on a pole. See page G–57 for the installed cost of a pole.

Technically and economically, low-pressure sodium is the best available lighting system for all public lighting applications where color rendition is not a limiting factor. Optimum lumen maintenance (on average, lumen output increases by 3 percent over initial value), non-insect-attracting color, and overall cool operation assure high maintenance factor. These luminaires, as manufactured by Norelco, have three lamp-socket positions for different distribution. Curves on page G–15 are based on position 1. See page G–17 for curves based on position 3.

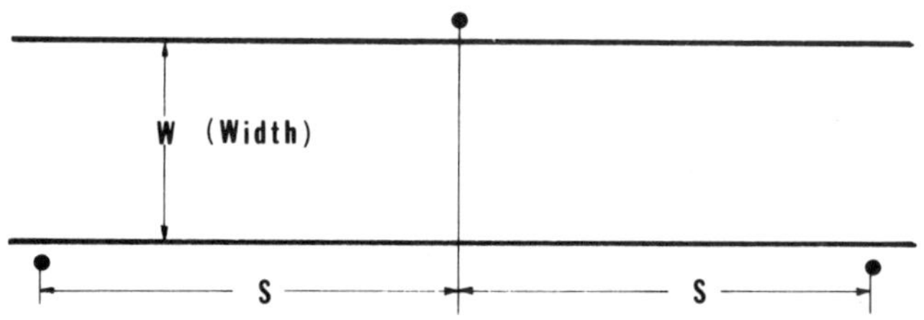

Staggered or One Side Spacing (S)

This information was based on ERL report 2503/2505, prepared for Norelco, Hightstown, New Jersey.

ROADWAY LIGHTING – LOW PRESSURE SODIUM, 90W

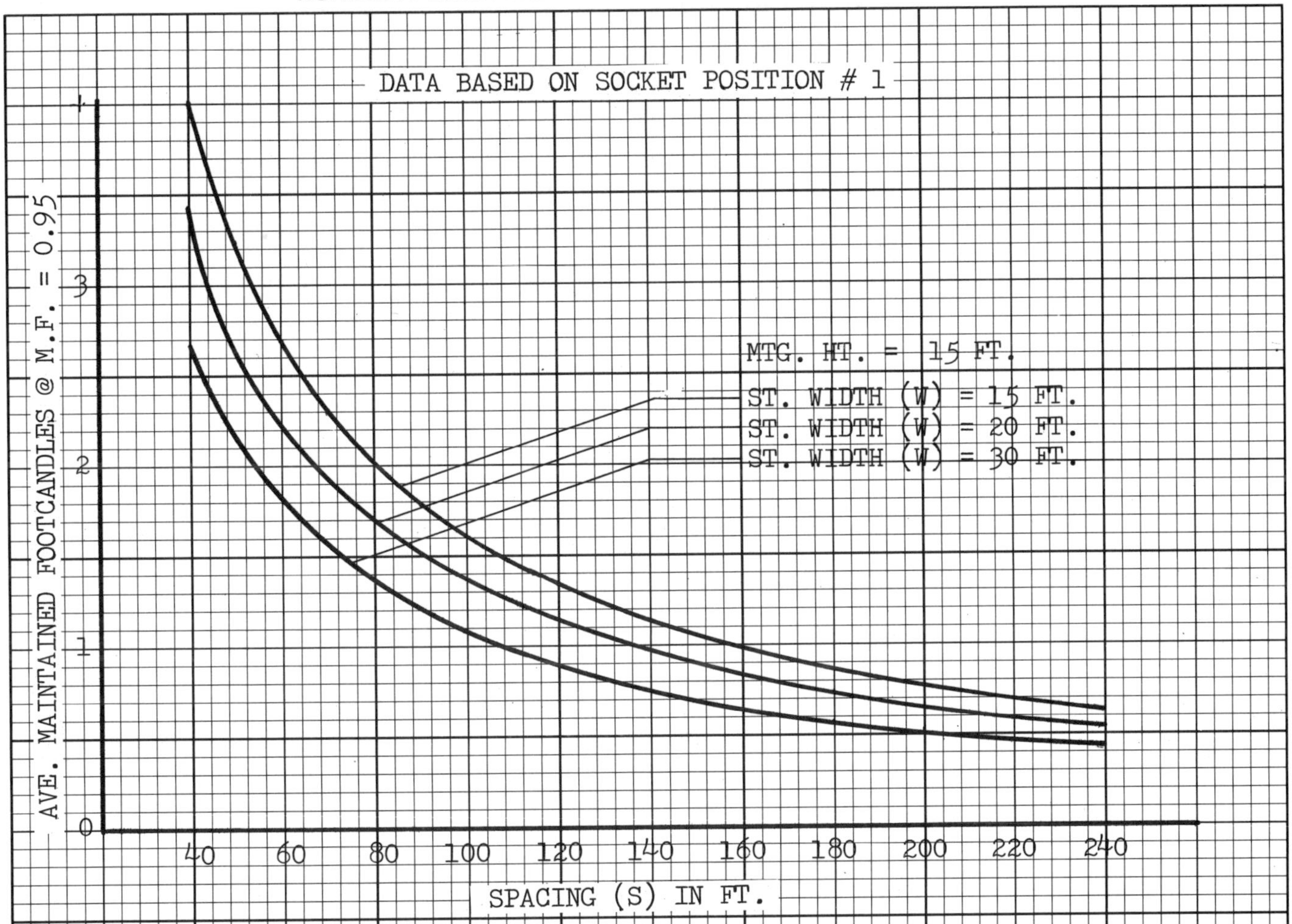

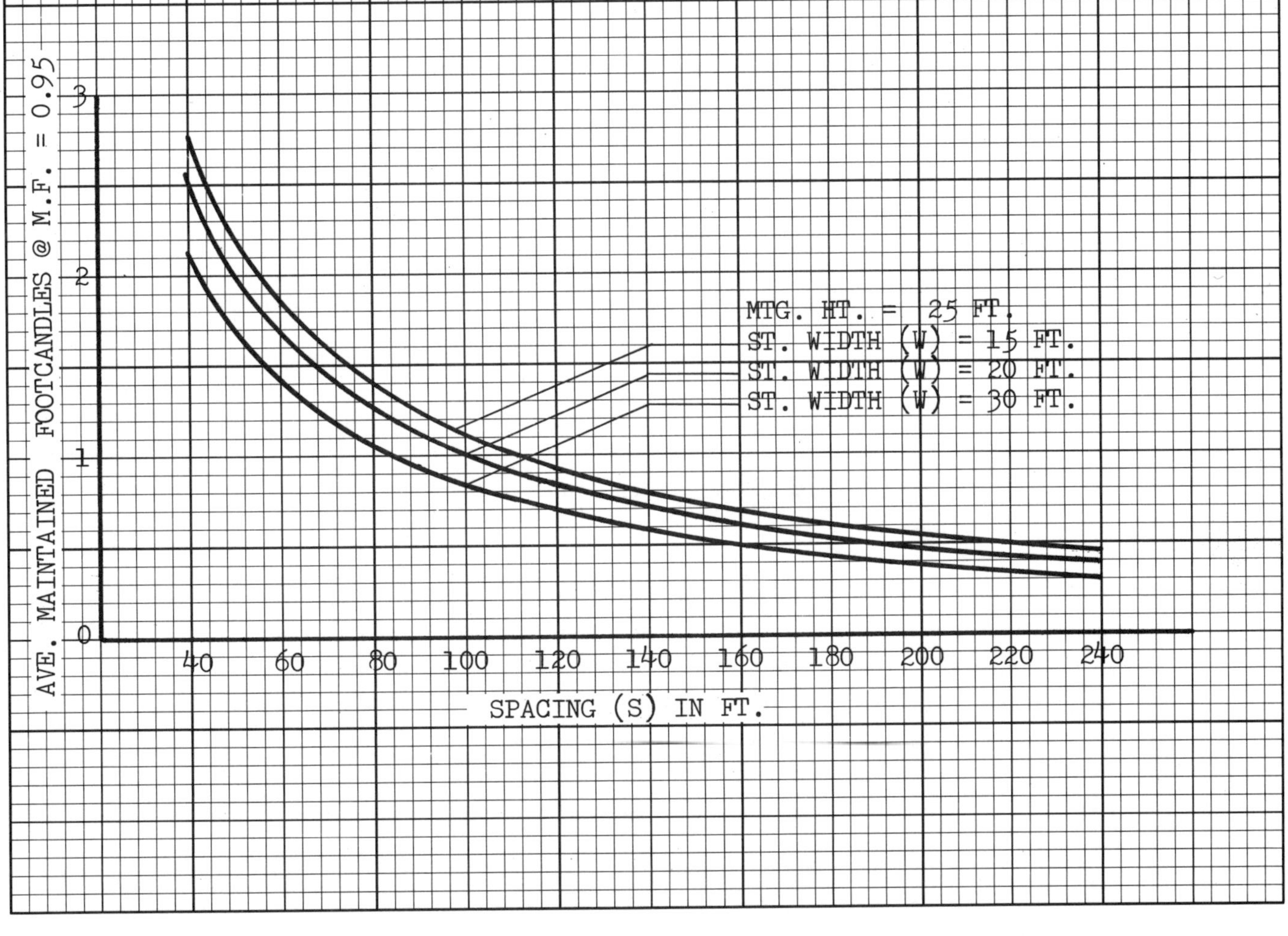

Low-Pressure Sodium Luminaire (Norelco), 90W:
(continued from page G–14)

Curves shown are based on lamp socket position 3. With this arrangement, the distribution is type IV, medium noncutoff, with maximum candle power at 75°. For other details, see page G–14.

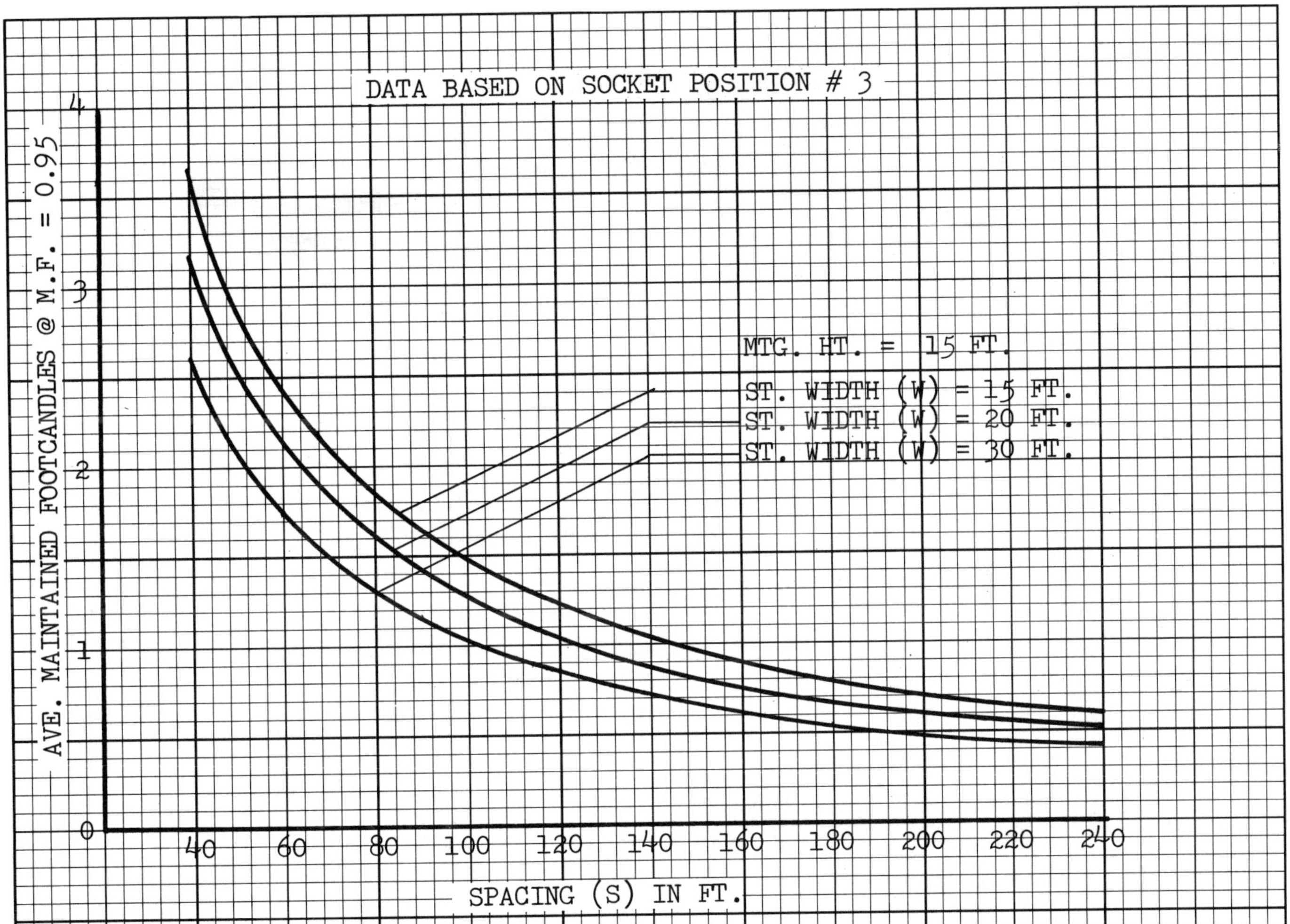
DATA BASED ON SOCKET POSITION # 3
AVE. MAINTAINED FOOTCANDLES @ M.F. = 0.95
0
1
2
3
4
40
60
80
100
120
140
160
180
200
220
240
SPACING (S) IN FT.
MTG. HT. = 15 FT.
ST. WIDTH (W) = 15 FT.
ST. WIDTH (W) = 20 FT.
ST. WIDTH (W) = 30 FT.

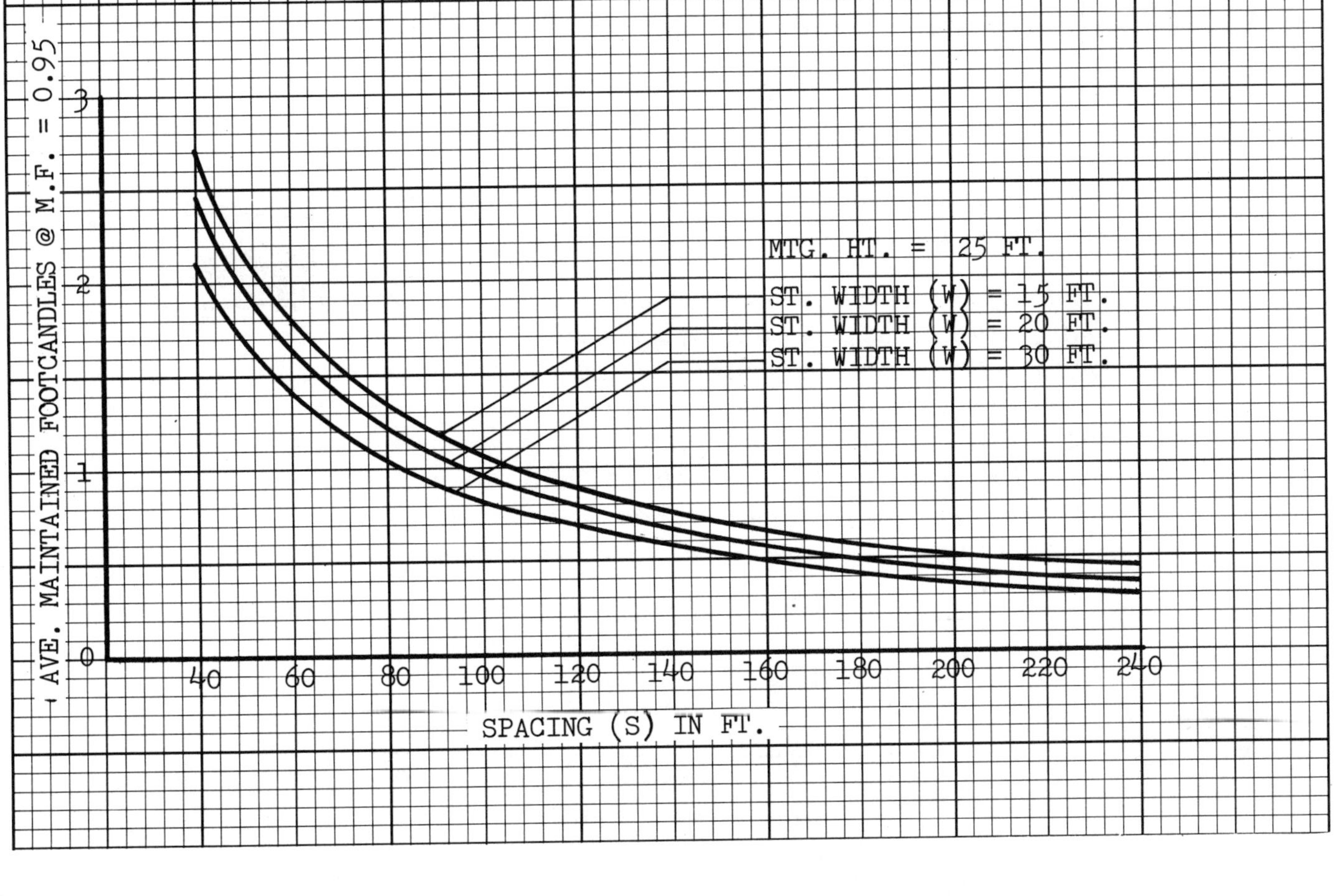
AVE. MAINTAINED FOOTCANDLES @ M.F. = 0.95
0
1
2
3
40
60
80
100
120
140
160
180
200
220
240
SPACING (S) IN FT.
MTG. HT. = 25 FT.
ST. WIDTH (W) = 15 FT.
ST. WIDTH (W) = 20 FT.
ST. WIDTH (W) = 30 FT.

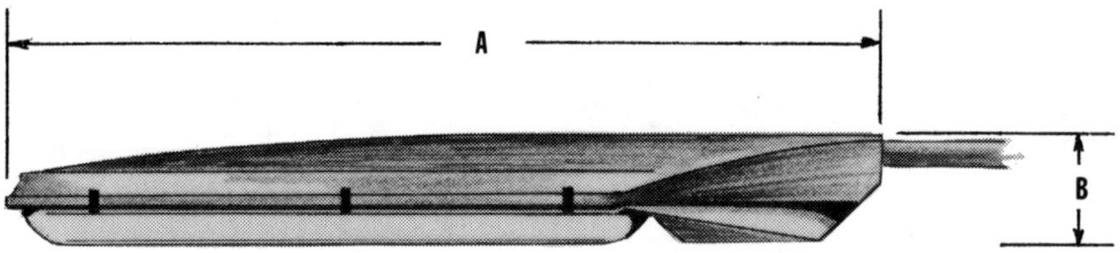

A = 55" (135W)
65" (180W)
B = 10"

Description	Low-pressure sodium luminaire (Norelco)
Lamp	One 135-W low-pressure sodium, 22,500 lm, 18,000 h
Refractor	Injection-moulded acrylic prismatic lens
Reflector	ABS gloss-white surface with 88 percent reflectance No. 1
Socket position	No. 1
Distribution	Type IV, short semicutoff, maximum candle power at 65°
Maintenance factor	0.95
Conversion factors	A. Unit with one 135-W low-pressure sodium lamp = 1.0 B. Unit with one 180-W low-pressure sodium lamp = 1.46

COST DETAILS PER LUMINAIRE

Type of unit	Input, W	Contractor's price	Installed cost
A	178	$241	$391.25
B	220	267	430.60

The installed cost includes published contractor's book price for the luminaire with ballast, lamp as shown, fastening devices, and the labor required for installation and connection on a pole. See page G–57 for the installed cost of a pole.

Technically and economically, low-pressure sodium is the best available lighting system for all public lighting applications, where color rendition is not a limiting factor. Optimum lumen maintenance (on average, lumen output increases by 3 percent over initial value), non-insect-attracting color, and overall cool operation assure high maintenance factor. These luminaires, as manufactured by Norelco, have three lamp socket positions for different distribution. Curves on page G–19 are based on position 1. See page G–21 for curves based on position 3.

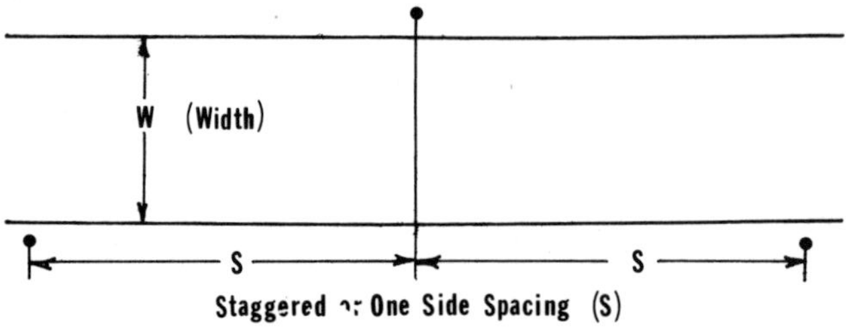

This information was based on ERL report 2500/2531, prepared for Norelco, Hightstown, New Jersey.

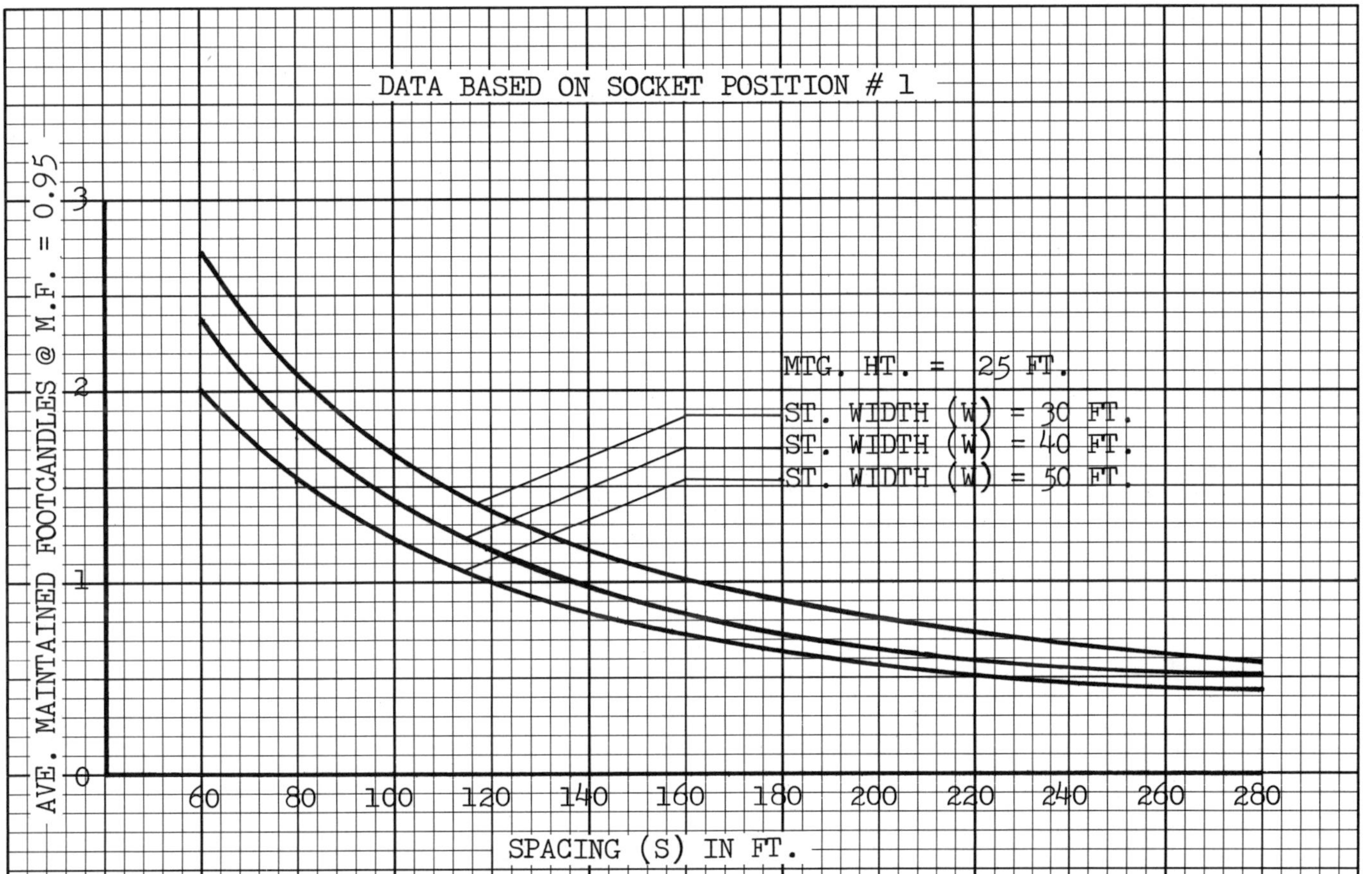
DATA BASED ON SOCKET POSITION # 1
AVE. MAINTAINED FOOTCANDLES @ M.F. = 0.95
3
2
1
0
MTG. HT. = 25 FT.
ST. WIDTH (W) = 30 FT.
ST. WIDTH (W) = 40 FT.
ST. WIDTH (W) = 50 FT.
60 80 100 120 140 160 180 200 220 240 260 280
SPACING (S) IN FT.

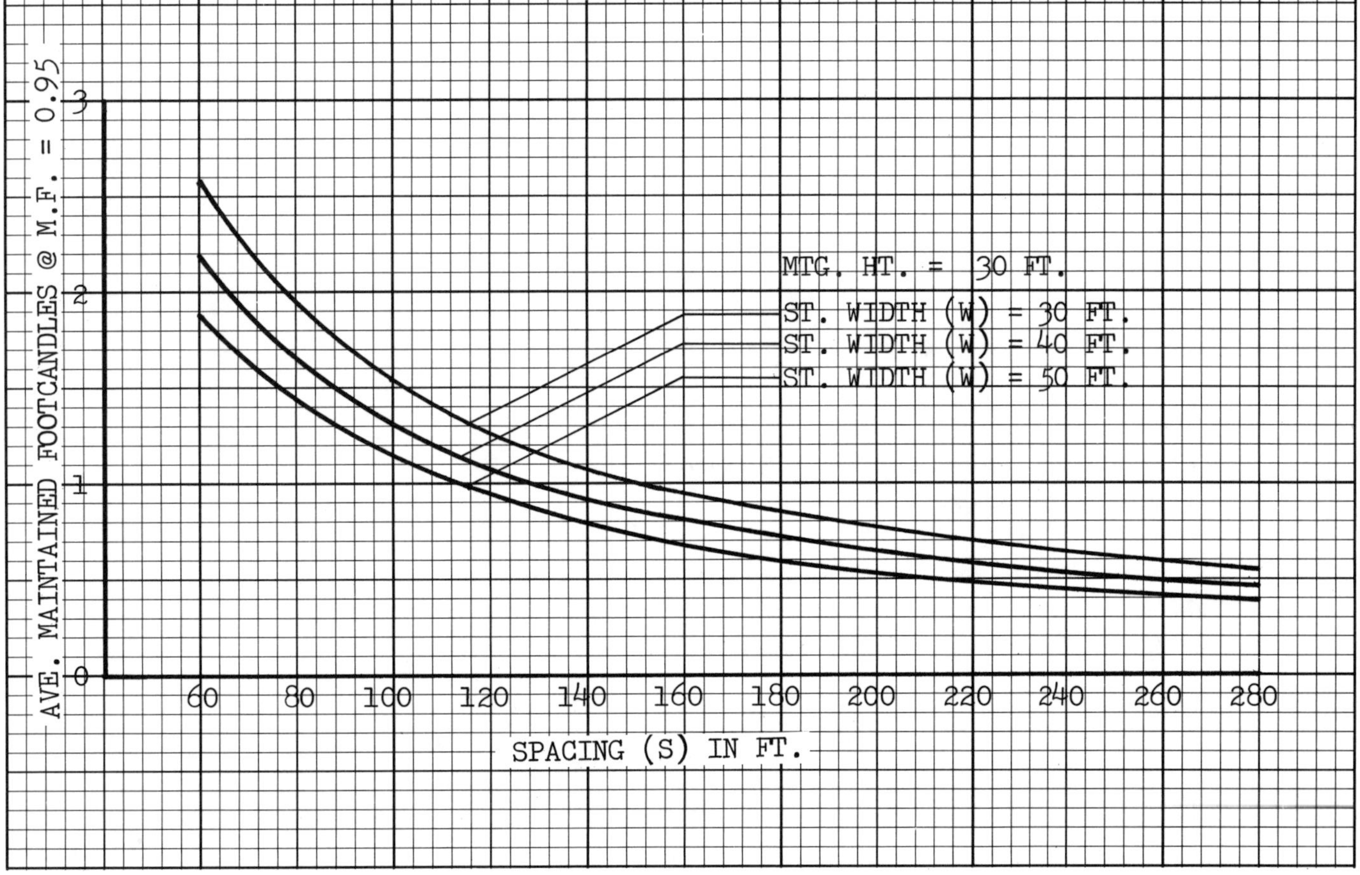
AVE. MAINTAINED FOOTCANDLES @ M.F. = 0.95
3
2
1
0
MTG. HT. = 30 FT.
ST. WIDTH (W) = 30 FT.
ST. WIDTH (W) = 40 FT.
ST. WIDTH (W) = 50 FT.
60 80 100 120 140 160 180 200 220 240 260 280
SPACING (S) IN FT.

Low-Pressure Sodium Luminaire (Norelco), 135W
(continued from page G–18)

Curves shown are based on lamp socket position 3. With this arrangement, the distribution is type IV, long noncutoff, with maximum candle power at 77½°. For other details, see page G–18.

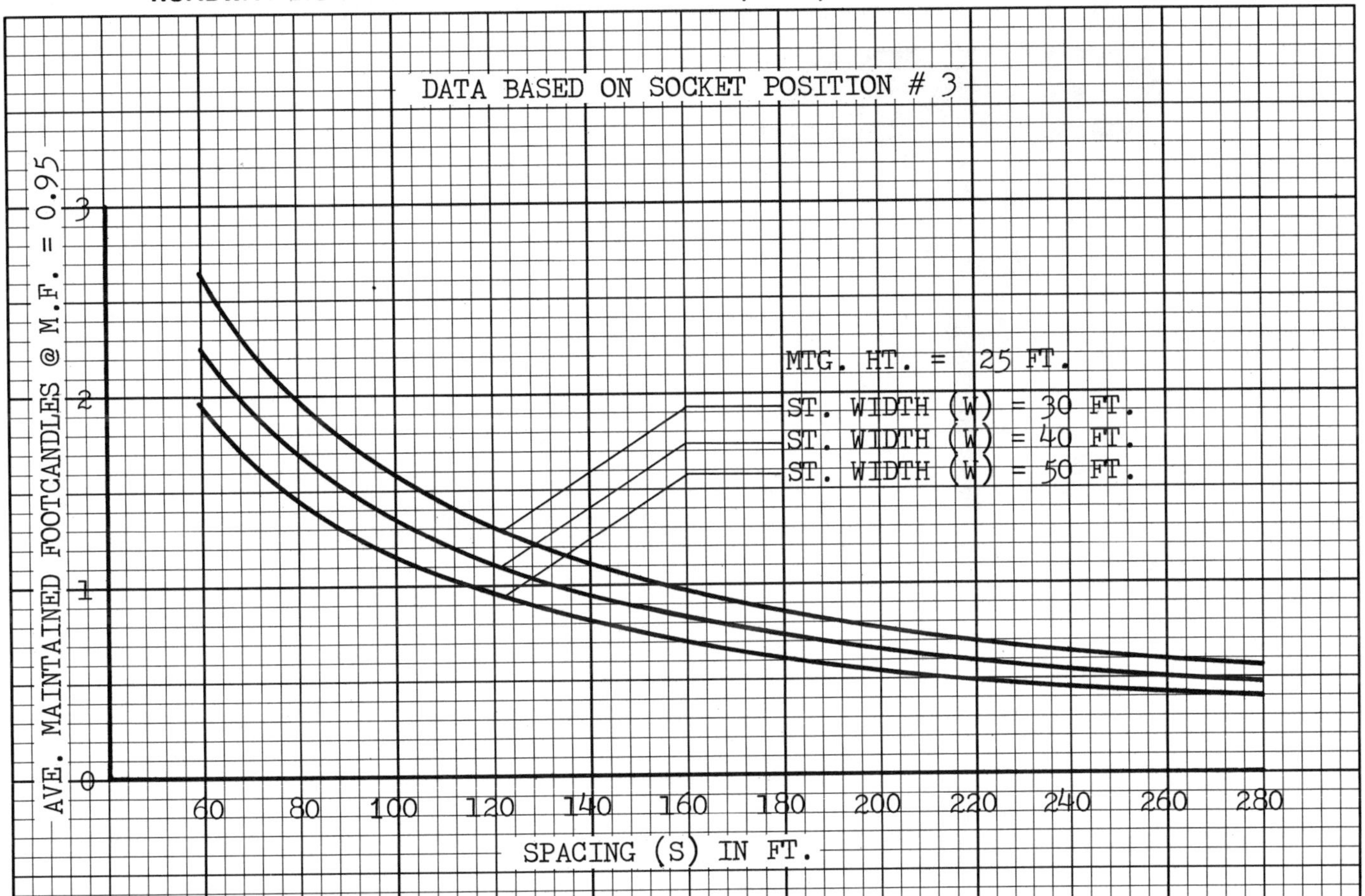
DATA BASED ON SOCKET POSITION # 3
AVE. MAINTAINED FOOTCANDLES @ M.F. = 0.95
MTG. HT. = 25 FT.
ST. WIDTH (W) = 30 FT.
ST. WIDTH (W) = 40 FT.
ST. WIDTH (W) = 50 FT.
0
1
2
3
60
80
100
120
140
160
180
200
220
240
260
280
SPACING (S) IN FT.

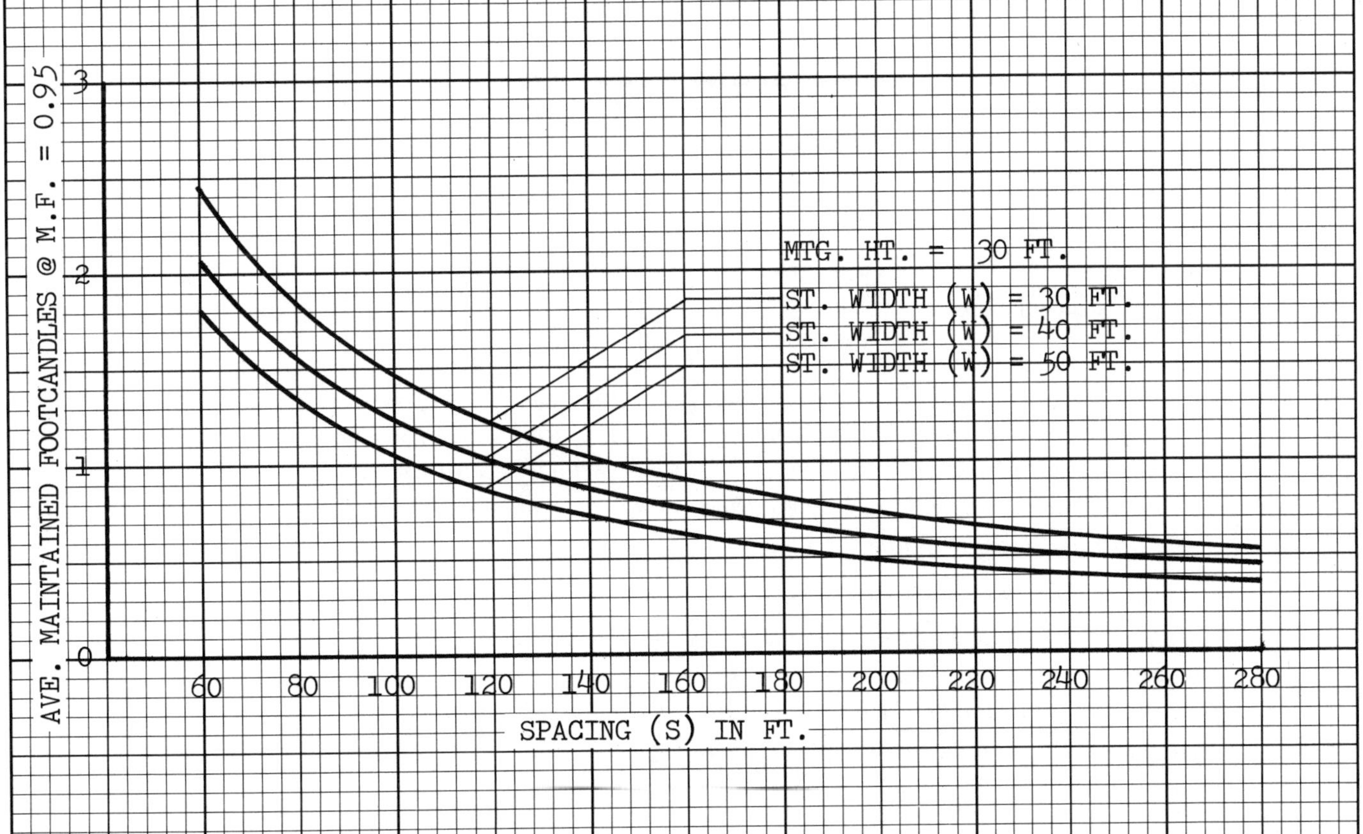
AVE. MAINTAINED FOOTCANDLES @ M.F. = 0.95
MTG. HT. = 30 FT.
ST. WIDTH (W) = 30 FT.
ST. WIDTH (W) = 40 FT.
ST. WIDTH (W) = 50 FT.
0
1
2
3
60
80
100
120
140
160
180
200
220
240
260
280
SPACING (S) IN FT.

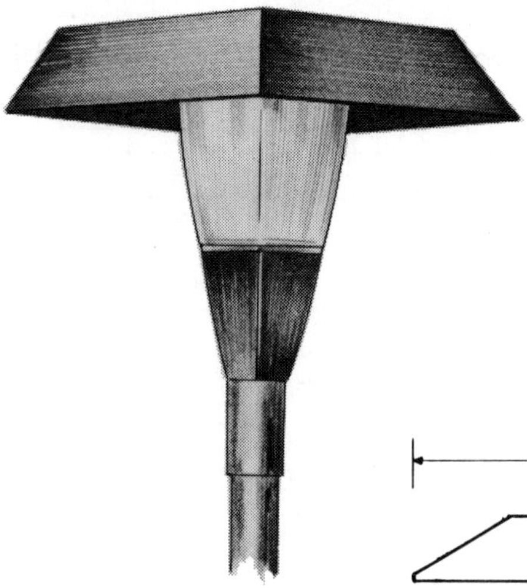

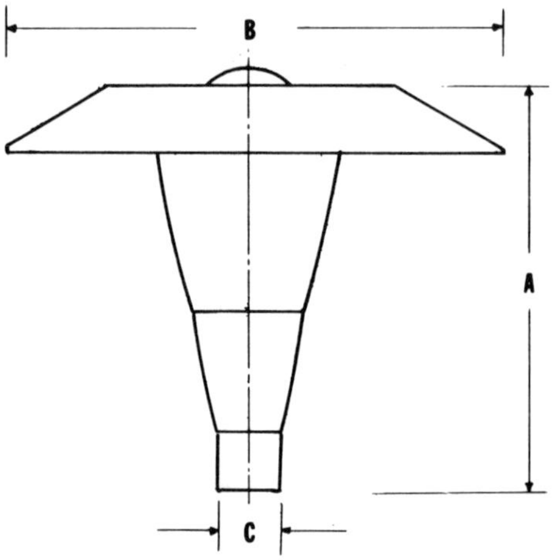

A = $24\frac{1}{4}$"
B = 24"
C = $3\frac{1}{16}$"

Description	Holophane square-postop
Lamp	One 175-W mercury (color-improved), 7300 lm, 24,000 h
Construction	Cast-aluminum body with prismatic, square glass refractor
Distribution	Type V
Maintenance factor	0.7
Input, W	200
Cost details per luminaire	Contractor's price = \$182 Installed cost = \$269

The installed cost includes published contractor's book price for the luminaire with ballast, lamp as shown, fastening devices, and the labor required for installation and connection on a pole. See page G–57 for the installed cost of a pole.

These popular luminaires with large refractor surface and specially designed prisms provide uniform luminosity with less concentrated glare spots. To obtain an average to minimum uniformity ratio of 3 : 1, do not exceed spacing 7 times the mounting height. For further information, refer to manufacturer's catalog.

This information was based on isolux chart (test 21644), published by Holophane Company, Inc.

AREA LIGHTING – HOLOPHANE SQUARE-POSTOP, 175W

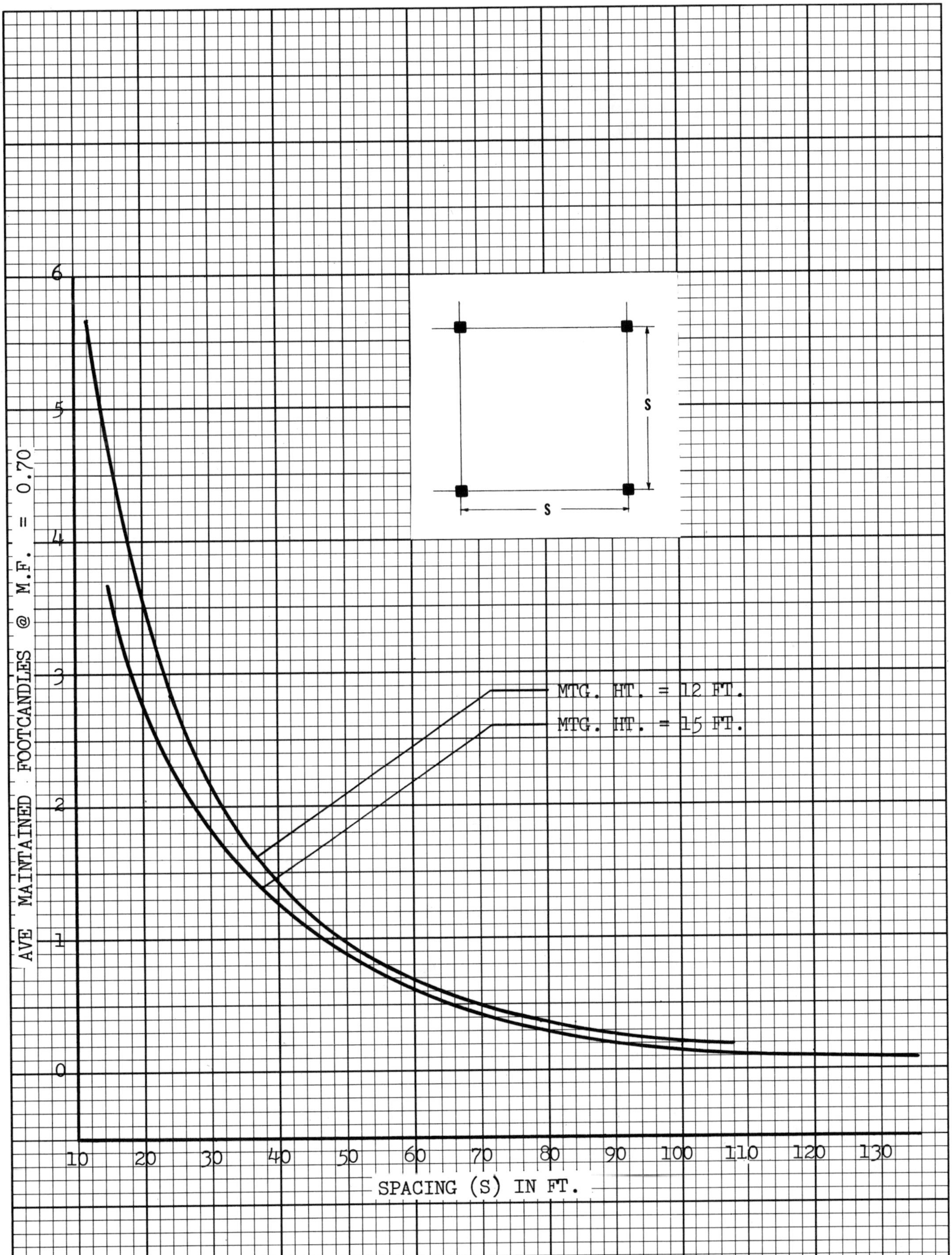

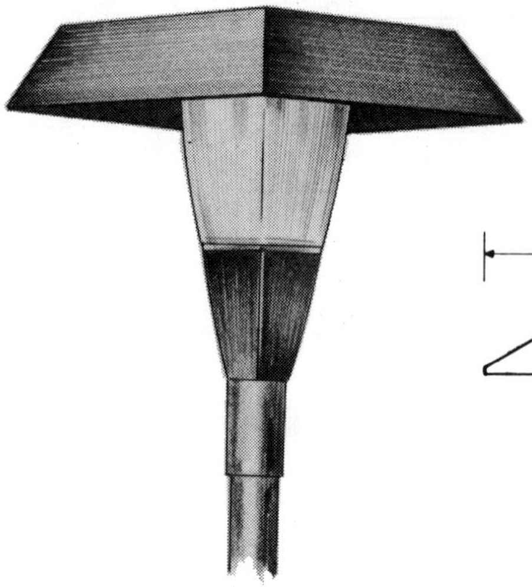

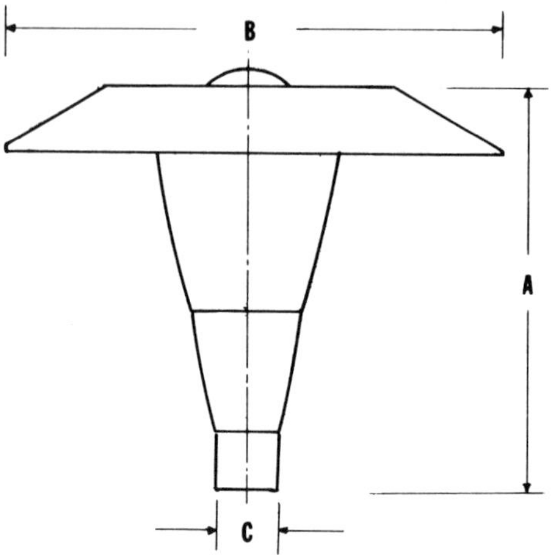

A = $24\frac{1}{4}$"
B = 24"
C = $3\frac{1}{16}$"

Description	Holophane square-postop
Lamp	One 250-W mercury (color-improved), 11,500 lm, 24,000 h
Construction	Cast-aluminum body with prismatic, square glass refractor
Distribution	Type V
Maintenance factor	0.7
Input, W	285
Cost details per luminaire	Contractor's price = \$187 Installed cost = \$286.75

The installed cost includes published contractor's book price for the luminaire with ballast, lamp as shown, fastening devices, and the labor required for installation and connection on a pole. *See page G–57 for the installed cost of a pole.*

These popular luminaires with large refractor surface and specially designed prisms provide uniform luminosity with less concentrated glare spots. To obtain an average to minimum uniformity ratio of 3 : 1, do not exceed spacing 7 times the mounting height. For further information, refer to manufacturer's catalog.

This information was based on isolux chart (test 20886), published by Holophane Company, Inc.

AREA LIGHTING – HOLOPHANE SQUARE-POSTOP, 250W

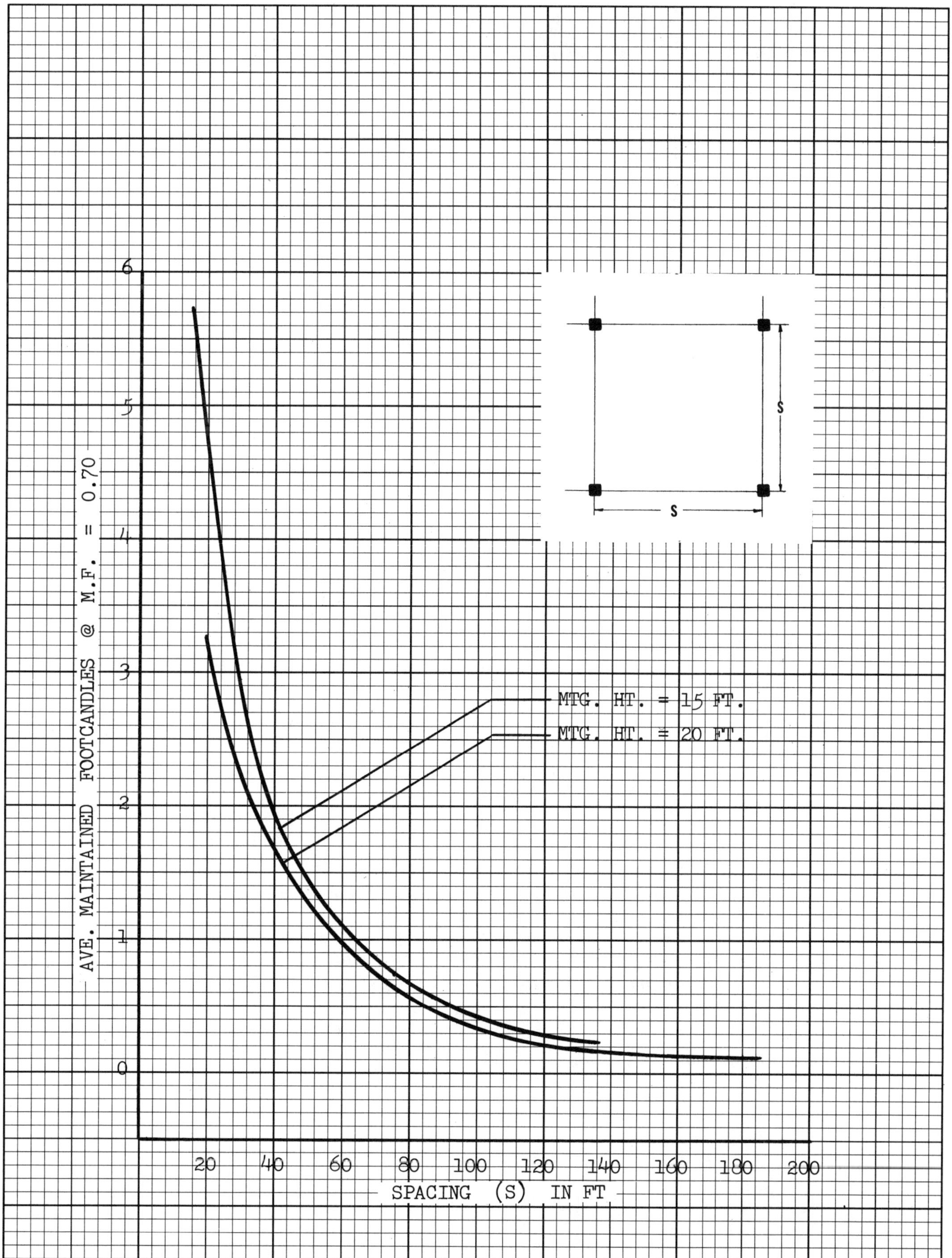

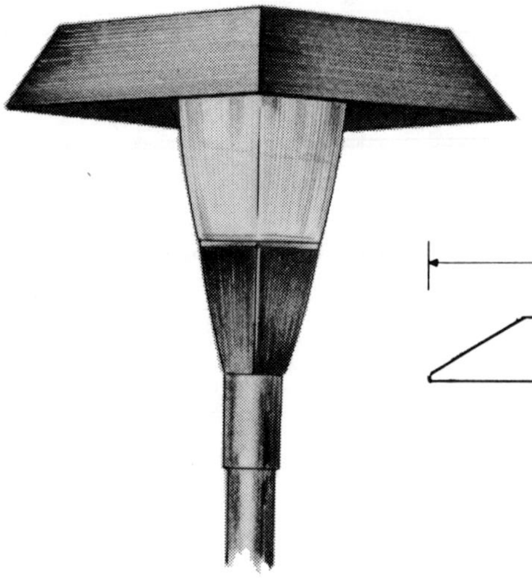

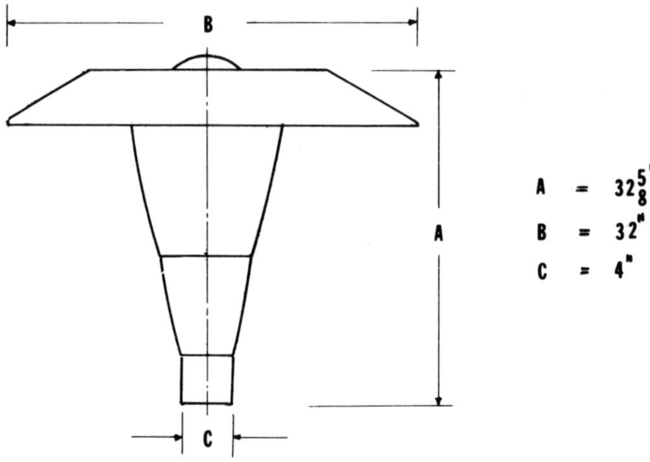

Description	Holophane square-postop
Lamp	One 400-W mercury (color-improved), 21,000 lm, 24,000 h
Construction	Cast-aluminum body with prismatic, square glass refractor
Distribution	Type V
Maintenance factor	0.7
Input, W	445
Cost details per luminaire	Contractor's price = \$250
	Installed cost = \$369

The installed cost includes published contractor's book price for the luminaire with ballast, lamp as shown, fastening devices, and the labor required for installation and connection on a pole. See page G–57 for the installed cost of a pole.

These popular luminaires with large refractor surface and specially designed prisms provide uniform luminosity with less concentrated glare spots. To obtain an average to minimum uniformity ratio of 3 : 1, do not exceed spacing 6 times the mounting height. For further information, refer to manufacturer's catalog.

This information was based on isolux chart (test 22278), published by Holophane Company, Inc.

AREA LIGHTING – HOLOPHANE SQUARE-POSTOP, 400W

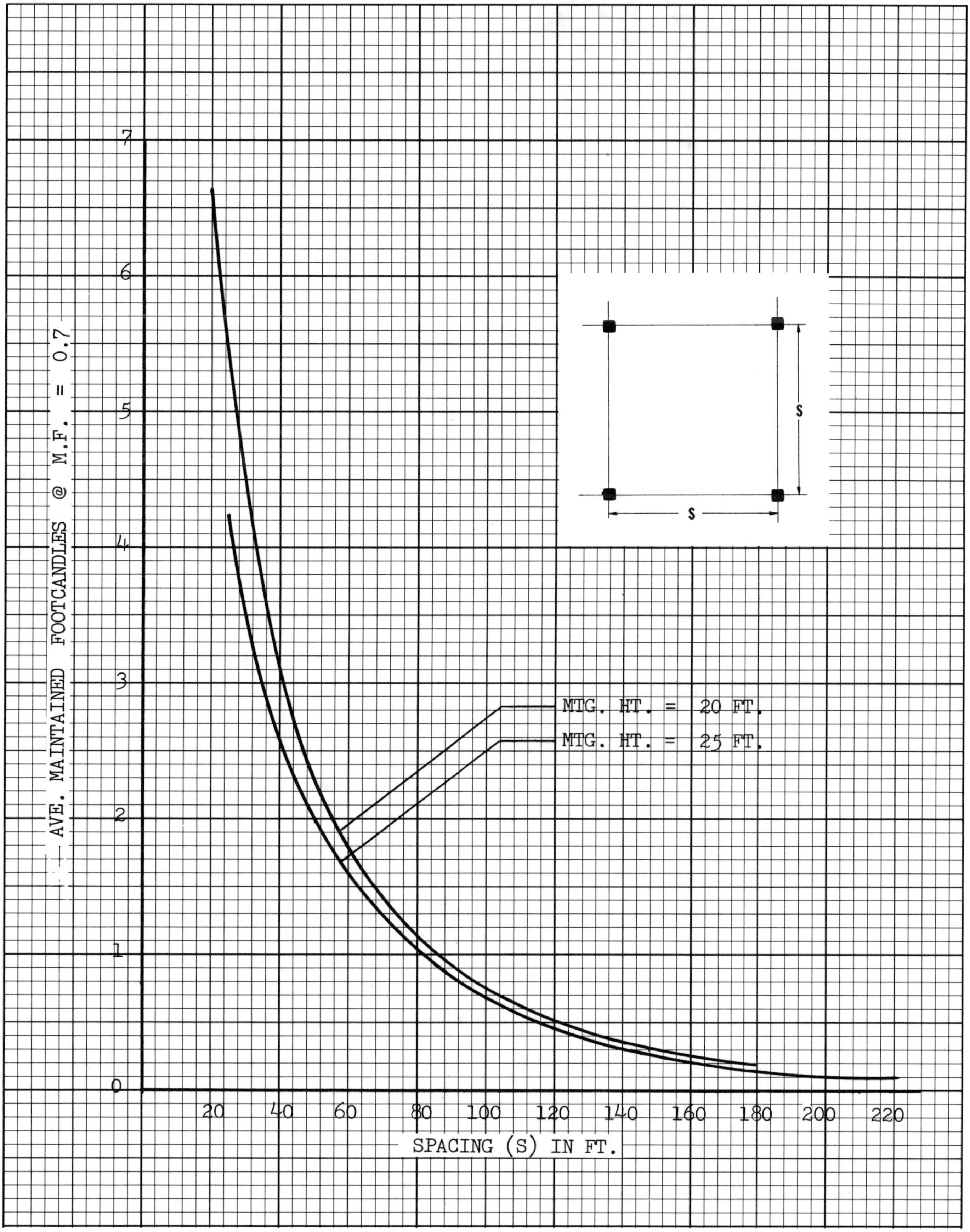

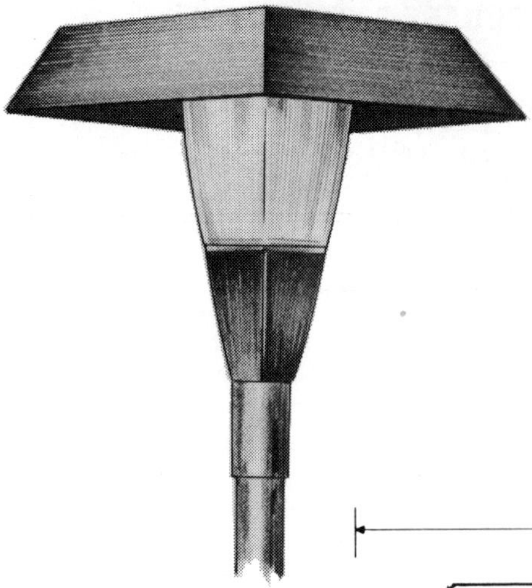

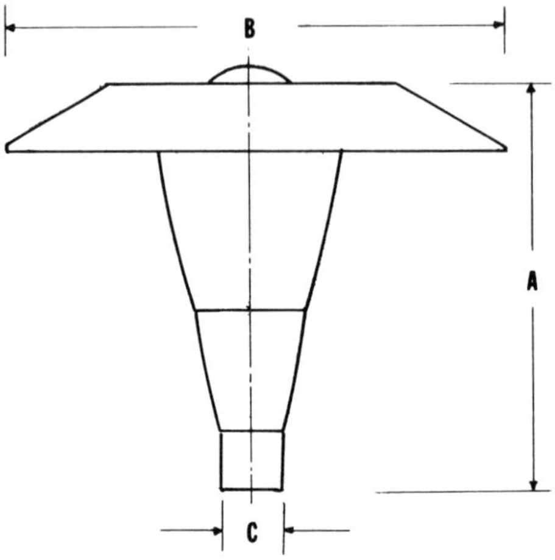

A = $38\frac{1}{4}$"
B = 32"
C = 4"

Description	Holophane square-postop
Lamp	One 1000-W mercury (color-improved), 54,000 lm, 24,000 h
Construction	Cast-aluminum body with prismatic, square glass refractor
Distribution	Type V
Maintenance factor	0.7
Input, W	1065
Cost details per luminaire	Contractor's price = \$364 Installed cost = \$550.75

The installed cost includes published contractor's book price for the luminaire with ballast, lamp as shown, fastening devices, and the labor required for installation and connection on a pole. See page G–57 for the installed cost of a pole.

These popular luminaires with large refractor surface and specially designed prisms provide uniform luminosity with less concentrated glare spots. To obtain an average to minimum uniformity ratio of 3 : 1, do not exceed spacing 5 times the mounting height. For further information, refer to manufacturer's catalog.

This information was based on isolux chart (test 22597), published by Holophane Company, Inc.

AREA LIGHTING – HOLOPHANE SQUARE-POSTOP, 1000W

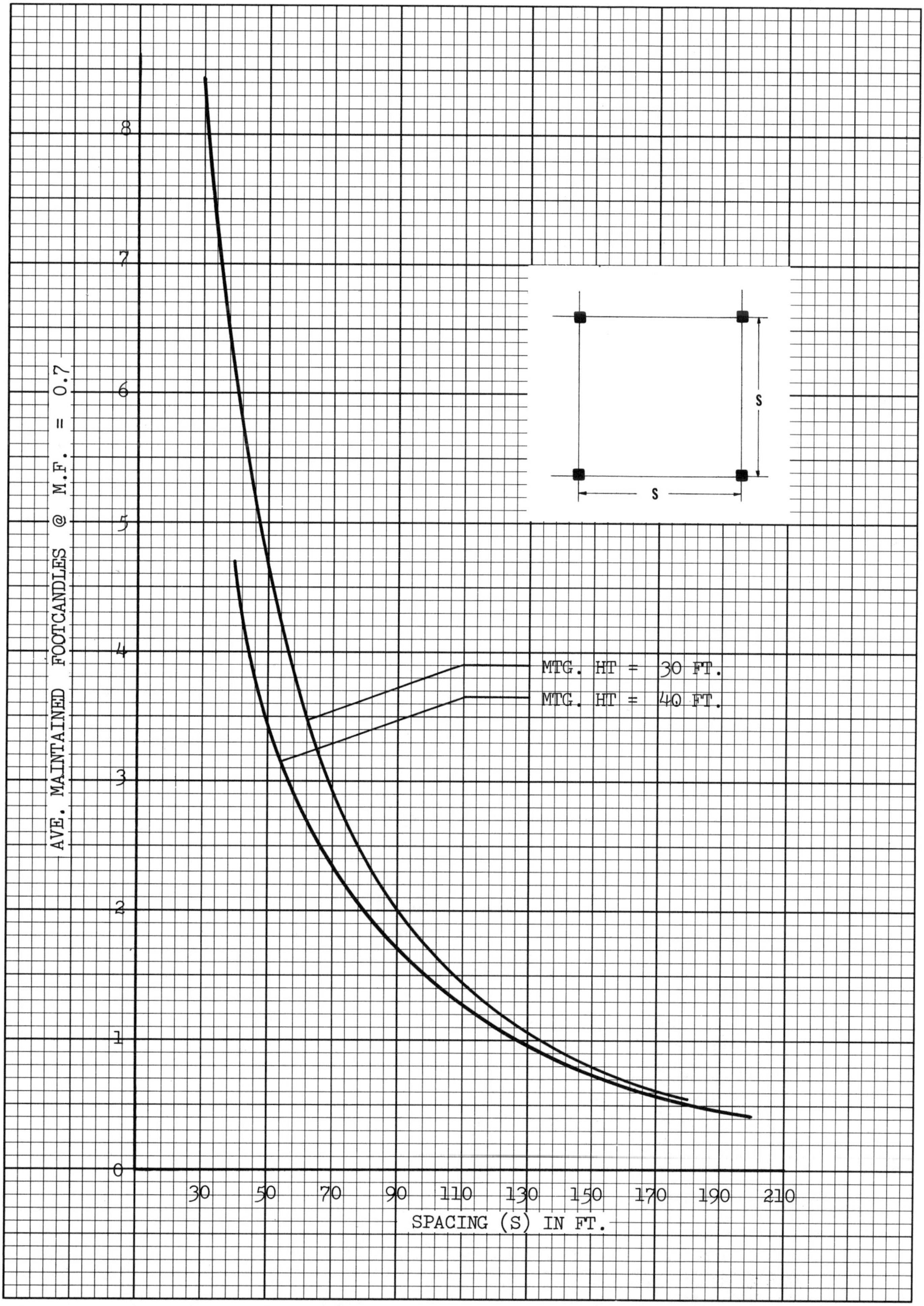

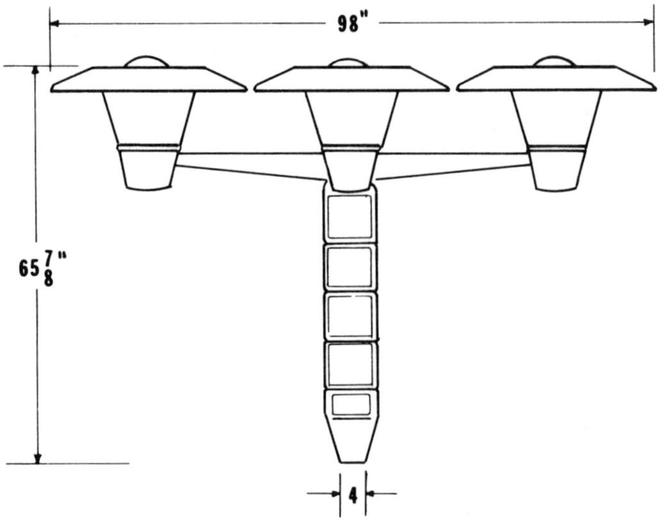

Description	Holophane square-postop
Lamps	Four 1000-W mercury (color-improved), 54,000 lm each, 24,000 h
Construction	Cast-aluminum body with prismatic, square glass refractor
Distribution	Type V
Maintenance factor	0.7
Input, W	4260
Cost details per luminaire	Contractor's price = $1526 Installed cost = $2180.25

The installed cost includes published contractor's book price for the luminaire with ballasts, lamps as shown, fastening devices, and the labor required for installation and connection on a pole. See page G–57 for the installed cost of a pole.

These popular luminaires with large refractor surface and specially designed prisms provide uniform luminosity with less concentrated glare spots. To obtain an average to minimum uniformity ratio of 3 : 1, do not exceed spacing 4 times the mounting height. For further information, refer to manufacturer's catalog.

This information was based on isolux chart (test 22597), published by Holophane Company, Inc.

AREA LIGHTING – HOLOPHANE SQUARE-POSTOP, (4) 1000W

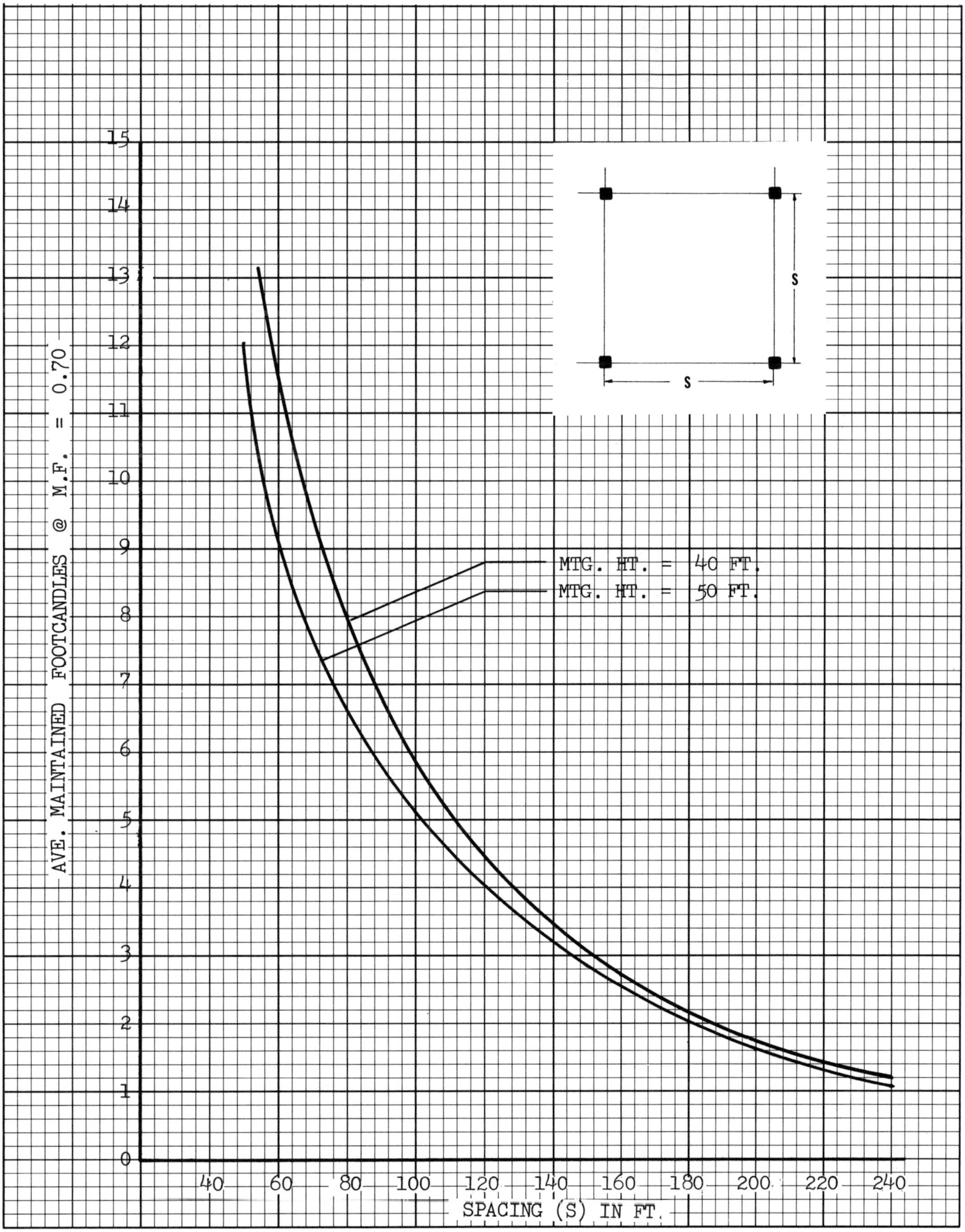

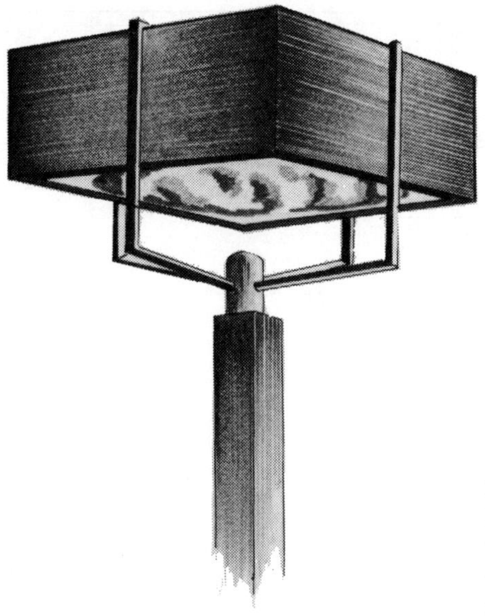

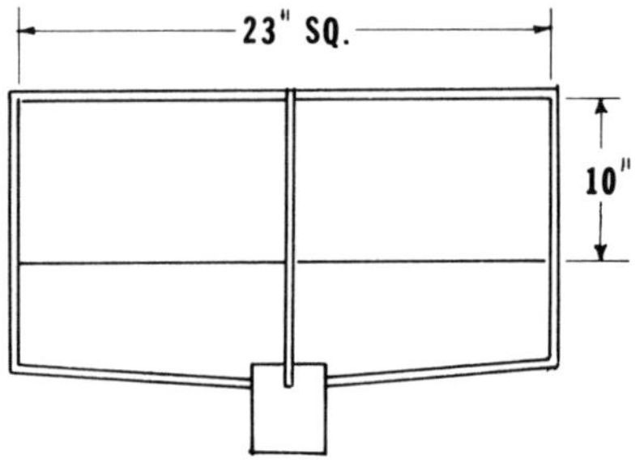

Description	Rectilinear luminaire
Lamp	One 175-W mercury (DX), 8150 lm, 24,000 h
Reflector	Clear specular aluminum
Distribution	Type V (square)
Maintenance factor	0.7
Conversion factors	A. Unit with one 175-W mercury (DX) = 1.0
	B. Unit with one 250-W mercury (DX) = 1.15
	C. Unit with one 175-W metal halide (clear) = 1.3
	D. Unit with one 150-W high-pressure sodium = 1.44

COST DETAILS PER LUMINAIRE

Type of unit	Input, W	Contractor's price	Installed cost
A	200	$410	$549
B	290	412	563.45
C	210	410	579.45
D	185	444	632.92

The installed cost includes published contractor's book price for the luminaire with ballast, lamp as shown, fastening devices, and the labor required for installation and connection on a pole. See page G–57 for the installed cost of a pole.

With square distribution (type V), these luminaires minimize light overlap and thus provide greater pole spacings. For uniformity, refer to the isolux chart of the specific luminaire under consideration.

AREA LIGHTING – RECTILINEAR LUMINAIRE (SINGLE), UP TO 250W

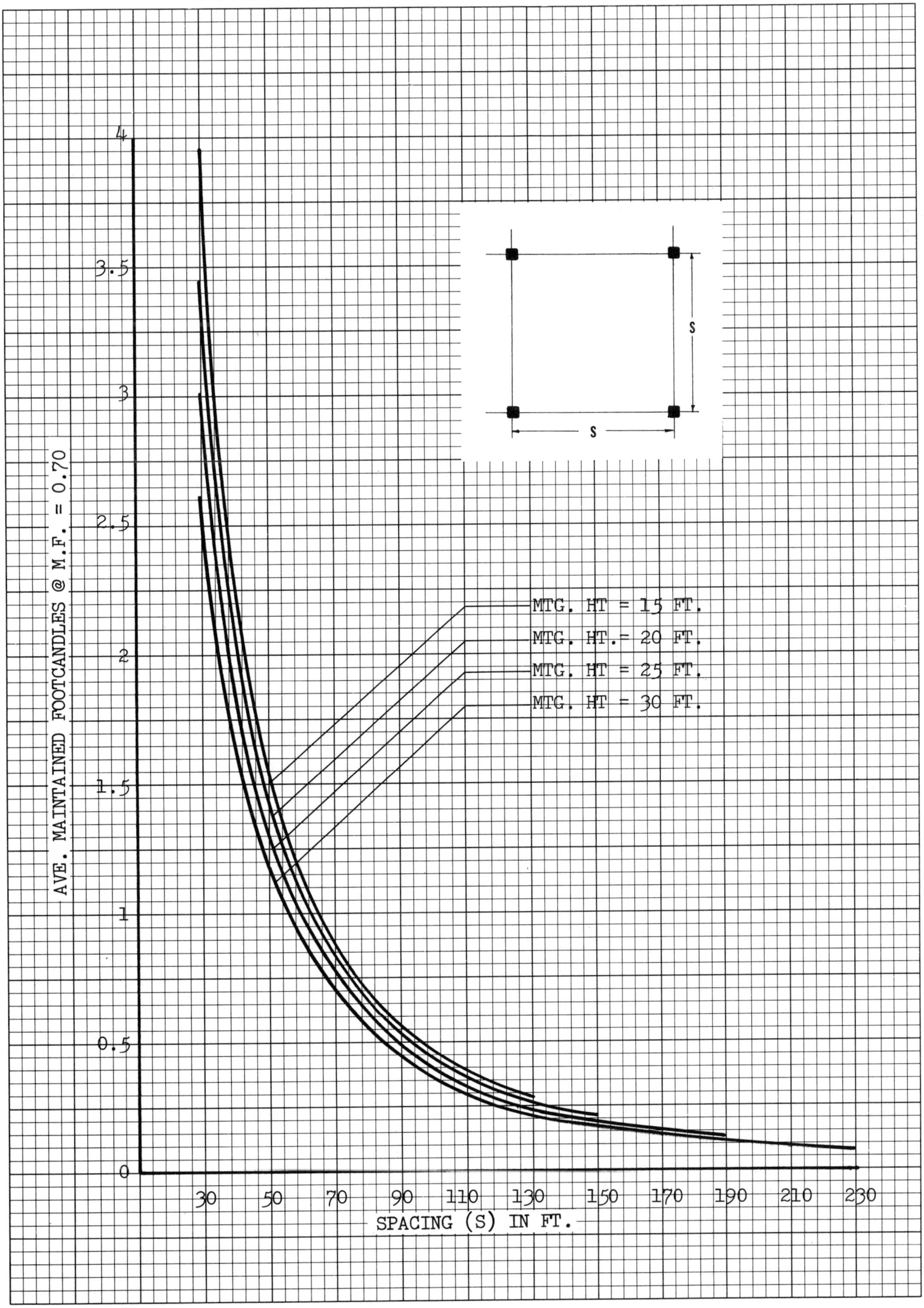

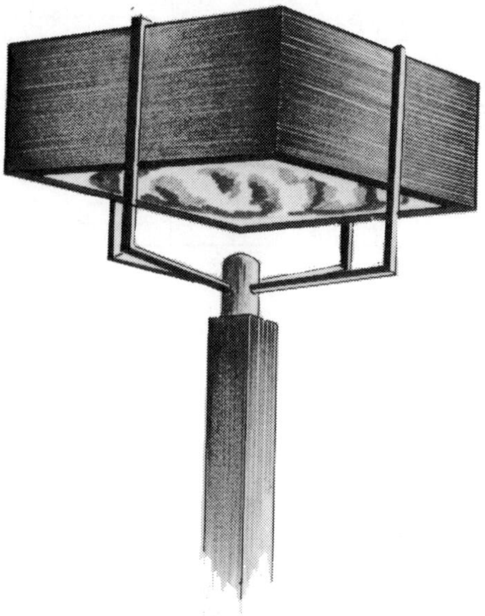

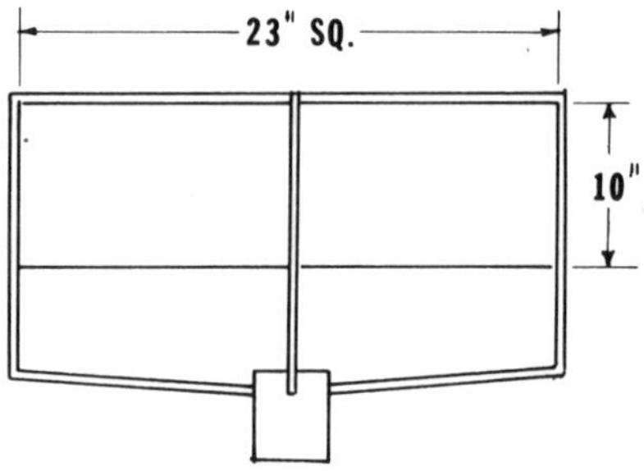

Description	Rectilinear luminaire
Lamp	One 400-W mercury (DX), 21,500 lm, 24,000 h
Reflector	Clear specular aluminum
Distribution	Type V (square)
Maintenance factor	0.7
Conversion factors	A. Unit with one 400-W mercury (DX) = 1.0 B. Unit with one 400-W metal halide (clear) = 1.46 C. Unit with one 400-W high-pressure sodium = 1.7

COST DETAILS PER LUMINAIRE

Type of unit	Input, W	Contractor's price	Installed cost
A	445	$425	$584.25
B	465	436	623.65
C	450	525	749

The installed cost includes published contractor's book price for the luminaire with ballast, lamp as shown, fastening devices, and the labor required for installation and connection on a pole. *See page G–57 for the installed cost of a pole.*

With square distribution (type V), these luminaires minimize light overlap and thus provide greater pole spacings. For uniformity, refer to the isolux chart of the specific luminaire under consideration.

AREA LIGHTING – RECTILINEAR LUMINAIRE (SINGLE), 400W

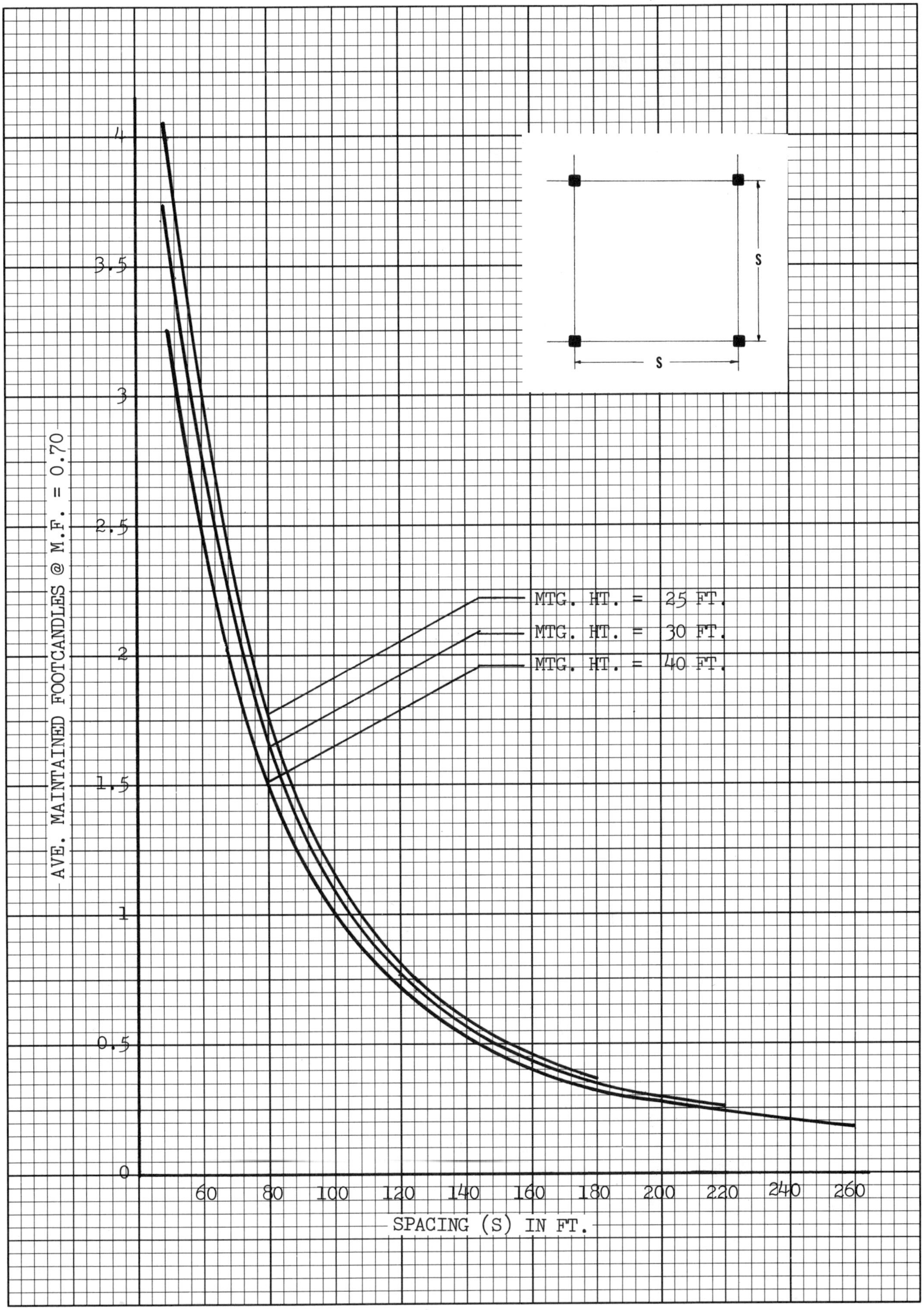

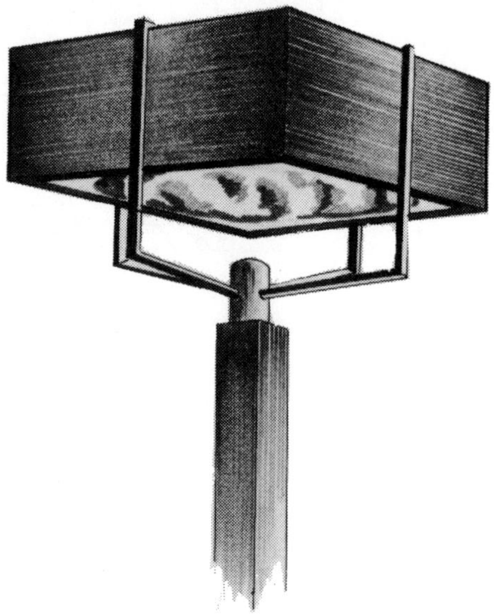

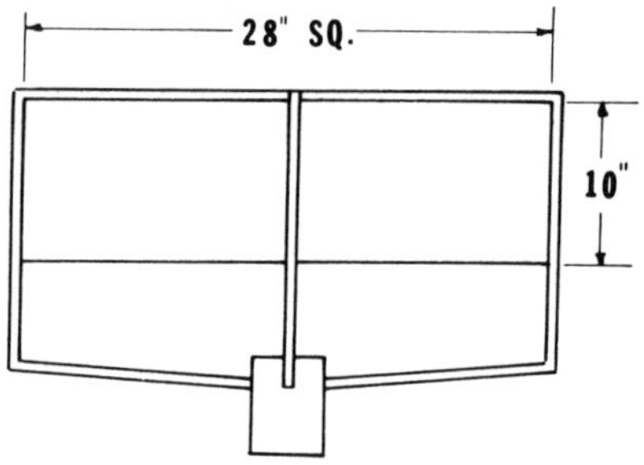

Description	Rectilinear luminaire
Lamp	One 1000-W mercury (DX), 60,000 lm, 24,000 h
Reflector	Clear specular aluminum
Distribution	Type V (square)
Maintenance factor	0.7
Conversion factors	A. Unit with one 1000-W mercury (DX) = 1.0
	B. Unit with one 1000-W metal halide (clear) = 1.42
	C. Unit with one 1000-W high-pressure sodium = 1.77

COST DETAILS PER LUMINAIRE

Type of unit	Input, W	Contractor's price	Installed cost
A	1065	$480	$693.40
B	1085	506	780.75
C	1068	694	1055

The installed cost includes published contractor's book price for the luminaire with ballast, lamp as shown, fastening devices, and the labor required for installation and connection on a pole. See page G–57 for the installed cost of a pole.

With square distribution (type V), these luminaires minimize light overlap and thus provide greater pole spacings. For uniformity, refer to the isolux chart of the specific luminaire under consideration.

AREA LIGHTING – RECTILINEAR LUMINAIRE (SINGLE), 1000W

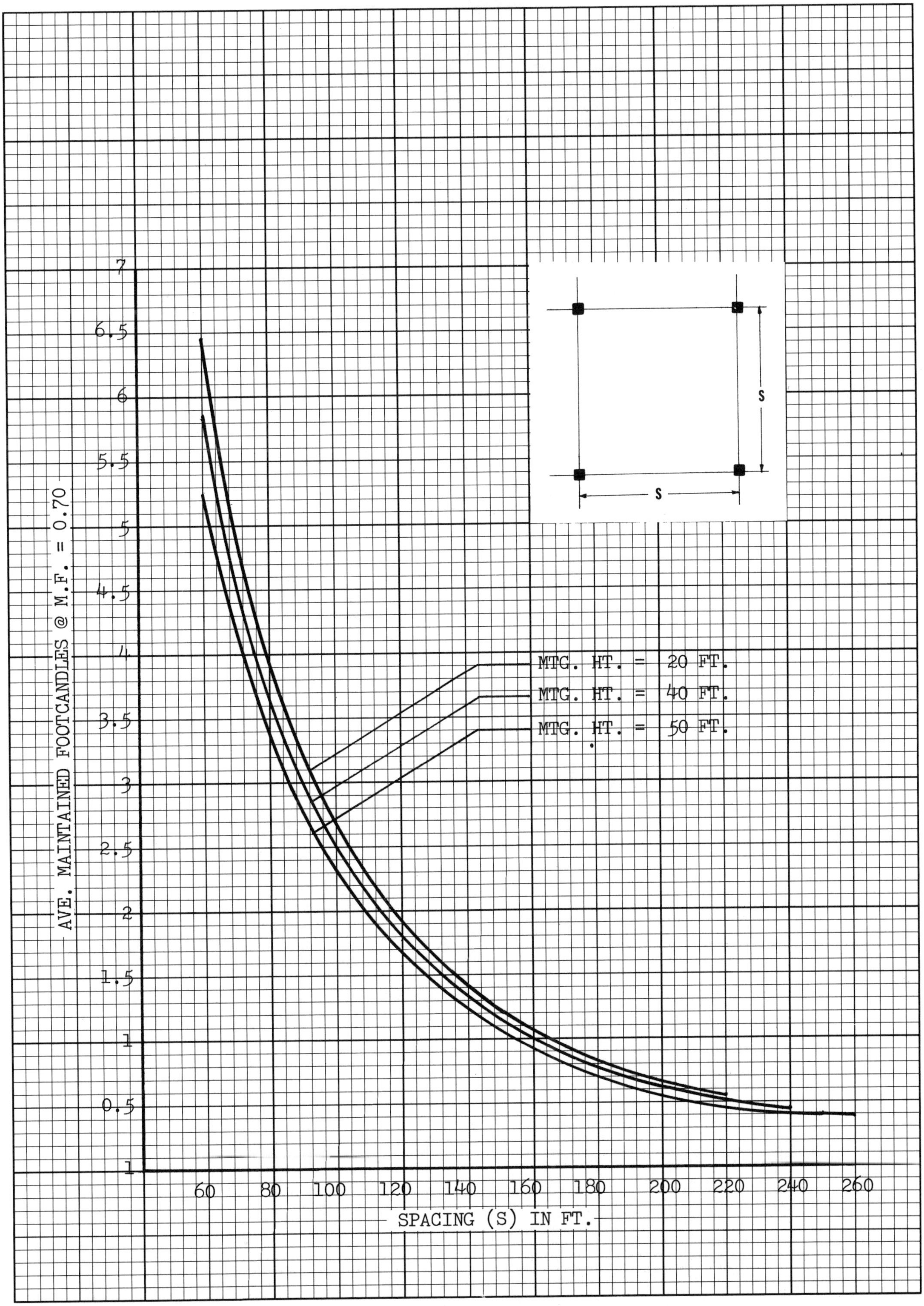

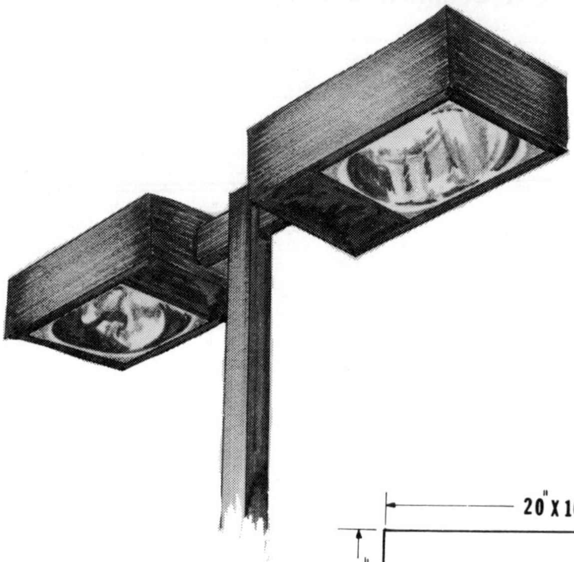

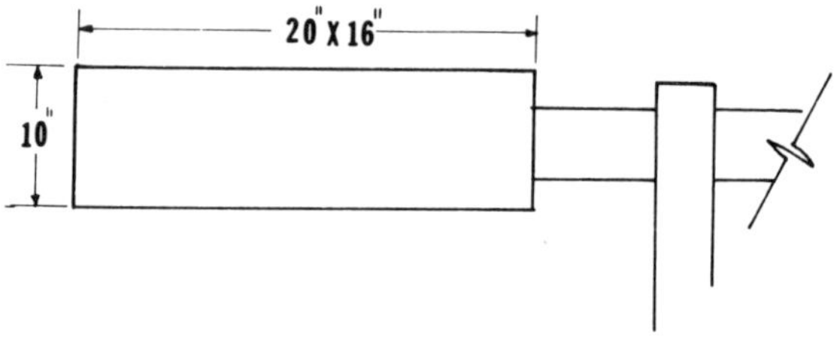

Description	Rectilinear luminaires
Lamps	One 175-W mercury (DX), 7750 lm each, 24,000 h
Reflector	Clear specular aluminum
Distribution	Type III
Maintenance factor	0.7
Conversion factors	A. Unit with two 175-W mercury (DX) = 1.0 B. Unit with two 250-W mercury (DX) = 1.21 C. Unit with two 175-W metal halide (clear) = 1.38 D. Unit with two 150-W high-pressure sodium = 1.41

COST DETAILS PER LUMINAIRE

Type of unit	Input, W	Contractor's price	Installed cost
A	400	$480	$663.54
B	570	490	697.00
C	420	508	749.64
D	370	578	867.72

The installed cost includes published contractor's book price for the luminaires with ballasts, lamps as shown, fastening devices, and the labor required for installation and connection on a pole. *See page G-57 for the installed cost of a pole.*

Luminaires of this rectilinear family represent today's popular area lighting. For uniformity, refer to the isolux chart of the specific luminaire under consideration.

AREA LIGHTING – RECTILINEAR LUMINAIRES (DOUBLE), UP TO 250W

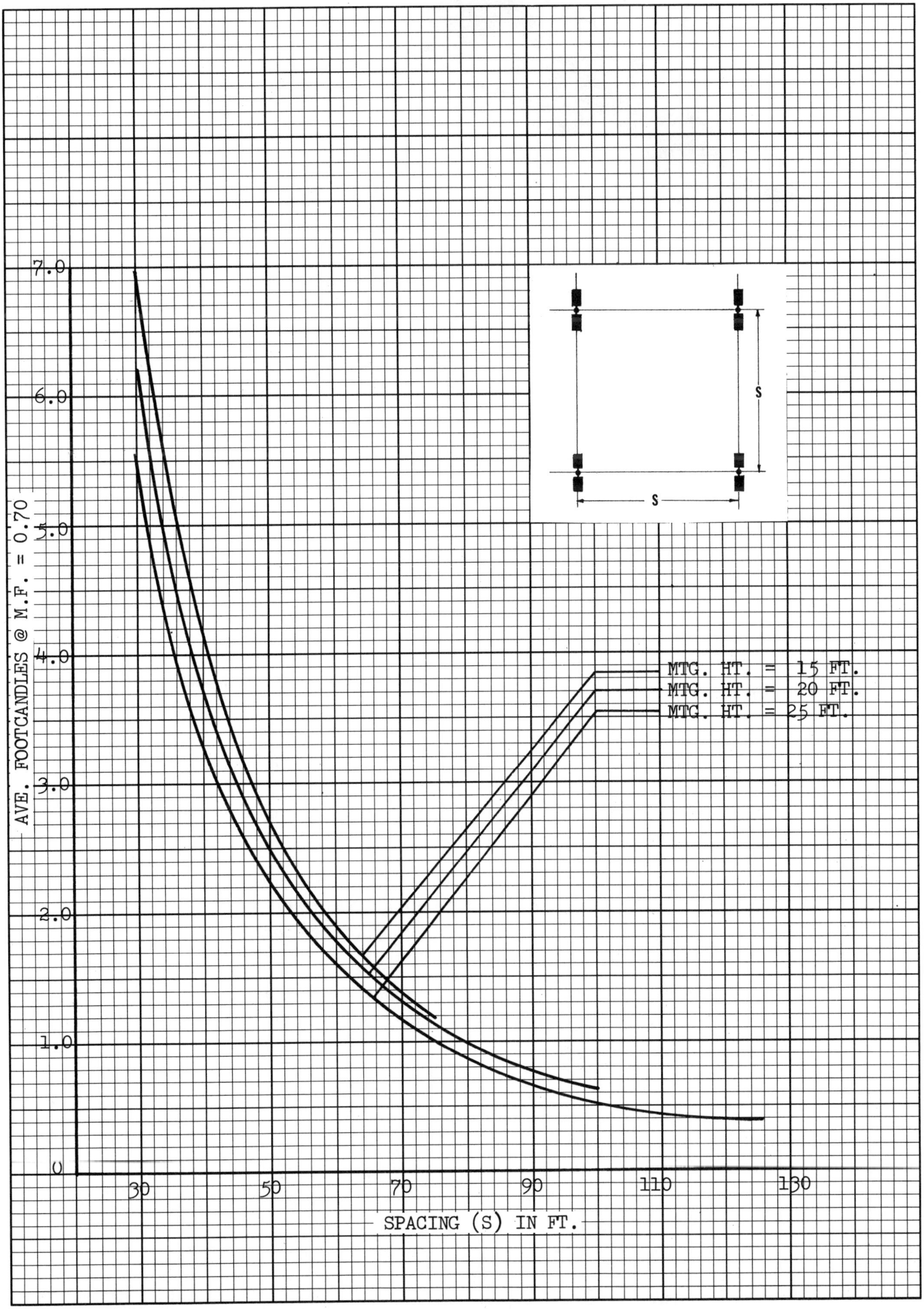

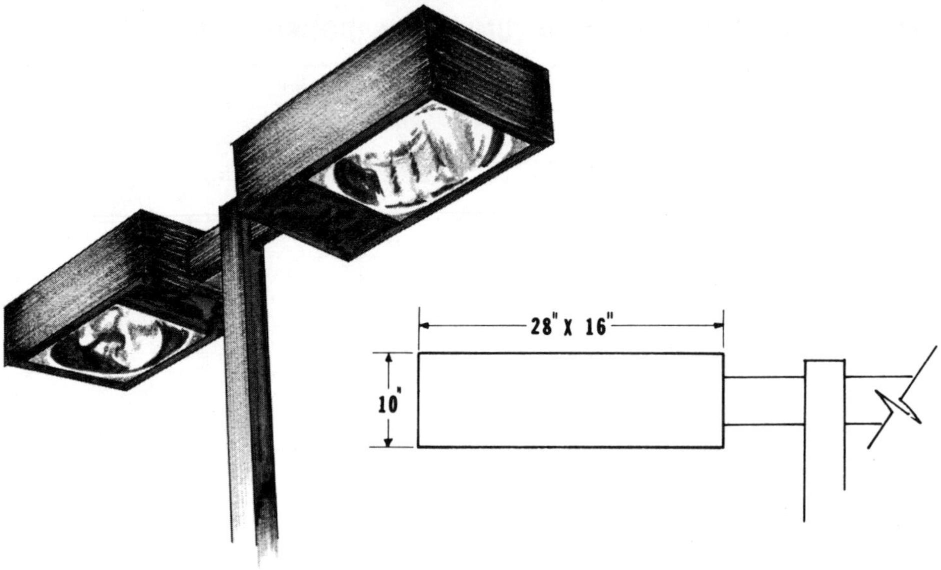

Description	Rectilinear luminaires
Lamps	Two 400-W mercury (DX), 21,000 lm each, 24,000 h
Reflector	Clear specular aluminum
Distribution	Type III
Maintenance factor	0.7
Conversion factors	A. Unit with two 400-W mercury (DX) = 1.0
	B. Unit with two 400-W metal halide (clear) = 1.34
	C. Unit with two 250-W high-pressure sodium = 1.38
	D. Unit with two 400-W high-pressure sodium = 1.7

COST DETAILS PER LUMINAIRE

Type of unit	Input, W	Contractor's price	Installed cost
A	890	$626	$857.20
B	930	662	965.44
C	590	680	1004.56
D	450	760	1117.96

The installed cost includes published contractor's book price for the luminaires with ballasts, lamps as shown, fastening devices, and the labor required for installation and connection on a pole. See page G–57 for the installed cost of a pole.

Luminaires of this rectilinear family represent today's popular area lighting. For uniformity, refer to the isolux chart of the specific luminaire under consideration.

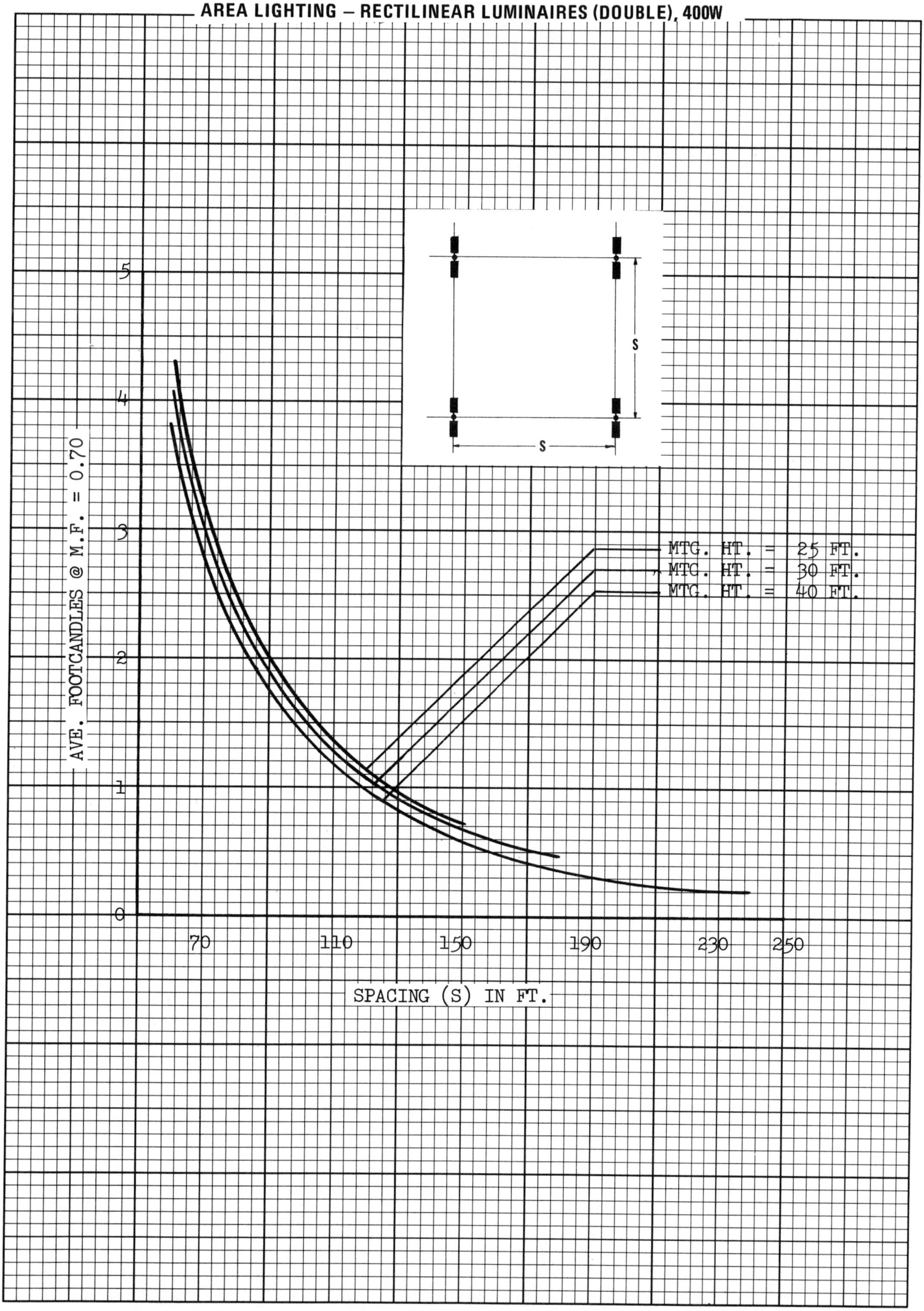
S
S
5
4
3
2
1
0
AVE. FOOTCANDLES @ M.F. = 0.70
MTG. HT. = 25 FT.
MTG. HT. = 30 FT.
MTG. HT. = 40 FT.
70
110
150
190
230
250
SPACING (S) IN FT.

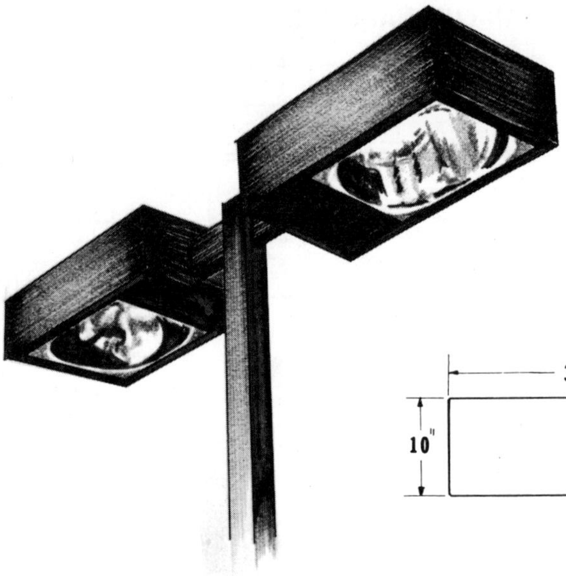

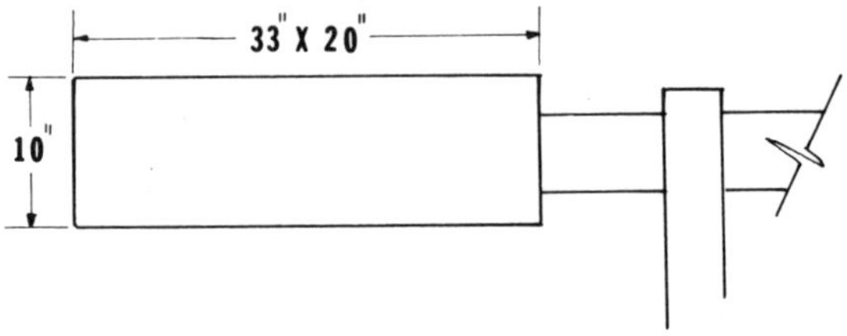

Description	Rectilinear luminaire
Lamps	Two 1000-W mercury (DX), 60,000 lm each, 24,000 h
Reflector	Clear specular aluminum
Distribution	Type III
Maintenance factor	0.7
Conversion factors	A. Unit with two 1000-W mercury (DX) = 1.0
	B. Unit with two 1000-W metal halide (clear) = 1.41
	C. Unit with two 1000-W high-pressure sodium = 1.54

COST DETAILS PER LUMINAIRE

Type of unit	Input, W	Contractor's price	Installed cost
A	2130	$ 754	$1097.20
B	2170	810	1276.79
C	2136	1160	1793.39

The installed cost includes published contractor's book price for the luminaires with ballasts, lamps as shown, fastening devices, and the labor required for installation and connection on a pole. See page G–57 for the installed cost of a pole.

Luminaires of this rectilinear family represent today's popular area lighting. For uniformity, refer to the isolux chart of the specific luminaire under consideration.

AREA LIGHTING – RECTILINEAR LUMINAIRES (DOUBLE), 1000W

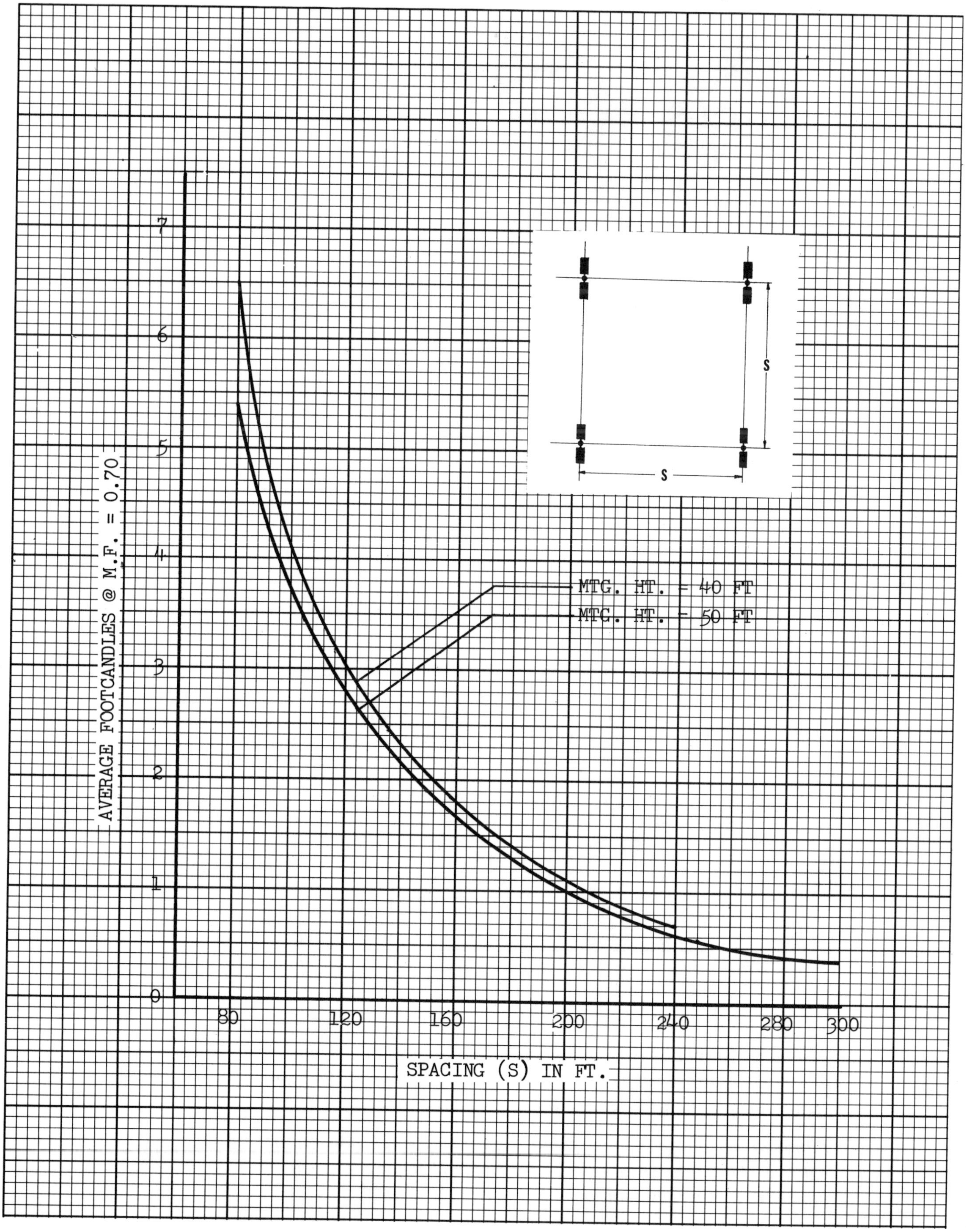

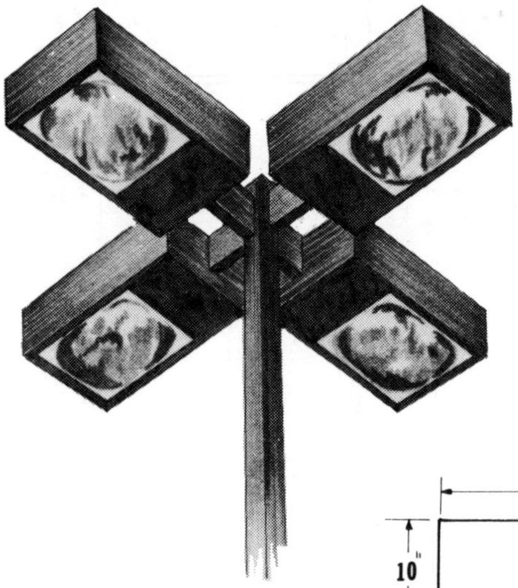

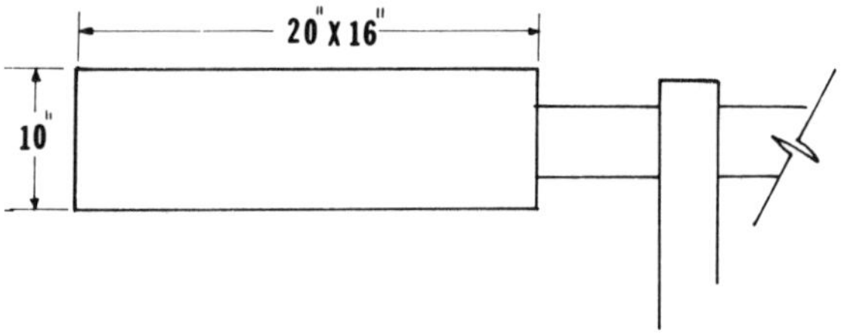

Description	Rectilinear luminaires
Lamps	Four 175-W mercury (DX), 7750 lm each, 24,000 h
Reflector	Clear specular aluminum
Distribution	Type III
Maintenance factor	0.7
Conversion factors	A. Unit with four 175-W mercury (DX) = 1.0
	B. Unit with four 250-W mercury (DX) = 1.21
	C. Unit with four 175-W metal halide (clear) = 1.38
	D. Unit with four 150-W high-pressure sodium = 1.41

COST DETAILS PER LUMINAIRE

Type of unit	Input, W	Contractor's price	Installed cost
A	800	$ 960	$1310.00
B	1140	980	1291.10
C	840	1016	1482.30
D	740	1156	1718.45

The installed cost includes published contractor's book price for the luminaires with ballasts, lamps as shown, fastening devices, and the labor required for installation and connection on a pole. *See page G–57 for the installed cost of a pole.*

Luminaires of this rectilinear family represent today's popular area lighting. For uniformity, refer to the isolux chart of the specific luminaire under consideration.

AREA LIGHTING – RECTILINEAR LUMINAIRES (QUAD.), UP TO 250W

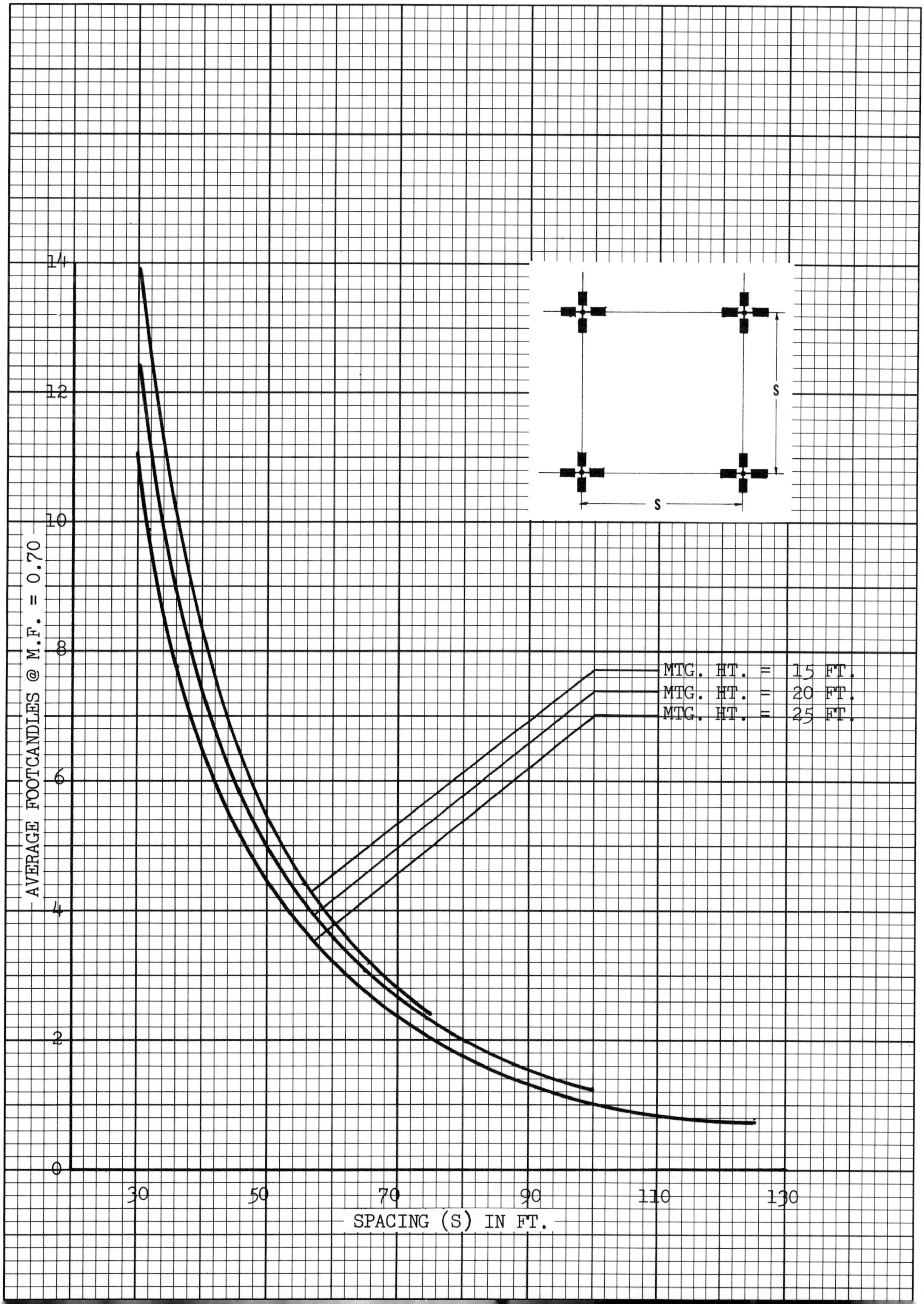

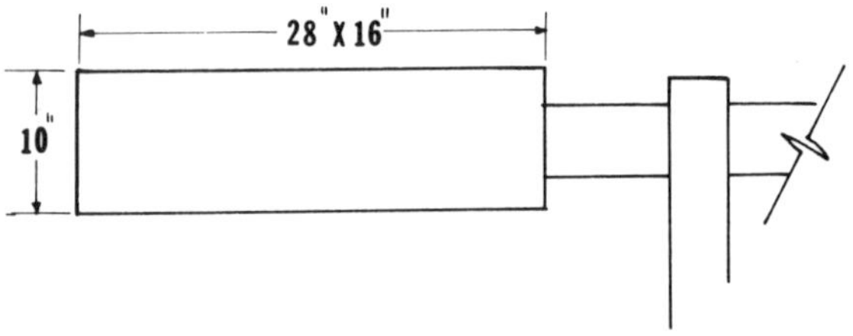

Description	Rectilinear luminaires
Lamps	Four 400-W mercury (DX), 21,500 lm each, 24,000 h
Reflector	Clear specular aluminum
Distribution	Type III
Maintenance factor	0.7
Conversion factors	A. Unit with four 400-W mercury (DX) = 1.0
	B. Unit with four 400-W metal halide (clear) = 1.34
	C. Unit with four 250-W high-pressure sodium = 1.38
	D. Unit with four 400-W high-pressure sodium = 1.7

COST DETAILS PER LUMINAIRE

Type of unit	Input, W	Contractor's price	Installed cost
A	1780	$1252	$1715.80
B	1860	1324	1907.67
C	1180	1360	1989.75
D	1800	1520	2212.70

The installed cost includes published contractor's book price for the luminaire with ballasts, lamps as shown, fastening devices, and the labor required for installation and connection on a pole. See page G–57 for the installed cost of a pole.

Luminaires of this rectilinear family represent today's popular area lighting. For uniformity, refer to the isolux chart of the specific luminaire under consideration.

AREA LIGHTING – RECTILINEAR LUMINAIRES (QUAD.), 400W

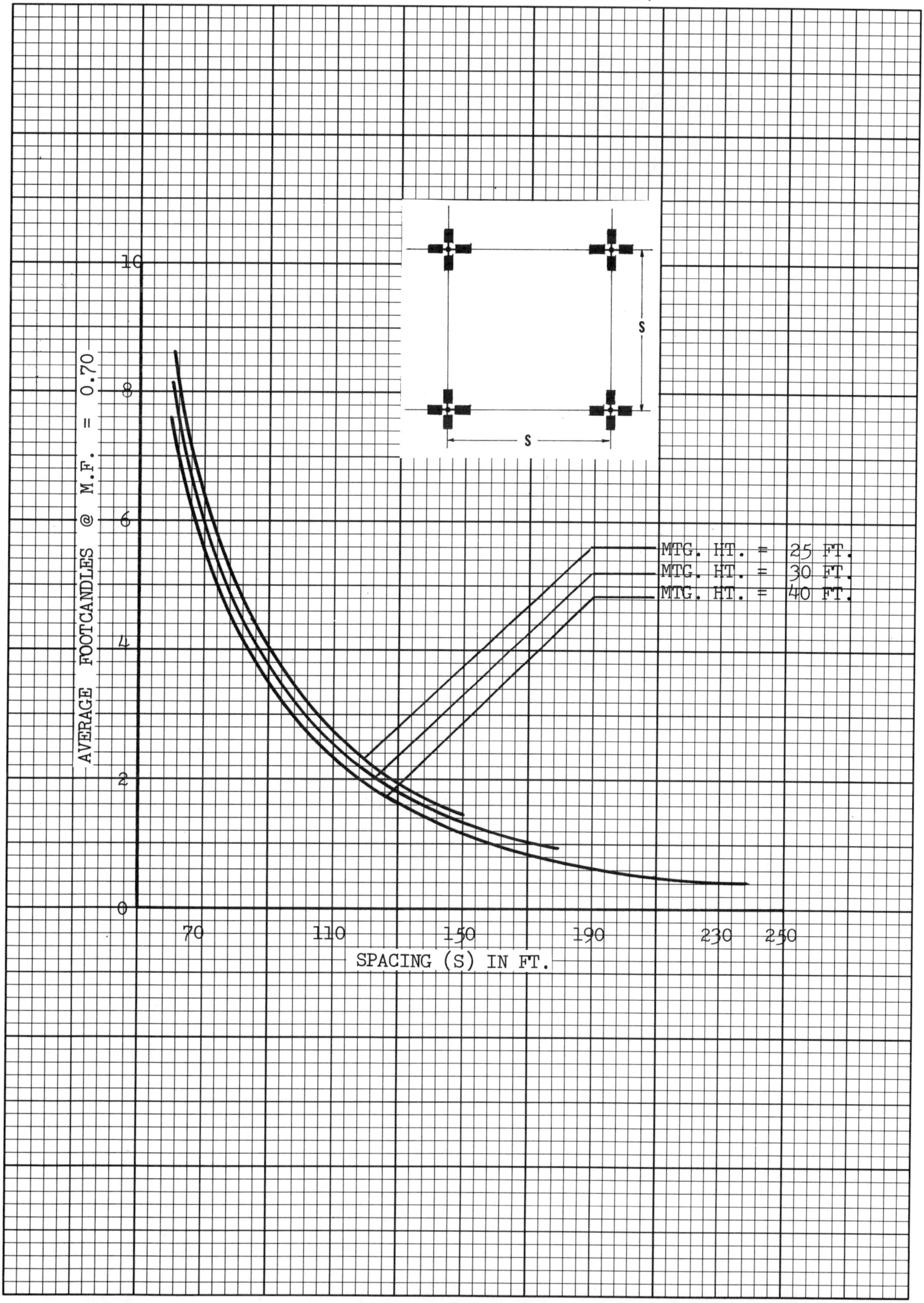

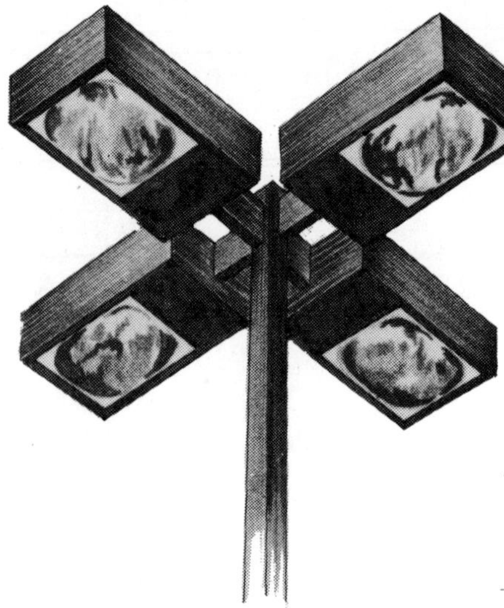

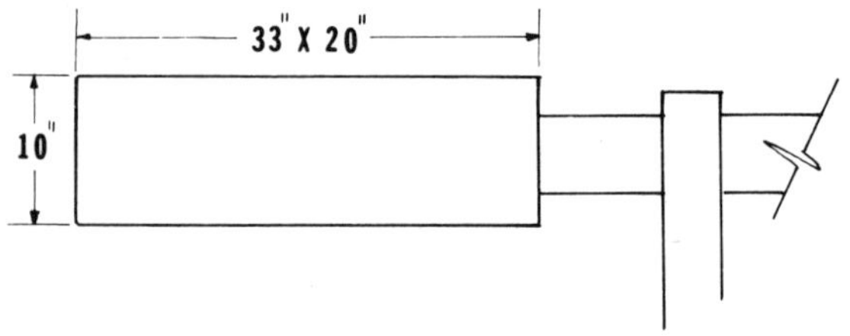

Description	Rectilinear luminaires
Lamps	Four 1000-W mercury (DX), 60,000 lm each, 24,000 h
Reflector	Clear specular aluminum
Distribution	Type III
Maintenance factor	0.7
Conversion factors	A. Unit with four 1000-W mercury (DX) = 1.0
	B. Unit with four 1000-W metal halide (clear) = 1.41
	C. Unit with four 1000-W high-pressure sodium = 1.54

COST DETAILS PER LUMINAIRE

Type of unit	Input, W	Contractor's price	Installed cost
A	4260	$1508	$2158.38
B	4340	1620	2517.54
C	4272	2320	3550.74

The installed cost includes published contractor's book price for the luminaires with ballasts, lamps as shown, fastening devices, and the labor required for installation and connection on a pole. See page G–57 for the installed cost of a pole.

Luminaires of this rectilinear family represent today's popular area lighting. For uniformity, refer to the isolux chart of the specific luminaire under consideration.

AREA LIGHTING – RECTILINEAR LUMINAIRES (QUAD.), 1000W

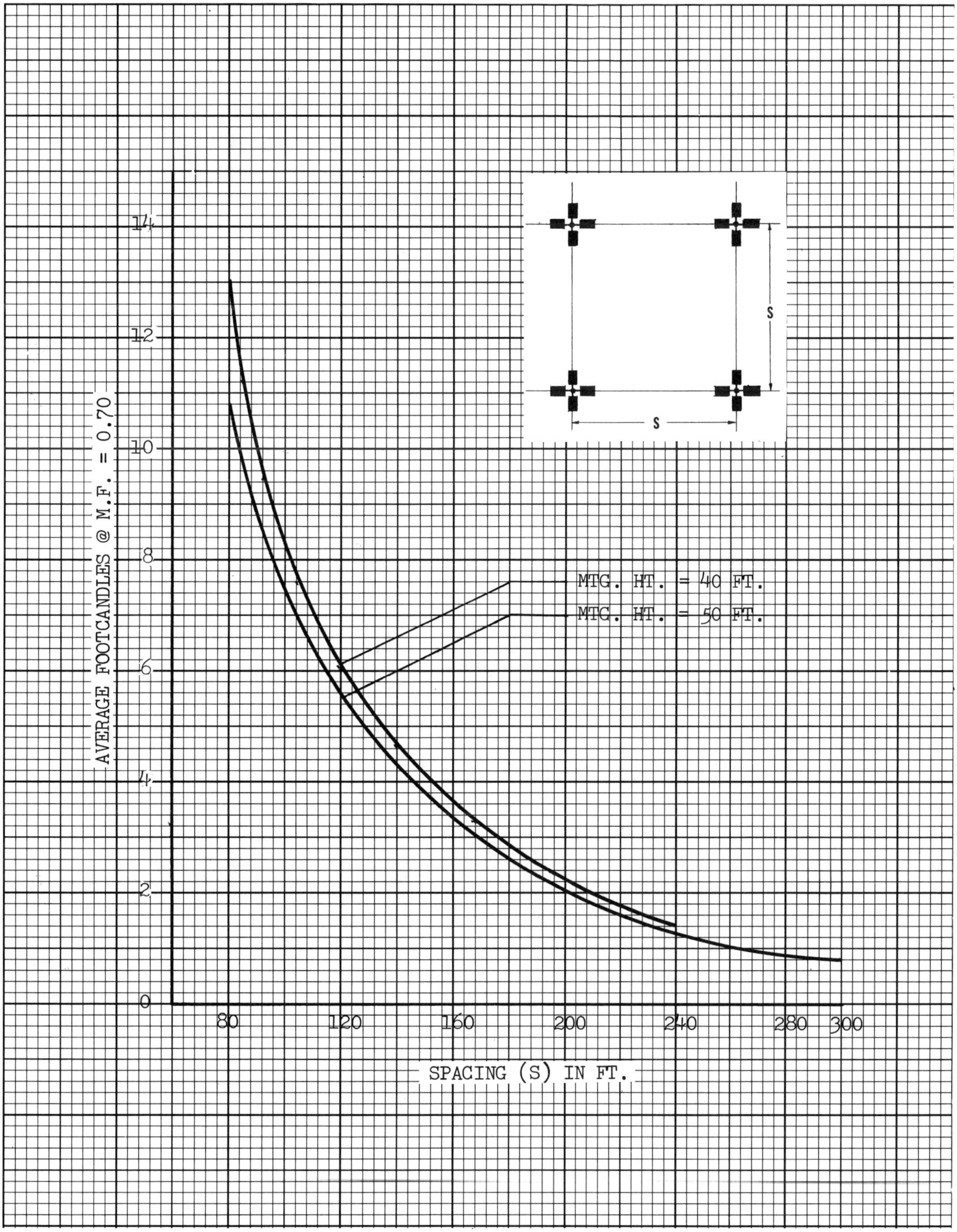

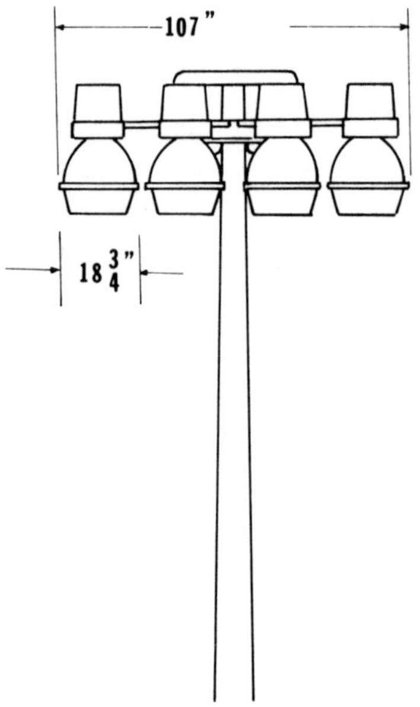

Description	High-mast luminaires
Lamp	One 400-W high-pressure sodium, 50,000 lm, 24,000 h
Luminaire	Glass reflector and refractor, open bottom
Maintenance factor	0.7
Conversion factors	A. Unit with one 400-W high-pressure sodium = 1.0
	B. Unit with one 400-W metal halide (clear) = 0.82
	C. Unit with one 400-W mercury (DX) = 0.67

COST DETAILS PER LUMINAIRE

Type of unit	Input, W	Contractor's price	Installed cost
A	450	$413	$612.75
B	465	280	431.75
C	445	240	356.75

The installed cost includes published contractor's book price for the luminaire with ballast, lamp as shown, fastening devices, and the labor required for installation and connection on a pole. See page G-55 for the installed cost of a high -mast pole.

The high-mast lighting system is used in extra-large parking lots, highway roadway interchanges, etc., for uniform lighting levels. High luminaire mounting reduces glare for the motorists and reduces halo effect that rain and fog create around luminaires mounted at conventional heights. For quick reference, do not exceed a spacing of 8 times mounting height for an average to minimum uniformity ratio of 3 : 1.

AREA LIGHTING – HIGH-MAST LUMINAIRES, 400W

THE CURVES SHOWN ARE BASED ON ONE LUMINAIRE PER POLE. AS MANY AS 12 LUMINAIRES CAN BE INSTALLED ON A POLE. FOR MULTIPLE CONFIGURATIONS, MULTIPLY FOOTCANDLE VALUES BY THE NUMBER OF LUMINAIRES PER POLE.

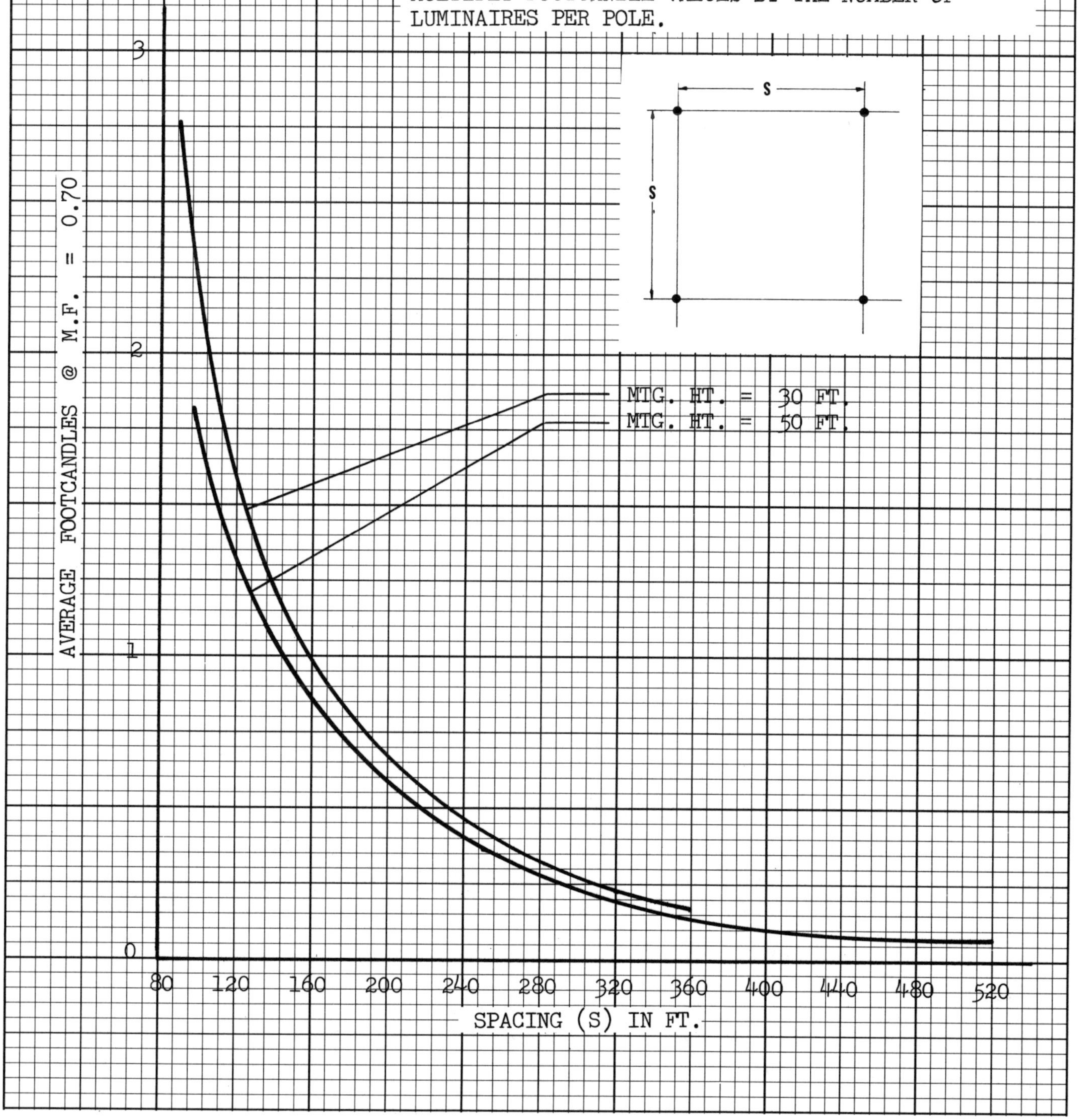

G

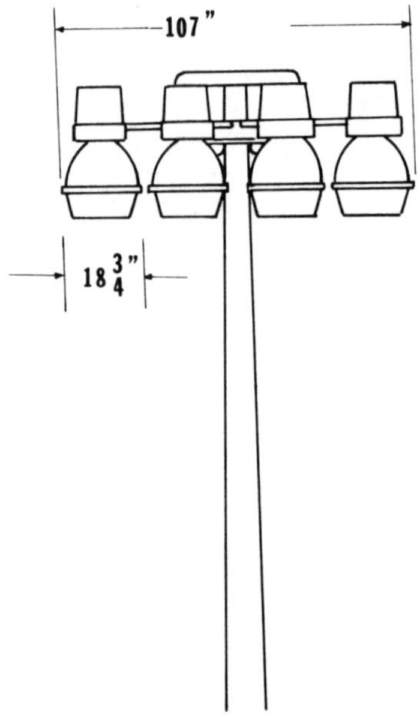

Description	High-mast luminaires
Lamp	One 1000-W metal halide (clear), 1000,000 lm, 10,000 h
Luminaire	Glass reflector and refractor, open bottom
Maintenance factor	0.7
Conversion factors	A. Unit with one 1000-W metal halide (clear) = 1.0 B. Unit with one 1000-W mercury (DX) = 0.8 C. Unit with one 1000-W high-pressure sodium = 1.1 For multiple configurations, multiply footcandle values by the number of luminaires per pole

COST DETAILS PER LUMINAIRE

Type of unit1	Input, W	Contractor's price	Installed cost
A	1085	$351	$590
B	1065	314	489.25
C	1068	536	860.75

The installed cost includes published contractor's book price for the luminaire with ballast, lamp as shown, fastening devices, and the labor required for installation and connection on a pole. See page G-55 for the installed cost of a high-mast pole.

The high-mast lighting system is used in extra-large parking lots, highway roadway interchanges, etc., for uniform lighting levels. High luminaire mounting reduces glare for the motorists and reduces halo effect that rain and fog create around luminaires mounted at conventional heights. For quick reference, do not exceed a spacing of 9 times mounting height for an average to minimum uniformity ratio of 3 : 1.

AREA LIGHTING – HIGH-MAST LUMINAIRES, 1000W

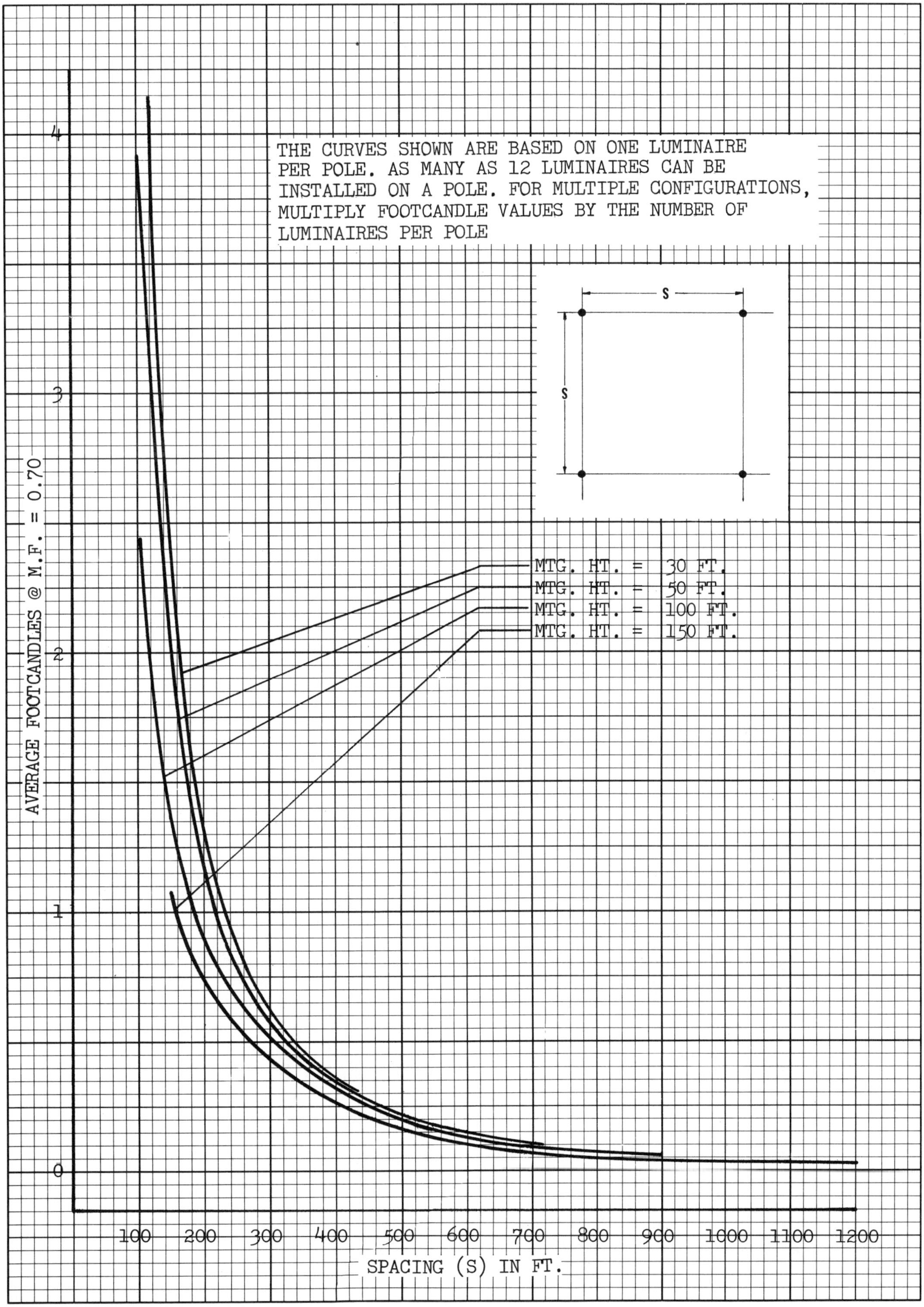

G

The installed costs shown for the 150- and 100-ft poles include a complete built-in lowering system, but no hoist motor is included. The poles are sectioned hot-dipped galvanized steel for use in 100 mi/h steady wind with 1.3 gust factor. A maximum of 12 luminaires can be installed on a pole. For the total installed cost, add the installed cost of the luminaires to the applicable installed cost of the pole.

Add an additional $1000 per site for a hoist motor, which can be moved from pole to pole to raise and lower the luminaires.

The 50- and 30-ft poles do not have a lowering system. The poles are galvanized steel for use in 100 mi/h steady wind with 1.3 gust factor. For the total cost, add the installed cost of the luminaires to the applicable installed cost of the pole.

COST OF HIGH-MAST LUMINAIRE POLES

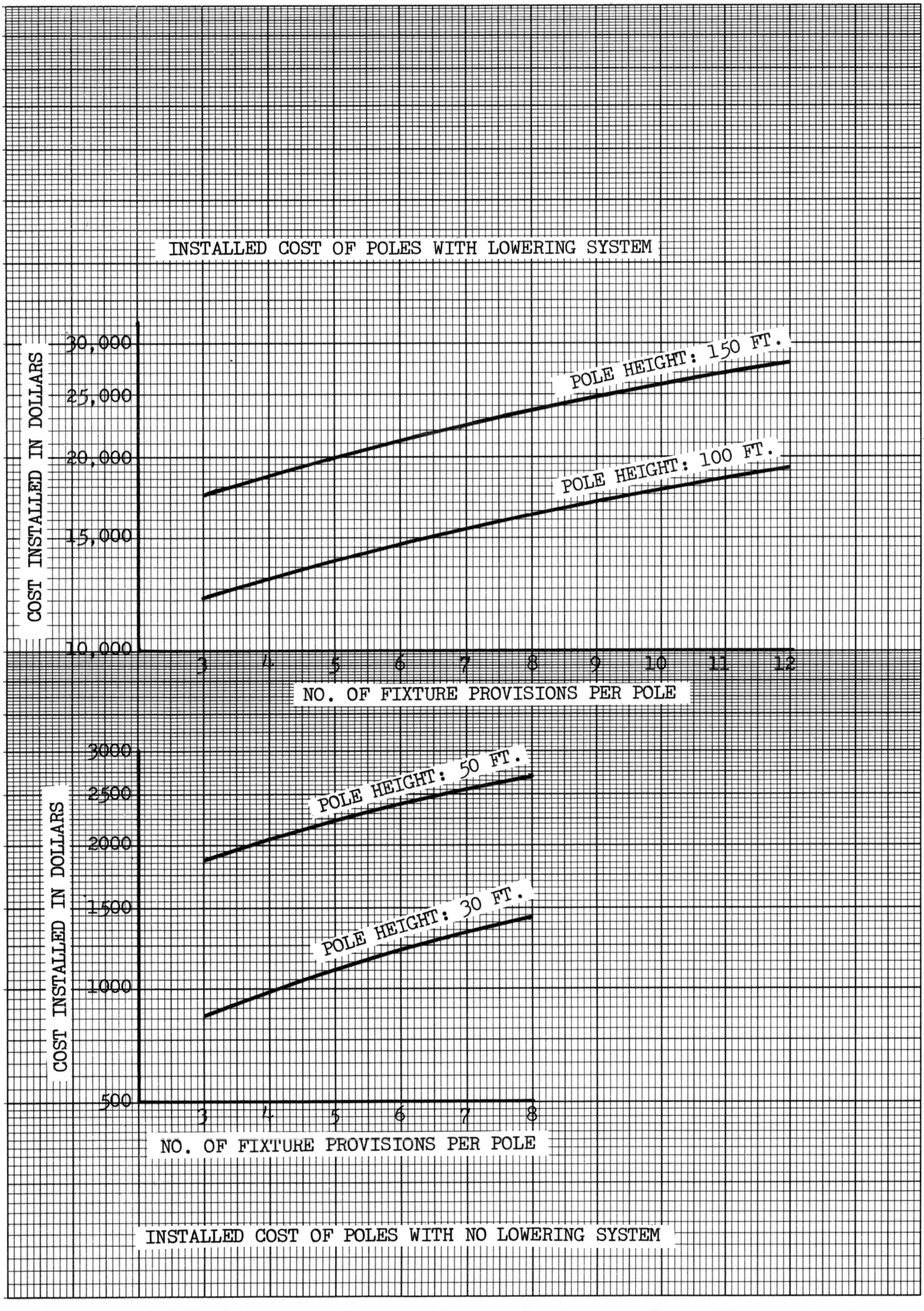

G

Each installed cost shown for the poles includes published contractor's book price for the pole (primed only), anchor bolts, ground wire, concrete base, and the labor required for installation. No luminaires, arms, or painting are included in these figures.

INSTALLED COST OF POSTOP AND FLOOD LIGHTING POLES

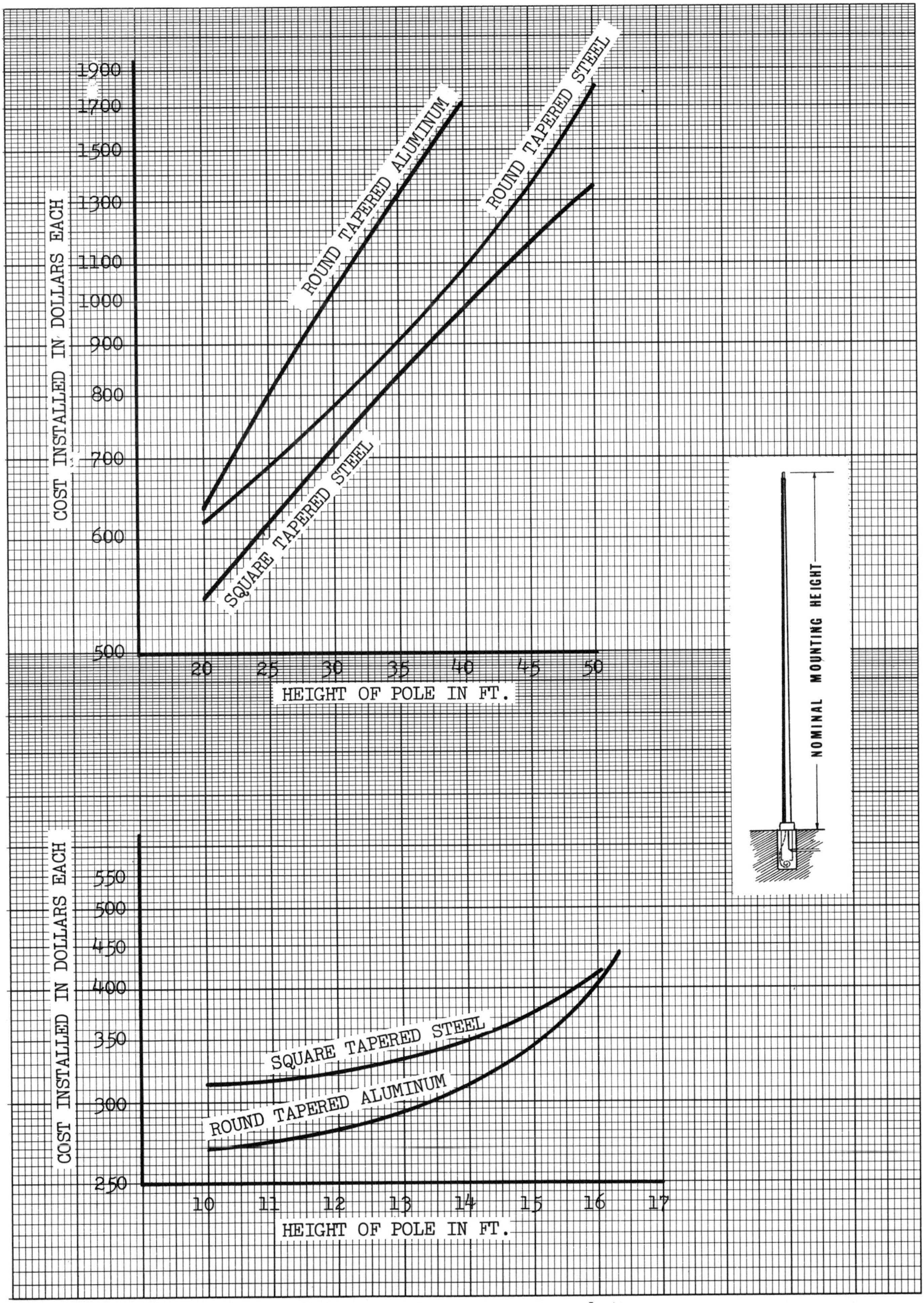

Miscellaneous

Installed Cost of EMT and GRC Conduits with Wires (Indoor) H-3
Installed Cost of GRC and PVC Conduits with Wires in a Trench H-5
Cost-Adjustment Formula H-7

RECOMMENDED LEVELS OF ILLUMINATION, IES

General Lighting H-8
Sports Lighting H-10
Roadway Lighting H-10

LAMP DATA

Incandescent H-11
Fluorescent H-12
Mercury H-13
Metal Halide H-13
High-Pressure Sodium H-14
Low-Pressure Sodium H-14

H

The installed costs shown for the EMT and GRC conduits with wires include the published contractor's book prices and installation of both conduits and wires.

INSTALLED COST OF EMT & GRC CONDUITS WITH WIRES, INDOOR

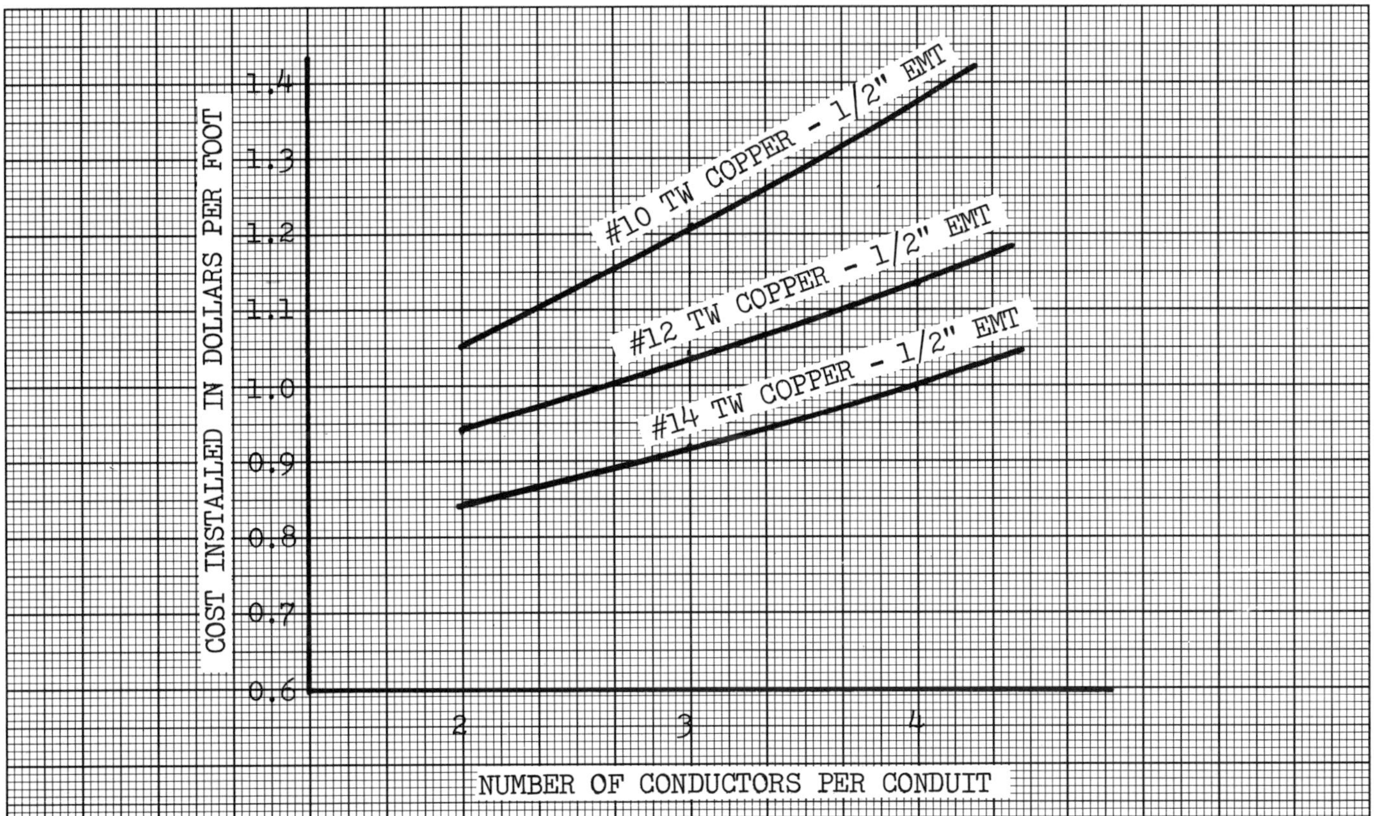

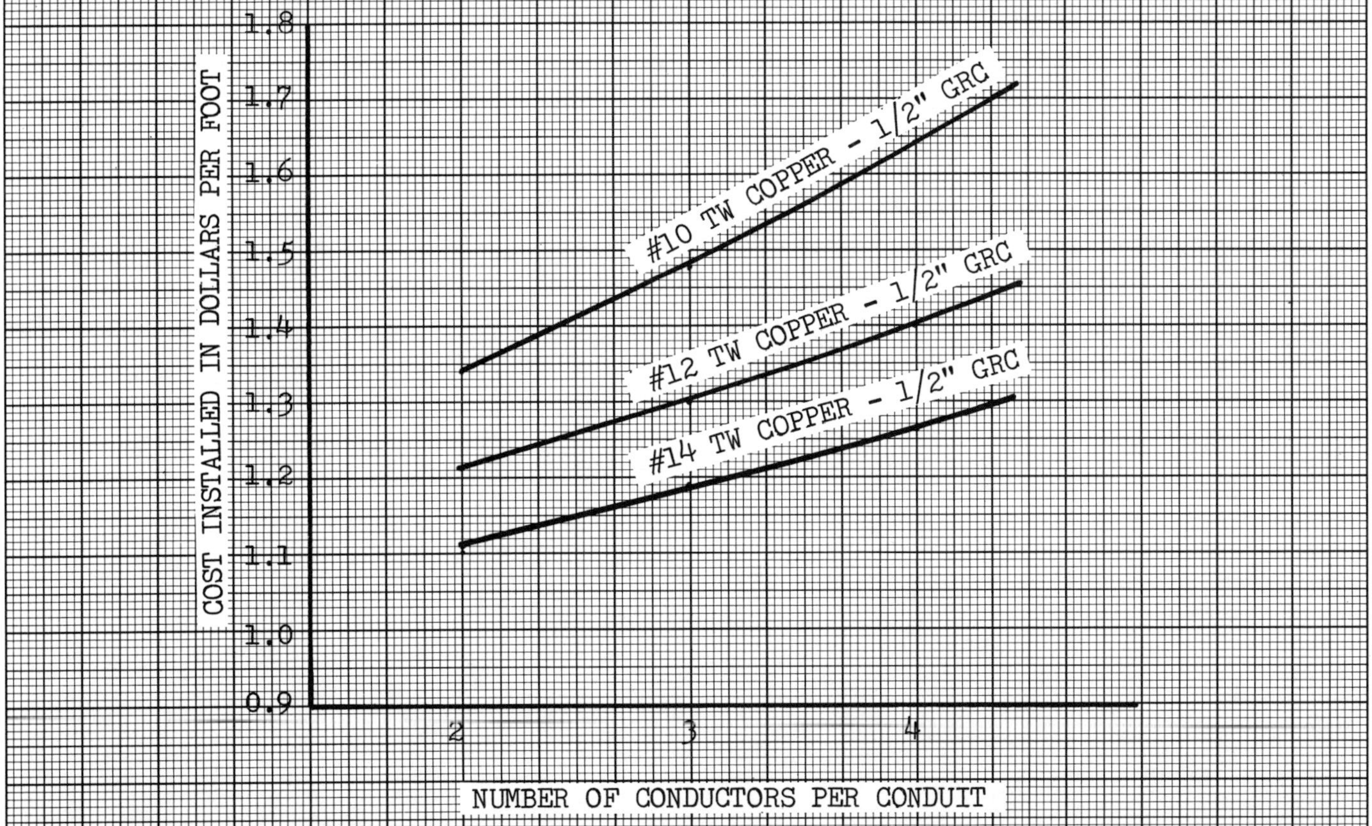

The costs shown are for the installation of a 3/4-in GRC or PVC conduit with the number of conductors as shown, in a trench of 6-in width and 18-in depth. It includes the price of trenching and backfilling, assuming a normal, average dirt-digging condition. For a difficult digging condition, a job factor must be added as necessary.

For PVC, where a ground wire is necessary, see the installed cost with an additional conductor in the conduit.

INSTALLED COST OF CONDUIT WITH WIRES IN A TRENCH

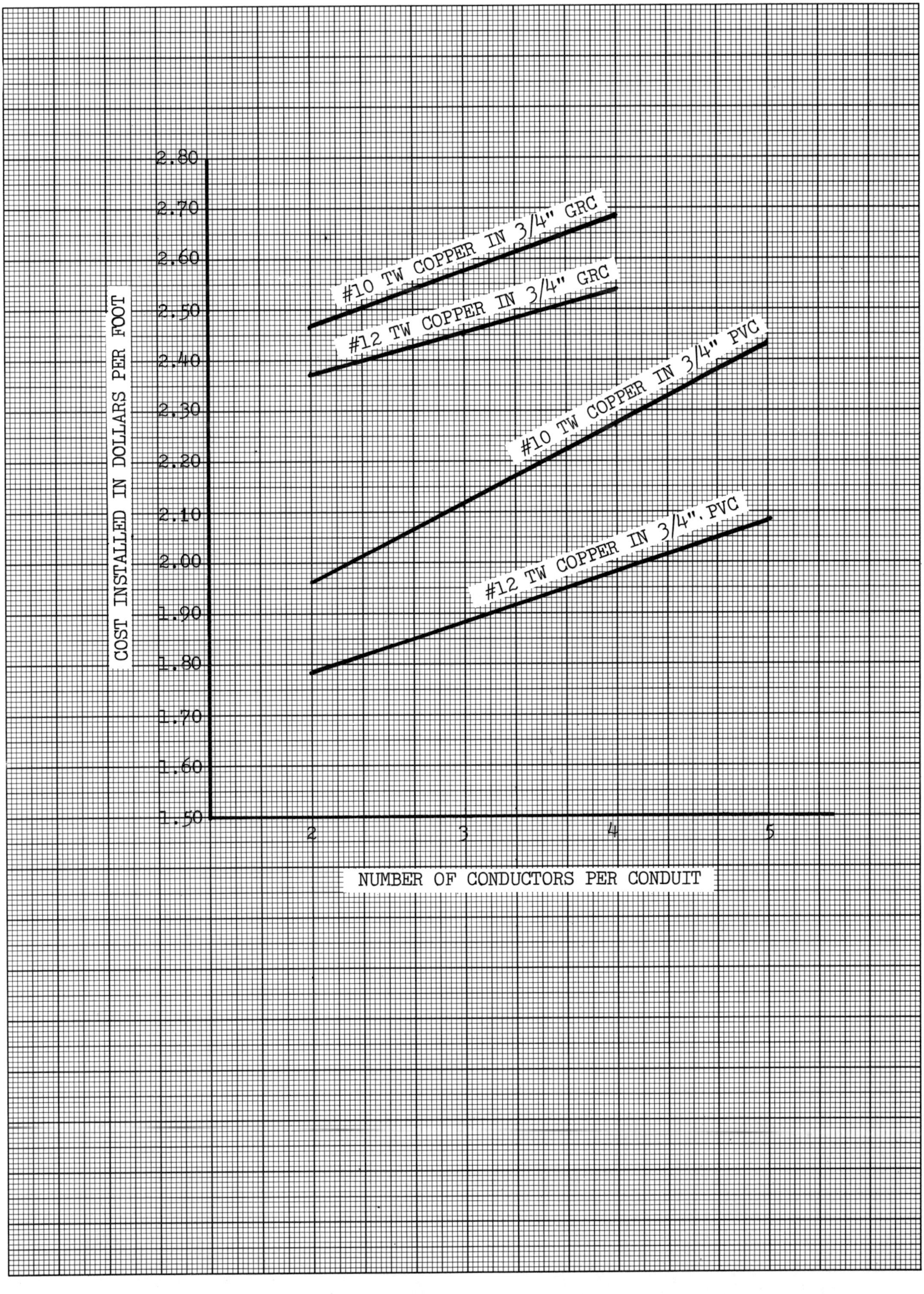

There are two variables in lighting cost estimation which directly affect the total price. The first is the labor rate which varies with place and time and the other, the material cost, which generally varies only with time. The total installed costs obtained from this book are based on a national average labor rate and the material cost at the time of publication. An adjustment has to be made for the labor rate and material cost of a specific area and time.

This is done with the help of the Cost Adjustment Formula, shown on page H–7, which has been carefully developed to take these changes into account.

COST ADJUSTMENT FORMULA

Total Price Multiplier = (0.0049 × Index) + (0.0136 × Labor)

Where Index = Latest Price Index for Industrial/Commercial Lighting Fixtures.

Labor = Total labor rate of your area including payroll taxes and fringe benefits.

Procedure:

1. *Find out the total hourly rate of your area which includes the payroll taxes and fringe benefits. Let us suppose it is $15.50 per hr.*
2. *Ask an electrical wholesaler to look in the latest issue of Electrical Marketing, published by McGraw-Hill, for the latest price index on the "Industrial/Commercial Lighting Fixtures." Let us suppose it is 174.*
3. *Apply these two data to the formula to obtain the total price multiplier. In our example it is:*

   $= (0.0049 \times 174) + (0.0136 \times 15.50)$

   $= 1.0634$

   This factor when multiplied by the total installed cost obtained from the book will give you the adjusted total installed cost of your area.

Note that the labor rate and the price index used in developing the installed costs in this book are $14.62 and 164 respectively. When these two data are applied to the formula, the Total Price Multiplier is 1.00.

IES RECOMMENDED LEVELS OF ILLUMINATION

The following tables give a partial list of minimum, maintained levels of illumination as currently recommended by the IES lighting handbook.

TABLE 2 GENERAL LIGHTING

Area	Light on tasks, fc
Art galleries:	
General	30
On paintings (supplementary)	30
On statuary and other displays	100
Auditoriums:	
Assembly only	15
Exhibitions	30
Social activities	5
Banks:	
Lobby:	
General	50
Writing areas	70
Tellers' stations	150
Posting and keypunch	150
Barber shops and beauty parlors	100
Breweries:	
Brewhouse	30
Boiling and keg washing	30
Filling (bottles, cans, kegs)	50
Churches and synagogs:	
Altar, ark, reredos	100
Choir and chancel	30
Classrooms	30
Pulpit, rostrum (supplementary)	50
Main worship area:	
Light and medium interior finish	15
For churches with special zeal	30
Courtrooms:	
Seating area	30
Court activity area	70
Garages, automobile and truck:	
Service garages:	
Repairs	100
Active traffic area	20
Parking garages:	
Entrance	50
Traffic lanes	10
Storage	5

Area	Light on tasks, fc
Library:	
Reading areas:	
Reading printed material	30
Study and note taking	70
Conference areas	30
Seminar rooms	70
Book stack (30 in above floor):	
Active stacks	30
Inactive stacks	5
Book repair and binding	70
Cataloging	70
Card files	100
Carrels, individual study areas	
Circulation desks	70
Rare-book rooms, archives:	
Storage areas	30
Reading areas	100
Map, picture, and print rooms:	
Storage areas	30
Use areas	100
Audio-visual areas:	
Preparation rooms	70
Viewing rooms (variable)	70
TV room	70
Audio listening areas:	
General	30
For note taking	70
Record inspection table	100
Microform areas:	
Files	70
Viewing areas	30
Locker rooms	20
Meat packing:	
Slaughtering	30
Cleaning, cutting, cooking, grinding, canning, packing	100
Offices:	
Drafting rooms:	
Detailed drafting, and designing, and cartography	200
Rough-layout drafting	150

Area	Light on tasks, fc
Accounting offices:	
Auditing, tabulating, bookkeeping business-machine operation, computer operation	150
General offices:	
Reading poor reproductions, business-machine operation, computer operation	150
Reading handwriting in hard pencil or on poor paper, reading fair reproductions, active filing, mail sorting	100
Reading handwriting in ink or medium pencil on good quality paper, intermittent filing	70
Private offices:	
Reading poor reproductions, business-machine operation	150
Reading handwriting in hard pencil or on poor paper, reading fair reproduction	100
Reading handwriting in ink or medium pencil or good-quality paper	70
Reading high-contrast or well-printed materials	30
Conferring and interviewing	30
Conference rooms:	
Critical seeing tasks	100
Conferring	30
Note taking during projection	30
Corridors	20
Post offices:	
Lobby, on tables	30
Sorting, mailing, etc.	100
Schools:	
Tasks:	
Reading printed material	30
Reading pencil writing	70
Spirit duplicated material:	
Good	30
Poor	100
Drafting, benchwork	100
Lip reading, chalkboards, sewing	150
Classrooms:	
Art rooms	70
Drafting rooms	100
Home economics rooms:	
Sewing	150
Cooking	50
Ironing	50
Sink activities	70
Note-taking areas	70
Laboratories	100
Lecture rooms:	
Audience area	70
Demonstration area	150
Music rooms:	
Simple scores	30
Advanced scores	70
Shops	100
Sight-saving rooms	150
Study halls	70
Corridors and stairways	20
Dormitories:	
General	10
Reading books, magazines, newspapers	30
Study desk	70
Service stations:	
Service bays	30
Sales room	50
Shelving and displays	100
Rest rooms	15
Storage	5
Theaters and motion picture houses:	
Auditorium:	
During intermission	5
During picture	0.1
Foyer	5
Lobby	20

TABLE 3 SPORTS LIGHTING

Area	Light on tasks, fc
Badminton:	
Tournament	30
Club	20
Recreation	10
Basketball:	
College and professional	50
College intramural and high school	30
Recreation (outdoor)	10
Bowling:	
Tournament:	
Approaches	10
Lanes	20
Pins	50
Recreational:	
Approaches	10
Lanes	10
Pins	30
Gymnasium:	
Exhibitions, matches	50
Gen. exercising and recreation	30
Assemblies	10
Dances	5
Locker and shower rooms	20
Handball:	
Tournament	50
Club:	
Indoor, four-wall or squash	30
Outdoor, two-court	20
Recreational:	
Indoor, four-wall or squash	20
Outdoor, two-court	10
Tennis, lawn (indoor)	
Tournament	50
Club	20
Recreational	20
Tennis, lawn (outdoor)	
Tournament	30
Club	20
Recreational	10
Tennis, table	
Tournament	50
Club	30
Recreational	20
Volley ball:	
Tournament	20
Recreational	10

TABLE 4 ROADWAY LIGHTING

Roadway and walkway classification	Area Classification		
	Commercial	Intermediate	Residential
Vehicular roadways:			
Freeways	0.6 fc	0.6 fc	0.6 fc
Major and Expressway	2.0	1.4	1.0
Collector	1.2	0.9	0.6
Local	0.9	0.6	0.4
Alleys	0.6	0.4	0.2
Pedestrian walkways:			
Sidewalks	0.9	0.6	0.2
Pedestrian ways	2.0	1.0	0.5

TABLE 5 INCANDESCENT LAMPS

Watts	Bulb/base	Initial lumens	Life, h
General-service lamps:			
60	A-19/med.	870	1000
75	A-19/med.	1,190	750
100	A-19/med.	1,750	750
	A-21/med.	1,690	750
150	A-21/med.	2,880	750
	A-23/med.	2,780	750
	PS-25/med.	2,680	750
200	A-23/med.	4,010	750
	PS-30/med.	3,710	750
300	PS-25/med.	6,360	750
	PS-30/med.	6,110	750
Projector (PAR) lamps:			
75	PAR-38/med. (SP)	765	2000
	PAR-38/med. (FL)	765	2000
150	PAR-38/med. (SP)	1,740	2000
	PAR-38/med. (FL)	1,740	2000
200	PAR-46/med. SP (NSP)	2,300	2000
	PAR-46/med. SP (MFL)	2,300	2000
250	PAR-38/med. (SP) (tungsten-halogen)	3,180	3000
	PAR-38/med. (FL) (tungsten-halogen)	3,180	3000
300	PAR-56/Mog. EP (NSP)	3,840	2000
	PAR-56/Mog. EP (MFL)	3,840	2000
	PAR-56/Mog. EP (WFL)	3,840	2000
500	PAR-56/Mog. EP (NSP) (tungsten-halogen)	7,650	4000
	PAR-56/Mog. EP (MFL) (tungsten-halogen)	7,650	4000
	PAR-56/Mog. EP (WFL) (tungsten-halogen)	7,650	4000
Reflector (R) lamps:			
30	R-20/med. (FL)	210	2000
50	R-20/med. (SP)	440	2000
75	R-30/med. (SP)	900	2000
	R-30/med. (FL)	900	2000
150	R-40/med. (SP)	1,870	2000
	R-40/med. (FL)	1,870	2000
300	R-40/med. (SP)	3,650	2000
	R-40/med. (FL)	3,650	2000
500	R-40/Mog. (SP)	6,500	2000
	R-40/Mog. (FL)	6,500	2000
Tungsten Halogen lamps (tubular):			
75	T-3/Min. Scr. (28V)	1,600	2000
200	T-3/RSC	3,460	1500
250	T-4/Min. Can.	4,700	2000
300	T-3/RSC	5,900	2000
	T-4/RSC	5,650	2000
325	T-4/Min. Can.	7,800	500
400	T-4/RSC	7,750	2000
500	T-3/RSC	10,700	2000
	T-4/Min. Can.	9,500	2000

TABLE 6 FLUORESCENT LAMPS

Watts	Bulb	Description	Initial lumens	Life, h
Rapid-start:				
40	F40 T-12	Cool white	3,200	20,000
	F40 T-12	Warm white	3,200	20,000
	F40 T-12/U	Cool white, U shape (3 5/8-in leg spacing)	2,900	12,000
	F40 T-12/U	Warm white, U shape (3 5/8-in leg spacing)	2,850	12,000
	F40 T-12/U	Cool white, U shape (6-in leg spacing)	2,900	12,000
	F40 T-12/U	Warm white, U shape (6-in leg spacing)	2,850	12,000
Slimline:				
75	F96 T-12	Cool white	6,400	12,000
	F96 T-12	Warm white	6,400	12,000
High-output:				
60	F48 T-12	Cool white	4,300	12,000
	F48 T-12	Warm white	4,300	12,000
110	F96 T-12	Cool white	9,200	12,000
	F96 T-12	Warm white	9,200	12,000
Very High output:				
110	F48 PG-17	Cool white	7,450	12,000
	F48 PG-17	Warm white	7,000	12,000
215	F96 PG-17	Cool white	16,000	12,000
	F96 PG-17	Warm white	15,000	12,000

TABLE 7 MERCURY LAMPS

Watts	Bulb	Description	Initial lumens (vertical)	Life, h
50	E-17	DX	1,575	16,000
75	E-17	Clear	2,700	16,000
	E-17	DX	2,800	16,000
100	A-23	Clear	3,700	18,000
	A-23	DX	4,000	18,000
	E-23½	Clear	3,850	24,000
	E-23½	DX	4,200	24,000
	R-40	Flood	2,850	24,000
	R-40	DX (WFL)	2,850	24,000
175	E-28/BT-28	Clear	7,950	24,000
	E-28/BT-28	DX	8,600	24,000
	E-28	Color-improved	7,250	24,000
	R-40	Flood	5,700	24,000
	R-40	DX (WFL)	5,700	24,000
250	E-28/BT-28	Clear	11,200	24,000
	E-28/BT-28	DX	12,100	24,000
400	E-37/BT-37	Clear	21,000	24,000
	E-37/BT-37	DX	22,500	24,000
	E-37	Color-improved	20,500	24,000
1000	BT-56	Clear	57,000	24,000
	BT-56	DX	63,000	24,000
	BT-56	Color-improved	55,000	24,000

TABLE 8 METAL HALIDE LAMPS

Watts	Bulb	Description	Initial lumens (vertical)	Life, h
175	E-28/BT-28	Clear	14,000	7,500
	E-28/BT-28	Coated	14,000	7,500
250	E-28/BT-28	Clear	20,500	7,500
	E-28/BT-28	Coated	20,500	7,500
400	E-37/BT-37	Clear	34,000	15,000
	E-37/BT-37	Coated	34,000	15,000
1000	BT-56	Clear	110,000	10,000
	BT-56	Coated	105,000	10,000

TABLE 9 HIGH-PRESSURE SODIUM LAMPS

Watts	Bulb	Description	Initial lumens (vertical)	Life, h
70	E-23½	Clear	5,800	20,000
100	E-23½	Clear	9,500	20,000
150	E-23½	Clear	16,000	24,000
250	E-18	Clear	27,500	24,000
	E-28	Coated	26,000	24,000
400	E-18	Clear	50,000	24,000
	E-28	Coated	47,500	24,000
1000	T-18	Clear	140,000	24,000

TABLE 10 LOW-PRESSURE SODIUM LAMPS

Watts	Bulb	Description	Initial lumens	Life, h
35	T-17	Monochromatic yellow	4,800	18,000
55	T-17	Monochromatic yellow	8,000	18,000
90	T-21	Monochromatic yellow	135,000	18,100
135	T-21	Monochromatic yellow	22,500	18,000
180	T-21	Monochromatic yellow	33,000	18,000

Index

Acrylic prismatic lenses:
recessed fluorescent troffers, B-2 to B-9
surface-mount fluorescents:
modular units, A-22 to A-29
wraparound, A-2 to A-15
(*See also* Surface-mount fluorescents)
Area lighting, outdoor (*see* Outdoor lighting, area)

Baffle downlights, incandescent:
recessed, F-16 to F-21
surface-mount, F-50 to F-55

Carolite Radialens, troffer with, B-26 to B-29
Commercial high-intensity-discharge units:
recessed units: ellipsoidal-reflector downlights, E-12 to E-19
open downlights, E-2 to E-11
parabolic-louvered, E-22 to E-23, E-28 to E-31
regressed lens, E-20 to E-21, E-24 to E-27
round regressed lens, E-32 to E-35
square regressed lens, E-36 to E-37
surface-mount units: cylindrical downlights, E-38 to E-39
modular lens units, E-40 to E-41
Commercial incandescents:
recessed units: baffle downlights, F-16 to F-21
ellipsoidal-reflector downlights, F-22 to F-35
open-reflector downlights, F-2 to F-15
parabolic-louvered, F-42 to F-43
regressed lens, F-36 to F-41
surface-mount units: baffle downlights, F-50 to F-55
open-reflector downlights, F-44 to F-49
Conduits, installed cost of:
EMT, H-2
GRC: indoor, H-2
in a trench, H-4
PVC, H-4
Corridor fluorescent wraparound, A-2 to A-3
Cost adjustment formula, H-6 to H-7
Cylindrical downlights:
high-intensity-discharge units, E-38
incandescents, F-44 to F-55

Day-Brite VIP lens, troffer with, B-30 to B-35
Downlights (*see* Commercial high-intensity-discharge units; Commercial incandescents; Cylindrical downlights)
Dropped-dish recessed fluorescent troffers, B-48 to B-51
Dropped-dish surface-mount fluorescent modulars, A-30 to A-33

Egg-crate louver [*see* Plastic cube (egg-crate) louvers]
Ellipsoidal-reflector downlights, recessed:
high-intensity-discharge, E-12 to E-19
incandescent, F-22 to F-35
EMT conduit with wires, installed cost of, H-2
Enclosed and gasketed fluorescent wraparound, A-16 to A-17

Floodlighting poles, installed cost of, G-56
Fluorescent lamps, data on, H-12
Fluorescent recessed troffers (*see* Troffers, recessed fluorescent)
Fluorescent strips (*see* Strips, fluorescent)
Fluorescent wraparounds (*see* Wraparounds, fluorescent)
Fluorescents:
industrial (*see* Industrial fluorescent units)
surface-mount enclosed (*see* Surface-mount fluorescents)

General lighting, IES recommended illumination level for, H-8 to H-10

Gibson EE system, troffer with, B-40 to B-43
GRC conduit with wires, installed cost of:
  indoor, H-2
  in a trench, H-4

High-intensity-discharge units, commercial (*see* Commercial high-intensity-discharge units)
High-intensity-discharge units, industrial (*see* Industrial high-intensity-discharge units)
High-mast luminaires, G-50 to G-53
High-mast poles, installed cost of, G-54 to G-55
High-pressure sodium lamps, data on, H-14
Holophane RSL Postop lighting, G-2 to G-7
Holophane Square-Postop lighting, G-22 to G-31

Illumination levels, IES recommended, H-8 to H-10
  general lighting, H-8 to H-9
  roadway lighting, H-10
  sports lighting, H-10
Incandescent baffle downlights (*see* Baffle downlights, incandescent)
Incandescent lamps, data on, H-11
Incandescents, commercial (*see* Commercial incandescents)
Industrial fluorescent units:
  general-purpose, D-2 to D-9
  heavy-duty-grade, D-14 to D-17
  premium-grade, D-10 to D-13
Industrial high-intensity-discharge units:
  full-profile: aluminum reflector, D-24 to D-25, D-28 to D-29
    prismatic glass reflector, D-26 to D-27, D-30 to D-31
  full-profile, twin units: aluminum reflector, D-32 to D-33
    prismatic glass reflector, D-34 to D-35
  low-profile: aluminum reflector, D-18 to D-19
    porcelain enamel reflector, D-20 to D-21
    prismatic glass refractor, D-22 to D-23

KSH 3-E lens, troffer with, B-36 to B-39

Lamps, data on:
  fluorescent, H-12
  high-pressure sodium, H-14
  incandescent, H-11
Lamps, data on (*Cont.*):
  low-pressure sodium, H-14
  mercury vapor, H-13
  metal halide, H-13
Louvers, plastic-cube [*see* Plastic-cube (egg-crate) louvers]
Low-pressure sodium lamps, data on, H-14
Low-pressure sodium luminaires, for roadway lighting, G-14 to G-21
Low-profile fluorescent wraparound, A-4 to A-7
Luminaires:
  ceiling outlets for, cost of (*see* Outlets, installed cost of)
  high-mast, G-50 to G-53
  rectilinear (*see* Outdoor lighting, area; Outdoor lighting, roadway)

Mercury vapor lamps, data on, H-13
Metal halide lamps, data on, H-13
Modular units:
  fluorescents (*see* Surface-mount fluorescents, modular)
  high-intensity-discharge, E-40 to E-41

Norelco low-pressure sodium luminaires, G-14 to G-21

Open downlights, high-intensity-discharge, recessed, E-2 to E-11
Open-louvered surface-mount fluorescents, A-18 to A-21
Open-reflector downlights, incandescent:
  recessed, F-2 to F-15
  surface-mount, F-44 to F-49
Outdoor lighting:
  area: by high-mast luminaires, G-50 to G-53
    by Holophane Square-Postop lighting, G-22 to G-31
    by pole-mounted rectilinear units: one head, G-32 to G-37
      two heads, G-38 to G-43
      four heads, G-44 to G-49
  roadway: by Holophane RSL Postop lighting, G-2 to G-7
    pole-mounted: by low-pressure sodium luminaires, G-14 to G-21
      by rectilinear luminaires, G-8 to G-13
Outlets, installed cost of:
  above ceiling, B-52, C-22, D-36, E-42
  flush-mounted, A-38, C-22, E-42, F-56

Parabolic-louvered troffers, fluorescent, B-10 to B-25
Parabolic-louvered units:
  high-intensity-discharge, recessed, E-22 to E-23, E-28 to E-31
  incandescent, F-42 to F-43
Plastic-cube (egg-crate) louvers:
  recessed fluorescent troffers, B-44 to B-47
  surface-mount fluorescents, A-34 to A-37
Pole-mounted rectilinear luminaires (*see* Rectilinear luminaires, pole-mounted)
Poles, installed cost of:
  high-mast, G-54 to G-55
  post-top and floodlighting, G-56 to G-57
    round tapered aluminum, G-57
    round tapered steel, G-57
    square tapered steel, G-57
Premium fluorescent wraparound, A-14 to A-15
Prismatic lenses, acrylic (*see* Acrylic prismatic lenses)
PVC conduit with wires, installed cost of, H-4

Recessed-baffle downlights, incandescent, F-16 to F-21
Recessed commercial high-intensity-discharge units (*see* Commercial high-intensity-discharge units, recessed units)
Recessed commercial incandescents (*see* Commercial incandescents, recessed units)
Recessed fluorescent troffers (*see* Troffers, recessed fluorescent)
Rectilinear luminaires, pole-mounted (*see* Outdoor lighting, area; Outdoor lighting, roadway)
Regressed lenses:
  high-intensity-discharge recessed units, E-20 to E-21, E-24 to E-27, E-32 to E-37
  incandescent, F-36 to F-41
Roadway lighting (*see* Outdoor lighting, roadway)
Round regressed lens, E-32 to E-35
Round tapered pole, installed cost of:
  aluminum, G-57
  steel, G-57

Scissors-curve fluorescent wraparound, A-12 to A-13
Sports lighting, IES recommended illumination levels for, H-10
Square regressed lens, E-36 to E-37
Square tapered steel pole, installed cost of, G-57
Strips, fluorescent:
  general-purpose, C-2 to C-13
  premium-grade, C-14 to C-21
Surface-mount baffle downlights, incandescent, F-50 to F-55

Surface-mount commercial high-intensity-discharge units (*see* Commercial high-intensity-discharge units, surface-mount units)
Surface-mount commercial incandescents (*see* Commercial incandescents, surface-mount units)
Surface-mount fluorescents:
modular: acrylic prismatic lens, A-22 to A-29
dropped-dish, A-30 to A-33
plastic-cube (egg-crate) louvers, A-34 to A-37
open-louvered, A-18 to A-21
wraparound: corridor, A-2 to A-3
enclosed and gasketed, A-16 to A-17
Surface-mount fluorescents, wraparound (*Cont.*):
low-profile, A-4 to A-7
premium, A-14 to A-15
scissors-curve, A-12 to A-13
traditional, A-8 to A-11

Traditional fluorescent wraparound, A-8 to A-11
Troffers, recessed fluorescent:
acrylic prismatic lens, B-2 to B-9
with Carolite Radialens, B-26 to B-29
with Day-Brite VIP lens, B-30 to B-35
dropped-dish, B-48 to B-51
with Gibson EE system, B-40 to B-43
Troffers, recessed fluorescent (*Cont.*):
with KSH 3-E lens, B-36 to B-39
parabolic-louvered, B-10 to B-25
plastic-cube (egg-crate) louvered, B-44 to B-47
Twin units, high-intensity-discharge, D-32 to D-35

VIP lens (*see* Day-Brite VIP lens)

Wraparounds, fluorescent:
corridor, A-2 to A-3
enclosed and gasketed, A-16 to A-17
low-profile, A-4 to A-7
premium, A-14 to A-15
scissors-curve, A-12 to A-13
traditional, A-8 to A-11